BEAT THE SYSTEM!

BEAT THE SYSTEM!

1,200 Tips for Coming Out on Top in Every Deal and Transaction

Edited by Jeff Bredenberg, Senior Editor, Rodale Books

Rodale Press, Inc.
Emmaus, Pennsylvania

Printed in the United States of America on acid-free ∞, recycled paper ♻

Library of Congress Cataloging-in-Publication Data

Beat the system! : 1,200 tips for coming out on top in every deal and
    transaction / edited by Jeff Bredenberg ; [adviser, Stephen M.
    Pollan ; contributing writers, Lisa Bennett . . . et al.].
        p.   cm.
    Includes index.
    ISBN 0–87596–388–9 hardcover
    1. Consumer education. 2. Shopping.   I. Bredenberg, Jeff.
    II. Bennett, Lisa.
    Tx335.B384 1997
    640′.73—dc21   97–549

Distributed in the book trade by St. Martin's Press

2 4 6 8 10 9 7 5 3 1   hardcover

─── OUR PURPOSE ───

*"We inspire and enable people to improve
their lives and the world around them."*

BEAT THE SYSTEM! Editorial Staff

Rodale Health and Fitness Books

Contents

PART 8: TAXES

PART 9: WORK

PART 10: OUT AND ABOUT

PART 11: LAW AND GOVERNMENT

PART 12: LIFESTYLE

Foreword

This book is truly a remarkable achievement. The pages that follow contain more inside information, more savvy advice, and more insight and wisdom on consumer issues than I've ever seen brought between two covers. All the tools and techniques that you need to win the game of life are outlined right here.

Yet even this wealth of resources isn't complete. There's one piece missing. Not because the authors and editors forgot it but because it can only come from inside you. That missing piece is a take-charge attitude.

After more than 30 years of consulting and advising, I've found that there's really only one difference between winners and losers. Winners act, while losers react. The people who are living life to the fullest, who are getting the most bang for their buck, are those who have taken charge of nearly every element of their lives.

Whether it's due to a lack of self-esteem, a misplaced fear of "rocking the boat," or a simple lack of knowledge, many people go through life reactively. They wait to be offered a raise, they think that store policies are etched in stone, and all too often they take "no" for an answer. Most of them bemoan their lack of control, thinking that there's nothing that they can do but roll with life's punches.

But there is something that they can do. They can become proactive. They can take charge. They can become the major player in their own lives rather than just a spectator. All that's required is taking the action. Life's winners ask for raises and promotions. They know that there are exceptions made to every rule. And they understand that "no" is a judgment based on the set of facts that were presented, not an infallible and irrevocable decision.

Combine the incredible store of information inside this book with the take-charge attitude and you're guaranteed to become one of life's winners. Don't let self-doubt get in your way. All that you need is the ability to absorb the information in these pages and to communicate with others. Sure, you may occasionally need to rock the boat. But winners always stand apart from the crowd.

Taking charge isn't easy. It takes real work. But the rewards far outweigh the costs. Just look at all that you have to gain. Taking charge will revitalize your career, revolutionize your consumer habits, and reinvigorate your whole life. Don't be content with being a passenger in your own life's journey. Grab the reins.

—Stephen M. Pollan

Introduction

Sometimes a book changes you forever.

A peculiar thing happened during the editing of this book. I purchased from a prominent department store a sofa and love seat, plus a "free" living room chair, paid for on a credit card. On delivery day the sofa and love seat arrived—without the chair. The delivery man was perplexed. So was the salesperson. So was the customer service person at the we-handle-all-problems toll-free number.

I placed dozens of frustrating calls. "Oh, yeah—your free chair," I kept hearing. As if we were discussing a trinket missing from the bottom of a cereal box. Not only did I get no answers but also I couldn't even get the store's employees to call me back. Customer service had taken a holiday.

The system worked fine for the department store, as my credit card bill attested. But it was failing me miserably.

After two weeks, I decided that extreme measures were warranted. I knew how to move up the lines of authority and soon had the ear of the store's manager and a vice-president of the parent company. I knew how to rally the credit card company to my defense. I knew to keep careful notes along the way—names, dates, information exchanged. I knew how to craft firm, effective, and professional letters to the right people.

I knew how to set an enforceable deadline for delivery of the chair, and finally it appeared in my living room with 10 minutes to spare. What's more, I got paid for my extra effort: The store was shamed into shaving an extra 10 percent off the entire purchase price of the furniture. And through-out the episode, I kept intact the genteel demeanor that I prefer.

How did I know how to do this? Having just edited the book that you are holding, I resolved never to play the pushover consumer again.

As marvelous as the American way of life is, there's a persistent element of treachery in store for the little guy. Hundreds of times a day, hundreds of the "systems" swirling around us—stores, repairmen, doctors, governments, schools, employers, and many more—invite us to open our wallets and hand over cash or expend some energy. But there's always information bene-ficial to you that the systems do not volunteer: that you can accomplish the same transactions faster, cheaper, or easier—if only you knew how. If only you knew what to say, where to go, whom to talk to, what reference to open, what button to push.

Thus, the philosophy of this book: The passive consumer will always lose money, time, and effort. The assertive consumer will come out ahead.

To identify these daily transactions and the insider information that pulls them to your advantage, we enlisted more than a dozen talented writing professionals who specialize in the subjects at hand. Among them are a lawyer, a certified public accountant, a master mechanic, a minister-psychotherapist, a renowned personal finance columnist, and other consumer journalists with decades of experience. And coaching this team along the way was attorney, financial consultant, and author Stephen Pollan, whom you may know from his many books and television appearances. Not only did Pollan prove to be invaluable behind the scenes but also his advice is quoted throughout the book.

The advice provided here is plainspoken, stripped of the jargon that industries use to cloud issues and intimidate you. The advice also is specific and within anyone's power.

Read this book front to back, and you will have fitted yourself with impressive armor as you go about your daily life. But it also serves as a handy reference, so dip in as specific occasions arise. Buying a car? Better read the Wheeling and Dealing chapter. Filling out the old 1040 for Uncle Sam? Better turn to Forging Your Audit Armor. To further assist browsers, we end each chapter with a "Bottom Line"—a handy summary, plus definitions of key terms and a rundown of organizations and helpful references.

You will find that this book is an invitation to a new lifestyle. Absorb this information and it will emerge when you need it, as I discovered with my mystery chair. As you put these ideas into practice and reap the benefits, you will wonder why you were ever a doormat. This philosophy is not harder— it's smarter. You can't afford not to live this way.

So read on. And get ready for a prosperous, confident, assertive new life.

—Jeff Bredenberg
Senior Editor

Part 1

THE BEAT THE SYSTEM TOOL KIT

Arming Yourself Mentally

Hone Two Basic Weapons for Your Arsenal: Attitude and Goal Setting

Striking a deal is like striking a balance. It entails finding that mysterious, teetering point at which a buyer is willing to buy and a seller is willing to sell. And regardless of which side of the equation you're on in any given deal, your input as to where that point lies is going to depend, in large part, upon two factors: the attitude you adopt and the goals you set.

Suppose, for instance, that you're going to a baseball game. A guy comes up and shows you two $20 tickets for seats right behind your favorite team's dugout. You couldn't possibly buy this kind of ticket yourself, because they're in the special, VIP section. He's asking $50 for each.

What should you think? What do you want? Well, by the time you finish reading this book, you'll know how to answer these questions and apply them to virtually any daily transaction, whether you're trying to buy a house, sell a car, get the ultimate bargain on a sweater, or trim your taxes.

Moreover, you'll learn that the same approaches used to maximize a financial transaction also give you an edge in the more abstract areas of daily life. These skills, for example, will save you immeasurable amounts of time, anxiety, and effort as you enroll your child in college, wrangle for a promotion, contribute to church or charities, confront bias, or improve your health.

So what about that ticket scalper? First, let's examine two of the basic tools you'll need to make that call.

Attitude: Balance Is Crucial

"Sadly, the vast majority of us are passive participants in most transactions. We tend to accept what's presented to us," says Mark D. Tilson, Ph.D., a clinical psychologist based in Portland, Oregon. This passivity endures through a broad range of daily experiences—the price on a baseball ticket, a mechanic's repair bill, or the quality of a restaurant meal.

And if we're being passive, that leaves the other party to be active, to call the shots. If we sit by quietly, they set the rules and dictate the cost and quality of whatever it is we're negotiating for or trying to achieve. They determine where the balance will be struck. And, with sagging shoulders and furrowed brow, we just go along with it.

JUST WHO DO YOU THINK YOU ARE?

There are three kinds of attitude that we can adopt when we're engaged in a transaction, explains psychologist Gila Saks, Ph.D., of Tucson, Arizona, an expert in assertiveness training. They are passive, aggressive, and assertive.

The passive person, says Dr. Saks, is like a blade of grass on a blustery day, yielding to whichever way it's blown and pushed. Without question or comment, without protest or negotiation, the passive person accepts the terms, costs, and limits of the transaction as defined by the other.

He is an abdicator, letting someone else write the rules and then quietly obeying them. He buys items he doesn't want over the phone, gives his mechanic carte blanche to fix his car's transmission, and quietly takes the obstructed seat at the theater. When the guy at the stadium offers him tickets to the ball game, his only question is how he can handle paying $100 for them. And when he does, he'll not only be out a lot of money, he'll be an easy mark for every hustler at every future game.

The aggressive person, by contrast, knows what he wants and is determined to pursue it at all costs, with absolutely no regard for the other. If it serves his purpose, he will bully, cajole, threaten, extort, and intimidate in order to win the day, Dr. Saks says. Not only will he write the rules, but he'll do so with a ruthlessness that would make a Hun blush.

He parks in handicapped spaces, talks during movies, and lights cigarettes in a smoke-free zone. When the seller offers him the tickets, he backs the guy into a parking garage and threatens to call the cops unless he can have the tickets for 10 bucks. If he succeeds, though, they'll be the last tickets he gets this way, because he'll be marked by every ticket seller as a guy to avoid in the future.

Key Questions before You Negotiate

Here are three crucial questions you need to answer for yourself before you pursue a specific negotiation. They were developed by Stephen Pollan, an attorney, financial consultant, and co-author of *The Total Negotiator*.

What do I want? Can you set a specific and definable goal for yourself? Include all reasonable detail. For instance, "I want to buy a house" is not a goal. "I want to buy a modern, four-bedroom, two-bathroom house in the Oakmont section of town" is a goal.

Is it worth my time? Decide if it's negotiable. Is there room to cut a deal with the vendor? A steak dinner listed on a restaurant menu for $18.95 is going to cost you $18.95—trying to negotiate the price down will be a waste of your time. But a steak dinner ordered medium rare that comes out well done may be worth negotiating.

Is it important to me? Every negotiation is give and take. Decide what you will have to give to the process (time, thought, emotional energy) and determine if the outcome you hope for is worth the certain investment.

The most balanced, effective, and savvy of consumers is the assertive person who, according to Dr. Saks, knows what he wants, knows how to assert his rights, and also knows that winning need not entail someone else losing. He sends back the steak that's overdone (and leaves a good tip), gets the school crossing guard hired for his corner, and finagles a refund while returning a garment to a store whose policy is "no returns, no refunds."

He is the one with the attitude for successful negotiation. When the seller offers the tickets, he decides they may be worth it but not at the stated price, and he's ready to negotiate a better deal. If he succeeds in doing so, he'll be able to recycle that talent at all future games. He's probably read this book.

In short, good negotiators are assertive negotiators. Stephen Pollan, an attorney, financial consultant, and co-author of *The Total Negotiator*, says that this means six things.

1. They show initiative.
2. They take an active and open disposition toward any transaction.
3. They assume that nothing is chiseled in stone.
4. They aspire to what is fair.
5. They know that they can probably get a better deal than is being offered.
6. They set their own rules rather than blindly obeying someone else's.

Goals: Know Where You're Going

After attitude (a willingness to negotiate), goal setting (defining the desired outcome of the negotiation) is the most critical tool in the transaction process. After all, how can you get what you want if you don't know what it is?

JUST TELL ME WHAT YOU WANT

While many people believe that getting the best deal simply means, say, getting the lowest price on a particular item or service, this isn't always the case. There will be times when a low price is only one component of the whole negotiation package, Pollan says, and when what you gain in one area may cost you in another.

For instance, your child needs a new bike, and the two of you know which one you want to get. The bargain-basement price at Bill's Bike-o-Rama may seem like a good deal, but not if it doesn't include a warranty. House of Hobbies, on the other hand, offers the same bike at a slightly higher price, with a warranty, but you have to wait 10 months for delivery. Bike City has about the same price, with the warranty and immediate delivery, but you have to assemble the thing yourself—all 657 pieces.

What you need to be able to say is: "I want the best price I can get on this bicycle, with a warranty and immediate delivery and fully assembled." Then, you're ready to go out and make your best deal.

Under other circumstances, your wants are even less financially driven—but just as thoroughly defined. Maybe you want the peace of mind a high-tech home alarm brings. Maybe you want assurance that every penny you donate is really going to that sad-eyed waif you see in save-this-starving-child advertisements. Maybe you want a doctor who really *listens* to you.

In those cases, too, think deeply. Get specific. The rule of thumb for actually achieving what you want is to define as detailed and comprehensive a goal as possible for yourself. The more specific it is, Pollan says, the more likely you are to end up with it. To see attitude and goal setting in action, let's go back to the ballpark.

GETTING TO FIRST BASE

You came to the stadium expecting to step up to the ticket booth and purchase the best available seats you could get. You budgeted $30 for the two tickets (one for you, one for your daughter), plus $25 for snacks and a souvenir. Now, you know the price of tickets at the booth is nonnegotiable. You also know that within your price range, there are only certain areas of the stadium where you'll be able to sit. It all seems pretty cut-and-dried.

When the individual seller approaches you, however, the rules suddenly change: Because the price of the tickets is somewhat arbitrary, it's a wide-open game. The value of the ticket is not predetermined by the ball club; it's whatever value you two assign to it.

Let's watch some of the tactics of the assertive negotiator at play.

Decide what you really want. You need to do some pretty quick goal setting. If your goal includes getting into the stadium for $30 or less, then you know that you will not pay more for the premium seats that he's offering to sell you.

However, if your goal now includes, say, giving your daughter a truly extraordinary once-in-a-lifetime experience at the ballpark, you then have to determine what it's worth for you to do so. You have to ask yourself if you're willing to spend a little more on the tickets and less on the food. And if so, just exactly how are you now willing to divide your $55 pie?

Maybe there's even more to your goal than this. Maybe your goal is to get into the ballpark, give your daughter an extraordinary experience, and have $25 left over for food and souvenirs.

Let's say it is. Let's say that you define your goal as follows: "I want for my daughter and me to see this baseball game. Further, I want to purchase those two premium seats from the individual seller. Finally, I want to pay him no more than $30 total."

Now, you haven't left yourself much wiggle room, but, as Pollan recommends, you have made it clear what it is that you want. And you know that if you don't get it, you can always go back to your original goal of taking your kid to the game and splurging for a few extras. Nothing ventured, nothing gained.

Make your counteroffer. Armed with an assertive attitude, a clear understanding of what you want, and a slew of other tips you'll find in the rest of this book, you tell the guy that you're interested in his proposition and that you want to make a counteroffer. He's willing to listen.

"I'll give you $25 for the two tickets."

"Why, that's not even face value," he says, incredulously, "and you can't even buy these tickets at the ticket office. They're worth $100."

"They're not worth $100 if you can't find anyone who will pay $100 for them," you tell him.

Make it clear that you have options. "Look," you tell the ticket seller, "if you won't take my price for your tickets, I'll just get back in line and purchase others. However, according to my watch it's now 12:45. The game starts at 1:30. That means in 45 minutes your tickets will be worthless. So while I'm guaranteed to get what I want, you're not.

"Now, I know that you didn't pay face value for them. (Scalpers never do.) So what I'm offering assures you that you won't be stuck with two worthless tickets at game time and, no doubt, promises you a tidy profit to boot!"

Factor in your opponent's needs. The guy selling tickets doesn't like your offer. He says that he'll take his chances with someone else. You reply,

"I'll tell you what. The normal price for good seats is $30 for two. I will agree to wait until 1:20 before I purchase my tickets. If you haven't sold yours by then, I'll buy them from you for $30. If you have, I'll simply get my own tickets."

He agrees, and 10 minutes before game time you do your deal. Congratulations—you're learning how to play hardball.

BOTTOM LINE

Arming yourself to get what you want doesn't mean equipping yourself to destroy someone else. It means that transactions—financial or otherwise—happen within the context of a system, and you have determined to put that system to work to your maximum personal benefit. It also means that you have decided to assert your rights when someone else might be trying to abuse them, you are willing to rewrite the system's rules when necessary, you know exactly what it is that you want, and, as you'll see in later chapters, you can think strategically as to how best to get it.

WORDS TO THE WISE

Attitude: The mental disposition you take toward any transaction. It will be the fundamental determinant in the outcome of the transaction.

Goal: In very specific terms, what you want to come out of any transaction and what you're willing to pay in order to reach your goal.

ALLIES

Awaken the Giant Within, by Tony Robbins (Simon and Schuster). Encourages readers to harness their internal power and inherent assertiveness and apply them to personal transactions.

The Total Negotiator, by Stephen Pollan and Mark Levine (Avon Books). Strategies for successfully negotiating your way through a variety of situations.

Communicating Effectively

Have Your Say and Get Your Way—
Without Being a Jerk

Jack and Betty have been married for a little more than 16 years now, and as is their custom, their day starts at the kitchen table with a simple breakfast of cereal and orange juice. The morning newspaper is there as well.

One morning when they sit down, Betty begins to give Jack a running inventory of some of the things she needs to do that day—attend a board meeting, have lunch with so-and-so, finish a report, pick up some dry cleaning—pretty mundane stuff. Simultaneously, Jack opens the paper wide and begins to read the sports section, in effect, creating a thin but impenetrable paper moat between the two of them.

Betty, incensed at being boxed out like this, pounds her fist on the table and, with gritted teeth, exclaims, "Jack, you just don't communicate with me anymore!"

Poor Betty couldn't be more right. Or more wrong. On the one hand, her flaccid husband was tuning out his life's partner by burying his nose in the trivia of last night's box scores. He was neither talking nor listening.

But on the other hand, Jack was indeed communicating, with all the subtlety of a tank at a tea party. What he was wordlessly saying was, "I don't care to deal with you, Betty. I would rather read a bunch of irrelevant drivel in the morning paper than hear about your impending day. So leave me alone!"

Jack and Betty's marital problems aside, the point here is that when we communicate with one another, we do so with a wide array of equipment at our disposal—voices, hands, feet, facial expressions, fists, even newspapers. Communication, as the eminent philosopher Mortimer Adler pointed out, is the art of making contact with the heart and mind of another person. And if we make that contact for the purpose of getting something we want from them, we'd best understand some of the basic do's and don'ts of effective communication.

Complaining: The Art of Change

Complain. Now here's a word that rings about as gently to the ears as fingernails across a grade-school blackboard, conjuring up as it does images of impossible-to-please bratty children—squeaky whiners incessantly nagging their parents for another ice cream cone, a puppy, or a bathroom break at the next gas station.

But in fact, shorn of its negative imagery, a complaint is a most necessary form of communication. Complaint is simply a feeling you register when there is a reasonable change you want to effect and there are possible obstacles to your effecting it, says Laurie Schloff, director of executive training for the Speech Improvement Company in Boston and author of the audiotape *Smart Speaking*.

Say, for instance, that you've gone to one of those glitzy, high-end restaurants where reservations are next to impossible and your table is next to the kitchen. Unless you want to blow a week's pay on a night's meal eaten amidst the bang and clatter of breaking dishes, you're going to have to communicate a—you got it—complaint.

Or suppose your horticulturally inspired next-door neighbor has taken to mowing his 2½-acre lawn at 6:00 A.M. on Saturdays, disrupting the one morning during the week you've permitted yourself to sleep past daybreak. Now, there are any number of ways to approach this situation. In all likelihood you'll rule out taking the drastic step of moving away from his noise or the defeatist step of living with his habit. You're likely to choose some kind of strategy that entails registering your objections with the hope that he will rearrange his schedule. In this case, you want to change a noisy Saturday morning to a quiet one, and the obstacle to your effecting it is your neighbor and his mower. In other words, you complain.

So, whether it's a good evening's meal, a good morning's sleep, or any other little pleasantry to which you're entitled and from which you're being kept, a legitimate complaint—artfully crafted, strategically timed, and properly enacted—can indeed be among the most usefully eloquent forms of communication, Schloff says. What are the key elements to keep in mind with complaint-oriented communication? Preparation, strategy, and action.

Four Secrets of Effective Communication

Philosopher Mortimer Adler identified these four rules for effective communication.

1. Remember that setting is important. Where and when a conversation is to occur can be as important as the conversation's content.
2. Know what kind of conversation you're going to have before you have it. It's like knowing what kind of book you're going to read before you read it.
3. When you're listening to the other party, do so with the same enthusiasm you have when you speak.
4. Remember that excitement can quickly transform itself into rudeness, so don't interrupt.

90 PERCENT PREPARATION, 10 PERCENT EXECUTION

There are four questions worth asking ourselves in preparation for registering any complaint, offers trial attorney Gerry Spence in his best-selling book *How to Argue and Win Every Time*.

What do you want? To make a change happen, we have to be able to clearly define both what we want that change to look like and what impediments must be removed.

What is the principal argument that supports you? That is, are we indeed entitled to insist that these changes be made? Are they reasonable?

What are the facts? Before we try to implement change, we must have a strong command of enough data to make our argument compelling and persuasive. "You have a chance of winning an argument only if you're an expert on your situation," points out attorney and financial consultant Stephen Pollan, co-author of *The Total Negotiator*.

What is your story? How are you going to convey your argument to whomever can help or hinder you in your effort to bring about change? What will your words be?

So when that lawn mower–head is ripping up the sod by the dawn's early light, you would do well first to prepare your argument before you wage it.

- What do you want? To be able to sleep uninterrupted on your weekends.
- What supports this? The truism that lawn-mowing schedules can be adjusted far more easily than sleep schedules.
- What are the facts? You know that most people are still asleep in the early morning hours, that your neighbor's noise clearly penetrates the

walls of your home, and that your neighborhood association has defined 11:00 P.M. to 8:00 A.M. as quiet time.

- Finally, what is your story? That he's entitled to take care of his property, but surely there's a way he can do that and not bother you.

CHOOSE YOUR TURF

The logical extension of preparation is strategy, a game plan tailored to maximize your effectiveness as a communicator. As Adler points out in his book *How to Speak, How to Listen*, the setting in which a discussion ensues is at least as important as the discussion itself. In fact, the fundamental elements of a good strategy for registering a complaint include the right place, the right time, the right attitude, and the right opening.

Find neutral ground. Let's say that you're now prepared to talk with your neighbor. You might ask him over to your house for a visit, but chances are that the minute he finds out what the subject of the invitation is, he'll feel ambushed, lured onto your territory, amidst your family, to discuss a fundamentally territorial issue. There's a strong likelihood that he's going to feel set up, uncomfortable, and defensive, especially if he sees himself as outnumbered.

You might avoid these discomforts by going over to his place. But what if his family is home? What are the chances that he'll feel embarrassed by what you have to say in their presence? A home is a powerfully symbolic place to most of us, a place where we feel safe and in charge, where any threats to that safety, however great or small, are likely to be met with intense resistance.

So you decide that a neutral place is the best arena in which to carry on this conversation. You invite him for a walk. That's a good move, Schloff says, because, by and large, confrontational conversations are most effectively conducted in a place where both persons can feel relatively safe, secure, and at ease.

Find a low-key time. Timing is the art of knowing when not to do something, and nobody seems to grasp this better than children. Kids seem to have an instinctive sense of when to present their parents with the news that their allowance is insufficient, that their report card is inexcusable, or that their mom's favorite vase is now unrecognizable. Call it manipulation, devilishness, or control, but there's no better master of timing than a seven-year-old with a sticky problem.

So learn a thing or two from kids. Don't be impulsive, be strategic. Choose your time, Schloff says. Make certain that your neighbor has it to spare, that he's not going to feel rushed or distracted. Choose a day when he hasn't cut his lawn so that it doesn't appear that you're simply reacting to something that's happened that morning. Avoid engaging him in the middle

Six Secrets of Effective Complaining

Attorney and financial consultant Stephen Pollan, co-author of *The Total Negotiator*, offers these six tips for effective complaining.

1. Confront reluctantly. Weigh the personal pros and cons before you decide whether to complain. Make sure that the net is worth it to you.
2. Set yourself up to win. Learn everything about your situation first.
3. Complain in person. Letters can be ignored, and it's easy for your opponent to be unreasonable over the telephone.
4. In complaining to a large company, start at the bottom. Respect their protocol and, as necessary, work your way up.
5. Stay cool. Remember that openly irate customers are less likely to be treated deferentially by their opponents.
6. Push the "up" button. When you aren't getting satisfaction from someone, request to speak to their supervisor. This often works like a cattle prod on a reluctant steer.

of a day, replete as it is with interruptions and impositions. Find time instead in the freshness of a morning or the calm of an evening, preferably when the streets are relatively quiet so that you can both enjoy a sense of privacy. Choose—or, if need be, create—a time when both of you are likely to give undivided attention to the issue at hand. This means not only that your schedules permit it but also that your frames of mind encourage it, Schloff says.

For attitude, easy does it. You want to create a safe mood, so decide ahead of time what your attitude should look like—that is, how you want to be perceived by your listener. Especially when dealing with a friend or neighbor, it's good to remember Adler's wisdom on the subject: "Communication is aborted when the confrontation of speaker and listener involves the suppression of one or the other."

So despite the fact that you might consider your neighbor's behavior exceedingly selfish, thoughtless, or invasive, and despite whatever measure of discomfort and grief it has caused you, you decide to approach him in a calm, conciliatory manner. Know that however angry or frustrated you might feel, the only attitudes and feelings worth revealing are those that will help the two of you change the thing you're trying to change, Schloff observes.

Find nonthreatening words. Having created the right mental and physical venues, you then want to devise the right opening line. Assume that your neighbor is oblivious to the problem, so your raising it might hit him like a bolt from the blue. Be gentle. Assume also that the more accusatory and the more personal you make your opening remark, the more likely he is to go on the defensive. Be exceedingly nonjudgmental. And assume that your first words will set the tenor and tone of whatever follows. Be encouraging.

WITH COMPLAINING, STYLE IS SUBSTANCE

When you actually get down to discussing your complaint with the other person, remember Jack and his newspaper fortress. The two of you are communicating with one another not just with text but with subtext, too—the intonations and subtle body gestures that accompany your words.

"The tone and inflection of our delivery is at least as important as the content," Schloff says. "These factors, in addition to the body language with which we communicate—gestures, postures, facial expressions—probably speak greater volumes to our audience than the words themselves."

A young child pounding her fists into the ground, a young adult weeping at the closing scene of *Romeo and Juliet*, an old man staring dejectedly as the doctor delivers some bad news—all of these are profound, if wordless, revelations of the deepest stirrings of the human heart. And any change you want to effect must be communicated from here as well as from your voice.

Thus, an opening line like, "Bob, I think that we have a surmountable problem," if delivered through clenched teeth with pointed finger, will be met with equal parts resistance, resentment, and rejection. And you'll have lost your argument before you even deliver it. But if they're spoken directly, compassionately, eye-to-eye, with a tone of voice that says, "I like you, I value our friendship, I want to work this out, and I believe we will," chances are that your next step will be figuring out not if the two of you can solve your differences, but how.

Remember, Schloff says, if the voice is saying one thing and the body another, your audience will be far more attentive to the unspoken signals than to the words. And only when the two are in sync can you possibly deliver an argument persuasive enough to get anybody to change anything.

Calls and Letters: Know the Limitations

Nothing can take the place of face-to-face communications. But technology has brought us into increasingly tighter spheres of interaction, notes Gavin Eadie, associate director in the information and technology division at the University of Michigan in Ann Arbor. On any given day it's no great wonder for a physician in Fargo, North Dakota, to consult on a surgical procedure by computer in Dallas, while a fourth-grade class in Sacramento, California, is being lectured by an astronaut in outer space. So instead of just fixating on the limitations of these less-than-ideal conversations from afar, we would do well to figure out how to use them to our advantage.

REACH OUT (SOMETIMES) AND TOUCH SOMEONE

If you're trying to beat the system, the telephone is one of your greatest assets and worst liabilities. If you were a horse trainer, you wouldn't use a thoroughbred to pull a hay wagon or a Clydesdale to run at Pimlico. Likewise, the phone is eminently useful to the system-beater who best understands its utility and its limitations. Here are some strategies for its most effective use.

Canvass the country. Shopping for the best price on a weight machine? Fax machine? Pasta machine? Not only can you comparison shop in your own neighborhood, but through the proliferation of catalogs, toll-free numbers and Internet Web sites, you can now scour the nation from coast to coast in search of the biggest bang for your buck. And it's axiomatic that the broader the marketplace, the greater the competition, and thus the lower the price. So if you live in Missoula, Montana, and you've worked the phones and found that you can order that fax machine from a warehouse in Little Rock, Arkansas, at one-third the price offered by a local supplier, show your local the Little Rock price, give them a chance to beat it (they very well might), and take your better deal.

Massage a client. If you're in a line of work that has you communicating with clients all over the nation or the world, use your phone to touch base with them, especially when you don't have business to discuss. Call them at random, ask how they are, stay on just long enough to let them know that you had them in mind and just short enough to keep from making a pest of yourself. The occasional massage, however brief or subtle, can nonetheless be of enduring worth.

Move like lightning. Remember that when you're considering negotiating any kind of a deal for yourself, you always need to ask whether it's worth the money and the time. While the phone can depersonalize personal interactions, use it as an expediter when time is of the essence and personal appeal isn't.

Beware the crutch. There's a danger in becoming too reliant upon the phone . . . not to augment face-to-face communication but to replace it. That's like replacing gourmet cooking with fast food. One has to distinguish between the phone as necessary and the phone as merely convenient. The same goes, naturally, for the telephone's offspring—fax, voice mail, and e-mail.

Remember what's missing. Telephone conversations are a form of disembodied communication open to all manner of diversion. Because the two parties are not physically present to one another, much of the nuance of communication (gesture, inflection, body language) is lost, on top of which, simultaneous to our conversing, our eyes and minds tend to wander, like moths toward a distant bulb, to any little distraction.

WHEN TO PUT IT IN WRITING

As with the telephone, the written word can be a boon or a bane, depending upon how it's employed. Here are a couple of reasons why.

Most apparent, of course, is the fact that a good letter helps to form a paper trail when one is needed. Say, for example, that you feel that you're being discriminated against in your workplace. As a later chapter will show, the written correspondences you exchange with your superiors can provide the kind of black-and-white documentation that will avoid the clumsy and embarrassing war of "he said, she said" later on, when the issue finally hits the surface.

In addition, written correspondence affords you the opportunity to compose your thoughts and arguments rather than having to ad-lib them. So while a disgruntled bride and groom who find the wrong meal being served at their reception might get some immediate cathartic satisfaction out of screaming at the caterer, if instead they cool off a little bit, write an articulate, convincing, and somewhat threatening letter to the head of the catering agency (with a copy sent to the local Better Business Bureau), chances are that they'll be able to give the offending party plenty to chew on.

On the other hand, Pollan notes, two serious limitations must be kept in mind as well. First, letters can be ignored, so they should never be the only weapon in your arsenal. And second, they can slow down a negotiating process so that what might take a few hours to work out face-to-face can take weeks through the mail. If you're in a hurry then, do what Schloff suggests: Compose your arguments in writing but deliver them in person.

Finally, of course, remember that sitting down in front of a piece of paper doesn't make you a scribe any more than sitting down in a garage makes you a car. If a letter is going to be effective, it has to be:

- Literate (otherwise, you discredit yourself)
- Brief (otherwise, it won't be read)
- Thorough (otherwise, you will only confuse your issue)
- On a letterhead, if possible (which conveys a certain level of maturity and authority)

REMEMBER, DIALOGUE IS EVERYTHING

Dialogue is the open and frank interchange of ideas in search of mutual understanding and harmony. What this means to the would-be system-beater is that nothing is lost as long as some form of communication is occurring. And nothing is gained as long as communication isn't occurring.

Remember, throughout this book you'll find suggestions of how best to communicate your complaints, desires, and needs in specific situations. And while those situations might drastically differ from one another, there is one constant: The only point at which dialogue no longer serves you any purpose is the point at which you have fully achieved that which you set out to achieve.

Against all odds and obstacles, no matter how long or frustrating the fight, keep the lines of communication open. More disputes die unresolved from apathy and attrition than from a protracted inability of negotiators to find that point of "mutual understanding and harmony" where deals can be made—and systems can be beaten.

BOTTOM LINE

Communication is a broad term that refers to all the tools at your disposal that can be used to exchange thoughts, feelings, and ideas with another person. As such, your ability to prevail in any transaction is inextricably tied to your ability to communicate effectively.

WORDS TO THE WISE

Body language: Refers to the myriad nonverbal movements and gestures we employ when communicating with another person. They are powerful, if often subconscious, communicative tools.

Telephone protocol: The difference between speaking with someone face-to-face and speaking with them over the telephone is the difference between watching a fireworks display in person and listening to it on the radio. Compensate by putting special emphasis on intonations, not allowing awkward silences to clog the phone lines and verbalizing feelings and thoughts that might otherwise be communicated physically.

ALLIES

Great American Gripe Book, by Matthew Lesko (Information USA). Quick, witty, and useful guide to complaining.

Making Things Happen—Your Way

Harness the Power of Information

You've had the dress rehearsal for beating the system. You're mentally and physically prepared. You know your cues, your lines, and the props. The rest of this book is about taking information and using it to stage a winning performance, and convincing others that you are who you say you are, know what you seem to know, and deserve what you think you deserve. In short, making converts out of skeptics.

Remember that whether you're selling a house, buying a car, planning a wedding, or suing your employer, your sole aim is to get from the transaction what *you* have determined to be in your best interest.

So here are some pointers before you take center stage.

Level the Playing Field

If you're facing an uphill battle, level your playing field. In any transaction, you want to garner as much power as possible to put yourself on an equal footing with your adversary, says attorney and financial consultant Stephen Pollan, co-author of *The Total Negotiator*. There are three ways to get at this power, the first involving little more than paying attention.

TURN INSIDE INFORMATION TO YOUR FAVOR

Let's say that Betty and Bob want to buy the house that Sam and Susan have on the market. As they consider the transaction, Betty and Bob learn two things: Sam and Susan have already purchased a new home in a distant city, to which they must move within five weeks, and the taxes on the home Sam and Susan want to sell are due to go up in the next fiscal quarter. These are useful little bits of information—both about the other party and about the item being negotiated—that Betty and Bob will employ to their advantage if they actually sit down to negotiate a deal. In this instance, then, a couple has leveled their playing field by garnering power in the form of "inside" information that can favorably affect the selling price of the home.

The second source of power is what Robert Bolton, Ph.D., calls cooperative problem solving. Dr. Bolton, a behavioral scientist in Cazenovia, New York; president of the training company Ridge Associates; and author of numerous books on human interactions, notes that even in contentious or adversarial negotiations, knowing what your opponent needs to get out of the deal can help establish the boundaries of the transaction. And it helps you decide whether it's in your best interest to pursue it.

STRIVE FOR HARMONY, LOWER THE DISSONANCE

Playing fields can be leveled simply by knowing how best to present yourself to the other. This is what Pollan calls lowering the dissonance between you and your opponent. Included in this technique is the elimination of anything that might serve as a barrier—perceived or real—between you and them. Here are some examples.

A business executive in an expensive Italian suit refuses to shake the grease-encrusted hand of the auto mechanic to whom he's entrusting his sports car for repair. This could engender such hostility that the mechanic will stall the work and overcharge him just as a form of retribution.

On the other hand, the executive who greets the mechanic by extending his hand and saying "Look, I may be an expert in finances, but you're the expert in cars. Perhaps you can do some work for me" has lowered the dissonance between himself and the mechanic. This creates an atmosphere of mutual professional respect instead of resentment.

Or take the example of Jenny, who has an appointment with her supervisor to discuss her request for a raise. Jenny could shuffle in, head bowed, and, in an effort to appeal to the supervisor's sense of pity, plead for the extra money on the grounds that she simply can't get by on what she's currently being paid. In other words, she can lower her own status by simultaneously elevating his, surrender any shred of power she might have at her disposal, and stake her financial future on the slender, oxymoronic reed of corporate mercy.

On the other hand, she could also strut into the appointment with an air of confidence; indicate that confidence with her words, her demeanor, even her choice of clothing; and then communicate in a persuasive manner why it is in both her best interest and the company's that she be given a pay increase. By putting her request in terms of her value to the company, and by implying that both she and her supervisor hold the company's interests at heart, Jenny is elevating her position of power to that of her opponent. At this point her raise becomes a matter of mutual self-interest rather than unilateral pity.

Who's in Charge Here?

You've purchased airplane tickets, but now, because of unforeseen circumstances, you can't use them. When you go to the airline's local ticket office, you're told by a clerk that he cannot refund your money for one or more of the following reasons.

- "It's against policy."
- "I'm just doing my job."
- "I don't make the rules; I just follow them."

Sound familiar? Sound frustrating? Then here's some sound advice: It's time for what Pollan calls pushing the "up" button.

WORK YOUR WAY UP TO THE DECISION MAKER

Beating a system entails knowing who's in charge of that system, the keeper of the keys, the guardian of the sacred rules. In the example cited above, a clerk sitting in an outpost office regurgitating company policy hasn't the power to decide his own lunch break, let alone what customer should get company money. At best he serves as a functionary, a buffer between the customer and the power brokers. He measures his performance in terms of how effectively he can keep the former away from the latter. Many people mistakenly accept his word as *the* word—final and irrevocable, a consumer's death sentence.

So how do you avoid him? You don't. That is, you recognize that, while he's not in a position to give you what you want, he certainly is in a position to either impede or expedite the process of getting you to the person who is. So instead of trying to get around him, you recruit him and get him to hit the "up" button for you. You say, for instance: "I understand that it's policy not to offer me a refund, and I understand that you're responsible for carrying out that policy. You've been very helpful in explaining that to me. Perhaps you can further help me out by directing me to the person here at Wing Nut Airlines that I might speak to about making an exception to the policy."

By addressing him in this manner you do three things, says Pollan.

1. You imply to him that you recognize and accept the limitations of his position.
2. You acknowledge to him that he has done his job in a good and responsible manner.
3. You give him another opportunity to be helpful to you, that is, to use what little power he does have.

Does this guarantee you success in your endeavor? Of course not. But it's sure to get you going in the right direction.

That clerk may only get you from the basement to the first floor, when, in fact, the real power lies in the penthouse. Your best bet is to remember that, as the English author Samuel Johnson once wrote, "great works are performed not by strength but by perseverance." Be ready to make your ascent one story at a time.

CHECK YOUR EMOTIONS AT THE DOOR

"A dialogue is more than two monologues."
—Max Kampleman, U.S. arms control negotiator

The single element common to all negotiations is that something is at stake for both parties. Thus, there's a temptation to approach negotiations with a kind of victor/vanquished mentality.

But as Dr. Bolton points out, when your desire is to win at any cost, "emotions get in the way of effective negotiations. We can get petulant and easily angered, because we have a personal stake in what we're trying to achieve. We'd do well to control those emotions, if for no other reason than the fact that they are barriers. They'll keep us from getting what we want."

"Remember, against all temptation, to stay calm," adds Curtis Loewe, manager of consumer services for the Minnesota Attorney General's office in St. Paul. "Don't personalize the process. It's business, so detach yourself and treat it that way."

As Kampleman's quote reminds us, negotiating implies a cool and patient ability to listen to and respect the position of the other, with the added knowledge that there's something they need from this process as well.

Let's say, for instance, that your neighbor's oak tree hangs over your backyard and you spend the better part of spring mornings raking its buds and fall afternoons raking its leaves. Irritated at the tree's incursion into your life and tired of cleaning up its seasonal castoffs, you're about two acorns shy of taking a chain saw to the beast. Instead, you go next door and pitch a fit with the neighbor, demanding that he take it down before things really turn ugly. He bellows back that the law is on his side, that the tree stays, and that if you don't like it, you can move. Back and forth you go, each screaming your righteous indignation to an increasingly deaf audience. Threat and counterthreat.

It may make for good street theater. But nothing's accomplished, in part because you've both personalized the situation, refused to dignify the other's position, and refused to hear the other's thinking.

Had you gone for dialogue instead of competing monologues, the neighbor might have learned that you don't necessarily want the tree gone, that you just want it to stop fouling up your springs and falls. You, in turn,

A Poker Master's Six Rules for Bluffing

Steve Fox, executive director of the National Poker Association, has been playing and winning poker hands for more than 40 years.

"Remember the adage 'You can't make a silk purse out of a sow's ear'? Well, winning a pot with a bluff seems to contradict that principle!" says the Boulder, Colorado, resident.

Bluffing is simply a matter of good timing, the right situation, proper psychology, and identifying your best target, says Fox. Here are some of his most important tips.

1. Bluffing is the art of knowing what to conceal and what to reveal.
2. What you have is less important than what your opponent *thinks* you have.
3. Your claim must be possible and plausible.
4. Bluff the right player. Identify the person that you think will fold under pressure, and then isolate that person. Don't bluff more than one person at a time.
5. Make your supporting evidence consistent with the bluff.
6. There must be tangible threat. Your opponent must be afraid of possible loss.

might have learned that the tree was a cherished part of his property with loaded emotional significance—that his kids learned to climb on it when they were young, just as his grandchildren do today. And that his own great-grandfather planted it four generations ago.

By respecting the legitimacy of the other's claim on the discussion, while not capitulating to it, you jointly create the possibility to reach a solution that you can both live with. "Negotiations are simply human relationships hard at work," Dr. Bolton says.

Special Tools:
Dig Deeper into the Arsenal

A number of years ago a group of residents living in a low-income section of Baltimore wanted to meet with the president of a local bank. Their complaint was that the bank was redlining their neighborhood, refusing to grant mortgages and other loans to people living and working there. After numerous failed attempts to get a response from the bank president, they decided they needed to get his attention.

So on a particularly busy Friday (payday, a high-volume day for banks), about 60 of the residents, all of whom had accounts at the bank, went down and stood in tellers' lines. When their turns came, each one would present the teller with a particularly complex transaction.

Some brought buckets of pennies to deposit. Some who spoke Spanish suddenly forgot how to speak English and tried to conduct business in their native tongue. Some asked the tellers for obscure information about their accounts and appeared to have a difficult time understanding the tellers' responses. Some brought in great reams of outdated documents in need of interpretation. As each concluded his business, he would then get back in line and wait for another such transaction.

As you might imagine, bedlam soon broke out in the bank. When the president came down from his office to see what was going on, the organizers told him that he had ignored repeated phone calls and letters and that they were doing what was necessary to secure a meeting with him.

They got their meeting. And, by the way, their loans.

If any of the 60 residents had tried to get the bank president's attention, they would have been treated like a fly in an elephant's ear—a minor irritant best ignored. But instead they networked—that is, they pulled together a group of people with similar interests and needs. They organized those people around clearly defined actions (disrupting business at the bank) in pursuit of a clearly defined goal (to get a meeting with the head of the bank). And the group accomplished what no one person could have dreamed of.

And, as Dr. Bolton notes, your network needn't always be *acting* as a whole to be effective: "People are naturally eager to help each other out. When you enter into a negotiation process knowing that you have the support of others, you are emboldened. The power you have in that negotiation is not only your own power but also the power of the people who are behind you."

So while a bevy of friends and supporters can't be physically present when you go in to, say, argue that speeding ticket, their collective wisdom, ideas, and encouragement can equip and embolden you when you step up to the judge and go it alone.

FIGHTING THE BAD FIGHT: DEAL WITH BIAS

It's not enough to equip yourself for a fair deal when your opponent is stacking the deck against you. The qualified employee passed over for a promotion because he's African-American, the elderly couple browbeaten by an unscrupulous solicitor for a bogus charity, and the young woman who's given a runaround by a sleazy plumber are all victimized by what Dr. Bolton calls unsubstantiated assumptions that need to be uprooted.

Know the stereotype. If you're going to uproot any bias in your own defense, keep an eye out in those places where it's most likely to sprout, says

Beware These Buzzwords

People who try to sell you goods or services can use impressive-sounding words that really mean little or nothing, says Curtis Loewe, manager of consumer services for the Minnesota Attorney General's office in St. Paul. Resist the lure of these buzzwords.

Sale: A sale can be a figment of your imagination. If a sale price is proclaimed every other week, it's not really a sale.

Low-maintenance: This means absolutely nothing. "Low" is in the eyes of the beholder—it can't be gauged, regulated, or legally challenged.

Limited warranty: Here's a similarly meaningless term, with the emphasis usually on "limited" rather than "warranty." It's a phrase that often excludes far more than it includes.

Company policy: This is an invention, an arbitrary concept presented as law. Company policy is always negotiable.

Sherry Kane, director of the New York area office of 9to5/National Association of Working Women, a nonprofit women's organization.

A gay man applying for a job, for example, needs to know what questions might be asked by a biased interviewer—things that wouldn't be asked of a heterosexual applicant. And if you're straight, Anglo, middle-class, and male, you may think yourself immune from bias. But just remember, you're going to be an old man one day. Think you'll be treated any differently then than you are now?

Remember: Conditions change. A recent graduate of an all-women's college may have experienced no visible bias during her studies, but the day she steps off campus to apply for a job, she may find herself in a whole new ball game, says Pollan. Similarly, a citizen of one country suddenly transferred by his company to offices in another might find himself measured not solely by the quality of his work but by the accident of his heritage.

Head 'em off at the pass. There may be times when it's both possible and useful to debunk the bias. People don't generally like having to justify their own existence, but there are occasions when, as Dr. Bolton suggests, uprooting the bias can play to your advantage.

Say you are a woman wanting to purchase a new car and a salesman has you pegged as someone who just cares about the cosmetics of the vehicle rather than its technology. Do your homework ahead of time. When you go in and the salesman's asking you if you like the cute little vanity mirror hidden under the sun visor, you can ask him in return if the engine block is aluminum alloy, whether the brakes are breathable disc ABS (antilock braking system), and whether the automatic overdrive employs the same gear ratio as the five-speed manual.

Be ready to cite the law. The racist home owner who refuses to sell his place to an African-American couple on the flimsy rationale that "I'll sell to whomever I want" is seriously misinformed. The Fair Housing Act outlaws this very practice, notes New York City civil rights attorney Michael Krinsky, and a bevy of other federal, state, and local antibias laws protects people from discrimination on the job, in lending institutions, in recreational centers, in private neighborhoods, in insurance and other benefits programs, and even (in some areas) in that age-old bastion of exclusivity, the country club. So regardless of whether you use the law, know it.

Bottom Line

Beating the system is not a passive exercise. It's an active pursuit that requires a healthy dose of personal initiative, with a little "sweat equity" thrown in for good measure. Your primary goal in any transaction is neither to defeat your opponents nor to capitulate to them. You want whatever is fair and necessary to attain that to which you are entitled.

Words to the Wise

Cooperative problem solving: Recognizing and respecting your opponent's stake in a negotiation and determining whether both parties' needs can be met.

Level the playing field: Gathering information on your opponent or the subject of your negotiation in order to minimize the real or perceived power of that opponent.

Network: A broad and connected community of people with a shared set of interests, values, and aims.

Push the "up" button: Finding the person who is vested with the power and authority to handle your complaint or honor your request.

Allies

Getting to Yes: Negotiating Agreements without Giving In, by Roger Fischer (Penguin). How to negotiate from a position of mutual self-interest.

Rules for Radicals: A Practical Primer for Realistic Radicals, by Saul Alinsky (Vintage Press). Offers clear advice on how to network and organize to produce change.

You Can Negotiate Anything, by Herb Cohen (Audio Tapes). A good starter audiotape, offering tips on basic negotiation tactics and dynamics. It can be ordered at your local bookstore.

Part 2

HOME LIFE

Trimming Your Household Bills

With Some Simple Changes, Tap Into Big Savings

They arrive every month, as surely as the lunar phases. Plop, plop, plop through the mail slot—phone bill, power bill, cable bill. Maybe the Amish have it right, you tell yourself wearily. How nice it would be to unhook those steel umbilicals from the corner of your house.

If you're like most Americans, you dutifully shell out at least $160 every month in telephone, electric, gas, and television fees. While that may not seem like a lot at first glance, those bills take a roughly $2,000 bite out of your annual take-home pay.

New competition threatens to turn plump monopolies into leaner, meaner price-cutting machines—which eventually will be good news for your wallet. Because of the landmark Telecommunications Act of 1996, for example, the cable industry, which in 1993 posted the highest profit margins in the communications industry (about 20 percent), faces new rivals eager for a crack at their multibillion-dollar market.

However, "The cable industry is a pretty big boat," notes Jim Lande, a Federal Communications Commission (FCC) industry economist. "Even major changes take a long time to work through." So despite regulatory upheavals that are pending in the utility and telephone industries as well, don't hold your breath waiting for lower rates for your basic household utilities. Monopolies are slow to break up.

Until there are competing utilities in place for you to bargain with, you're in no position to lower the basic rates that you're being charged. But you can still take a few simple steps to trim each of your monthly bills. Make wise decisions to get the best service that companies offer. When you do, the savings will pile up by year's end and you'll be a more satisfied customer.

Energy: Reduce Those Shocking Expenses

Energy efficiency is the classic win-win situation. Not only does it save you money but also it benefits the environment.

The average household spends almost $1,300 per year on energy, including electricity, natural gas, oil, and other fuels. The U.S. Department of Energy estimates that without sacrificing comfort, a family can readily save 30 percent on home energy bills. That's almost $400 a year.

And because energy conservation is still a hot national issue, information and cash incentives are easy to come by.

First, Plug the Leaks

What you need is a pared-down list of energy-saving tips: where to start, what you can realistically accomplish (in light of your busy schedule), and how to get your utility company and others to work for you. By focusing your efforts you can save your 30 percent—and then some.

Note: All references to electricity prices are based on the U.S. average price per kilowatt-hour (kWh), 8.4 cents.

Batten down the attic. Almost half of that $1,300 a year in total energy costs goes to heating and air-conditioning. The least expensive and most effective way to trim that expense is to avoid wasting precious warm and cool air.

"A well-insulated attic is Energy Efficiency 101," says John Morrill, co-author of *Consumer Guide to Home Energy Savings.* "It's an area that's screaming for the home owner's attention." Add fiberglass batting (rectangular insulation strips) between the joists to contain cool air in the summer and to keep heat from following its natural escape route. Be smart, though: If there is already partial insulation and if the attic is floored and drywalled, it's probably not worth the effort.

Before purchasing the insulation, you'll need to determine your area's recommended R-value—an insulation material's resistance to winter heat loss or summer heat gain. (The higher the R-value, the more effective the insulation.) You can ask for assistance at your local lumber or home-improvement center. Based on your location and type of heat, they will tell you the U.S. Department of Energy's recommended value for your area.

Button up your house. Sealing leaks is another highly effective step. Think of it this way: The typical leaky home has the equivalent of a two-foot square hole in its shell.

First, take stock of hidden air leaks, Morrill advises. Either have a professional energy auditor inspect your house (utility companies sometimes send auditors free of charge) or do it yourself by feeling for drafts around problem spots. Some of the most common culprits are windows, doors, chimneys, attic hatches, water pipes, electrical outlets, and window-unit air conditioners.

What you plug the holes with depends on the size and location. Fill cracks less than ¼" wide with caulk. If it's a visible joint, choose a paintable caulk. For larger gaps, use a flexible foam tubing, called backer rod, or crack filler. It's sold in coils and is available at hardware stores. Around windows and doors, apply thin spring metal, rolled vinyl, or adhesive-backed foam weather stripping (all low-cost, easy-to-install items). Seal larger holes with rigid foam insulation.

For once, welcome a setback. Sure, you occasionally nudge the thermostat down a notch when you hop into bed. But be honest: Do you remember to do it often enough to reap substantial savings? What you need is a setback thermostat, which automatically adjusts itself depending on when you need more or less heating or cooling, Morrill says.

Widely available, these clock thermostats generally cost $50 to $100 and can be used for heating and cooling. The investment can pay for itself in less than a year of use, Morrill says.

ATTACK THE MAJOR POWER HOGS

Appliances account for half of your monthly electric bill. But don't waste your time worrying about the coffeemaker, the microwave oven, and other low-use items. Go straight for the electricity gluttons: the refrigerator and the water heater. Together, they cost about $300 per year to run.

The best way to save is to buy one of today's state-of-the-art energy misers. "When you buy a major appliance, that's sort of just a down payment," says Morrill. "Then every month when you pay your gas bill or your electric bill, that's additional installments." Compared with a model from the early 1980s, today's refrigerator will cost about one-third as much to operate. That means savings of about $100 a year.

Cool the kitchen. Contrary to popular opinion, studies show that cleaning a refrigerator's coils does not result in noticeable energy savings. However, keeping the kitchen cool can. A rise in kitchen temperature of 15°F can double a refrigerator's energy use. No, don't turn up the air-conditioning. Rather, consumer experts recommend that you ventilate the kitchen and give the refrigerator's motor ample room to breathe. If possible, place the fridge out of direct sunlight and away from the stove and dishwasher, which create heat.

Tame the hot-water tap. Annual water heating costs average $180, according to the U.S. government. For every 10°F you lower your water heater's thermostat, you'll save 3 to 5 percent of that cost. A setting of 120°F is sufficient for most families. If your heater has both upper and lower heating elements, make sure that they are both adjusted to the same level. Otherwise, one might bear the workload and wear out sooner. When you leave for vacation, turn the heater off.

You probably use one-quarter of your hot water on showering. Technical improvements in low-flow shower heads mean that you can cut water use in half without losing much pressure, according to consumer experts. Ask your utility company if they'll give you one free of charge. Some utility companies have special programs for high-usage customers or lower-income households.

Only about 25 percent of all home owners have insulated water-heater tanks. "The blankets cost $10 to $15 at hardware stores," Morrill says. "Installation takes a half-hour, tops. It's a simple way to save." Savings can mount to $20 per year.

Open the front door. Look for the new generation of front-loading clothes washers. These high-efficiency units use about one-third as much water as a top-loader, which means hot-water savings; and they spin faster, cutting down on drying time. Plus, they use less detergent—even more savings in the long run, says Morrill.

Just ask for powerful savings. Deciding that it costs less money to conserve energy than to build new power plants, utility companies may actually pay you to save energy. Some give away compact fluorescent bulbs. Others do more.

For example, the Public Service Electric and Gas Company, one of New Jersey's top two power companies, offers its customers a number of incentives. Purchasers of energy-efficient central air conditioners and furnaces can receive rebates. They help sponsor low-interest loans up to $4,000 to customers who spend money on conservation measures. They provide free home energy audits (which normally cost $50 to $100). For lower-income customers, they provide referrals to a community program that will caulk around windows and doors, install up to $250 worth of plastic to cover windows, and provide other weatherization measures. So call your utility company and ask what it will do for you.

See the light: Go fluorescent. Don't let the sticker price of compact fluorescent lightbulbs scare you away. Not only do they use less electricity—about two-thirds less—but also they last longer. So long, in fact, that technicians at *Consumer Reports* magazine had to pull the plug on some compact fluorescents that they were testing—after more than two years of constant use.

Telephone: Ring Up Big Savings

The average American is a pawn in the long-distance price wars. Despite all the shouting in advertisements about rock-bottom rates, the long-distance carriers still maintain high profit margins—at your expense, says Lande. And long-distance service is just one part of your monthly phone bill.

New competition brought about by changes in federal laws might cause a drop in prices in coming years, but not without confusing matters for the consumer. In the meantime, there are a number of ways to save on long-distance and local phone charges. So take action now and rise above the din of the telecommunications clash.

First, let's revisit an old basic that you might have let slide. Suppose that you had a peculiar car that cost nearly twice as much to operate during the daytime, Monday through Friday. You'd run more errands at night and on the weekends, right? Well, remember that the long-distance billing for your telephone really *does* work that way.

"It's surprising how we've forgotten about that," says Sam Simon, legal counsel for the Telecommunications Research and Action Center (TRAC), a Washington, D.C., nonprofit organization. Evening rates are generally 40 percent less than daytime rates, and night/weekend rates are almost half off. Although rate periods may differ slightly, they usually look like this:

- Day rates: Monday to Friday, 8:00 A.M. to 5:00 P.M.
- Evening rates: Sunday to Friday, 5:00 P.M. to 11:00 P.M.

It Figures

Fluorescent versus Incandescent

The following table compares the real costs over time of incandescent and fluorescent lightbulbs that are comparable in light output. The life span of the fluorescent bulb listed is so long that it takes more than 13 incandescent bulbs to match it. A timely tip: Since much of this investment's return comes in the form of energy saved, a fluorescent bulb will pay for itself faster if it replaces a light that stays on much of the day.

	20-watt compact fluorescent (lasts 10,000 hours)	75-watt incandescent (lasts 750 hours)
Energy costs for 10,000 hours	$16	$60
Purchase price	$25 (1 bulb)	$10 ($0.75 × 13.33 bulbs)
Total cost	$41	$70
	Total saved by buying a fluorescent bulb: $29	

• Night/weekend rates: Monday to Friday, 11:00 P.M. to 8:00 A.M.; Friday, 11:00 P.M. to Sunday, 5:00 P.M.

You Gotta Have a Plan

Never settle for the standard rates for long-distance service—they're almost always the most expensive. Also known as dial-1 rates, these are what your carrier sticks you with unless you ask for something better. "Sixty percent of people are paying basic rates, which is like paying the sticker price for a new car," says Simon. It's up to you to know the difference.

The difference usually comes in the form of a discounted calling plan. You've probably heard advertisements tossing around names like AT&T True Reach Savings, Sprint Sense, and MCI Friends and Family. But even if the aggressive campaigns seem like smoke and mirrors, the savings are real. So to ring up some real moola amidst the hoopla, Simon recommends that you takes these steps.

Assess your calling pattern. Long-distance calling plans usually offer discounts based on the number of calls that you make, the time of day when you place your calls, or which area codes and numbers you call. To settle on a plan, you'll first need to know which one best suits your lifestyle. So here's how to analyze your long-distance bill to determine what type of caller you are.

Take a close look at three of your typical monthly long-distance bills. Armed with a calculator, pencil, and paper, answer the following questions: When do you call most frequently—days, evenings, nights/weekends, or some combination of these? How many minutes do you typically talk? Where do you call—just a few numbers or all across the country?

Once you have figured out your family's calling pattern, you can shop for rates. Call the carriers and ask about their various plans. If they make you an offer, have them send it to you in writing, then read the fine print.

Each of the services has a toll-free telephone number. To obtain the numbers, call toll-free directory assistance.

Weigh the extras. Rates are the most important factor to consider when comparing plans, but there are other incentives. Some carriers award frequent-flier mileage points for every dollar you spend on calls. Others give points redeemable for products or deeper discounts on future calls. Be sure to ask about such extras when you call for rates. But don't simply sign on because of a one-time offer. Long-term discounts are what you're after.

Bargain for even better prices. Considering how actively the long-distance carriers recruit, they might put up a fight to keep you in the fold. Here's one approach: If a competing carrier calls and offers, say, $50 to switch to their service, call up your own carrier and ask for $50 to stay. They will often agree to pay, most likely over a period of several months, to give you incentive to stick around.

Get credit for switching. Most local telephone companies charge their customers $5 to $15 every time they switch primary long-distance carriers. If you do switch, ask your new carrier to credit your long-distance account the amount of the fee. They should gladly agree.

Check rates regularly. Once you have chosen a plan, don't let your guard down for long. The competition never sleeps—and they've probably figured out a way to undercut prices. Remember that plans change often.

Also, reassess your calling pattern at least two times a year.

Avoid "casual" calling. Maybe you never committed to a long-distance carrier—you just dial one of those access codes each time you phone your uncle in Guam. Casual calling, as the practice is called, has in the past been permitted, usually for no extra charge (but billed at standard rates). But to encourage consumers to commit, carriers have begun charging flat fees of around 80 cents per casual call. Surcharges like that could stack up quickly.

LOCAL SERVICE: MAKE THE RIGHT CALLS

Your receiver keeps humming with that reassuring dial tone, and you send the local phone company a check each month. What could be simpler? While there may not be a mind-boggling array of plans to choose from, there actually are a number of money-saving moves that you can make when dealing with the local outfit.

Consider local calling options. Most telephone companies offer options for local calling, usually either a flat-rate service (unlimited calling for a fixed monthly sum) or measured service (per-minute or per-call charges). The flat-rate service is the simplest and, in general, the best deal, says Lande. Ninety percent of Americans choose it.

However, if you are a low-volume caller, measured service can save you money. Based on an FCC study, a caller that makes 50 five-minute local calls in a month would save money with measured service. That's not a lot of calls, especially for a family with teenagers. But, under certain circumstances, choosing measured service makes sense: for second lines that are not frequently used, for lines devoted to fax machines, or for vacation-home phone lines.

Wiring plans can trip you up. Until 1987, telephone companies charged a standard monthly fee for inside-wiring maintenance insurance. Because of an FCC rule, you now have a choice.

You can forgo such plans or you can choose one of several different types, all of which vary from region to region. The gist of the most basic inside-wiring maintenance plan is this: A small monthly payment (the nationwide average is 85 cents) covers future repair costs involving telephone wiring on your premises. These plans often stipulate that if a technician makes a house call and finds that a telephone is the problem, not the inside wiring, you will be charged at least $30 for the service call.

Beware the Strange Pay Phone

Most pay telephones are owned by the local telephone company in the region. Others, known as customer-owned, currency-operated telephones (COCOTs), often team up with alternative operator services (AOSs) to offer what appears to be comparable service. But such phones tend to charge inflated rates for local calls, operator assistance, and, for long-distance calls, up to 10 times the rate that you get from a standard long-distance carrier.

When you approach a pay phone, utility experts suggest that you look for the logo of your area's telephone company, which signifies that the phone is not a COCOT. AOSs sometimes tack on ridiculously high surcharges, even when you bill to a calling card. If you're making a calling-card call, try to bypass the AOS by first dialing your primary carrier's equal access code. AT&T's is 10288, MCI's is 10222, and Sprint's is 10333.

This basic plan is not a big expense. Still, you might be able to do without it. If your telephone wire runs inside the walls, chances are that it will never go bad. If you only have one outlet and it's very close to where the main service comes in, there's not much inside wiring to pose a problem.

"On the other hand, if you have an old house with wiring that has been done by 12 different people on 12 different occasions," says Lande, "then maybe it's a good idea." Or, if some of it runs on the outside of the house, "then sooner or later the squirrels are going to chew it up and the phone company is going to come out and fix it."

Don't order "deluxe." Inevitably, the telephone company will try to talk you into a deluxe maintenance plan. Avoid these, says Lande. For instance, one company offers a plan called wire-plus: Repair to inside wiring is covered for $1.59 per month, and the company waives the service charge if the technician discovers a phone problem rather than a wiring problem. But the company's "full-service" plan, at $3.21 per month, seems designed for the unsavvy consumer. It's basically the wire-plus plan with a loaner phone thrown in for 60 days. Hardly a bargain, considering how easy it is to find an inexpensive telephone these days.

Hang up those optional services. Take a good hard look at those phone-service extras, like call waiting, call forwarding, and call tracing. They may sound nifty and inexpensive when the phone company representative describes them, but each one can run you $40 per year or more, say consumer advocates. Never pay for features that the average telephone has, such as speed dialing and call hold.

Television: Cable versus Satellite

The United States is, indeed, a TV nation: Ninety-nine percent of all U.S. households use a television, the government says.

A majority of those households rely on a cable company for their programming. But, according to one survey, a quarter of all cable subscribers are dissatisfied with their service—a sure sign of an unhealthy monopoly.

Two developments are already weakening the cable industry's grip on the TV-viewing market: new federal law governing the industry and a new generation of small, user-friendly satellite dishes.

Competitors are probably gearing up to muscle in on your local cable provider's territory. And the satellite services have already joined the fray, which leaves you with one question—stick with cable or aim for the stars?

TUBE TACTICS: KNOW THE OPTIONS

You're probably familiar with cable TV. The cable user rents a converter and pays a range of prices for different channel packages.

Satellite dishes allow viewers to sidestep the cable companies and grab the programming straight from the sky. That means that you buy a dish and get free TV, right? Wrong. Signals are scrambled, and you must pay a programmer, much like a cable company, a monthly fee to unscramble the channels.

Until the new compact style of satellite dish hit the market in 1994, the only dishes available for home use were 6 to 10 feet in diameter. Those behemoths are bulky and awkward to use because they have to rotate to track different satellites. "Plus, when the original dishes first came out, you could get tons of programming for nothing," says Bill McGuire, an assistant editor on the staff of *Consumer Reports* magazine. "Now, it's practically all scrambled." You must pay programming fees, therefore, which are comparable to fees required to use small, dedicated dishes.

So your choice is actually between the compact dishes and cable.

WEIGH THE PROS AND CONS

Industry experts offer these considerations that will help you choose between compact satellite dish TV reception and cable.

- The monthly programming fees for both cable and the compact dish are about the same.
- Of the two, cable is the easier to use. You make no capital investment for cable service and pay a minimal installation fee, usually about $60.
- The dedicated satellite dish is small. Of the two models that have been around longest, the RCA Digital Satellite System (DSS) is 18 inches in diameter, and the Primestar system is 26 inches. Unlike the early satellite dishes, these remain fixed, which means no tweaking to get better reception. In fact, excellent reception is a major benefit.

- With cable, the number of channels is limited to about 70. And cable-viewer frustration stems, in part, from the general lack of custom-designed viewing packages, which means that subscribers often pay for unwanted channels in order to receive others.
- Satellite dishes offer more channels—more than 150 channels with the RCA system and 100 with the Primestar system—and more flexibility to create custom programming packages.
- Satellite dishes mean equipment costs. RCA's DSS costs $300 to $1,200, plus either $200 to have it professionally installed or much less for a do-it-yourself kit. The Primestar equipment requires a mandatory installation of about $200. And once you have either system installed, there's the programming fee. Monthly packages range from $15 to $55, depending the format and programming that you choose.
- Compact satellite systems do not receive local programming. In order to pick up your area's public television station and network affiliates, you must use an antenna or subscribe to basic cable. Or for an extra charge, you can pick up network affiliates and PBS from a few big U.S. cities. With the DSS system, you must subscribe to one programmer for most of the standard cable fare and another programmer if you want HBO and other premium add-ons.

Now Make Your Move

With that background in mind, here are notes on how to proceed.

Define your TV needs. Are you a die-hard sports nut? Then satellite service might be worth the investment. Among the many sports channels and event specials is the 200-game NFL Sunday Ticket, which costs a flat fee of about $160 per season, and the 700-game NBA League Pass for about $150.

The same goes for movie buffs. With the satellite systems, viewers can order more premium movie channels and pay-per-view channels.

Do you live in rural America, beyond the reach of the nearest cable provider? "Out in the boondocks, I would say run out and get a dish," McGuire says, "because it will probably be 10 years before somebody comes along and gives you a real choice."

Are there huge trees or other cover obscuring your house? Unless you're willing to clear the way, you might be forced to stick with cable. Dishes must have a clear southern exposure. Keep in mind that if you purchase a dish and it won't pick up the satellite signal, you're stuck with it. No refund.

Keep an eye on the market. Increased competition among TV providers might alter the current outlook dramatically. When RCA and Primestar introduced their satellite systems in 1994, for instance, regulations allowed them a limited monopoly—after one million of their units sold, others could join the fray. Once other outfits joined the space race, prices quickly began to drop. "I would imagine that it would go the way of all electronics, and it will come down some more," McGuire says.

While you're away, don't pay. You may have learned to turn down the thermostat and the water heater when you go on vacation. But some cable companies say that you can save your TV service, too—without disconnecting the service. Next time you take an extended vacation, call your cable company. Some offer a reduced rate for absences of one to six months.

BOTTOM LINE

On energy savings, focus on the big energy users—heating and air-conditioning, refrigerators, water heaters, and lighting. Ask your utility company and state energy office what they can do for you.

On long-distance phone service, get on a calling plan and call nights and weekends. You'll save 30 to 50 percent.

On television programming, the choice is between cable and the new small, dedicated satellite dishes. There are pros and cons for each, but the monthly programming costs of each are about the same. Watch the market closely—technology and competition will work in your favor.

WORDS TO THE WISE

Calling plan: Discount programs offered by long-distance carriers. The way to beat standard rates.

Dedicated satellite dish: New generation of mini-satellite dishes that are giving cable TV a run for its money.

Setback thermostat: Programmable timer that replaces standard thermostat. Great way to avoid heating and cooling waste.

Switch-over fee: What local telephone companies charge when customers switch primary long-distance carriers. Ask your new carrier to pay.

Water-heater blanket: Insulates your water heater, one of the top two power-eating appliances.

ALLIES

Energy Efficiency and Renewable Energy Clearinghouse: P.O. Box 3048, Merrifield, VA 22116. Free information on saving energy, buying energy-efficient appliances, and using renewable energy technologies such as solar power.

Telecommunications Research and Action Center (TRAC): P.O. Box 27279, Washington, DC 20005. Nonprofit research organization that analyzes long-distance rates for consumers and small businesses. For a copy of "Tele-Tips," send a self-addressed, stamped, business-size envelope and $5.

Building a Better Home Life

Don't Get Rooked When You Upgrade Your Castle

Home, snug home. That's what today's home owners are after, according to one survey.

Most Americans consider today's home a fortified comfort zone, a safe and soothing place to escape the bumpy ride of the modern world. More than just a place to hang one's hat, the home is a refuge where the family spends quality time.

The rooms—especially kitchens and baths—are bigger and more pleasantly furnished, according to the National Association of the Remodeling Industry (NARI) in Alexandria, Virginia. Dens are now high-tech entertainment centers. And because of the changing workplace, more people have home offices where they work all or part of the time in order to be closer to their families.

A lot goes into creating the ideal family refuge. If you live in an old house, you might need to enlarge your kitchen or add a master bedroom suite. If you have a new house, or you want a new look, you must decorate. And external forces—say, a rash of burglaries in your area—might disturb your peace of mind.

By following these tips on remodeling, decorating, and home security, you can improve your home life without wasting time and money and without trading in your welcome mat for one that reads "Don't Tread on Me!"

Mastering Home Improvement

No pain, no gain. Most people who take on home-improvement projects surrender to this unfortunate philosophy.

But hiring a contractor and living through the tearing down and building up does not have to be punishment. And even though remodeling can require a big investment, by increasing the resale value of your house, it can pay off in the long run.

"The number one reason that people remodel is to add extra living space," says Bryan Patchan, executive director of the Remodelers Council of the National Association of Home Builders (NAHB). "We love our neighborhoods, but we like many of the features of the new homes."

WHEN CHOOSING PROJECTS, THINK RESALE VALUE

Done properly, every bit of home improvement should add to the value of your house, but not all remodeling projects were created equal. Sure, you know what needs to change in your own home. But knowing what appeals more to today's home buyer—what will pay off when it comes time to sell—can help you prioritize.

According to an annual study conducted by *Remodeling* magazine, minor kitchen remodeling—repainting, installing a resilient floor, replacing countertops, and refinishing cabinetry—topped the list in terms of resale payback. Home owners recouped an average of 98 percent of the projects' costs in the increased sale price of their houses.

Bathroom addition was next (89 percent of the costs were recouped), followed by a two-story addition (a family room and bedroom tacked onto a house) and major kitchen remodeling (each at 85 percent), the addition of a family room (83 percent), and the addition of a master bedroom suite (82 percent). Last on the list were new siding (68 percent) and the addition of a home office (58 percent).

LIST POTENTIAL CONTRACTORS—AND CHECK IT TWICE

If you decide that you need help with a remodeling project, let your fingers do the walking—away from the Yellow Pages. The phone book alone is no place to look for a remodeler. There's too much at stake to pick randomly. Ask cousin Betty or your colleagues at work for suggestions. Call one of the remodeling associations for a referral. Try to assemble a list of three or four strong candidates.

Interview the contractors. Do not let a contractor intimidate you. Ask as many questions as you need to and take notes. You'll need them when making final comparisons.

Judge not only on work experience but also on trustworthiness and sincerity, says the NAHB. During the interview, did the contractor pay attention? Did he respond well to your questions? Did he offer insights into your particular project? A contractor who communicates well is less likely to misinterpret your ideas and less likely to make a mistake.

Make sure that you like him. Depending on the job, this person might spend weeks or months working in your home.

Ask for bids. When you solicit bids for a project, make sure that each candidate is bidding on the same thing. Give them each the same set of plans or specifications. Ask for a detailed breakdown of costs—labor, materials, and any markups on materials. Where applicable, ask for specifics on materials, industry experts suggest: quantity, brand name, color, size, weight. This will help you compare the bids.

Beware the bargain-basement bid. The point of the bidding process is not necessarily to find the lowest price possible for a job, Patchan says. In fact, a lowball bid might be a red flag that the contractor plans to use cheap materials and labor. Or, it could mean that a contractor misunderstood your plans and bid on a different job than the others.

What Do I Say?

Calling a Contractor's References

Checking a contractor's references is a crucial part of making a wise choice. But you have to get past the small talk and the generalities. Here are some pointed questions suggested by the National Association of the Remodeling Industry in Alexandria, Virginia. They will help you learn those all-important details about how the contractor handles himself and his crew, how honest he is, and what sort of job he does.

- Did the contractor begin work on time?
- Were the workers well-supervised? Polite? Respectful of your property and privacy?
- Did the crew keep the job site neat?
- Did the contractor stay in touch throughout the project?
- Were the final details finished in a timely manner?
- Would you use this contractor again? (If there is any hesitation to this question, dig deeper.)
- Do you mind if I see the finished project? (It is extremely important to check the quality of the work yourself. Other people's standards might not be up to your own.)

Play the sleuth. While you are waiting on the bids, learn what you can about the contractors. If he is a real professional, he will expect you to, Patchan says.

Ask the contractor for three or four customer references, people for whom he has recently worked. Call your local Better Business Bureau to see if anyone has filed a complaint about the contractor.

Ask to see a copy of his certificate of insurance or for the name of his insurance agency to verify coverage. Most states require that contractors carry workers' compensation, property damage, and personal liability insurance. If someone whom you hire does not have adequate insurance, you're liable.

Ask for a warranty. Negotiate for at least a one-year warranty on the finished product, including materials and labor. Put the terms in the contract.

Protect yourself against delay. Add the phrase "Time is of the essence" to your contract. This is legal language that will bolster any complaints against late work. "It supports the concept that if there is any delay, there probably should be penalties," says Jack Brock, president of NARI.

Missed schedules can mean more than just lost time. Say that you've taken out a short-term improvement loan (they usually come at higher rates than a long-term mortgage) and it matures after six months, but your contractor still has two months to go on the work. The bank might charge you to reissue the loan. Using the "Time is of the essence" phrase might help recoup those losses.

Don't let subcontractors "lien" on you. If your general contractor stiffs his suppliers or subcontractors—the independent electricians, plumbers, and other specialists that he hires—they can put a lien, or legal claim, on your house until you pay them, even if you have already paid them through your contractor. A "waiver of lien" is your protection against such measures. By signing this simple legal document (usually one-page long), subcontractors and suppliers hired by a general contractor waive their ability to put a lien against your property.

Ask your contractor to provide you with a signed lien waiver from all subcontractors before he hires them and from major suppliers before he buys materials from them, suggests Pollan. In the contract, include a phrase committing the contractor to do so.

Don't sign for deliveries. It's almost instinctual in this age of overnight couriers and mail-order shopping to greet delivery men at the front door and quickly sign for packages. But that delivery release form is a small legal document that shifts responsibility for the shipped goods—lumber, glass, kitchen cabinets, and other materials, in the case of a remodeling job—into the hands of the signer. If you have hired a general contractor, says Pollan, it is his duty to inspect and sign for the delivery of materials to your home.

Sign the contract at home. By federal law, you have three business days to back out of a signed contract, Brock says, as long as it was signed away from the contractor's place of business—your home, for example. This protects home owners from overaggressive contractors. The rationale is that if you make the effort to go to a contractor's office, you have made up your mind to hire him.

Plan your payments wisely. Never pay too much up front. On short-term jobs (a week or less), try to pay a deposit of about 10 percent of the total fee. On longer jobs, you may need to pay more for materials, say, 20 to 30 percent of the total. Once the work starts, tie the payment to stages of construction—the completion of the foundation, the framing, and the hanging of drywall, for instance.

"The best position for a home owner to be in," says Patchan, "is to have more labor and materials in the job than the home owner has paid for."

Let your contractor get the permit. The permit holder is usually liable for the work if it fails to comply with local building codes. Besides, local rules and codes can be complicated, and a good contractor will be familiar with them, Patchan says.

Interior Design: Consider a Pro

To some people, interior designers seem like an unnecessary expense. Besides, these skeptics might add, shopping is one of life's great pleasures. Why pay someone else to have all the fun?

For one thing, interior design involves more than just shopping. And considering the importance that most of us place on creating our "comfort zone" and the overwhelming number of decorating choices available—colors, fabrics, rugs, furniture, furnishings—hiring a professional can be a smart decision. Interior designers bring a discerning eye and years of experience to the table. In the long run, they can even save you money.

"It's more than just picking out a pretty blue sofa," says Charles Gandy, past president of the American Society of Interior Designers (ASID). "Where I think you can save money is by not making mistakes."

DECISIONS, DECISIONS: FINDING HELP

Do it yourself and you risk redoing it in a few years. The right designer, on the other hand, will help you buy furniture and furnishings and establish a look that will last. Here are some tips.

Know the difference. Many people believe that "interior designer" is just a fancy way of saying "interior decorator." While the two are similar, they are not synonymous.

"A decorator is one who puts in a piece of furniture and upholsters it in a nice fabric," says Gandy. "They're selling decorative objects that make a room look good. Interior designers will do that also, but before they put those decorative objects in the room, they will help shape the space."

Interior designers might change the lighting or, with the help of an architect, alter a ceiling's height or the direction of a wall. Most professional designers have a two- to five-year degree in interior design, which usually includes studies in drafting and art and antique history. Twenty states require interior designers to be licensed, according to the ASID. Decorators, on the other hand, are not required to carry a license.

The way decorators and designers charge clients varies. Traditionally, decorators have charged on a "retail" basis, which means that they make their money by marking up furnishings they buy at wholesale prices (without revealing the markup). Designers tend to charge a fee, either flat or hourly, and buy furnishings on a cost-plus basis, which means that they tack a commission onto the purchases.

Note: If the person you hire buys furnishings on a cost-plus basis, ask for copies of the invoices of all purchases for your own records. This helps ensure that the base price you pay for an item was the price actually charged.

Choose wisely. The fact that anyone can hang out their shingle and call themselves a decorator makes finding a competent professional tricky. For this reason alone, you might want to stick to hiring a designer, one who is a member of the ASID. To become a member of the ASID, the country's oldest and largest interior design association, designers must have college degrees in design and must pass a rigorous qualifying exam. The association offers a referral service, which will provide you with a short list of member-designers in your area. Also, ask friends for recommendations. Try to find three or four designers to interview.

Show and tell. Use interviews with prospective designers as show-and-tell time. Clip pictures of rooms and furnishings that you like (and don't like) from home-decorating magazines. Personal taste is an abstract concept, and this is one of the best ways to communicate it, Gandy says. The designer should show you a portfolio of previous work and explain his work methods.

Don't let 'em pull the chintz over your eyes. Any time that the concept of taste enters the picture—and it's your opinion against the opinion of a professional—there is room for aesthetic intimidation. Use common sense. So what if blank canvases are all the rage these days? If it seems to you that the emperor is wearing no clothes, say so. It's your money. "If it feels like they're trying to sell you a bill of goods, then they probably are," says Gandy.

Make it letter-perfect. Never enter a relationship with a designer without some form of a contract. A long, drawn-out contract is not the norm. Usually, all that is needed is a detailed letter of agreement signed by both parties that outlines the scope of services, schedules, costs, and payments.

A Student Can Bring You Some Class

If you are adventurous and fairly sure of your own taste, hiring a design student might save you money. There are hundreds of interior design programs at colleges and universities around the country. School administrators say that many capable design students work as freelancers to support themselves and to gain experience. The fees that they charge can be a fraction of those charged by established firms, where you pay for overhead and reputation as well as for services rendered.

In New York City, design students charge $10 to $30 per hour for freelance work. Compare that to professional fees in New York City, generally $75 to $250 an hour.

In addition to low fees, design students can also bring a youthful freshness to a project. And they tend to be more in tune with the latest styles, products, and technology. For instance, a student might be more likely to design a room layout on a laptop computer, then bring the laptop to your house and make quick adjustments on the spot, saving time and money.

The downside is, of course, that you sacrifice experience when you hire a student. But there are ways to decrease your risk. First, save the big-budget jobs, including remodeling design, for the pros. Hire a student for smaller jobs that involve mainly decorating.

Note: In states that require interior designers to carry a license, be careful about whom you hire. You may have to hire the student as a consultant rather than a designer.

Hire seniors, not freshmen. Common sense says that they'll know more. Look for older students who might have gone back for a graduate degree after a few years of work experience, the ASID suggests. Contact a design school faculty member who might be able to recommend the top students. Look for a design firm that employs student interns or recent graduates. If they segment their fees, you might be able to get the best of both worlds: the overall experience of the firm and the lower cost of a young designer.

Burglary: An Alarming Trend

Every 10 seconds in this country a home is robbed. Over a year, that makes almost 13 million homes—1 in every 20. With crime as bad as it is these days, a man's "castle" better come complete with an alligator-infested moat.

By questioning convicted burglars, researchers have been able to determine how they think and to predict their moves. You can protect your home by beating thieves at their own game. Here's how.

Don't Be a Target

Burglars usually spend 30 to 45 minutes picking a target. They case houses from the street and, to give themselves a swift exit, often choose a home near a main neighborhood access road.

"Once a burglar has chosen a target, he'll pursue it," says Simon Hakim, Ph.D., professor at Temple University in Philadelphia and an expert in home security. Studies show that entry usually takes about 60 seconds. Even the best locks can be kicked in, jimmied, pried with a crowbar, or drilled out in a matter of minutes.

"The idea is to have enough signs that somebody is at home and that the home is well-protected so that a burglar does not choose it as a target," Dr. Hakim says.

Here are more suggestions from Dr. Hakim and other security experts.

Remove their cover. Cut down on potential hiding places around your house by trimming hedges and trees. Replace burned-out lights in your yard. Install infrared, motion-sensitive floodlights. These not only startle prowlers by turning on at their approach but also save energy. And although they sound complicated and expensive, they generally cost less than $50 and do not require professional installation.

"Gone fishing" won't do. The rate of home break-ins skyrockets during the summer vacation months. When you travel, leave no signs that you're gone. Park cars in the driveway. Use timers to turn lights on and off, varying the pattern to create an occupied look. Stop mail and paper deliveries. Turn your telephone ringers off—unanswered phones tell a potential robber that you're not home. Have a friend or neighbor mow the lawn. Keep drapes and shades open as normal. Closed blinds during the day are an obvious sign no one is home, and they provide cover to a burglar if he enters your house.

Defend the ground floor. Most break-ins occur on the ground floor. One study showed that nearly half of all burglars enter through the front door, 32 percent choose the back door, and 22 percent enter through a first-floor window. Only 2 percent of burglars choose a second-story window. The solution is to secure, expose, and illuminate the ground floor.

Beware daylight. Don't let your guard down when the sun comes up. Most burglaries take place between the hours of 9:30 A.M. and 4:00 P.M., when you're at work and the kids are at school. After all, more husbands and wives both work, and thieves know this. Therefore, take extra precautions during the day. Set timers for lights and radios. Have neighbors that stay home during the day keep an eye on your house.

Keep valuables out of the bedroom. Once they enter a house, crooks typically head for the bedroom. They know that this is the place where most people keep jewelry, extra cash, cameras, and other valuables.

GET WIRED FOR A BIG SOUND

Studies show that burglars attack homes without burglar alarms three times more often. And when they do hit a house with a loud alarm, they get away with less loot. The average property loss as a result of burglary is $1,300, but for those with alarms, that figure drops to $900.

Because of statistics like these, more Americans are turning to home security systems: Between 1990 and 1995 there was a 40 percent jump in the number of homes with alarms.

Home security systems have three basic components.

1. A control panel
2. Sensors, which range from magnetic switches for windows and doors to breaking-glass detectors to infrared motion detectors
3. Reporting devices, like sirens, strobes, and autodialers

Hard-wired, professionally installed alarms that include a 24-hour monitoring service offer the most protection. They cost $1,000 to $3,000 to install, plus a monthly monitoring fee. The monitoring system works like this: When the alarm is tripped, a telephone autodialer calls a security-service operator who hangs up and immediately calls back. If no one picks up, or if the person who answers does not give the proper code, the operator calls the police.

A less expensive alternative is a do-it-yourself system, available at electronics stores, hardware stores, and home-supply stores. Usually wireless, these cost $200 to $500 and do not include a monitoring service.

Scare up the best alarm company. If you decide to have a system professionally installed, don't just pick the company with the largest phone-book ad. Compare the costs and services of three or four companies. Meet with their representatives, check up on their work, and ask each to provide a detailed price estimate.

Start by asking friends and neighbors for recommendations. Contact the National Burglar and Fire Alarm Association (NBFAA) in Bethesda, Maryland, for referrals in your area. The NBFAA is the oldest and largest trade association for the security industry. Its 4,000 member-companies must pass the approval of other members in their respective states and adhere to a code of ethics.

More than half of all states require alarm companies to carry some type of license. Check license status—and ask about any legal or disciplinary action taken against a company—by calling the state licensing board.

Look for companies that screen their employees. When a company representative visits your house to give you a price quote, ask to see his company identification, says the NBFAA.

When discussing prices, make sure that you understand the company's equipment policy. Some companies sell you the equipment, and others lease it. Often people sign security contracts thinking that they own the equipment, when, in fact, they must give it back when they move or cancel service. Read all contracts carefully and ask your salesperson for a detailed explanation.

Install your alarm wisely. If you invest in a home security system, get the most from it. Cover the entire perimeter of your house, keeping in mind the statistics that show that almost all burglars enter on the ground floor. Do not install the siren near the control panel. A seasoned burglar will follow the noise and disable the alarm.

Post lawn signs and window decals to let prowlers know that you have an alarm. Remember that the most important method of burglar prevention is deterrence. If most people in your neighborhood have alarms, you put yourself at risk by not having one or not advertising the one you have.

Use it or lose it. That sticker in the window may deter a lot of bad guys, but back up that warning with a truly functioning alarm system. Believe it or not, a study in Connecticut showed that in almost half the alarmed homes successfully burglarized, the security system was not turned on.

Beat burglars to the punch. Most people wait two to four years after moving into a home to install a burglar alarm. Burglars know this and break into newly built homes shortly after they're occupied. If you're going to install an alarm, do it right away, the NBFAA says.

Make like a disco. Install an outdoor strobe with your alarm. Otherwise, if you do not have an automatic dialer that alerts the local police, the only way for anyone outside of your house to know that it is being broken into is the loud buzz of your siren, which might not be so loud by the time it reaches the street. A yard strobe causes more of a stir. Not only does it alert your neighbors but also it can help a police cruiser home in on your address more quickly.

Ask for an insurance break. By installing an alarm system, you are making an investment in your home's security. Most insurance companies recognize this by offering discounts of 2 to 30 percent on premiums. Talk to your insurance agent before you decide on a system. You may decide that buying a more expensive system—one that leads to a greater discount—pays off in the long run, the NBFAA says.

BOTTOM LINE

When considering home improvements, remember what will add to the resale value of your house. Check up on potential contractors by calling your state licensing board. Hammer out a clear, comprehensive contract.

To make your home secure, concentrate on deterrence—on not becoming a target—by giving your house a lived-in, well-protected appearance. Install an alarm, and advertise it with decals and lawn signs.

WORDS TO THE WISE

Interior decorator: Recommends color patterns and buys furniture and furnishings. In general, attends to what goes into a room. Does not need a license to work.

Interior designer: Does all the things that a decorator does, plus shapes space and makes structural changes, often with the help of an architect. In 20 states, required to carry a license.

Waiver of lien: An agreement signed by subcontractors and major suppliers that waives their rights to put a lien on a client's house. Used to protect home owners when a contractor fails to pay his subcontractors.

ALLIES

American Society of Interior Designers (ASID): 608 Massachusetts Avenue NE, Washington, DC 20002-6006. Can refer you to member-designers.

National Association of the Remodeling Industry (NARI): 4900 Seminary Road, Alexandria, VA 22311. Can refer you to member-contractors.

National Burglar and Fire Alarm Association (NBFAA): 7101 Wisconsin Avenue, Suite 901, Bethesda, MD 20814. Can refer you to alarm-installation companies in your area. Ask for a copy of the booklet "Safe and Sound," which includes a chart that helps you compare companies' bids.

National Kitchen and Bath Association: 687 Willow Grove Street, Hackettstown, NJ 07840. Can refer you to member-contractors.

Buying for Less, Selling for More

The Rules May Change, But Owning Your Home Is Still a Wise Move

Buying a home is the biggest investment that most Americans will ever make. But the word "investment" is something of a misnomer. In the 1970s and 1980s, real estate values rose dramatically and people bought property like it was some kind of hot stock. "Hey, they're not making any more of it—prices can only shoot up," went the thinking. When an owner outgrew a home or needed to relocate, he could count on two things—selling quickly and making a profit.

The old rules of buying and selling residential real estate no longer apply. The go-go 1970s and 1980s were replaced by an economy that struggled with a stock market crash, recession, and corporate downsizing. In most areas of the country, home values fell or stagnated. The best that owners could hope for was that housing prices would continue to rise at the rate of inflation. This has held true through most of the 1990s.

Despite this new reality, buying a home is still the dream of most Americans, and rightfully so. Beyond its value as an investment, home ownership has many psychological and emotional benefits, including security, pride, and pleasure. And for most people, it makes far more sense financially than renting, the most common alternative.

With the rules changed, buyers and sellers must bring an assertive approach to each step of the process. Location, affordability, financing, establishing a price, and marketing are all issues that must be researched and analyzed.

What Can You Afford?

Determining how much you can spend on a home is the most crucial decision that you'll face as a prospective buyer. The whole concept of affordability has changed dramatically in recent years. People once bought a starter home in the belief that it would appreciate in value, that they could sell it, and with all of this swelled equity, that they would be able to pay for a larger home where they would raise children and spend their retirement. But now, more people are renting first, choosing to wait until they can afford to buy their "forever" home.

Unlike the 1- to 3-year starter home their parents bought, first-time buyers today are likely to be making a 5- to 15-year commitment. And this can be a stretch for those first-time buyers. Even if they don't have children now, they'll want a home with enough bedrooms (or one that can be easily expanded), in a school district that they respect, and where the economic base of the community is sound.

Determining exactly what you can afford is not easy. Real estate brokers tend to say one thing, banks another, parents and friends yet another. A bank determines affordability by judging your ability to pay the mortgage, which it bases on current income—not what you'll be earning in the future. You, on the other hand, need to predict the future by judging what your income stream might look like in the next 5 to 10 years.

"Every buyer must develop a comfort level in terms of how much they're able—and willing—to spend on a home," says Michael Trombley, mortgage consultant for Skyscraper Mortgage Company, one of the largest mortgage brokerage companies in New York City. He suggests asking yourself the following questions.

- How much money will be left over after monthly mortgage payments are made?
- Will the leftover money be enough to cover emergencies?
- Is there enough money to pay for replacing big-ticket items like a furnace, refrigerator, or stove?
- What other expenses are likely to come up in the next few years, such as tuition or a summer camp for a child?
- Will your lifestyle change because more of your income is being spent on shelter, and can you live with that?

HOW TO RUN THE NUMBERS

In terms of numbers, affordability boils down to two factors: your ability to meet monthly payments (for both mortgage and living expenses) and coming up with the down payment. So now it's time to get out a pencil and paper.

Lenders have particular formulas for calculating how much they would be willing to lend you. But they are based on national averages that have nothing to do with your own situation. We'll discuss these later. For now, you need to figure out how much *you* are willing to spend each month on a house. Here's one way to do that.

First, calculate what you currently spend for shelter. Next, make a list of all your other monthly expenses and ask yourself: "What can I easily do without?" Can you cut down your monthly restaurant costs? Can you do without two traveling vacations a year? Can you buy less expensive presents on birthdays and holidays? Can you buy fewer clothes? Odds are that you can trim 15 to 20 percent from what you now spend without any serious compromise to your lifestyle. Take the savings that you estimate and add that figure to your current shelter costs.

Next, take a look at the amount that you are saving each month. Are you accumulating money for no clear purpose, or are your savings clearly earmarked, say, for a kid's college tuition or your retirement? You need to determine if there are monthly savings that can get channeled into a home payment and, if so, how much. If there's money there, add it to the mortgage pot.

Next, you need to account for the fact that the interest in your mortgage payments will be tax-deductible—a savings that you don't get while you rent. How much you actually save will depend on your tax bracket. Say that your "adjusted-rent" figure calculated above is $1,500. Compare that to a monthly mortgage payment of $1,500—remembering that a mortgage payment is nearly all interest at the beginning. If you're in the 28 percent tax bracket, a $1,500 monthly mortgage payment saves you about $420. So add that tax savings to your monthly adjusted-rent figure, too.

It's smart to adjust your sum to reflect property taxes and insurance. That's not easy, since both vary enormously city by city, state by state. To be prudent, assume that 20 percent of your monthly payment will go to these two costs. So multiply your adjusted-rent figure by 0.8 to get the amount that can go purely toward the mortgage.

Okay. You now have a ballpark number of how much you can pay each month for a home mortgage. Next, get a mortgage chart (available at some libraries, banks, or realty offices), and look up 30-year fixed-rate mortgages to see the maximum loan that you can pay off based on that sum you've come up with.

Finally, add the amount of that total mortgage to whatever down payment you can raise (the amount of front money that you'll need is typically 20 percent of the price of the home). And there you have the maximum amount that you're willing to pay for a house.

WRANGLING THAT DOWN PAYMENT

The most common reason people give for not buying a home is that they can't afford the down payment. So how do you get one? You beg or borrow. Here are some ways to go about it.

Ask your parents. For many younger people, the first and best place to turn is their parents. You needn't be ashamed or embarrassed. Parents know the score. They realize that young people today need all the help that they can get.

Make it a loan. Your parents might be more comfortable if they help you raise a down payment by loaning you money rather than giving it to you. For example, if your parents have money tied up in accounts or funds that pay them interest, offer to pay them whatever they would be making on the money if they hadn't lent it to you.

Keep in mind that lenders know that many first-time home buyers get their down payment funds from their parents. They look most favorably on money given as a gift, or at least a loan that doesn't have to be paid back immediately, real estate experts say.

Get an early inheritance. If parents and grandparents intend to leave you money when they die, convince them to give it to you now. This way, they'll get the added pleasure of seeing you enjoy what they've given.

Find investors. If parents are not an option, approach relatives or friends. If they can't or won't loan you money, perhaps they'd "invest" in your home. Offer a 20 percent or 25 percent ownership interest. You'll get to live in the home and pay for its maintenance. And when it's time to sell, your "investors" will receive their percentage of the profits.

Get with a program. Some lending programs, such as those tailored for veterans or low-income people, require little or no down payment or offer below-market interest rates. Ask lenders about the special programs that you may qualify for.

• If you're a veteran, look up the local Veterans Affairs office in the phone book.

• Check with the federal Department of Housing and Urban Development about its Section 235 program for low-income people and the Farmers Home Administration about its Section 502 program for rural families with low or moderate incomes.

• Check whether your state has a housing finance agency that offers favorable terms for low- and moderate-income home buyers.

• Ask lenders whether there are special redevelopment zones in the areas where you want to buy. Some government programs offer financial incentives to prospective home buyers—and some of the neighborhoods involved are rather nice.

Join the union. Check whether you're eligible for one of the country's 13,000 credit unions. Mortgages are available at about a third of them. Membership is typically arranged through your employer, a church, or some other association that you belong to. This means that you won't be able to shop around among credit unions. However, because these are non-profit institutions, they often offer better terms than commercial lenders—

Location Is Where It's At

The real estate market may have been turned on its ear over the last couple of decades, but this rule remains constant: The three keys to real estate acquisition are location, location, and location.

Here are some things to consider when choosing a house, real estate professionals say.

The tax base. Be wary of any locale with little or no economic base. If there's no industry or downtown district and the area is strictly a suburban community, taxes will go up as the population goes up because they'll have to build new schools and other facilities to support that growth. In these areas, the residential population will take on the whole burden of supporting the municipality.

The commuting factor. Homes in municipalities closer to inner cities typically cost more than those farther away. So weigh the quandary of modern life: If you're commuting into the city, the longer you have to travel from your job, the less expensive your house will be.

The surrounding homes. Never buy the most expensive house on a block. A cheaper home in a desirable location has a far greater potential to appreciate in value.

Track the trends. Trends in value tend to continue. If prices in an area are stagnant or declining, they're likely to continue to do so. However, if values in a community are rising, it's a good bet that they'll keep going up.

particularly in respect to closing costs and the amount of down payment required, which can run as low as 5 percent.

Borrow from the future. It may be painful to watch cash piling up in the old 401(k) plan that you have at work while you desperately need a lump of cash for the down payment on a house. If you withdraw money before you're age 59½, you'll probably be slapped with a 10 percent penalty. But that account may be able to help you out after all. Many 401(k) programs allow you to borrow against your own retirement fund without penalty. Wouldn't you prefer paying interest to yourself rather than to someone else?

Hit up the seller. If the seller weren't under some pressure to strike a deal, he wouldn't have his house on the market in the first place, right? So look for opportunities for the seller, or even his agent, to solve your down payment problem. The seller may be willing to front you the cash that you need as long as you pay him back later. Similarly, the agent may be willing to throw his commission into your down payment pot in exchange for repayment in the future. Tell them both that you may not be able to buy the property without such an agreement.

Getting a Mortgage

When real estate prices were soaring during the freewheeling 1980s, mortgage loan officers were in an enviable position. They knew that the value of the property you wanted to buy was going up, so that took a lot of risk out of the lending business.

But the recession that ended that decade also put an end to the human element in the mortgage business. The economy tightened, savings and loans collapsed, and the real estate market sagged. Lenders became more restrictive about the way in which they granted loans and closely monitored the practices of their loan officers. Now, loan applicants are judged by "credit scoring" systems that coldly rate such criteria as your income, credit history, and length of employment.

This is not to say that you are powerless over the home-mortgage system. It's just that the rules have changed, and you need to make yourself look good to the lender—even if he's ignoring your charm, your firm handshake, and your best suit.

"Preparation, preparation, preparation are the three rules for getting a loan," says Trombley. "If the bank discovers a problem later on in the application process, it may be too late to recover."

Before you jump into the fray, here are some more things that you need to know about the process.

How Lenders Size You Up

A bank's decision to lend money boils down to three elements.

1. The borrower's ability to pay back the mortgage
2. The borrower's willingness to pay it back
3. The value of the collateral that secures the loan—meaning what the home in question is worth

Banks look at your income and evaluate your ability to pay the monthly mortgage by using what's called debt-to-income ratios. This means that they compare your housing expenses and your overall expenses to your income. The average debt-to-income ratio is 28:36. That means that no more than 28 percent of your income can be used to pay your shelter expense, including mortgage, taxes, and insurance. No more than 36 percent of your income can be devoted to all fixed expenses—including household—plus such consumer debt as credit cards, car loans, and student loans.

In addition, the bank may have special income qualifying guidelines if you are self-employed, receive large bonuses, or are paid on a commission basis. In these cases, banks generally require a minimum of two years of income tax returns to verify your income. They usually average your income over the last two years, which lowers your mortgage affordability.

Banks also like borrowers to have plenty of cash—at least enough to cover the down payment, closing costs (generally 1.5 to 2.5 percent of the sales price), points on the mortgage, and two to three months of mortgage payments.

Next, banks judge your willingness to pay a mortgage by looking at your credit history. First, they order reports from credit agencies. It's quite common for credit reports to contain inaccuracies, such as erroneous past-due balances or missed student-loan payments. Legitimate debts and missed or late payments will also appear on the report. Generally, these problems are relatively simple to correct. However, the process can take time. So regardless of what you think of your credit profile, it's best to check it with all three of the major bureaus—Equifax, Experian (formerly TRW), and Trans Union—before you apply for a mortgage.

If you discover an error or an overlooked debt, write a letter of explanation to the credit agency, informing them of the mistakes or that you've negotiated a payment plan with legitimate creditors. Be sure that creditors submit a clearance letter to the agency to wash away the negative entry from your report.

Also, be careful not to carry too much credit. Unused credit cards or credit lines are viewed by banks with disfavor because they represent potential debt.

IF YOU DON'T QUALIFY, KEEP TRYING

Don't throw in the towel if you don't qualify for a mortgage based on your income, poor credit record, or low cash. It will take more work, but knowing your weaknesses in advance and implementing a strategy to offset them will give you the best shot.

Explain in advance. Banks don't like surprises. Attach a supplement to your mortgage application to explain any deficiencies. Also speak with a bank representative directly before you submit your application. Although there are certain standards for income and credit, they are not etched in stone and might be overcome with the right argument. For example, a gap in employment shouldn't be ignored. Explain that you "freelanced" for a period to gain additional experience, or that you took time off to get more training to enhance career opportunities.

Straighten out your affairs. Here are some more ways to improve your financial portrait.

- Put more cash into the deal (if insufficient income is the problem).
- Get rid of unused credit cards and pay off outstanding credit card debts or student loans.

- Demonstrate that income averaging is unfair in your case. Get a letter from your employer or accountant stating that your recently increased income is expected to remain at a high level.
- Demonstrate that certain expenses that were included when calculating your debt-to-income ratio were actually one-time expenses and should not be included.

Rejected? Appeal. If the bank still denies your application, remember that rejection doesn't necessarily end the process. By law, a mortgage lender must give a written explanation of the reason for the decision. Once you know the reason, you can concentrate on cleaning up the problem.

Call the loan department and ask about the appeals process. If there is no established procedure, you'll have to create one. Make an appointment to see the head of the bank's mortgage department. Go armed with facts that shed new light on your application. Don't insist that the loan officer was wrong but emphasize your willingness and ability to repay. If bad credit is the sticking point, submit a revised, sanitized report to the bank after working with the creditor to resolve the problem. If income was the problem, consider asking a relative to co-sign the loan.

The key is to be persistent. Meet with as many people at the bank as possible. Speak to superiors if you get no satisfaction.

FINDING THE BEST MORTGAGE RATE

Mortgage rates are very competitive, so comparison-shopping is a must. What's more, the availability of certain mortgage features—such as fixed rates and variable rates (and hybrids of the two), maximum loan amounts, points, and closing costs—vary greatly from lender to lender.

Get a rate list. To get your feet wet, contact a company that tracks interest rates. For about $20, these mortgage-listing agencies will send you a report detailing the rates being offered by banks in your area.

Pick a loan type. Before you begin your search, settle on a particular type of mortgage so that you can make direct comparisons. You can always change your mind later.

Grill the lenders. Compile a list of all the financial institutions in your area that offer mortgages, including commercial banks, savings banks, savings and loans, and mortgage bankers. Call several and ask to speak with a mortgage specialist. Be prepared with a list of questions. Ask for the annual percentage rate (APR), which is the effective rate of interest factoring in all loan-related costs. This allows you to compare the actual cost of one loan to another.

If you're looking for a fixed-rate loan, ask how long the term is and what the aggregate points are, if any. If you're considering a variable-rate mortgage, find out what types they offer. Ask how long the terms are, the rates for each, what the points are, how often and when the rate will change, what the maximum allowable "bump" is in each change period as well as over the life of the loan, which index is used as the basis for adjusting the rate, and whether the loan can be converted to a fixed-rate in the future— and at what cost.

Check what loan-to-value ratio the bank will allow. That is, the maximum amount of the loan they will approve given the value of the property as appraised by the bank.

Ask about the bank fees: application, points, appraisal, credit check, and closing attorney. Find out if the loan is assumable (if rates go up, this can be a valuable feature when it's time to sell your home) and whether there are any prepayment penalties.

Ask how long it will take for the bank to approve your loan.

Go for a broker. Here's another way to get a mortgage or to shop for rates: Use a mortgage broker, a person who matches up lenders and borrowers. The broker's fee is usually paid by the bank, so the service costs you nothing.

Like real estate brokers, a good mortgage broker can save you time and energy. What's more, a broker with close ties to local banks and other lenders can mean the difference between approval and rejection of your mortgage application. They can be especially useful if your situation is sticky—for example, if you have credit problems, if you need more than an 80 percent loan, or if you're self-employed and it's more difficult to verify income.

Improve on the deal. Once you've narrowed the field of potential lenders, don't be afraid to negotiate for a better rate. Banks have some flexibility, so be prepared with quotes from other lenders to bolster your request. If you're a qualified borrower, banks want your business.

Get advance approval. Prequalifying yourself for a loan can be a great strategy. In this process a lender can tell you how much money you can borrow—*before* you submit and pay for a formal application—just by looking at your income, assets, and debts. Not only will this help you in your search for a home but also once you've found one, the fact that you are prequalified will make you that much more attractive to the seller.

Monitor that PMI. Lenders usually require a borrower to pay for private mortgage insurance (PMI) when the loan exceeds the bank's normal loan-to-value ratios (typically 80 percent of the purchase price). This insurance guarantees to the bank that your loan will be paid if you fall into default. Annual premiums for PMI can run as much as 1 percent of the total amount of the loan, depending on the size of the loan, amount of the down payment, and the type of the loan. In most cases, borrowers will be asked to pay part or all of the first year's premium on the day of the closing.

The good news is that you'll only need this insurance until the size of the loan is brought down to the bank's normal levels, which usually takes three to five years. But be warned: Not all lenders tell you when PMI is no longer required. So it will be up to you to contact them to check. Also, be wary of lenders that include PMI in the interest rate that you're charged. If yours does, ask for a breakdown of actual premium costs.

FIND A LOAN THAT SUITS YOUR CIRCUMSTANCES

The desirability of fixed-rate versus variable-rate mortgages is a perpetual debate. Most experts agree that the one you choose should make sense given how long you plan on owning your home, the stability of your current income, and your personal attitude toward risk.

Fixed rates offer predictability. For the next 30 years, or until you sell or refinance, you'll know precisely what your payment obligations are. Here are some other reasons to get a fixed-rate loan.

- You think interest rates are unusually low.
- You can't count on your income going up, so you want to lock in at a comfortable payment level.
- You live on a fixed income or are near retirement, and you couldn't afford your house if your payments went up.

On the other hand, adjustable rates are always offered at a lower rate of interest in the early years. If you know that you'll be struggling to make payments, some relief early on might make sense. Also, if you're buying a starter home that you know that you'll grow out of in 3 to 7 years (some banks even offer variable rates that are fixed for 10 years), getting the lowest rate possible could be an advantage.

Do You Need a Broker?

Like it or not, brokers are an integral component of residential real estate transactions in America. While system-beaters are often tempted to cut out the commission-earning middleman, working without a broker can be self-defeating.

Many buyers mistakenly believe that by avoiding brokers they'll be able to knock 6 percent (the typical commission) off the cost of the house. But the fact is that brokerage commissions are built into the economies of virtually every home purchase. Most properties today are listed through multiple-listing services, so even if you shop around on your own, the sellers that you find will already be obligated to pay a commission to a broker anyway.

What's more, brokers perform several important functions. "An experienced broker has incredible knowledge about real estate in the area that most people simply could never get unless they immersed themselves in the process for a very long time," notes George De Voe, a Litchfield County, Connecticut, broker with more than 20 years of experience.

Yes, on paper the broker is usually paid by the seller. But the savvy buyer can still use a broker to get valuable information about the seller, his house, and why it's being sold.

HOW TO FIND AND WORK WITH A BROKER

For the home buyer, the system-beating strategy involves making a broker work to your advantage. The best way to find a broker is through the recommendation of people that you trust. Gather a few names and schedule interviews with each. Make sure that the broker you select specializes in the vicinity that you're interested in and is part of a multiple-listing service. This way, you'll have access to a lot of homes.

Stick to full-time brokers. Part-timers or moonlighting brokers are not as motivated. You'll want the added experience of a licensed broker rather than just a salesperson.

Test your broker out early in the house-hunting process by telling him what you're looking for in a home. If the first one that he shows you doesn't match up with what you discussed, a siren should go off inside your head. Either the broker is incompetent, wasn't paying attention, or has nothing to fit your needs. And it's time to find another broker.

Keep price to yourself. Avoid telling the broker what you can afford to spend on a home. While you'll need to provide some idea of price range, it's a mistake to get too specific. That information could be used against you when it's time to negotiate price.

Similarly, if you walk into a home that you immediately like, remain calm. It's too early in the process to tip your hand.

Ask for some legwork. Insist that your broker prescreen every house before showing it to show you. This way, if the broker is doing his job, you won't be wasting your time with homes that are way off the mark.

Be an observant passenger. Always let the broker drive you around. On the way to the next house stop, ask the broker the following questions.

- What type of person is the seller?
- Why is the home being sold?
- How long has the house been on the market?
- If it's been listed for sale a long time, at what price was it first offered?
- Did the seller's broker help set the price?
- Have any offers been made that were rejected?

Carefully examine the areas that you pass on the way to the house. Are there highways or train tracks close by? How far away are schools and stores? Do you see any factories, industrial sites, or garbage dumps? Remember that the broker will take you to the home via the most picturesque route possible, so drive around the area on your own to get the true lay of the land.

Never see more than five houses in one day or else you'll begin to confuse them.

Remember who's paying whom. Keep in mind that even though the broker is taking you around, his commission is paid by the seller. Therefore, the broker doesn't represent you. Unless you specifically hire a "buyer's broker" (for which you pay a fee), the broker is legally bound to represent the seller's interests.

The most that you can hope for is that the broker will concentrate on bringing you and the seller together to strike a deal that benefits you both. But remember that anybody with a stake in the transaction is not an objective viewer.

Negotiating a Price

Evaluate whether the seller's offering price is fair, meaning within the market range. How do you calculate this? First, find out what comparable houses are selling for in the area. There's typically a variable of 10 to 15 percent.

ANALYZING THE LOCAL MARKET

Start with the broker. An experienced one will have a good grasp on the marketplace and how homes are being priced. Ask to see the broker's multiple-listing book to get a feel for yourself. Consider consulting a local appraiser about the neighborhood.

After you've settled on a range, begin to focus on the variations within that range. These will depend on things such as configuration of the property, location on the block, and, most important, the condition of the house. According to De Voe, the condition of a home is so important that "less than one in four buyers opts for homes that require a lot of work."

Some people list houses at outrageously high figures, either because they've priced it without the advice of a broker or because they believe that starting high will give them room to negotiate for what they eventually hope to get. If you find that the asking price is completely out of whack, then your first offer should be more of a statement: "We'd like to make an offer on your house, but we need you to reconsider your asking price because we don't want to insult you." Confronted with this, sellers and brokers will often bring the price down.

If the asking price is reasonable, your goal should be to pay a shade less than the market. Don't make your offer absurdly low. Lowballing often results in something worse than a rejection—no response. Then, if you really want the house, you have to go back with a much higher offer just to get the seller to counteroffer. In effect, you're bidding against yourself.

HOW TO CONTROL THE GIVE-AND-TAKE

If your first offer is respectable and the seller then reduces his price, you'll get a pretty accurate idea of where the seller wants the negotiation to

---

Inspection Can Save a Flood of Trouble

Here's an instructive tale about the need for detective work when you're buying real estate.

Dan Michaels, a regional sales manager for a major communications company, was thinking about buying a co-op in a swank area in New York City (where nearly 80 percent of owned apartments are co-ops). But the first time he saw the apartment, Michaels noticed a raised, bubblelike area on the living room floor. By the time he went for a second look it had mysteriously vanished.

Michaels smelled trouble and hired an engineer to look at the apartment. The engineer determined that the buckling had been caused by flooding between the floors of his unit and the ceiling of the apartment downstairs. Michaels spoke with the building's doorman and learned that every time the building's air-conditioning system was switched on for the season, certain apartments in the building experienced some flooding.

"I don't know what I would have done if I hadn't gotten the engineer," Michaels says. "Can you imagine my carpet, furniture, and other property being ruined every summer?"

---

end up. Stephen Pollan, an attorney, financial consultant, and co-author of *Stephen Pollan's Foolproof Guide to Selling Your Home*, calls this process the great unzipping.

"Sellers generally broadcast where they want to go when they come back with that first price reduction," Pollan says. Usually, the price that the seller has in mind is midway between your offer and the seller's first counteroffer. To take control of the negotiation, says Pollan, make your subsequent offers in increasingly smaller increments.

For example, say that the asking price for the house is $150,000 and your first offer is $120,000. The seller drops his price to $143,000. You then know that the seller has in mind a midpoint of about $131,500. Your second offer could be $125,000, to which the seller might respond by dropping to $138,000. Any further increases in your offer should get progressively smaller—that is, less than the $5,000 increase that you last made. If you stick to this strategy, you'll end up with a price more favorable than the midpoint that the seller had targeted. You avoid that traditional trap of "splitting the difference."

What's more, you'll be sending the seller a clear message: You're willing to negotiate, but there's a limit to how high you'll go.

If you're still far apart and you really are stretching the limits of your budget, consider asking the seller to "take back paper," meaning that he lends you the difference between his offer and yours. Usually, this can be done on favorable terms, at little or no interest for two to three years.

It's often a good idea to combine your last offer with a nonfinancial concession. For example, if the seller wants to close quickly, agree to accommodate him. By doing this, you'll make a lower price more palatable.

Selling Your Home

Selling a home was once a slam-dunk proposition. When the time came for an owner to sell, he'd call up a broker, list the property, entertain several quick offers, and choose the best one. That your house would sell quickly was a given. That you'd sell for a profit was just as automatic. Now homes are often on the market for several months or even years. While there is nothing that an individual seller can do to change market dynamics, there are many things that can be done to increase the chances of selling quickly.

INSPECT YOUR HOME THROUGH A BUYER'S EYES

The first order of business when preparing to sell a house is to conduct a thorough inspection. As you look around your home, ask yourself these questions: Do all the lights work? Are there cracks in any walls? Is paint chipping or wallpaper peeling? Do any faucets leak? Are there stains on the carpet?

Try your best to see things through the eyes of a potential buyer. You may miss things because you've been living in the house a long time. Ask a friend to help. Make a checklist of everything that needs repair. You won't necessarily make all the repairs that you write down, but the list will be a good starting point.

Have a pro inspect. Having your property inspected by a professional inspector—before putting your home on the market—can play to your advantage. This way, you'll have time to decide what to do about problems before the buyer finds out about them. If you wait for the buyer's inspection report (almost all buyers have one before a deal is finalized), problems will become part of the negotiation. Either you'll be asked to reduce the price or you'll be expected to make repairs before the closing.

By getting the inspection in advance, you can decide whether to repair the problems or adjust the price to reflect the existing condition. As a rule, it's best only to take care of material objections before a buyer might discover them.

Arm yourself with bids. If you're selling a home and your preliminary inspection reveals that a major item, such as a roof or boiler, should be replaced, get several bids for the job from contractors. You won't actually have the work done, but you'll be armed with the lowest bid when the time comes to tell the buyer—which you'll do before they conduct their own

---

Sometimes, Renting Pays Off

Sure, owning your home can be a pain. If the toilet clogs or the roof springs a leak, there's no handy landlord to put on the case. But for people who can afford it, the financial and lifestyle advantages of owning a home usually far outweigh the disadvantages.

Nevertheless, real estate experts say that there are some situations where renting makes perfect sense.

- If you know that your life will be changing or that you'll be moving in less than five years. Five years is the minimum stay needed to offset the initial costs associated with buying a home.
- If you're just starting your career and you want the flexibility to go wherever and whenever opportunities become available.

---

inspection. This way, you can explain that the asking price reflects the existing condition.

Showcase the house. The most important thing in showing the house is that it look clean, light, and spacious. So preparation may consist of a simple paint job if the walls are stained or cracking. Get rid of marks on the refrigerator or scratches on kitchen counters and cabinets (white correction fluid is particularly effective).

But what people really notice first in a home is space and light. Fortunately, these are illusions that you can create. Create space by removing furniture, thinning out closets, and getting rid of any signs of clutter. Keep kitchen counters empty and don't leave newspapers or magazines lying around. Create light by increasing bulb wattage, leaving drapes open, and putting a fresh coat of paint on walls. Also, add to the ambience with fresh-cut flowers, preferably ones that smell nice.

Take yourself out of the picture. Buyers must be able to picture themselves living in your home, so depersonalize things as much as possible. If you decide to redecorate—paint walls, replace wallpaper, or reupholster furniture—be sure to choose neutral colors and patterns. Remove any obvious symbols that advertise your political or religious views.

Invest in the kitchen. The most important rooms in the house are kitchens and bathrooms. In fact, kitchens often make or break a house, so if you're going to put any money into a house, put it into the kitchen. There's a good chance that you'll get back every penny.

Move some furniture. Rearrange furniture to improve the flow of traffic through the house. Don't leave furniture in the middle of rooms.

Place couches and chairs flush against walls to open up rooms. If your floors are in good shape, consider removing carpeting and rugs. Not only will rooms look bigger but also someone with different taste than yours will be less put off.

Move some junk. People love a lot of storage room. But if your basement or attic is packed to the gills, buyers won't appreciate the space that's there. Rent an off-site storage space to hold your excess stuff or hold a yard sale.

ESTABLISHING THE PRICE—AND GETTING IT

Setting a price is the most difficult thing for a seller to do. Most sellers take the historical cost and add to it every penny that they ever put into the house. Then they add some more because they figure that the whole market has gone up or that the area is hot.

That's not the way to do it. The cash that you've sunk into a home has nothing to do with its present value. Your house is simply worth what the market says it's worth—nothing more, nothing less.

So the first step is establishing what the market price is for your home. Generally, what you'll find is that the "market" isn't a set dollar amount but a range. Your goal is to determine your home's value, within a range of 10 to 15 percent, and then to fetch the higher end of that estimate.

"You'll never know the market unless you do everything in your power to track recent sales in your area," says Trombley. Check with the county clerk's office, real estate pros, friends, and bankers to gather names of the top real estate companies in your area. Then call those businesses, ask for the top seller in the office, and make an appointment. "They'll have a much better sense of market value and will be in a position to provide valuable advice and insight."

Here are more notes on how to go about finding your home's market range.

Get "comps." Ask three experienced real estate brokers to provide several written comps—meaning a detailed printout of recent sales of comparable homes in your area. These will show you a home's asking price, how long it has been on the market, the number of bedrooms and bathrooms, square footage, and the eventual selling price. They may even come with photos of the houses.

Take several of the most recent comps for homes with characteristics that are closest to yours, then write down the range of prices at which the homes actually sold. Aside from just the bottom line, try to get a sense of market trends in your area. Pay particular attention to how long they were on the market before they sold. If they were sold quickly, the market is very active. If they were listed a long time, the market is probably slow.

Consider an appraisal. If you still doubt the numbers after working with comps, you may want to have your home formally appraised. Your attorney or a local banker should be able to recommend an appraiser.

Make a final check. Think about the brokers who provided you comps. Whose judgment do you respect most? Make a final check of your numbers with this person. Ask if there is any information or features about your home that you may have misjudged or forgotten.

Pick a number. After you've decided on a range of prices for your home, it's time to attach a specific price tag. Decide whether your home falls at the top, middle, or bottom of the spectrum that you've established. Take another look at the comps focusing on the homes whose features most closely resemble yours. What did they sell for?

Don't be greedy. Overpricing is the biggest obstacle to selling a home. In fact, Pollan says, "there is no such thing as a problem home—only problem sellers." Any home can be sold for the right price, but a home priced too dear can sit on the market for months or years with little or no activity. That's what brokers refer to as a stale listing.

If you've made this mistake, the only way to rehabilitate a stale listing is to take the house off the market for one full selling season. Then relist it at a proper price. If you've set a realistic price and done your homework by preparing the house for sale, it *will* sell.

INCORPORATE A BROKER INTO YOUR MARKETING PLAN

After establishing a price and preparing the house for sale, your third major strategy is making good use of the right real estate broker. Face it, when it comes to selling your own house, you're a poor salesman. You're too emotionally tied to the transaction.

What's more, there are several psychological advantages to using a broker, such as privacy for the buyers when they walk around the property, the appearance of an independent point of view, and a buffer during the tough negotiation process.

Don't be put off by the fact that you'll have to pay the broker a commission. If you try to sell your home without one, most buyers will mentally reduce your asking price by the 6 percent that you think you're saving.

Pick the right agent. Just as with buyers, word of mouth is the best place to start hunting for a real estate broker to help you sell. Speak to neighbors, friends, your real estate attorney, and banker. Drive around your community and count how many houses are listed with the agents or companies that have been mentioned to you.

Make sure that your broker works full-time, has several years of experience, and belongs to the National Association of Realtors.

Meet the candidates. Once you've narrowed your list to two or three candidates, set up appointments to meet with each and tour your home. Listen to what each says about your home. Ask them for an honest assessment and don't be swayed by flattery—it won't get your house sold.

Ask each broker for a detailed description, in writing, of what kind of marketing program they intend to utilize—open houses for other brokers, multiple listings, advertising, inclusion in company brochures, and perhaps a sign in your yard.

Go with the broker that you feel is the most professional and will do the best job of marketing your home. When you've selected one, agree to give him a limited, exclusive period of time to sell your home—say, 30 to 60 days—as an added incentive. Assure him that if he's doing a good job, you'll renew the arrangement. Always get the broker to put the listing arrangement, including terms of the commission, in writing.

Check that payoff clause. Watch out for the timing of payment of the broker's commission. In most states, brokers "earn" a commission when they've produced a buyer who is ready, willing, and able to buy. This can cause big problems if, for whatever reason, the deal never closes. Make sure that your agreement specifies that the broker will be paid a commission "if, as, and when the title actually closes."

LET A BOOK TELL YOUR STORY

A "seller's book" can be an extremely effective marketing tool. This is a book that the seller compiles telling about the house and surrounding community. Include pictures of the inside and outside of the house, a floor plan, a historical summary of the home's major systems (such as electric, plumbing, roof, heating, air-conditioning, and well or septic system). Include features that reflect positively on those items, such as upgrades, replacements, and new warranties.

If appliances are new or top-of-the-line, mention it. Remember that buyers want to know about utilities and other costs of operating the home. So include information on average utility costs, electric, oil, and garbage collection.

Also, provide a detailed description of the community, including a list of schools, shopping, recreational facilities, parks, cultural spots, and popular restaurants. Consider including a map of the area. The local chamber of commerce may already have assembled much of the information that you need. For information concerning schools, contact your local school board and be sure to include any impressive statistics regarding the school's reputation.

Make about 100 of these books so that when potential buyers leave your house, they take with them something permanent. Remember that house hunters have looked at four or five other houses on the day that they visited yours. They can't possibly recall everything they've seen.

BOTTOM LINE

Buying or selling a home is the biggest financial event in most people's lives. At first glance the process can seem overwhelming. But it doesn't have to be. The secret is knowing how to handle each step, what information you'll need, where to get it, and how to find and select experts to help you. Ultimately, the knowledge and confidence to close the deal means the difference between sitting on the sidelines and sitting inside a home that you can call your own.

WORDS TO THE WISE

Annual percentage rate (APR): The figure to look at when comparing mortgage rates. It's the effective rate of interest factoring in all loan-related costs.

Prequalifying: In this process a lender looks at your finances and tells you how much money you can borrow—before you submit a formal application. Being prequalified will make you more attractive to the seller.

ALLIES

Stephen Pollan's Foolproof Guide to Selling Your Home, by Stephen Pollan and Mark Levine (Simon and Schuster).

Kiplinger's Buying and Selling a Home, by the staff of *Kiplinger's Personal Finance Magazine* (Random House).

Credit reporting agencies: There are three major credit reporting agencies. When you contact them, you'll need to provide your date of birth, Social Security number, home address, daytime and evening telephone numbers, and verification of your name and address (a copy of a driver's license or utility bill).

- Equifax: P.O. Box 740256, Atlanta, GA 30374
- Experian (formerly TRW): P.O. Box 8030, Layton, UT 84041-8030
- Trans Union: National Consumer Relations Disclosure Center, 760 West Sproul Road, Springfield, PA 19064

Getting It Done Right—And on Time

From Plumbers to Comedians, How to Hire the Right Professional

In many ways running an efficient home is like managing a small business. You have an annual budget and a variety of short- and long-term goals. Instead of dollars, your profits are measured in quality family time, comfort, and a minimum number of household headaches.

To be time- and money-efficient, you'll need to manage outside help for a variety of projects, including everything from technical repairs to landscaping your yard. But hiring the right person and brokering the right deal can be a challenge.

Whether you need a service contractor (like an electrician, plumber, or appliance repairman), an architect, a landscaper, a caterer, or an entertainer, you'll want someone who is trustworthy and competent. "The screening mechanism really isn't that different across different home services," says David Hollies, president and founder of Home Connections, a home-service referral company based in Silver Spring, Maryland. "There are a lot of people who get hung up on technical details, when the key is customer satisfaction."

Many of the methods, therefore, for locating and hiring the best person to do a particular job are the same across the spectrum of specialties. Professional associations, for example, are a good place to start. Be it the American Institute of Architects (AIA), the Association of Bridal Consultants (ABC), or the National Association of Catering Executives (NACE), a professional society will often provide a list of members in your region.

Another universal tip for hiring home help is talking to previous clients. "I stress references, references, references," says architect Don Jacobs of Irvine, California, who is chairman of the housing committee for the American Institute of Architects. "I don't think that there is anything better to help you get an understanding of how this person is really going to operate."

Service Firms: Hire the Right Help

If it ain't broke, don't fix it. If it is, call somebody.

Ah, if it were only that simple.

When you call a repairman to fix, say, a television set, a broken sewage pipe, or a burned-out electrical circuit, you put yourself at the mercy of the expert. You must trust that person to do a good job and charge a fair price. The same goes for exterminators, carpet cleaners, painters, and other service contractors.

GATHER PROMISING CANDIDATES

These jobs—minor improvements, repairs, and cleaning—do not warrant an involved bidding process. However, home owners often hire the company with the first listing or best-looking ad in the Yellow Pages—the other extreme. There are steps you can take to choose a trustworthy expert—even if you are pressed for time by an appliance that needs to be fixed right away. Here's how.

Get several recommendations. "Most people choose home-service firms based on the recommendation of one neighbor," says Hollies. "We figure, 'Well, gosh, if you can please Mrs. Thompson, you have to be all right.' Then we hire them, and it doesn't work out."

Even if most contractors are honest and hard-working, some of them don't have their act together as businesspeople. When it comes to scheduling and juggling jobs, some fall short. They might please customers, say, only 35 percent of the time. You want a skilled professional who is also a smart businessperson with a customer-satisfaction rate of 98 or 99 percent.

Look in small social circles. A tradesman or contractor who markets himself in a very small circle—a church or synagogue congregation, a civic organization, a condominium association—is probably going to care about reputation. If the contractor does shoddy work, word's going to get around quickly.

Use a referral service. If you can't find several people to vouch for a particular plumber or exterminator, Hollies recommends using a referral service, which beats the Yellow Pages throw-of-the-dart approach. These companies maintain up-to-date lists of proven professionals, who pay a small commission for each referral. The service is free to the home owner.

Not all cities have them, however. Look under the primary home-service heading in your Yellow Pages—usually "Home Improvements" or "Contractors-Alterations."

Check licenses. Not all states license all service contractors. If yours does license the type that you are looking for—you can find out by calling your state licensing board—ask to see a license. While it does not assure quality work, a license shows compliance with the law. Unlicensed firms in states with licensing laws are marginal. Rule them out.

Check insurance. "If a contractor is operating without liability insurance, he's betting his company—his life's work—every day," says Hollies. "If you're dealing with a contractor who doesn't have insurance, you can assume one of two things: He's either stupid or broke. In either case he's not a candidate that you want to hire."

Ask to see the contractor's certificate of insurance, or ask the contractor to have his insurance company send it to you directly.

Make a Smooth Exchange

Once you've settled on the right service person, Hollies suggests these steps that you can take to make sure that your business transaction goes smoothly—cash paid for a job well done.

Know the price of a service call. Plumbers, electricians, repairmen, and other service contractors typically do not give free estimates. If they make a house call, even just to assess a situation, their meter is probably running. Some companies charge you an hourly rate, beginning when they arrive and ending when they leave. Others start the clock when they leave the previous job. Still others charge you an hourly rate, plus a flat service-call charge of, say, $30. Get it straight from the start—that is, when you first call, not when they arrive at your door.

Remember that price isn't everything. Hiring an incompetent plumber because he charges less than a competent one is like buying a broken radio because it costs less than one that works. The best price may not mean the best deal. Try your best to choose quality. Rather than hire the cheaper company, use its bid as leverage to bargain for a lower price.

Pay only when the job is finished. Since in most cases you will not sign a detailed contract, withholding payment is your protection if something goes wrong. Although there are exceptions, you will probably not be asked to pay a deposit, because service jobs do not typically involve an up-front outlay for materials.

Settle disputes quickly—and in your favor. The moment a problem arises on a job, start taking notes, including a record of important dates and other details: when a contractor promised to complete a job, for example, and when he actually finished.

Beat the Clock: Getting the Most from a By-the-Hour Service Call

You're as tense as an expectant father—pacing, glancing down every few minutes at your watch. Relax. That's the first tip. And whatever you do, don't hover. A repairman with a nervous Nelly peeking over his shoulder will find it hard to concentrate.

When you're paying an expensive hourly rate for a home repair or other job, it's difficult not to focus on the imaginary meter clicking away. There are, however, steps you can take to save time and money and decrease your anxiety. Organization is the key. Next time, try the following, recommended by David Hollies, president and founder of Home Connections, a home-service referral company based in Silver Spring, Maryland.

Discuss details over the phone. If you've thoroughly talked out a project over the telephone, that's before the clock starts ticking. This saves time, plus it helps the repairman know which tools to bring.

Make a list. Your to-do list should include everything you want the repairman to fix. This will save you even more time when the technician arrives.

Include related problems. Since many companies front-load the first hour with additional charges, you want to get as much done in one trip as possible. In other words, if you call a plumber to unclog a toilet, ask him to tighten the leaky pipe in the basement, too. While making your list, walk through the house and consider other needed repairs.

Prepare the work area. If the work will take place in the kitchen, for example, make sure that all dishes are washed and put away. Clear clutter. Remove breakable objects.

Do the cleaning yourself. Contractors often do not clean up after themselves as thoroughly as you would like anyway—and you have to follow up with a broom and mop. So why not ask the repairman to leave all the cleaning to you? You'll save time and money.

Try first to resolve the dispute with the company. Move your way up the chain of command if your first attempts are fruitless (unless, of course, it's a one-person show). If that doesn't work, contact your city or county office of consumer affairs, which might have the kind of clout it takes to get a favorable response from the company. Ask for a mediator (often provided free-of-charge by the government) who will lead a solutions-oriented discussion between you and your contractor.

Also effective at pressuring contractors are the Better Business Bureau and the chamber of commerce. And, most trades have at least one national association, which probably has a local chapter that will help mediate disputes.

Make legal action your last resort. Hiring a lawyer and filing a suit is the most expensive means of dispute settlement. Small-claims court is a less expensive alternative because no lawyer is required. But each state limits its small-claims settlements to about $3,000.

Architects: Invest in Quality

Many people consider an architect an unaffordable luxury. But using an architect to design a house or home addition pays off in the long run—when you put your house on the market. According to an annual study conducted by *Remodeling* magazine, the average home owner recouped at least 80 percent of the cost of an architect-designed remodeling project in the increased sale price of his house.

Besides that, a good architect can save you money in a number of other ways: A well-conceived house can be built more economically, and a home designed for maximum energy efficiency will cost less to heat and cool.

HIRING TIME: FOLLOW THIS BLUEPRINT

How, then, do you hire a good architect? Here are some tips recommended by Jacobs.

Find the right fit. Not only should you try to find a professional who is talented and reliable and whose tastes meet your demands, but you also need one with whom you are comfortable working. "You, the client, should feel like you can pretty much bare your soul to this person—because you're going to at some point during this process," says Jacobs. "If you don't have the chemistry to begin with, it's not going to develop over time."

Drive around the neighborhood where you plan to build, and look at other homes. Decide which ones you like. Houses and additions that went up recently will usually carry the architect's sign. Knock on doors. Most people are willing to tell you about their experience working with an architect.

Contact one of the 300-plus local chapters of the American Institute of Architects for a list of member architects in your area. Many local chapters have resource centers that keep architects' portfolios on file. To find the local chapter nearest you, contact the national office: AIA, 1735 New York Avenue NW, Washington, DC 20006.

Visit the architect's office. Call for an appointment. Check out the operation. Look at pictures of the architect's work, and ask him to take you to houses that he has designed. Show the architect pictures from magazines of houses and features you like. The better you communicate your feelings and ideas, the better the architect will understand what you want in a design. Some architects charge for this initial interview. Be sure to ask if there is a fee.

Ask for references. First of all, be wary of an architect who has a hard time coming up with references. It usually means that he either lacks experience or has left a trail of unhappy clients in his wake.

Ask the references if you may visit their homes. Are they happy with the architect's work? Did the architect design a house that fit their budget? If not, what was the reason? Was it the architect's fault?

Talk to contractors. Builders who have worked with architects that you are considering will have a different perspective than the client references. Be sure to ask the contractor if the architect is known for bringing projects in on budget.

Consider licenses. All states license architects. While having a license can't guarantee the type of service you will receive, checking these licenses is a basic form of client protection.

To determine which state government division issues architecture licenses, call your state or local AIA chapter. To find the local chapter nearest you, contact the AIA's national office.

List the details. When you settle on an architect, include all of the important negotiated details—services, schedule, construction budget, and architect's fees—in a contract.

PICKING A SITE? ARCHITECTS HAVE A LOT TO OFFER

If you are deciding between several lots for building a new home, hire an architect as a consultant for a few hours to help you make the decision. The cost will be relatively low—usually $50 to $100 per hour—and the consultation might save you money in the long run. It's also a good way to get a feel for an architect before hiring him to design your house.

The architect can offer crucial insights, like whether one lot is going to be more expensive to build on because it has a water problem or a grade problem. He can help you consider your house's orientation: Will you be able to leave the trees on the property, for example, and still be able to soak up the morning light? If the architect is familiar with the microclimate of a particular neighborhood or area, even better.

Landscapers: Raising Your Home's Value

It used to be that taking care of the yard meant paying your teenager a weekly allowance, or hiring a kid down the block, to mow the lawn once a week.

These days, landscaping is big business. And well it should be: According to one survey, landscaping, or ornamental plant cover, increases the value of a house by an average of 15 percent.

That's because landscaping gives your home curb appeal. It's the first thing that neighbors and potential home buyers see when they pass your house. Broad-leafed shade trees, a flower-lined stone path, and a tall hedge for privacy also make your yard a more pleasant place to spend time.

First, Do Some Ground Work

Yard work is still a popular do-it-yourself domain. Even with major landscaping renovations, many people do part of the work to save money. But when the design, implementation, and upkeep of a landscaped yard is too time-consuming or technical, you might need to hire a pro. Here are some tips from experts for picking the best yard specialist.

Call your cooperative extension. All states have cooperative extension systems, run by state universities, which make available agricultural information to all citizens. The information is free, and there is usually an extension office in each county. For most landscaping projects, including major overhauls, this is a good place to start.

Along with publications and fact sheets on plants, insect control, disease control, and other horticultural topics, the extension may be able to provide you with lists of licensed arborists, pest-control companies, and other landscape experts in your area. They should also have someone on hand to answer technical questions.

First, ask yourself two questions.

- Do I want a low-maintenance yard, or would I prefer maples and oaks even though they shed leaves?
- Do I want a native grass, or do I want a hassle-free lawn alternative?

With the help of your extension office, create a two-page plan. Have them review the plan, then show it to the landscape firms you interview. You will be more prepared and look like less of a pushover.

Decide what help you need. Are you looking for regular yard maintenance, like lawn mowing, weeding, and hedge trimming? Or do you want to overhaul everything between the exterior walls of your house and your property limit? The options are endless. When hiring help, first choose the best type of landscape professional for the work you want done. Here are brief explanations of several popular types of pros.

Landscape architects. These professionals plan outdoor living space. Trained in building codes, land-use laws, grading, irrigation, and plants, they design sites, often integrating features such as driveways, paths, and walls. About 40 states have licensing requirements for landscape architects, which include passing a rigorous national exam. Look for a landscape architect who is a member of the American Society of Landscape Architects (ASLA). For a

Yard Planning: Call a Family Powwow

The success of a large-scale landscaping project depends on knowing what you and your family want.

"The key is to get the family engaged," says Tom Dunbar, a landscape architect in Des Moines, Iowa, and president of the American Society of Landscape Architects. "In many cases, the family does a lot of the construction. If they are engaged in the design, they understand the construction a little better."

Call a family meeting to discuss future landscaping projects. Give each participating family member a piece of paper and a pen, and have them list the things they like and dislike about the yard. Then have everyone list what they would like to have in a new yard.

"You might not like the cold wind or a smell coming from a certain direction," says Dunbar, "or a view to a neighbor's yard, or the fact that some kids cut across the yard, or that there is a wet area over here, or you can't get grass to grow over there. You might like to sit in a sunny area or a cool area in the yard. You might like the fact that it's private."

Ask the following questions in the meeting, says Dunbar.

- What do you want in your outdoor space?
- Should the yard be private and shaded or wide open with lots of light?
- What do we want to do in the yard?
- Will we raise children and pets?
- How long will we be here? (In other words, don't plant three-foot cedars if you plan to move in a few years.)
- What does a long-term stay mean in terms of changing lifestyle, and how can we plan the evolving yard to reflect that?

free list of members in your area, contact the ASLA at 4401 Connecticut Avenue NW, 5th Floor, Washington, DC 20008.

Landscape designers. Like landscape architects, landscape designers also design outdoor space—but with an emphasis on plants. They typically have less engineering and structural training and are not licensed by states. They often work for nurseries or full-service garden centers.

Landscape contractors. These are the builders of the landscaping business. Using blueprints, they dig, plant, lay paths, and build patios. Their jobs vary as widely as the kind of work people do in their yards. They can be specialists, like irrigation installers and deck builders, or general contractors.

Landscapers. Call on landscapers to do yard work, like mowing, weeding, pruning, and planting as well as limited design.

It is common in the industry to find landscape firms or full-service garden centers that provide a combination of the above specialists.

Hiring Someone to Dig In

Now that you're on solid ground as to what you want done in your yard, here are prudent tips from landscapers for getting the work rolling.

Hire a consultant. Save the cost of a full-time landscape architect or designer by hiring the same person to examine your own ideas and plans. They can answer questions about technical issues, like land-use laws and water drainage, and keep you from making costly mistakes, like planting shade-loving azaleas under trees too young to cover them or drowning water-shy junipers by planting them in a low-lying flood zone.

The same goes for hiring a landscape contractor, especially if you, like many Americans, enjoy gardening. Let them do the heavy work, like bulldozing a grade or laying a patio, and you do the digging and planting.

Get a second and third opinion. Have the biggest, best-known firms come by first to look at the job. Hear them out, learn from them, and get a cost estimate for the work. Then call in smaller (and probably more reasonably priced) companies and ask their opinions. When choosing among the companies, base your decision on previous work, reputation, trustworthiness, and price.

Ask to see examples of work. If it's a big job and you're interviewing landscape architects, designers, or contractors, this is important. Look at portfolios. Call references and ask to visit their yards.

Put it in writing. For most large-scale jobs (anything more than weekly lawn mowing), you'll want some form of contract or letter of agreement. Include all the important details regarding service, schedule, and fees.

Get the best deal on plants. Be aware of landscape designers who work for one nursery and who might limit your plant choices and competitive pricing. On the other hand, a designer might be able to land plant discounts. It boils down to trust. From the outset, try to hire a designer you can rely on.

Caterers: Delivering the Goods

Someone once defined caterers as quiet chefs who work miracles in ridiculous venues and get noticed only when things go bad.

These days everybody is calling himself a caterer, which means that finding one who will work miracles without "getting noticed" is no piece of cake.

"Anybody can open a catering company," says Michael Roman, director of education at CaterSource, a national catering consulting and training company based in Chicago. "If you have a pot, water, and a stove, you can open a catering company." So casually selecting a caterer for your business function could land you in hot water.

PICK FROM A LARGE MENU

When you decide that you need a caterer—for a business dinner, a wedding reception, or some other occasion—take these steps recommended by Antoinette Benjamin, a caterer in Ann Arbor, Michigan, and co-chair of the catering committee of the International Association of Culinary Professionals.

Consider several caterers. The nature of the business means that comparison shopping is difficult. Ingredients differ and menus differ, making it hard to compare applesauce to applesauce.

Word of mouth is the best way to find a good caterer. Try to recall where you had exceptional catered food. Was it an awards banquet? Or a relative's party? Also, ask friends and acquaintances for their suggestions. When asking around, try to find friends whose occasion and budget resemble yours.

For a list of licensed caterers in your area, contact the National Association of Catering Executives (NACE), 60 Revere Drive, Suite 500, Northbrook, IL 60062, which will refer you to your local chapter.

Ask for estimates. An experienced caterer should be able to give you a detailed, bottom-line price estimate. Most caterers charge a fee based on the number of people they are feeding. Prices for food-only pick-up orders and buffets can cost as little as $7 to $15 per person. Sit-down meals that include service and dinnerware setups can cost $50 per plate and more. (One caterer in New York City charges a $300-per-person minimum!)

Typically, the costs fall under three categories: food, rentals (china, silverware, tablecloths), and staff. Ask for a breakdown. It will give you a better idea of what you're paying for. And it will help you avoid sticker shock when the final bill arrives.

When comparing caterers, however, don't simply pick the lowest bidder. Hotels and restaurants, for example, will almost always underbid private caterers, but the personal touch of a private caterer might make his service a better value.

Sample the cooking. Before you hire someone, arrange a tasting. This can be as casual as dropping by the caterer's kitchen and trying a few dishes or picking up a meal to take home. If you are hosting a major event, a caterer might prepare an elaborate tasting. It's one final way to be sure that you're getting good food.

Note: In some cases, a caterer might charge you for these samples. Be sure to ask in advance.

Check the caterer's license. Catering is an attractive start-up business. "People think: 'I'm a pretty good cook. I could do for 10; that means I could do for 100,' " says Benjamin.

"Well, the whole ball game changes. You have to be educated in sanitation. You have to know that food reacts differently in large quantities. Unfortunately, a lot of people get into catering because they think that it's a quick way to make a buck."

As with restaurants, the facilities and equipment of a caterer must pass inspection by the local board of health. In most cases, municipalities and counties license caterers. There are about 43,000 licensed caterers in the United States, but just as many are unlicensed.

Ask to see a copy of the caterer's food-vendor license or the latest record of inspection from the health department. A tax-ID license is not good enough. If that's all a caterer offers you, think twice. Or, call the health department directly and ask about the status of a specific caterer.

Visit the kitchen. See for yourself what sort of operation this person is running. It does not have to be big. But it should be clean and professional-looking, and it should have adequate refrigeration.

I'LL TAKE ONE CHEF TO GO, PLEASE

So you've found a chef-on-wheels that will wow 'em at your luau. Now take these steps for closing a deal.

Be honest about your budget. You're better off giving as much information as possible about what you want and what you can afford. "Most people think that it's like going to a car salesman. You don't want to tell a car salesman anything," says Roman. "But most reputable caterers will always

What Do I Say?

How to Interview a Caterer's References

Checking up on a caterer's references is a crucial step in making a wise hiring choice. To find out how a caterer handles himself, industry experts recommend that you ask these pointed questions.

- Would you hire the caterer again? (If they have any hesitation, dig deeper. Ask them to explain the doubt.)
- Does the caterer have any weaknesses?
- What were the best things they served? What were the least successful things?
- How did you hear about them? Was it another satisfied customer?
- Did you feel you got a fair price?
- Were there any surprise add-on charges?

work with people up and down on a budget. They can't give them A food at B prices, but they can come up with some very nice B menus. An example would be a frozen salmon versus a fresh salmon. In the hands of a good chef, when you put it in a buffet, it's hard to tell the difference."

Put it in writing. Include all of the important details regarding service, schedule, and fees in a contract or letter of agreement.

Rent your own. Chances are that if you ask a caterer to provide set-ups—china, silverware, tablecloths, and the like—he will simply rent them himself and charge you on a cost-plus basis. If your caterer agrees, consider renting your own supplies separately. Look under "Party Rentals" or "Party Supplies" in the Yellow Pages.

Talk (leftover) turkey. When it comes to catering, there is more to left-overs than meets the plate. In fact, because the issue can be quite contentious, hash it out before your event begins. Don't just assume that because you've paid for the food it's yours to take home. Because caterers are liable for any illnesses caused by their cooking, they must decide at the end of the evening if the food is safe to keep. If it has been sitting out on a buffet table for several hours at an outdoor event, the caterer may decide that it must be thrown away. It's their call.

Leave a paper trail. Remember Nannygate? It involved people who were caught failing to pay taxes on wages paid to nannies. By paying a caterer cash "under the table," you break the same laws.

"A lot of caterers say, 'Oh, just pay our staff directly,' or 'Just pay me cash, and I won't charge tax,' " says Roman. "That's a violation of the federal law."

Not only is it a matter of obeying the law, but part of what you're buying when you hire a licensed caterer is the caterer's liability. If something goes wrong—a guest gets botulism, a food server falls and breaks a leg—a licensed caterer carries the insurance necessary to protect their client. If you hire an unlicensed caterer or pay cash under the table, you're probably not getting that liability coverage.

When paying your caterer, use a check or credit card. Ask for a receipt detailing the services rendered.

Entertainers: Working Magic

When hiring an entertainer, what you don't want is a guy whose best song and dance is his sales pitch.

Choosing a good entertainer is not easy. They're like caterers. Anybody can claim to be one, but only a true professional will put on an impressive show. And it's not just what they serve up—be it jazz, comedy, or a magic show. How they handle themselves as businesspeople and service providers can make or break a performance.

WEEDING OUT THE BOZOS

When selecting an entertainer for a children's party, a wedding reception, a holiday bash, or some other event, you'll need to consider talent and professionalism. That involves more than just listening to a demonstration tape. What about appearance? You probably don't want a band to show up wearing only tights and tattoos for your daughter's Sweet Sixteen dance. And behavior? A drunk clown is nobody's idea of fun. Here are some tips from entertainment experts for choosing a performer who is talented, safety-conscious, and considerate.

Scout out the talent. Before you turn to the Yellow Pages, ask around for recommendations. Call civic clubs, churches, or synagogues. If it's children's entertainment that you need, call your children's schools or scout leaders for suggestions. In most cases you will deal directly with the entertainer, but occasionally you might need to work with an agency.

Look for entertainers committed enough to join some type of professional association—a musician's guild or magician's society, for example. But don't worry unnecessarily because an entertainer is a part-timer. In the entertainment business, this is common. A high school music teacher might play in a band on the weekends. A magic shop owner might perform twice a month at birthday parties.

The Association of Bridal Consultants, whose members include bridal consultants as well as entertainers, has a network of state and local chapters that can provide lists of entertainers in your area. Write: ABC, 200 Chestnutland Road, New Milford, CT 06776.

Ask for a video. It used to be that "demo tape" referred to an audiocassette sample of a band's music. These days, however, the best demo tapes—for musicians and other performers, like jugglers, comedians, and magicians—are ones you can watch as well as listen to. Do not expect all entertainers to have video footage of themselves. But if they do, not only is it a good way to judge a performer but it's also a sign of professionalism.

CATCH THEM IN THE ACT

Once you've arrived at a candidate or two, go beyond demo tapes. By all means use them. But because the demo tape is probably going to be one of the best jobs they have ever done, or a collection of highlights, you need to dig deeper. Here's how.

Speak to recent references. Do not settle for just any names a performer provides. Ask for the names and numbers of their last three clients. This will allow you to hear from a random, up-to-date sampling of clients, not just the most satisfied ones. An entertainer unwilling to provide the names of the last three clients raises a red flag of warning.

Check the performer's calendar. If possible, see your prospective entertainer perform. Maybe they have a regular gig at a local watering hole. Or, in the case of a magician or other children's entertainer, perhaps they are appearing at a local public school. If so, ask if you can drop by to check them out. This is the best way to get a feel for their talents.

Consider appearance. Even rock musicians can be expected to maintain an air of professionalism. First impressions and behavior count, especially when you are trying to choose between performers you have never seen perform. Don't expect the members of a group called The Screechers to show up for an interview in business suits. Professionalism is relative, after all. But they should be punctual, sober, and reasonably attentive.

Ask about the treatment of animals. If you're hiring a magician, a farmer who gives pony rides, or some other type of children's performer, animals might be part of the act. If so, ask about them. How are the animals transported? Where are they kept? How are they used in the act? Are they treated humanely?

Frank DeMaria of Queens, New York, who is a member and former officer of the Society of American Magicians, founded by Harry Houdini, remembers one case when a magician hired to entertain a child's birthday party made a fatal error regarding his rabbit. "It was a hot summer day, 100°F or more," DeMaria says. "By the time he pulled the rabbit out of his hat, it had died from the heat. He looked up at the kids and said, 'Oh, Mr. Rabbit must be sleeping.' That's horrible for children. He should have known better."

Ask about safety. When it comes to children's parties, safety is essential. Make sure that the entertainer you hire has experience working with children. For example, impressionable youngsters might try to imitate a magician who does a dangerous trick.

"There's a beautiful effect of sticking a foot-long needle through a balloon without it bursting," says DeMaria. "However, it's dangerous for kids. They might not find that exact pin, but they can get their hands on a regular pin, a pair of scissors or knitting needles."

THE CLOSING REFRAIN

So you've decided you want Cory and the Corvettes to play at your office barbecue. Take these steps to close the deal.

List times and fees. A simple letter of agreement will do, as long as it includes key details—how long the show will last, method of payment, overtime charges. Because many entertainers request payment in cash, the contract is your paper trail. If you will be paying cash, make sure that the letter of agreement says so. This further legitimizes the deal.

Clarify overtime. Make sure that it's clearly identified how many hours someone will be performing and when and how long breaks are. Ask if the performer will agree to overtime and what the overtime rates are. Include the details in the letter of agreement.

Watch for the old switcheroo. "Make sure that the letter of agreement spells out who is going to be performing," says Gerard Monaghan, president of the Association of Bridal Consultants. This is especially true when you hire an entertainer through an agency. "You may like a certain person, whether it's a live performer or a disc jockey, but unless the contract specifies that person will be there, they may be able to substitute someone else."

Agree on appropriate attire. Don't just focus on the talent aspect of a performer. Says Monaghan: "You listen to a tape, the performance is great, but the guy shows up looking like a scuzzbucket for a formal wedding."

The reverse holds true, too. You don't want a singer to wear white tie and tails for a beach party. Talk it over, decide on what's appropriate, then specify it in the letter of agreement.

Hire a consultant. If you are throwing a big party, like a wedding reception, a consultant might be worth the extra fee. "A consultant will know who's good because that's his business," says Monaghan. Not only do consultants increase your chances for success but also they alleviate stress, which allows you to enjoy yourself at your own party.

Consultants usually charge an hourly rate or a flat fee. Expect the cost to be 10 to 15 percent of the event's total cost.

For a free list of party consultants—and not just for weddings—contact the ABC. To choose among them, use the same screening mechanism you would for the entertainers themselves: Check references, conduct interviews, and ask for a detailed cost estimate.

Bottom Line

When hiring professionals to do work for you, first ask for references and check them out. Then sample their work—for a musician, for instance, drop in on a live performance. In an interview, ask pointed questions, such as: Do you have the time and interest to devote to my project? Put details of your agreement in writing. Consider hiring a pro as a consultant only—to review your landscaping design, for instance—if you'd like to do the hands-on work yourself.

Words to the Wise

Cooperative extension office: Run by state universities, these nonprofit centers make available agricultural and horticultural information to all citizens. There is usually an extension office in each county.

Demo tape: No longer just an audiocassette sample. These days, the best demo tapes are videos.

Food-vendor license: Like restaurants, caterers must be approved by their county board of health, which issues one of these (or a similarly named permit) to catering companies that pass inspection. When hiring a caterer, ask to see a copy of the company's license or permit.

ALLIES

American Institute of Architects (AIA): 1735 New York Avenue NW, Washington, DC 20006. The AIA can put you in touch with one of its 300-plus local chapters, which provide lists of member architects in your area. Many chapters have resource centers that keep architects' portfolios on file.

American Society of Landscape Architects (ASLA): 4401 Connecticut Avenue NW, 5th Floor, Washington, DC 20008. Write for a free list of members in your area.

Association of Bridal Consultants (ABC): 200 Chestnutland Road, New Milford, CT 06776. Members include bridal consultants as well as entertainers. They have a network of state and local branches that can provide lists of entertainers in your area.

National Association of Catering Executives (NACE): 60 Revere Drive, Suite 500, Northbrook, IL 60062. Contact the NACE for a list of licensed caterers in your area.

Part 3

SHOPPING

Wringing Cash Out of the Retail System

How to Shop Wisely When an Army of Marketers Have Their Eyes on Your Wallet

There's no doubt about it. Americans are world-class shoppers. But whether it's to save money or time, more than half of us are shopping less. As we plunge into the twenty-first century, what was the national pastime of the 1980s is now a tiresome chore. The average consumer spends three hours a week shopping—two for food and necessities and one for apparel and other goods, according to a National Retail Federation survey.

And more than half of consumers agree with the statement, "Shopping is a hassle I try to avoid."

This is bad news for retailers who have saturated the country with too many stores and too much stuff. Retail-space growth has outpaced population growth by a 10-to-1 ratio. The number of U.S. shopping centers has grown from 2,000 in 1957 to more than 30,000 today, according to the International Council of Shopping Centers. And considering that one of the keys to this growth has been a proliferation of outlet malls, off-price stores, discount chains, and warehouse clubs, it's no wonder that the consensus among today's consumers is: If you paid retail, you paid too much.

"There's nothing precise about shopping," says Sue Goldstein, in her book *The Underground Shopper*. "My battle cry is, 'Never pay retail.' There are alternatives to paying full price for everything."

Recent surveys of consumer attitudes about retail shopping show that a staggering 90 percent felt that they paid too much when they paid full price. Still, retailers racked up $2.2 trillion in sales in 1994. Sounds impressive, but the reality is that retailers are feeling the pinch of stagnant sales fueled by the growth of discounters.

Survey after survey shows that shoppers are discontented, are buying less, and are switching brands. In a scramble to offset these trends, retailers are constantly studying consumer behavior, trying to figure out ways to get you to spend. Their basic one-two strategy, though, has always been the same: Get them in the store and then keep them in the store, because the longer they stay, the more they spend.

Their theory is simple. The longer you linger, the more likely you are to buy on the spur of the moment. This basic act—the unplanned purchase—is the foundation of retail profit-making and a prime consideration in store layout, in the advertising that draws you into the store, and the gimmicks and come-ons used to get you to buy once you're there, such as sales, coupons, or free gifts. Even the VIP treatment (holding your packages or greeting you when you come in the door) has come into its own as a sales gimmick.

Once you're caught in the feel-good experience of impulse spending, retailers will whisper in your ear, "Just charge it." That $100 dress is suddenly a very affordable $10 a month. Of course, once you're done paying for the dress plus interest, it will probably cost an additional $20. In 1993, Americans charged $422 billion, up 25 percent from 1992. The average cardholder now carries 8 to 10 credit cards, owes about $2,500, and pays about $450 in interest annually. Once they're financed, all those great bargains that you found on sale aren't such a deal after all.

Everything about the typical retail store is calculated to generate more sales per square foot for the retailer by getting you, the consumer, to buy on the spur of the moment. Studies show that about 53 percent of groceries and 47 percent of hardware store purchases are impulse purchases. When you realize that half of the retailer's bread and butter comes from our unplanned purchases, it's no wonder that so much effort is spent just getting you into the store.

Advertising: The Ins and Outs

If consumers are the horse pulling the cart of the retail system, then advertising is the carrot dangling in front of the horse's nose, perpetually goading, enticing you to buy, buy, buy. Experts estimate that the average American who lives 75 years will spend almost three full years of waking life just watching television commercials and one additional year listening to radio ads, viewing print ads, and talking to telemarketers.

Sales pitches have invaded almost every aspect of our lives, turning up in once-noncommercial places—public schools, home telephones, sporting events, movies, school buses, public restrooms, even the bottom of holes on putting greens.

Here's the bottom line. While advertising can serve to inform, it also soaks up a great deal of our time and money.

ARE YOU READY FOR THE PITCH?

Marketers spent more than $150 billion in 1994 to persuade consumers to buy their products—which amounts to $565 per person. Ultimately though, those advertising expenditures are paid for by consumers in the form of higher prices. About 10 percent of the cost for products such as cosmetics, CDs, or games goes for promotional costs. These advertising premiums are as high as 50 percent on items like national-brand breakfast cereal.

"Companies marketing national brands strongly prefer to compete on the basis of advertising, not price. That strategy—which keeps profit margins high—is obvious any time you go to the grocery store," says Michael Jacobson, founder of the Center for the Study of Commercialism in Washington, D.C., and co-author of *Marketing Madness*.

In response to this unrelenting onslaught of commercial claims, Americans have grown increasingly skeptical and cynical. A 1995 survey published by the Consumer Network found that 73 percent of consumers agreed that "knowing what to believe is harder than ever these days."

Understanding advertising and the buttons that advertisers push to get you to buy can help you to filter out fact from fiction when making your purchasing decisions.

"One has to use one's judgment all the time and always be skeptical," says Jacobson. When it comes to weekly specials at local grocery stores, sale items at the local shopping center, and new products that are on the market, ads can be a useful source of information. But the majority of marketing messages crafted by these professional sellers puts most of us amateur buyers at a distinct disadvantage. Here are some pointers that Jacobson recommends to put you on firmer ground for making purchasing decisions.

Separate the facts from the glitz. Once you get into the habit of picking advertising apart, you will find that most ads have little or no factual information, such as price, value, or quality of a product. Ask yourself: Does the ad tell you any facts about the product? Do you really need the product? Would you really use it? Could you find another product of the same quality? Are there products of the same quality for a lower price?

Help to clean up the system. Scrutinize ads for false claims. It is illegal for ads to knowingly misrepresent a product. Report suspected advertising fraud to your local Better Business Bureau, your state consumer protection

How Ads Push Your Buttons

Here are some of the most common appeals that advertisers use to influence your buying decisions. When you hear such pitches, activate your B.S. (that stands for *Beat the System!*) antennae and start separating the facts from the hype.

- Be like others.
- Be different.
- Be sexy.
- Be young.
- Be like the stars.
- Love yourself.
- What a bargain.
- Our tests prove it.
- If we're funny, you have to love our product.

office, or the Federal Trade Commission, or call toll-free directory assistance for help contacting the National Fraud Information Center. If you want such practices to stop, you have to do your part.

Limit your exposure. The average person is exposed to nearly 3,000 ads a day. Even the savviest of consumers is not immune to influence from this level of exposure. Ads encourage a brand-name mentality—buying on the basis of the maker rather than the quality or the price of the product. To combat this, change the radio or television station when an ad comes on and rely more on public television and public radio and on newsletters and magazines with little or no advertising. Better yet, hit the "off" switch on your channel changer more often. The average American will spend 13 years of his lifetime watching TV. Grant yourself a reprieve.

WHEN IS A SALE REALLY A SALE?

The word "sale" used to mean something. There were end-of-season price slashings for leftover goods and January "white" sales, tactics used by retailers to attract customers during the slow season. Shoppers heading home with an armload of marked-down merchandise knew that they were getting a bargain.

Today's proliferation of sales—the sale mania started with the recession of the late 1980s—has clouded the standards of retail pricing. You can walk into a department store on virtually any day of the year and find a sale promising discounts of 20, 30, or even 60 percent. But the question is, How much are you really saving? How can you tell a real bargain from a bogus one?

"You can never be sure unless you're an industry insider. It's a nightmare. The more that discounting flourishes, the more convoluted those markups and markdowns are going to be getting," writes Goldstein.

The fact is that sales are no longer the exception, they're the rule. Department stores sold 60 to 80 percent of all merchandise on sale in 1994. A substantial percentage of this merchandise was not really sold at bargain-basement prices. If it was, retailers wouldn't be able to stay in business. Items are often offered just briefly for the "regular" price, then are put on sale. The sale price—usually 25 to 30 percent off—is closer to the true retail price.

Consumers may not be aware of these practices. Most of the complaints alleging deceptive sales advertising are actually lodged by retail competitors, not consumers, according to Lynne Collins of the national advertising division of the Council of Better Business Bureaus, in Arlington, Virginia. But here are a few consumer-friendly tips to help you recognize deceptive sale practices.

Know your store's merchandise. If you regularly familiarize yourself with a store's stock, you'll know if a product was ever really sold for its "regular" price. Most fellow retailers sell the same merchandise—that's how they can spot a phony sale. This doesn't mean that you have to do a price inventory of the whole store. Just keep your eyes on the things that you're likely to buy.

Compare prices, not percentages. Know your prices and always compare the bottom line. This is the best defense against phony sale prices. An item that sells for 30 percent off in ABC Goods may actually cost more than the same item offered by XYZ Stuff at 15 percent off.

Don't buy just because it's on sale. If it's a can of peas on special at the grocery store, go ahead and splurge. But if it's a $200 suit that you hadn't given a thought to before you walked into the store, hang on to your wallet.

Plan meals around supermarket specials. According to the U.S. Department of Labor, the average household spends nearly $4,300 a year on food. Experts estimate that you can save up to a quarter of your costs—or about $1,100—by shopping supermarket specials, using coupons, buying less processed food and meat, and using store brands.

Lean on the "loss leaders." Supermarkets and discount chains commonly offer advertised sale items at or below cost. You can get a genuinely great deal on that item. But loss leaders are used to get you into the store on the theory that once you're there, you'll buy additional items at regular prices. So don't play into the retailer's hands.

Beware of the bait and switch. It's a trick as old as retailing itself. But retailers still use it because consumers still fall for it. Bait and switch works like this: The retailer advertises an item at a low price. You go to the store to buy the item, and the retailer says that it's sold out. But he is only too happy to show you another—usually more expensive—item that's in stock. This kind of deceptive advertising is against the law. If this happens to you, immediately report the retailer to the local Better Business Bureau.

QUALITY AND VALUE VERSUS AD HYPE

The image-conscious 1980s produced a bonanza of designer goods with bloated price tags for status-conscious consumers. But now the buying mood has turned from image to thrift. Surveys show that consumers today care more about getting their money's worth than anything else. They want good value for good products. Consider the following:

• Figures show that consumers care less about fashion and more about value. In 1995 only 22.9 percent of consumers agreed that it is important to wear fashionable clothing, down from 31 percent in 1994 and 28.1 percent in 1992.

• Private-label and store brands continue to gain acceptance in consumer minds. In 1995, 53 percent of all consumers indicated that private-label clothing was a better value, in terms of price, than well-known national brands—up from 29 percent in 1992.

• Shoppers expect everyday low prices and seek sales. More than half decide which stores to shop based on advertised sale prices.

• Surveys of consumer trends show that brand loyalty has eroded substantially. In 1976 more than 75 percent of all supermarket shoppers considered themselves brand-loyal. Today fewer than 25 percent do.

Although we're buying into image less and value more, American consumers have been conditioned by manufacturers and retailers to equate brand names and higher prices with good quality. Whether it's blue jeans or coffee, brand-name goods have always conveyed the image of superior products, while the lowly store brands with their plain packaging were left for the penny-pinchers. In their quest for value, consumers are putting aside these longstanding images of quality. It's become chic to be cheap. Retailers know this and have responded by promoting value in their appeals to consumers. So the savvy shopper should beware: The image of value is becoming one more hype-laden marketing tool.

These approaches will steer you toward honest-to-goodness value.

The golden rule: comparison-shop. Retailing techniques may come and go, but knowing your prices is still the only way to know whether you're getting value for your money. It sounds like an obvious thing to do, yet salesmen state that they are continually surprised by the number of people who fail to comparison-shop. To determine whether the store where you shop gives you the best value for your dollars, make a list of the items that you frequently buy. Then go to your supermarket and at least one other store and compare. Even a difference of a few percent can add up to several hundred dollars over a year.

When the Full Retail Price Is the Best Value

Sales and bargains are not always a best buy. *Money* magazine polled economists, professional shoppers, retail analysts, marketing gurus, and penny-pincher newsletter editors to find out when it's worthwhile to pay premium prices—even when you can get it cheaper. They came up with six scenarios.

1. It'll last forever.
2. It beats all the competition.
3. It's one of a kind.
4. It solves an urgent problem.
5. It gives peace of mind.
6. It's a reward.

Buy store brands. You can save 15 to 21 percent off your grocery bill by choosing no-frills brands instead of nationally advertised brands. This adds up to about $110 per person per year. Discount brands developed by super-market chains now account for 18 percent of all grocery purchases. Increasing attention is being given to the quality and image of store brands. Today's store brands enjoy prominent shelf placement, more promotion, and generally higher manufacturing standards.

Look high and low for value. In a store, the high-rent district is the shelf space at eye level. It is occupied by the manufacturers who have the most clout, meaning the nationally advertised brands that sell the most products in the store. Since these are also often the most heavily promoted brands, you'll find yourself paying more to cover the advertising and packaging costs. Eye-level space is also occupied by products with a higher profit margin. That's why you'll find specialty instant coffees and single-serve coffee at eye level and the three-pound economy size slumming it on the bottom shelf. Your strategy, then? Keep your eye on the higher and lower shelves for the true values.

Check the unit pricing. If you have the storage space and the extra cash, it pays to buy a bigger quantity of something to save on the unit price. Dog food, for instance, may cost nearly double per pound in the handy 5-pound bags than in the cumbersome 20-pound sacks.

Shopping: Buyer, Beware

Do you know the difference between shopping and purchasing? Well, keep a firm grip on your wallet until you've learned. Mary Hunt, reformed spender and editor of *Cheapskate Monthly*, explains it this way: Shopping is moseying around with a vague notion of wanting to buy something. Purchasing is knowing what you want and finding the best deal.

"Walking into the store with only a vague notion is as silly as trying to build a house without a blueprint," Hunt says. "It's a haphazard way to live and a very dangerous way to manage your money."

MAP OUT YOUR SHOPPING STRATEGY

Without a purchasing plan, you are prey for dozens of retailing tricks that you will encounter as soon as you enter a store.

"I was a blank canvas waiting to see what would strike my fancy," Hunt says of her wanton spending days.

These techniques will help you shop wisely.

Always shop from a list. Retailers want you to buy impulsively, and they know that consumers have a weakness for it. Remember that about half of all sales are impulse buys. A study by the International Mass Retail Association found that 45 percent of men and 54 percent of women make unplanned purchases. If an item is not on your list, don't buy it. If you really want it, put it on next week's list.

Pay cash. "It's a lot harder to lay a $100 bill down on the counter for a dress than to write a check or use a credit card," says Hunt. "Credit cards skew our thinking. A $300 suit isn't $300. It's $15 dollars a month."

Research items in consumer magazines. If you plan to make a major purchase, consumer and specialty magazines can provide a wealth of general information on features, performance, and price. Learn enough to recognize a good deal when you see one.

Keep a permanent price book. For groceries, list the prices of everything that you normally buy from three stores that have good prices. Record the unit price, too, since many stores vary the sizes that they carry. Keep the book with you at the store or while perusing ads.

"Over a period of time, you'll develop a new habit of price awareness," says Hunt. She recommends extending the book to include clothing items that you routinely buy, such as men's shirts, socks, underwear, or bedding items. Record specific sales, noting the dates and the savings.

Sleep on it. Think twice about your big-ticket purchases. Whether you're considering a $150 dress or a $3,800 camcorder, you may change your mind in 24 hours.

Never miss a grand opening. To attract a lot of customer attention, merchants often have special storewide discounts and double-coupon deals at grand openings.

At a spectacular sale, stock up. When you find a truly good sale price on expensive items that you routinely use, buy extras, suggests Goldstein. Retailers do exactly the same thing when manufacturers offer them limited-time discounts on certain brands.

Tricks of the Retail Stores

Retail stores are laid out to attract you with a minefield of sensory cues. Here's a sampling of techniques stores use to keep unwary patrons spending. Being aware of these tactics will help you resist unnecessary spending.

Trail of temptation. Patrons usually have to pass through a gauntlet of goodies that stimulate impulse buys before they get to the "demand" departments tucked away on an upper floor or in a far corner of the store—the places that customers originally set out to visit, such as furniture, appliances, audio equipment, or the linen department. Cosmetics, a department store's most profitable area, is nearly always near the ground floor entrance. Hosiery, scarves, handbags, and jewelry—other high-impulse items—are located nearby.

The checkout trap. Supermarkets and department stores strategically place impulse buys near the cash register—items like hair bows and costume jewelry in department stores and candy, film, and magazines in the grocery store. What's another $5 or $10 as long as you have the wallet open? It's no coincidence that these items usually have high profit margins.

The bin invitation. Even upscale stores will display small items like gloves, scarves, and leather goods on a table or "dump bin" to make it appear that buyers are getting a bargain. This bazaar approach implies markdowns that aren't necessarily in effect. Supermarkets try the same ploy with end-of-aisle displays and island displays to make you think that the products are being sold at reduced prices.

Coming and going. Escalators are the center stage of many stores, which makes them ideal locations for promotional items and signs.

HIT 'EM OFF-SEASON

You pay the highest prices for products during the peak of their shopping season. So if you can anticipate your needs—sometimes this means almost a year in advance—you can get savings of up to 75 percent by shopping off-season. There is usually a limited selection and availability of items. But the savings, especially on big-ticket items like appliances, is usually worth the trade-off.

While there are usually some preseason promotional sales with markdowns of 20 to 30 percent to get merchandise moving, the real bargains will usually come during postseason clearance sales when retailers want to get rid of the old to make room for the new.

Check the hot prices on summer stuff. Buy summer items in late August and September. You'll save on things like window air conditioners,

Making you see red. Red excites. Retailers maintain that it stimulates buying. That's why many sale signs use red. Color is also used in the dressing room, where warm pinks, peaches, and corals make people feel good about themselves and (retailers hope) what they've just tried on.

Scatter the basics. Supermarkets are laid out so that you'll have to hike through the entire store to pick up staples like milk, eggs, flour, and bread. Milk, for instance, is always in the farthest corner from the entrance door. The retailer's hope is that you'll pick up more than just a gallon of milk as you're sailing down the aisles.

Surveys have revealed that consumers tend to shop the periphery of the store, which is why the store has it's most profitable items such as meat and produce along the edges. Logic might tell you that the produce department should be the last you come to, so these items don't get squashed by all the heavier things you buy. However, studies show that placing produce near the front boosts sales by 1 to 1½ percent.

Time is money. Supermarkets know that the more time that you spend in the store, the more money you spend in the store. Every extra minute roaming the aisles or twisting through displays results in an average of $2 more spent. Store planners put obstacles—such as salad bars, floral shops, bakery goods, and other high-profit specialty items—in shoppers' paths near the store entrance. There, customers are less likely to be annoyed by them and are more likely to buy, since they aren't already looking at a cartload of groceries.

fans, lawn furniture, grills, lawn mowers, pool equipment, and camping gear. As a bonus, you may be able to get additional discounts on display models at this time of year.

Look for cool savings on winter stuff. Look for bargains on winter necessities in January, February, and March. Items like space heaters, Christmas decorations and wrapping paper, coats and boots, sweaters, and snow tires can typically be had for 40 to 60 percent savings postseason.

THE LOWDOWN ON MARKUPS

Forget the manufacturer's suggested retail price, or MSRP. In his book *The Total Negotiator*, attorney and financial consultant Stephen Pollan explains that, while a manufacturer may advertise a suggested retail price, it is really meaningless. Each retailer bases his price first on what it cost him to buy the item, then on what it costs him to do business, next on what other retailers are selling the item for, and finally on what he thinks someone is willing to pay for the item.

To wring extra cash out of the retail system, it is essential that you have working knowledge of typical retail markups. This will enable you to discern several things before deciding whether you want to buy an item.

- Am I getting a good value for my money?
- Is there room for negotiation?
- Am I paying too much for this item?

Markups or profit margins, however, are one of the most closely guarded secrets of the retail industry. While they will vary from store to store and chain to chain, here are some common ranges, according to retail insiders.

Appliances. Small appliances like microwave ovens are usually marked up about 30 percent. Large ones—such as refrigerators, ranges, washers, and dryers—are marked up about 15 percent. To help appliance and electronics salespeople, retailers often put a special alphanumeric code on their price tags, indicating how much the item cost or the lowest price that it can be sold for without management approval.

Automobiles. A new car will normally carry a markup of 5 to 10 percent already built in to the sticker price. But don't be misled by a seemingly modest margin. Dealers also make money from factory incentives, financing, and so-called holdbacks—payments from the manufacturer of as much as 3 percent of the car's retail price. Dealers also make a nice profit on extras like CD players and sunroofs, which are typically marked up 15 to 25 percent.

Clothing. You'll find markups as high as 100 percent on most types of clothing and even higher on designer clothing or licensed items. When it comes to apparel, markups are a game of musical prices complicated by the perpetual "sales" that have become a fixture in American department stores and specialty stores. Seven in 10 consumers say that they buy nearly everything on sale.

Furniture. The standard furniture retailer's profit margin is known as fifty and ten. *Fifty and ten* literally means a markup of $55 on each $100 of the suggested retail price. It works this way: Fifty percent of $100 is $50. To find the wholesale price, subtract and additional 10 percent from $50, which reduces the original $100 to $45. So if you're paying full retail for a $500 chair, the markup adds up to $275.

Groceries. Supermarket markups generally range from 5 to 20 percent. High-profit items such as produce and meat are found around the periphery of the store and at eye level on shelves. The store may make less than 1 cent on every dollar of sales on staples such as bread, milk, coffee, and flour while cashing in on a hefty 30 percent profit on those magazines and candy bars located at the checkout.

Salespeople:
Sidestepping Smooth Talk

You're contentedly thumbing your way through a rack of men's ties in a department store when, out of the corner of your eye, you spot a salivating salesman homing in on you. You'd like to whip out a crucifix and chant, "Back, vampire, back!"

Yes, a large number of shoppers hate dealing with sales staff, and retailers know it. In the minds of many consumers, salespeople are slick, carnivorous pitchmen who will push merchandise that you don't want so that they can earn big commissions. The well-worn caricature of the pushy salesman with his loud suit and transparent sales pitch may be the stuff of late-night commercials, but it's not what you're likely to encounter on the sales floor of your favorite retail establishment.

HOW SALESPEOPLE SIZE YOU UP

Instead, you'll find sales techniques that are much are more subtle in their attempt to get you to buy. As a shopper, always remember that the salesperson is in the business of selling. Throughout the interaction between you, the salesperson will be continually sizing you up—trying to figure exactly what will make you buy the product and, if at all possible, buy it today. This is done by asking you such questions as the price range that you're willing to pay, the features that you're looking for, and the color that

---

Tracking the Seasons, Retail-Style

So you thought that there were four seasons in a year. Apparel retailers divide the calendar into eight seasons—more changes than the weather warrants. Within each season manufacturers create groups of clothes whose colors and fabrics are meant to be worn together. Look for markdowns about eight weeks after the merchandise hits the sales floor.

Season	Starts in
Early spring	Mid-January
Late spring	March
Early summer	Mid-April
Transition	Early June
Early fall	Mid-July
Fall	Early September
Holiday	Mid-October
Resort/cruise wear	December

you'd prefer. The salesperson's goal is to clear the path for the sale by addressing (or appearing to address) all your needs.

Which salesperson you end up with is usually a matter of chance. Most stores have an "up" system, which means that the sales staff take turns approaching new customers. In sizing you up as a potential sale, the first thing that the salesperson will do is determine whether you're a buyer or a browser. They don't want to waste their time with someone who has no intention of buying. At this point the salesperson is likely to ask you several questions about the type of product that you're looking for. This is called qualifying the customer. Once you've passed the test, it's time for the salesperson to close the sale.

You don't have to fall prey to the salesperson's art. The final decision of whether to buy should rest on whether the store has satisfied your product requirements, not that you fell for a convincing sales pitch. So here's how to deal with salespeople.

Read up. Research your product enough to keep the salesman honest. It's a good idea to read *Consumer Reports* and any specialty magazines that cover the product that you're interested in. Don't take the information as gospel, however, since most magazines lag behind the industry by a few months. Features and model numbers are likely to change. If you go into a store brandishing *Consumer Reports*, you're playing right into the salesmen's hands. Salesmen are trained to deflect information published in these reports.

Make your getaway. Make your buying decision away from the glitz and pressure. The sales floor is designed to get you to want to buy, and the salesperson is trained to induce you to buy. So make the decision of whether to purchase in the quiet of your own home.

Extract the expert. Appeal to the expert side of the salesperson. Most people who sell big-ticket items work primarily on commission. To succeed they need to be expert salespeople and experts in the products that they are selling. To bring out the product expert in your salesperson and suppress the commercial instincts, approach the situation as a nice, confused consumer looking for information. Say that you've read a little about the products and would like to learn more. If you approach the situation as a know-it-all ready to do battle, the salesman side of him will sharpen his pitch for the attack.

HASSLE-FREE HAGGLING

Negotiating price is common in other countries. And to most Americans the thought of haggling is exactly that—something foreign and unfamiliar. But experts estimate that you can save 10 to 20 percent on major purchases by following a few basic guidelines for the age-old practice of haggling.

Most of the items that are negotiable fall into three categories—vehicles, major appliances, and consumer electronic equipment. Most of the products in these categories are big-ticket items worthwhile of some negotiating effort, says Pollan. A good rule of thumb is to stick to items that cost more than $250. Don't overlook the value of negotiating away extras—like delivery charges, installation charges, or additional features on an item—to bring down the overall cost.

To decide what type of retail outlet to negotiate with, keep your specific goal in mind. Is it finding the lowest price? Then negotiate with regional

Tricks of the Sales Trade

Here are some techniques commonly used by salespeople, according to consumer advocates Ralph Nader and Wesley J. Smith, co-authors of the book *The Frugal Shopper*. Being aware of them will put you a step ahead of the average consumer.

Just say yes. One sales theory holds that the more you say yes while you're listening to a sales pitch, the more likely you will be to say yes when the salesperson "asks for the sale." Watch for questions that are couched to generate yes answers.

The dialog might start with a simple. "So you're looking for a new washer and dryer?" Yes.

"Do you have a color in mind?" Yes.

And the conversation builds to, "So you are shopping for a large capacity, white washer and dryer, with an extra rinse cycle that sells for under $950?" Yes. "I have just the model for you. We'll be delivering in your area on Tuesday. Is that a good day for you?" Yes. And so on. Beware of these "yes" mode tactics and don't hesitate to say no when the salesperson asks, "Should I reserve one in your name?"

Putting you on the defensive. Some salespeople might try to make you justify why you won't buy a product. Then the salesperson attempts to knock down your defenses. For instance, if you say, "I just can't afford it," the salesperson might say, "You'd be surprised. Did you know that you can have this computer for only $35 a month?" Don't play this game with a salesperson. If you are not ready to buy, then don't.

Appealing to your emotions. Trained salespeople know that the decision to buy is often an emotional one. They will begin the sales pitch with logic and then try to close the sale on an emotional note: "This car has all the features that you're looking for—good gas mileage, excellent warranty, and good service history. Don't you think you deserve a new car?"

An emotional state can lead to irrational buying decisions. Get away to neutral ground if this happens and then make your decision.

and national specialty chains. If you are interested in an ongoing relationship where the retailer provides service, stick with a local specialty store. Department stores, discount stores, and catalog showrooms don't offer much opportunity to negotiate. Prices in these stores are often fixed.

Once you find the right store, you need to find the right person to negotiate with. This often means starting with the salesman and then working out the final price with the manager. You'll know that you've gotten a good price if it requires the manager or owner's approval, says Pollan. And remember one of the key tenets of haggling: The more expensive and widely available an item is, the more negotiable it is.

Shop on weekday mornings. Weekends are much busier for retailers, so salespeople will be under more pressure both to deal with more customers and to close more sales. On a weekend, salespeople will spend less time with you and, therefore, have less investment in you. On a weekday, when very few customers are in the store, a salesperson will be happy to spend as much time as you want explaining the store's products. Mornings are less pressure-filled than afternoons and evenings. In the morning, salespeople are optimistic and not worried about what they haven't sold that day.

Shop at the end of the month. Discounts are more likely to be had at the end of the month in order to meet sales quotas.

Let them know that you're ready to buy. If you make it clear that you're about to make that big purchase, this will distinguish you as a buyer, not a shopper. Salespeople don't negotiate with shoppers, but they know that negotiating with buyers may mean closing a sale, which is all that they're really interested in.

Tell them that you're comparison-shopping. By letting the salesperson know that you'll be shopping their competitors, the pressure is on the salesperson to come up with their best price.

Ask for a good price. Don't immediately accept or reject the salesperson's first offer, suggests Pollan. Ask him to do better. Say that you really like the product and would like to buy it from him but that you just can't afford the price. You can follow it up with some suggestions of just how he might improve his offer.

Get a discount for paying cash. Do this near the end of the negotiation, when you believe that the salesman has offered you his lowest price. Then ask him to ask his manager if you could get an additional discount for paying cash. This is more likely to work in smaller establishments, because it frees them from having to pay credit card fees, says Pollan.

Remember: Haggling pays. If the idea of haggling makes you cringe, just remember that the worst thing that can happen is that the other person will say no. On the other hand, there's a good chance that you will save 10, 20, maybe even 25 percent on your purchase.

Coupons and Rebates: Payback Time

There's a divided camp of consumer experts when it comes to coupons and their industry cousins, rebates and refunds. Diligent clippers maintain that you can routinely shave 10 to 20 percent off your weekly grocery tab. Others, like consumer advocate Ralph Nader in his book *The Frugal Shopper*, say that coupons are a gimmick promoted by manufacturers to entice you to buy overpriced, name-brand products that you normally wouldn't purchase.

From a retailer's perspective, coupons are one way that manufacturers get stores to stock new products—and there are more than 17,000 of them each year. A retailer who is reluctant to stock a new product need only be reminded that a major coupon drop is scheduled for his area. He has to consider the consequences of disappointing all those coupon-clutching customers.

When manufacturers offer coupons on high-profit impulse items like a new rice mix, people buy 50 percent more than if the product wasn't promoted. That's why manufacturers find it worthwhile to distribute 310 billion cents-off coupons per year, even though 292 billion of them will go unredeemed. Besides introducing new products, coupons are also used to protect or strengthen a product's share of the market, usually by encouraging some brand switching to create new loyal customers.

However, surveys show that since 1992, coupon redemption has declined steadily. It may signal a trend that mega-manufacturers like Proctor & Gamble (P&G) are picking up on. Consumers are getting fed up with coupons, gimmicks, and come-ons. The result could be that coupons go the way of the dinosaur. In 1996, P&G and other major manufacturers began testing no-coupon policies in various regions of the country. Instead of creating brand loyalty, coupons have undermined the perception of name brands being a good value. A growing consensus among shoppers seems to be "If I don't have a coupon, I'm not going to buy it."

Retailers are getting on the coupon bandwagon, albeit a little late. In recent years, department stores, specialty stores, and even off-price stores have begun offering coupons. Unlike their grocery store cousins that offer savings on a specific product, these retail gimmicks are designed to draw you into the store—usually by offering 5 to 20 percent savings if you shop on a certain day, or on your first purchase. Some feature a lottery-style aspect where you rub off a patch on the coupon to reveal your "savings," which is usually expressed in percentages. But surveys show that these types of coupons may cause customers to avoid making purchases.

SAVING AT A GOOD CLIP

Whatever your "big picture" view of the coupon biz may be, it's still a thriving institution that—for the time being, at least—offers substantial savings to savvy shoppers. So here are some wise couponing techniques.

Five Steps to a Better Price

Start any negotiation process by letting the salesperson know that you'll be comparison-shopping and that you are interested in buying today. Once a price is quoted, say attorney and financial consultant Stephen Pollan and Mark Levine, co-authors of *The Total Negotiator*, don't accept or reject the offer. Instead, ask for a better price. Here are some suggestions to get the seller to lower the price further.

1. Consider the extras. Ask if it's possible to get the full-featured model for close to the price of the stripped-down model. You are, in effect, asking the retailer to throw in options free of charge.
2. Plead poverty. Say that you need more money to buy some extras and then mention what they would be. This gives the salesman the opportunity to throw them in for nothing.
3. Say that looks don't matter. Tell the salesperson that appearance really isn't a factor so that it's possible that he could sell a demonstration model or floor model to you for a lower price.
4. Roll back the calendar. Ask for last year's model, explaining that you really don't need a state-of-the-art product. This gives the salesman the chance to sell something that he needs to get rid of or to give you a discount.
5. Look to the future. Imply that you'll be coming back for other products and will become a regular customer or that you represent a group of other potential new customers.

Start small. If you're new to couponing, start out by using a few each week for items like cereal and detergent that you always buy. When you see the savings, you'll be hooked.

Stick to your regular grocery list. Only clip coupons for items that you normally use. Keep them filed alphabetically by product category (not brand name) in a file or envelope and note the expiration dates. Most coupons expire after 90 days, and nearly all expire within six months.

Double your savings. Look for stores that will double a coupon's value. Some stores only offer double coupons on a certain night of the week. This is the time to shop. But beware: Some stores that offer double coupons have higher everyday prices than stores that don't, so it pays to compare prices.

Calculate the value. Coupons usually are a marketing gimmick for higher-priced national brands. Make sure that you are paying less for the national brand with the coupon than you would for a store brand.

Get a double discount. Use manufacturer's coupons in combination with store coupons found in those weekly circulars or in combination with weekly specials.

First, run the numbers. Before shopping, gather advertising circulars from all the stores where you might shop. Make lists of the sale items that meet your family's needs, then check your coupon file to see if you have coupons for any of the items. Add up the savings and decide which stores are worth the trip.

Watch for castoffs. When you drop newspapers off at the recycling bin, keep an eye out for discarded coupon inserts from Sunday newspaper supplements, suggests refunding expert Susan Samtur, author of *The Super Coupon Shopping System* and publisher of *Refundle Bundle*. Keep in mind that fewer than 4 of every 100 coupons that are distributed are used. Recycling bins can be a gold mine of coupon opportunity.

REBATES: CHECKS IN THE MAIL

Couponing has a couple of cousins—rebates and refunds. These are the cash, credits, and gifts that you can receive from manufacturers and retailers for purchasing their products. Most of us ignore those $2 rebates offered if we send in two proofs of purchase from a box of cereal or a pack of batteries. It isn't worth the time and postage that it will take to redeem the offer, right?

Well, Samtur earns an average of $100 to $150 per month from refunding. In the last 20 years, she has paid for winter heating costs, funded a trip to Florida for her family of five, and paid for $35,000 worth of college education costs—all with money earned from refunding. As a bonus, cash refunds are considered discounts by the federal government and are, therefore, tax-free.

Many credit card companies now offer rebates with their cards. For each dollar charged on these cards, the issuer gives you anything from cash to credits toward free airline tickets, to discounts on telephone calls, to cents off at your favorite store. About 100 million of the 387 million Visas and MasterCards that Americans carry are rebate cards—up from about 40 million in 1992. Most of the rebate cards introduced in 1995 were from retailers, such as Egghead Software, Toys "R" Us, and Waldenbooks.

The more you charge, the bigger your rebate with these cards. The problem is that the pennies that you "earn" rarely outweigh the high interest rates, which average one or two points above the typical 18.2 percent of other credit cards and up to 11 points above the rate of the lowest cards. You would, for instance, have to charge a whopping $25,000 worth of stuff on most airlines' cards within three to five years to earn a free domestic flight. The bottom line is that none of these cards is an extraordinary deal unless you are a big spender and pay your bill in full every month, says Pollan.

Here are more tips that Samtur recommends for savvy rebating.

Follow the refunder's SOS. "S" is for save—save everything that might be useful and helpful, such as cash register tapes and packaging (about 80 percent of offers require proof of purchase or a universal product code). "O" is for organize—set up a simple system for managing your rebates, including a regular time for doing the work. And "S" is for send—put those rebate forms in the mail on a regular and consistent basis.

Find the forms. Refund offers are rarely distributed as aggressively as coupons. You have to look for them. Six common sources of rebate forms are:

- Stores—near the customer service center, on a bulletin board near the entrance or exit, or in the aisles
- Newspapers and magazines
- Directly from manufacturers
- Refunding newsletters
- Direct mail
- For the die-hard, clubs and conventions

Know when to look. Look for rebate forms in stores in the middle of the week—usually on Tuesdays or Thursdays—when the manufacturer's representatives are most likely to be restocking them. Forms run out quickly because some people take large quantities to sell and trade.

Make direct contact. Contact the company directly if you have a problem. Most rebate offers are processed through clearinghouses and take about 6 weeks. If you still have not received your rebate after 12 weeks, pick up the phone. Toll-free phone numbers often appear on product packaging, and that's your best bet. Forget that address that you sent the refund to.

Read 'em and reap. Subscribe to a refunding newsletter. There are about 10 in the United States, with a combined readership of about 150,000. You will find information on current rebate offers, and you will have the opportunity to trade forms and qualifiers (that's rebate lingo for labels, packaging, and cash register tapes) with other subscribers. Samtur estimates that you can miss up to 90 percent of refunding opportunities if you don't consult a newsletter. A typical bimonthly issue of her *Refundle Bundle* includes information on approximately 500 rebate offers totaling $700. For information on *Refundle Bundle*, write to P.O. Box 140, Centuck Station, Yonkers, NY 10710.

Faulty Goods: Know Your Rights

Although the credo "the customer is always right" seems to have lost all meaning in today's retail world, retailers do want to keep your business—which means that they're more inclined to set things aright when you aren't happy with merchandise you've bought.

In the sale mania of recent years, stores have concentrated on low prices, losing sight of the role that service plays in promoting customer loyalty.

Where to Find Coupons

A crack coupon user leaves no stone—or magazine page—unturned when it comes to locating the best deals. Make sure you habitually tap these coupon opportunities.

Sunday newspapers. More than three-quarters of all cash-off coupons are distributed in glossy Sunday newspaper inserts.

Within newspapers and magazines. Nestled between news stories and advertisements are what the industry calls ROP (right on the page) solos. These usually appear on food day of the local papers, which usually falls in the middle of the week when local stores distribute their advertising circulars. Women's magazines such as *Family Circle, Woman's Day, McCall's,* and *Ladies Home Journal* are also a source of coupons. Look in the stacks of magazines at the doctor's and dentist office.

Home mailers. Nearly everyone has received Carol Wright mail packets in a plain brown wrapper. Don't ignore such savings opportunities.

In-store coupons. One of the most direct ways that manufacturers use to develop customer loyalty is bounce-back coupons. Coupons are printed on a product's package or inserted in the package for customers to use on that or a subsequent purchase. Some stores also have dispensers in the aisles that offer coupons for nearby products. The back of your cash register tape also may be printed with coupons, which are only redeemable at that store or chain.

The Select Coupon program. More than 100,000 shoppers belong to this program, which specializes in providing large quantities of product coupons to its members by charging one-third of the face value of the coupon. For an annual membership fee of $19.95, you receive $19.95 worth of coupons. For information on this program send a self-addressed, stamped business-size envelope to Select Coupon Program, Box 141H, Scarsdale, NY 10583.

Faced with stagnant sales during the early 1990s, talk in the retail industry is now shifting back to customer service. A national survey by the International Mass Retail Association in 1995 found that a store's return policy, for instance, ranked seventh among the top 10 reasons women choose a store.

HOW TO ENSURE HAPPY RETURNS

Don't overlook a store's return policy when purchasing an item. After all, you don't want pay for defective goods, clothes that don't fit, food that is spoiled, or something you simply don't like. Under the law, a store is not required to exchange or make refunds on items that perform as advertised. But many stores will do so simply because it's good public relations.

Most department stores, specialty stores, and chains such as JCPenney and Sears have generous return policies. Even if you don't have a receipt, most of these stores will accept returns.

On the other hand, outlets and off-price stores usually make it more difficult for you to return goods. Most impose a time limitation, such as 10 days, and require a receipt. Some only offer a store credit instead of a refund.

The bottom line is this: Don't shop at stores that have a no-return policy. Here's how to make sure that your returns go smoothly.

Keep all your receipts. A good rule of thumb is to keep receipts for 30 days. You'll need a receipt to get full credit for a return if that item has since gone on sale. Also, if you buy an item at full price and it later goes on sale, you'll need the receipt to get a refund for the difference.

Use that plastic. Using a credit card is one of the best safeguards against unsatisfactory purchases, says Pollan. The Fair Credit Billing Act says that you can withhold payment for goods or services that don't satisfy you if three conditions apply.

1. You show that you tried to resolve the dispute with the seller.
2. You made the purchase in your home state or within 100 miles of your billing address.
3. You paid more than $50.

Meet the maker. If a retailer won't back up his merchandise, go straight to the source. Most manufacturers are willing to accommodate you by either replacing the product, repairing the product free of charge, or offering coupons for a new one. Most products have information about the location of the manufacturer right on the item.

For clothing, hit the books. To the layman, most garments would seem to lack any information about who manufactured them. However, there is a trick to deciphering garment labels. The federal government requires each label to contain information on fiber content, care instructions, the country of origin, and a manufacturer's name and address or their registered number (RN) or wool products label (WPL) number. These are numbers assigned by the government to each and every clothing manufacturer.

You'll find that most garment labels have an RN or WPL number, not a name and address. A directory called the *RN and WPL Encyclopedia* lists all the manufacturers and their numbers. The directories, though, are hard to find in most local libraries. The surest route is to locate the nearest college of textiles and call the reference desk of its library to track down a manufacturer.

WARRANTIES: CHECK THE FINE PRINT

Unless an item is clearly sold "as is," every new product has an implied warranty that offers protection if the product doesn't work when it's used as intended. Each state has its own laws about implied warranties, including how long they are in effect and whether the seller must repair the product, replace it, or give you a refund. Contact your state's consumer protection office to find out the laws in your state.

Although they are not legally required, most products also come with a written warranty from the retailer or the manufacturer. These warranties fall into two categories: limited, which specifies what repairs will be covered for free and for how long, and full warranty, which has no limitations.

Or you may purchase a product that has a combination of both. For instance, an item may carry a full warranty for the first year and a limited warranty for the next three years. A true tip-off to quality is an unlimited lifetime warranty.

Check before buying. Be sure that you understand the extent of a product's warranty before you buy—not after you get it home and out of the box. For instance, will you have to ship a faulty television set to Japan or a malfunctioning computer to the West Coast, or will the retailer take care of all shipping and handling? This can be especially important when you purchase electronics equipment, which is costly to fix.

Get it in writing. If the salesperson makes any promises at the time of the sale, like, "If it breaks, we'll fix it for free," get it in writing.

Play your cards right. You can double your warranty coverage by purchasing with certain credit cards. Items purchased with American Express cards and gold Visa and MasterCards as well as some standard cards automatically double the time allowance of the manufacturer's warranty, if the warranty period lasts one year or less.

EXTENDED COVERAGE: THINK TWICE

Extended warranties, also known as service contracts, are rarely worth the money that is spent on them, says Pollan. That's because usually if a product is defective, it will break down while the manufacturer's warranty is still in place. Only 12 to 20 percent of the people who buy warranties ever use them, yet it is estimated that consumers buy extended warranties for 30 to 40 percent of all appliances and electronic goods sold.

And here's why. Extended warranties are big moneymakers for retailers, often bringing in more profit than the merchandise. For every dollar that a retailer makes on a warranty, an average of just 4 to 15 cents is spent fixing the product. This means big commissions for salesmen, who can talk a good line about the necessity of protecting your investment.

A study by the National Science Foundation found that you often pay more for the contract than you would for the repair that it covers. Most warranties on retail merchandise cost $50 to $500. Normally, you will be pressured to purchase the extended warranty right after you decide to purchase the product (in effect, making an impulse purchase). But the fact is that you can usually purchase an extended warranty at any point in time, not just when the product is brand-new.

Another problem with extended warranties is that they tend to exclude coverage on almost everything that could go wrong. And warranty companies too frequently go out of business, leaving the consumer with a worthless piece of paper.

Consider, carefully, a safety net. Some experts cautiously advise that extended warranties could be good protection for electronic goods. You might want to consider a contract that offers loaner equipment or 24-hour repair service if you work at home and can't be without your computer, for instance. But be sure to read the fine print and evaluate exactly what is covered. Take into consideration the length of the warranty and the life of the product. Computer technology advances so quickly that it may not be worth repairing high-tech equipment three to four years down the road.

Follow the 10 percent rule. A rule of thumb is to only consider buying an extended warranty if its cost is 10 percent or less of the purchase price of the product, suggests Pollan. This doesn't mean that any warranty at this price is a good value. Steer clear of warranties on long-life, easy-maintenance products like refrigerators and dishwashers. Stick with electronics products that have costly maintenance histories, such as camcorders. You still must read the fine print to see exactly what type of repairs and parts are covered for the fee.

BOTTOM LINE

Getting the best deal on a product requires planning, research, and comparison shopping. For accurate product information, you cannot rely on advertising or sales personnel. Arm yourself against retailing ploys designed to get you to buy impulsively. And pay cash. Not only will it save you high monthly interest charges, but it might also stop you from making an unwise purchase.

WORDS TO THE WISE

Keystone: A phrase used in retailing to describe the standard markup on an item. In clothing, for instance, the keystone, or standard markup, is 100 percent above wholesale cost.

Loss leaders: Products priced at or below wholesale cost to draw consumers into the store. Retailers make up for the loss when consumers buy other items at regular prices in addition to the loss leaders.

RN and WPL numbers: The registered number or the wool products label number commonly found in a garment label. These numbers will help you track down the manufacturer.

ALLIES

Center for Media Literacy: 4727 Wilshire Boulevard, Suite 403, Los Angeles, CA 90010. This advocacy group publishes a workshop kit that helps parents and kids watch TV with a critical eye.

Center for the Study of Commercialism (CSC)—Stop the Calls: For a kit on how to stop unwanted calls from telemarketers, send $3 to CSC, 1875 Connecticut Avenue NW, Suite 300, Washington, DC 20009-5728.

Consumers Union: 101 Truman Avenue, Yonkers, NY 10703-1057. Publisher of *Consumer Reports*.

Council of Better Business Bureaus: 4200 Wilson Boulevard, Suite 800, Arlington, VA 22203-1804. On advertising issues, write to the National Advertising Division at 845 Third Avenue, 17th Floor, New York, NY 10022.

Public Citizen: 1600 20th Street, Washington, DC 20009. An activist group formed by consumer advocate Ralph Nader that focuses on consumer rights in the marketplace and citizen empowerment.

Sidestepping Retail Stores

Grab Up Big Savings through Nontraditional Sales Channels

Thrift and value are the buzzwords of today's savvy shopper. As prices continuously climb, our dollars have to stretch further. Bargain hunting has become so commonplace that paying full price at the checkout is now the exception to the rule. In other words, retail is out.

The explosive growth in the last decade of nonretail shopping alternatives—mail-order shopping, outlets, warehouse stores, electronic shopping, TV shop-at-home channels—reflects our desire for quality products at cut-rate prices. Whatever you're shopping for—clothing or food, tools or appliances, furniture or housewares—you don't have to look far for an opportunity to sidestep traditional retail stores and retail prices.

Sidestepping the retail system has become big business. Some avenues offer true bargains, while others are merely retail dressed up like a bargain.

Saving money usually involves a trade-off—and generally speaking, the bigger the savings, the bigger the trade-off.

- If you shop mail-order or its electronic cousins, TV and online services, you give up getting to "try it before you buy it."
- If you shop the outlets, you're likely to spend a lot of time driving to faraway outlet centers to get discounts on merchandise that might not be first-rate.
- If you shop the warehouse clubs, you'll get value, but not selection.

- If you buy used instead of new, you'll get a great price, but you're also likely to spend a lot of time finding what you need. And once you buy it, there are no guarantees—you're buying "as is."

Which bargain-hunting technique works best for you depends to a large extent on what you're willing to give up to get quality products and services at the best price.

Shopping from Home: Far from the Crowds

You can't beat the convenience of mail-order shopping: No fighting for a parking space at the mall. No need to stand in long lines at the cashier. And prices are generally 25 to 30 percent lower because mail-order companies aren't burdened with the high operating costs of the typical retailer.

Whether it's to save time or money or for the sheer convenience of it, more than half of American consumers shop by mail at least once a year. From 1990 to 1995, consumer catalog sales grew a healthy 5.5 percent per year to $38.6 billion, according to the Direct Marketing Association.

CATALOGS: BEAN AND BEYOND

While nearly everyone is familiar with old standbys like Lands' End and L.L. Bean, there are thousands of mail-order companies out there offering everything from gourmet sausages to prescription drugs to antique hardware.

But the best mail-order deals are not found in the glossy catalogs that clutter your mailbox each week. Many companies that sell a wealth of merchandise and sell it at wholesale prices don't even publish catalogs because of the added cost. Others offer catalogs for a fee, such as Baby Clothes Wholesale, which will charge you for the first three catalogs (a total of $3) and then send you subsequent catalogs for free.

Several resource books have a comprehensive listing of mail-order companies offering great deals. Among them are the *Wholesale-by-Mail Catalog*, which is updated every year, and *Great Buys by Mail (and Phone!)* by Sue Goldstein. The listings include addresses and phone numbers, methods of payment, and a description of the range of products offered. The mail-order outlets listed in these books typically offer discounts of 20 to 70 percent off retail prices.

Never pay cash. If your order gets lost, there is no proof that you have paid for the product if you pay with cash. When ordering, it's best to use a credit card. While personal checks are also acceptable, many companies will wait until the check has cleared to process your order. That can mean a delay of two to three weeks.

Get the size right. Clothing is the most mail-ordered item. To avoid fitting problems, send your measurements in with your order, or refer to the

How the Price-Quote System Works

Many of the companies listed in mail-order directories like the *Wholesale-by-Mail Catalog* and *Great Buys by Mail (and Phone!)* have access to thousands of products at discount prices. But if they were to publish a catalog, the result would be an unwieldy volume twice the size of the Los Angeles Yellow Pages. The cost to produce a book this size, and then continually update it, would result in higher operating costs for them and higher prices for you.

Instead, these companies have chosen a less expensive way to do business—that is, to quote prices to people who call or write.

Price-quote firms are not as glamorous or well-known as catalog companies, but they offer some unbeatable bargains and savings that can add up to hundreds or even thousands of dollars on major purchases. As Sue Goldstein explains in *Great Buys by Mail (and Phone!)*, the price-quote system is an extremely cost-efficient way to let you know what the current price is and whether the item is available.

"Don't be afraid of price quotes—the system is simple," Goldstein says.

Here's how it works: Contact the company by mail or phone and give the specifics of the product that you're interested in—manufacturer, model number, style number, color, size, quantity. (This may require some legwork on your part.) The company will then provide a price quote. If you like the quoted price, go ahead and order.

It's that easy. Remember to include a self-addressed, stamped business-size envelope with your inquiry if you are obtaining a quote by mail. This will speed up the quote process.

company's sizing chart if it's provided in the catalog. Each manufacturer cuts garments differently.

Save a tree. One of the pitfalls of being a frequent catalog shopper is finding that your name and address have turned up on dozens of additional mailing lists of companies that you've never heard of who clog your mailbox with an almost-daily barrage of specialty catalogs. You can remove your name from mailing lists by sending your name, address, and ZIP code to Mail Preference Service, Direct Marketing Association, P.O. Box 9008, Farmingdale, NY 11735-9008. As a service, many companies will refrain from renting your name if you request it. Look for details on the catalog order form.

TELEVISION: SHOW SOME REMOTE CONTROL

Combine the two things that Americans love most—television and shopping—and you get the concept for today's home shopping channels.

Back in 1977, the Home Shopping Network (HSN) started TV retailing in Florida, hawking factory overruns and discontinued items. By 1995, home shopping channels were selling $3 billion worth of merchandise a year. The two major players, HSN and QVC, alone generate $2 billion a year in sales.

The standard fare of these network selling machines is much the same—jewelry, collectibles, clothing, small electronics, and housewares—sold against a backdrop of incessant patter from exuberant host salespeople.

Shopping ease and convenience are favorite home shopping channel buzzwords. (Just sit on your couch with the remote control in one hand and the telephone in the other!) But depending upon how you go about it, TV shopping can be extremely time-consuming. A *Glamour* magazine reporter, for instance, decided to put together an entire outfit this way, complete with accessories. It took 40 hours of shopping and cost $741.62. It could literally take days of TV watching before the specific item you are looking for is aired.

As with catalogs, TV shoppers can order by credit card by calling a toll-free number and giving an order-taker the identification number of the item that they are interested in purchasing. And like mail-order shopping, TV shopping doesn't enable you to touch the merchandise or try on an outfit. Unlike catalogs though, you can't go back and take a second look at the merchandise, unless you had the foresight to tape the program.

As for value and price, it is hard to generalize. A 1995 *Consumer Reports* comparison of brand-name products found that prices were higher on the home shopping channels than in retail stores. They also found that prices for some things, such as sports collectibles, were highly inflated. Because much of the merchandise sold on these channels is from exclusive lines and private labels (nearly half is jewelry), viewers can't comparison-shop.

Take your time. Don't get caught up in the TV shopping frenzy. Like their mall-bound retailing cousins, TV retailers calculate every move to trigger an impulse buy. From the close-up shots of the merchandise to the endless patter of the hosts to the call-in testimonials from happy buyers to the countdown clock—all are designed to get you to buy, buy, buy. Which is why you shouldn't, shouldn't, shouldn't . . . at least not right away. Take the necessary information down and take some time to think about it before placing the call.

Don't waste your time. Why sit through two hours of cubic zirconia programming when all you're really looking for is a clock radio? Call the network to request a copy of its program guide.

Keep it loose. To avoid sizing problems when ordering clothing, stick to loose, untailored styling generally found in small, medium, large, and extra-large sizes. While this won't guarantee a perfect fit, it leaves a little room for error.

Stick to styles you know. TV shopping networks seem to specialize in items that you won't find in your local stores. When it comes to clothing,

---

Infomercials:
Not Sold in Stores—Not Yet Anyway

Home shopping channels are just one way to shop by television. Paid programming, or infomercials as they've come to be called, are filling up those late-night spots previously reserved for old movies and *Three's Company* reruns. They've also begun to creep into daytime program slots, particularly weekend mornings.

These half-hour commercials, produced to resemble legitimate shows, offer a vast array of items "not sold in stores"—baldness remedies, kitchen gadgets, wrinkle creams, cosmetics, diet treatments, exercise equipment, furniture refinisher, and more.

Generally, infomercials are used to launch new products. If the pitch generates enough sales, the product moves on to the stores. And as a rule, store prices will be less because the manufacturer has already recouped its start-up costs.

So if you see something that you just gotta have, wait a while. If it's a good product, chances are that you'll find it months later in Wal-Mart or Kmart for a fraction of the cost. For example, *Consumer Reports* found BluBlocker sunglasses, which sold for about $50 a pair on an infomercial, for about $19 at Wal-Mart.

---

avoid styles that you've never tried before. If you've never worn sequined hot pants, then TV is probably not the best place to give it a try.

Tune in at the top of the hour. At the beginning and end of each hour, the shopping networks preview the major items that will be sold during that time slot and were sold during the previous time slot. You can save time by deciding at that time if anything interests you.

Compare prices. With expensive items, comparison-shop when possible. Ask the order-taker for the model number and call local retailers for comparison prices. This may be difficult, since many items are exclusive to the shopping channels and won't be found in any store.

Avoid clearance shows. As with department store sales, you'll usually find limited sizes, colors, and quantities during shopping network clearance shows. Typically, clearance merchandise is nonreturnable unless damaged.

ONLINE SHOPPING: CLICK AND BUY

With the Internet, one thing is for sure: The quantity and quality of the information available is changing moment by moment—mostly for the good. In the not-too-distant past, shopping with your computer via the Internet or online services such as CompuServe, America Online, and Prodigy was a spotty experience in terms of the value, convenience, and selection that smart consumers want. But that's quickly changing.

By the end of 1995, there were more than a million products and services available to online users. To mention just a few: appliances, books, cars, clothing, gourmet foods, insurance, recorded music, and, naturally, software.

Shopping online takes the convenience of catalog shopping one step further. When you find the product that you want, you don't even need to make a phone call. Just click your mouse button to place the item in your electronic shopping cart and head to the electronic checkout where the whole transaction takes place with just a few keystrokes. You can shop through the electronic mall, searching by store, manufacturer, product category, or even product features.

Still, shop with your eyes open and your brain engaged. While it may be at the cutting edge of technology, don't assume flat-out that your computer has located the best bargain available. For one thing, selection of the product that you're interested in may or may not have caught up with the array that you'd find in a retail store. While one online bookstore may offer only a few hundred titles at ho-hum conventional prices, for instance, another electronic bookshop might offer a million titles with discounts and low-cost delivery. (A typical mall bookstore carries more than 20,000 titles.)

In the major appliance department of one online service that we checked, there were several brands of dryers for sale but no washers. Delivery charges were astronomical on some products. One upright freezer, for instance, had a member price of $497.33 and a $126.50 delivery charge.

On the other hand, fervent online shoppers point out that even if you don't make your purchase online, you can use your computer to conduct extensive product research. With an easy search, one shopper found the Web site of the manufacturer of the refrigerator that he wanted to buy. There, he got more extensive technical specs than in-store salespeople could offer—and he discovered a $100 manufacturer's rebate that no store had ever mentioned.

Online bargains are especially extensive in the electronics and computer software area, where the selection is staggering and prices are competitive, even with the delivery charges.

Before you fill your electronic shopping basket with goodies, keep in mind the following smart-shopper tips.

Compare, compare, compare. Stick with the tried-and-true golden rule: Compare prices. Before you click that button, know what the going rate is at other online sources and at your local retailer.

Better safe than sorry. Be aware that the security and privacy of electronic transactions is still open to question. Antitheft measures have been integrated into the popular Netscape Navigator, for instance, to keep cyberspace thieves from gaining access to your credit card numbers. But such security has not been proven impenetrable. Several proposed solutions are under development. Contact your online service or credit card company periodically to find out about the ongoing changes in the antitheft arena.

Deep Discounts: Outlets and Clubs

Before they went mainstream, factory outlets were nondescript, bleak warehouse buildings with bare walls, concrete floors, and communal dressing rooms. Bargain hunters sifted through racks and bins of the manufacturer's problem merchandise—seconds, irregulars, overruns, or last season's fashions that just didn't sell.

And the prices were unbeatable, usually ranging from 50 to 80 percent off retail for name-brand goods.

But outlets have changed. Nowadays, they're big business, moving about $13 billion in merchandise a year. They've evolved into first-quality merchandise centers that more closely resemble your typical local mall, complete with food court, tasteful decor, and private dressing rooms.

OUTLETS GAINING IN POLISH—AND PRICE

By 1996, there were more than 10,000 outlet stores across the country representing 500 manufacturers—names such as Levi's, Lee, Nike, Liz Claiborne, Nine West, Reebok, and Ralph Lauren. Many of these stores are housed in outlet mega-malls, such as Potomac Mills Mall in northern Virginia. The 200-store mall has drawn more than 100 million shoppers since it opened in 1985 and has become the top drawing destination in Virginia.

Unfortunately, the bargains that you find in outlet malls are starting to resemble the bargains that you'd find in any mall or department store sale. The bargains typical of the original factory outlets of yesteryear are fading.

While most outlet centers promise savings of up to 70 percent off retail prices, typical discounts average 20 percent off retail prices. However, figuring out these "savings" becomes even more blurry when you realize that 15 to 80 percent of the merchandise is manufactured strictly for the outlets and was never intended to sell retail. Since the merchandise is never sold at full price, manufacturers determine the savings by listing a "compare at" or "suggested retail" price, says Stephen Pollan, an attorney, financial consultant, and co-author of *The Total Negotiator*.

The problem is that you're not comparing apples to apples. Products manufactured strictly for the outlets may not meet the same standards as those sold at retail.

"There are some legitimate bargains to be had at the outlets. Some of the bargains are simply the depth of the merchandise," says Goldstein, author of several bargain-shopping guidebooks. You may find the designer's complete line in an outlet, while a department store will only carry a few styles.

Seasoned outlet shoppers say that the best deals may be on housewares, since this is the same merchandise stocked in conventional stores. Major manufacturers like Mikasa, Lenox, Gorham, and Dansk offer discounts of 30 to 50 percent off their outlet store merchandise.

THE INS AND OUTS OF OUTLETS

Before you make the trek to your nearest outlet center, there are several shopping guides available that may make your trip more productive. *Outlet Bound*, a 175-page magazine with details on 12,000 factory outlets, sells for $7.95 (plus shipping) and can be ordered by writing to Outlet Bound, P.O. Box 1255, Orange, CT 06477. Check your local bookstore for *Lazar's Outlet Shopper's Guide* by Elysa Lazar and Eve Miceli (Lazar Communication Group). And the annual *The Joy of Outlet Shopping* can tell you where to find the store that you're looking for. Order by writing to The Joy of Outlet Shopping, P.O. Box 17129, Clearwater, FL 34622-0129.

Keep these tips in mind before you head to your nearest outlet center.

Time your trip. Since many outlet centers are located near vacation areas, they schedule sales for around holiday periods. You can expect to find additional price reductions on President's Day, Memorial Day, Labor Day, and Columbus Day weekends as well as after Christmas.

Know the store type. Is it really a factory outlet or just a store selling cheap copies and defective merchandise? How do you know if you are getting an item made specifically for the outlet store? Most manufacturers won't label their products that way. One way to find out what you're getting is to find out how many outlet stores the manufacturer operates. If it is only a few stores across the country, then it is probably all overstock.

On the other hand, if the designer has a store in every factory outlet center, at least some of the merchandise is going to be made especially for the outlet. True factory outlets are usually located adjacent to the factory that manufactures the products.

It's worth the wait. Some outlets carry goods that arrive just six to eight weeks behind the department stores at a 30 to 70 percent savings. You can get the best selection of the current season's styles if you peg your shopping trip to coincide with these shipments. For instance, the bulk of current fall fashions would arrive in outlet stores from mid-September through October.

Try on several sizes. Some garments end up in the outlets because they are sized incorrectly. Don't let your vanity stand in the way of great bargain. If you're a size 10, don't pass up a deal on a size 12 dress that fits perfectly just because it says it's a bigger size than you normally wear.

Buy out-of-season. Just like in retail, the best deals are on off-season items, so plan. Why pass up a great buy on a coat or a bathing suit just because you might have to wait a few months to use it?

Examine items carefully. Even stores that highlight flaws with stickers may have missed a defect. Count anything that comes in a set, such as cutlery, napkin rings, or even shoes. The box may contain two different sizes or two left shoes. You don't want to get home and be faced with a 45-mile drive to return a stained shirt. Most outlets are not equipped to handle mail-in returns, and most set a time limit on how long you have to return an item.

WAREHOUSE CLUBS: MINIMAL MARKUP

If you're willing to spend a little extra time, muscle, storage space, and a $25 to $35 membership fee, you can save by shopping at one of the nation's 850 or so warehouse clubs. Within the no-frills walls of these 100,000-square-foot caverns of consumerism, you'll find a limited selection of first-quality, brand-name merchandise, usually available only in big packages and sold at cheap prices.

Low prices are the appeal of these clubs, which mark up merchandise just 2 to 13 percent over wholesale, about one-third the typical discount markup. A 1995 study by *Consumer Reports*, which compared the prices of 20 household products, found that warehouse clubs generally sell merchandise for less than their primary competitors. In the case of big-ticket items, such as televisions, exercise equipment, and computers, the prices were dramatically lower.

Half of all American households shopped at a warehouse club in 1994, according to a survey by the Home Improvement Research Institute, and about 90 percent of 24 million club members nationwide belong to either Sam's Club or Price Costco.

Club membership is usually limited to businesses and certain groups, such as senior citizens, employees from various member organizations, government workers, or members of a credit union. But the criteria are so broad that almost anyone qualifies. The member fee assures clubs a strong customer base and also tends to weed out the browsers.

To maintain low prices, clubs cut costs to the bone. There's no service to speak of, little advertising, and no promotional sales.

While supermarkets typically stock about 15,000 products, warehouse clubs carry only 3,000 to 5,000, which are usually limited to the top-selling product brands in any one category. Merchandise turns over rapidly, so selection on items like appliances and office equipment can be hit-or-miss.

Try it out. Visit the store to decide whether you'd like to become a member. Sam's Club and B.J.'s will issue a temporary pass if you qualify, which will allow you to purchase merchandise with a 5 to 10 percent surcharge. If you like what see, you have the option of joining and purchasing items at the member rate during your first visit.

Compare grocery prices. When it comes to grocery items, remember to check unit pricing. Warehouse clubs are known for their low prices, but some grocery staples, such as coffee, juice, and bacon, are cheaper in the supermarket. Keep in mind that not everything is cheaper by the dozen.

Check seasonal bargains. Warehouse clubs are a bargain source for seasonal merchandise such as school supplies in the fall and lawn furniture in the spring.

Know the ways to pay. Since the average shopper can easily tally up $100 at the checkout, it pays to know which methods of payment the clubs accept. Cash and checks are fine if you are a member. Some don't accept MasterCard, Visa, or any other major plastic—except for Discover Card, which is accepted at all three clubs.

Beat the crowds. Shop during the week, when checkout lines are shorter. But remember that some stores reserve one or more mornings a week for business customers, which make up about 70 percent of club sales revenue.

Buying Used: Tried-and-True Goods

There's no longer a stigma attached to buying used merchandise. The downscaled 1990s produced a whole new breed of shopper. Buying used or "nearly new" merchandise isn't just for bargain hunters or people with limited financial means anymore. It's the new retail trend.

Depending on how used an item is, you can expect to save 50 percent or more over the original retail cost. Buying used may also afford you the opportunity to buy better-quality goods. In her book *Save Yourself a Fortune*, author Jody Bamel points out, "I'd rather have quality goods, used, than mediocre new."

SPECIALTY SECONDHAND STORES BOOMING

Stores specializing in used merchandise are increasing at a rate of 20 percent per year, according to the National Association of Resale and Thrift Shops in Detroit. And the stores that are sprouting up aren't just your conventional secondhand storefronts. Franchised chain stores devoted to quality used goods—such as sporting goods, computers, and baby gear—are popping up in strip malls across America.

Grow Biz International has almost 1,100 outlets nationwide under five specialty names—Play It Again Sports (where you can buy $170 Rollerblades in mint condition for just $90), Computer Renaissance (where you can buy a reliable 486 personal computer for just $600), Once Upon a Child (where you can get used car seats for less than 50 percent of the new price), Music Go Round (which sells musical instruments for about half their retail price), and Disc Go Round (which sells used compact discs for $6 to $8). You can get their numbers by calling the toll-free directory or checking the Yellow Pages of your phone book.

There are some trade-offs to consider when you buy used merchandise. You will usually have to look longer and harder for something than if you bought it new, but avid secondhand shoppers say that this is part of the fun. Also, once you find the item that you are looking for, it is doubtful that it will come with a warranty or guarantee, although some used cars sold through dealerships now come with warranties.

And you can usually forget about returning something that you're dissatisfied with, since most merchandise is sold "as is." This longstanding policy, too, is changing with the growth of franchised resale stores, which will allow a customer to return an item with a receipt.

Sizing Up Those Bargains

Remember that the goal in secondhand shopping, Bamel says in her book, is to buy good value at a low price. Keep these tips in mind when you go on your bargain-hunting expeditions.

Learn to spot quality. Turn an item over and look for markings, signatures, or logos of manufacturers or designers. Read labels to see if they bear a name that you recognize. Educating yourself either through collectors' guides or repeat shopping trips is the best way to learn to spot top-of-the-line goods.

Check for damage. Check clothing for rips, snags, and stains. Look at furniture for scratches, dents, or irreparable damage. Check dishes and glassware for chips and cracks. In short, don't buy it if it is beyond repair.

Low price isn't enough. Don't buy something that you have no use for just because it's a bargain. This is one of the most common mistakes that novice secondhand shoppers make, Bamel writes. It may be hard to pass up a $3 blouse. But if it doesn't match anything in your closet, chances are that you won't wear it.

Sharpen your sight. Seasoned secondhand shoppers know how to scan a jumbled store for items that they might be interested in buying. According to Bamel's book, first you scan, then search around. And then finally dig around in hidden corners.

Pick it up. If you see something that you like, pick it up—until you decide whether you want to buy it. Possession is nine-tenths of the law, and when it comes to buying secondhand, there's usually only one to a customer.

Resale, Thrift, and Consignment Shops

These days you'll find people from all walks of life combing the thrift-store racks for a bargain. "There was a time when there was a stigma about

Shopping for Used Goods?
Gather This Gear

Before you head out to the flea markets, thrift shops, and garage sales, make sure that you have the following supplies on hand.

Cash: Most places do not accept personal checks or credit cards. Some of the larger thrift chains, such as Goodwill Industries and the Salvation Army, do accept major credit cards.

Shopping bag: Bags are usually on short supply, especially at flea markets.

Moist towelettes: After rummaging through used merchandise, you definitely need to clean your hands.

Tape measure: You'll need to know if an item that you've found is the right size for the job. An alternative is to learn the measurements of your feet and hands.

Magnifying glass: Helps you read hard-to-see labels or markings on an item.

Magnet: Test metals in lamps, jewelry, and collectibles. Magnets won't stick to brass, silver, bronze, or gold but will stick to iron and cheap base metals.

thrift shopping. My mother used to say, 'Don't tell anyone where you got that!' " Bamel says.

If you're new to the techniques of secondhand shopping, resale, thrift, and consignment stores are a good place to get your feet wet. The merchandise in these stores is usually organized, and the prices are basically fixed. Unlike flea markets and tag sales, there isn't a sense of urgency that you need to sift through the merchandise quickly in order to get the best pick.

There are differences, however, between the three types of stores: in prices, in how they obtain their merchandise, and in where the profits go from the sale.

Consignment stores. Merchandise is usually one or two seasons old. The consignment store does not own the merchandise but acts as a middleman between the consignor and the buyer. The consignor and the owner then split the profits—usually 50-50. Prices vary. You will generally pay 50 to 70 percent off what the product sold for new.

Resale stores. These are not much different from consignment stores—except that they buy their merchandise outright. Resale stores also may sell donated merchandise. Since resale stores operate on a for-profit basis, prices are higher than in thrift stores but still at least half off the retail selling price.

Thrift stores. These stores are nonprofit and run by charitable organizations. There are 22 national charity organizations that operate thrift stores. Most people are familiar with Goodwill Industries, one of the largest, which operates about 1,400 stores nationwide. Since thrift stores sell strictly donated merchandise, prices are low—only about 5 to 10 percent of the original selling price. You'll also find a wider range of merchandise spanning several decades of trends and fashion.

THRIFT-STORE STRATEGIES

While you're sure to find good deals in these stores, these shopping strategies will help you avoid some of the pitfalls of thrift shopping and maximize your savings.

List the locations. Keep a list of store sightings and locations. With the exception of the larger chains, most resale, thrift, and consignment stores aren't located in shopping centers. You'll usually find them on the fringes of a town's commercial district. Looking in the phone book will help you to locate some but not all, since a listing in the Yellow Pages costs at least $100 per month.

Check in frequently. Merchandise turnover is constant, and store owners never know what is going to come in next. So drop into your favorite shops frequently, especially if you are looking for a particular item. If you become one of the regulars, store personnel may even give you a call when something that you've been looking for arrives.

Dress in form-fitting clothes. Most thrift stores don't have dressing rooms, so wear form-fitting clothes like leggings and a lightweight shirt so that you can try clothes on over what you're wearing.

What Do I Say?

Bargaining Dialogue

The first rule of bargaining is this: Never tell the seller how much you're willing to pay for an item. It may be more than what the seller is willing to take. Stumped for the right approach? These phrases will help get you started and open up the negotiating process.

- What is your best price?
- What would you take for this?
- Will you come down on that?
- Why don't we split the difference?
- What if I take all of this merchandise?

Check the neighborhood. There is a direct correlation between the affluence of the neighborhood and the merchandise in the store. This is even true in thrift chains that warehouse merchandise at a central location and then ship out to appropriate stores. In transient areas, there tends to be an abundance of good merchandise in thrift stores as people clean house before moving away.

Do some window-shopping. Often the most unique items are found in the window displays, where they will attract customers. These display items usually go up for sale the day the display is changed. If you want a window-display item, you can come back when the item goes up for sale. Or even better, pay for your selection right away and then return for it when the display is taken down.

Ask about the back room. Before you leave a secondhand store, ask if they have a designer or "back" room. These boutique sections are not open to the general public without an appointment, but many stores keep their better merchandise there.

Watch for special sales. Many thrift stores hold their best merchandise for pre-Christmas sales, which are held to generate money for the charity's Christmas fund. Many also hold annual fashion shows where you will find better merchandise. However, you may have to request an invitation for this type of event. A favorite is bag sales where, for a preset per-bag price, you may fill a bag with any merchandise in the store.

Dig for buried treasure. "Look where no one else wants to look," advises Bamel. "Go into the most horrible box in the dirtiest corner with all kinds of junk on top. Nobody is going to look in that because it's repulsive."

TAG SALES, GARAGE SALES, AND FLEA MARKETS

If you are ready for some down-and-dirty shopping, you'll find dozens of opportunities every weekend at local tag sales, yard sales, garage sales, and flea markets. You'll find highly useful goods (clothing, toys, housewares, and furniture), unused merchandise, an odd assortment of bric-a-brac, collectibles, and just plain junk.

Generally, merchandise at these private sales is priced at 10 to 30 percent of its original price. If you want to get the best price, "Come with cash and look like a schlepper," says Goldstein, who also wrote *The Underground Shopper*. "You don't drive up in a Mercedes and all your finery."

To find out how much you should pay for goods, consult *Price Guide to Flea Market Treasures*, by Harry L. Rinker, Jr.

Private sales of all sorts are listed in the classified section of your local paper. Check the listings on Thursdays and Fridays for weekend sales. Highlight the ones that interest you with a pen. You can't expect miracle finds at flea markets anymore. Sellers nowadays generally know the value of their wares. To find out about the locations of flea markets near you, check *The Official Directory to U.S. Flea Markets*, by Kitty Werner.

Start out by following these tips.

Be early. Get the pick of the day by arriving just prior to the start of the sale. Most of the selling will take place during the first few hours of the sale. By afternoon you're left with the leftovers.

Test everything. Be careful when you buy appliances, toys, tools, or electronics. Ask the owner to plug it in and test it to see if it works. Bamel once bought a chrome Oster blender for $8, but by the time she had it repaired three times, it cost $60—the same as it would have cost new.

Always bargain. No matter what the price is, try to bargain down. Generally, you should pay about one-tenth to one-fifth of what the item costs new, says Bamel. Always make an offer and remember to be fair. You'll find your best buys on rainy mornings and late in the day.

Flash the cash. The sight of a $20 bill may persuade someone to part with a $30 item.

Dress down. You will enhance your bargaining power if you dress casually. If you're dressed to excess, flaunting designer duds, sellers will presume that you can afford to pay top dollar.

FROM SEEDY BEGINNINGS, PAWNSHOPS BLOSSOM

For most of us, the word "pawnshop" conjures up an uninviting image of a dimly lit store on the seamy side of town cluttered with merchandise (some of it "hot"), complete with iron bars on the window. A place for only the bravest of bargain hunters.

But pawnshops have changed. Since 1988 the number of pawnshops in the United States has doubled to 14,000. This mini-boom is being fed, in part, by a bounty of no-longer-earning-their-keep goods from the excess-as-success 1980s. The new breed of pawnshops looks much like a regular store—well-lit and spacious, with tasteful displays of merchandise.

Besides being a source for quick cash loans (usually in the $50 to $100 range), pawnshops are a good place to find bargains, especially on musical instruments, electronics, and jewelry. You can save 30 to 50 percent or even more off retail prices.

About 70 to 80 percent of all items pawned are redeemed by the owners. The term of the loan is usually 60 to 90 days. If it is not paid back in time, the pawned item goes up for sale. According to the National Pawnbrokers Association in Dallas, less than 0.5 percent of all loans are identified as stolen goods.

Buy a well-known brand. Since used goods aren't guaranteed, buy a brand that you know performs well, especially with electronics. This way you'll have some assurance of product reliability.

Get an appraisal. Jewelry is a very popular item in pawnshops. If you decide to buy an expensive piece, get an appraisal to determine its authenticity and value.

Intriguing Alternatives

On occasion it makes more sense to rent or lease a product instead of purchasing it. While tools, tuxedos, baby cribs, and party supplies have long been staples of the rental trade, you can now find almost anything for rent. If you can buy it, you probably can rent it somewhere, too.

A 1994 Gallup poll conducted for the American Rental Association showed that 41 percent of the American population uses rental shops. A good rule of thumb: "The more specialized a piece of equipment is, the more likely you may be to rent it," says Sandy Howell, director of public relations and marketing for the American Rental Association in Moline, Illinois.

FOR SHORT-TERM NEEDS, RENTING PAYS OFF

Renting provides an opportunity to try before you buy when it comes to many big-ticket items, such as boats, campers, and exercise equipment. Renting a $600 treadmill for $65 a month on a trial basis may help you decide whether you'd be investing in exercise equipment or a costly clothes rack that ends up in the bedroom corner in six months.

Other items that have recently come into vogue as rentals, such as evening gowns and jewelry, allow you to sidestep the expense of buying an item that you may use only once or twice.

Still other for-rent items, such as artwork and books, offer the opportunity to enjoy something for a period of time at a fraction of what it would cost to own it. The Albright-Knox Gallery in Buffalo and the Seattle Art Museum rent paintings, prints, and sculptures to their members. You'll pay $17 a month for a painting valued at $751 to $1,000 from Albright-Knox.

Beware rent-to-own. Steer clear of rent-to-own scenarios. On the surface, these arrangements may sound too good to be true—no credit check, no hassles, and a 20-inch color television for $14.99 per week. But to actually own that television, you will spend four to five times what the item sells for in a typical retail store. So a $250 television may end up costing $1,000.

Branch out. Renting isn't just for rental stores. All types of stores and organizations offer merchandise for rent. Have a taste for art? Check local museums for rental programs. Want to go camping? Check with your local recreational vehicle dealer.

Rent some expertise. Describe your home projects to rental-center personnel. Most rental centers have thousands of specialized tools and items

---

When Renting Makes Sense

Renting is a way to save money if you only plan to use an item temporarily. But it also has some other advantages to consider, says the American Rental Association in Moline, Illinois.

No maintenance costs: Rental contracts generally cover all maintenance costs, so you won't need to worry about fixing broken equipment.

No storage: Rather than wasting valuable space in your home or garage to store idle equipment, you can return it when you're done using it.

No obsolete equipment: Inventory is updated often at rental centers so that you have the benefit of state-of-the-art equipment without state-of-the-art prices.

No botched jobs: You can save hours of time on do-it-yourself projects when you have the proper equipment.

---

for rent. They can advise you on exactly what kind of equipment you need to get the job done—equipment that you may not even know exists.

Get it together. Before you rent, get organized. Rental equipment is available by the hour, half-day, day, week, or month. You are charged by how long you have the product, not how long you use it. You can save yourself some money by organizing your project so that you are able to use the equipment right away. For example, don't rent a carpet shampooer until you have moved all of your furniture out of the way and are ready to clean.

BARTERING: TRADE ON YOUR TALENTS

If you're short on cash but long on talents, give bartering a try. The practice of trading goods and services is as old as history itself, yet still a little unfamiliar to most of us, acclimated as we are to cash and credit card commerce.

"Look at your skills. Barter is a way to get things in your life without having to pay cash. It's very commonsense. It means that you like to babysit and that your neighbor likes to carpool. It's informal swapping," says Goldstein.

In the world of business, barter has become big business. More than 240,000 businesses use barter and trade exchanges to transact $10 billion in goods and services annually. It's a way for companies to preserve cash and swell business 10 to 15 percent by using excess services and inventory.

The same principle can work for you and your household.

Most of the 400 or so barter networks, such as the International Reciprocal Trade Association in Alexandria, Virginia, cater to businesses. They charge membership fees and monthly transaction fees in exchange for providing a computerized network of goods and service for barter.

However, public barter fairs, barter parties, and barter potlucks aimed at individuals are now widespread. At monthly meetings, members distribute lists of skills for trade—one of the hottest skills traded is organizing papers and files.

Identify the give-and-take. Decide what you want and what you're willing to give in return. First make a list of what you can trade (carpool services, errand services, organizational skills, space in your house, typing services) and then make a list of what you need (such as car repairs and lawn mowing). You can't barter without knowing what you have to offer and what you need in return. And remember, don't sell yourself short. You probably have more skills than you realize.

Check out the value. Find out what your trade or service is worth. Check the want ads and talk to friends and associates to find out going rates for both sides of the trade so that you can work out the particulars of the swap.

Start out simple. Start out with something easy. Trade a skill that you enjoy, such as gardening, for a job that you hate—maybe ironing.

Search for partners. Find a group of individuals such as yourself who want to barter. Barter groups have become widespread. Look in your newspapers, on supermarket bulletin boards, or at community centers for information on local groups. If you can't find any in your area, post a notice asking people to contact you.

Put it in writing. By having a written agreement, both sides understand the swap. Outline the particulars. If it's services, indicate whether it's an hour-for-hour trade. If it's a product or object being traded, list who delivers and when. Don't overlook issues concerning insurance or what happens if one side defaults on the agreement.

Bottom Line

To get the best deals, savvy consumers have to weigh the trade-offs and analyze their priorities to determine what's a bargain for them. Is low price the most important thing? Are time and convenience the top priority? Will a used item do the same job a new one would? And remember, just because something is sold as a bargain doesn't mean that it's a bargain.

Words to the Wise

Barter: An age-old practice of swapping goods and services. Instead of using cash to transact a purchase, you offer something for trade.

Overruns: Excess merchandise produced for retail stores that is then marketed in manufacturers' outlets.

Price-quote firm: A mail-order firm that, instead of publishing periodic catalogs of the merchandise it carries, will tell you by mail or phone if it has a product and will quote you a price on that product. Prices are generally 20 to 70 percent lower than retail.

ALLIES

American Rental Association: 1900 19th Street, Moline, IL 61265. For information on local rental establishments.

Direct Marketing Association: Mail Order Action Line, 1111 19th Street NW, Suite 1100, Washington, DC 20036-3603. Helps resolve difficulties with mail-order purchases.

National Association of Resale and Thrift Shops: 20331 Mack Avenue, Detroit, MI 48236. For information on locations of local resale, thrift, and consignment shops.

Cheapskate Monthly Newsletter: P.O. Box 2135, Paramount, CA 90723-8135. For tips on hundreds of ways to shop wisely.

Buying Luxuries on a Budget

Spend Like a Pauper, Live Like a Prince

We all like nice things. Purchasing a luxury item now and then transports us beyond the daily grind and makes us feel that we are at least a little bit special.

It could be a fine wine to mark an occasion. An air conditioner instead of a fan to get through a humid summer. A real piece of art on the wall rather than that framed poster that you've been carting around since college. A watch that will last a lifetime, maybe two, rather than the discount-store watches that you replace every other year.

Not all of us are in a position to buy these fine things, of course, and none are essential to a happy life. Chasing material dreams is not time well spent, most anyone with wisdom would counsel. But to treat yourself to something nice every now and then, particularly if you are not sacrificing too much, is a basic pleasure of life.

Of course, nice doesn't have to be expensive. Just as you can be a savvy grocery shopper, so can you be a savvy shopper for the niceties of life. And the more savvy you are, the less of a financial sacrifice you will make. Which could mean more nice things.

Experts on high-end consumer products agree that by shopping smart, you can save considerable money. So if you find yourself in the market for a high-end item—and we've defined that broadly in this chapter, starting with high-quality alcohol and then moving on to appliances, antiques, collectibles, art, and jewelry—read on. Finally, we'll tell you how to sell your luxury items to maximize your gains.

Alcohol: Sobering Thoughts

Alcohol can be good for you, no matter what Carrie Nation said. "Studies show that abstainers have four times the mortality rate of moderate drinkers," says Morris E. Chafetz, M.D., author of the book *Drink Moderately and Live Longer*. Those who imbibe a modest two drinks a day "are less prone to strokes and cardiac disease."

Still, Americans' use of alcohol has been, in drink lingo, mixed. We spent $96 billion on alcohol products in 1995, up 0.8 percent from the year before, according to *Wine and Spirits*. Yet we actually drank a few barrels *less*, continuing a trend toward reduced consumption that actually began in the 1980s. So we're drinking better, pricier stuff. The trick is to buy it at less than the priciest prices. Let's see how.

WINE: TRACKING A TASTE

"Most Americans don't seek out wine for the pleasure of collecting or of studying what makes a wine taste the way that it does," says David W. Dickerson of Wine and Spirits Wholesalers of America. We do seek it out, though. Wine is the all-around winner of the numbers games, since volume went up 2.1 percent in 1995 and dollar sales climbed 1.6 percent.

Now suppose that you want to find, say, the ultimate $6 bottle of wine. First, Dickerson says, pick your type: zinfandel, Merlot, Chardonnay, or whatever. Buy a few bottles. When you find one you particularly like, remember the label.

Find a good wine store. Rick Genderson, co-owner of Schneider's of Capitol Hill, a liquor store in Washington, D.C., says that seeking recommendations from friends is a good way to find a vintner. The first thing to look for when you cross the threshold is "a big selection. If the store doesn't have many bottles, it isn't serious and you're not going to get good merchandise or a good deal. Big isn't automatically good, but a store with a larger selection will have an easier time fitting your taste and pocketbook."

Target that taste. "Talk with the dealer," Genderson says. "Show him the labels of the wine you like and ask if he can duplicate the taste at a price you're willing to pay. There are plenty of good, inexpensive brands, and a $6 bottle of Chardonnay that is equal to or better than one costing $10 is not hard to find. He should also guarantee that he'll buy the wine back from you if you're not satisfied."

Look to the futures. Wine futures offer a way of buying good—maybe even great—wines at a discount as deep as 35 percent. Allen Murphey, wine consultant for Calvert Woodley Liquors in Washington, D.C., explains that the deal is available from any vintner.

"The choices are limited to the Bordeaux wines of France and some California varieties," Murphey says. "You put up the money two years in advance. You can, in theory, buy any amount you want, though most dealers keep it to a minimum of half-case lots—six bottles. You can pay from $50 to $800 or even more for the six.

"There are people who buy futures as an investment," Murphey says, "speculating that in five to six years these wines will quadruple in price." But he estimates that for $500 you will likely get a case of wine that would retail for at least $680. Even if you're not getting rich in the wine business, you are getting a fine wine at a fine price.

BEER: SLOSHING THROUGH THE HYPE

Beer keeps foaming from the tap. In fact, beer accounts for 88 percent of all alcoholic beverage sales. Even though beer consumption declined 0.4 percent in 1995, most of the individual categories—imports, light beers, and microbeers—actually gained.

Variations in state laws can make consumer advice chancy. Some require, for instance, that the seller post his retail price with a state agency, meaning that it can't be reduced. Some states allow deep discounting by way of newspaper coupons. Others do not, and if you're in such a benighted state and far from the border of a friendlier place, options can be limited.

You do have some factors on your side. Remember that over half of all beer consumed in the United States is made by only three brewers. It's expensive to shelve, so the retailer wants to move it. And the competition is brutal. Keeping an eye on the beer bins at the liquor store and the supermarket can turn up deep discounts.

Start a beer cellar. Beer is generally cheaper in the summer months. So save money by stocking your own beer cellar each summer. While it is true that beer's taste is at its peak when it's freshest, it's also true that if you store a supply in a cool, dark place and—this is important—don't move it until you open it to drink, it will maintain near-maximum taste for six months.

Once you're in cellar-stocking habit, explore beers like those Belgian varieties that are brewed to age in the bottle.

Don't drink the label. Those wily advertising agencies have managed to convince us that what the suds taste like isn't as important as the sort of person you'll be if you drink this brand (*cool!*) and the sort of "beautiful people" you will attract (*major hunks and babes!*). One beer industry expert calls this the difference between "taste drinking" and "image drinking," and laments that brands that consistently win the blind taste tests—he mentions Old Milwaukee and Pabst—don't sell well because they lack image.

And they can cost as much as 50 percent less than the image brands.

Hold a taste test. Don't take the experts' word for it that "imageless" beers can taste better than their highly hyped cousins. Try your own blind taste test. It's a perfect excuse for a party. Stock a minimum of four brands, make sure that the person pouring is the only one who knows what's in those glasses, and forget that nose-in-the-air terminology—use your own words to describe the flavor. "Good!" means that it's a keeper and "tastes like shellac" means that it isn't.

LIQUOR: CUT OUT THE MIDDLEMEN

Liquor, or distilled spirits—what we used to call the hard stuff—declined 1.8 percent in volume, while we spent 0.2 percent more on it in 1995. That means that the prestige drinks, like single-malt Scotches and small-barrel bourbons, attracted our wallets. It also means that some subcategories, like the "white whiskies"—rum and tequila—did well.

Wipe away those tiers. Name-brand alcohol products are "tiered." That is, they are the creations of an enormously complex and expensive distilling, distributing, wholesaling, and advertising system that packs in a profit at every step. Eventually, somebody has to pay for all of it, and that tends to be the consumer.

It is possible to take advantage of "nontiered" brands, often less well-known labels brought in directly by the liquor dealer and retailing $3 to $6 less per fifth. As with the ultimate $6 bottle of wine, the secret is a collaboration with a dealer.

"Taste things and define what you like," Genderson says. "Then ask the dealer for the nontiered brand of Scotch, bourbon, gin, or whatever that duplicates the taste. Your dealer might also buy a lot of good products—ones that don't sell because they're not known—and offer good buys."

Get a refund. For those who have no interest in the mid-priced brand that tastes sort of like the expensive tipple, there *is* a way to get the good stuff for less. In fact, there is a method of saving as much as 20 percent on *all* alcohol products, including beer and wine, says refunding expert Susan Samtur, author of *The Super Coupon Shopping System* and publisher of *Refundle Bundle*.

Refunding works for alcohol as well as food, though there is less to work with. Couponing, the other half of the paperwork arsenal, is minimally present in alcohol sales. The few coupons available tend to be attached to the bottle and offer $2 to $3 off the price when you carry it to the cashier. But distillers prefer refunding: They hope you'll take the bottle home, look at the paperwork and postage involved in getting money back, and decide that it's too much trouble.

Hunt down the forms. Refund forms are available only where the alcohol is sold: liquor stores and liquor departments in pharmacies, grocery stores, and discount outlets. The forms are attached to the product, on a pad underneath the product on the shelf, or pinned to a board somewhere in the store. You must buy the product, fill out the form, and mail it with proof of purchase—label, bar code, or register receipt—and wait, explains Jean Kwiatkowski, publisher of *Moneytalk*.

"Refunding is fairly new in this world," says Samtur, "and for now, it's chancy and unpredictable. Some stores are better geared for it than others: A store in a lower-end area where customers are not educated about refunds will have few of them. Also, a supermarket will likely be more 'consumer-friendly' and up on this. Liquor stores are more often dominated by men, and men may not realize the value of rebates. So you may have to do a little legwork in finding the best deals in the drinks that you buy."

Pressure the retailers. Availability of refunding forms is dependent upon quirky state laws and quirky owners, who will say that they carry only those rebate forms passed along by distributors. "You can write your state representatives and ask why people who live here are being punished," says Kwiatkowski. "You can tell the liquor store owner that your business depends on those forms. It's amazing how well those approaches work."

Appliances

Major appliances—such behemoths as dishwashers, clothes washers, refrigerators, and stoves—need not mean major money. No, they don't come cheap. But never forget that the figure that you see on the price tag is invariably too high.

Let's explore ways to bring these prices down to a reasonable, er, range.

DON'T STICK TO THE STICKER PRICE

That sticker price on the appliance "is just a figure that the manufacturer thinks we should sell it for," says Barry Krasney, owner of Cole's Appliance and Furniture Company in Chicago. It's a markup based on factors that need not interest you as much as ways to lower it.

Rule number one: Never step into a salesman's lair without knowing exactly what you want. "You must spend the time to decide what model you want," advises Corky Pollan, shopping columnist for *New York Magazine*. "Then comparison-shop. That's just a matter of calling at least three stores and mentioning the prices that you've seen on this model and asking if they can do better. Almost always, they can. Even high-end stores that deny that they give discounts will usually negotiate."

To dig deeper, get the toll-free numbers of the major manufacturers, where you can learn of discontinued models and their model numbers, Pollan says. Especially with appliances like stoves and refrigerators, discontinued lines are likely to have all the features that you could want anyway. With other appliances, you may find the new models superior.

If you tend to throw up your hands in the face of research and comparison-shopping, at the very least shake a few dollars out of a salesperson right there on the floor. "Don't be afraid to ask the salespeople for the best price that they can give you on the appliance you're pointing at," says Krasney. "You might be surprised at what you hear."

AIR CONDITIONERS: COOL SAVINGS OFF-SEASON

It's only natural: When you get that first hot lick of summer heat, you remember that it's time to replace the old window air conditioner. But when you rush to the appliance store with the rest of the sweaty horde, that's when you're most apt to get taken.

"Preseason, like late winter, is a good time to buy an air conditioner," says Ed Dooley, vice-president of communications and education at the Air Conditioning and Refrigeration Institute in Arlington, Virginia. "It's the time when they have the most units in inventory, and it's before the big rush, so they're poised—ready to install."

You can manage 20 percent off the summer price if you buy preseason. Even better is postseason, which begins roughly at the end of August. That period can offer savings as deep as 30 percent.

And look for a "utility rebate," adds Dooley. "Check with the utility company to find out if they offer a rebate depending upon the seasonal energy efficiency rating (SEER). They do this to encourage people to get more efficient air conditioners, which means that the utility doesn't have to provide as much power at peak-use times and that they can defer plant construction. So the higher the SEER, the bigger the rebate."

There are details that a salesperson should know before advising you about models.

- How many people use the room?
- Does the room have a lot of windows?
- Is the room on the first or second floor (heat rises)?
- If it's on a top floor, is it covered by a flat roof (which draws more heat) or a peaked roof?
- Are there computers (which require cooling) in the room?

DISHWASHERS: CLEAN UP WITH A REBATE

There are surges of interest in dishwashers during holiday times—especially Christmas—and Mother's Day. So those are reliably the times of peak prices, too, just as with air conditioners in midsummer. But manufacturers have begun to compete for your dollars during these prime buying times with rebates. Since the interval between Christmas and Mother's Day is a long one, rebates are beginning to appear in late summer and early fall.

The dealers automatically get rebate forms sent to them by the manufacturers. The percentage that you can have mailed back to you can run from 1 percent to 30 percent, or from $25 to $100.

Here are some questions to answer before you visit the dealer.

- How many loads of dishes do you do each week?
- Does everything go in there? Fine glassware as well as pots and pans?
- Do you wash the dishes *before* you put them in the dishwasher?
- Does sound matter to you?

WASHERS AND DRYERS: DISCOUNTS ON DISCONTINUED

Washers and dryers do not have seasonal sales cycles. However, new products are typically introduced in January and June, so discounts—usually about 30 percent—can be achieved on discontinued lines. Rebates on washers and dryers are available, but they tend to be modest—about 20 percent.

Here are some things you'll want to know about washers and dryers.

- The greater the horsepower of the washer's motor, the fewer problems there'll be during the life of the product. Shoot for at least one-half horsepower.
- With the dryer, one of the keys is cubic feet per minute (CFM), meaning the amount of air that is moving through the dryer. Average dryers move 140 to 150 CFM. The best move 214 CFM.
- Another key to dryer quality is frequency of tumble. The higher the number, the more air gets to the clothes. The average dryer is 40 tumbles per minute, and the best offer 50.
- The dryer can be gas or electric. An electric dryer usually costs $40 to $50 less than a gas dryer. Offsetting the initial savings, though, is the cost per load: roughly 8 cents for gas-powered versus 25 to 27 cents for electric. These figures vary, depending on your part of the country, but typically gas prices are less than electric.

Here are some questions to answer before you visit the dealer.

- How many people are doing laundry? If it's the whole family, you'll need a heavy-duty set that can take a lot of use and abuse.
- Do you wash delicates in the washer? If so, then you'll need a multispeed machine.

REFRIGERATORS AND STOVES: CASH IN ON COMPETITION

Fifty percent of all refrigerators sold are sold in May, June, July, and August. The manufacturers seek to meet summer competition by offering rebates worth up to 25 percent of the appliance's cost. As this is written, refrigerator manufacturers are beginning to offer these rebates in January, February, and March as well as summertime.

In the past, gas stoves have outsold electric ones, partly because of gas's quick response: It's ready when you twist the knob, while electric burners had to heat themselves before they could heat anything else. But now, according to

Amana spokesperson Ann Humbert, advances in electric cooking technology are making them quicker, and sales of the electrics are catching up.

The bargain-hunting shopper must know, though, that gas is cheaper to operate. Electric's traditional advantage is that it's cleaner and easier to maintain. Stoves of both kinds are sold in the highest numbers in the fall, when people are thinking about holiday cooking. That's also when dealers compete by mounting specials that can save you 10 to 15 percent.

Antiques: Old Reliables

Let's see . . . it's durable, it looks great, it might be valuable someday. . . . Of course you know what an antique is. It's what Grandma had throughout her house. So why are the experts confused about definition?

One has it that an antique is a sort of upscale collectible—a collectible that puts on airs. Another expert says that an antique is something made before 1945. Uncle Sam's attempt to clarify things for tax purposes only made them murkier: He says that an antique is anything at least 100 years old.

Quibbles aside, you can at the very least say that an antique is something from an earlier time that was ambitious in design (no Beatles lunch boxes here), was built to be functional rather than diverting (no matter how old Barbie dolls get, they will *still* be collectibles), and was probably made by hand rather than machine.

So antiques can range from Queen Anne writing desks, which only J. P. Moneybags could afford, to the items in Grandma's house. If she was wily or lucky—or if she was Mrs. J. P. Moneybags—they are the sorts of things that you'll find now at estate sales and in antique shops, awaiting a buyer.

They may be good deals, and you might be able to make those deals even better. But this is a very tricky business, so experts suggest these tips for keeping yourself on the smart side.

It's Not a Purchase, It's a Lifestyle

By all means, visit estate sales. But do so with the right mind-set. Be willing, for instance, to spend a year or so looking for one item, advises Amy Dacyczyn, author of the book *The Tightwad Gazette.*

"Estate sales are attended primarily by dealers," Dacyczyn says, "and there are no amazing deals, no discounts. But think of it as buying wholesale, because items are cheaper than at antique shops."

Concentrate on bigger pieces such as beds, tables, bureaus, and chests of drawers. "There, the quality of a medium-range antique is equal to that of the best new furniture that you can buy. You can get a very nice old bureau at an estate sale for $350. A particleboard bureau at a department store costs about the same," she says.

Serving Up Savings on China, Crystal, and Silver

There are two times of the year when department stores *always* offer their tableware on sale: August and January, according to Hannah Davis of the Buschemeyer Silver Exchange of Louisville. Discounts as deep as 60 percent are available.

Fork it over early. Some stores have presales. That is, the sale itself starts, say, August 4. The presale will start in July. You pay for it with credit card only. The store will deliver it for an additional fee after the sale starts, or, for no charge, you can come back and pick it up. This is a way of extending the period of the savings.

Check out an outlet. Outlet malls are factory stores owned by the tableware manufacturers. Some are limited to one particular line, and others have a mix of fine silver and china. They claim discounts of 40 to 70 percent.

The professional advice is to have your mind made up about what you want when you walk into the store, says Milton Singer, president of Jamar, a jeweler in New York City. Question the salesclerk closely; otherwise, you may unknowingly pick up a discontinued line or factory seconds. Both can be difficult to replace if something gets chewed up in the garbage disposal.

Go by the book. For the ultimate in savings, insiders say, you'll need a little time, patience, and diligence: Browse through the store to get the name, the pattern, the manufacturer, and all other relevant information on the items you want. Then browse the mail-order catalogs and begin calling. Your energy can be rewarded with savings as deep as 70 percent.

"Looking at it that way, the antique is a good buy. It will never go out of style. It will keep its value, maybe even go up. None of this is true of the new stuff," says Dacyczyn.

BUY WHAT YOU LIKE, BUT LIKE GOOD STUFF

You're going to have to live with what you buy, and a life lived surrounded by good things is more pleasant than the other kind.

"Buy everything as if you're going to sell it some day," advises George Michael, who hosted the PBS series *Antiques and Americana* for more than 20 years and wrote *The Basic Book of Antiques and Collectibles*. He knows the trap in the buy-what-you-like argument: "When it comes time to sell the piece, you're in tears because nobody *else* likes it. Spending this kind of money purely on aesthetics is for the wealthy. The rest of us should be more practical."

Buy functional antiques. "Get things that other people can use in their houses," Michael says. "Tables and chairs, I mean, and chests of drawers. The moment that you start collecting salt and pepper shakers or Jim Beam bottles, you're playing with stuff that could go up or go down or disappear altogether. But good furniture has no place to go but up."

Learn the periods. "Learning furniture periods is the most important step that you can take when you start out in antiques," Michael says. "These were the largest things in the house, and all other decorator items were made to complement them. If you don't learn the designs within furniture periods, then you'll be a hopeless collector because you won't have things that relate to one another."

You can attempt to learn about antique furniture by reading the trade magazines and the price guides, but the former can be obscure and the latter overspecialized and out-of-date the day after they appear.

"The best way to learn is to take classes, through extension services or museums, if you can. Go to seminars and forums. Learn from the experts," says Michael.

Scout the market. Next, to get an even better handle on the antique furniture market, start going to auctions, Michael says. "Auctions have inspection times. Ask questions of the auctioneer and his helpers about condition, age, and repairs," he says.

"You'll see maybe 400 items pass over the block in just a few hours. What are they? How old are they? Was there much bidding for them? What did they sell for? Now *that's* an education—do it for six months and you'll be pretty well sharpened up about what things are worth.

"Then you can go into an antique shop and negotiate," he says. "Just walking in and offering $50 for a $100 item is a good way to get shown the door. That's not negotiating. But to be able to say, 'The veneer on this table-top should not be more than ⅝ inch. This is ¾ inch, so the table is worth only. . . .' That's negotiating."

OLD FURNITURE, NEW TRICKS

Nobody knows how much money moves through the antique market every year. As with fine art, many transactions are private. Hundreds of millions of dollars would be a conservative guess.

"After the drug trade, antiques and collectibles are the single greatest source of hidden cash," says Harry L. Rinker, a consultant and author based in Emmaus, Pennsylvania, specializing in antiques. Treachery abounds in both these worlds, but antiquers, since they usually do not carry Uzis, must spot deceit in advance. Here, according to Rinker, are a few things to watch out for.

Beware digital deceit. "The Internet has introduced the need for extra caution," Rinker says. "A computer image of an item for sale can be enhanced—cracks smoothed over, chips covered. You can be snookered. Don't buy from somebody you don't know."

Watch for the cover-up. "A disturbing trend in antiques is an overemphasis on condition," Rinker says. "It's a spillover from 'in the box' standards for collectibles. A chip on an antique item used to take 10 percent off its value. Now it's 50 percent. That means that we're seeing a lot of hidden restoration work and phony enhancements."

Get the date in writing. Don't buy anything from an antiques dealer who won't give you a receipt or who refuses to fill out the receipt with "a full description of the piece including a condition report and a date—when he believes the object was made," Rinker says. "The date is the fraud element. He could be describing a reproduction rather than an original, and the wording would be the same except for the date. If he won't put that down, back away."

Get a guarantee. "Stay away from a dealer who doesn't have a money-back-no-questions-asked policy," Rinker says. "You need to be able to take an item to an expert to check it out." And you need to be able to return the item if it's not what you thought you were getting.

Collectibles

Collecting is a tricky business. While stamps and coins may be tried-and-true, the future value of a collection of 1950s lunch boxes is rather dependent upon the whims of a fad-loving public. Collecting is best done, the experts say, if you have a passion for the things that you're gathering. If it's really a passion for money that's driving you, go feed your 401(k) instead.

"I'm wary of using collectibles as investments. I'd rather see people invest in a mutual fund," says Jane Sarasohn-Kahn, columnist for *Toy Trader* magazine and author of *Contemporary Barbie*. "Having said that: There are collectible categories that are hot now. Like animation cel art. They were done by hand, while the new stuff is computer-generated. Disney cels especially are *really* hot."

What else is hot? Beatles posters. Kiss dolls. Barbie dolls. Early James Bond paperbacks (first printing only). Elvis Presley's Sun label 45s. Golden Age movie posters. . . .

"The baby boomers are behind this," says Pam Danziger, author of the annual *The Collectibles Industry Report*. This pig-in-the-python population bulge wants reminders of its youth, which managed to last from the mid-1950s to the mid-1970s.

IN THIS MARKET, THERE'S ROOM FOR EVERYONE

Each year, $25 billion is spent on collectibles, Danziger estimates. With a little guidance, you can locate items that will satisfy the yearning for nostalgia and at least hold their value through the next generation.

There are basically two types of collectors, says Danziger. "The first is served by the contemporary collectibles industry," she says. This industry posted sales of $8.2 billion in 1995, an increase of 13 percent over the year before. "These are new products, but they're appealing to the same motivation as the vintage items. That is, loneliness for vanished youth. The most popular area here has a Christmas theme—those lighted and snow-covered miniature cottages. People buy them with an eye to appreciation."

The second type of collector works the memorabilia market—old stuff with a high nostalgia factor attached. The experts say that the days of serendipitous finds are waning as the public grows savvier about collectibles, and the boomer demand for such items makes the dwindling supply ever smaller. They sigh for the days when they could find the Beatles' butcher cover, the one that posed the boys amid decapitated dolls and bloody chunks of meat, for a buck at a garage sale. (At this writing, a fine copy fetches $6,000.)

"Stamps and coins are holding their value," says Bob Tierney, president of Annapolis Marketing in Maryland, which arranges and promotes collectibles' dealer fairs. "So are Tiffany lamps and Boy Scout memorabilia. Some vinyl collectibles are expected to falter, like those 1950s doo-wop 45s by groups with names like the Orioles and the Magic Tones. They go into four figures now but probably won't forever. But the Beatles' *Yesterday . . . And Today,* with the butcher cover, that one just keeps going up."

CONTEMPORARY COLLECTIBLES: JOIN THE CLUB

Dolls and teddy bears, animals and angel figurines, Americana and folk art—contemporary collectibles may be a sprawling field, but some of the basics apply across the board. Here's what industry experts suggest in general.

Find a "deep" dealer. Knowledge is crucial in collectibles, and the best beginning sources are dealers. To find them, check with friends and the phone book. Judge the dealers by the lines they carry, and look especially for depth—not that they have 25 lines but that they've invested heavily in the three or four lines that they do stock.

Join and save. The dealers will also know about collectors' clubs, some of them sponsored by manufacturers. The prices in this primary market are not negotiable, but the clubs can offer information about couponing, which is appearing in nearly all areas of retailing.

Watch for signings. "One thing that people in the know are also aware of is signings," Danziger says. "Collectors will have favorite artists, who go to the shows and sign the pieces, and those signed pieces often have value."

Take it easy. The percentage of appreciation is not really calculable. Unlike mutual fund managers, this industry doesn't keep a performance record. The novice is advised to do a lot of schmoozing before thinking of this area as an investment.

Read up. Keep learning, say the experts. Two appropriate magazines, *Collector Editions* and *Dolls,* are published by Collector Communications

Corporation, 170 Fifth Avenue, Suite 1200, New York, NY 10010-5911. Sample copies are $5 each.

Watch for the ad advantage. Know when and how your favorite producer of collectibles offers cut-rate deals. For instance: Toward the end of the year, the primary manufacturer of Christmas cottages, Department 56, takes out a full-page ad in *USA Today* to announce the lines that it is discontinuing. Discontinued lines are bought up for their appreciation potential.

Vintage Collectibles: It Pays to Specialize

For vintage collectibles, knowledge is paramount, and so is specialization. This is a business that, so far, doesn't know it's a business: There are no headquarters, no company spokesmen, no central clearinghouse of information. But you can create order out of this chaos.

First, identify the area—out of the dozens available—that you are most interested in, be it comic books or detective stories or *Rolling Stone* magazines or science fiction. That's the easiest part: You already know your favorites, or you wouldn't be reading this.

Then go to the library reference room and get, via interlibrary loan if you have to, *Maloney's Antiques and Collectibles Resource Directory* by David J. Maloney, Jr. It lists, alphabetically and by category, thousands of collectors and collecting societies and reference books for every facet.

Do you like spy novels? There's an espionage society, even a James Bond society. Sherlock Holmes? There's a society for him, too. And for autograph collectors. And for collectors of war relics.

"Buy what you like, of course," says Kyle Husfloen, books editor for *The Antique Trader* in Dubuque, Iowa. "But buy the *best* items that you can afford. Spend a little more money to get the basis of a good collection, because you'll be living with it. And because someday you may wish to sell, and it's easier and more profitable to move good things. Learn as much as you can. Invest in reference materials and periodicals that specialize in your field. Soon you'll learn enough and gain enough confidence to buy, sell, and trade on your own."

The experts offer these tips for specific areas.

Track those first editions. "If you are drawn to book collecting, you can look up the prices of writers' first editions and cross-reference them for the past five to seven years," says Allan Stypeck of Second Story Books in Washington, D.C. "You'll see that in cases like Hemingway, the catalogs show increases of 400 to 500 percent over a five-year period." Consider investing your money in these "high points"—the book collectors' equivalent of blue-chip stocks, say, a perfect copy of *The Maltese Falcon* or *The Great Gatsby*. Or consider authors of more recent renown—perhaps first editions of early works by Patricia Cornwell, Sue Grafton, Elmore Leonard, or John Grisham.

Hold signings by mail. You can write to modern authors in care of their publishers and ask if they will inscribe their books by mail if you handle the packing. Some will, and this will increase the books' values substantially, although a percentage can't be calculated.

Stick with the stalwarts. "There are whole areas of books that maintain their value," Stypeck says. "Photography. Travel and exploration. Americana. Children's books. Remember to buy the best books in the best condition. All of these should increase in value in proportion to the inflation rate."

Keep it under wraps. If your collecting tastes run toward toys and such, try to keep the original packing intact, says Pollan. Toys and dolls from the 1950s and 1960s are holding their value, she notes. "It's best if they're in their original boxes, even better if they've not been used at all."

Move fast, electronically. Collectors, dealers, and collecting clubs are busy exploring the possibilities of the Internet. Dealers are putting their catalogs online, and collectors are swapping information, buying, and selling on online services like CompuServe and America Online. Enthusiasts say that the information to be found here is more up-to-date than anything in a catalog and look forward to a time when digitized photos of items for sale are routinely flashed across several continents in a nanosecond.

Art: Investing a Pretty Penny

A work of art, be it a painting or a drawing or a sculpture, can prettify a room. It can also, sometimes, strike chords within you that you didn't know were there. And with a little luck and acumen, it can make you some money.

Benjamin Doller, director of Nineteenth Century European Paintings, Drawings, and Sculptures at Sotheby's in New York City puts it plainly: "You have some money to spend, and you want to spend it on art. Obviously, you have places on your wall that you want to fill. Now, a good thing about an art investment is that it's not just money in the bank and a balance statement to look at. You get to live with it and enjoy it."

Understand first that you have some negotiating power. An artwork does not have a shelf price, like a can of peas. Once you have entered the art gallery and spotted a painting that you fancy, feel free to dicker.

What should you do to get a discount? "Ask for it," says Ronald Greenberg, operator of the Greenberg Van Doren Gallery in St. Louis. "Usually, there is a courtesy discount if you've bought before, sometimes 10 percent and sometimes more."

AT LEAST KNOW WHAT YOU LIKE

You should know a bit about yourself, though, before going in to haggle. "Ask yourself if you think that you could be sufficiently interested in the art world to develop a real understanding of it," advises Marc Rosen, a New

York City art consultant. If you depend too heavily on the advice of gallery owners, "you're letting someone else play with your money, and you're unlikely to do well with it."

If you conclude that, yes, you do want to do more than hang a decorator asset, here are some tips to guide you through what is—remember!—a buyer's market.

Narrow your focus. You have to specialize, says Greenberg. "You must pick a specific area and stay with it. It is too time-consuming, and there is too much to know to be a generalist. The more expert you can become in the one little area, the more fun you're going to have and the better your collection will be."

Make it a habit. "Focus on what you like," elaborates Doller. A particular artist. A particular school. Impressionist or Expressionist or Native American. Then educate yourself with your eyes: This is easy, it's free, and it's fun. "Look at items in this area as much as you can. Take your time. Go to exhibitions and auctions. Go to museums. Go to galleries."

Hit the books. "Read," Doller says. "Learn when the artist—or artists—was painting. Was he alone in his field? Was it a recognized movement? And how have the prices done?"

There are furrow-browed ways of doing it, like digging through catalogs and price guides in library archives. You will surely have to do this as your interest—and your investment—grows. But there is a less daunting way to start.

"Whatever city you live in, there is likely an art museum there or in a nearby community," says Greenberg. "Feel comfortable going and talking to the curator. He won't charge you for it. Start a dialogue." Let him know your interests. He can guide your researches into the history of your specialty.

BUSINESS SENSE CAN STILL APPLY

All the experts advise buying artwork that you like and feel good living with. But there is so much money swirling around this world that you can be forgiven for being curious about value. After all, it's even easier to live with something that's growing in value moment by moment.

There's no escaping the fact that there's the element of a crapshoot in buying artwork. You don't need that much money to get into the game. A few thousand dollars will give you access to a choice: you can spend it on a Picasso lithograph or a full-scale work by an unknown. Five years later—which, by the way, is the minimum time you should plan to hold on to something for appreciation—the Picasso will have done its blue-chip growth. And the unknown? It will be worth a little less. Or a little more. Or 10 to 20 times more, and you can congratulate yourself on your farsightedness.

Tip: When you go to buy, the work by the unknown characteristically has a larger percentage of markup than the Picasso and thus is more susceptible to haggling.

If you don't want to treat the art world like commodities trading but you do want to feel a modicum of security in your choices, here's how.

Buy the best that you can. Of course, the Ferrari is more likely to appreciate than the Ford Escort. It looks better, too. But there's more: Choose an artist who has some significance yet whose *best* works you can afford to buy. Ask the curator and the gallery staff if it's plausible to get good things with whatever money you're starting with. Is it $100 to $5,000, $5,000 to $10,000, or more? Keep asking questions and "kicking tires"—eventually, they'll line up your interests with your pocketbook.

Stick to the typical. Stay with items by that artist that are typical of that artist. Do not be seduced by a piece that looks interestingly offbeat. As Rosen puts it, "You want to be sure that you have something that anyone can recognize as a work by that artist. You definitely don't want the one thing that doesn't look good, that nobody would guess was by him."

Plan your collection. Make a plan that gives you room to acquire over time a meaningful body of material, either by one artist or one school or one type, whether Renaissance bronzes or Victorian landscapes or Dutch fruit bowls. "Some people do it by having one major drawing by each artist they're interested in," Rosen says. "Others like to get a small collection of works by one or two artists."

If you're a beginner, act like one. Here's a checklist of things to do until you're an art expert.

- Buy from a dealer for now, not an auction house. As Greenberg says, as a beginner "you will not always be able to tell if the auction house is passing along something that has been damaged and repaired. It may have been in a fire and is now the property of an insurance company, which creates too many unknowables."
- Make sure that the dealer is one to whom you can go back if there's a problem.
- Don't believe that you're going to get a $100,000 painting for a few dollars just because someone has taken a liking to you. "You'd be surprised how often that happens," says Rosen.

Luxury Items

Many of us grow up skeptical of "flash," of "conspicuous consumption." But then one day we feel silk against the skin or catch the flash of sunlight on gemstones and another sort of thought comes. Hmmm . . . there's that special anniversary coming up. Or your wardrobe could stand that one special touch of finery to project the right professional image. So you break down: Let us have a little of the good stuff.

There are ways to obtain it without blowing all the grocery money. Here's how to buy wisely in two categories—jewelry and fine watches.

JEWELRY: THE INVESTMENT THAT YOU WEAR

When you're buying fine jewelry, how do you weigh your means against the cost of what may be a once-in-a-lifetime purchase? The industry has a rule of thumb.

"Somebody who wants to buy a diamond should consider spending two months' salary to buy something of value," says Guido Giovannini-Torelli, a diamond consultant in New York City and editor of the monthly newsletter *Diamond Insight.* We're speaking here of not just any jewelry purchase, of course, but a diamond for a "momentous" occasion like a wedding or anniversary—something intended to be a family keepsake. "So if you are earning $40,000 annually, you should consider buying something costing between $6,000 and $7,000," he says.

That's a lot of money for anyone. So take some time to learn a bit. Start by learning a minimum of terms.

Costume jewelry is what you don't want if you're looking for an investment-quality, image-building purchase. These are phony jewels like rhinestones set in coated, cheap metal.

Fine or precious jewelry is more like it. It's pure metal—gold or platinum—holding real or synthetic stones.

Some of the synthetics can be quite beautiful, but it's the real stuff you want, advises Keith Shaw, vice-president of St. Louis jewelers Elleard B. Heffern. "Things made by nature rather than man are rarer, and people feel better knowing that they have something natural," he says.

Time it right. Go shopping in January and February or July and August. Jewelers object to the commonly held belief that the markup in fine jewelry is around 300 percent. They attribute this notion to the plethora of scams routinely advertising "50 percent off!" The profit among legitimate jewelers, they say, is somewhere between 50 and 75 percent.

And you can get 20 to 25 percent off that by shopping after the Christmas season or during the summer slump.

Brush up on your gems. If you're not seeking a diamond, the dealer should be willing to give you a short course in alternatives, says Deborah Hiss-Odell, spokesperson for the Gemological Institute of America in Santa Monica, California. "If you want a green stone, you should know that there are more than just emeralds out there," she says. "And know that some stones can take wear and tear, while another, such as an opal, needs to be handled with care."

If you *are* after a diamond, request a grading report that states the characteristics of the diamond: weight, clarity, and color.

Establish the return route. Clarify the dealer's position on returns. You should be able to return the item you purchase within two or three days and get all your money back.

Ponder the future. Ask about appreciation potential. A jewel, like a new car, is all of a sudden not worth what you paid for it. But the jewel has a chance of regaining its value and perhaps more if you can hang on to it for 20 to 30 years. It depends upon rarity, quality, and setting. Single stones will appreciate faster than more elaborate pieces. Gold and other metals tend to lose, not gain, in value.

Arrange for an appraisal. Before you make any big-ticket jewelry purchase, write to the American Society of Appraisers at 555 Herndon Parkway, Suite 125, Herndon, VA 20170-5226. They will help you locate an appraiser savvy about jewels in your area. Tell this person that you are going to be jewelry shopping and ask if you could drop in for a visit.

Get it inspected. Visit the jeweler with whom you've decided to do business. After all your questions have been answered, say that you wish to leave a check for the full amount and submit the jewel—and the grading report, if there is one—to outside appraisal. A reputable dealer will comply. Take the item to the appraiser. Chances are that he won't charge to tell you that the price is fair or to give you ammo for further negotiation.

Get a second opinion. On your way back to the jeweler, stop at a second jewelry store and ask for a quick appraisal. While jewelers must go along with this routine, they dislike it because they fear the second jeweler will see a chance to offer you a sweeter deal.

It would be terrible if that happened, wouldn't it?

WATCHES: YES, TIME IS MONEY

Fine watches cost a lot of money. For $7,500 you will get no more than the simplest gold watch with a leather strap, according to Shaw. If you want to qualify for high-roller status and wear a name like Piaget or Patek Philippe, you may have to pony up as much as $20,000.

Or you may not. Bob Beumer, president and owner of Hamilton Jewelers in St. Louis, offers a few things to know.

"The markup in fine watches is between 30 and 40 percent," he says. "So you won't get anywhere offering $10,000 for a $20,000 watch. But if you say, 'I'm really interested in this watch. Would you take a fair offer of—15 percent off? Or 10 percent off?' you might be told yes half the time. For other considerations—how long has the watch been sitting there, for instance, and how well does the dealer know you?—the cut might be as deep as 20 percent."

For a still deeper discount, he suggests reconstituted watches—quality tickers that have had their innards reworked. They can go for as much as 50 percent off the price of a new watch and carry a two-year warranty, too.

Selling Fine Possessions

You don't have to be dead to have an estate sale. There can be a number of reasons: You've inherited a houseful of property that you must unload.

You or a relative are moving into a nursing home. You must relocate and don't want to schlepp all that stuff across the country.

Whatever the reason that you're "downsizing" your possessions, you want to get the most that you can for these items. The only variable is time: If you want your money fast, you may have to settle for a bit less. Getting top dollar takes a while. Still, speed has its own economies: Sell your things fast enough and you've avoided paying another month's rent or another month on the mortgage.

DON'T THROW ANYTHING AWAY

There's a customer for just about everything, says Paul Quinn, president of the Auction House of Falls Church, Virginia: "Old newspapers. Old advertisements. Even old family photographs and letters."

Marylouise Day, who handles estate sales out of Bethesda, Maryland, adds that "a lot of people don't know that they have valuable things, like early-twentieth-century furniture or silver or porcelain."

Consider an appraisal. The American Society of Appraisers (ASA) will give you a free referral to an appraiser near you. An appraiser's services should start at $150 an hour, says senior member of the ASA Richard Driscoll.

Hold your own tag sale. Using an appraiser's inventory, you could put a price tag on every item and conduct your own tag sale. Arrange your possessions in a way that you hope will help sell them. Then place an ad in the

Danger Signals

The Perpetual Sale

Avoid jewelry stores that are forever having "Going Out of Business" and "Lost Our Lease" sales or similar come-ons. These places tend to mark up a lot, then mark down a little, consumer advocates say.

And beware of stores that offer to set a stone that you've purchased somewhere else. There's a risk of damaging the stone in setting it, and only the schlockiest jewelers will take the risk.

Mail wholesalers of jewelry are a minefield: You may tread safely, or you may get blown up. Before entering it, have a talk with an appraiser and perhaps contact the Jewelers Vigilance Committee, 401 East 34th Street, Suite N13A, New York, NY 10016.

newspaper noting your specialties—antiques, collectibles, household items—and sit inside the front door with a cash box.

Out of all your options, this strategy could net you the most money, since you're not paying sales professionals. But there are drawbacks. Thieves have been known to follow ads and use a sale's open-door policy to case the building. It's also a good idea to have a friend stationed in each room of the house to deter shoplifting. Also, make sure in advance that you are up for dealing with the sale junkies and professional hagglers who will be paying you a visit.

INVOLVING PROFESSIONAL SELLERS

If you decide to turn the sale over to professionals, begin by telephoning attorneys and trust departments at banks, asking who they recommend to sell such holdings as yours. You're going to have to make a choice between two methods of selling—auctions and estate sales. There are advantages to each.

An estate sale is a tag sale run by an expert. The agent will appraise your possessions (saving you the cost of an appraiser), tag them, and advertise the sale, which will be held on your property. They'll also handle the cash box for you.

Estate sales are a slower process than auctions, but you're likely to make more money, insiders say. Keep in mind that some items are better suited to an auction house—first-edition books, fine art, and oriental rugs, for instance—and a competent estate sale manager will pass them along. Expect an estate sale to take a few days. The estate sales agency should pay for advertising, outside appraisals, and even security. The money will come out of their fee, which should be 25 percent of the take.

Auction houses offer some red-blooded action and the chance to score nice bucks on a wild night, but such nights are rare. Ask in advance about the fees these houses charge for hauling, insuring, and advertising the properties and for returning items that don't sell. Expect the auction house to take 25 to 40 percent of the money. The advantage is that an auction is faster than an estate sale and better at handling really splendid items.

An auction house may be willing to set a "reserve" on your items—a price below which they will not sell. But if the piece doesn't sell, the auction house will charge you a fee. Reserves are getting rarer because they are unpopular with buyers, who go to auctions wanting bargains.

For art, consider the source. To sell your paintings or sculptures, go back to the dealer who sold them to you, advises Greenberg. The dealer may specialize in works by the artist, meaning that he sells to the artist's audience and thus can move yours quickly. If not, any dealer would probably do, so talk to as many as possible to find your best deal. If your piece goes on consignment, the dealer should take 15 percent.

For books, weigh the hassle factor. If you have a rare-book collection to sell, a dealer is likely to offer you one-half the value of your library, says Stypeck. You might be happy with that, since the dealer will do the packing and hauling and you'll have it over with. If you have more time and if you live in a fair-size urban area, do some phone work and find the auction house that specializes in this material.

If you're really willing to sweat and want maximum return for your rare books, sell them yourself, Stypeck says. "You'll need access to a good reference librarian who can get you information about dealers, catalogs, and collectors' clubs. Put together the best information you can, and begin running your ads in magazines like *AB Bookman's Weekly*. Be sure to include a price. Saying just 'best offer' will have people thinking that you're not serious," he says.

Letting the gold go. Selling your jewelry is likely to be a disappointing experience, particularly if there are no precious stones involved. "You are probably going to be able to sell gold jewelry for 25 to 30 percent of what you paid for it," says Shaw. "Whatever labor went into the piece is a wash—if it's gold, all you're going to get is the weight of the metal. Jewelry shows wear, so it can never be sold as new."

But if it's gotta go, it's gotta go. For a $20,000 to $30,000 item, auction houses are an option, Shaw says, but that's a two-edged sword: You may have two or three parties bidding, or it might be an off night with no interest.

You can sell it back to the original jeweler and take your lumps, but they may not be so lumpy: If you need the money in a hurry, you can at least get cash quick rather than waiting for what is only a possible bonanza weeks ahead.

Bottom Line

You can live beyond your means—without actually blowing your household budget—by being a savvy buyer. Learn the seasonal fluctuations of supply and demand. Use research to gain bargaining strength. And learn when you're being asked to pay for less quality and more advertising hype.

Words to the Wise

Appraiser: A seasoned pro in the field of art, jewelry, antiques, or other fine goods. You'll usually pay to have an item appraised, but this unbiased opinion can save you from making a major mistake, whether you're buying or selling.

Taste drinking: Choosing a beverage based on its taste rather than its marketing hype. The opposite of image drinking.

Utility rebate: A rebate that some utilities offer to buyers of energy-efficient air conditioners, based on their seasonal energy efficiency ratings.

Allies

American Society of Appraisers: 555 Herndon Parkway, Suite 125, Herndon, VA 20170-5226.

Jewelers Vigilance Committee: 401 East 34th Street, Suite N13A, New York, NY 10016.

Collector Editions and *Dolls:* Published by Collector Communications Corporation, 170 Fifth Avenue, Suite 1200, New York, NY 10010-5911.

Maloney's Antiques and Collectibles Resource Directory, by David J. Maloney, Jr. (Chilton Book Company). Available from The Antique Trader, P.O. Box 1050, Dubuque, IA 52004, or your local bookstore may have a copy.

Part 4

HEALTH

Slimming Down the Doctor Bills

In This Consumer's Twilight Zone, You Can Still Save a Healthy Sum

Take your car to a mechanic, and you'll often see the shop's hourly labor rate posted on the wall. Before they begin work, they'll typically give you a written estimate of the cost, based on the shop's hourly rate, an estimate of how long the repair will take, and the price of parts. In many states, by law, the shop must get your approval before doing anything that will substantially increase your bill.

Surely, it's an imperfect system; but at least as a consumer you know what to expect. And you can be reasonably sure that the next guy's going to pay the same price.

Now imagine that your legs break down instead of your wheels and you have to visit a doctor. Enter the Consumer's Twilight Zone: No one voluntarily tells you how much anything's going to cost. And if you're like most people, you don't think to ask. The exchange of financial information is strictly a one-way street. You tell the receptionist how you're going to pay.

You can't be certain that the doctor's going to charge his next patient the same amount, even if he performs essentially the same service. And what he charges depends not on your ability to pay but on how you're paying and who is helping you—that is, what type of insurance you have.

Ironically, while limiting medical spending has become a national obsession, some doctors routinely charge uninsured patients—those least likely to be able to afford a large bill—more than patients whose care is paid for by a large insurance company or health maintenance organization that has the leverage to negotiate lower rates.

The explanation for this situation is complex, but it can partially be summarized in two letters that inspire many consumers to abandon all pretense of rational economic decision making: M.D.

"Most people are intimidated, especially by the old-style doctor," says James F. Fries, M.D., professor of medicine at Stanford University School of Medicine and co-author (with Donald M. Vickery, M.D.) of *Take Care of Yourself*, a self-care manual that has sold more than 10 million copies since it was first published in 1976.

Controlling Medical Fees

Intimidated or not, we spend vast amounts of money. In all, Americans spent about a trillion dollars on medical care in 1995, a 45 percent increase in only five years, according to the federal Health Care Financing Administration. That figure is projected to increase to nearly $2.2 trillion by the year 2005.

In 1994, the typical American family with children spent $2,049 on out-of-pocket health care costs, including insurance, medical services, drugs, and supplies. But that figure represents less than 20 percent of the true cost of medical care. American families spend more than twice as much as supporting programs like Medicare and Medicaid. Those costs are part of your federal and state taxes.

With the much-publicized arrival of managed care, insurance companies control, to varying degrees, what doctors you can see and how doctors treat their patients. However, managed care has not cut individuals' out-of-pocket medical costs.

"What is driving this health care reformation is not the hospitals, not the government, not physicians, not insurance companies, but employers who are picking up the tab for health care," says Gray Tuttle, a certified business consultant in Lansing, Michigan, who specializes in helping physicians to manage their practices. "They're demanding higher quality at lower costs. Doctors and hospitals who don't heed this are going to find themselves in trouble."

Are You Paying "Full Fare"?

In many ways, health care works like an airline. To maximize his income, the physician wants to fill all the "seats" (appointments) on his "plane" (daily office schedule) with "passengers" (patients) who pay full fare (the doctor's fee).

But in today's economic climate, large insurance companies, health maintenance organizations (HMOs), and the federal government all use their extensive leverage to negotiate lower fees in return for a potential stream of patients. Few if any physicians can fill their appointment books with the equivalent of the airline's last-minute business traveler—visits for which the insurance company pays 80 percent or more of the doctor's full fee, with no questions asked, and the patient promptly pays the remainder.

When flying, different passengers pay wildly different fares, depending upon such variables as when they reserve their seats and when they're going to return. Similarly, a typical physician fills his calendar with several different types of patients, all of whom pay different fees, usually through their insurance companies or HMOs.

- The patient with traditional "indemnity" insurance that pays 80 percent of the doctor's fee and related charges while the patient pays the rest. Many such plans, however, have a schedule of approved fees. If the doctor charges more than your insurance company wants to pay, you're responsible for the balance.
- A patient whose insurance company includes the physician in its "preferred provider" network and will pay as much as 100 percent of the fees that the company has negotiated in advance.
- The patient who belongs to an HMO, which pays the doctor a set monthly fee for providing all the patient's primary care.
- The patient with government insurance, either through Medicare (usually someone over 65) or Medicaid (a poor single mother, for example).
- The patient with no health insurance who pays for himself.

"The price that the medical provider will accept is dramatically affected by who's paying the bill," says Mark Kaiser, chairman and chief executive officer of Medirisk, a private firm in Atlanta that tracks physicians' fees. "We know because we have the data."

Except perhaps in the plastic surgeon's office—where insurance rarely covers face-lifts and other services—relatively few patients today pay the doctor's "standard" fee. "Five to 10 years ago, a large number of patients would pay the standard fee, in full, and their insurance companies would pay the standard fee," says Tuttle. "As managed care has grown, the physician's standard fee has become irrelevant, except for people who don't have insurance coverage for those services—what we call self-pay. There the doctor can still charge his full fee, but the patient has to dig into his jeans and pay it. What's also changed is that the number of people without health insurance is growing at an alarming rate. However, we still see physicians applying appropriate discounts for self-pays, based upon ability to pay."

ARM YOURSELF WITH INFORMATION

If you belong to an HMO or a doctor belongs to your insurance company's preferred provider network, that's good news for you—at most, you'll

It Figures

Avoiding the "Balance Bill" Trap

Unless your doctor agrees to abide by your insurance company's price structure, you could end up paying substantially more out of pocket for a medical procedure. Here's how the charges can quickly stack up.

Say that you live in Los Angeles and have heart disease. You go to the hospital for angioplasty, a common procedure in which a physician uses a catheter to inflate a balloon inside your clogged artery, opening up the passage and allowing more blood to flow.

You have traditional "indemnity" insurance (which pays 80 percent of your bills), but your carrier's fee schedule is lower than your doctor's charge. The doctor might easily send you a balance bill of $1,000—or more.

Doctor's fee for angioplasty	$4,100
Company's assigned fee	$3,150
Company pays 80 percent of $3,150	$2,520
You owe	$1,580 ($4,100–$2,520)

SOURCE: *Medirisk*

On the other hand, if you've discussed fees with your doctor in advance, and he's agreed to accept your insurance company's assigned fee, you save a bundle.

Doctor accepts assigned fee	$3,150
Company pays 80 percent of $3,150	$2,520
You owe	$630
You save	$950

SOURCE: *Medirisk*

And remember, this is just the doctor's fee. You'll have a hospital bill to reckon with, too.

This demonstrates why you should always discuss a doctor's fees before you undergo treatment. Legally, in most cases you're liable for the difference. Most doctors ask patients to sign a paper saying that the patient is responsible for whatever charges his insurance company does not pay.

usually owe a small co-payment. But if you're uninsured or the physician's not in your preferred provider network, you'll usually end up paying more. And given the high cost of medical care, even if you're paying only 20 percent, the bills can add up quickly, especially if you go to see a specialist or need an expensive procedure.

As in all negotiating relationships, the more you know about both your physician and his competition in the area, the more leverage you have. Ideally, you'd like to know the sort of information in the tables accompanying this chapter—what's typical for your area, what's high, and what's low. It would also help to know what your doctor charges other patients.

Alas, this sort of information is difficult to find: Physicians, unlike auto mechanics (at least mechanics in regulated states like California), rarely post fees on office walls. Medirisk, the company that provided our figures, offers similar information to subscribers by phone. A subscription to the service, which is called Mediguard, costs an individual about $70 per year.

Even without such detailed data, though, you might be able to use this basic knowledge of how the system works to negotiate a lower fee. "If you're a savvy medical consumer, you want to know why you're being charged 50 to 100 percent more than the patient in a preferred provider organization," says Kaiser.

Here's some advice from Medirisk and the People's Medical Society, a nonprofit organization based in Allentown, Pennsylvania, that provides information and advice to its members about consumer medical issues.

Begin at the beginning. The best time to discuss a doctor's fees is at the start of your relationship—when you "hire" the physician. If, for example, you have traditional indemnity insurance, at least make sure that the physician accepts your insurance company's established fee schedule. If the doctor does not belong to your preferred provider network, ask him to accept your company's preferred provider rates. You won't have to haggle over every bill, and you'll avoid the "balance bill" trap—that overwhelming balance due notice that you'll get after a medical procedure.

Of course, you can completely avoid this dilemma by choosing doctors within the network.

Whether you discuss fees with your doctor or his business manager is partly a matter of preference. The nonprofit consumer health organization People's Medical Society recommends discussing fees directly with the physician or with the physician and his business manager together. (Surprisingly, some doctors don't even know their fee schedule—they delegate complete responsibility for billing to others.)

Remember that for most doctors the standard fee is essentially a fiction created for bookkeeping purposes—it's the amount that he'd like to charge if market forces had not intervened. In today's economic climate, few physicians have the economic freedom to charge all their patients a standard fee.

What Do I Say?

Renegotiate That "Balance Bill"

You've already had angioplasty, you're back at work and recovering nicely when—boom!—you're hit with a larger-than-expected bill for the balance not covered by insurance. Suddenly, you feel ill all over again. Here's how you might handle the problem.

Ideally, you'd like to know the full range of fees that doctors in your area charge. In Los Angeles, doctors' fees for angioplasty vary tremendously.

Maximum "reasonable" charge	$4,101
Typical reimbursement	$3,157
Managed care (high)	$1,404
Managed care (typical)	$1,161
Managed care (low)	$1,104
Medicare reimbursement	$1,021

Source: Medirisk

Here's how Mark Kaiser, chairman and chief executive officer of Medirisk, a private firm in Atlanta that tracks physicians' fees, recommends addressing the problem.

Be reasonable. Doctors and business managers are human—they don't like someone screaming that they charge too much.

Instead, Kaiser says, try saying this: "Please help me understand. You've charged me $4,100 for my angioplasty. If I belonged to an HMO (health maintenance organization) in this city, you would get between $1,100 and $2,000. Medicare pays $1,021."

Or this: "My insurance company already paid you $3,150. That's $1,150 more than you'd get in the highest-paying managed system and $2,136 more than you'd get from Medicare. Why isn't that $3,150 enough?"

Adds Kaiser, "We know, because we do this every single day of the week and year, that physicians will work with you. They will either waive the balance due, reduce it, or at least come up with a payment plan. In 95 percent of cases, the physician will work with you."

They (or someone from their office) routinely discuss, justify and negotiate fees, albeit with insurance company and HMO representatives. All that you're asking for is similar treatment.

And remember to ask again about fees each time you and your doctor discuss a new procedure, treatment, or test.

If you're on Medicare, ask the doctor to accept Medicare's "assignment"—the fee that the federal government deems appropriate for a given procedure.

Another strategy, albeit a less common one, is to ask your doctor to waive the co-payment—the portion of your bill for which you're responsible.

Check your regular doc first. Before you go to a specialist, consult with your primary care physician, recommends the People's Medical Society. He knows you, can handle many problems himself, and is trained to look at your overall health, not just one part of your body. Similarly, don't rely on a specialist as your primary care provider—his fees are usually higher, and he's not necessarily qualified to treat problems outside his specialty.

But there are exceptions. If, for example, you suffer from a complex chronic disease like rheumatoid arthritis, you want your primary medical relationship to be with a rheumatologist.

Before a test, know the score. Question the need for any test. Why is your doctor recommending it? What will a positive result tell him? A negative one?

Many medical tests are expensive. Some are unnecessary. Make sure that you understand fully what the test is intended to do and that you're convinced that it's truly necessary, advises the People's Medical Society. For this, a good medical reference can be invaluable.

Save the ER for emergencies. The emergency room (ER) might be a hot set in Hollywood, but it's an expensive place to have a doctor treat a cut or sprained ankle. If you're in a bad car wreck, you obviously need to go to an emergency room; if your doctor's office is closed and your problem is relatively minor, go to an urgent care center instead, advises the People's Medical Society. As with medical tests, educate yourself: A good self-care manual, which helps you know when you should and should not see a doctor, will easily pay for itself.

Pick up the phone. If you're not sure whether you need to see a doctor, don't be shy. Call the doctor's office or an advice nurse. Often you'll save money and time—for yourself as well as your insurance carrier.

Selecting Doctors

You've moved across the country and are without a regular doctor for the first time in 20 years. You want to find someone new—before anyone in your family gets sick. Where to begin?

Ask First: Medical Fees Vary Wildly

Here's another example of why you should discuss doctors' fees in advance. Even for a simple procedure like a skin biopsy (the doctor removes a small piece of possibly damaged skin to test for cancer), the difference in price can be staggering.

City	Lowest Charge	Highest Charge	Variation
Boston	$27	$215	696%
Dallas	$30	$200	566%
Atlanta	$40	$180	350%

SOURCE: *Medirisk*

Make lists. Gather names from a variety of sources—friends, colleagues, the company personnel office, your insurance company, the Yellow Pages. Think about your needs and habits. Can you get to the office quickly? Are the hours convenient?

Then interview potential doctors as you would any other person who might provide you an important service. Is the staff polite and efficient? Does the physician have the appropriate training? And don't overlook the obvious: Is the doctor licensed?

What's the doctor's philosophy—does the physician believe in preventive care? The People's Medical Society advises consumers to set up a get-acquainted visit specifically for this purpose—a time to talk, fully clothed, without the worry of a medical problem hanging over you.

FIND A PHYSICIAN THAT YOU CAN TRUST

Depending on your family and its needs, you might choose a family practitioner, osteopath, pediatrician, or specialist in geriatrics. A woman of child-bearing age may well see her gynecologist more than a generalist. Whomever you choose, you want someone that you trust—someone who knows you and can both help you remain healthy and treat you when you're ill.

The most important qualities in a personal physician, say Dr. Vickery and Dr. Fries, are communication and anticipation. You want a doctor who listens to what you have to say. And who's able—and willing—to explain things clearly and concisely. One measure of this willingness is the doctor being available to talk on the phone.

A good primary physician also anticipates the future, trying to address potential problems before you get ill. If you're 50 years old and 50 pounds overweight, you want a doctor who can help you with diet and exercise.

As you get to know your new physician, be alert to signs of poor medical care. One of the most obvious is how he uses medication. "You want a physician who uses medication sparingly, who discontinues medication as soon as possible, and who uses the lowest possible dose," says Dr. Fries. The worst-case scenario: a doctor who spends only a few minutes with you, doesn't want to hear about your problems, quickly scribbles a prescription, and says good-bye.

SPECIALISTS: A BREED APART

Specialists are, in many respects, much like your primary care physician: Most charge widely varying fees, which depend largely on who's paying. But specialists are also different.

Sure, it would be nice to have a heart surgeon who took the time to discuss your fears before you went in for a quadruple bypass. What's more important is that he has the skills and experience to do the job right.

In most cases, your primary physician will be the one who sends you to a specialist. Dr. Vickery and Dr. Fries suggest two basic tests for choosing a specialist.

Weigh your options. Be sure that your primary physician trusts and approves of the specialist. Ask your doctor about other possibilities and discuss their advantages and disadvantages. Here's where it helps to have established a good, trusting relationship with your personal physician.

Study the history. Ask how much experience the specialist and hospital have in performing recommended procedures. Usually, doctors who perform technical procedures regularly have better results than those who do them only occasionally. Likewise, the hospital's degree of experience affects the success rate. As a general rule, Dr. Fries and Dr. Vickery say, the doctor and hospital should perform the procedure at least 50 times a year. For more complicated procedures like bypass surgery or angioplasty, you'll want both the surgeon and hospital to have even more experience.

The People's Medical Society suggests these further steps when you need a specialist.

Check credentials. Within many specialties, physicians maintain their own board, which oversees educational requirements. Board certification— for example, by the American College of Cardiology (ACC)—is no guarantee of competence, but at least you'll know that the doctor has undergone the necessary additional training. You can check many but not all specialists' credentials by calling the American Board of Medical Specialties certification line at 1-800-776-2378.

Talk, talk, talk. Now more than ever, ask questions about all tests. Ask what the doctor hopes to accomplish, how much it will cost, whether it will be painful, and whether there are alternatives.

Ask about ownership. Ask who owns the equipment or lab to which you are being referred. About half of the states require physicians to disclose ownership, which represents a conflict of interest. Be wary of doctors who order extensive and expensive tests on their own equipment: A 1994 study by the federal accounting office found that doctors who owned their own equipment ordered more MRIs (magnetic resonance imaging), CT (computed tomography) scans, x-rays, and other tests than those who did not.

Treatment Costs: The Big Bucks

Here's where being a smart consumer really pays off. If you're charged $63 for an office visit while the next guy's HMO pays only $32—the price range in Minneapolis—it's not that big a deal. If your insurance company pays 80 percent, it costs you only an additional $6.20 (20 percent of $31).

But have open-heart surgery in the same city and the potential difference in the doctor's fee alone swells to several thousand dollars. And that, depending on your insurance coverage, might cost you at least several hundred dollars.

YES, AN OUNCE OF PREVENTION...

Your first line of defense, obviously, is to stay out of the operating room. Ask about nonsurgical alternatives. Some experts estimate that 10 to 20 percent of all surgery is unnecessary.

Be an informed patient. Libraries and bookstores are filled with accurate, clearly written medical books written for the layperson. The more you know, the better prepared you are to ask questions and make decisions. And, some studies suggest, the less likely you are to have surgery.

If, after reading about your problem, you're not sure that you want to undergo surgery, seek a second opinion. It's usually best to consult someone who's independent from the first doctor—preferably one who's not a surgeon. And be sure to read your insurance policy. Some require a second opinion before they'll pay for nonemergency surgery.

With major surgery and major medical treatment, more than ever you'll want to check your doctor's qualifications. The ACC and the American Heart Association (AHA), for example, recommend that surgeons perform a minimum of 100 open-heart surgeries a year, most of them coronary artery bypasses. The organizations also recommend that at least 200 open-heart surgeries be performed in the hospital each year.

With angioplasty, the ACC and AHA recommend that cardiologists perform at least 125 angioplasties in training, including 75 in which they are the primary operator, and at least 75 procedures a year to maintain competence. For hospitals, 200 procedures a year, the organizations say, are "essential for the maintenance of quality and safe care."

With heart surgery, at least, it's no exaggeration to say that your life may be at stake. Mortality rates differ dramatically from one hospital to another.

Don't Take Your Hospital Stay Lying Down

What is it about a hospital that makes an ordinary adult feel like he has regressed 30 years in age? Is it the paper-thin gown? The food, so often reminiscent of a junior high school cafeteria? Indeed, the entire experience seems to infantilize the patient.

That need not be the case, consumer advocates say.

Do your homework. If you research your medical condition before entering the hospital, you'll be prepared to be an active, involved patient. You'll be more likely to protect yourself against human errors, such as improper medication.

Remember: It's your body. You may be the patient, but you're in control. Wear your own clothes. Do little things for yourself. Get to know the nurses and staff who are taking care of you—they, in turn, will see you as more than the condition.

Act like a customer—which you are. You deserve good service at a hospital, just as you do at a restaurant. Nurses should visit every few minutes if you're seriously ill, every few hours if you're not. They should answer your calls at once, at least by intercom. They should spend time with you and listen to you.

If you aren't satisfied, take your complaints up a ladder: to your nurse, the head nurse, the hospital administration. Many have a patient representative or ombudsman who's responsible for such matters.

Read your insurance policy. If your policy requires you to pay, say, 20 percent of hospital charges, the fees add up quickly. That's why you should begin thinking about financial matters before you go to the hospital. Sure, your policy is as tedious as the tax code, but you need to know what it covers and what rules apply to your situation before you check in.

Do you need a second opinion? Preauthorization from your insurance company? If you're insured through a preferred provider organization, do all doctors—including anesthesiologists—participate? If you have indemnity insurance, will your doctor and hospital accept your insurance company's fee?

A Bitter Pill: Prescription Fees

Prescription drugs can be a significant part of the annual health care bill, especially when a family member has a chronic condition like high blood pressure. Depending upon what type of insurance coverage you have, several converging trends may well point to even higher costs.

Under pressure to control costs, many doctors are increasingly treating patients with medication rather than surgery and other expensive treatments. And while the general trend is for insurers to pay more of the cost of

Get an estimate. Ask the hospital in advance to estimate how much the procedure or operation will cost. When you examine your bill, this will help you spot the most egregious errors.

Time it right. Check in late and leave early. Hospitals are like hotels, charging for rooms by the day. And don't check in on weekends.

Keep a log. As much as possible, write down everything that your doctor and the hospital staff do—every intravenous line they insert, every pill they give, every specialist who examines you. If you're not well enough to do it, ask a friend or relative to help. This will help you spot errors on your bill, says the People's Medical Society, a nonprofit organization based in Allentown, Pennsylvania, that provides information and advice to its members about consumer medical issues.

Question the need for tests. Doctors and hospitals sometimes perform x-rays, blood tests, and other diagnostic tests that are unnecessary, according to the People's Medical Society.

Consult on consultations. Ask your primary physician to discuss with you the need for any consultations by other specialists. Then make sure that the consultation is needed. Otherwise you may be charged hundreds of dollars by doctors that you barely remember.

Pack a bag. Bring necessities to the hospital, including tissues, hand lotion, and vitamins. Speak to your attending physician or nursing staff for approval to bring your own supply of drugs for chronic conditions. The hospital staff will gladly provide all of these things for you—at an inflated price. But tell your doctor about any medicines.

Just say no thanks. Don't assume that anything's free and don't accept anything that you don't need. The best way to avoid being charged $16 for a pacifier or $15 for a pair of paper slippers is not to take them in the first place.

Recover at home. If you face a long recovery period, ask about home health services. It will be cheaper and, in many cases, better for you.

medication than in the past, they still pay for only 58 percent of retail prescriptions, according to the magazine *Drug Topics*.

And the cost of prescription drugs is rising. *Drug Topics* says, for example, that in 1994 and 1995 wholesale drug prices rose an average of nearly 7 percent a year—more than twice the rate of inflation.

For many consumers, this means that prescription drugs are a good place to save money without sacrificing the quality of medical care. Here's some basic advice from the People's Medical Society and other experts.

Buy generics. Each year drug companies spend many millions of dollars to market their medicines, mostly to physicians. New drugs are patented and can be manufactured only by the company that developed them (or bought the rights to do so). But older drugs, for which the patent has expired, can be manufactured by other companies, which generally don't spend money establishing and promoting a brand name. As a result, you can see one of the most basic principles of capitalist economics at work: Competition drives prices down.

On average, you'll pay about 30 percent less for generic drugs than you'd pay for their name-brand counterparts. Your best strategy is to ask for a generic as soon as your doctor reaches for his prescription pad. If you forget—or if your doctor doesn't know whether a generic is available—be sure to ask your pharmacist. Unless the prescription says "dispense as written" (or similar words, depending upon the state), most pharmacists can and will replace name-brand drugs with generics.

And don't be fooled by drug-company propaganda alleging that generic drugs don't work as well or are dangerous. By law, generics must have the same active ingredients as the name-brand version and must be absorbed into the body at a similar rate. But there are exceptions: "In some instances, the name-brand drug works better than the generic," says Nicholas Popovich, Ph.D., professor of pharmacy practice at Purdue University's School of Pharmacy in West Lafayette, Indiana. The moral is to find a pharmacist whom you can trust to tell you when the generic is not up to speed.

Even when buying generics, shop around. While some states require pharmacies to pass along wholesale savings on generic drugs, few require them to pass along the full savings. Nor do all pharmacies carry the least expensive version of a generic drug, which may be manufactured by more than one company. As a result, the cost of generics can vary from one pharmacy to another.

Sample the merchandise. Ask your doctor if he can give you any samples of the drug that he has prescribed—especially if there's no generic equivalent. Drug company salesmen sometimes give doctors free samples of medicines, so it'll cost your doctor nothing to give you several days' supply. Also, if you have an adverse reaction to the drug, you've saved yourself the prescription cost.

Count 'em up. Some newer prescription drugs are phenomenally expensive. In 1996, 14 Cipro pills—a week's regimen of this powerful antibiotic—cost $54 at CVS. That's $3.86 apiece, for a total of $7.72 each day of treatment. So make sure that those little gems are all there when your druggist hands the bottle over.

Shop around—within reason. Though competition has almost uniformly driven prices down—and driven many neighborhood pharmacists out of business—the cost of drugs varies, depending upon location and the type of pharmacy. Sometimes prices even differ from one chain outlet to another.

 **It Figures**

Generic Drugs versus Name Brands

Buying generic drugs will save you money—sometimes a *lot* of money. To illustrate the point, we dropped in at a grocery store pharmacy in Minneapolis. Depending upon where you live and the amount of local competition, you may save more or less, but the principle remains the same. Your average savings on these five drugs is 29 percent.

Drug	Brand-Name	Generic	Savings
Amoxil/amoxicillin (antibiotic) 30 500 mg. capsules	$15.69	$11.69	25%
Capoten/captopril (blood pressure regulator) 100 25 mg. tablets	$66.89	$41.79	38%
Motrin/ibuprofen (painkiller) 100 800 mg. tablets	$22.29	$20.39	9%
Tagamet/cimetidine (antacid) 30 800 mg. tablets	$88.69	$47.89	46%
Veralan/verapamil (blood pressure regulator) 30 240 mg. tablets	$38.49	$27.99	27%

But be prudent. In general, you'll find better prices at chains and better service at a neighborhood store. You may discover that one pharmacy has a better deal on one drug but a second store has lower prices on another.

But shopping around is not always a good idea. If you're allergic to any drug or take more than one medication, jumping from one pharmacy to another for each new prescription removes a crucial safety net. A good pharmacist acts as a safeguard, making sure that your doctor hasn't made an error or prescribed one drug that might conflict with another. If you're going to move back and forth between pharmacies, you must assume added responsibility: Be absolutely sure to ask your doctor and pharmacist about side effects and possible conflicts with other medications.

Order by mail. By some estimates, you can save 20 to 30 percent on mail-order drugs, though the savings are generally smaller when compared to prices at large chains and pharmacies in competitive markets. If you have a chronic condition that requires regular medication, though, the savings can add up.

But don't be penny-wise and health-foolish. Ask questions and be sure not to order by mail a drug that conflicts with something else that you bought from your local retailer. If you do use more than one pharmacist, make sure that both—and your doctor—know what other medications you're taking. Each time you visit your doctor, take your medicines with you to help him remember what he has already prescribed.

Sign up for a plan. Buy a drug card or prescription insurance plan. Many insurers offer prescription coverage for a small additional premium. Large employers often have prescription drug cards that allow you to pay at most a few dollars for a prescription.

DRUG SAVINGS ARE ON THE HOUSE

For prescription drugs, you buy generics at a huge savings. Similarly, when you buy over-the-counter medicines, look for house brands instead of the highly advertised name brands.

A 150-pill bottle of the leading nonprescription painkiller, Tylenol Extra Strength Gelcaps, was priced at $11.45 when we checked at a chain drugstore, while the same drug, acetaminophen, cost $6.69 in the house-brand package—more than 40 percent savings. Similarly, you would have paid $9.99 for a bottle of the leading name-brand aspirin, but only $3.79 (a whopping 62 percent less) for the store's house brand. Sudafed, the popular name-brand decongestant, sold for 125 percent more than its house-brand equivalent.

Don't be afraid to ask your pharmacist about specific over-the-counter medicines. Some simply don't work. Many involve some risks and side effects.

"We want people asking questions," says Dr. Popovich. "We need them to get in the habit of seeing over-the-counter products for what they are: They are drugs, and they can get people into trouble."

And finally, when possible, buy in bulk. The same Tylenol Extra Strength Gelcaps that cost 17 cents apiece in a box of 24 cost only 8 cents apiece in a bottle of 150.

That is, of course, a lot of Tylenol. You should not buy more than you can use before the expiration date comes around. You'll save nothing if you have to toss out half your medicine when it has gotten too old.

Brush Up on Dentistry

Want a glimpse of impact that preventive dental care has had in the United States? Just visit England, where it's not uncommon to see adults with a mouthful of brown, rotting teeth. It's a scary sight—enough to send even those who quake at the prospect (by some estimates, 10 to 14 percent) scurrying to the dentist's office.

The widespread use of fluoride in drinking water, health education, and innovations in dental care have dramatically changed the practice of dentistry in the United States. The average patient has far fewer cavities to drill and fill today than 15 years ago.

Remarkably, this change happened largely without the help of dental insurance, which only 41 percent of Americans have. In 1995, for example, Americans paid for half the cost of dental care out of their own pockets. For physicians' services, only 17 percent paid their own way. The bottom line is this: Here's a place where you can take a bite out of health care bills.

ASK THEM TO FILL YOU IN ON FEES

The basic advice for hiring a dentist is the same as for M.D.'s: Think about fees before you get treated. If you have traditional insurance, which pays the dentist for services rendered, make sure that he accepts your insurance company's rates—at least for simple procedures like cleanings and fillings. Otherwise, you get stuck in the same balance bill trap that haunts many medical patients. Alas, it's hard to avoid this trap entirely: Few dentists accept as full payment insurance company fees for complex procedures like root canals and caps.

Say that your insurance policy is supposed to pay for half the cost of a crown. But the insurance company says that it should cost $400 and your dentist says it's $600. Then you're stuck.

Dentist's fee: $600

Company pays 50 percent of $400: $200

You owe: $400

Remember, too, that dentists (or their business managers) routinely negotiate fees with insurance carriers, if not to the same degree as physicians. Why should you pay more just because you heard about your dentist from a friend rather than some insurance company's list of approved dentists? Ask whether the dentist participates in a preferred provider plan. If so, ask to be billed at that rate.

Or, join a dental plan such as a preferred provider network, which pays 100 percent of your routine costs and states clearly what you'll pay for additional services like crowns and root canals. But remember that there's an important difference between dental insurance and regular medical coverage: In dentistry, the focus is on preventive care.

"The best dental plans have no cost to the consumer for diagnostic checkups, tooth cleanings, fluoride treatments, and basic fillings—no deductible and no payments. That's the measure of a good plan," says Don Mayes, D.D.S., a dental benefits consultant based in Hershey, Pennsylvania. "The best plan has participating dentists and tells you what you'll have to pay. You get a schedule that says, 'If you need a crown, you'll pay X.' "

DENTAL HMOS: SHOULD YOU BITE?

As an alternative to traditional insurance, which pays separately for each service, look into dental HMOs, which pay the dentist a monthly or annual fee for each patient. A good HMO, Dr. Mayes says, can cost 15 to 30 percent less than fee-for-service insurance, with no deductible. It will pay for all your preventive and routine dental care.

But do your homework. "A well-designed, well-managed dental HMO will provide higher-quality dental care at less cost than a well-designed, well-managed fee-for-service dental plan," Dr. Mayes says. "On the other hand, a poor dental HMO is a greater menace to dental health than a poor fee-for-service plan."

Here's the danger. In its quest for profit, a poorly managed plan might make it difficult or impossible for you to get needed care.

How do you tell a good dental HMO? Here are some of Dr. Mayes's criteria.

• It pays the full cost of checkups, cleanings, fluoride treatments, and basic fillings.

• The plan doesn't erect what Dr. Mayes calls artificial barriers to getting care. For example, you don't have to wait more than four weeks for a non-emergency visit, and the dentist schedules as many services as possible at the same time. (They don't expect you to have your teeth cleaned at one appointment and examined a month later.) Nor should you have to wait a long time in the office to see the dentist.

Dentists belong to the American Academy of General Dentists, and specialists are either board-certified or board-eligible. Neither is a guarantee of competence, but both are evidence of the dentist's commitment to providing quality care, since they require additional training or education.

The Signs of a Good Dentist

Before you open your mouth, open your eyes. The following signs are indications of a good dentist, says Don Mayes, D.D.S., a dental benefits consultant based in Hershey, Pennsylvania. He has evaluated hundreds of dentists for health care providers.

• The office is clean and neat. "If it's not clean and neat out front," Dr. Mayes says, "the chances are that it's not in back, where you can't see."

• The dentist (or an employee) takes your health history, updating it each time you return.

• The dentist wears gloves, glasses, and a mask when treating you. He examines each tooth thoroughly and probes for gum disease.

• The dentist heat-sterilizes the drill and keeps handheld instruments either in a bag or on a covered tray while working.

• In a good plan, administrative costs and profit are less than 15 percent of revenue. This means that 85 percent of premiums are going to the dentist. Some divert as much as 41 percent to other uses.

• Dr. Mayes also worries when any insurance plan requires a dentist to get approval before referring a patient to a specialist, such as an endodontist for a root canal. Sometimes administrators routinely approve referrals, but if they don't, you risk having your regular dentist perform a service that he feels he's not capable of doing.

Dental HMOs, which have become more popular in recent years, are available only through employer-provided insurance. If you're self-employed or your employer doesn't provide insurance, look for a prepaid or discount dental plan. Their details vary, but typically you pay an annual fee to the company, then get free or discounted services from the plan's dentists.

But do the math first: You can't predict how much care you'll need, but if you've never had a cavity in your life, you may spend more on the plan's annual fee than you would if you went to a dentist on your own.

Here's another caveat. Some plans don't oversee the quality of care their dentists provide, so take extra care to make sure that yours is up to speed.

Here are some other tips for nibbling at your dental bills.

Pay as you go. Some dentists give a discount of, say, 5 percent if you pay at the time of your appointment. That way they don't have to send you a bill.

Be skeptical. If a new dentist wants to replace old fillings and crowns that aren't bothering you, think twice. At the very least you should get a second opinion before letting him drill away.

Transfer records. If you switch dentists, have your old dentist send records and x-rays to your new provider. He's ethically bound to do so; in some states, he's required to by law.

Remember Mom's advice. Yes, the longtime advice still holds: The best way to limit dental bills is to brush and floss your teeth regularly and limit the sugary foods that you eat.

FLUORIDE EACH DAY KEEPS THE DENTIST AWAY

Fluoride, which was first introduced to U.S. drinking water supplies in the 1940s, has been proven to reduce tooth decay. Despite that fact, even some major cities still don't have fluoridated water. What should you do if you live in such a place? Here are some tips.

Cover your kids. Start giving fluoride supplements to your children when they're 6 months old, says Barry Dale, D.M.D., assistant clinical professor of dentistry at Mount Sinai Medical Center in New York City. Consult your pediatrician. He'll want to evaluate the fluoride in your drinking water to be sure that your child doesn't get too much.

Brush it on. Adults as well as children should use fluoridated toothpastes and mouth rinses that carry the American Dental Association's seal of approval. If you're prone to tooth decay, ask about topical fluoride treatments, which are administered in a variety of different ways.

"As your teeth are forming, the fluoride that you ingest is incorporated into the tooth structure, which offers cavity resistance," says Dr. Dale, who also has a private dental practice in Englewood, New Jersey. "Topical fluoride works from the outside in. It penetrates into enamel in very small amounts, but it can be beneficial in preventing cavities."

Consider sealants. Plastic sealants are another preventive tactic to use with children, says Dr. Dale. If administered when the child's adult teeth come in, sealants can provide extra cost-effective protection against tooth decay. Dr. Dale says that sealants can be very helpful for some adults as well.

Focusing on Optical Options

Do you wear eyeglasses or contacts? The cost is enough to make you see red. That's true, in part, because many retailers charge a high markup on frames and services like tinting. What this means is that you can save $100 or more on a pair of glasses by shopping around.

And we do mean shop. Prices vary greatly, not only between private doctors' offices and chain or franchise outlets but also between individual chains. In Washington, D.C., for example, *Checkbook* magazine, which is published by the nonprofit Center for the Study of Services, found that the most expensive optical outlet charged almost three times as much for the same glasses as the least expensive shop. The high-priced culprit: a giant chain.

PREPARE TO COMPARE

One of the first tasks that you'll face is sorting through the vast array of choices. Unless you know exactly what frame you want to buy—typically the frame represents more than half the cost of a pair of glasses—you won't easily be able to make direct comparisons.

You're also dealing with a confusing industry. While some chain and franchise outlets offer lower prices than independent offices, others actually charge more than independent practitioners, according to surveys conducted by both *Consumer Reports* and *Checkbook*. *Checkbook* even found independents who had prices lower than the average chain. So comparisons are imperative.

Then there's the issue of quality. Both surveys found that customers of independent optometrists and ophthalmologists were more satisfied than those who bought at chains or franchises. But the *Consumer Reports* survey—which covered 71,000 subscribers who had recently purchased glasses—found that nearly as many customers of the highest-rated chains (Price Club Optical, For Eyes Optical, and Frame-N-Lens) were "highly satisfied" with the service that they received—as much as customers of the independent practitioners. The moral of the story is this: Contrary to what you might have guessed, you can get low prices at independent optometrists and ophthalmologists and good service at some chains.

In all, the optical business is a tough system to beat, but here's some advice for doing so.

Check credentials. Ask about an optician's training and experience. Surprisingly, many states don't license or regulate opticians—all you have to do is hang out a sign saying that you're an optician. A state license or certification by the American Board of Opticianry may be a sign of proper training, though neither is any guarantee.

Study your policy. This may be a tough one if you're in dire need of glasses, but do read the fine print. When it comes to paying for eye exams and glasses, insurance benefits vary wildly. If the language seems unclear, ask.

Compare apples to apples. Some companies charge extra for things like antiscratch coating and oversized lenses, while others don't. So when you're quoted a price, be sure to ask what's included.

Contact Lenses: A Soft Market

Glasses or contacts? Soft or hard? Once you've made these basic decisions—in most cases, matters of taste and comfort—you still face a bewildering array of choices. Actually, even the basic choices aren't so simple. The conventional hard lens has gone the way of the dinosaur, replaced by rigid gas-permeable lenses, which permit oxygen to reach the cornea (and are thus safer than hard lenses).

If, like some 26 million other Americans, you choose contacts, the first thing to realize is this: Contacts are different. You're putting a piece of plastic on the surface of your eye, which is potentially dangerous. Among other things, you risk infecting the cornea, the clear window that covers the front of the eye. An infected cornea is a serious matter, because the tissue is not reached by white blood cells that fight most bodily infections, says John Sheppard, M.D., spokesperson for the American Academy of Ophthalmology and an ophthalmologist in Norfolk, Virginia. So whatever type of contacts you wear, carefully follow instructions about cleaning and sterilization.

Although they're initially more expensive—$150 to $250, and even as much as $500 a pair—rigid gas-permeable lenses are usually the cheapest option, even when you add $50 to $80 a year for cleaning supplies. This is because they can last several years (if you don't lose them). But the vast majority of users choose soft contacts, and it's here that you face the real choices.

In essence, your choice with soft contacts boils down to this: You pick between lenses that must be removed and cleaned every night (daily-wear) and those that can be left in your eyes for as long as a week or two at a time (extended-wear).

Cleaned properly, the sturdiest daily-wear soft lenses last six months to a year, while others are designed to be thrown away after a week or two. Basically, you pay for a more convenient way to manage the risk of putting a piece of plastic on your eyeball: Instead of cleaning your contacts—a ritual that some people find tedious—you toss them out.

By being a smart consumer, you can cut down the cost of convenience. Here's how.

Run the numbers. In choosing between types of lenses, look at the total cost, including the price of cleaning solutions, not just the initial or first-year costs. Over the course of a year, the cost of solutions can be substantial—$50 to $80 for soft daily-wear lenses that you clean every night.

Get the paperwork. Ask at the outset whether your optometrist or ophthalmologist will release your prescription after the prescribed follow-up period (typically 90 days). In some states, they're required by law to do so; in others they're not. You want the freedom to shop for the best prices, but if the doctor won't release your prescription, you have no choice about where to buy replacement lenses.

It Figures

A Close Look at Contacts

What will shopping around for contact lenses do for you? Plenty. To illustrate the point, here's a sampling of prices for one brand of disposable soft contact lens, Johnson & Johnson's Acuvue, which is supposed to be worn for one to two weeks.

Company	Per Pair	Annual Cost (average 42 pairs)
Lens Express	$7.50	$315 (if you order a year's supply at one time). Includes $25/three years' membership fee plus $9 for shipping and handling.
Lens Express	$8.50	$355 (if ordering 6 pairs at a time). Includes $25/three years' membership fee plus $9 for shipping and handling on the first order and $5 on additional orders.
Sears Optical	$9.10	$363
Independent	$8.70	$365
LensCrafters	$8.50	$355

The moral of the story: If you're going to order by mail, plan ahead.

Some doctors require patients to sign a release if they want to buy their contacts elsewhere. "We're not willing to accept responsibility for what somebody else does," explains Dr. Sheppard. "It only makes sense. If you're a car mechanic, you don't guarantee the carburetor that someone else installs."

Whatever you do, don't skip your follow-up visits. Make absolutely sure that your eyes have adjusted properly to your contacts. If not, you risk paying a steep price. "If the car mechanic makes a mistake," Dr. Sheppard adds, "you have to walk. If someone messes up your contact lenses, you can't see."

He's not exaggerating: Used improperly, contacts can cause infections that may lead to sight loss.

Order in bulk. At a mail-order firm like Lens Express, you'll pay 15 to 25 percent less for your contacts and save on shipping and handling costs.

Weight Control: Shed the Gimmicks

Ah, you're thinking, if only we were all as fortunate as Oprah Winfrey and could hire a cook and personal trainer when we wanted to shed excess pounds. Surely there would be fewer overweight Americans.

But Americans do spend heftily on weight-loss—$33 billion a year, according to the nonprofit Institute of Medicine, which is affiliated with the National Academy of Sciences. And all of this expenditure produces demonstrably poor results: One in three Americans between the ages of 20 and 74 is overweight, according to the National Center for Health Statistics.

That amounts to tons of wasted money. When it comes to weight loss, you're not just up against a mere bureaucracy—you're dealing with the intractable laws of physics. *That's* a system that you're not going to beat.

The basic math is simple. You gain weight when you take in more calories than your body metabolizes. The average man takes in 2,500 calories a day, and the average woman consumes 2,000 a day. When you consume 3,500 calories more than you burn, you gain one pound. Eat 3,500 fewer calories than you usually consume, and you're a pound lighter. No fancy diet in the world is going to alter that basic fact.

But actually, experts say, it's not hard to lose weight. The hard part is keeping it off for a year or more. "There are lots of ways to take off weight quickly," says James O. Hill, Ph.D., professor in the Department of Pediatrics and Medicine at the University of Colorado Health Sciences Center in Denver. "There aren't any good ways to keep it off, unless you modify your lifestyle."

But that doesn't mean that you have to be resigned to carrying 50 extra pounds for the rest of your life. What you have to do is change the number of calories that you consume, the number that you burn, or both.

Here are some basic principles.

Eat less fat. The average American consumes about 34 percent of his calories in fat, according to the National Center for Health Statistics. The most basic problem is that each gram of fat contains nine calories, more than twice as many as a gram of protein or carbohydrate. Think of it as putting 11 gallons of gas in a 10-gallon tank—your body has to store the excess somewhere.

The best way to decrease your fat intake is not through a fancy diet but by eating plenty of high-fiber grains, fruits, and vegetables.

Exercise. The most effective approach to exercise is to combine aerobic exercise, such as walking or cycling, with muscle-building exercise. During aerobic exercise, you burn additional calories; if you lift weights you increase your muscle mass. "Fat uses less energy than any other tissue," Dr. Hill explains. "If you have more muscle, you're going to require more energy."

Look at it as turning your car into a gas guzzler.

Lose weight slowly. Many experts suggest a goal of losing a pound a week. Dr. Hill thinks that even that might be unrealistically high. He suggests a far-more-modest pound a month.

Skip the gimmicks. Managing your weight, over the long term, is difficult. Anyone who says otherwise is exaggerating, at best. Diet shakes are fine for the occasion when you can't eat well, but if you rely on them to lose weight, you're probably going to fail in the long run, says Dr. Hill.

Still tempted? Try this mantra: A liquid fast won't last. A liquid fast won't last.

WEIGHING THE REDUCTION PROGRAMS

Of course, if losing weight were as straightforward as a physics equation, there'd be fewer overweight Americans. And there wouldn't be a $33-billion-a-year weight-loss industry.

For many people, successfully losing weight—and keeping it off—means addressing behavioral and psychological issues that are entangled with purely physical ones. They need help.

If you're thinking about buying more than a pair of walking shoes to help you lose weight, consider this grim statistic from the Institute of Medicine's *Weighing the Options*: Those who complete weight-loss programs typically lose about 10 percent of their weight but regain two-thirds of it within a year and almost all of it within five years.

Whether you're shopping for a diet aid, a commercial weight-loss program, or a live-in one like the Pritikin Center, look for products and services that help you make lifestyle changes that you can sustain over the long term rather than products that will simply help you to lose weight quickly.

In its 1995 report, the institute said that a good weight-loss program should:

- Give prospective customers a clear description of its approach, as well as detailed lists of goals, staff credentials, total costs, and results

- Assess its clients' overall physical and psychological health
- Teach you how to eat a diet that is lower in calories but is still nutritious
- Encourage physical activity
- Advise you of potential risks

"You want to look for programs that have outcome measures," says Dr. Hill. "And I'm not talking about photos of Mrs. Jones who lost 300 pounds. I want to know how many people lost weight and kept it off a year, two years, five years down the line. What percentage of their clients succeeded?"

Bottom Line

Don't be blinded by the myriad degrees—the alphabet soup of M.D.'s, D.D.S.'s, D.O.'s, Ph.D.'s, and others—that accompany the names of those who provide your medical care. Sure, medicine is different than the auto repair shop—the risks are higher and hit much closer to home. But you're still a consumer purchasing a service and deserve to get your money's worth. Demand it.

Words to the Wise

Generic drug: A less expensive version of a highly promoted name-brand drug. Generics contain the same active ingredients as the name-brand version and are absorbed into the body at a similar rate.

Indemnity insurance: The traditional health insurance that pays 80 percent of the doctor's fee. You pay the rest. But many plans have a schedule of approved fees. If the doctor charges more, you pay the balance.

Rigid gas-permeable contact lenses: Over the long haul, this type of contact lens is the least expensive option. They can last several years.

Allies

National Health Information Center: P.O. Box 1133, Washington, DC 20013-1133. Run by the U.S. Department of Health and Human Services, it offers free literature about AIDS, asthma, cancer, insurance, alcohol abuse, and other health-related topics and can help people find organizations that can answer their questions. Also, search for their World Wide Web site on the Internet.

People's Medical Society: 462 Walnut Street, Allentown, PA 18102. A nonprofit membership organization, it bills itself as "America's largest consumer group working solely for your medical rights." The organization publishes a newsletter, books, and pamphlets about consumer medical issues and health care.

Putting the Doctor on Hold

Good Health May Be Its Own Reward—But It's a Monetary One, Too

In life as in football, the best offense is a good defense. In health terms this means that if you really want to trim your medical bills, forget the doctors and hospitals, insurance companies, and health maintenance organizations. Instead, take responsibility for keeping yourself healthy.

The savvy medical consumer knows, in effect, that the best consumer is often no consumer at all. But not always.

By incorporating a handful of simple practices into your lifestyle—by exercising, for example, and eating a healthy diet—you can dramatically decrease your chance of developing some of the most deadly diseases to afflict human beings in modern industrialized societies. And in the process, you'll almost certainly cut your medical bills.

Look at it this way: If you don't get high blood pressure, you don't have to worry about whether you're getting a good deal on Vasotec. (A month's supply of the drug costs about $35.) And if your arteries don't clog, you won't have to worry whether the surgeon's fee for a bypass is $4,600 or $3,300.

But it's inevitable that problems will eventually arise, some of them serious. That's why following a schedule of tests—medically sound tests that are prudent for someone your age—can literally mean the difference between life and death.

So don't write off the doctors. Instead, use them intelligently, when you really need to. And when you do get ill—with chronic conditions like arthritis, especially, which can greatly affect your lifestyle and well-being—educate yourself and help yourself. Research shows that knowledgeable, informed patients tend to choose less intrusive—and usually less expensive—care. And they tend to get better results than passive patients.

Over the course of a lifetime, you can do more for your health than the best doctor in the world. And good health is its own reward.

Prevention: The Best "Cure" of All

Think of it in gambling terms. If you were at the racetrack and a trusted friend showed you a simple, straightforward—and legal—way to vastly improve your chance of picking a winner, would you do it? Of course you would.

Now imagine that someone whispered in your ear a different kind of secret. Shhhh! I can tell you how to greatly improve your chance of escaping this terrible disease. (Pause.) It's a real killer—it got more than 700,000 Americans in 1994, more than any other disease.

The difference, obviously, is that you're betting against the grim reaper, not the house. And these aren't secrets whispered in a shadowy corner at the racetrack: They're modest lifestyle changes that have been proven effective in preventing a host of afflictions, from heart disease (which did indeed kill 734,000 Americans in 1994, according to the National Center for Health Statistics) and lung cancer to diabetes and arthritis. Shelves full of books and magazines have been written—publishing empires have been built—to help people incorporate these principles into their everyday lives. But in fact, the truths are quite simple.

Here, in short, is the real secret to beating the medical system: Stay healthy.

THE TOP 10 HEALTHY PRACTICES

Exercise. We're not talking about marathon running and triathlons. Aim to burn 1,600 calories a week through exercise, says Don R. Powell, Ph.D., a clinical psychologist, president of the American Institute for Preventive Medicine in Farmington Hills, Michigan, and author of *Self-Care: Your Family Guide to Symptoms and How to Treat Them*. Research conducted at William Beaumont Hospital in Birmingham, Michigan, found that a group of overweight people who were able to work off that many calories lost weight and kept it off. If you weigh 130 pounds, that means walking an hour a day, five times a week, at a modest 4-miles-per-hour (mph) pace. Or run for 34 minutes at 10 mph five times a week. Play basketball. Jump rope. Take an aerobics class. Pick an activity that you enjoy. The more you like what you're doing, the easier it will be to reach your 1,600-calorie goal.

Can't set aside that much uninterrupted time? Work out for 30 minutes three or four times a week and fill in with 30 minutes of activity during the rest of your day, suggests Dr. Powell: Climb stairs instead of using the elevator, mop the floor, mow the lawn.

For the best results, do 20 minutes of resistance training (also known as weight lifting) three times a week in addition to your aerobic exercise, says Dr. Powell. Aerobic exercise strengthens your heart and helps you maintain a healthy weight; weight lifting strengthens and tones your muscles.

Eat a healthy, well-balanced diet. The federal government's ubiquitous food pyramid is a good place to start. Eat lots of fruits and vegetables and eat little fat and sugar.

Control your weight. Do the first two things on this list and, in most cases, you'll have no problem. If you're overweight, the pounds will slip away naturally (if slowly).

How important is this? In one 22-year study of more than 19,000 men, those who were just 20 percent over their ideal weight had a 2½ times greater risk of dying from heart disease than men who were trim.

Don't smoke. In 1990, 418,000 Americans died from smoking-related diseases, according to the federal Centers for Disease Control and Prevention. Nearly 120,000 died of lung cancer, 134,000 of heart disease, and almost 15,000 of bronchitis or emphysema.

Think it's tough to quit smoking? Ask someone with emphysema, tethered to an oxygen tank, how tough it can be to smoke.

Drink only in moderation. Moderate drinking means—at most—two drinks a day, says Dr. Powell. Cirrhosis of the liver is almost nonexistent among those who don't drink. Excess consumption of alcohol also has a host of trickle-down effects on your health. For example, it's harder to eat well, exercise, and sleep.

Use common sense. Wear seat belts, for example—they reduce the risk of injury or death in an auto accident by 75 percent. Similarly, you can reduce the risk of accidental injury or death to family members by such simple steps as installing smoke alarms and wearing life preservers on small boats.

Sidestep disease. Protect yourself against AIDS and other sexually transmitted diseases. The only surefire defenses, clearly, are abstinence or monogamous sex with an uninfected partner. Barring these, use condoms.

It almost goes without saying that you shouldn't share hypodermic needles. For that matter, avoid illegal drugs altogether.

Ease up. Reduce stress, or at least learn to relax.

What modern Americans call stress is actually your body's "fight-or-flight" response: In response to a perceived "threat" (in our modern world, things so relatively benign as traffic jams and deadlines), your body releases a flood of chemicals, causing your heart to race and muscles to tense. Uncontrolled chronic stress can have numerous ill effects on the body. Among them are headaches, asthma attacks, elevated blood pressure, and a weaker

Improving Your Odds: 10 Diseases That You May Be Able to Avoid

Some people hate numbers. Others love them.

If you belong to the first group, turn the page. If you're among the latter—if you find few arguments so compelling as a good statistic and want to see the impact a few lifestyle changes can have on your health—then check out the table below, which was compiled by James F. Fries, M.D., professor of medicine at Stanford University School of Medicine, and Donald M. Vickery, M.D., co-authors of the book *Take Care of Yourself.* Overall, say Dr. Fries and Dr. Vickery, you can reduce your risk of disease and injuries by about 70 percent if you incorporate healthy behaviors into your day-to-day living.

Disease	Action	Risk Reduction
Heart attack, stroke	Exercise, eat healthy diet, and control weight; don't smoke; treat high blood pressure.	70%
Lung cancer	Don't smoke.	90%
Breast cancer	Eat healthy diet, control weight; examine breasts; have regular doctor's exams, recommended tests.	50%
Colon cancer	Exercise; eat low-fat, high-fiber diet; have recommended tests.	50%
Cervical cancer	Have regular pap smears.	90%
Emphysema	Don't smoke.	90%
Cirrhosis	Eat healthy diet; drink alcohol in moderation.	90%
Arthritis	Exercise, control weight. *Note:* You may not be able to prevent arthritis, but you can often limit its disabling effects.	50%
Osteoporosis	Eat high-calcium diet; do weight-bearing exercise; perhaps take estrogen.	50%
Tooth decay, gum disease	Eat low-sugar diet, brush and floss teeth; have regular checkups; don't smoke.	80%

What Tests to Have When

Preventive screening once amounted to this: Your physician would haul you into the office for a physical once a year, look you over, and pronounce you fit (or not). No longer.

Today, medicine is blessed with numerous high-tech tests that can detect illness in its early stages—and save lives. Modern medicine is also cursed with dozens if not hundreds of high-tech tests that can make your medical bills soar, without providing any real information that will help you stay well.

So what tests should you have—and when?

Think of this list not as a bible but as a blueprint—a list compiled using information from the U.S. Public Health Service and the American Institute for Preventive Medicine that can help you help your doctor make sure that you're healthy. Depending on your genetic history and circumstances, your physician might recommend other or more frequent tests. If, for example, you're a woman and your mother or sister had breast cancer, he might suggest that you begin getting annual mammography exams at age 40 instead of 50. Or if you live in an old home and have young children, your doctor might recommend that you have them screened for lead poisoning.

Also, remember that medical knowledge—and experts' recommendations for testing—change rapidly. For example, older men once uniformly advised to get a prostate-specific antigen test every year, are now being told that screening may not be necessary due to the condition's slow progression and high survival rate.

Caution: Once you've had a test, don't just forget about it, assuming that no news is good news. Though rare, labs and doctors do make mistakes—sometimes deadly ones.

Be sure to call and get the results of any test. Discuss the results directly with your doctor. Ask questions. Make sure that you understand both the purpose of the tests and the results. This will assure that you're better informed and that your doctor reviewed the results personally. You might also want to ask for a copy of any lab report to keep with your medical records.

immune system. Anger and depression likewise compromise the immune system.

The antidotes to stress are numerous and often very personal—music or meditation, a bath, a massage. How you relax isn't important. What's crucial is that each day you find time to relax.

Some of the most powerful antidotes to stress are the most simple. Here's one: Talk to a friend. It's true. Research shows that a supportive network of

Type of Immunization, Test, or Screening	Who Needs It When
Immunizations	Children should be vaccinated against hepatitis B, polio, and other diseases as recommended; some are required in order to attend school. Adults should get a tetanus shot every 10 years, pneumococcal vaccine at age 65, and annual flu shots after age 70.
Physical exam	Every 2–3 years; every 1–2 years after age 50.
Blood pressure	Check every 1–2 years.
Cholesterol	Check every 3–5 years.
Vision	Check every 3–5 years to age 40, every 2–3 years after age 40, and every 2 years after age 70.
Hearing test	Every 3–5 years, increasing frequency after age 70.
Pap smear	Every 1–3 years.
Breast self-exam	Monthly.
Mammography	One mammogram by age 40; every 1–2 years up to age 50; annually thereafter.
Professional breast and pelvic exams	Every 2–3 years to age 40; annually after age 40.
Testicular self-exam	Monthly.
Digital rectal exam	Annually after age 40.
Sigmoidoscopy (colon cancer)	Every 3–5 years after age 50.
Stool blood test	Annually after age 45.
Urinalysis	Periodically after age 65.
Dental	Annual exams, especially after age 50.
Glaucoma	Every 2–3 years after age 50.
Chest x-ray, electrocardiogram, exercise stress test	Not recommended for people without symptoms who are not at high risk.

people may strengthen your immune system and improve your outlook on life.

Make contact. Connect with other people—family, friends, neighbors, colleagues. Research suggests that social isolation increases your risk of illness or early death as much as smoking, high blood pressure, high cholesterol, obesity, and a sedentary lifestyle. Look at it another way: Evidence suggests that being lonely may be as dangerous as smoking.

Buy a Book (Or Two, or Three)

One of your best defenses against unnecessary trips to the doctor or the emergency room is a mini-library of self-help medical references. We consulted a host of medical experts to compile these recommendations.

GENERAL MEDICAL REFERENCE

Columbia University College of Physicians and Surgeons Complete Home Medical Guide (Crown Publishing).

The American Medical Association Family Medical Guide (Random House).

Johns Hopkins Symptoms and Remedies: The Complete Medical Reference, edited by Simeon Margolis, M.D., Ph.D. (Rebus).

SELF-CARE AND HOME REMEDIES

The Doctors Book of Home Remedies, by the editors of *Prevention* Magazine Health Books (Rodale Press).

Take Care of Yourself, by Donald M. Vickery, M.D., and James F. Fries, M.D. (Addison-Wesley).

Self-Care: Your Family Guide to Symptoms and How to Treat Them, by Don R. Powell, Ph.D. (People's Medical Society).

MEDICATIONS

USP DI Volume II, Advice for the Patient: Drug Information in Lay Language, by the United States Pharmacopeial Convention (United States Pharmacopeial Convention).

Complete Guide to Prescription and Nonprescription Drugs, by H. Winter Griffith (The Body Works).

MIND-BODY

Healing Mind, Healthy Women: Take Control of Your Well-Being Using the Mind-Body Connection, by Alice D. Domar and Henry Dreher (Henry Holt and Company).

Keep checking. Get yourself tested—at the recommended times. Catching a serious illness, such as breast cancer, in time can literally mean the difference between life and death.

Self-Help: Before You Call the Doctor

You're out jogging at dusk one evening and inadvertently step on a root. Your right ankle turns sharply outward. It hurts immediately. Fortunately, you're only a few hundred yards from home. You hobble back to the house.

The Wellness Book: The Comprehensive Guide to Maintaining Health and Treating Stress-Related Illness, by Herbert Benson, Eileen Stuart, and the Mind-Body Medical staff (Carol Publishing).

CHILDREN

Caring for Your Baby and Young Child—Birth to Age 5, by the American Academy of Pediatrics (American Academy of Pediatrics).

Caring for Your Adolescent: Ages 12 to 21, written and published by the American Academy of Pediatrics (American Academy of Pediatrics).

HEALTH NEWSLETTERS

Harvard Health Letter, Harvard Medical School Health publications, P.O. Box 420300, Palm Coast, FL 32142-0300.

University of California at Berkeley Wellness Letter, P.O. Box 420235, Palm Coast, FL 32142-0235.

Mayo Clinic Health Letter, P.O. Box 53887, Boulder, CO 80322-3887.

Nutrition Action Health Letter, Center for Science in the Public Interest, 1875 Connecticut Avenue NW, Washington, DC 20009-5728.

ALTERNATIVE MEDICINE

The Encyclopedia of Natural Medicine, by Michael Murray and Joe Pizzorno (Prima Publishing).

Fundamentals of Complementary and Alternative Medicine, edited by Marc S. Micozzi (Churchill Livingston).

Alternative Medicine: What Works, by Adriane Fugh-Berman, M.D. (Odonian Press).

New Choices in Natural Healing, edited by Bill Gottlieb (Rodale Press).

Inside, you take off your shoe and sock. Your ankle has already started to swell. Your first instinct is to rush to the emergency room (ER).

Don't.

HIT THE BOOKS FIRST

Hop or crawl to your bookshelf and pull out a copy of a book like *Take Care of Yourself*, written by James F. Fries, M.D., professor of medicine at Stanford University School of Medicine, and Donald M. Vickery, M.D. Look up "ankle injuries" in the index and turn to the appropriate page. Read the general information—it'll take you only a few minutes. Then go step-by-step through the flow chart.

- The first question from Dr. Fries and Dr. Vickery: "Is the ankle deformed or bending in an abnormal fashion?" If so, they advise you to see a doctor immediately. If not, an arrow directs you to the next box.
- Here the authors advise you to see a doctor today if you feel "tenderness on the tip or rear of either bony bump on the ankle's sides." They give similar advice if the pain has prevented you from putting weight on the ankle for more than eight hours.
- Meanwhile, Dr. Fries and Dr. Vickery advise you to rest the ankle, keep it elevated, and apply ice. (After 24 hours, apply heat.) If you still find it difficult to put weight on the ankle 48 hours after the injury, they say, go to see a doctor.

By then, however, your ankle will more than likely feel better, since most strains and sprains respond well to simple home treatment. And you'll have saved yourself the cost of a visit to the hospital emergency room.

The point is that many visits to doctors and emergency rooms are unnecessary—by some estimates, 25 percent of doctors' visits didn't have to happen, while 55 percent of ER patients do not require urgent care. By educating yourself, you can decrease your family's unnecessary visits, thus eliminating the accompanying cost.

"People go to the doctor's office because they don't know what to do," says Dr. Powell, "They're concerned that there might be something major wrong. They've not been educated to make those decisions. We were brought up to think the doctor is all-knowing."

Of course, more than money is at stake. "Any medical visit that doesn't help you hurts you," says Dr. Fries. "You waste half a day of your time. The magazines are old. You have to get naked in front of a stranger. Even doctors are nervous when we go to see other doctors."

DIALING SAVES DOLLARS

Not sure whether you should see a doctor or go to the ER, even after consulting a self-care manual? Pick up the phone. Call your doctor or, if one exists, your health plan's advice nurse. Research shows, for example, that people who call for advice before visiting the ER tend to choose a lower—and less expensive—level of care (such as an urgent care center, or appointments with their doctors the next day, rather than a hospital ER).

In reality, you can often do far more for your health than simply put ice on a minor ankle sprain. Whether that means regular aerobic exercising to help control diabetes or high blood pressure or reaching for the right medicine when you have a cold, knowledge, patience, and faith—trust in your body's ability to heal itself—are essential.

You'll sometimes miss the comfort of a good physician's hand on your shoulder and the placebo effect of his take-two-aspirin-and-rest advice. But you'll gain more control of your health. And you'll save on your medical bills.

Alternative Medicine: Tread with Care

In a landmark study published in 1993 by the sober-minded *New England Journal of Medicine*, Harvard Medical School professor David M. Eisenberg, M.D., and his colleagues described the startling results of a national survey. In the previous year, one in three respondents had sought help for a medical problem through some sort of "unconventional therapy"—everything from relaxation techniques and chiropractic care to acupuncture and hypnosis.

Extrapolating to the entire U.S. population, the authors estimated that Americans made 425 million visits to providers of unconventional therapy in 1990, more than all visits to primary care physicians. By the authors' estimate, Americans spent $13.7 billion on such treatments in 1990—three-quarters of it from their own pockets.

Their conclusion was that far more Americans use unconventional therapy than had previously been reported. The message to physicians was to take alternative medicine seriously, if for no other reason than the fact that many patients take alternative medicine seriously.

And so might you. Sometimes. Cautiously.

A WILD MIXTURE OF SCIENCE AND CHICANERY

The difficult questions, of course, are the obvious ones: Which alternative treatments should be taken seriously? When? And how should they be used? By whom?

Beneath the vast umbrella of what is loosely described as alternative medicine, you'll find a number of serious researchers eager to stretch the boundaries of what is known about how the body heals and the connection between the mind and body. You can also find many charlatans and quacks.

Which means that if you have recurring headaches, you can do more than swallow handfuls of painkillers. And if your coronary arteries have clogged, you have more choices than the knife (bypass surgery) and the balloon (angioplasty, in which a balloon opens up the narrowed artery). The difficult part is distinguishing between the promising, medically sound alternatives and the legions of bogus "cures."

Indeed, some alternative treatments do appear to help, even with serious illnesses like heart disease and cancer. Here are some.

• In California, Dean Ornish, M.D., president and director of the Preventive Medicine Research Institute in Sausalito and assistant clinical professor

(continued on page 186)

How to Stock a Medicine Cabinet

There ought to be a saying that goes, "Patient, heal thyself." Sometimes you just need help, if not actually to heal then to help you cope with symptoms while your body does its job. And one place to turn is your drugstore.

The problem, of course, is that the typical American drugstore carries hundreds of products, many of them heavily promoted. And some simply don't work.

Below we've compiled a list of over-the-counter (OTC) medicines recommended by Nicholas Popovich, Ph.D., professor of pharmacy practice at Purdue University's School of Pharmacy in West Lafayette, Indiana, that do work. Some, like syrup of ipecac, you'll always want to keep in your medicine cabinet for emergencies—at least if you have children. Others you may want to buy as needed so that you don't have a medicine chest full of outdated (and thus useless or even dangerous) products.

Rather than give you brand names, we've listed active ingredients. Although this might force you to do a little label reading, you'll find the savings pile up when you buy those house or generic brands. For example, with a product like Sudafed, the popular name-brand decongestant, you can cut your cost in half by purchasing its house-brand equivalent, which contains the same active ingredient, pseudoephedrine hydrochloride.

Don't rely solely on this list. In recent years, the Food and Drug Administration has switched a number of drugs from prescription to nonprescription status, a trend that seems likely to continue. In some cases, that might enable you to save money, but it also worries experts like Dr. Popovich because consumers sometimes forget that OTC medicines are still drugs, which can be dangerous if misused. The dual morals: Ask your doctor or pharmacist about new OTC products that might help you. And work with them to make sure the OTC medicine is appropriate for you and does not conflict with any prescription drugs that you're taking.

Remember to read and follow directions carefully. Used improperly, all OTC products can be harmful.

COLDS AND FLU

For colds and the flu, choose one medicine (or, if necessary, several medicines) with a single ingredient that treats your specific symptom, rather than a product that takes a shotgun approach, says Dr. Popovich. Here are several.

Saline nasal spray. These nasal sprays can help keep your nose clean; restore moisture; relieve dry, crusted nasal passages; and prevent sinus infection.

"Long-acting" nasal-spray decongestant. Look for products that work for 8 to 12 hours—the label will tell you how often to take them—and contain ingredients such as oxymetazoline hydrochloride or xylometazoline hydrochloride. But don't use them more often than directed or for more than three days: You risk experiencing a rebound effect, in which your congestion gets worse as you continue using the spray.

Oral decongestant with pseudoephedrine. For nasal stuffiness. But be careful: If you have heart problems, high blood pressure, or thyroid problems, oral decongestants can cause problems.

Cough suppressant containing dextromethorphan. You can buy it in capsule form, as a liquid, or as lozenges. Use for a dry, hacking cough, not one that's bringing up mucus. (In that case—a so-called productive cough—use a product with guaifenesin.) If the cough is keeping you up at night, take a product that contains these two ingredients at bedtime to help you sleep.

Sore-throat lozenge containing benzocaine or dyclonine hydrochloride. See a doctor if you have swollen lymph nodes and fever along with your sore throat. You may have an infection.

OTHER AILMENTS

For allergy symptoms. Look for oral antihistamine products that contain chlorpheniramine. All antihistamines can cause drowsiness, but chlorpheniramine causes less than most.

For an upset stomach. Try antacids that contain magnesium hydroxide along with either aluminum hydroxide or calcium carbonate. If you take them in caplet or gelcap form, they may be easier to swallow.

Newer drugs, called histamine H_2 antagonists, take a different tack but have a similar effect: They prevent the secretion of acid that causes many stomach problems. Look for the ingredient famotidine. But if you need either medicine more than occasionally, consult a doctor—you may have a more serious problem, such as an ulcer.

For constipation. You can often find relief with a high-fiber diet—fruit, vegetables, whole grains, and legumes. If you need extra help, try a bulk-forming powder laxative that contains psyllium.

For diarrhea. The best remedy is rest and fluids. If you simply must work or play, use an OTC product with loperamide or bismuth subsalicylate—as long as you don't have bloody diarrhea, a temperature above 101°F, or take a medicine that interacts with these ingredients. See your doctor if it lasts for more than 48 hours.

(continued)

How to Stock a Medicine Cabinet—
Continued

For cuts and scrapes. Use mild soap to clean the area. Then apply triple antibiotic ointment (polymixin B sulfate, neomycin, and bacitracin)—it works better than iodine or hydrogen peroxide.

For athlete's foot. Look for the ingredients tolnaftate, clotrimazole, or miconazole nitrate.

For hemorrhoids. For relief, sit in a bathtub of warm water for 15 to 30 minutes. Zinc oxide ointments will provide temporary relief while you heal.

For rashes. Use a product that contains hydrocortisone. But apply it sparingly, and not for more than two weeks—otherwise, your skin can become damaged. Don't use hydrocortisone products on children younger than age 2: Their thinner skin and greater skin/body mass ratio means that they'll absorb more into their system, possibly causing serious problems.

CHILDREN

For kids, you'll want a few additional, or at times slightly different, products. Be sure to give them medicines that have been formulated for children. Usually, they're not as concentrated as the adult version. In any case, they're formulated to match a child's metabolism.

For aches, pains, and fever. Use acetaminophen. Don't give aspirin to children under 18. If a child needs acetaminophen for more than three days, contact a doctor.

For stuffy nose. Children's decongestant nasal drops that have "long-acting" or "12-hour" used on the label.

For dry coughs. A children's formula cough suppressant that contains the ingredient dextromethorphan. If the cough is producing phlegm, use guaifenesin.

For allergy symptoms. An antihistamine that contains chlorpheniramine in a children's formulation.

For inducing vomiting. Syrup of ipecac. But call your poison-control center first: Depending upon the poison ingested, causing vomiting may be harmful.

For diaper rash. Ointment with zinc oxide.

of medicine at the University of California, San Francisco, has shown that patients can actually reverse the progression of heart disease—that clogged arteries will begin to open—through a comprehensive lifestyle program that includes an extremely low fat diet, moderate exercise, relaxation, and social support.

• At centers across the country, patients who suffer from chronic headaches are learning to use biofeedback and relaxation techniques to control and at times virtually eliminate headache pain. Biofeedback is a process in which you learn consciously to influence bodily functions such as heart rate and blood pressure by use of special temperature-sensitive equipment. It's also being used to help in the treatment of other medical problems, such as diabetes and urinary incontinence.

• The ancient Chinese practice of acupuncture is being used to treat an array of ailments, including asthma, bronchitis, arthritis, chronic pain, and addiction. Though not yet conclusive, the evidence of acupuncture's effect is compelling, especially in the treatment of chronic pain and addiction.

• In a study conducted at Stanford University School of Medicine in the late 1980s, women with breast cancer who took part in group therapy along with standard medical care lived significantly longer than those who received only traditional medical treatment. In other words, the acts of confiding in and listening to others may be potent weapons against cancer.

SEPARATING THE QUALIFIED FROM THE QUACKS

Alas, the evidence to support most alternative treatments is far less compelling even than for acupuncture, which still deeply troubles some Western medical experts. At times—with treatments like homeopathy, for example—evidence is all but nonexistent. And advocates of other, potentially useful treatments like chiropractic (some evidence suggests that it's effective for back pain) sometimes wildly exaggerate its potential benefits.

So how's the ordinary consumer to tell the difference? And once you've ventured outside the normal bounds of Western medicine, how can you at least be sure that you're not hurting yourself?

Sometimes it's easy to recognize a quack. A few years ago, for example, the TV newsmagazine *20/20* showed a chiropractor flexing a woman's leg— as a way of "diagnosing" a problem in her young son. If you find yourself in such an office, you'll want to politely excuse yourself.

Unfortunately, quackery is usually harder to spot. Here's some advice from John H. Renner, M.D., president of the Consumer Health Information Research Institute, director of the resource center for the National Council against Health Fraud, and author of the book *HealthSmarts*.

Keep your M.D. in the loop. First, look up your medical problem in a self-care guide. If a doctor's visit is recommended, do visit your personal physician first. Alternative treatments like homeopathy are not by themselves harmful, although in the opinion of many experts they're useful only as a placebo. The danger is that you'll delay or avoid medical treatment for a serious condition.

Tell your doctor when you're using an alternative treatment. In the *New England Journal of Medicine* survey, fewer than 30 percent of those who used unconventional therapies mentioned it to their physicians. That, the authors warn, can be harmful. "I don't like my patients to take medicines of any kind unless I know what they're taking," says Dr. Renner.

Put skepticism in gear. Imagine that you're buying a new car and the seller has made extravagant claims—say, that it will go 300 miles on a gallon of gas. Skeptical? Of course you are. Carry the same attitude with you as you "shop" for medical care.

Some people find that difficult. "I can get them to talk about cars very unemotionally," says Dr. Renner, who uses the 300-miles-per-gallon (mpg) analogy in speeches. "But when I start talking about medical things, I can't get them to talk about it unemotionally."

Do some research. If you were going to buy that imaginary wonder car, you'd surely look in *Consumer Reports* or a similar publication for evidence that it indeed got 300 miles to the gallon. Medical journals and popular health magazines are aggressive and highly competitive, so it's extremely unlikely that a potentially useful alternative treatment has entirely escaped notice.

In fact, Dr. Renner says, you're likely to find the opposite—that potentially useful treatments often get more attention than the available evidence warrants. "I see a profound distrust in our society for what's familiar—the government, the American Medical Association, the hospital," he says. "Rather than being hesitant to adopt something new, I think that we're apt to bring on something new before it's ready. We tend to be optimistic about 'the next new thing.' If anything, the press tends to overreport treatments that are not ready yet."

Most consumers have neither the time nor the expertise to make an absolute judgment about a treatment's effectiveness. But that doesn't mean that you have to take a blind leap of faith.

Look for solid evidence, if not absolute proof—studies by credible scientists or organizations that suggest that a treatment is effective for someone with your ailment. To some extent, you must inevitably enter a land of mystery; otherwise, a treatment would not be considered unconventional or alternative. And even with a treatment like acupuncture, which has gained some acceptance, no one can yet explain, in Western terms, how it works.

You can easily find vast amounts of information about health and medicine in print, on the Internet, and on commercial online services. The problem is that you can find bad information as well as good information.

So consider the source of all that you read. A public relations handout might look nice, but don't rely on it. And an obscure, low-circulation publication that you've never heard of might essentially be a cheerleader for alternative health care providers.

A number of newsletters and magazines generally publish reliable information about health and medicine. Conduct your research in magazines like *Prevention*, *Health*, and *American Health*.

How do you distinguish a reliable publication? One sign is a panel of medical advisers, which usually appears up front, near the masthead. Another sign is writers discussing scientific research, not just anecdotal evidence, to evaluate claims.

Having trouble finding information? A reputable health care practitioner—whether an M.D. or someone who's trying to sell you the newest would-be cure for cancer—should be willing and able to point you to reliable sources that discuss the benefits and risks of the treatment that you're considering.

Think critically. You may or may not have fancy letters after your name like M.D., Ph.D., or M.S. But you have a brain. Use it. Ask questions. Was that 300-mpg wonder car tested in the Rocky Mountains—going downhill? In the Mojave Desert—with a solar energy panel on top?

Get a referral. If you're going to seek alternative treatment, at least get a referral from a reliable source. Some M.D.'s, for example, work with and will recommend chiropractors for back problems.

Other sources of referrals include the National Association for Chiropractic Medicine and the American Academy of Medical Acupuncture.

Give 'em the first degree. As with a traditional doctor, interview an alternative health care practitioner before you submit to treatment. What sort of training does he have? What degrees? To be fair, you'll find plenty of quacks with M.D.'s—Dr. Renner considers them the most dangerous kind—but the lack of a degree, or a mail-order Ph.D. from an unaccredited school, should at least cause you to ask more questions.

Danger Signals

Five Signs That a Quack's a Quack

1. He offers a quick and painless cure.
2. He promotes a "special," "secret," "ancient," or "foreign" formula, available only through the mail and only from one supplier.
3. His only proof consists of testimonials or case histories from satisfied users.
4. He promotes a single product as an effective treatment for a wide variety of problems.
5. He claims that his treatment is a scientific breakthrough or miracle cure that has been repressed or overlooked by doctors.

SOURCE: U.S. Department of Health and Human Services

No matter what type of treatment you get, you want a practitioner with the education and training to recognize signs of a serious problem—and the wisdom to know his limitations.

Watch for warning signs.

- A practitioner who boasts of treating a vast array of ailments when your research showed evidence that suggests that his treatment may be effective but only in limited circumstances.
- A practitioner who aggressively tries to recruit family members and friends as patients, or tries to sign you up for an extensive series of regular treatments. Here's one of Dr. Renner's rules of thumb: The more a provider makes, the warier you should be.

Trust your body. With acupuncture, for example, you should notice improvement after 5 to 10 treatments. If you don't, stop.

BOTTOM LINE

Patients who have educated themselves about their own health tend to choose less extreme, and usually less expensive, care. And they generally get better results than patients who surrender all decision making to medical professionals.

WORDS TO THE WISE

Aerobic exercise: Activities like running, cycling, and swimming, which strengthen your heart.

Alternative medicine: A broad term encompassing serious researchers and practitioners who are eager to expand knowledge about the body's ability to heal. Unfortunately, it also includes any number of charlatans and quacks.

Resistance training: Weight lifting, which strengthens your muscles and helps you maintain a healthy weight.

ALLIES

The American Academy of Medical Acupuncture: 5820 Wilshire Boulevard, Suite 500, Los Angeles, CA 90036. Can provide a list of physicians who practice acupuncture in your area.

The National Association of Chiropractic Medicine: 15427 Baybrook Drive, Houston, TX 77062. Member-chiropractors adhere to certain guidelines. In essence, they accept the limits of their craft and treat only musculoskeletal problems.

Part 5

EDUCATION

College Admissions

How to Ace the Test of All Tests

Getting into college has become such a competitive business, it may seem that schools are trying to keep you out.

Since cutbacks in federal funding of higher education during the 1980s, many colleges and universities have stepped up their efforts to recruit the best students they can. That means that more schools are competing for the best and the brightest students.

College-Bound? Lay the Groundwork

At the same time, students are getting more competitive about getting into college. With the loss of millions of jobs over the past decade, many students and their parents have become worried about career prospects. The result is increased pressure to get into the best schools.

"Getting into college has become much more competitive than it used to be, and it will continue to be this way for some time," says Roger Swanson, associate executive director of the American Association of Collegiate Registrars and Admissions Officers in Washington, D.C.

It's a tough system, all right. But the good news is that you can beat it and get into a school that's right for you. Here's how.

TAKE HIGH SCHOOL SERIOUSLY

It used to be that high school students began thinking about college in the eleventh grade. Now that's considered the eleventh hour. Here are some things that you need to take care of before then.

Enroll in the right courses. It would be awful to find out in your senior year that while you were out enjoying yourself in Dog Walking 101, you skipped the courses that most colleges require. "It's amazing how often families wake up too late," says Joyce Smith, associate executive director of the National Association for College Admission Counseling in Alexandria, Virginia.

Take These Courses

Most four-year colleges require applicants to complete at least 32 high school credits in a specific set of courses, according to the College Board, a New York City–based nonprofit association that provides educational services to students, families, high schools, and colleges. So ace these if you can.

LANGUAGE ARTS
8 credits in literature, writing, and/or speech

MATH
6 to 8 credits in algebra, geometry, algebra II, trigonometry, and/or calculus

SCIENCE
6 credits in lab science, including:

2 in biology

2 in chemistry and/or physics

2 in chemistry, physics, earth/space sciences, advanced biology, advanced chemistry, and/or advanced physics

SOCIAL STUDIES
6 credits, including:

2 in U.S. history

1 in U.S. government

1 in economics

1 in world history or geography

1 or more credits in the above or other areas

PHYSICAL EDUCATION
1 credit (2 semesters)

HEALTH/SAFETY
1 credit (1 semester)

ELECTIVES
8 additional credits from the above core or the following electives:

Foreign languages

Arts (art, music, or drama)

Computers (computer applications or programming)

Career area (courses in a technical career area)

You should start talking about college to your guidance counselor in junior high school and keep talking every year after that. Ask: What courses do I need to prepare for college? How do I enroll? Is there anything else I need?

Always be sure to take the most rigorous courses you can. Above all, if you want to give yourself the best shot, take four years of English, all the mathematics and science courses your school offers, and at least one foreign language. Colleges like students who challenge themselves.

Go easy on the extracurricular. From the schedules some high school students keep—band on Monday, soccer on Tuesday, cleaning up the environment on Wednesday—you'd think that they got paid by the hour.

They think a long list of extracurricular activities on their college applications will help them get accepted. In fact, it may hurt their chances. A jam-packed schedule can sap the energy they need for the activities that really count.

Asked what they considered the most important facts about a college application, college admissions officers ranked extracurricular activities ninth out of 11 items, according to one survey. Three out of four said that extracurricular activities are of only limited to moderate importance.

The best strategy is to get deeply involved in one or two activities through which you can show some leadership and commitment.

Get a jump start with early decisions. If you don't want to bite your nails from December until April waiting for a response to your college application, you might apply for an early decision. An increasing number of students are, according to the College Board, a New York City–based non-profit association that provides educational services to students, families, high schools, and colleges.

Under an early-decision program, you can apply to college during your junior year of high school and, assuming that you maintain your grade point average until you graduate, have a college seat held for you before your peers have even filled out their applications.

"Early decisions make a lot of sense for students who really know where they want to go," says Swanson. But stay away from them if you think you might change your mind about where you want to go or if you need to know about financial aid before you can commit to a school.

Here's why. Once colleges give you an early decision, they require you to withdraw all your applications to other colleges. Moreover, you won't be able to find out about financial aid until about April, the same time that all your peers will be getting their acceptance letters. Then it will be too late to change your mind.

SO WHAT DO YOU WANT ANYWAY?

Before you begin looking at colleges or filling out applications, you need to figure out what you want out of the experience—to decide what factors are important to you.

What Ranks inside the Admissions Office

From the outside, how admissions counselors decide whom to admit seems only slightly less mystifying than an Agatha Christie novel. But from the inside, there's little mystery to the process.

Here, in priority order, are the top ten factors college admissions counselors use in evaluating an application, according to a survey published by the National Association for College Admissions Counseling in Alexandria, Virginia. Score well on the top ones and you'll improve your chances.

1. Grades in college preparatory courses
2. Admission-test scores
3. Grades in all subjects
4. Class rank
5. Essay/writing sample
6. Counselor recommendations
7. Teacher recommendations
8. Interview
9. Work/extracurricular experiences
10. Ability to pay

Ask yourself these questions, which Shirley Levin, an independent college counselor and president of College Bound, based in Rockville, Maryland, recommends to students and their families.

- What subject do you want to study or which field would you like to work in? This will help you focus on the schools that offer what you're interested in.
- Where do you want to live for the next four years? Do you want to be within driving distance of home or is farther better? Do you get depressed in cold weather or would you rather be skiing? Do you prefer the bustle of a city or the relative isolation of a rural area?
- Which extracurricular activities do you want to continue? If mountain climbing is truly important to you, you'll want to make sure that the school you choose isn't in Iowa.
- What kind of social environment do you want? Do you want to join a fraternity or sorority? Do you want to be part of a big team school? Or would you rather be a loner? There's something for everybody.
- How important is the name of the school to you? There are plenty of good "no-name" schools, but if you've always dreamt of Harvard or Yale, you're probably not going to drop the dream before you apply.
- How do you deal with competition? Some students thrive on it. Some cave in. Decide what you do before you decide where to go.

- How do you learn best? If you need personal attention to do your best, then you'll want to go to a small school. If you would rather be part of a large class—even as large as 500 students—then choose a large school.
- How much are you willing to spend? College is expensive. But you don't have to spend top dollar if you don't want to. Weigh how important graduating with little debt is to you, as opposed to getting exactly the education you want no matter the cost.

So Here's Your Research Assignment . . .

There is no shortage of information about schools. The real trick is to find the right information quickly. Here are a few tips.

Be wary of popular rankings. Every year, *U.S. News and World Report* publishes a popular ranking of colleges. But many admissions counselors warn students against relying too heavily on these reports.

The rating system may encourage colleges to enhance their data, says Levin. Indeed, in recent years, several schools have been accused of altering the facts they report for surveys.

Your safest bet is to take the time to do your own research and make your own judgments.

Surf the Internet. Check the World Wide Web for sites about the colleges or universities you are interested in. Many have Web sites posted now. If you can't easily locate the site, call the admissions office and ask for their Web addresses. Or look in their publications: Many list it along with their mailing address.

Also, sign onto College Board Online, a program available via the Internet that allows you to search for information about colleges and careers, register electronically for the Scholastic Aptitude Test (SAT), and post your questions and get a personal answer from a resident counselor. For example, you might ask: What are my chances of getting into Yale? Should I apply to a community college? Or, how should I answer the essay question on the application?

Ask about ExPAN. Ask your guidance counselor how you can get access to ExPAN, a College Board computer program that some high schools provide for their students.

Once you sign on, it will instruct you on how to access an electronic library of statistics on more than 3,000 colleges, search for colleges that meet your needs, and request college publications, which are mailed to you free.

Make a trial visit. Most college guides recommend that you visit the campus if you can. But you'll get a lot more out of the trip if, instead of taking the traditional tour, you spend a day as if you're a student attending that school.

That means that instead of visiting the campus during your family's summer vacation, schedule your visit when classes are in session. Also, before you arrive, tell an admissions counselor that you would like to:

Check Out These Books

Dozens of books on the market advise students who are considering college. Here are three that are generally considered among the best.

Barron's Profile of American Colleges. Provides basic facts and statistics about more than 1,650 schools.

The Fiske Guide to Colleges. Provides basic information and descriptions based on an annual survey of students and administrators. Also discusses quality-of-life factors, such as extracurricular activities.

Peterson's Handbook for College Admissions. Provides basic facts and extensive information about how to choose and apply to a school.

- Take a tour of the grounds and facilities
- Eat a meal in the college dining facility
- Take a tour of a dorm and, if possible, spend a night in one
- Sit in on classes and meet with a few professors
- Visit local coffee shops where you can meet and speak with students

Be sure to ask students what they think of the college, its dorms, classes, faculty, and extracurricular activities.

Ask Pointed Questions

Regardless of whether you visit the college you are considering, there are a number of specific questions you should ask an admissions counselor before you make a decision.

Remember that schools in the business of recruiting students are going to put their best foot forward and may not volunteer information about their blemishes. You have to ask to find those out.

Here are some of the most important questions, Smith says.

Who would teach my courses: professors or teaching assistants (TAs)? Teaching assistants are graduate students. Many colleges, and especially universities, rely on them to teach introductory-level courses. But TAs shouldn't teach the majority of your courses—at least not so many that you feel shortchanged.

Who would my peers be? These are the people with whom you will be spending the next four years. So find out if they'll interest you by asking about their academic background, experience, interests, and hometowns.

Which graduate schools do students get admitted to? If you plan to attend graduate school, you'll want to know whether they tend to like undergraduates from the school you are considering.

Which employers visit the campus? Many employers visit college campuses to recruit, or at least meet, graduating students. Ask which companies have visited lately to find out whether the school attracts the kinds of firms you are interested in.

How readily available are computers? Many college campuses have computer laboratories, but sometimes there aren't enough computers to go around. Ask if you will actually be able to depend on the use of one when you need it.

Deciding: The Final Exam

Once you have figured out your needs and gathered all your information about schools, you'll need to make some choices. Here are three tips to help you sort through all that data you've collected.

AVOID THE "BEST" TRAP

Almost everyone wants to get into a school that has a reputation for being the best. But rankings of the best colleges and universities can be a very misleading way to choose a school, according to Levin.

Why?

"Because it's so subjective. One school may be right for one student and totally wrong for another," says Levin. In other words, colleges and universities vary greatly, and so do learning styles. What counts is finding the school that's best for you.

Moreover, say many experts, a lot of students don't need to attend what others consider the best.

"It's true that at the more selective schools, you can hobnob with the rich and famous," says Smith. "But at what cost?"

Many students do just as well at a lesser-known school, without having to pay the same cost or fight the fight it takes to get admitted to a big-name school.

In fact, unless you are geared to a very specific high-level graduate school or professional school, a big-name undergraduate degree is not likely to make or break your career success, according to Swanson.

NARROW YOUR CHOICE BY TYPE

One good way to narrow your choices from among the 3,400 open to you is to understand that colleges and universities come in types, just like sneakers, sports, and TV shows.

Decide which type sounds like the best match for you, and you can skip the rest. Here are four types described by the College Board.

1. Liberal arts colleges. These emphasize undergraduate education. Good for students who want small classes and personal attention. Also good for a broad base of courses, rather than narrow career preparation.

2. Universities. Typically a cluster of schools that includes a liberal arts college, professional colleges, and graduate programs, universities are best for students who want large classes, a great range of academic choices, access to extensive resources, and faculty members who are actively involved in research. Students should be able to live without a lot of personal attention and be willing to have some classes taught by TAs.
3. Professional or technical schools. These emphasize preparation for specific careers. Good for students who are sure of what they want to do.
4. Community or junior colleges. These offer the first two years of a liberal arts education and specialized career preparation. Good for students who are not ready to attend a four-year school.

WEIGH THE FISH FACTOR

So do you want a college only slightly larger than your high school? Or one as big as a small city? It's a critical decision—and one you will have to make for yourself. The question it comes down to, says Levin, is: Do you want to be a big fish in a small pond, or a small fish in a big pond?

If you think that it is important to have an opportunity for personalized attention, time with faculty, and a chance to be heard in class, then choose a small college.

On the other hand, if you want to belong to something big, like the University of Michigan, which enrolls some 25,000 students and has a sports stadium that seats 105,000 people, then choose a large university.

Now, Sharpen Your Pencil

At last, it's time to fill out the application. Is there anything you can do at this stage to improve your odds? You bet.

Emphasize your individuality. Let's say that you graduated at the top of your class, that your recommendations make you sound like the next Albert Einstein, and that your essay is worthy of the Nobel Prize in literature. Your application still could get rejected because a college campus is not just a holding pen for brilliant kids. It's a community with a diverse set of needs.

That's why you should think about what makes you different, or how you can contribute to the community, and emphasize that, says Swanson.

If you're a minority, mention it. Identify yourself as a member of a racial, ethnic, or sexual preference minority group, if you can.

The reason: Ever since the 1960s, colleges and universities have been making an effort to recruit more members of minority groups, says Swanson.

But it's not enough just to say: "I'm African-American," "I'm Latino," or "I'm gay."

Meeting Multicultural Needs

If your child is African-American, latino, a member of some other ethnic minority, or gay, he may want to know whether there are 2 or 200 students like him on campus before he decides to spend the next four years in that environment.

How can you help him find out?

Most college reference books offer little information that is specifically addressed to minority students. But one is focused on just this subject. And it's worth looking up in a library or bookstore. Ask for *The Multicultural Student's Guide to Colleges, Revised Edition: What Every African-American, Asian-American, Hispanic, and Native American Applicant Needs to Know about America's Top Schools*, compiled by Robert Mitchell, an English teacher at Chelsea High School in New York City.

If your child is gay or lesbian, you probably want to help him or her find a college that is safe, comfortable, and supportive of different sexual orientations. Go to the college section of a bookstore or library and look up *The Gay, Lesbian, and Bisexual Students' Guide to Colleges, Universities, and Graduate Schools*, by Jan-Mitchell Sherrill and Craig A. Hardesty.

Ask yourself how being a minority might help you contribute to the college community—say, for example, by bringing a different perspective to classroom discussions—and emphasize that.

Claim connections. Last but not least, if you or your family knows a president, trustee, faculty member, or major alumni donor of the school you're interested in, by all means use your connection by asking that person to put in a good word for you.

It's not likely to get you admitted if you have nothing else going for you. But it might help nudge them in your favor if you're a borderline case, says Swanson.

It's essential, however, to be tactful. If your Auntie Matilda paid for the college's new 400-seat theater, try not to brag about it in your cover letter—they might peg you as an extortionist. Instead, have her write a nice letter, pointing out what a promising drama student you are.

BOTTOM LINE

You can substantially improve your odds of choosing the right college, and having the right college choose you, if you understand how the system works, and you work it. Start discussions with school counselors as early as junior high school. In high school, emphasize the tough course work and go light on extracurricular activities. Tackle selection of a college like a research project—finding the best fit for you.

WORDS TO THE WISE

Early admission: Often confused with early decision, early admission refers to being admitted as a full-time college student before completing high school.

Early decision: This applies to students who apply to college before December of their senior year and are informed of a decision before April. Students accepted through an early decision are required to withdraw their applications to all other schools.

ALLIES

The College Board: 45 Columbus Avenue, New York, NY 10023-6992. A national nonprofit association of educator organizers that provides educational services to students, families, high schools, and colleges.

Peterson's: 202 Carnegie Center, Princeton, NJ 08540. A publisher of reference books and computer software focusing on careers and education.

Trimming Tuition Costs

Don't Pay "Sticker Price" for That College Diploma

The key to your children's future could also be your key to the poorhouse.

Tuition costs increased for the fifteenth consecutive year in 1995–1996 at four-year colleges, both public and private.

Tuition averaged $2,860 for one year at four-year public schools, and $12,432 at private schools. Add in room and board, books and supplies, transportation, and other personal expenses and the annual budget was $9,285 at public schools and $19,762 at private ones.

At some of the more elite colleges and universities, the cost soared even higher, to more than $30,000 a year in 1996–1997—the equivalent of buying a fancy new car every 12 months.

But the good news is that you can spend a lot less than this if you know how to beat the system.

"What you have to understand is that $30,000 tuition is a sticker price, just like it is on a car," says Lisa Lazarow, director of college counseling at Friends Seminary School in New York City.

"Would anyone with consumer savvy be foolish enough to simply pay the sticker price on a new car? Of course not. It's the same thing with college tuition."

Do I Sacrifice Aid If I Save Cash?

Some people believe that they will be eligible for more financial aid if they have no college savings at all. And they may be right. But it's a poor reason not to save, experts say.

The truth is that no one can predict how much college aid will be available in the future, or whether your child will be one of the students that schools will want to pay to join their class.

In either case, if you are turned down for financial aid, you could end up leaving your child with no money at all to attend college.

"It's penny-wise and dollar-foolish," says Kalman Chany, founder and president of Campus Consultants, a fee-only financial-aid consulting firm in New York City, and co-author of *The Princeton Review Student Advantage Guide to Paying for College.* "The amount of aid you would lose by having savings is really minuscule."

Only 5.6 percent of parents' savings are expected to be used for college tuition costs, and that is after setting aside a certain amount of money for living costs, depending upon the age of the elder parent.

Yes, Sock Away Some Cash

You can do many things well at the last minute. But financing a college education is not one of them. Here is what you should do, before your child begins talking about the school of his or her dreams.

START A COLLEGE FUND

It pays to start a college fund as early as you can: Whether your child is still in grammar school—or even in the cradle—it can't be too soon.

The reason is that "it's much better to earn interest than to pay it," says Kalman Chany, founder and president of Campus Consultants, a fee-only financial-aid consulting firm in New York City, and co-author of *The Princeton Review Student Advantage Guide to Paying for College.*

In other words, families without college savings often end up taking out loans and paying far more in interest, in the long run, than families that have interest-earning savings accounts set aside for college costs.

In fact, Chany says, you may be able to pay the family's share of college costs just by tapping interest earned.

Set aside what you can. Many experts warn that you may need $100,000 to pay for your child's tuition 18 years from now. But it's a mistake to think about it that way.

How Much Should I Save?

If college costs continue increasing as they did in the mid-1990s—6 percent, on average—four-year tuition costs in the year 2014 are likely to be more than $100,000 at a public school and more than $200,000 at a private school.

How much do you have to put aside now to save that much by then?

If your child is now one year old, and you want to save $100,000, you need to put aside $256.33 monthly, or $512.65 monthly to save $200,000.

If your child is now 10, you'll need to put aside about $780 a month to save $100,000, or about $1,560 for $200,000 (savings calculations are based on a fixed 7 percent interest rate).

"Looking at the big numbers tends to just paralyze people. Then you think that there's no possible way you can set that aside, so forget it," says Chany.

But just put aside what you can—whether it's $20 or $100—on a regular basis, and it will definitely pay off more than nothing at all will.

Put the college fund in your name. Your child is born. You know about college costs. So what smarter thing to do than immediately start a college fund in his or her name, right?

Wrong.

"If you want to have any hope of getting financial aid, don't put money in your child's name," says Chany. The reason is that colleges assess assets in students' names far more heavily than assets in parents' names.

For example, if your child has $20,000 in savings at the time she applies for financial aid, the college will expect her to spend 25 percent of the savings, or $5,000, during her freshman year. And another 25 percent during each of the following three years until she has spent the entire $20,000.

And spending that money, say, on a nice new car won't help. Colleges will expect your child to contribute the amount held in savings at the time she first applies for financial aid, regardless of whether she later spends it on something else.

On the other hand, money put in the parents' name will be assessed at no more than 5.6 percent. That is, in contrast to the full $20,000, colleges may expect only $1,120 to be used toward college costs.

Keep the money away from Grandma. Some people think that the best way to keep a college from knowing how much money you have and diminishing the amount of financial aid you may receive is by sheltering it in an account in the name of the student's grandparents. Don't believe it!

That's a very risky move, because the government may end up tapping these funds for the grandparents' medical costs. Or, if the grandparents happen to die before the child reaches college age, the funds could get mixed up in a financial tangle that might take years to straighten out.

Always keep control of your own money.

STUDYING FOR DOLLARS

Help your child become an academic superstar. It doesn't have to cost you anything, and it can pay off big-time in tuition savings.

Seek a merit scholarship. Encourage your child to get A's, graduate at the top of the class, and take the Scholastic Aptitude Test (SAT) and American College Test (ACT) a second or third time if it may help boost scores. Pull that off and you've masterminded the most painless way to reduce college costs. Students with the best grades have the best chance of getting financial aid because schools use financial aid as an incentive to attract the students they most want.

Take AP tests. Get your child to take an advanced placement (AP) course and pass the standardized test, and he can win up to a semester's worth of college credits.

Here's how it works. AP courses are those classes designed to prepare high school students for college by allowing them to do college-level work while still in high school. For example, a fourth year of mathematics is often considered an AP course. At the end of these courses, students have the option of taking a standardized AP test to demonstrate what they learned.

Now here's the real payoff. If your child scores four out of five on one of these tests, he can skip the course in college and receive credit for it. If your child does this in four or five subject areas, you can save a semester's worth of tuition, or between $5,000 and $7,000.

Develop a specialty. The truth about college students is that they're not all brilliant. The truth about financial aid is that schools aren't interested in A's alone. They also pay for students who bring other qualities to their school that they're looking for.

"I had a C+ student who played lacrosse. You'd think that he couldn't get any financial aid," says Chany. "But he got 90 percent covered because the school was looking for lacrosse players."

Encourage your child to develop a special talent while in high school, or even earlier, and it can lead to money in college. For example, you might encourage your child to play a musical instrument; act, swim, or skate; or become an expert in engineering, architecture, or medieval France.

Planning Your Plea

Financial-aid rules are complex and growing more complex all the time. So to whom should you go for advice?

The school's financial-aid office, clearly, is a necessary stop. But making it your only stop would be foolish.

"It's like going to a tax-planning seminar sponsored by the IRS," says Chany. "You have to remember that it's not in the best interest of the financial-aid office to show you what you can do to maximize your eligibility for financial aid. They work for the school, not you, and they won't show you the keys to the kingdom."

FOR THE BIG PAYOFF, DIG DEEPER

For the lucrative financial-aid secrets, then, you're going to have to look beyond the obvious.

Do your own research. The best and cheapest way to find out about financial aid is to do the research for yourself in libraries, bookstores, and high school guidance offices, says Joyce Smith, associate executive director of the National Association for College Admission Counseling in Alexandria, Virginia. There is plenty of information available through books, the Internet, and college literature.

Hire a college consultant. If you want to invest in the advice of an expert, make it a college-aid consultant who makes it his business to keep up with financial-aid trends.

Like a visit to a good accountant, it's an investment that could save you thousands of dollars. Campus Consultants in New York City, for example, usually charges $750 (depending upon the information needed) but has saved clients thousands of dollars.

Beware of scams. During the past several years, companies have sprung up that proclaim: You pay us $250, and we'll find you $6,000 of financial aid.

Be skeptical.

There's a good chance that they'll just repeat the information you could find for yourself in the back of most college catalogs.

Other organizations promise to find you financial-aid money, with a money-back guarantee, so long as you fulfill their conditions.

The only problem is that "they'll say, 'Here are 2,000 places you can look,' and if you don't look into all 2,000 places, you don't get your money back," says Lazarow.

CHOOSE THE RIGHT SCHOOL

Deciding where to apply is a lot like comparison shopping for dresses. You can get quality products for less if you know where to go.

Get the facts. The first thing to do is find out what resources a school has available to help with financial aid. Ask a financial-aid officer these key questions, suggest some experts.

- What's the endowment per student? This tells you how much money the college has set aside to help students meet financial aid.

Crack These Books

You'll find dozens of books about financial aid in bookstores, libraries, and high school guidance offices. These two are considered among the best.

College Costs and Financial Aid Handbook. Published annually by the College Board, a New York City–based nonprofit association that provides educational services to students, families, high schools, and colleges, it provides extensive information about college costs, advice on how to meet them, and worksheets for calculating expenses.

Princeton Review Student Advantage Guide to Paying for College. Published annually by the Princeton Review, this book provides extensive detail about how to make short- and long-range preparations for college tuition, how to get the most out of your money, and line-by-line tips on how to fill out financial-aid forms.

- Do you meet full need as established by the financial-aid application forms? If so, for what percentage of students? If they meet it for 75 percent of the students, that probably means the top 75 percent according to the school's admission preferences. So if you are in the bottom 25 percent, you'd be better off looking elsewhere.
- Is financial aid guaranteed?
- What's the average size grant that students get? Schools usually talk about their "financial-aid packages," but these include loans and work-study funds. You want to find out how much free money they give away—and that means grants.
- If you don't guarantee to meet full need, do you admit/deny (admit the student to the school but deny aid), "gap" (cover partial aid), or deny (on the basis of financial need)?
- Is there any merit money?
- For whom is it set aside?
- What is the position you take on divorced and separated parents? Some schools will expect both sides of the family to contribute. Some expect it only of the custodial parent.
- What's the average SAT score of incoming students, and where do we fit into that pool? If your student is at the bottom of the barrel, your chance of getting aid will be very low.
- What is the school's demographic distribution, and is my hometown heavily represented? The rare bird is rewarded more generously than the common one.

Surfing for Dollars

Here are ways to hunt down tuition money with a computer.

Nail the Board. Call up the College Board's home page on the World Wide Web, called College Board Online, for financial-aid information and worksheets as well as for information about scholarships and other aid opportunities. The College Board is a New York City–based nonprofit association that provides educational services to students, families, high schools, and colleges.

Get with the program. Ask a school guidance counselor about how you can get access to a software program called the College Board Fund Finder, which allows students to create a personal search profile to find scholarships and other financial assistance from more than 3,000 sources.

Ask about ExPAN. Ask a school guidance counselor how you can use the College Board's ExPAN, a computer program that provides up-to-date information on individual college costs and financial-aid offerings. It also allows families to determine what they would be expected to contribute to college costs and helps calculate how different types of loans and payment schedules would affect the family budget.

There are no standard answers to these questions, but it pays to compare answers from the schools you are considering and choose the best option.

Be a big fish. To improve your odds of getting the best financial-aid package, don't apply to schools where your child has to struggle even to get in. Apply where the school will be happy to get him.

"Most colleges employ preferential packaging," says Lazarow. "The kids they want the most will get the best offers."

The second advantage of this strategy is that if your child then is lucky enough to get into Harvard, you can use the financial-aid offer from one school as a bargaining chip with the other.

To determine which schools would be happy to have your child, compare student-profile factors, such as average class rank and SAT scores, in the books that list them. Then select the ones where your child would be an above-average student.

Work for the college. Get a job at a college or university, and you may save 100 percent on tuition costs for your child. These benefits often apply to the children of professors as well as the children of technicians, secretarial staff, and cleaning personnel. But beware—there are risks: Your child may not want to go to that school, or he may not be admitted.

If he is not admitted, you're out of luck. But if your child wants to go to a different school, you may still save money. Many colleges and universities offer a discount of 25 percent or more to the children of employees of other colleges and universities.

Applying for Financial Aid

In 1995, $47 billion in financial aid was awarded to college students. How can you get some of it?

"The theory," says Chany, "is that financial aid goes to the people who need it. The reality is that it goes to the people who know how to get it."

HOW TO LOOK GOOD ON PAPER

The key is to keep the family contribution as low as possible. Here's how.

If you rent, keep it up. If you have always rented your home, that's to your advantage. Don't try to buy a home when your child is applying for financial aid.

The reason is that the higher your income bracket, the lower your odds of getting financial aid. If you have always rented your home, schools are likely to group your application among families with a combined income of less than $25,000.

Wait on that second home. If you have a chance to buy a second home, and your child is about to apply for aid, wait. Or you will walk into a financial-aid minefield.

Many families applying for aid don't even own one home. If you have two, a college will expect you to pay for your child's education.

Surrender your car keys. Instead of letting your child buy his own car, let him drive yours. Students who own their own cars may prejudice the financial-aid officer against their applications.

Hold off on wedding bells. If you're divorced or a single parent and you're considering getting married for a second time, congratulations! But consider waiting. Schools will look at the new family member as another source of tuition funding.

Talk to the department. Call the academic department that your child plans to major in and ask if it has any financial aid available.

"Departments do have discretionary money in varying amounts," says Roger Swanson, associate executive director of the American Association of Collegiate Registrars and Admissions Officers in Washington, D.C. And this source is often overlooked.

Your best bet is to appeal to departments that have strong connections to the outside world. Engineering and agriculture departments, for example, are more likely to have available funding than philosophy and literature departments.

File early. File as early as you can—at least a month before the deadline—if you want the best chances of getting financial aid.

The reason is that these funds are limited and are awarded on a first-come, first-serve basis. So make your bid before they run out.

Check with the institution for deadline information. Deadlines vary.

NEGOTIATING THE BEST DEAL

Here's the first rule of bargaining with a school's financial-aid office: Recognize that you're in an adversarial relationship, just like car buyer and car dealer. They want you to spend as much money as you can, and you want to spend as little money as you can. Here's how to play it.

See through the propaganda. For years, schools have been saying that parents are too greedy, that they're not willing to make sacrifices, that they're robbing aid from the people who truly need it. It's important not to fall for that propaganda, says Chany.

Remember that choosing a college is a business transaction. Many schools spend $2,000 to $4,000 per student in marketing costs. And they hire consultants to find out how to improve their profit yield by spending as little as possible in financial aid.

But many parents get swept up in the emotions of the whole thing and forget their consumerism.

Stay rational, warns Chany.

Put on a poker face. If you want the financial-aid office to compete for your student, act as if you have all the choices in the world—and if they don't give you a good package, you'll go elsewhere.

"A lot of parents get worried that if the financial-aid people don't like them—if they're too pushy—their child will be rejected," says Chany.

But, in fact, these schools look for indicators of how badly you want to go there. The more indicators you give them of how much you want to go there, the less money they think they have to give you.

Start a bidding war. When you receive a financial-aid letter from a school, consider it a starting point, not a final offer—especially if you have other schools to choose from.

To try to increase an aid offer, send your best offer from one school to another school and ask: Now what can you give me? Often, they'll increase their package.

"It definitely pays to negotiate at the back end," says Lazarow. "I had a student who got zero aid from Tufts University and $18,000 from Cooper Union for the Advancement of Science and Art. We wrote a cover letter to Tufts and sent it with a copy of the offer from Cooper Union. And he got a better package."

Write an appeal. Another approach is to write to the financial-aid office, explaining any extraordinary conditions that they may not have taken into consideration when they saw your financial-aid forms.

If you feel that expenses are high in your part of the country, write a letter outlining why. If your husband was laid off for six months or is about to be; if you are supporting an elderly mother or father; or if your child is handicapped, write a letter explaining your situation.

"Financial-aid officers have quite a bit of discretion," says Swanson. "It's worth it to make a personal appeal."

Just say no to early decisions. If you need financial-aid money, forgo the early-decision admissions option. Early-decision admissions programs are designed for students who want to find out in December of their senior year—that is, months before everyone else—whether they have been accepted at the school of their choice.

But students who apply for an early decision automatically get smaller financial-aid packages than students who wait. The reason is that early decisions tell the college that you really want to go there, and that tells them that they don't need to give you as much money to entice you.

BOTTOM LINE

The cost of college tuition is like the cost of a new car. You can bring it down if you know how to work the system.

WORDS TO THE WISE

Admit/deny: This is a practice that some schools use to admit an applicant to their school but deny them financial aid. It is used most frequently for foreign students because they are ineligible for federal government funding and the college must, therefore, shoulder the entire financial-aid bill.

Financial-aid package: Financial-aid offices use this phrase to describe a combination of grants or scholarships, loans, and student employment. Grants and scholarships represent aid that does not have to be repaid. Loans, of course, must be repaid.

ALLIES

The College Board: 45 Columbus Avenue, New York, NY 10023-6992. Publishes free publications about financial aid.

Federal Student Aid Program Center: P.O. Box 84, Washington, DC 20044. Write for a free copy of the annual student guide, "Student Aid Programs Sponsored by the U.S. Department of Education."

Part 6

AUTOMOBILES

Keeping Your Car on the Road

How to Steer Clear of Costly Breakdowns and Repair Scams

Your car is a money pit on wheels. As if the purchase price and insurance weren't enough, you then have to routinely bestow upon it fuel, oil, antifreeze, fan belts, tires, transmission fluid, wiper blades, and wiper fluid. Not to mention car washes and Christmas tree–shaped air fresheners. And when the old jalopy breaks down, of course, you find yourself in a whole new financial arena.

To keep these expenditures under control you have to walk a fine line, automotive experts say. Servicing your car prematurely means wasting perfectly good materials and paying for unnecessary labor. But waiting too long to service your car can be expensive, too—in the form of big repair bills.

No one but you is going to call the shots about maintaining your car. So in defense of your wallet, educate yourself about your automobile: what it needs, what you can do for it yourself, and how to find reliable mechanics to do the rest for you. With some common sense and preventive maintenance, you can add years of life to your car and thousands of dollars to your bottom line.

Do-It-Yourself Preventive Maintenance

Most drivers are their own worst enemies when it comes to making their vehicles last. Here's a rundown of things that automotive experts say that

---

Women, Take a Silent Partner

A special note to women: Sure, you can take care of just about anything without a man's help. But if you have a man in tow while a mechanic is looking over your car, you just might save yourself a lot of money and aggravation.

Unscrupulous service people still see women as easy marks. So find a male friend who looks experienced and distinguished—maybe like Mr. Clean in TV commercials. He doesn't have to say a thing—just observe the process.

Having a silent observer can make a big difference in how you're treated. If he says something, he may tip off the mechanic to his lack of knowledge. If he remains silent, the mechanic will have no way of knowing what Mr. Clean knows or if he's in any position of authority.

---

you can do yourself to make your car last longer and to avoid those costly towing and repair bills.

GLANCE UNDER THE HOOD—REGULARLY

Once a week, pop the hood of your car. With the engine off and cold, have a look around the engine bay. While you may not know what everything is, become familiar with the general layout and looks of the machinery. It is important to know the location of the oil dipstick, transmission dipstick, coolant reservoir, brake fluid reservoir, and windshield washer reservoir. If necessary, consult your owner's manual.

This way, if something frays, tears, breaks, or leaks, you will be able to spot it. If *you* don't check around and look for problems, who will?

Check the dipstick. The most important liquid in your vehicle is the oil in your engine and drivetrain. Check your engine oil level every week before you start the car for the first time in the morning. It only takes a moment. You don't even need to wipe off the dipstick. For accuracy, the vehicle should be on a flat surface.

Checking the drivetrain oil is better left to your mechanic—it's difficult to get to, often requiring putting the car up on a lift. Ask your mechanic to look the next time you change motor oil.

How's the rubber? Check the hoses connecting the motor to the rest of the car. Are they cracked or bulging or are there any leaks? Using a flashlight, carefully examine the condition of the fan belt or belts.

Look at the liquids. Find the brake fluid, coolant (also called antifreeze), and windshield washer reservoirs. Many cars have see-through, plastic liquid containers, allowing you to observe the fluid levels without touching anything. If your vehicle is so equipped, you can check their levels at a glance.

Over time, the windshield washer fluid should be the only level that goes down. If any other fluid level drops, there may be a leak, so have your mechanic take a look. Leaking coolant or brake fluid can be a real disaster.

Know your battery's age. Battery replacement isn't a time to go cheap. Always buy and install the biggest and best battery, with the longest warranty, that will fit in the battery tray. The longer the life and bigger the battery, the easier job the alternator has keeping it charged—and the better the starter will work, especially on cold starts.

Replace the battery six months before its warranty expires. During the twilight of its life, a marginal battery will require the charging system to work full-time, possibly burning out the alternator. If you've decided to hold on to an aging battery, be sure to have its capacity and specific gravity (if applicable) checked six months before the warranty expires. In the end, both the alternator and starter will thank you.

Clear the air. The thin material of an air filter is the only thing between dirt in the outside air and your engine. So replace the air filter every 30,000 miles—more often if there's a great deal of sand and dust where you drive. Consider installing a reusable, long-life air filter. These filters can be cleaned and reused indefinitely and do a better job of filtering the air.

Screen out debris. Here's an easy way to keep your radiator clean: Simply install a piece of nylon window screen in the front area of the radiator. This will serve as a trap for bugs and leaves, keeping them from becoming lodged in the delicate fins of the radiator. Use plastic wire ties to hold it in place.

GAS TANK TACTICS

Did you know that premium gasoline can actually *decrease* engine performance? According to the General Motors (GM) Research and Development Center, many premium gasolines are refined from lower-volatility feedstocks. Translation: They're actually heavier grades of gas that the average car can't vaporize as well. The unburned gasoline gets pushed out into the exhaust, wasting it and increasing emissions. This leads to poor combustion, stalling, and hesitation.

Experts on engine performance offer these additional gas tank tips.

Don't go too low. If you vehicle has fuel injection, keep the gas tank at least a quarter-full. This supplies plenty of fuel for the electric pump, which depends on a constant supply of fuel to lubricate its internal parts. Running it low on fuel causes the pump to wear out more quickly.

Store it full. The gas tank must be kept full when you store a vehicle. This limits the amount of condensation—water droplets—forming in your gas tank. It's also a good idea to add a gas preservative if the vehicle is going to be stored for more than a few months.

Jump-Starting: Soften That Spike

When you jump-start a vehicle, disconnecting the cables can cause voltage spikes. These spikes can destroy the computer, cellular phone, stereo, digital dash, or any solid-state module on board.

Prevent this by turning on the rear-window defroster, the heater fan on high, and low-beam headlights. Switching these accessories on will help reduce the voltage spike when the jumper cables are disconnected.

Don't top it off. Over-filling the gas tank causes saturation of the charcoal evaporative emissions canister (a coffee can–shaped device that holds gas fumes from the tank to keep it from polluting the air). This component can cost $100 to replace. So always stop fueling at the first click of the pump nozzle.

HABITS: DRIVING FOR THE LONG HAUL

Want to literally double the life of your car? Wise driving habits will do that. By far, this is the easiest and least expensive way to beat the car maintenance and repair system, mechanical experts say.

Use the parking brake. Parking brake, emergency brake—call it what you will, if you don't use it, you'll lose it. The parking brake cables will rust in place and fail to work when you need them. So apply the parking brake at least once a week to prevent that. On many vehicles, using the parking brake adjusts the rear brakes. Not using it can lead to a low brake pedal.

Flex your ABS. We're not talking about abdominal muscles. Cars with an antilock brake system (ABS) need this safety device exercised once in a while, experts say. So once a month make a sudden emergency stop on an empty parking lot or deserted street. This keeps the ABS from getting sludge in it and cycles the brake fluid through it. Also, be sure to change the brake fluid every two years or 30,000 miles, whichever comes first.

Start your air conditioner on high. Your air conditioner's compressor will last longer with a little help from you. Start it with the fan on as high as you can stand it and at the coldest setting. Then turn it warmer as the interior cools down. This puts less of a burden on the compressor, while using the evaporator more efficiently. This also saves on fuel. At the start, also crack a window to let out the hot air and close it when the interior of the car starts to cool off.

Beware too much idling. Excessive idling accelerates wear on the engine and creates unneeded emissions. It also produces zero miles per gallon. So if you need to sit more than a minute or two, turn the engine off.

PROTECT YOUR INVESTMENT, INSIDE AND OUT

The effort you put into caring for a vehicle's interior and exterior pays a double benefit. You'll avoid costly fix-ups as the car ages—a whole new paint job, for instance. And you'll have that all-important good first impression when it comes time to sell the car. So here are things that the car experts say you should pay attention to before it's too late.

Buy protection. When you purchase a new car, pay for a paint-protection treatment at the same time. Then apply a coating of paint protection designed for new finishes every six months (three months in polluted areas). Your paint job will last longer, and this will help prevent acid-rain damage. If you are a do-it-yourselfer, you can buy the same paint protection from an automotive paint supply store and apply it yourself—with a considerable savings.

Get a clean routine. Wash your vehicle often and apply a high-quality wax to the paint every season to protect it. Use a shop vacuum cleaner to suck out leaves and other debris from the air plenum (grille) in front of the windshield. While you're at it, lubricate the bushings on the wiper motor transmission using silicone spray, and if you have an automatic antenna, lubricate that at the same time.

Give 'em the brush-off. Automatic car washes can be very damaging to your paint. Avoid those that use spinning brushes or cloth, which will leave swirl marks on your paint. Either wash it by hand or frequent a brushless car wash.

Save your sight. If you do use an automatic car wash, remember that they use a liquid wax in their rinse water to help water run off the car and to aid the air-drier blower in removing the water droplets at the end of the wash lane. This wax will get on the windows, leaving a coating behind that causes streaking, hazing, and poor nighttime visibility. To prevent the problem, clean the windshield with wadded-up newspaper and glass cleaner as soon as you exit the car wash.

Drain the rain. Hill dwellers who park their cars on a slope often have the front or rear of their lower door panels rust out. It may be necessary to unplug the forward or rearward drain holes on the bottom of the door panel in order to prevent water accumulation. If necessary, drill new holes.

Don't lose your cool. Don't leave pencils, coins, or other small objects rolling around on the dash where they can fall down into the ductwork. They can clog the heating/air-conditioning system and cause the air-blend doors to jam. The labor to remove these items can be very expensive.

The key to lock maintenance. Frozen car door locks should be thawed using a lock de-icer. While a penetrating oil like WD-40 does work, it will also wash the graphite lubricant out of the mechanism, causing it to jam and fail soon after. If you must use penetrating oil, be sure to re-lubricate the lock mechanism with lithium spray lube or another product made for that purpose.

If it's your car door that's frozen shut, pour windshield washer solvent over the door for an instant thaw.

Save your hide. Leather seats must be treated properly or else the leather will turn brittle and crack. Leather is very porous and must be able to breathe to remain pliable. Use only products designed for leather, such as Lexol leather cleaner and Lexol leather conditioner. Avoid polymer-based vinyl conditioners like Armor-All for this purpose.

Shut out the rodents. Rodents can easily enter a vehicle's heating and ventilation system through the fresh-air duct. Once they enter, they can cause thousands of dollars of damage to the heater and air-conditioner components by jamming them with nesting materials. To prevent this, leave the vent controls set on the "recirculate" position when not is use. This closes the outside-air door.

Cover the stripping. Rubber weather stripping could use the occasional spritz of silicone spray to prevent the rubber from sticking and tearing when you open the door. Do the trunk and hood rubber, too. Annually, treat all the rubber weather stripping on your car with a coating of silicone grease. This will prevent the rubber from cracking from summer heat and splitting from freezing rain.

Free the drains. Sunroof water drains must remain unclogged or else water can back up and cause unseen damage—especially when freezing. Once a year, open the sunroof and blow compressed air backward through the drains to keep them free. Be sure to cover the upper end of the drains before blowing out the debris or else it will come out all over the interior of the car.

Run from the sun. Sunshine dulls interiors and causes the vinyl and leather to crack and fade. So park your vehicle facing a different direction every day. Even better, use a sunshield or a car cover. For best results, park in a garage.

Carpet the territory. Lay outdoor rubber-backed carpet on both the trunk floor and its sides. This will protect the trunk by preventing things from sliding around and denting the sides.

You and Your Mechanic

To keep your car running smoothly and prolong its life, you need to keep it well-lubricated and make sure that each type of filter is operating properly and not getting plugged up. Also, each part will need service after a certain number of miles or years.

How do you keep track of all that? In general, your owner's manual is the best source of service interval information. What if you don't have a manual? And what if you've discovered, as is often the case, that not all the items that need regular care are listed in the owner's manual? (Some are left out by the manufacturer in order to get a better rating on cost comparisons.)

What Car Parts to Replace When

Lost your service manual? Wondering what needs to be done to your car and when? Wondering if your mechanic is selling you a bill of goods?

This table lists when, generally, certain parts of your car should be replaced. But remember, this is a generic table. If the manufacturer of your car calls for more frequent intervals, follow that recommendation.

Also, the type of driving that you do will have a big effect on how often to carry out the services listed. If you drive fewer than 10 miles per trip, follow the more frequent intervals. If you drive mostly long distances (50 miles or more per trip), follow the longer intervals.

Car Part	Replacement Interval
Battery	2–6 years
Belts and hoses	60,000–150,000 miles
Brakes, front	24,000–50,000 miles
Brakes, rear	40,000–100,000 miles
Clutch (manual transmission)	80,000–150,000 miles
CV (constant velocity) joints	100,000–150,000 miles
Fuel injectors and fuel pump	100,000–200,000 miles
Headlight bulbs	50,000–150,000 miles or 3–8 years
Muffler and pipes	60,000–150,000 miles
Radiator	100,000–200,000 miles or 10–12 years
Shocks and struts	25,000–75,000 miles
Suspension, tie-rods, and ball joints	50,000–150,000 miles
Timing belt	60,000–90,000 miles
Timing chain	100,000–150,000 miles
Tires	30,000–60,000 miles
Universal joints	150,000–250,000 miles
Water pump	100,000–175,000 miles
Windshield wiper blades	1–3 years

Here's a collection of general recommendations assembled by master mechanics. These guidelines are best used as a supplement to an owner's manual, so dig it out of the glove box or contact the manufacturer if it sprouted wheels of its own and took off.

VISIT A GARAGE REGULARLY

The inner mechanical workings of your car are a delicate balance of many things that operate in concert. If one goes out of whack, it can adversely affect some other part and wind up costing much more than just correcting the original fault. If only you had caught the first item before it destroyed several other expensive items.

Here's an example. Replacing the timing belt is done as part of a regular maintenance service. Because this item is not replaced until your vehicle reaches 60,000 to 90,000 miles, it is often left out of the service manual. But, if you fail to replace it, the result can cost thousands of dollars for cylinder head work—maybe even an entire engine. Ditto for tire rotation and alignment—ignoring this can cost you a set of tires.

Overlap your repairs. One big way to save money is to find a shop that will do several maintenance items at the same time. This is called doing overlapping repairs. For example, when you're having the hoses changed, get the coolant flushed. When changing the timing belt, replace the water pump. If the shop doesn't want to overlap repairs, go somewhere else.

Tune-ups aren't everything. Of course, you should follow your owner's manual's instructions for regular tune-ups—typically every 30,000 miles. But beware: Some of the newer cars can go 60,000 and even 100,000 miles between tune-ups. This doesn't mean that you can ignore other regular items, like fuel filters and transmission service. If you hold off on these important things until tune-up time, you may have already damaged your vehicle.

Modern engines keep mum. In the old days, you could tell that your car needed a tune-up, because the engine became hard to start. Modern cars don't let you know anymore. Instead, if you miss your service interval, the ignition module might fail as a result of a worn spark plug, wire, cap, or rotor. And some ignition modules cost $400.

Because some cars require valve adjustments and special equipment to properly set the mixture and timing, tune-ups are best done by a mechanic who specializes in your car make or by your dealer. Using a quickie tune-up place may really cost you. Their mechanics are often in too much of a hurry to get on to the next job and can carelessly create more problems.

Replace the rubber. Have a mechanic check the condition of the belts and hoses annually and replace them every five years or 60,000 miles. The timing belt should be replaced, typically at 60,000 to 90,000 miles.

Many modern engines have timing belts that *must* be replaced at 60,000- or 90,000-mile intervals. On many cars, especially the Asian imports, if you fail to change the timing belt and it breaks, there will be extensive engine damage. Consult the dealer for the proper service interval for your engine and find out if it will be damaged if the timing belt breaks.

Be careful where you cut corners. Just because a replacement part looks the same and sells for less doesn't mean that it's a bargain. Sometimes inferior car parts can wreak havoc. Here are some examples.

Spark plug wires. The spark plug wires on an engine that's controlled by computers are very important. Cheap wires can cause misfire, especially at high speeds. Wires not placed in their holders can send stray voltage into nearby sensor wires. Using nonresistor (solid-core) wires can shut down a computer completely.

Belts and hoses. Inferior-quality drive belts, timing belts, and hoses can fail prematurely and, in some cases, damage other parts of the engine. Your best bet is to stick to brand-name parts, such as Goodyear, Dayco, and Gates.

Blower motor. Cheap blower motor replacements may be a disaster. The more expensive blower motors contain voltage spike–suppression diodes that protect the onboard computer and other electronic devices from voltage spikes.

Rotate regularly. Find a local tire dealer willing to make a deal that includes periodic rotation, balancing and alignments. You'll want this done every 7,000 to 10,000 miles to get your money's worth from your tires. Some shops give free alignment checks by driving your car over a metal plate. Also, have your tires examined for nails or cuts and checked for proper air pressure at every oil change.

Retighten those lug nuts. When mechanics take your wheels off, they replace them with the use of an air-driven impact gun, which often over-torques the lug nuts. This can warp the brake rotors and permanently damage them. So retighten your own lug nuts any time the wheels have been off. A torque wrench is inexpensive and easy to use.

LIQUIDS AND LUBRICANTS: CHANGE FOR THE BETTER

Contrary to what many people (especially oil companies) would have you believe, you don't need to change your oil every 3,000 miles.

The change interval depends on several factors, engine experts say: how many cylinders your engine has, how far you drive per trip, how many miles you drive every year, and the operating conditions under which you drive. Some people driving long distances with V-8 engines can go 7,500 miles between oil changes. Others driving stop-and-go in small four-cylinder cars might need to change the oil four times per year, regardless of mileage.

The best way to know if your motor oil is holding up is to have your oil analyzed every year. A $5 lube oil analysis can tell you if your oil-change intervals are okay, and, more important, it can detect potential problems long before they cause major engine damage. (See "Allies" on page 231.)

Save with synthetic. Consider using a synthetic oil, such as Redline, Mobil, or Western Auto, among others, in your engine and transmission. The longer engine life and better gas mileage you'll get more than compensate for the extra expense. While petroleum oil is usually changed every 3,000 miles, synthetic oil will last 7,500 miles or more. If you can't afford to use a synthetic oil, using one quart of synthetic oil along with your regular oil will give you much of the added protection of synthetic oil without the extra cost. Synthetic oils are available through most auto supply stores.

10W-30 will usually do. In most parts of the country, 10W-30 oil is the stuff to use. Don't use 5W-30 oil unless the temperature drops below freezing. Even then, use 10W-30–weight oil the rest of the year. If the temperature rises to over 90°F, avoid using 5W-30 and 10W-40 oils, because they do not provide adequate high-temperature protection.

Quarts are better. Oil in quart containers is better quality than bulk oil dispensed from storage tanks. So if you see your brand on sale, stock up. Then, when you're having your oil changed, take your own and ask for a discount because you are supplying your own materials.

Brand loyalty pays. Mixing brands of oil will cause the protective components of the oil to prematurely break down, leaving the engine vulnerable. If you want to change brands of oil, you must drain your present oil completely and change the oil filter before adding a new brand.

Don't forget the filter. Replace the oil filter at every oil change, or every six months if you're using synthetic oil. If there is room under the hood, consider installing a bypass oil filter. Bypass filters clean the oil extremely well, making the engine last much longer.

Service the transmission, automatically. Front-wheel-drive cars, especially automatics, have very expensive transmissions. Because of the low hood profiles used today, these units run hot and need more service. It's cheaper to have the transmission serviced than to have it fixed—with repair costs ranging up to $3,000. Most front-wheel-drive cars need service every 25,000 miles—shorter intervals are recommended for city driving. Rear-wheel-drive vehicles can go 50,000 miles between services.

Know your filter requirements. Many automatic transmissions have transmission filters, which should be replaced when the transmission is serviced. However, some cars don't require transmission filter replacement but instead have filters that are merely cleaned and reused.

Find out which type your vehicle has by asking the dealer's parts department if they clean and reuse the transmission filters. Don't pay for a filter replacement if the filter is supposed to be reused, and don't let them reuse the old filter if it should be replaced. The best place to go for this service is a transmission specialist or dealership.

Manual transmissions and differentials require much less maintenance and can withstand more abuse. Also, they don't have filters to replace.

Manuals need it, too. Manual transmissions on front-wheel-drive cars also have transaxles—an integral differential located in the front axle. Rear-wheel-drive vehicles have separate differentials, located in the rear axle. Don't forget to have the differential or transaxle (whichever you have) serviced, too. This generally needs to be done every 50,000 miles.

Steering fluid: cheap insurance. Most carmakers don't call for power steering fluid changes, but dirty fluid can cause power steering failure. Change the power steering fluid every 30,000 miles—including the filter, when applicable (as with Volvo and Mercedes-Benz). Power steering repairs are very expensive, but power steering fluid changes are cheap insurance against major problems later on.

Stop brake damage. Having the brake fluid changed may prevent expensive brake repairs or catastrophic brake failure. Flush the fluid and inspect the brakes every 30,000 miles or two years, whichever comes first. Some ABS parts are easily ruined by old brake fluid and cost about $2,000 to replace.

Be a cool customer. Engines are made today with a great deal of aluminum, which requires a proper mixture of coolant and additives to prevent aluminum corrosion and acid buildup. If you skimp on periodic changes, you increase your chances of a blown head gasket or ruined cylinder head. Coolant turns acidic from combustion gases leaking into the cooling system.

So change your coolant every two years or 25,000 miles, whichever comes first. This service should be done by the dealer or someone experienced with your type of car. If it is done improperly, an air bubble can become trapped and cause a blown head gasket.

Shop for a Shop: Goober, Where Are You?

On the *Andy Griffith Show*, all the cars in Mayberry ran great, thanks to Goober. He could just pop a car's hood, listen for a moment, and diagnose properly without the aid of computerized equipment. Using only a screwdriver, he would dive under the hood, make a tiny adjustment, and—poof!—the car was fixed.

No one expects a magician in the real world of auto repair. But are there still places where you can count on top-notch treatment, low prices, and honest service? The answer is yes, provided that you know where and how to look.

Start your search by asking friends, neighbors, co-workers, relatives, teachers, bankers, the policeman, priest, and the postman. If you're in a strange city, go ahead and ask people in parking lots at shopping centers. Remember, though, that this is an age of specialization. Be sure to ask whether the shop that they recommend works on your particular make and model. It moves the process along if you collar people who have the same kind of car you have.

While it's tempting to find a mechanic who is known for rock-bottom prices, that shouldn't be your guiding principle in choosing a garage. For a shop to make repairs at a great discount, "9 times out of 10 the shop is cutting a corner—using a less skilled person to do the job or using poor-quality parts," says Larry Moore, former president of the Automotive Service Councils of California, located in Sacramento. "Or they're saying that it's cheaper, but when you go out the door, your bill is more expensive. It's a fact that everyone in the same geographical area has about the same cost of doing business."

How to Size Up a Repair Shop

Automotive experts recommend that you use these diagnostic routines when you're looking for a mechanic.

Stable is better. "Pick a shop that has been in a neighborhood for quite a while," says Moore. "Look for a small-community setting—a neighborhood. If that shop had not been a good shop, by now would it be gone. It wouldn't be surviving on the people who live around there, who talk to each other." The exception is a shop that sits along a main highway and can survive on passers-by regardless of its reputation.

Look for order. Is the shop you're considering well-lit and properly ventilated? Or is the air foul, and is junk piled to the ceiling? Take a good look at the shop floor: Is it covered with a decade's worth of grease and grime? That muck will probably wind up inside your car, on the carpet.

Conversely, if the shop seems more like an operating room than a garage, look out. The mechanics may not have anything to do but clean floors all day. A busy and efficient shop will be somewhat messy—especially by the end of the day—but not festooned with debris and worn-out parts.

Check the displays. Good repair shops are involved in their communities. Look for signs of involvement: photos, plaques, and trophies. Look for membership in groups like Lions Clubs, Rotary Clubs, the Better Business Bureau, Little League Baseball, and Boy Scouts and Girl Scouts. A shop owner who cares about the community usually takes extra measures.

Professional and trade organization memberships are also a plus. Look for signs that acknowledge their affiliation with groups such as the American Automobile Association (AAA), Automotive Service Excellence (ASE), Automatic Transmission Rebuilders Association, and Automotive Service Association.

Being a member of a trade association is no guarantee of a good shop. "But it ups the odds tremendously," says Moore. "No shop is going to spend money to be part of an organization that has a code of ethics, knowing that they don't abide by that code of ethics. At least you eliminate the rip-off artists from your choices, who are there strictly to take your money."

Look for certification. If the shop does not have a technician who's certified to perform the work you need, leave. ASE, for instance, only certifies mechanics in dozens of areas, from automatic transmissions to recycling refrigerant. The skills necessary to pass any given test are the bare minimum. The ASE credential expires after five years, and recertification is required.

Caution: ASE does no policing of repair shops advertising that they employ certified mechanics. "Ask to see ASE certification that the person working on your car knows how to work on that car," Moore says.

Check the diagnostic equipment. Equipment is an important measure of any service facility. Does the shop have modern diagnostic machines? Do the machines appear to be in good working order? Does the equipment look like it is in use, or is it just shoved into a corner out of the way? Look around the service desk area for the credentials of the mechanic staff. Ideally, there should be certificates that match the name-brand of the diagnostic equipment. For example, if the shop has a CAS Engine Analyzer, there should be at least one mechanic with a training degree from CAS.

Scan the lot. Check out the other cars parked in the lot. Are there any cars like yours, or does your car stand out like a horse among donkeys? Is yours the only imported car in a lot full of domestics, or vice versa? Is your car the only new one, while the rest look ready for the scrap heap? If the lot is fairly deserted, what do you suppose chased all the other customers away?

Size up the staff. Get a feel for the staff's attitude. Do they seem helpful? Ask them a few simple questions: How much is an oil change? What about a tune-up? What length of time does a simple repair take? If the person waiting on you is in a bad mood and barks at you or gives you an uneasy feeling, take your business somewhere else.

KNOW YOUR SHOP'S PROCEDURES

Finally, before choosing a repair shop, get a solid feel for its procedures.

Check the length of the guarantee on the parts as well as labor. Some shops give the standard 90-day guarantee. Others offer guarantees for six months or even a year. If you don't ask, you may get stuck with a "taillight guarantee"—meaning that the job is covered only as long as they can see your taillights.

Ask about parts. Ask about the parts that the shop intends to use on your car. Does it use original equipment parts, rebuilt or remanufactured parts, or name brands? If you aren't sure about the quality of the brand, check with several parts stores and ask about the quality of that particular brand of part. If you are told that brand is second-rate, choose a different repair shop.

How does pay work? Find out how the mechanics are paid. The best shops employ salaried mechanics, so there is no incentive to cut corners. However, most shops pay piece- or flat-rate. The mechanic is only paid for work as it is completed, making it to his advantage—and your disadvantage—to rush through one job and on to the next.

Chain stores and mass merchants pay both commission and flat-rate. This means that the more parts the mechanic replaces, the more commission he gets on the sale of those parts. This situation encourages mechanics to rush through the job, replacing as many parts as possible. Even worse, many shops of this type also have quotas. This means that the mechanic must sell a certain amount of parts and put in a minimum amount of repair

---

Send Them a Dozen Doughnuts

Don't forget to thank everyone who is involved in the auto service shop that you frequent. They all have hard jobs and will most likely respond quite well to a bit of positive feedback.

Believe this: A little appreciation will go a long way toward ensuring that you get great service for your vehicle. A gift at holiday time is a good idea, and a thank-you note has monumental impact.

---

time every day. If the mechanic is running behind the quota, he is under pressure to hurry and "create" more repairs.

Repair Rip-Offs: Know the Signs

About 40 percent of all car repairs made in 1995 were unnecessary, according to a federal study. And about 10 percent of those repairs were never even conducted. The government estimates that fraudulent auto repairs are ripping off the public for more than $20 billion every year.

Automobile service and repair can be big cash makers for scam artists. Anyone can rent a garage, pull on some overalls, hang out a "Mechanic on Duty" sign, and start fixing cars. In most states, licensing of mechanics is not a requirement and will probably never be one.

How do you protect yourself from rip-offs? The following recommendations come from auto repair experts, including a task force created by the National Association of Attorneys General.

PROTECT YOURSELF WITH PRECISE COMMUNICATION

When you're dealing with a mechanic, rule number one is to protect yourself by communicating effectively. With honest mechanics, this will prevent misunderstandings. With less-than-honest mechanics, this will allow them less "wiggle room" to misinterpret instructions in their favor.

Remember, says Moore, that "most repair technicians are in this business primarily because they are not very good with interaction with others. They preferred to work on cars and machinery and may not be the best communicators when talking with their customers, especially when you are talking about high-tech problems."

Work face-to-face. Find a shop where you can talk with the mechanic directly. If you can't, prepare a neatly printed or typed page describing exactly what is wrong with and what you want done to the car. Attach it to the dash.

Get a written estimate. Ask for an estimate written on shop stationery or a work order. Scribbled numbers on a notepad are useless in court. Many states require a written estimate, but you must request it. Make sure that they tell you how much the total job will cost—including incidentals like solvents, shop rags, environmental fees, and surcharges. Be sure to keep these records in a safe place for future reference. Don't leave them in the glove box or where they can be misplaced.

Pay for diagnostics. Guesswork is free. It also has a much lower likelihood of being correct. Proper diagnostic work will determine with a high level of certainty that such-and-such a repair will cure your problem. So be willing to pay for diagnostic time. Look out for Mr. Know-It-All who is ready to replace expensive parts without even looking under the hood or going for a test-drive with you.

Get a backup estimate. If the repair is going to cost more than about $100, shop around for other estimates. Be sure to tell the shop that you intend to do this. This will put them on notice that you are a shrewd consumer.

Speak to any subcontractor. If the job involves interior work, paint, or body and frame work, ask whether the shop plans to subcontract the work. Go to the shop and talk with the subcontractor. Say that you will not settle for anything less than top-quality work.

Get an escape hatch. If the shop tells you that there is no way to provide a realistic estimate for your repair job, get costs for teardown and reassembly alone. This will provide you with a ballpark estimate and a built-in escape hatch if you decide that you don't want to go through with the repair.

Save the old parts. When signing the repair order, write neatly across the bottom, "Save replaced parts for customer inspection." This alerts the mechanic that he had better be careful. For all he knows, you might be from the consumer protection division of the State Attorney's Office or the Better Business Bureau.

Leave no blanks. Make sure that the repair order is completely filled out. You will need the date, mileage, a complete description of the work performed, and who did the work. Also make notes on whom you talked with and the date and time you had the conversations.

HOW TO SPOT A RIP-OFF IN THE WORKS

If you know the signs of a scam in the making, you can withdraw quickly or at least employ some damage control to minimize your losses. If you suspect that something is amiss after work has begun on your automobile, it is vital that you carefully document everything that happens. Make meticulous notes as you go along. Write down the names, dates, and people you deal with. This will help if you wind up in court.

Repair experts offer this field guide to common rip-offs.

Parts? What parts? You ask for the return of replaced parts—a law in most states—but the repair shop fails to return them or returns only some of the items.

The $1 Honesty Test

Here's a simple way to test the honesty of a garage's employees. Leave four quarters in strategic locations inside your car when you leave it for repair. When you pick it up, check to see if the quarters are still there.

If someone took them, be sure to make the management aware of it. Someone who will stoop low enough to steal a quarter will steal even more. By risking a little pocket change, you could save yourself a bundle in the future.

Self-defense: Write on the work order that parts should be saved.

"Value" added. When you ask for a certain type of repair to your vehicle, the service rep automatically adds another type of service or labor operation. Or, after the customer leaves, additional repairs are added to the work order.

Self-defense: Write on the work order, "Only perform worked authorized by vehicle's owner."

Zapped. A relatively minor electrical repair is being performed, and suddenly the shop calls saying that the car has major electrical problems. The shop will try to scare the vehicle owner into having several items replaced because the charging system is "too weak to keep the new battery charged." The vehicle didn't exhibit these problems when it was brought into the shop, but now it is discovered that several expensive items need to be installed.

Self-defense: Only authorize replacement of the item that you agreed on and ask for proof that the other electrical items are faulty. If necessary, get a second opinion.

Clean those injectors, sir? Many cars don't benefit from the cleaning of fuel injectors, and new injector designs don't get dirty. Some unscrupulous dealerships are cleaning injectors even though the carmaker says not to. These service departments are making extra money on a service that is neither called for nor needed. What's worse, the cleaning solvents can shorten the life of many types of injectors.

Self-defense: Consult your owner's manual, contact your dealer, or call the manufacturer's customer service hot line and ask if your engine's injectors should be cleaned—or if they will be damaged by cleaning solvent.

Milking the cow. A vehicle won't start and is towed to a garage for starter problems. The garage lists several items needed to repair the vehicle in addition to the starter.

Self-defense: Have the vehicle inspected by a different shop.

While we have it apart... Replacing a clutch or transmission is often used as an opportunity to sell a new engine, even though the engine is in perfect working order. The shop calls the owner and says that the engine will need a replacement in the immediate future. The shop encourages the owner to replace the engine now, since the vehicle is already apart.

Self-defense: Authorize only those repairs necessary to cure the problem.

Beyond warranty. A repair is covered under warranty, and therefore, the owner doesn't expect any cost. But the shop insists that other repairs are necessary to carry out the warranty work.

Self-defense: Write on the repair order, "Only warranty repairs are authorized."

Line up the loot. Alignments are one of the biggest scams. The vehicle owner may be told that an alignment was performed, but the steering still pulls or the tires wear out quickly.

Self-defense: Ask for a printout of the vehicle's alignment specifications before and after the alignment is performed. If there is still something wrong with the alignment, you will have printed evidence of it, especially if the alignment wasn't carried out properly and some alignment angle wasn't adjusted.

Missing pieces. You drop off the vehicle without any body damage or missing parts. When you pick it up, there is a missing hubcap or a new dent in the door. The shop claims that the problem was there before you left the vehicle.

Self-defense: Bring the vehicle in during working hours. In the presence of the service adviser, walk around the vehicle and point out to the service adviser that there are no physical problems and that all the wheel covers are present.

Automatic dollars. Be careful when getting your automatic transmission serviced. Many times, the shop scares the owner by showing the drain pan, claiming that the material in the pan is reason to rebuild the transmission. Remember, it is normal to find some solid material such as clutch pieces and metal shavings in the drain pan.

Self-defense: Have the transmission inspected by a different shop.

BOTTOM LINE

A mechanic who looks out for your best interest is golden. He should be totally familiar with you and your driving habits as well as the quirks of your car. Such a person will help you make the right service decisions and provide the best preventive maintenance. He will know what is an immediate problem, what can wait a little while longer, and how to stretch your dollars. He will make judgment calls in your favor much more often than some stranger in a strange shop.

Words to the Wise

Silicone spray: A lubricant that can prolong the life of rubber weather stripping on your car.

Synthetic oil: A more expensive engine oil, its cost is more than off-set by longer life of the oil and less wear on your car.

Allies

Car Care Council: Department UH, One Grand Lake Drive, Port Clinton, OH 43452. Send a self-addressed, stamped envelope and ask for information on their free publications.

National Association of Attorneys General: 444 North Capitol Street, Washington, DC 20001. Ask for their "Auto Repair Task Force Report." There is a charge of $35 for the report.

National Automobile Dealers Association Automotive Consumer Action Program (NADA Autocap): 8400 West Park Drive, McLean, VA 22102. This arbitration board deals with problems with certain brands of new cars.

Oil analysis test kits: Nutz & Boltz, P.O. Box 123, Butler, MD 21023. For $5 (at-cost), you get a mail-in kit for testing your engine oil. The lab responds with a technical report, plus suggestions for what to do if problems are spotted.

Wheeling and Dealing

When Buying a Car, You're in the Driver's Seat

When you walk onto a car dealer's lot, you expose yourself to some of the worst treatment known to consumers. You face high-pressure sales practices executed by slick, experienced salesmen who use chain saw sharpeners on their teeth.

"The second-largest consumer transaction an individual enters into is more than likely his automobile," says J. Joseph Curran, Maryland Attorney General. "In our office, 25 percent of all calls that come in are auto-related."

Indeed, a mistake made when buying a car can be devastating. To beat the car sales system, you'll need to know a little more about car salespeople and how they operate. Then you'll be able to turn the tables and make their tactics actually work to your favor.

New Cars: Don't Be a Floor Mat

Most people are impulse buyers—even when it comes to cars. But this is one of the largest expenditures that you'll ever make. Should you really do it on a lark?

Car dealers depend on rampant whim purchasing in the general population and are masters at using this propensity against you. If you are prone to impulse buying, take a friend along on any car-shopping expedition, with instructions to not let you be pressured into buying. If necessary, your friend must drag you out the door and splash cold water in your face.

232

Is there anything else that you can do fend off car-lot piranhas? Plenty. Take a tip from car industry insiders: Car salesmen have quotas and time constraints. At regular intervals the total sales made by each sales person are tabulated, and bonuses are paid accordingly. During the last few hours at the end of each time period, the sales staff is trying to rack up as many sales as possible. If they don't meet the quotas, they might not even have a job.

Take advantage of this fact to get a better deal. The end of the sales week is typically Saturday. The last day of the month is the end of the sales month, and the last day of the year is the end of the sales year. Try to buy on one of these days, preferably on the first Saturday in December.

Also, arrive late in the day. It takes a couple of hours for the salesman to complete his routine—that is, to complete the paperwork and to soak the most money out of you. To avoid his planned pressure tactics, go into the dealership one hour before closing and make your purchase. This will make it very difficult for the salesman to "rake you over the coals," trying to wring more money out of you—and you are more likely to wind up getting the price you are offering.

MAKE UP YOUR MIND BEFORE YOU GO

Before you walk onto a car dealer's lot, do some homework. Have a firm idea of what you want to buy, for instance. Here are some basic considerations: When picking a new car, stay away from innovations. (Do you want to be the guinea pig to test out a new design?) And be careful about purchasing last year's model—especially if a new model is about to be released. This will affect the resale value of the car. (However, if you don't plan on selling it for more than five years, buying last year's model can work to your advantage. Insist on a big price reduction on it.)

Take in a show. Consider going to a local car show to compare cars. You will be able to sit in one, then walk over to another and compare them directly. You will not be pressured into buying, and you can see the different choices without having to travel to various dealers' lots.

Always put it to the test. One of the biggest mistakes that car buyers make is skipping the test-drive, says Shelly Warsaw, owner of a Chrysler Plymouth and Suzuki dealership in Catonsville, Maryland. "You wouldn't buy a suit without trying it on first," he says. "Why buy a car without driving it first?"

If the dealership you're visiting doesn't have exactly the car you're interested in buying—particularly the same engine-transmission combination—find a dealer who does have a demo car. Otherwise, you could be ordering an engine that is too small to properly power the vehicle or one with too much power for your taste. And you may hate the way the seats or the suspension feel.

"Any dealer worth his salt will have a predesigned demo driving route to test out the car," Warsaw says. "The test route should have a slow drive through a neighborhood and a drive on the superhighway to get up to 65 miles per hour."

GETTING SERIOUS: STEPS TO BUYING A CAR

When you decide to buy a new car, first make a list.

- What will the vehicle be used for most? Work? Shopping? Transporting children? Pleasure? As a second car?
- How many passengers will it need to hold comfortably?
- What are your priorities in a vehicle? Performance? Economy? Comfort? Safety? Luxury?
- Will there be any major changes in your life soon? Marriage? Children? New job? Retirement?
- How much can you spend on fuel a month?

The second step is comparison-shopping. Go to the library and look over car price guides to find out what is available within your budget. These price guides will also give you suggested retail and dealer cost so that you can be informed about what you want to buy.

When you have your choices narrowed down a bit, find out:

- What it will cost to insure each car
- What kind of repair history it has
- How it fared in the crash tests

Next, check out what the car buff magazines have to say about the cars that have caught your fancy. Car reviews will give you an idea of the strengths and weaknesses of each model. Some periodicals offer car evaluations in terms of repair history, insurance costs, warranties, and safety features. Among the helpful publications to study are *AAA AutoGraph*, *AutoWeek*, *Consumer Reports*, *Consumers Digest*, *Intellichoice Complete Car (and Truck) Cost Guide*, and *The Car Book* by Jack Gillis. While you're perusing these publications, keep your eye out for the toll-free numbers that many offer where you can order detailed reports on specific models for $10 to $15 per report. Similar reports also are available on the World Wide Web—at Microsoft's CarPoint service, for instance, where downloadable reports cost about $5.

SORTING THROUGH YOUR OPTIONS

Before you step foot onto a dealer's lot, know what options you want on your car. Keep in mind what options will have a positive effect on the resale value. *Consumers Digest* says that these are the most desirable options in terms of value in dollars after five years of ownership: automatic transmission, air-conditioning, aluminum/chrome wheels, moonroof, leather upholstery, premium stereo, sunroof (power), CD player, power windows, and power steering.

When comparing car makes, be sure to compare which options are considered standard on the model that you choose and which cost extra. And when you buy, make sure that the options you choose are spelled out in the contract. Just because you see that item on the car at the dealership doesn't mean that you will get it with the car. Be aware that some manufacturers may require you to purchase a costlier model to be able to have items such as an antilock braking system (ABS) or electric mirrors. (A few options such as remote lock systems and costly stereos may still be purchased separately as options.)

Here's what automotive experts have to say about some of the common features on the market.

Adjustable (tilt) steering. Offers better and easier access to the driver's seat but raises expenses of steering column repairs.

Air-conditioning. A must for hot weather, improves window defogging and helps resale value. But it can reduce fuel economy by up to 10 percent.

Antilock brakes. More expensive and difficult to maintain, but they are a lifesaving feature, especially where roads tend to be slippery.

Automatic/manual transmission. Automatic is nice for a lot of city driving and will give a higher resale value. Overdrive helps increase fuel economy. Manual transmissions have better pickup and fuel economy and are less expensive to maintain but more difficult to operate. Manuals are better in snow and ice.

Cellular phone. A must-have item for some commuters as well as women who want the added security. The best ones are concealable to prevent becoming a target for thieves.

Central and remote locking system. Increases safety and is a very desirable option but adds mechanical complexity. It will increase resale value.

Cruise control. Reduces driver's fatigue and increases resale value but can cause loss of control on slippery roads.

Electric mirrors. Convenient and easy to adjust if more than one driver uses the car. Some cars offer heated mirrors for cold climates and autodimming interior mirrors. However, the added costs are not recovered at resale.

Engine size. Get a larger engine if you drive a lot of long distances. Small engines are better for short-trip/around-town driving. Turbos and superchargers are better for high-altitude operation.

FWD versus RWD. Front-wheel drive (FWD) is safer (especially on snow, ice, and mud) but can be more expensive to service. Rear-wheel drive (RWD) is better for towing.

Mayday systems. These add value and security to the car and are highly desirable. They allow the driver to call for help in the event of an accident, holdup, or breakdown. Some systems will automatically call for help if the air bags are deployed.

Passive restraints. These proven lifesaving devices are highly recommended. The more air bags you can afford, the better. Keep an eye out for a new generation of air bags designed to reduce the danger to children sitting

How Car Dealers Turn Up the Pressure

The tricks that car salesmen use cost you money. Know them in advance and you won't fall prey. Here are some of the more common ones in use today, industry insiders say.

Lowballing. One of the oldest tricks in the trade. When you walk on the lot and ask about a car, you are offered an unbelievably low price—much lower than the posted sticker price. You will be told that if you buy today or if you can qualify, you can get that price. This is a way to get you into the salesperson's office, where you're pressured to pay the lowball price, which is pure fiction. The salesperson will invent a reason why you don't qualify.

Stripped-down cars. In order to remain price-competitive, car companies are resorting to "decontenting" their vehicles. In other words, they are "stripped down." Here, the normal features that have been standard are now considered as options: such things as seat adjustments, wiper-speed functions, dash gauges, cruise control, floor mats, passenger side mirrors, and air-conditioning are no longer standard.

Bait and switch. The bait and switch is another old tactic used to push cars. The ad in the paper announces a very low price for the car that you want. When you arrive, you are told that someone else already put a down payment on it and that you must buy a different car. You are "bumped up" to a higher price.

Bumping up. Whatever price you negotiate, you are going to be subjected to at least three efforts to get you to pay more. This is standard operating procedure. You will be told that the sales manager has to approve the deal. The salesman will leave to get the approval and come back each time saying that the manager would not approve the deal. In reality, the sales manager is not even approached until efforts have been made to bump you up three times. This tactic also works psychologically against you—making you believe that you got the best deal possible.

License trick. The salesman asks to make a copy of your driver's license. Don't do it. Not only will a copy be made but also your credit report will be

in the front passenger seat. If possible, get door-mounted bags, too. Avoid door-mounted seat belts: They discourage use, are unwieldy, and provide no protection if the door flies open.

Power steering. A must for city driving, it is needed on large cars—not on lighter, subcompact cars. You should test-drive a car with and without to determine your need.

Power windows. Add weight and complexity and can injure children. If you drive mostly alone, they are a must.

accessed and they will study your credit history. Every time your credit report is accessed, the name of the business accessing the report is added to the report. This gives the dealer a list of the other dealers that you have already visited, telling them how much you have shopped around. Also, knowing your credit history will help salesmen decide how to negotiate with you.

Old car tricks. While you are out taking a test-drive, your present car may be searched for clues to tell them more about you. Don't leave anything in plain sight that will act as a tip-off about who you are or where you have been shopping before you arrived there. Park across the street and walk over, or ride in a friend's car.

"It's yours." You are offered the car for a weekend—without consummating the deal. When you return to close the deal, you are told that your credit was not good enough. Now the price is higher because of the added interest finance charges. Be ready and willing to walk away from it if this trick is pulled on you. Take advantage of the opportunity to have a long test-drive at their expense, but don't become attached to that car.

Turnover trick. If the salesman is having a difficult time getting you to make a deal or can't talk you into paying their price for the car, you may be turned over to a different salesman. The second salesman may try to sweet-talk you into buying, saying that he has the "authority" to cut you an even better deal. Between the two of them, you will become worn down and cave in to the high-pressure sales tactics. Get up and leave.

Phantom discounts. These sleights of hand rely on your confusion about how discounts work. Car companies will "package together" several popular options and offer them as a package for less than they would cost if purchased separately. This is done as an incentive to get you to purchase those extra options. But the dealer may hide the details of the discount, and you wind up paying full-price for the options. Remember that the dealer is not required to pass on the discount to you.

Rear-window defroster. Recommended everywhere except arid climates. It is essential for safe driving in cold climates. Rear-window wiper/washer is recommended for most hatchbacks, wagons, and sport utility vehicles.

Stereo/CD player. A nice option, because it makes the vehicle more user-friendly. The best systems have a CD changer installed in the trunk and removable faceplates that make them less appealing to thieves.

Sunroof/moonroof. Both add resale value. They can increase headroom. Sunroofs can help ventilate without using the air conditioner. However, when closed, they can reduce headroom. Moonroofs brighten the interior of the car.

Theft-deterrent system. Recommended in high-crime areas, especially on desirable cars. The drawback is that they can have embarrassing false alarms. Be sure to affix window warning stickers to fend off thieves.

Towing packages. Will not help resale value. If you do any sort of towing or tote a large cargo with you while driving in the mountains, this option will save the drivetrain. Trailer hitches should have a removable receiver to prevent injury to anyone walking by.

Trip computer. An expensive gimmick that can distract the driver's attention. A poor value.

STRIKING YOUR BEST DEAL

If possible, make your deal with the owner of the car dealership, industry insiders say. He doesn't have to pay any commissions and can give you the very lowest price. Getting to the owner may be impossible, however, so you may have to settle for a salesperson.

Call up and ask for the name of the top-selling person on the sales staff and try to deal with him. This person is not struggling to meet quotas and doesn't need to fight with you over the price as much as a hungry, low-volume salesperson. He can afford to let you walk away with the best deal.

To save valuable time, always work with the same salesperson each time you visit the dealership. Shop during peak times so that the salesperson can't concentrate his efforts on you. Don't let him rush you. Never talk price during your first visit to the dealership. Tell him that you are still shopping around and will let him know when you are ready to work out a deal.

Tell the truth about the prices you have been quoted. The salesman knows what the true price is, so don't hurt your credibility with a fib. You want him to believe you when the time comes to make your offer. He will know that you mean business and that you will do what you say.

When you are finally ready to buy, call the salesman that you have been dealing with and tell him that you are ready to buy that car today. Have your financing in order and know what you can afford in monthly payments. Make arrangements with your bank or credit union for financing ahead of time. Once in his office, take out your checkbook to show that you mean business.

The price that you offer should be $300 to $500 over factory invoice for the car. (Unless it is a luxury car, which should have a $500 to $1,000 markup.) Tell the salesperson that you've been hitting the books and have done your research. You will offer no more than X amount for the car.

Be firm and don't waver in your offer. If you get a great deal of resistance, simply get up and say that you will take your business elsewhere. Then leave—but make sure that the salesperson has your phone number in case he changes his mind and decides to sell at your price.

At Pickup Time, Inspect the Merchandise

When you finally strike a deal, here are points to remember about taking possession of the car, consumer advocates say.

- Never accept delivery of your new car at night. You won't be able to see imperfections in the paint. In the bright daylight, look for dents, scratches, acid blotches in the paint, cracked taillights or headlight lenses, and imperfections in the glass. Sight down the length of the car, looking for irregularities in the paint finish or discoloration of a door, fender, or hood.
- Check for paint overspraying on chrome or rubber trim on the sides and top of the car and on the undercarriage beneath it. Remember that factory-applied paint leaves no overspray.
- Check for badly fitting doors, windows, or hood. Open and shut everything. Close a dollar bill in the door along its perimeter to check for proper weather-strip sealing. Ask to borrow a hose and douse the car to check for water-tightness.
- Check the tires for bulges or slits—signs of transit damage. Run the car for a few minutes over a dry spot on the pavement and look for leaks underneath. Only the air conditioner should leak condensation.

If you find a fault in the car and the dealer tells you that all those models have the same defect, check out another one on the dealer lot and see for yourself. If there is a problem, get an agreement in writing that it will be fixed.

Never accept delivery without test-driving it first and checking the operation of all the functions.

Watch for those add-on charges. Some dealers have a sneaky way of tacking charges onto the agreed-upon sales price for a car after the deal has been struck. Among these charges are advertising and processing, dealer prep, pre-delivery inspection, documentation fees, destination charges, title processing fees, and fuel charges. These all add to the dealer's profit margin. Remember that these are all part of the dealership overhead operating costs and are reimbursed by the manufacturer via a separate bonus account.

On the other hand, destination charges are legitimate and are found on all cars and trucks sold today. Additional destination charges (not from the factory) are bogus and should be refused.

"If there are any fees that were unexplained or are questionable, feel free to ask about them. If you are not comfortable with the answer, either don't agree to pay it or take your business elsewhere," says Steven Sakamoto-Wengel, a Maryland assistant attorney general.

Track those rebates. Dealers do not want you to know this, but the car companies routinely pay the dealer 2 to 3 percent of the manufacturer's suggested retail price when the vehicle is sold. If a dealer is advertising that "all vehicles must be sold at cost," the dealer still gets paid the holdback, as it's called, and still makes a profit. Similarly, manufacturers will pay the dealer additional rebates and sales incentives to help move a certain model of car. It is up to the dealer whether he passes this discount on to you. To keep track of manufacturer rebates, check with industry publications such as *Automotive News* or *AutoWeek*.

Warranties and Financing

All cars come with at least a one-year, bumper-to-bumper warranty. During that period, everything is covered. After that time, only the drivetrain is covered, typically for another 3 years. After 3 years, nothing is covered except the powertrain computer and catalytic converter, since the Environmental Protection Agency mandates that these items must be covered for 10 years.

Extended warranties and service contracts are basically the same thing. The only difference is who offers them. Car companies offer extended warranties, and private underwriters offer service contracts. Because of the spotty history of service contract underwriters (going out of business and leaving the holders of these contracts with no coverage), the best policies to buy are underwritten by the carmakers.

How Much Repair Insurance Do You Need?

Should you purchase an extended warranty? It depends on three factors.

1. How much you drive
2. How long you plan to keep the car
3. How many electronic accessories it has

Look at your driving record. Extended warranties are based on both mileage and time. Obviously, if you are going to get rid of the car before the extended warranty expires, save your money and don't purchase one. Also, if you drive a lot—more than 15,000 miles per year—an extended warranty may not be a good value. You will use up the mileage too fast to make it worthwhile. In addition, long-distance driving eats up lots of mileage but is very easy on the car.

Short-trip driving, on the other hand, is very hard on the vehicle and is a good reason to buy an extended warranty. If the car has ABS, traction control, power windows and seats, a digital dashboard, or an electronic leveling suspension, it is a good candidate for extended coverage.

Check for overlap. "Many times the extended warranty overlaps some or many of the same provisions that the manufacturer's warranty covers," Curran warns. "What additional protection are you getting—if any? How much overlap is there?"

For example, if you are buying a five-year extended warranty, and the car already has a three-year manufacturer's warranty (called the express warranty), you are, in reality, getting only two years' worth of coverage. If you pay $800 for that coverage, in reality you are spending $400 per year on coverage for two years.

Buy it later, earn interest. It is best to wait until the factory bumper-to-bumper warranty is about to expire before buying an extended warranty. Why pay for double coverage? What happens if your car is stolen or totaled in an accident before the extended warranty coverage kicks in? Your insurance company will not reimburse you for the cost of the extended warranty, and you will lose your investment. You're probably better off investing the money and earning dividends rather than locking it up for five years.

Read about rustproofing. Before purchasing rustproofing or undercoating, read the warranty coverage section of the owner's manual. In many cases, the carmaker will void your factory rust-out warranty if any rustproofing or undercoating is applied. If there are any questions about this area of factory coverage, call the manufacturer and ask. Do not listen to what the salesman tells you about how it affects the warranty.

FINANCING: HOW MUCH IS TOO MUCH?

Do you have a clear idea of how much car you can really afford to buy? Don't be hyped into buying more car than you can afford. If you can't afford to pay for it in about three years, the car is too expensive for you. Stay away from five-, six-, or seven-year car loans. The interest costs are way too high. The car might be ready for the junkyard about the time it is paid off.

Here's one easy way to find out how much you can afford to finance, including a down payment: Stop by your bank and have a friendly chat with a loan officer. This will help prevent you from falling prey to a high-pressure salesman who will try to talk you into buying more car than you can afford. If the monthly payments are too steep, you could wind up hating the car or, worse, having it repossessed.

Don't tip your hand. If you are planning to finance your car purchase with a source other than the dealer, don't tell the salesman. They get a commission from financing the car. If they know you will be doing your own financing, they might try to get extra cash out of you on the selling price. On the other hand, financing with the dealer has one advantage: If you have a big problem with the car, you can put the payments in escrow and use that as leverage to get the car fixed.

Buy down the financing costs. Put down as much money as you can afford on your new car. This is called capitalized cost reduction, and it will lower the total finance costs a great deal.

Look at the loan structure. Be sure to read finance contracts very carefully. Shrewd shopping for the least expensive method of financing can save you several thousand dollars. While the dealer's finance rate may be lower than your bank (which offers simple interest), the loan may be arranged so that your payments are first devoted to paying off solely the interest. Once the interest is paid, then you pay off the principal. Why is this bad? What happens if you decide to sell the car before it is paid off? What if it is stolen or totaled in a wreck? The amount that you still owe on the vehicle will be enormous. Insurance only pays for the fair market value of a car and will not pay off your loan. You will have to cough up the difference.

Pass on the payoff. Don't pay for "credit life and disability insurance," which pays off the car loan if you die. Many people already have this coverage in life insurance policies. If you don't, you can buy it cheaper from your insurance company than from the car finance company.

Try home equity. Home equity loans are a promising alternative to financing with the dealer or getting a bank loan. If you can qualify for a home equity loan, you are better off no matter what the interest rate offered by the dealer. Home equity loans are tax-deductible—unlike car loans. The only drawback of financing this way is that your home equity loan will typically be a long-term loan, much longer than the depreciating time limit of your car. So to beat the system, finance your car with a home equity loan, but pay the loan off as quickly as possible. Figure out how much you will need in order to pay it off in a maximum of four years. Remember that the faster you pay off the loan, the less you pay in interest.

Used Cars: Weigh Your Priorities

What's your priority in buying a used car—price or protection? The very best deals on used cars are found in classified ads posted by private parties. On the other hand, if you have a problem with a used car sold to you by a dealer, the dealer will still be there to appeal to for help. That's never true when you buy from a private party.

A licensed dealer also will make the sale much easier by handling the title and licensing paperwork for you, helping to arrange financing, and arranging for the manufacturer's express warranty to be transferred into your name if it's still in effect. Sometimes dealers will offer their own warranties.

First, Work the Phones

Whatever route you choose in buying a used car, first you need to make some decisions about what you're looking for.

Begin with a legal-size pad and list the things that you feel are necessary, in order of your priorities. List the price, options, size, number of doors, engine size, type of transmission, color, and anything else that comes to mind. Study the newspapers for what is being offered in your price range. Clip out the interesting ones and paste them on your pad.

Call the most appealing ones and get more information—this is for research, not serious buying. Gather enough information about the market in your area so that you'll know a good deal when you find one. Call as many

ads as possible and study the market for at least a week before beginning
your search in earnest. Get to know the used-car lots' ads by becoming familiar with their phone numbers. Cars that are not the best buys or have serious hidden flaws often wind up at used-car lots.

Once you have a good idea of the market, here's how automotive experts
recommend that you proceed in buying a used car.

Time it right. When answering a classified ad, don't call too early in the
morning or too late at night: 7:00 A.M. to 10:00 P.M. is fine. Most sellers start

What Do I Say?

Buying a Privately Owned Used Car

When you're shopping for a used car, ask private owners these questions before you dash off to see the vehicle in person. You'll save yourself loads of frustration and unnecessary trips, consumer advocates say.

- What condition is the car in? What is wrong with it?
- Why are you selling it?
- Do you sell many cars? (If the answer is yes, don't waste any more
  time—this "private" advertiser may have a sideline of selling prob-
  lematic cars.)
- Are you the original owner?
- How long have you owned the car?
- Have you maintained the car according to the manufacturer's
  schedule in the manual? How often has the oil been changed?
- Do you have repair receipts that I can look at? Where did you usu-
  ally take the car for service?
- When was the car last inspected? (Highly important in states where
  the car must pass inspection before the title can be transferred.)
- Where did you buy the car?
- Where did you generally drive the car. City? Long trips?
- What is the mileage? Is the odometer correct?
- Has the car ever been painted? If so, why?
- Has the car ever been recalled? If so, may I see verification that the
  problem was corrected?
- Would you object if I took the car to my mechanic for inspection?
- Are there any liens on the car?
- What is needed to put the car in tip-top condition?

their ads on Saturday or Sunday, and the best deals are gone by 10:00 A.M. To beat the system, then, find a newsstand or store that sells an early edition of the paper a day early. Get Saturday's paper on Friday afternoon and Sunday's on Saturday afternoon. Then examine the next day's paper and compare the advertising with your notes. You should be able to easily spot new listings. With your new knowledge of the market, you will be able to quickly identify the best buys.

Grill the owner. If a person advertising a used car tells you that it's been sold already, don't hang up. Ask what the final selling price was. This will add to your knowledge of the market.

If the car's still available, ask about the mileage—one of the most important facts, say mechanical experts. A car reaches the twilight of its life at around 100,000 miles for a four-cylinder car, 125,000 for a six-cylinder car, and 150,000 for an eight-cylinder car.

Always try to find out as much about the car over the phone as possible. Ask about each of the items on your priorities list. Ask why the car is being sold. And ask bluntly: "What's wrong with it?"

Act quickly. If you find a car of interest, call the seller immediately and ask to see it. Be prepared to make an offer on the spot. If you are unsuccessful in reaching the seller that day, start calling at 7:00 the next morning. If there is no phone number—only an address—go see the car right away.

Give That Used Car a Thorough Checkup

Arrange for your mechanic to be on call in case you need to drop by on short notice to have him check out a car. If no mechanic is available, arrange with your local American Automobile Association (AAA) or local dealer (for the corresponding brand of car) for an unbiased analysis of the drivetrain. You may have to make the sale contingent upon the car passing the mechanic's examination.

It is a good idea to have the exhaust gas analyzed for proper mixture, which tells a great deal about the engine's condition. If possible, inspect the receipts for proper service intervals. Note the mileage and dates of service. And watch for inconsistencies in the mileage.

If you decide to check the car out yourself, master mechanics say, at the very least make these inspections.

Cooling system. With the engine cold, remove the radiator cap and inspect the coolant. (*Caution:* Never remove the cap when the engine's hot.) If it is rusty, has a milky color, or an oily film on top, it probably has major cooling system problems. Next, allow the engine to run long enough for the temperature gauge to come up and stabilize. Does the electric cooling fan come on (if it is so equipped)? Does it overheat?

Leaks. Look for puddles underneath after running the car for 20 minutes parked in the same spot. Oil leaves dark oily stains; coolant is a yellow or

A Car's Title Can Speak Volumes

Don't hand over one penny for a used car until you have carefully examined the title, consumer advocates say. The following title problems are potential signs of a rip-off in the making.

- If the title is not in the same name as the seller, ask why. Ask if the person is authorized to sell that vehicle. Contact the owner listed on the title before proceeding. If the dealer's name is on the title, the car may have been bought at an auction—a bad sign. The history of an auction car can be very difficult to trace.

- Does the vehicle identification number (VIN) on the title match the car? Make sure that the numbers on the title are clear and not altered. Ditto for the VIN stamped on the metal plate located on the left front side of the dash. That plate is supposed to be held on by two special clover-shaped rivets—not "pop" rivets. The mileage entered on the mileage disclosure should match the title. Contact the previous owner to confirm this and to validate the length of ownership.

- If the title lists an owner from another state, has a post office box for an address, or is an auction company, be very suspicious. This could be a car with a history of problems.

- Make sure that there are no liens listed on the title. You do not want to be held responsible for someone else's debts.

- Be suspicious if the title is new for a car that is already several years old. Beware if it is stamped "duplicate," because it could be a fake. Look for staple marks purposely covering up alterations or any changes in the original printing on the document. Look out for any decimal points added to the odometer reading.

- If there are any rubber-stamped codes on the title, check with the Department of Motor Vehicles to determine what the code means. That stamp on the title (called branding) could mean the vehicle was damaged, salvaged, a lemon, or stolen and recovered. It could also mean that the odometer has already turned over 100,000 miles or that the odometer reading has been altered.

green liquid; transmissions leave a red fluid; power steering fluid is either red or clear; brake fluid is colorless and dissolves in water.

Check the door seals for leaks by closing the door on a dollar bill. It should not pass through easily. Take it through a car wash to check for leaking window glass and body parts.

Electrical. Turn on all the electrical accessories, including lights, turn signals, four-way flashers, and blower (on all the settings). Check the battery for corrosion. Check the operation of all the bulbs—all around the car, inside and out. Also inspect the lenses for cracks or patch-up repairs.

Shock treatment. Go around and bounce each of the vehicle's four corners. It should rebound but not continue bouncing. If it does continue bouncing, the car will need shocks or struts.

With the car in park and the engine running, watch the steering wheel. If it moves at the same time you bounce the front end, the steering system probably has a worn component. Listen for rubbing or squeaking noises indicating other worn suspension components. Open the hood and watch for engine movement while a friend shifts the transmission into drive then reverse. (Do this with the brakes on, of course. If the car is a stick shift, let the clutch out in first and then in reverse with the parking brake firmly applied.) Worn engine shocks (also known as struts or upper engine mounts) or broken motor mounts will allow the engine to rock back and forth.

Tires. Tires tell a real tale. Are all four tires the same size and type? Brand-new tires could be covering up alignment problems. Be sure to check the spare, which may provide a clue about alignment problems. Run your hand along the tire tread. Wear on one side or ragged, sharp edges usually indicates alignment problems—or, even worse, that the vehicle could have been in a major accident and have a bent frame.

Body. Carefully examine the body in the bright daylight, never at night or when it is wet. Sight down the sides looking for signs of patchwork repairs or poorly fitting body parts. Use your hand to measure the distance between each tire and the surrounding body. Any discrepancies between the left and right sides indicates major body flaws. Do the same thing, this time checking the distance from each side of the car to the ground. A difference in car height from side-to-side indicate problems with the springs or a major suspension problem.

Tap with your knuckles all over the body, especially on the doors and fender areas. Differences in how the body sounds from one side to the other indicates the presence of a thick layer of body plaster. Bring along a small magnet to confirm your suspicions that the body is covered with filler—the magnet will not stick to plastic. Check the windshield for small cracks, chips, and visual imperfections in the driver's visual area.

Dash bulbs. Turn on the ignition key and check all the warning bulbs for proper operation. There should be a warning bulb for every major electronic function that the vehicle has been equipped with (for example, "ABS," "Check Engine," "Fasten Seat Belts," "Traction Control," and "Automatic Level Control"). Almost all vehicles made since the mid-1980s have a "Check Engine" light. If this lightbulb doesn't work, someone may have removed it to hide an expensive problem with the engine emission system.

Odometers: Miles to Go before They Cheat

Low mileage on a car, of course, translates directly into a higher price tag when the auto is sold. Here's how to spot whether someone's been tampering with the odometer of the used car that you're thinking of buying.

- Test-drive the car. Does the odometer move properly?
- Check the dash for missing screws, scratches or misaligned dashboard parts and covers. Look for marks or paint on the numerical display numbers. Do the numbers line up?
- Look for service stickers under the hood or on door posts. Look for a service book. Are there any mileage readings to check against? Look for service receipts and tire or muffler warranties for mileage. Also look for tire and emission warranty papers detailing dates and mileage notations.
- Ask where the tires on the car were purchased in case you have a problem with them. If possible, visit that tire store and check their records, or go to the local dealer and check emission records. Are the mileage readings on those documents consistent with the readings on the car—when taking into consideration elapsed time?
- In what shape is the driver's seat? Are the seat springs worn? Is the fabric newly stitched? Check the pedal covers for wear. Are they newly replaced? Is the floor mat new—or is it covering up a worn rug? Does the kick panel have wear and scuff marks from usage? Compare the seats, carpets, and kick panel from side to side.
- Check to see if the windshield has been replaced. Does it look too new (or too pitted) to belong to a car with that odometer reading?
- Are all four tires the same brand? A late-model car with fewer than 30,000 miles should have original tires—usually radials.
- Contact the original owner and try to verify the mileage. Check whether your state's Department of Motor Vehicles will supply the address.
- Some titles have the odometer reading entered on them. Look out for ink stamps or staples over the reading, obscuring the numbers. Beware of an entry showing tenths of a mile. For example, the mileage shown as 37,564.2 was actually 75,642 before the fraud.

Test-drive. Start the engine cold to determine if it stalls or emits an excessive amount of exhaust smoke. If the engine has already been warmed up when you arrive, be suspicious. There may be a problem that is being hidden from you. Come back when it is cold and test it again. Take the car up to 65 miles per hour and hold it there for a few minutes. Listen to the engine for noises like pinging while accelerating and knocking when letting off the gas. Feel the steering for shimmying or vibration. Does it pull when accelerating or decelerating?

Have a friend follow you to see if the car is tracking straight. When viewed from behind, the rear tires should be in line with the front ones. Find an expressway cloverleaf and test the suspension by going up and down the ramps, both to the left and the right. Any problems found during the test-drive will warrant a closer inspection by a mechanic.

Drivetrain. Have a friend slowly rev the engine while you listen under the hood for the telltale sound of bad engine bearings. Bearing problems will make a rumble deep down in the engine. Check the engine oil and transmission (automatic only) dipsticks. A low oil level indicates neglect or an oil burner or leaker. If the transmission oil smells burnt, there are very expensive problems looming. The transmission oil should be red.

Does the transmission shift smoothly? Try shifting from forward to reverse. Do you hear a clunk? This could mean worn CV (constant velocity) or universal joints. If the car is a stick, does the clutch work smoothly? From a stop, put it in fourth gear and try it. It should not slip and the engine should quickly stall. If it slips or if the clutch engages right at the end of its travel, there are expensive clutch problems.

Brakes. Make a sudden emergency stop. Let go of the steering wheel and note if the car pulls to one side when braking. Look for skid marks leading up to all four tires, meaning that all four brakes are functioning properly (except on ABS vehicles, which will not skid). With the engine off, hold the brake pedal down for a few minutes. Now start the engine while pressing the brake pedal. It should sink slightly and then become firm. If it is mushy or sinks to the floor, this indicates expensive brake problems.

Exhaust. After completing the above items, the engine should be hot. Have a friend rev the engine several times and check the exhaust for smoke. White smoke means a blown head gasket. Blue smoke means burning oil. Black smoke means an overly rich fuel mixture (which can also make the exhaust smell like rotten eggs).

Run your finger along the inside of the tailpipe. (*Caution:* It may be hot.) It shouldn't be oily. Normal exhaust conditions leave a tan, gray, or charcoal-colored film on the tailpipe. Check for exhaust leaks by *momentarily* plugging the pipe with a wadded-up rag. This should cause the engine to falter and even stall. If there is a leak, you may hear it, and the engine will continue to run normally.

Hidden stuff. Look for signs of hidden damage and rust inside the trunk, doors, and under the hood and trunk lid. With a flashlight, inspect the inside of each wheel well. Peel back the carpet under the dash and pedal covers and look for rust—a sure sign of water damage.

Does the color of the paint match the color inside the hood and under the trunk lid? Are there signs of paint overspray on the rubber weather strips and door moldings? A fresh paint job on a car that is only a few years old is a sign that someone is trying to hide something.

Now, What Do You Do with Your Old Car?

What you do with your used car depends on who you are and how much time you have to dispose of it. The easiest way to sell it is to use it as part of a trade-in for a new car. The hardest and most risky way is to sell it yourself, automotive experts say. Do you mind dealing with strangers who come to your house? Are you willing to get telephone inquiries at all hours? On the other hand, selling it yourself is also the way to get the most money.

To find out the resale value of a particular used car, contact your bank or insurance agent and have them look it up for you. Or drop by a dealer and have it appraised (you will only get the wholesale value from a dealer). Several publications, such as *The NADA Official Used Car Guide Book* and *Edmund's Used Cars Prices and Ratings*, list vehicle values, so buy a copy or drop by the library.

Here are more helpful tips that auto experts recommend for beating the used-car selling system.

Size up the market. Study the weekend papers to get a realistic idea of what cars like yours are worth. Call some of the sellers to find out exactly what condition their cars are really in. If it has been sold, ask how much it finally sold for. This will also give you an idea of how fast cars like yours are selling.

Go over used-car price lists and decide what your asking price will be. Also decide what, at the very minimum, you will accept. Your listed price should be within 5 to 10 percent of what you are willing to settle for.

Doll 'er up. Put as much time, money, and effort into making your car as attractive as possible. Be sure that the oil and air filters are clean, that it starts right up and that the gas tank is full. A clean engine compartment and interior are helpful, too. Buyers are frequently more concerned about a clean car than a perfectly tuned engine. Put an air freshener in the car, too.

A fresh state vehicle inspection sticker can make it more appealing. Do this only if it is feasible for your state. If not, be sure to have the buyer sign an affidavit stating that the car is being sold "as is."

Get the papers in order. Gather up the repair and service receipts and offer them as evidence of proper upkeep. Make certain that the title is free and clear at the time of the sale.

Wow them with your ad. Get familiar with the jargon used in auto ads. Those abbreviations will help keep your ads short. Describe all of your car's aspects, accessories, and extras—you want to grab the car hunter's attention. Don't skimp when describing the positive things that your car has to offer. What may seem mundane or ordinary may be the thing that causes someone to call you.

Don't mention problems in your ad. It's best to tell the buyer about those things face-to-face.

Hang around the phone. Most car buyers will call only once and don't like to respond to answering machines. So be home to answer the phone and have someone continue to take calls while you are outside showing the car.

Reel them in carefully. When talking to a caller about the used car that you're selling, the object is to get the buyer to overcome inertia. You must motivate the caller to drive over and actually see the car. This part is your biggest battle.

Be just a little on the positive side of neutral with each caller. Be brief and to the point. Encourage the caller to see the car in real life.

Always go along for the test-drive. For safety, first look at the buyer's license and ask for a second piece of identification. Check the expiration date and make sure that the picture matches. Copy down the license number and leave it with the person answering the phone.

Get cash on the barrel head. Never accept a check as payment. Cash, cashier's check, or money order only. Make it clear to the buyer that you will sell the car to the first person who pays in this manner.

Never agree to time payments, and only take a deposit under the stipulation that you keep the car until you are paid in full. Make up a bill of sale that lists the selling price, buyer's and seller's names and addresses, a sentence stating that the car is being sold "as is," the make, model, year, vehicle identification number, and mileage.

If the buyer wants to take the car to a mechanic, try to secure the deal with a deposit. (Always go along, by the way, and question the mechanic about every detail of the report.)

Bottom Line

Before you walk onto a car dealer's lot to buy a car, have a firm idea of what car you want—not only the model but also the options. This is achieved by thoroughly analyzing your needs, researching in car and consumer publications, and comparison-shopping. Thus armed, you will be less vulnerable to the car salesman's pressure tactics.

Words to the Wise

Car show: Your local car show is not just a place to indulge your fantasies. Look at them as a place where you can comparison-shop dozens of models under one roof—without a salesman salivating on you.

Extended warranty: Repair coverage for your car, beyond the standard warranty. The value of this depends upon how much you drive, how long you plan to keep the car, and how many electronic accessories it has.

Allies

Auto Service Contracts: FTC Public Reference Branch, Sixth and Pennsylvania Avenues, Washington, DC 20508. Free brochure on auto service contracts.

Avoiding Shakes, Rattles, and Rollbacks: How to Buy a Used Car: Consumer Protection Division, 200 St. Paul Place, Baltimore, MD 21202. Cost: about $2.

Buying a Safer Car: American Automobile Association (AAA), 811 Gatehouse Road, Falls Church, VA 22047. Free with self-addressed, stamped envelope.

Nutz & Boltz: P.O. Box 123, Butler, MD 21023. Automotive consumer newsletter.

Part 7

MONEY

Whipping Your Cash Flow into Shape

For $60,000, Wouldn't You Pass Up the Pizza?

In the 1950s, almost every man wanted to be Errol Flynn, the movie star with the on-screen derring-do and the offscreen life of luxury.

In the 1990s, when it comes to their spending habits, far too many people *are* like Flynn, who once noted, "my problem lies in reconciling my gross habits with my net income."

It doesn't take extravagant habits to have cash-flow problems, just the wrong mix of expenditures and income. Making ends meet—and getting ahead—is not hard.

"You either make more money or spend less cash. It's that simple," says Tracey McBride, publisher of *Frugal Times: Making Do with Dignity*. "Of course, if you can't earn more money, then you have some choices to make; but if you look at everything calmly and clearly, you will find a lot of ways to get more out of the money that you make now."

Improving your cash flow, in general, is a matter of self-evaluation, common sense, and a few simple changes. Here's what to do.

Get a Grip on Your Spending

There's a reason they call it cash "flow." Money spends like water—in the palm of your hand one minute and slipping between your fingers the next.

To improve your cash flow, start by examining where the money goes now. This can be as simple as reviewing your credit slips, canceled checks, and receipts on a daily or weekly basis or by keeping a detailed logbook. The more detailed the account of your spending, the more useful your spending review will be.

TAKE A SLICE OUT OF THOSE EXTRA EXPENDITURES

It might not seem like a dollar dropped on a soda in the office or a pizza on the way home could ever amount to much money, but those extra expenditures are missed opportunities.

Take that pizza habit. Suppose that a family resolves to stop eating two large pizzas per week. Instead, they put the savings—call it $100 per month—into an investment account with an 8 percent annual return. The savings over 20 years would amount to $60,000.

"If you keep a spending record, it's harder for money to slip away unnoticed," says Paul Richard, director of education at the National Center for Financial Education in San Diego. "When you lay out your receipts or your ledger and see where the money is going, you will notice any disturbing patterns about your spending right away—like the guy that I once did this with who saw that a big problem was his three trips to the convenience store every day. By waking up early and packing a lunch, he saved $30 a week—but only after he recognized where the problem was."

Once you're armed with information about where and how you spend your money, break that information down.

SORT OUT THE NECESSITIES AND THE LUXURIES

Your expenses fall into three primary categories.

Fixed costs. These are the most difficult to curtail. They include your rent or mortgage, loan payments, utility bills, car payments, food, and, in general, anything for which you must pay money every month.

If you intend to save each month—perhaps through automatic deposit plans from your bank account—include that money as part of your fixed costs so that you are paying yourself first, or at least with the same priority you reserve for the mortgage.

Periodic expenses. These costs are typically fixed in nature but don't occur every month. These would include car repairs; medical or insurance bills; dues to civic, social, and religious organizations; and more. These need to be saved for so that they don't derail your cash flow when they hit.

Discretionary spending. Your spending record may show your habits, but it can't determine how much you really have to spend on entertainment or clothing or fun.

To get that amount, forecast what your periodic expenses will be for the next year and divide by 12 to get the monthly amount. Add that figure to your monthly fixed expenses. Then subtract that amount from your monthly

(continued on page 258)

Monitoring Your Cash Flow

Improving your cash flow starts with knowing how much money comes in and where it goes once it gets there. This exercise will help you figure that out.

Wherever possible, use actual monthly expense and income amounts. Otherwise, use averages or divide annual fees by 12 to break costs down into their monthly average. Do not double-count expenses (for instance, health insurance or savings deducted directly from your paycheck, or gas purchases made with a credit card).

You will note that savings plans are part of your spending habits, too. That being the case, there is nothing wrong with expenses that equal—but do not surpass—your income, provided that you are saving adequately for the future.

Your Monthly Disposable Income

| Take-home pay from salary #1 | $_____ | Take-home pay from salary #2 | $_____ |

Other monthly income

| Source | $_____ | Source | $_____ |

Interest/investment income

Checking account	$_____	Pension (if applicable)	$_____
Savings account	$_____	Individual retirement account	
Money market account	$_____	or Keogh (if applicable)	$_____
Other	$_____	401(k) withdrawals	$_____
Other	$_____	Gifts	$_____
Stock dividends	$_____	Alimony	$_____
Investment income	$_____	Other	$_____
Loans receivable	$_____	Other	$_____

TOTAL INCOME $_____

Your Monthly Expenses

Credit cards (use minimum due or the amount you pay regularly)

| Card #1 | $_____ | Card #3 | $_____ |
| Card #2 | $_____ | Card #4 | $_____ |

Housing

| Mortgage/rent | $_____ | Out-of-pocket tax payments | $_____ |
| Second mortgage/ vacation home | $_____ | Other | $_____ |

Household costs

Child care $_____
Maid service/dry
   cleaning/laundry $_____
Clothing $_____

Groceries $_____
Medicines/personal care $_____
Pet supplies $_____
Subscriptions $_____

Insurance

Property and Casualty $_____
Auto $_____
Life $_____

Health $_____
Long-term care/disability $_____
Home owner's/renter's $_____

Motor vehicles

Car #1 (monthly payment,
   if any) $_____
Car #2 $_____

Other vehicles $_____
Gasoline/service costs $_____

Savings (enter monthly deposits,
excluding monies taken direct from your paycheck)

College fund $_____
Retirement plan $_____

General savings $_____

Utilities

Cable TV $_____
Electric/gas $_____
Telephone $_____

Trash removal $_____
Water/sewer $_____
Yard care/snow removal $_____

Entertainment

Dining out (include meals
   at work) $_____
Babysitters $_____

Movies/theater/sports/
   museums/culture costs $_____
Other $_____

Other expenses

Alimony $_____
Church/synagogue donations $_____
Other charitable contributions $_____

Miscellaneous $_____
Miscellaneous $_____

TOTAL EXPENSES $_____

Your Bottom Line

Total monthly income $_____
Total monthly expenses $_____
Monthly cash flow   ± $_____

take-home pay. The remainder is what you will have for discretionary spending each month. If the number is less than zero—so that your discretionary spending outstrips the discretionary portion of your earnings, chances are that you have a negative cash flow. But, with your spending record in hand, you also have enough information to make your cash flow better.

EVALUATE AND ELIMINATE THE "EXTRAS"

As noted, the two easiest ways to improve cash flow are to earn more money and spend less. Cutting your spending is a cross between practicality and value.

"Many people think that they must sacrifice quality in order to save money," says Harry Clarke Noyes, Ph.D., head of Psychological Motivations, a consumer research firm in Dobbs Ferry, New York. "There are trade-offs to be made, but there are also many ways to look at them. If people look at the real value that they are getting—if they currently spend a dollar at the candy machine every day—they might find a lot of easy ways to cut their expenses without feeling like they are ruining their lifestyle."

Discretionary spending is the easiest to cut, although it also tends to yield the smallest savings. It might mean packing a lunch instead of eating out, cutting the trips to the convenience store, reducing your purchases of new clothes, and limiting your entertainment budget.

In many instances, however, there are creative solutions that can stretch your dollar—for instance, forming a babysitting co-op where you trade off child care time with friends and neighbors so that a night on the town is not made doubly expensive by the help that you have at home.

You also want to eliminate wasteful or redundant spending. That means canceling the subscriptions to magazines that you have no time to read or can get at the office. Or it means carrying a cup of coffee from home rather than paying for one during your morning commute. Instead of buying books, you can borrow them from the library. Instead of buying new goods, buy high-quality used ones.

"It's a matter of your priorities," says McBride. "If you value saving money, you can do that and still have nice things. If you value owning something that is shiny and new, you can do that—but you might not be able to save money."

Remember that the example of the "$60,000 pizza" required just $25 in savings a week. So trimming $2 a day in snack foods and $3 a day by packing a lunch can generate the same $60,000 nest egg in 20 years.

An easy way to keep discretionary spending in line is to set up an account from which you take a monthly allowance. The amount might be the dollar amount that you came up with while evaluating your expenses, or it might be less, depending upon your needs and goals. Fund the account at the start of the month and use it for your pocket money—knowing that the monthly spending stops once the account and your pockets are empty.

"It's a good motivator because you really want to save money so that you can do more with it; and you become very careful about spending it because you know that there will be something else you want later in the month," says Eric Gelb, author of *The Personal Budget Planner*, who keeps a separate account for his own monthly fun money.

Necessities: Are They, Well, Necessary?

The bigger place to improve your cash flow—and also the more difficult—is in your fixed and periodic expenses. This is where your lifestyle may change.

On the surface, the task of altering fixed expenses—mortgage, car payment, and the like—seems impossible, because those costs are fixed. The question that must be asked about each of those regular expenditures is whether they are necessary.

"If what you want is to improve your cash flow so that you can cut your debt or to save more so that you can reach your long-term goals, it won't change your necessities, but it might change how you look at them," says Shawn M. Connors, president of the Financial Literacy Center, a Kalamazoo, Michigan, group that works with employers to improve the money skills and awareness of workers.

"You still need to get to work, but you might be able to do it on public transportation. Or you still need a car, but you might be able to get by with a used car that you can either pay cash for or pay off more quickly.

"Watching your debts come down and your net worth improve is a rewarding process," Connors adds, "and far more rewarding than spending your money on stuff that you may not really need or appreciate."

MORTGAGES: SAVINGS ON THE HOUSE

The rule of thumb is that you don't refinance your home unless you can shave two points from the mortgage rate, but investment experts say that that's outdated advice. Given no-points, no-closing-costs mortgages, refinancing can pay off if you cut the rate by as little as half a point.

Of course, you may have a mortgage rate that is so good that you can't find something better, says Marc Eisenson, publisher of *The Pocket Change Investor*, a quarterly newsletter. Even so, consider shortening the mortgage duration from, say, 30 to 15 or 20 years. It may not cost much money in additional monthly payment, and it will save thousands of dollars over the life of the loan. In anticipation of being able to refinance if mortgage rates become favorable, you might even prequalify with a local lender, who can then track rates on your behalf and call when money becomes available at the rate that you seek.

INSURANCE: SOME PROTECTION ISN'T WORTH IT

You hear all the time that cutting your insurance protection is penny-wise and pound-foolish, but it is worth doing the math. By raising your deductibles and making sure that you have adequate—but not overgenerous—coverage, you can save hundreds of dollars a year.

For example, if you drive an older car—particularly one where the value would be $1,500 or less—you might be better off not carrying collision damage protection and comprehensive coverage, suggests Gelb. You would have to pay the deductible for damage done during an accident, and that would eat up a sizable percentage of your claim. If the same deductible could put a nice down payment on a car of similar value—a car that could be paid for quickly—it might be worth the risk of reducing your coverage.

Similarly, inquire about the cost of raising your deductible on your auto and home owner's insurance. Willingness to part with a few hundred dollars extra in the event of an incident could save you thousands of dollars in premiums between rare claims. Be sure to weigh the likelihood of needing the insurance coverage: Paying the premium might be worth it if you drive hundreds of miles in heavy traffic each week. But doing without the coverage might be an acceptable risk for a hundred miles of suburban driving.

Consider carefully the insurance that you carry on valuables. For example, an heirloom ring may have $1,000 in appraised value but be priceless to you in terms of sentiment. If that is the case, a $750 check from your insurer (the ring's value minus a deductible) can't replace it.

Now factor in the likelihood that the ring will be lost or stolen and the cost of the insurance. Consider whether you wear the ring or keep it in a safe-deposit box, and whether you live in a low-crime area.

You may be paying a lot of money for insurance that is inadequate because the ring's value is predominately intrinsic. Since the ring cannot be replaced—throwing money at a new ring would not bring back the one for which you have feelings—you might be better off saving the insurance money for situations where a cash settlement will repurchase your lost goods.

As with discretionary expenses, eliminate redundancies.

For example, your home owner's insurance will rebuild your house in the event of catastrophe, and your life insurance will protect your family in the event that you die. Which makes "mortgage insurance"—which pays off the mortgage in the event that something awful happens—unnecessary for most people, advises Gelb. Similarly, health insurance policies sold through a child's school tend to overlap the health care coverage offered by many employers and, as a result, aren't worth the expense.

TRY SOME CARD TRICKS

Here are more ways that you can easily trim some fixed and periodic costs.

Save on the cost of debt. Sure, reducing debt is one reason why many people examine their cash flow to begin with. But saving money on what

Does It Pay to Refinance?

With no closing-costs, no points mortgages, refinancing your mortgage can mean big savings, even when the interest rate drops by just a little. Here's how to determine how long it will take to break even on a new mortgage. This exercise assumes a fixed interest rate for the life of the loan.

1. Enter your current monthly mortgage payment
   (principal and interest only). $_____

2. Subtract your new mortgage payment (principal
   and interest only).   − $_____

3. Your monthly savings   = $_____

4. Add up all refinancing costs.

   points   + $_____

   appraisal   + $_____

   title search   + $_____

   legal fees   + $_____

   miscellaneous/other   + $_____

Total   = $_____

5. Divide refinancing costs by your monthly savings.

   Refinancing costs (step 4) $_____

   divided by savings (step 3)   ÷ $_____

Result   = $_____

The result is the number of months that it takes to break even on the new loan.

you owe is a good way to improve cash flow and reduce your debt at the same time. Just as you refinance a mortgage to save on your housing costs, you can also refinance your credit cards and personal debts.

"Every $1,000 that you don't spend on debt means $1,400 that you don't have to earn," says Eisenson. "And that is a savings that is real, not taxed; so cutting your debt pays for itself very quickly and can really improve your cash flow."

The habit of constantly managing your credit debt to keep the lowest possible interest rate in place is known as credit surfing, and all that it requires is a decent credit rating and a telephone. For most people, it starts with a mail solicitation, preferably for a no-fee credit card with a low "teaser" rate, which the issuer offers as an incentive to sign up for six months to a year.

Refinance higher debt by using the available balance from this new credit card, thereby cutting your payments. (Be sure to close your old credit accounts, because open credit cards will count against you when lenders review your credit history.)

Shortly before the teaser period ends, call the card issuer and ask for an extension—or an even better rate, suggests Robert McKinley, president of RAM Research Group in Frederick, Maryland. Explain that you will close the account and transfer the debt elsewhere if an extension is not possible—and have new card offers in hand so that you are prepared to do it. Most lenders will extend the rate, provided that you have been a good customer. Some may ask that you transfer additional balances to the account, which may further your efforts to consolidate debt. (If the card issuer will not extend the initial low rate—or if you can get a better teaser rate somewhere else—go ahead and make the switch.)

Come to terms with your cards. It is important to know the terms of the credit cards you use to cut your debt. Many offer a low rate for cash advances and balance transfers and a higher rate for purchases—and purchases flow to the bottom of your pile of debt, meaning the high-rate debt gets paid off last. If this is the case, you will want to use the card as a refinancing vehicle only and not for new purchases.

"If you take a $3,900 balance at 18 percent and transfer it to a 12 percent card, you'll save $234 that first year," says Ruth Susswein, executive director of the Bankcard Holders of America, a consumer group based in Salem, Virginia. "If you switch to a 7.5 percent card, you'll save $409. And you didn't even have to cut back or do anything different to save that money."

Even out those power bills. If your electric or gas company has an average monthly bill program—where you pay an average amount rather than for the specific amount that you used in a month—sign up. These programs even out your cash flow and allow you to plan more carefully.

Saving at a fast clip. Eating is an obvious necessity, but veteran shoppers report saving 20 to 30 percent on their grocery bills simply by clipping coupons and shopping at wholesale clubs. As with most cash-flow savings, small amounts add up—and a 25 percent savings on a $100 weekly grocery bill is worth the same amount as cutting out those two large pizzas a week.

BOTTOM LINE

If you can't go out and earn more money, then the only way to improve your cash flow is to make your current income go further. That means examining—and changing—your spending habits.

WORDS TO THE WISE

Cash flow: The money that you have flowing in right now and where it is going. A positive cash flow means that you have money to save or invest at the end of each month or pay period, while negative cash flow means that spending outstrips your income.

Net worth: The value of everything you own minus everything you owe. Start with a total value for all of your assets—home, car, bank accounts, investments, cash-value life insurance, retirement and pension savings, collectibles, ownership stake in a business, and so on. Then subtract your debts, including mortgage, car, student and personal loans, credit card debts, and anything else that you foresee paying out. The remainder equals your net worth.

ALLIES

American Savings Education Council: 2121 K Street NW, Suite 600, Washington, DC 20037-1896. A not-for-profit group funded by some of the nation's biggest corporations. Produces free worksheets, brochures, and a number of guides to improve your savings and spending habits. Send a self-addressed, stamped business-size envelope, with two first-class stamps.

CardTrak: P.O. Box 1700, Frederick, MD 21702. Published by RAM Research Group, offers a list of the nation's best available credit card rates. For a sample copy, send $5.

National Center for Financial Education: P.O. Box 34070, San Diego, CA 92163-4070. Offers several worksheets, all for the cost of a self-addressed, stamped business-size envelope (for each additional request, add one first-class stamp to the envelope). Ask for "How to Set Up and Implement a Spending Plan," "Signs and Symptoms of Money Troubles," or "Spending by Choice." The literature is also available from their site on the World Wide Web.

The Personal Budget Planner: A Guide for Financial Success, by Eric Gelb (Career Advancement Center). Available by writing to Career Advancement Center, P.O. Box 436, Woodmere, NY 11598. Cost is about $20, plus shipping and handling.

Climbing Out of Debt

Time to Make a Cold, Calculated Change in Lifestyle

No one needs help getting *into* debt.

People with any hint of a decent credit rating always find a way to finance the next big purchase, no matter what the new debt does to the family cash flow.

But buying something and paying it off are two different things, and there are few shortcuts to getting out of financial trouble.

"It's like walking down a hill," says Harry Clarke Noyes, Ph.D., head of Psychological Motivations, a consumer research firm in Dobbs Ferry, New York. "You spend and spend, and then look up and realize that you have a long, hard climb back to the top. It is much tougher saving and going up the hill than spending on the way down."

It's not just overspending that is the problem. Many people live on the financial edge, only to be pushed over by some catastrophe like a health problem, layoff, or accident.

Terrell Hayes, assistant professor of sociology at Davis and Elkins College in Elkins, West Virginia, who studied members of the group Debtors Anonymous, noted that many were "people who were paying their debts regularly until something happened to throw them behind. Once they went from being on the edge to being over it, they couldn't recover. It's very easy to lose control of your finances if you are stretched to the limit."

No matter how financial problems were created, there are few solutions.

The starting point is obvious: Don't borrow more money. But actually paying off thousands of dollars in debt is much harder, requiring changes in habits, lifestyle, and values in order to erase the problem and never fall behind again.

Making Change: Five Battle Plans

Credit counselors typically break the solution down into five parts, and while they may argue about the order in which to follow these steps, the idea is to cut living expenses, sell assets, increase income, restructure debts, and evaluate bankruptcy.

None of those solutions is attractive, but each can be a key ingredient toward getting out of debt.

Cut Living Expenses

"If you have run up tremendous debts, you have surrendered the opportunity to have certain choices," says Mary Hunt, reformed spender and editor of *Cheapskate Monthly*. Hunt knows a little something about sacrificing to get out of debt. She and her husband once had unsecured debts—credit card bills, lines of credit, and personal loans—of more than $100,000. She spent 13 years paying them off.

"When your debts are so big that you can't see how to repay them, you have to make unpleasant choices," Hunt says. "That means that if your child gets into Harvard, you may have to send him to a state school instead. Or if you want to send him to Harvard, you may have to move into a smaller house or sell the second car to afford it."

Sale of Assets May Erase the Problem

Selling assets is a crucial part of the recovery process, because it generates cash. Unless you are selling something that is leveraged—a car with an outstanding loan, for example—the entire proceeds of a sale can pay off debt. Even in the case of assets on which there are loans—such as a second home on which there is a mortgage—selling should take the debt off the books, thereby improving cash flow.

But surrendering possessions is not easy. Some people look at it as an admission of defeat and a surrender of their hopes and dreams.

"When you are staring down the barrel of a potential bankruptcy, you're going to have to decide what you really need and what you can do without," says attorney Robin Leonard, author of *Money Troubles*. "You may want to keep something, but you are better off selling it than losing it to the bankruptcy court, which is what will happen if you can't make the hard choices."

Inventory your stuff. Just as you have evaluated your living expenses to see what you can do without and how you can reduce outlays in order to better service your debt, so must you inventory your holdings, small and large.

"If you haven't used it in a few years or don't see yourself using it, see what you can get for it," says Leonard.

Put those big-tickets up for sale. Look for goods that have a significant market value, including jewelry, automobiles, property, collectibles and antiques, furs, and other big-ticket items. Experts also suggest unloading heirlooms lacking in sentimental attachment.

Hang up the high life. Many of the assets that can raise the most money are part of the reason for the debt in the first place. Hunt recounted the tale of a couple with a good income and a debt problem caused almost entirely by the husband's love of classic cars.

"He didn't want to sell them because he felt that he couldn't get what they were worth," says Hunt. "He was talking about trying to transfer the title so that he could keep them after the couple went bankrupt, which probably wasn't going to work. He finally agreed to sell. He complained about the price but got enough for the cars that they didn't have the debt problem."

"It's hard to convince yourself that things are so bad that you have to bring your lunch to work, let alone sell your second car or some heirloom," says Mel Stiller, executive director of Consumer Credit Counseling Service

Danger Signals

There's No Easy Fix for Your Credit

If someone says that they can "fix" your credit report and have accurate-but-negative information removed from your credit files, they're lying. So says the Federal Trade Commission (FTC), which says that there is no way for a "credit doctor" to fix something that legitimately belongs in your file.

Credit-repair firms may be able to help get incorrect information from your report and know that the rules allow "catastrophic" situations to be stricken from your record, but they can't help you if your report shows that you once stopped paying the bills for five months.

"We haven't seen anything but time that can clear up negative information in your credit file," says Don d'Entremont, an attorney in the FTC's Division of Credit Practices in Washington, D.C., who investigates credit-repair fraud. "They have some tricks that may take accurate information off your file for a few days or weeks, but the credit bureau will put the data right back on once they know that it is correct. Until the information becomes obsolete—generally 7 years for late payments and 10 for bankruptcy—there's no honest way to get it out of your file."

Both credit-repair firms and agencies that sell you copies of your credit reports are doing work that you can do yourself. You can arrange to get copies of your credit reports, protest information that is inaccurate or that was caused by catastrophe, and do the legwork needed to clear up file mistakes.

of Massachusetts in Boston. "But if you don't see any way to continue living the way that you do now and still pay down the debt, then you had better stop living the way that you do now."

WORK MORE—IF IT REALLY PAYS

Most people figure that the easiest way to cut their debts is simply to earn more money, and this is where they turn for help first. The problem is that additional income by itself is not enough to shrink the debts unless it is accompanied by reduced spending and a repayment plan.

Besides, making more money is not easy, especially in today's tight economy. Some people are already working two jobs, piling on overtime at their current employers or facing a tight local economy. Others have the skill to start a sideline business or earn extra money but not the cash to get the ball rolling. Just because you want to earn more doesn't guarantee that you can actually do it.

Still, make a realistic appraisal of how you can bring in more cash to make ends meet. If you don't want to declare bankruptcy and you don't want to change your lifestyle, aspirations, and dreams, earning more money is the only option.

There is one major caution, however: Make sure that a second job truly generates enough money to be worthwhile. In some cases, the costs of going to work—which can include everything from child care to heightened insurance to wardrobe—can be nearly as much, and in some cases more, than the second job actually brings into the home.

RESTRUCTURE YOUR DEBTS

If you can't meet your minimum payments, it's time to ask for some help. This assistance comes in one of two ways: either through refinancing to lower interest rates or through restructuring the outstanding debts.

Reduce your rates. On the refinancing side, look for low-rate credit cards or other cut-rate borrowings, making sure to close old accounts and not to add any new spending to the new ones.

Lean on the lenders. Most lenders offer some assistance, provided that they have reason to believe that they will be repaid over time, says attorney, financial consultant, and author Stephen Pollan. Banks and credit card issuers will not forgive loans but may be willing to waive penalties, cut interest rates, or stop the debt clock while you get your finances in order.

Typically, creditors will do this with average customers—although some do not offer this kind of treatment until you are delinquent in your payments, thereby qualifying for special circumstances. If you don't want to negotiate this kind of deal yourself, seek the help of a credit counselor, most of whom work for little or no fee. Generally, they get a small piece of your repayment to the creditors as the payment for their services.

Consolidate carefully. In restructuring debt, there are several traps to avoid, advises Pollan. For example, debt consolidation is a terrific idea but only under certain circumstances.

- A debt-consolidation loan must have a lower interest rate than the separate debts that it replaces.
- The payoff time on the consolidation loan must be within four years so that you have a set time when the debts will be paid off and are not simply shifting debt from one vehicle to another.
- You must be on a plan to cut spending and take on no more debt. If you haven't created a repayment plan—and cut up your credit cards—you run the risk that the consolidation loan makes you feel free to spend again.
- A debt-consolidation loan should not turn unsecured debt—such as credit cards—into secured debt. Many people consolidate their debts by taking out a home equity loan, a move that makes their houses the security for their debts. That means that if they can't repay their debts, they could lose their homes.

Unsecured debts are backed by your word and honor that you will repay. There is a limit as to how far an unsecured creditor can go to collect the debt from you, especially in a bankruptcy situation. If you secure a consolidation debt with a piece of property, you will need to be prepared to lose the property, even if you wind up declaring bankruptcy.

Bankruptcy: No Magic Wand

Many people mistakenly think that bankruptcy is like a get-out-of-jail-free card, forgiving debts with little or no cost. But a personal bankruptcy can be reported to the credit agencies and can stay on your credit files for 10 years, making it difficult to re-establish yourself financially for years to come. Clearly, there is a stigma with going bankrupt, particularly because the public views it as a combination of overspending and shirking financial responsibilities.

When to Pull the Plug

"The advice on when to declare bankruptcy is conflicting, usually because people who give it have conflicts of interest," says Ed Mierzwinski, consumer advocate for the U.S. Public Interest Research Group in Washington, D.C. "They don't want you to file, because they are hoping to get some money back or to help someone else collect; or they want you to file bankruptcy, because they will get a fee for helping you do it. There's a lot of misinformation out there, a lot to think about, and no quick answers."

Experts have a rule of thumb on when it's time to pull the plug and declare bankruptcy. "Sit down, rationally and honestly, to evaluate your finances," says John M. Caher, co-author of the book *Debt Free!* "If you say, 'There is no way that I am going to be able to pay these bills within the next three years,' then bankruptcy is a smart and ethical tool to consider."

Bankruptcy should be approached on a cold, hard financial basis and used only where the benefits outweigh the drawbacks.

Don't fan the flames. Most bankruptcy lawyers and credit advisers are against people racking up credit with the plan of declaring bankruptcy to dodge the creditors. Just as important, the courts are not particularly tolerant in those situations, which can lead to difficult settlements. Debt that has been run up after a point when someone knows that they cannot repay it may be considered fraud and might not be forgiven by the court.

Stop the clock with Chapter 13. A Chapter 13 bankruptcy filing—which stops the interest clock from increasing old debts and allows for scheduled repayment, possibly with some debt forgiveness—is typically the best route for individuals who have a job, assets to protect, and a realistic possibility to pay the bills off over three to five years, says Pollan.

But if you had a hard time cutting expenses and selling assets on your own, don't expect Chapter 13 to make you particularly happy. The court will mandate your budget and may force the sale of some assets to help reduce debts, and the plans typically aren't easy. Expect a once-a-month trip to McDonald's to be a big night on the town.

Liquidate for a clean start. Without the property to protect or any hope of repaying the debt, then a Chapter 7 bankruptcy filing—liquidation of assets—is typically the most sensible route to a clean start, especially if the event was emotionally destructive, says Pollan. Many people start by filing for Chapter 13 but convert to liquidation when they can't uphold the court-mandated repayment schedule.

In both cases, the loss of your home to the bankruptcy court depends on the rules of the state in which you live and the specifics of your debt situation. Laws tend to support the American dream, and the courts try hard not to strip home ownership while selling other assets. But find out the rules where you live before a bankruptcy situation turns even more unpleasant.

Prepare for the emotional toll. The drawbacks to bankruptcy are the soiled credit record and the emotional turmoil of throwing up your hands. Credit can be re-established, especially using secured credit cards, where the cardholder puts money up front to cover expenses run up on the card. The emotions can be tougher to overcome.

"It is hard for people not to look at themselves as a failure after they file for bankruptcy," says Dr. Noyes. "Even though they get a clean start, that's a burden that they carry around—and one that has constant reminders for the people who have trouble re-establishing credit. No one likes to admit failure or to suffer the consequences of failing."

While bankruptcy is a last-resort solution, it is something that should figure into the calculations of everyone with a serious debt problem.

"Bankruptcy is the price you pay if you can't reduce your debt through other means," says Leonard. "So look at it as an option, and you will see that you will lose less by cutting your spending, selling some assets, and creating a repayment plan than by simply filing for bankruptcy. When you look at what bankruptcy will cost you, it becomes a pretty good motivator not to do it unless you absolutely have to."

PUT A PLAN INTO ACTION

Having reviewed ways to cut spending and living expenses, earn additional income, sell assets to pay down debts, and restructure borrowings, there are two choices. One, as discussed, is bankruptcy. The other is trimming your debt burden.

Having taken steps to restructure and refinance debt, structure a plan in which the debts with the highest interest rates are paid off first. This ensures that your repayment picks up steam, wiping out the most costly borrowings and then moving to debts that can be eliminated quickly.

"Once you see progress—when you create a plan, stick to it, and see it starting to work—that is when you will know that you can do it," says Hunt. "The bad news is that it's not easy to dig yourself out of big debts. The good news is that it's not impossible."

BOTTOM LINE

The only way to reduce mountains of debt is to live below your means—and to use the extra to pay down your bills. The best time to start was yesterday.

WORDS TO THE WISE

Bankrupt: This is a legal condition that may occur before a person or business is actually insolvent. Individuals or businesses declare bankruptcy under the rules of the federal bankruptcy code, asking for the court either to hold off creditors from adding interest to or collecting interest on old debts during a financial reorganization or to liquidate holdings to pay creditors as fully as possible and forgive any remaining debts.

Insolvent: This describes you if the sum total of all your assets—from your home to investments to valuables—is less than the value of your total debts, so that you would still owe money if you sold everything tomorrow in an attempt to wipe out your debt.

ALLIES

Bankcard Holders of America: 524 Branch Drive, Salem, VA 24153. For $15, will analyze your debt as part of its Debt Zapper program.

Based on how much you can pay each month, the program suggests a plan that will repay your current debts in the least amount of time.

Credit reporting agencies: There are three major credit reporting agencies. When you contact them, you'll need to provide your date of birth, Social Security number, most recent home address, daytime and evening telephone numbers, and verification of your name and address (a copy of a driver's license or utility bill).

- Experian (formerly TRW): P.O. Box 8030, Layton, UT 84041-8030
- Equifax: P.O. Box 740256, Atlanta, GA 30374
- Trans Union: National Consumer Relations Disclosure Center, 760 West Sproul Road, Springfield, PA 19064

Debt Relief Institute: Suite 1010, 611 Pennsylvania Avenue SE, Washington, DC 20003-4303. Offers a debt-relief kit, which includes all the forms necessary to help consumers combine monthly bills "into one convenient and often lower monthly payment." After returning the creditor list to the institute, you will receive a personal debt-reduction proposal. The kit is free, but there is a $5 charge for postage and handling.

National Foundation for Consumer Credit Counseling Services: Call 1-800-388-CCCS for the office nearest you. Will help you beat back your debt. But be aware that most credit counselors are aligned with creditors and can actually function like collection agents, getting a cut of the monies that they convince consumers to repay. That apparent conflict of interest does not demean their services but is something that you should ask about before entering a debt-repayment plan.

Debt Free!: Your Guide to Personal Bankruptcy without Shame, by James P. Caher and John M. Caher (Henry Holt and Company). Explains the bankruptcy process in straightforward, nonlegal language.

Money Troubles: Legal Strategies to Cope with Your Debts, by Robin Leonard (Nolo Press). Contains sample letters to collection agencies, credit-reporting firms, credit issuers, and more and includes worksheets on how to work out a reasonable budget to dig out of debt.

Insuring Yourself Shrewdly

If You Can't Afford to Lose It, Cover It

For most people, insurance is like a leaky roof.

When it's raining, it's too late to fix it.

When it's sunny, it works as well as anyone else's.

And when the time comes to make repairs, it can feel like a chore, best taken care of quickly and then forgotten again.

But if you can't afford to replace your car, home, income, livelihood, or lifestyle, insurance is just as necessary as your roof. And with a little bit of common sense, you can get a terrific security blanket without having the cost go through that roof.

"Most people are sold insurance—told what they need and what coverages they should have—instead of going out and buying it," says Jack Ramirez, president of the National Association of Independent Insurers. "You can buy insurance coverage that gives you just what you need and do it relatively easily without paying more than you have to."

To insure yourself shrewdly, experts agree that the operative phrase to remember is: "Insure only what you can't afford to lose."

For example, most people would want to insure a brand new car against collision damage so that if their investment gets wiped out in an accident, they don't need to pony up $15,000 or more to get a new set of wheels. But when that car is eight or nine years old, its value is much less and replacing it would not be such a financial hardship. That's when cutting collision protection becomes an option.

The same goes for life insurance. Many people need coverage when they are young, but can forgo it in retirement because they no longer need to protect their survivors.

"You become a self-insurer," says Ramirez. "You take the risk that you can replace the car if something happens. And you know your own driving situation and can decide in your own mind how likely you are to have that accident and have to replace the car.

"With every type of insurance, that's the decision to make," Ramirez adds. "Do you want to pay someone for insurance, or can you do it yourself?"

Buying Insurance

Before turning your attention to the types of insurance that you want or need, consider how to buy it. Increasingly, for standard policies like auto coverage or term life insurance, regional or national quote services and direct-to-the-customer insurers offer low-cost alternatives.

Buy Direct or Work through an Agent?

Unlike agents who work for only one company, the quote lines are essentially shopping services. Behind the phone lines are independent insurance agencies representing many companies. They get the same commission as the local agent who comes to your home to talk insurance over the dining room table.

While they have certain economies of scale, that is no guarantee of the best available prices.

No service works with all insurers, so you will want to compare different phone quote lines. In addition, the services sometimes play favorites, either with insurers they like dealing with or with those who offer the juiciest commissions.

As long as you are on the phone, consider insurers who sell their products straight to the public, using direct marketing to cut sales costs and to make the policies cheaper than those offered by agents. This so-called low-load coverage—there is less commission than on a policy sold by an agent—can be cost-effective, but you will have very little contact with the company's representative in the future.

Most telephone services either walk you through a number of questions or have you fill out and return a questionnaire to determine your needs. Some quote services use only insurance agents to answer the phones; others use sales representatives. It pays to ask whether the person that you are dealing with on the phone is a licensed agent so that you can gauge how comfortable you are with his advice.

Not every type of insurance is available from the quote services. And even companies that sell direct to the consumer may not be licensed to sell in your state.

Be sure to compare the results of your phone search with what is available from your local agent. If prices are in the same ballpark, you may prefer the service of your agent, someone that you know personally who can answer your questions instead of a faceless voice on the phone. In addition, part of insuring yourself wisely means managing your coverage carefully in the future, and having an established agent typically makes that process easier. In addition, your local agent may be able to offer a cost break that the phone providers can't. Many insurers offer discounts for customers who have several types of coverage with the firm. Typically, this means buying home owner's and auto insurance from the same firm, but it can extend to life and liability policies as well.

Do You Really Need Life Insurance?

Life insurance is not for everyone. Typically, people need life insurance if they have children or others who depend upon their income for daily living, are the sole income source for a family with significant mortgage debt or with plans to send young children to college, or if their survivors could not pay for the cost of burial.

People without dependents or debt, or whose survivors could get along without the lost income, should skip life insurance, says attorney, financial consultant, and author Stephen Pollan. That includes children, singles, and couples either with no kids or whose children are grown, and retirees with sufficient savings to generate income and pay funeral costs.

As for how much protection to buy, there are several rules of thumb, all too general to really work. That leaves the rule being that there are no short-cut rules.

Experts advise doing a well-reasoned analysis of your family's cash needs and flow over time. Keep in mind what your family would face without you and it's hard to make a poor decision. You aren't likely to skimp if you picture them with a bleak future.

Where's the Value in "Cash Value" Policies?

The next choice comes down to "term versus cash value." Those are types of life insurance, with term being straightforward coverage for a set period of time and cash value being one of several policy types that doubles as an investment.

Term policies typically cost about 10 percent of whole-life and other cash value policies. Unless you pay to lock in premiums, payments rise as you age and, statistically speaking, move closer to death. In later years—if you will still need coverage—those premiums can become prohibitive.

Whole-life policies offer level premiums for a lifetime and build a cash value. The money grows tax-deferred and may be borrowed against. In whole-life policies, the investor typically does not control how the premi-

Got Enough Life Insurance?

Here's a simple way to determine if you have enough life insurance. It is not adjusted for inflation but is designed to give you an idea of how much insurance you need *today*. Working with an agent, you can flesh out this basic number to get a policy that meets your long-term needs.

Money you need to reach your goals

Annual living expenses for your survivors	_____
Number of years they would be without you	× _____
Total anticipated living expenses	= _____
Education expenses/college tuition	_____
Mortgage payoff	_____
Funeral expenses	_____
Other debts to be paid off (list)	_____
	_____
	_____
Miscellaneous needs (list)	_____
	_____
Total money needs	_____

Money you have now to reach your goals

Current investments (include retirement plans, individual retirement accounts, 401(k)s, savings, brokerage and mutual fund accounts, etc.)	_____
Pension—annual pay to your survivors	_____
Number of years they would be without you	× _____
Total pension payout	= _____
Social Security—annual pay to your survivors	_____
Number of years they would be without you	× _____
Total Social Security payout	= _____
Spouse's annual earned income	_____
Years he/she plans to work	× _____
Total spousal income	= _____
Other assets	_____
Less estate taxes, if applicable	_____
Total money available	_____

Subtract the money available from your money needs. The difference is the minimum amount of insurance protection you need. If your current life insurance policy provides less than that, you do not have enough insurance protection for your family. Remember that this is a snapshot of your current needs. Policies are designed to account for inflation and other factors, which is why it is common to be "overinsured" for current needs.

ums are invested. Universal and variable life policies—which have slightly different premium rules—do allow for investment control.

But cash value policies can be complex and hard to compare. Inflated assumptions on investment returns can distort the real value of a policy.

In general, financial advisers suggest buying term insurance and investing the difference. Cash value policies make the most sense for people who need the policy to develop savings discipline or who will need insurance late in life.

The insurance business is competitive and prices change almost daily, so insist upon current quotes.

Covering Your Car

Auto insurance is easier to shop for because policies vary little from one firm to the next. In many states, coverage is heavily regulated, making virtually every policy the same. Still, it pays to call around, including the direct-market insurers as part of the process.

DON'T LOAD UP UNNECESSARILY

You probably can reap the most savings on auto protection by carefully reviewing your needs. "Depending upon your state, there are certain levels of protection that you must have," says Ramirez. "Beyond that, you can do a lot of things to save money."

Raise your deductible. A small fender-bender with $300 in damage is not the same kind of catastrophe as a complete wreck.

Raising your deductible means self-insuring against the small stuff. By moving from the standard $100 or $250 deductible to $500, you can cut premiums in half. Deposit the premium savings in a bank account to cover emergencies and you will have created a self-insurance fund that is more than sufficient to cover future small incidents.

Cut collision and comprehensive coverage on older cars. Collision coverage pays for repairs in the event of an accident, while comprehensive protects you from theft, vandalism, and other events. Together, they make up 30 to 40 percent of the typical premium; most lenders require both before making a car loan. But if the car is five or more years old, trimming or eliminating this protection may make sense, since you could self-insure against replacing a car worth a few thousand dollars, says Pollan. Remember that as the car's resale value falls, so does the need to insure it.

Check out any and all available discounts. Typically, you get price cuts for insuring more than one car with the same company, adding anti-theft devices and safety features like air bags, parking in a garage rather than on the street, taking a state-approved defensive driving course, and more. There are discounts for nonsmokers, good students, and for people who have had their policy with the same company for several years.

You may also be able to get a discount by having monthly insurance premiums automatically deducted from your checking account.

Revisit the policy as your lifestyle changes. Insurers use characteristics and lifestyle to put you in a peer group. Rates are based on the accident history of that group. Any time that you have a major life change, it may pay off in your policy. Young singles, for example, pay more for coverage than married people the same age. A person who stops commuting a long distance to work is in the car less and, hence, becomes a lower risk. And if you quit smoking, see how long you must be smoke-free to earn the non-smoker's discount (which should also be available for your life insurance).

DISCONNECT THOSE BELLS AND WHISTLES

Some policies offer insurance in the event that your car needs towing, which most auto club members probably don't need. Similarly, rental coverage pays for a rental if you have a crash, not if the car needs routine maintenance. If you can carpool, take public transportation, or use a second car to get to work for a few days, save the money.

Some auto policies extend collision coverage to any time that you drive a rental car. Depending upon your credit card, that coverage may be redundant. Even if it isn't, a "nonowner's liability policy" is a low-cost alternative for people who rent cars for 20 or more days per year.

But don't be too hasty in trimming auto premiums, says Pollan. There are two common mistakes worth avoiding.

First, liability coverage protects you from claims brought by others alleging that you caused an accident. A bare-bones policy has low premiums but could leave you naked on liability claims. Stripped-down policies are only suitable for people who own older cars or have little or no assets and should be upgraded as personal holdings grow.

Similarly, uninsured motorist coverage—protection in the event that you have an accident with someone who has insufficient coverage to pay for your damages—is generally not the place to save money. It's another form of liability coverage. If the wrong person bumps you, insufficient protection could leave you paying for everything that medical insurance doesn't cover.

Covering Your Castle

The key words to remember for home owner's insurance are "replacement cost," as that is the standard for buying coverage that is both sufficient and yet not excessive. Coverage that simply repays your outstanding mortgage debt actually is declining in value at the same time that the cost of rebuilding the home is rising.

Similarly, insuring a home for its market value leaves a lot to chance. A large, older home in a neighborhood on the decline might fetch, say,

$100,000 on the open market but could cost $150,000 to rebuild. And if you live in an area where housing prices have soared, you could be overinsuring your property, because the market value of the home includes the actual land, something that's not likely to be wiped out by catastrophe. It might only cost $100,000 to build a home with a market value three times that high, thanks to a popular location.

THE CRUCIAL TERM: REPLACEMENT COST

Replacement value insurance pays whatever it takes to replace your items with something of a like quality and type. "Actual cash value" policies pay the replacement cost minus depreciation.

Think of this in terms of your bed. If you bought a top-quality mattress five years ago, a new replacement would cost a lot more than your used model.

Full replacement cost coverage is only available if you set your limits at 80 percent of the value of the home. You could protect your home more cheaply but probably wouldn't want to.

Barbara Taylor, writing in *How to Get Your Money's Worth in Home and Auto Insurance*, notes the "unexpected and unpleasant consequences" of insuring your home for just half of its replacement cost. If a windstorm knocks two trees through the roof and causes $10,000 damage, the insurer will give you the greater of "a percentage of the total loss, based on the amount of coverage you carry" or "the actual cash value of the roof, which is its replacement value minus depreciation for its age."

The first choice amounts to $5,000, or half of the $10,000 in damages, because your policy covers just half of the home's replacement cost. The second option will depend upon the age and life expectancy of the roof, but figure that you will wind up in a severe hole—especially if you have an older roof nearing the age when it needs to be replaced.

FIND YOUR COMFORT LEVEL

The more that you have in the way of possessions, the more comprehensive a home owner's policy you will need. The most simple policies cover the house and its contents against dangers like lightning, vandalism, fire, and felled trees. The next coverage level adds specific risks, such as freezing pipes, power surges, and ice buildup on the roof. The most advanced home owner's policies protect you against virtually everything but earthquake, flood, and nuclear war—although you can get coverage for those, too, if you believe it necessary.

Flooding is actually the most common home disaster in the United States and yet one of the least insured. One of three flood-insurance claims comes from outside of areas typically considered "flood-prone," so be sure to ask an agent about the flooding experience in your community.

Typically, your belongings are covered for up to 50 percent of the value of the house, but have limits on the total value allowed for jewelry, collectibles, and art. A "personal articles floater" will provide the extra coverage necessary to replace those goods.

Renter's insurance gives the same kind of personal property protection as a home owner's policy, typically with the same limitations. Coverage makes sense for any renter who could not afford to replace his belongings.

There are riders for almost everything, so check with your agent if you have special circumstances. A freezerful of meat, for instance, might require "refrigerated products coverage," a cheap add-on that protects food in a way that freezer wrap can't.

To save on your home owner's policy, here are more things to consider.

Raise the deductible. It works the same way as with auto insurance. The standard deductible for a home owner's policy offering $100,000 to $250,000 of coverage is $250. Raise it to $500 and you can expect to cut your premiums by 5 to 10 percent. Hike it to $1,000 and the premiums will fall by 15 percent.

Install protective devices. Just as car alarms and air bags cut auto premiums, so do smoke detectors, sprinkler systems, and burglar alarms. There may also be discounts if your home—or new additions—are made of fire-resistant materials.

Quit smoking. Many insurers offer discounts if no one in the family smokes.

Retire. Since retirees as a group have more time to maintain their home and spend a greater portion of the day at home than their working contemporaries—which makes it statistically more likely that they will spot a fire early—some insurers drop rates for older customers.

And just as with your auto insurance, find out if there are discounts for having more than one line of insurance with the same company as well as a discount for being a longtime customer.

Other Coverage

Insurance, in all of its forms, can be confusing. With every policy offering, ask "Do I need this protection?" and "Is this cost reasonable, given the likelihood that I will need it?" This way you can eliminate a lot of the muddle that makes people think of insurance shopping as just another chore.

GOOD BETS FOR REDUCING YOUR RISK

Here's a look at other kinds of insurance that experts say are worth considering.

Umbrella coverage. If you have both car and home owner's insurance, adding an umbrella policy ups your liability protection more effectively than raising the limits of your existing coverage. This does not mean going with stripped-down auto and home policies—which would raise the price on umbrella coverage or make it impossible to get altogether. Rather, it implies that there is a balance point where umbrella makes sense. People with high net worths, valuable holdings, or high-profile jobs—wherever someone might think that there are deep pockets to take aim at—are likely to want the safety of an umbrella policy.

Disability insurance. This makes sense for people who can't afford to be without a paycheck for any length of time. People between the ages of 35 and 65 are more likely to be disabled than to die, so a disability policy functions like paycheck replacement coverage.

Typically, disability coverage pays 60 to 70 percent of your pre-injury salary. The policies can be written to apply for the rest of your life but are cheaper if they are for a finite term. Most people do not need to carry disability coverage into retirement.

Before buying a policy, find out first what the terms are of any disability coverage offered by your employer. Allowing more time between injury and when you start taking benefits cuts your premiums, so let employer-sponsored coverage do its job and then pick up where it leaves off.

Long-term care insurance. This type does not draw a consensus from the industry. The argument against it is that two out of three people over age 65 never enter a nursing home, or they stay in one for less than three months. Just one in four people who stay in a home is there for more than a year. Still, if you have a family history of debilitating diseases, have no family members to care for you at home, or have less than $1 million in assets—or if you want to protect your assets for your heirs—a long-term care policy is worth considering.

Long-term care premiums typically remain level, but the difference between buying when you are 60 and 70 is substantial. These policies generally are best purchased by someone between age 55 and 60—and if you already have a condition such as the early signs of Alzheimer's, you can probably forget about getting coverage altogether.

This is one area where whole-life insurance might bail you out, as you can borrow from the cash value of the policy to pay for long-term care. If you are terminally ill and, for obvious reasons, can't get long-term care coverage, many whole-life policies allow you to receive benefits in advance.

As with disability policies, you can cut long-term care premiums by extending the period between the need for coverage (when care starts) and when insurance kicks in. And if you have no interest in home health care—say that you live far from relatives who could help you in the home—consider coverage that pays only if you check into a nursing home. It will be about one-third cheaper.

WITH SOME COVERAGE, JUST SAY NO

Avoid paying for protection that you simply don't need.

Flight insurance. This is one of the most expensive and least valuable forms of coverage for anyone who pays for life insurance. Because it is in effect for just a few hours, it is among the most costly coverage available. And because of the big settlements that airlines offer crash victims and their families, most experts consider it unnecessary regardless of your other coverage.

Accidental death coverage. This is another expensive, unnecessary form of insurance. Accidents account for just 4 percent of deaths and are almost always covered in ordinary life insurance policies. If someone is offering specific protection against disease—cancer, for instance—or crime (yes, there are policies that protect you from muggings), check out your life policy first and you will likely find that you are covered.

Sports-injury protection. While your school district or sports club may offer you coverage, it typically kicks in only after your health care has been exhausted. If you have a decent health plan at work, neither you nor your family will need this coverage.

Credit card insurance. This offers to protect you in case your cards are misplaced or stolen. By law, reporting the lost cards promptly limits your liability to a maximum of $50 per card anyway. That limit plus homeowner's coverage—which protects against personal property loss away from the home—should suffice.

Mortgage insurance. Your bank may require this when you purchase a home, but that usually is waived once your home equity equals 20 percent of the home's value. Once you hit that bogey, try to replace mortgage insurance with a cheaper term life policy offering more coverage and greater flexibility.

BOTTOM LINE

When it comes to insurance, be an assertive buyer and take the time to shop around and ask questions. That's the best way to understand how policies work and to make sure that you pay only for what you need.

WORDS TO THE WISE

Term life insurance: Written to offer protection for a specific period of time. Requires the policyholder to pay only for coverage against the event of death. Premiums tend to rise each time that the policy is renewed, because the holder has aged and is statistically more likely to die. Still, policies can be sold with terms of 20 years or more, with level premiums throughout. Term life insurance policies build no cash value but offer a significant savings in premiums.

Whole-life insurance: Builds investment value and offers lifetime level premiums unless the policy is canceled or lapses. The policy's cash value grows tax-deferred and may be borrowed against. The holder typically has no input as to how premiums are invested.

ALLIES

How to Get Your Money's Worth in Home and Auto Insurance, by Barbara Taylor (McGraw-Hill). A comprehensive shopper's guide. It was sponsored by the Insurance Information Institute.

Insurance News Network: If you have a computer and want to check out the financial strength of your insurer, look up the Insurance News Network's site on the World Wide Web. It provides instant access to Standard & Poor's and Duff & Phelps financial strength ratings of insurance companies.

Chapter 20

Socking It Away

To Make Your Greenbacks Grow, Plant Them in the Right Place

Money spoils.

Left inactive in a safe place, like your mattress, it actually erodes over time.

It's not the paper that's the problem—that is good for as long as bankers can recognize the currency and exchange new for old. It's the value of the money that, thanks to inflation, loses buying power over time.

As a result, money is a perishable good.

The Saving Attitude

Think of it in terms of a food like nuts. Kept in a safe place, nuts will be edible for a long time. But if you had to find your own food and could not gather enough for a lifetime—accounting for the fact that an increasing amount of what you have gathered will go bad the longer that you let it sit—you would have to plant some. In the right kind of soil, your nuts yield more, eventually providing sustenance for a lifetime.

So it is with money. Unless you can earn so much of it that you could never spend it all regardless of what inflation does to buying power, you have to make your dollars grow.

When it comes to safely growing your money, however, you have little choice but to dive into highly sophisticated "systems"—the world of stock exchanges, mutual funds, brokerages, and banks. This is not a bad thing. The U.S. investment system, thanks to tight policing by the government and the participants themselves, is safe, reliable, and, in many important ways, predictable. It is also extremely inflexible in how it operates. You might be able to get a department store to personalize its care for you, but don't expect the New York Stock Exchange to bend the rules for how you buy stock with it.

Sure, you could try to beat the system by mastering it—becoming an aggressive player, trading, calculating, timing your ins and outs with a stopwatch. But becoming a market player has huge drawbacks: It's an extremely risky way to manage your money, to start. It's also expensive, since all those trades cost money. And it's enormously time-consuming, since it takes tons of reading and study.

In fact, almost every bit of research shows that a patient, calm, long-term approach to investing is often the most lucrative over time. Put your money in smart places and let it grow and, in time, it almost always does.

For average people, then, the best way to beat the system is to look for low-cost ways to invest regularly and to let time and the market do the rest. This means understanding the various ways of buying into an investment and understanding the various ways that those investments benefit you.

In investing, as in farming, you reap what you sow. If you plant seeds early and the conditions are right, you will have a bumper crop; but if you procrastinate, you can miss much of the growing season and wind up hungry.

To get the most growth and the fewest effects of spoilage from your money, you will need a mix of stocks, bonds and mutual funds. Here is what to consider as you sow your financial seeds.

EVERY LITTLE BIT HELPS—IF YOU'RE REGULAR

"What I hear from people most often is 'I can't afford to save,' " says Ross Levin, president of the Minneapolis-based Accredited Investors and former president of the International Association for Financial Planning. "They have it backward. They can't afford *not* to save, because it only gets tougher to reach your goals if you wait to get started on them."

Say that you saved $1 every day—which certainly doesn't seem prohibitive, no matter how hard you think it is to "save"—and invested your $365 bounty at the end of each year. Assuming that you get the average long-term return of the stock market—the round number used by most experts is a 10 percent annualized average return—and reinvest your dividends, your $1 per day would be worth $69,632 after 30 years and would grow to $195,524 after 40 years.

So while it is helpful to be socking away big chunks of money, the important thing is that you set aside something, no matter how small, at all times. The best chance to become measurably wealthy, notes Ted Miller, editor of *Kiplinger's Personal Finance Magazine*, is by "developing the habit of adding something to the pot on a regular basis and putting it where it can do the most for you."

COMPOUND INTEREST: A POWERFUL ALLY

The big deal about "saving now" revolves around what experts call the time value of money. That's another way of saying compound interest.

Small Adjustments Mean Big Yearly Savings

There are several ways to squeeze more savings from your income, but they boil down to this: Spend less.

Here are examples of a few things that you could do to save hundreds or thousands of dollars a year.

- Cut out the soda at lunch, drinking water instead and conservatively saving 60 cents per workday. Over a year, that saves about $150.
- Likewise, brew your own coffee. Allowing for your own costs, you should still save at least 60 cents per workday, good for another $150.
- Give up the magazine subscriptions. Your library card is free—or requires a small donation—but the five subscriptions at $20 a pop are costing you $100 a year.
- Watch commercial television. Premium movie channels can add $100 to $150 apiece to your cable television bill, while a two-video-per-week habit at $2 per movie is a $200 annual expenditure.
- Brown-bag your lunches. If you pay $4 for a deli lunch per workday, you're spending roughly $1,000 per year. Smart shopping can cut that in half.

"It becomes easier to start saving when you are conscious of what you are spending and what you have to show for your money," says Gerri Detweiler, policy director of the National Council of Individual Investors, based in Washington, D.C., and author of *The Ultimate Credit Handbook*. "You don't have to save in big lumps. You simply have to be looking at what you can do to regularly set aside something and let it work for you.

"What people don't realize—because they don't look at the ways in which they can save by cutting frivolous spending and generating real returns for that money—is that saving is almost always possible. What can be impossible is catching up if you let the years slip by."

Compounding creates wealth by racking up current interest on top of previous interest, and its power is most clearly seen over long time periods. For example, if you gave a gift of $2,500 to celebrate the birth of a newborn, and that money earned 10 percent compounded annually, it would be worth more than $1.2 million when the child reached retirement age.

But compounding also highlights the need to shop around for different vehicles for your money. Say that two investors each have $25,000 to meet identical monetary goals with a 20-year time horizon. One picks an investment that compounds at 6 percent monthly, while the other does a point better and gets 7 percent. On paper, using simple interest, that difference would appear to equal $5,000—1 percent of $25,000 ($250) times 20 years.

But in reality, at the end of 20 years, the first investor has $82,755; the second has $100,968. The reason for the $18,213 difference—instead of the $5,000 simple-interest projection—is that with compounding, you earn interest on the entire pot of money, not just the *initial* investment. Previous earnings, in other words, rack up even more earnings in the future.

The big swing in value between those two investors underscores the need to make savvy financial decisions. But simply saving—gathering your proverbial acorns—is not enough. You must use the money you save wisely, leaving some of it as "savings"—best defined as ready cash for emergencies and other current needs—and making the rest "investments," which is where you make your money grow.

As a result, it is possible to save longer than necessary, beyond the level of your current cash needs. At that point, you should be investing.

Investing: Spreading It Around

When it comes to investing your hard-earned savings, there are four basic options: money market or bank accounts, stocks, bonds, and mutual funds. The last option, as already noted, may be ultra-safe, but it returns so little money on a comparative basis that it is really for small contingency funds rather than the investment portion of your holdings.

Bank investments require very little work on the investor's part. In exchange, they have almost no risk.

WITH STOCKS AND BONDS, MEASURE THE RISK

Stocks, on the other hand, can be high-maintenance and high-volatility investments. When buying stock, you buy a piece of the company. Your profits are based on the performance of the company. But unless you can buy into a number of companies, you essentially are an eggs-in-one-basket investor, with most of your hopes and dreams riding on the fortunes of no more than a few companies.

The workload in buying individual bonds varies depending upon what kind of security you want to purchase. So, too, does the risk level.

Bonds are debt instruments, meaning that you loan your money out, with the bond representing the promissory note showing how and when you will be repaid and at what rate of interest.

The risk is that the borrower never repays you at all or does it at a rate that is below what you could earn if the money wasn't tied up in bonds.

Bonds vary from the ultra-safe—such as savings bonds or U.S. Treasury bonds that are backed by the full faith and credit of the government—to junk bonds, which are securities where an independent rating agency fears that the money might never be repaid. Junk bonds are referred to as high-yield bonds because the borrower's questionable credit translates into accepting a deal providing hefty interest payments.

Queasy? Try the Treasury

Treasury securities are considered almost risk-free investing. The money is backed by the full faith and credit of the U.S. government, which makes it the safest form of financial instrument. (Your principal is not at risk, although you do face inflationary risk, where a rising cost of living erodes the buying power of your fixed-interest-rate notes.)

Treasuries are also one of the least expensive forms of investing.

Treasury securities can be purchased directly from the Federal Reserve Bank through a program called Treasury Direct. Unlike mutual funds, where investors pay ongoing management fees or face sales charges, there are no significant costs associated with purchasing Treasury securities straight from the government. (If your account exceeds $100,000, there will be a $25 annual maintenance fee, still less than you would pay if you purchased the bonds through an intermediary.)

Treasury bills are short-term securities, maturing in 1 year or less, issued in minimum denominations of $10,000, with $5,000 increments above that. Treasury notes, meanwhile, are intermediate securities in amounts from $1,000 to over $1 million, maturing in 1 to 10 years. Last, Treasury bonds are long-term debt instruments, maturing in 10 years or more, issued in amounts of $1,000.

You can participate in Treasury Direct through the nearest branch of the Federal Reserve Bank, which should be listed in your telephone book. If not, you can send for information on the Treasury Direct program by writing to the Bureau of Public Debt, Capital Area Servicing Center, Washington, DC 20239-0001.

What most investors are looking for from bonds is a steady source of income—in the form of interest payments on the money being loaned out—at a reasonable return that outpaces inflation.

MUTUAL FUNDS: STRENGTH IN NUMBERS

By comparison to individual stocks or bonds, mutual funds are like investing in a ready-made portfolio, complete with a professional manager.

A mutual fund is an investment pool, allowing many people to bring their money together, paying an accomplished money manager and achieving the kind of diversification—and, hopefully, performance—that they most likely could not afford individually. Funds invest your money in anywhere from a few dozen to several thousand securities. The price of your shares in the fund is based on the underlying value of the stocks and bonds that the fund holds.

While funds are diversified investment portfolios, they do not work on a one-size-fits-all basis. Instead, the idea is to construct a portfolio using different fund types, each concentrating on a specific investment arena.

For example, you would invest in a small-company growth fund—which purchases high-risk, fast-growth stocks—with the portion of your money that you designate as aggressive and would select a bond fund for the more tame, steady-income-stream portion of your holdings.

"There are mutual funds that specialize in pretty much everything that you could want to have in your portfolio," says Michelle A. Smith, managing director of the Mutual Fund Education Alliance in Kansas City, Missouri. "If you can accomplish it with individual stocks and bonds, you can do it with mutual funds but at a lower cost, in less time, with more diversification, and, as a result, less risk."

For those reasons, most people have made mutual funds their investment vehicle of choice.

How—And When—To Diversify

Still, the long-term return of your portfolio depends more on the way that you divvy up your money between funds—your asset allocation strategy—than on the individual funds that you pick.

With that in mind, Stephen Pollan, an attorney, financial consultant, and author, offers this guidance for building an investment portfolio.

Start off steady. As you start out—with no more than $5,000 to invest—you will be limited in the number of funds that you can buy. That increases the temptation to purchase one hell-bent-for-leather aggressive-growth type of fund, but experts suggest starting out with a broad-based fund to give you a solid footing and steady, long-term performance. Chances are that your best choices for that will be either an index fund that tries to closely follow the performance of the stock market or a less aggressive balanced fund that splits its portfolio between stocks and bonds.

Diversify at the right time. Once you have about $10,000, you may want to split your money further, separating the stock and bond portions of your money so that you can control the percentage of your holdings allocated to each. With the core funds in place, you can start to add to your holdings with more specialized funds.

As you grow, refine your strategy. By the time that you have $20,000, you should own four to six mutual funds, each dedicated to a different type of asset. This is where you start to develop an investment strategy tailored to your goals and risk tolerances. If you are an aggressive investor, your portfolio will be weighted toward a small-company growth fund and a fund made up of midsize company or "mid-cap" stocks. If you are more income-oriented, you are more likely to focus on a municipal bond fund to your core stock-and-bond fund holdings.

Put a lid on it. Beyond $20,000 your holdings will continue to expand. While there is no one answer for how many funds to own, most experts suggest keeping things simple and limiting your holdings to no more than 10 funds.

In this way, you can also avoid duplication, which can reduce the efficiency of your portfolio. If you have more than two funds of the same type, you start to lose your potential for above-average performance within that category of assets.

Consider individual stocks. Also beyond $20,000 you may decide to purchase some individual stocks and bonds to round out your portfolio. Since stocks tend to be more volatile than funds, advisers suggest that individual issues—including shares in your employer's company—should not be allowed to exceed 20 percent of your stock market holdings.

The same goes for sector funds, which are mutual funds that invest only in companies within the same industry. Sector funds—which could be limited to technology, banking, utility, or other industry groups—are less diversified than other funds and generally should account for no more than 20 percent of the value of a portfolio.

Smart Saving: Investor Tactics

Most people need to invest to meet several goals, with the standard big-ticket items being their own retirement and the college education of their children.

That being the case, they must invest to meet each goal, a process that almost always starts at work with employee-benefit savings plans. Where previous generations had pension programs that took care of them for life, today's workers must contribute to their own retirement savings. Typically, this is done through a 401(k) plan.

THE 401(K): EASY AND POWERFUL

Named for the section of the tax code that allows it, the 401(k) allows workers to contribute money to an assortment of funds and lets the money grow tax-deferred. The money comes directly out of your paycheck, untaxed, and works for you until it is withdrawn. The idea is that a retiree has no continuing income and will pay taxes at a lower rate when the time comes to pull the money from the retirement plan.

While 401(k) plans are common, there are similar concepts for government agencies (457 plans), nonprofit agencies (403(b) programs), small companies (SIMPLE plans), and people who are self-employed.

There are several benefits to contributing to these plans, starting with the tax benefits. Essentially, a 401(k) or similar plan allows you to leverage your paycheck. Not only does it let you save without having taxes taken out but also the amount that you set aside cuts your current taxable income as well. That's a complicated way of saying that the amount that you set aside will actually be worth more than what comes out of your take-home pay each week. Consider it an IRS subsidy to make you want to invest.

The second big benefit of many employee savings plans is the "employer match," where the company contributes an amount based on how much you kick in. Some companies pay 25 cents for every dollar, others match you dollar-for-dollar up to a certain percentage of your income.

This is "free money," a guaranteed return on your investment. And because it, too, is paid on a tax-deferred basis, this little bonus is worth more to you than if the cash were given to you directly.

INVEST AUTOMATICALLY

Direct-deposit programs available from most employers allow money from your paycheck to be directed in many ways, including to banks and mutual funds.

In addition, many mutual funds have automatic monthly purchase plans that take a set amount of money from your bank account on a monthly basis. This regular investment forces you to "dollar-cost average," a winning investment technique that can boost long-term gains and, just as important, removes the emotions that might drive you out of the market during market gyrations.

Another benefit to signing up for automatic monthly investments is that most fund groups waive minimum initial investment requirements for investors who agree to make regular investments. This makes any fund—even some with $25,000 or more initial investments—accessible. Because the waivers are not universal, call a fund to see whether it offers this option.

Another way to make your money grow painlessly is by automatically reinvesting dividends and capital gains.

This last option is also available with individual stocks that have a dividend reinvestment program (DRIP). Most firms offering DRIPs reinvest your dividends for free, which makes for a savings on commission that, in turn, helps you accumulate money faster. While it's not worth picking a stock simply for the availability of the DRIP, it's an appealing option that is available on about 1,000 stocks.

CUT OUT THE MIDDLEMAN

Another appealing option is buying stocks and mutual funds without a broker on what is called a no-load basis. Typically, investors pay loads, or sales charges, as a way of paying for the advice of a broker or financial adviser. If you do not need that help and feel confident that you can pick a fund, a no-load fund puts all your money to work immediately instead of giving some of it to the intermediary.

Look for no-load stocks. Most stocks require the use of a broker, although an increasing number are allowing direct purchase, effectively functioning as no-load stocks. That universe is limited to about 100 companies

It Figures

Here's Proof:
Investing Regularly Pays Off

Dollar-cost averaging is an investment system designed to beat the system by playing it regularly. It involves investing money—usually the same amount—at regular intervals in order to reduce the overall cost per share of an investment.

Say, for example, that you are interested putting $100 a month into a mutual fund currently selling for $10 per share. You make your initial investment and buy 10 shares. A month later, the stock has dropped to $8 per share, and your $100 buys 12½ shares. Another month passes, and the price rebounds to $8.33 per share, meaning that your $100 buys another 12 shares. And the fourth month, the price jumps to $11.11 per share so that you buy 9 shares.

After four months, you have invested $400 to buy 43½ shares, for an average share price of $9.19. Your profit after the four months stands at $85.

Had you simply invested the money in a lump sum at $10 per share, you would have 40 shares, and your paper profit would be just $40 and change.

If prices rise consistently—and you obviously must believe that the investment is a long-term winner—you buy in at regular intervals, buying more during the rare down periods and profiting throughout.

Dollar-cost averaging allows you to buy more of an investment when the price is down and less when prices rise, says Stephen Pollan, an attorney, financial consultant, and author. In addition, many mutual funds waive their minimum initial investment for people who have a set amount automatically withdrawn from their checking accounts and put into the fund each month. Thus, dollar-cost averaging allows you to have access to more and better mutual funds, to save money on a regular basis and to stick with a disciplined investment approach that many experts believe is the key to long-term investing success.

but is growing quickly. As with DRIPs, a direct-purchase plan should not be the sole reason to buy a stock.

"You can set up an impressive portfolio of stocks without paying any commissions at all or by paying a minimal amount to buy your first shares and then enter the company's DRIP," says Charles Carlson, editor of both *DRIP Investor* and *The No-Load Stock Insider* newsletters. "The big thing that you need is to feel comfortable picking stocks on your own."

Go for a discount. If you aren't comfortable making your own stock buys, you will need a stockbroker. But even that has its money-saving options. If you need advice, then the logical choice is a full-service broker. If you pick stocks on your own and simply need a company to process the trades, then examine the discount or deep-discount brokerage houses, where the savings on large trades can be substantial. (On small trades, however, there will be times when a full-service broker is less expensive than the discounters. It has to do with the way that fees are charged but applies to trades of up to roughly $1,500.) Get price comparisons and find out what level of service each type of firm offers to get the best deal.

Consider your low-cost bond options. Brokerage firms are also the route to pursue for individual bonds, with two notable exceptions. The Payroll Savings Plan is a paycheck deduction to purchase U.S. Savings Bonds, government bonds that do not pay interest until reaching maturity. It is offered by some employers. If yours does not have it, you can buy savings bonds at most financial institutions.

U.S. Treasury bonds can be purchased direct from the Federal Reserve Bank, a program that eliminates all sales costs on the safest bonds of all. (Government bonds are backed by the full faith and credit of Uncle Sam and are considered risk-free by most money-management experts.)

Picking Investments

Look at how long this chapter has been before it got to the actual investments themselves. That's because the process of selecting investments is more about saving, setting and meeting goals, and being money-savvy than it is about buying Stock A or Fund B.

In fact, the rules for picking investments have less to do with specific selection than with making sure that you are on track to meet your goals.

"The stock market doesn't know when you plan to retire or when your next tuition payment is due," says Don Phillips, president of Morningstar, the Chicago firm that is considered the leading monitor of the mutual fund industry. "If you only strive to beat the market or if you only try to pick the hottest funds, you are missing the point. The idea is to develop a strategy that meets your goals. If you wind up with more than enough, that's a bonus. But don't wind up with less because you spent all of your time trying to pick only the so-called best investments.

"The investments that do the best today probably won't do that well tomorrow, so pick something that does well today and that has reasonable expectations for tomorrow. That's a lot easier to find, and it's a lot easier to be satisfied with your selections," says Phillips.

FIVE RULES FOR SAVVY SELECTION

That being the case, here are the rules to follow to pick investments that will help you reach your goals.

Buy investments that you understand. "If it takes 10 minutes to explain it to you, chances are that you have wasted 9 minutes," says Kurt Brouwer, a partner in the San Francisco investment advisory Brouwer and Janachowski. "If you don't understand something yourself, get help from someone who does. And if you don't understand the adviser, change to someone else. This isn't brain surgery. Investing in something that you can't explain to your mother or your kids is asking to make a mistake."

Buy and hold. The ideal investment strategy is explained in four words: "Buy low, sell high."

All investments go through cycles and periods when they are down. Market timing is the art of trying to be on the sidelines when the market tanks, and in the game only when things are on the rise. For the average investor, it is a fruitless pursuit.

Most market timers fall short of their mark. Most mutual funds run by professional timers, for example, offer performance that is below average for their peers. And those are guys who earn their living trying to do this stuff.

By comparison, the average long-term return of the stock market is roughly 10 percent; and if you stick with a sound investment and let your

Danger Signals

Resist the Rush to Invest

Every investment sounds good, especially if you haven't been putting your money away. But just because you haven't started is no reason to rush into things.

If a stockbroker or adviser is pushing you to make a decision with which you are not comfortable, back away. And if someone wants to send a courier by to get your money—rather than having you mail a check—hang up the phone and call the authorities. There is no investment that can't afford to wait another day, and anyone unwilling to use the postal system is probably afraid of committing mail fraud.

It Figures

How Quickly Will My Investment Double?

The Rule of 72 is a rough measure of how quickly investments double. Divide 72 by the rate of return on your money, and the answer is how many years it will take to double your money, assuming a constant rate of return.

Because the rule functions based on a constant return, rather than an average return, it is most accurate when used on bank accounts and fixed-income instruments where rates do not fluctuate. For stock and mutual fund investments, its accuracy is best with stable holdings, rather than volatile securities where values and growth rates tend to fluctuate wildly. In all cases, the actual speed for doubling an investment varies depending upon the method of compounding.

And if you want to see how quickly your money will triple, use the Rule of 115. It functions in exactly the same fashion, but with 115 rather than 72.

---

strategy work, you should be able to see solid gains that smooth out the rough periods, says Pollan.

Even if you are capable of figuring out when to get out of the market, you have to have the savvy to know when to get back in. Missing the uptick means being on the sidelines during the sunny periods when you should be making hay.

Over the short term, timing can produce better returns; but through years and many market cycles, buy-and-hold is a better bet.

Shoot for consistency, not the moon. Last year's hot fund may get the deep freeze this year. In fact, any fund that is capable of being atop the chart is equally capable of finishing dead last, thanks to some of the riskier strategies that many chart-busting funds use to edge their peers.

That being the case, look for investments with a smoother ride, those that regularly outpace peer funds without necessarily shooting off the charts, suggests Pollan.

Keep an eye on your progress. Many people want "widow-and-orphan stocks," investments that are supposed to take care of you for a lifetime. But the original stocks that met those criteria were railroad companies, most of which wound up merged or out of business after the Great Depression.

Every investment requires monitoring, not only to see whether its performance measures up but also to see how well it fits in with your portfolio.

One key to help maintain your perspective on investments is to write down the reasons why you bought something and to revisit them annually. Key factors include not only performance but also whether you believe in a market sector or needed a low-minimum investment, for example.

You can then consider whether those factors or your needs have changed. And ask yourself what most experts believe is a crucial question: "Would I buy this again today?" If the answer is no, then it may be time to make a change.

Adjust to your changing goals. When you are young, there is more time to recover from the fallout of high-risk investments. As you near retirement—or the purchase of a home or other big-ticket item—you may not be able to rebound.

Periodically readjusting your investments—changing your asset allocation to reflect the progress that you have made or to account for different needs or goals—is essential to having a sufficient nest egg.

Remember, too, that if one investment does very well, your portfolio tilts in the direction of that issue. Even if none of your goals change, you may need to rebalance your portfolio to stay within your preferred asset allocation.

"Don't make things more complicated than they need to be," says Brouwer. "Save it, invest it, manage it, all with an eye toward what you realistically want the future to hold, and there is no reason why you can't achieve your goals."

Bottom Line

Saving and investing aren't hard if you take advantage of the ways that you can maximize your money and then develop a strategy for reaching your goals.

Words to the Wise

Compounding: Creating wealth by racking up current interest on top of previous interest. Its power is most clearly seen over long time periods.

401(k): Savings plan that allows workers to contribute money to an assortment of funds and lets the money grow tax-deferred. The money comes directly out of the paycheck, untaxed.

Mutual fund: An investment pool that allows many people to bring their money together and pay an accomplished money manager to achieve the kind of diversification and performance that they could not afford individually.

No-load: A "load" is the broker's sales charge for handling the purchase of a stock or fund. For the confident, no-load purchases eliminate the middleman.

ALLIES

Mutual Fund Education Alliance: Department 0148, P.O. Box 419263, Kansas City, MO 64193-0148. Produces "The Mutual Fund Investor's Kit," which includes a plain-English explainer on investing in funds, as well as "The Investor's Guide to Low-Cost Mutual Funds," enough statistical data to help you sort through the world of no-load funds.

A Commonsense Guide to Mutual Funds, by Mary Rowland (Bloomberg Press).

DRIP Investor: Monthly newsletter that tracks dividend reinvestment plans and offers model stock portfolios. Write to NorthStar Financial, Inc., 7412 Calumet Avenue, Suite 200, Hammond, IN 46324-2692. One sample issue free.

The No-Load Stock Insider: Bimonthly newsletter that covers which companies are offering their shares direct to the public. Write to NorthStar Financial, Inc., 7412 Calumet Avenue, Suite 200, Hammond, IN 46324-2692. One sample issue free.

Treasury Direct Public Information: Bureau of the Public Debt, Capital Area Servicing Center, Washington, DC 20239-0001. For information on using the Treasury Direct program to buy government securities straight from the Federal Reserve or to order "Information about Marketable Treasury Securities," a pamphlet that offers information on government bonds.

Part 8

TAXES

Trimming Your Taxes

Exercise Your Right to the Write-Offs

"Nobody owes any public duty to pay more than the law demands."
—Federal Judge Learned Hand, 1947

There it is: confirmation—from the federal bench, no less—that paying the government the least that you can legitimately pay doesn't mean that you're unpatriotic or an evil miser. So go to it: Beat the formidable tax system by prying out every applicable deduction the IRS doubtlessly hopes lies buried in its tax code. Then you can turn that five-pound, 7,000-page paperback into a reliable doorstop.

Tax Planning 101

Here's what tax-trimming experts say that you need to know about keeping all the cash that you legally can in your own pocket and not Uncle Sam's.

First of all, claim each and every exemption that you are due. Each one that you took in 1996, for instance, resulted in a write-off of $2,550.

An exemption is a fixed amount that the IRS allows you to deduct for yourself, your spouse, or a dependent claimed on your tax return. Who is a dependent? You can probably bet that a minor child who lives in your home qualifies, but there are strict rules about the amount of support that you must contribute before you can claim someone else (say, a nanny, an adult child, or a parent) as a dependent. Check the rules under "Exemptions" in the instructions with your tax return.

TO ITEMIZE OR NOT TO ITEMIZE?

Itemized deductions are those that taxpayers report on Schedule A: medical expenses, state and local income taxes, real estate taxes, mortgage and investment interest expenses, charitable contributions, and "miscellaneous itemized deductions." Should you comb your records for every deduction that you can find, or is it better to take the "standard deduction"—a flat amount that every taxpayer can subtract from his total income, thereby reducing his tax bite?

In 1996, the standard deduction for a single person under the age of 65 was $4,000; for a married person, $6,700. It makes sense to itemize only if your allowable expenses add up to more than the standard deduction.

If your deductions regularly fail to exceed the standard deduction by a small amount, take a short financial leap into the future. Pay January's tax, mortgage, or medical bills, or make additional charitable contributions, before the tax year ends. If those payments hike your expenses and contributions above the standard deduction, your foresight will save you tax dollars.

Jump the gun. Fork over state and local income taxes early. "If you pay these taxes before the end of the year, you'll give yourself one of the biggest deductions that a middle-income taxpayer usually gets," says Martin Geller, head of the New York City accounting firm Martin Geller CPA P.C.

So, before year-end, make a projection of your state tax liability by using a commercial software package or by filling in income and expense estimates on your state tax return and computing your projected tax due. If you pay any balance of state tax due before year-end, you can deduct it on your federal tax return.

Warning: You're an exception to this rule if you're one of those unlucky folks who is subject to the federal Alternative Minimum Tax (AMT), a separate tax calculation generally applied to high-income taxpayers. If you're subject to the AMT, payment of your state tax bill before year-end probably won't translate into a write-off. Those who must pay this tax would be prudent to seek the advice of a certified public accountant (CPA).

Subtract real estate and personal property taxes. Save the stubs sent by the state or local government as proof that you've paid taxes on your real estate or on the value of personal property like a boat or a car. You can deduct these taxes on your federal return.

Scrutinize your mortgage interest statement. Form 1098, the statement that your bank sends each year detailing the mortgage interest that you've paid, may not reflect all the mortgage interest that you've paid in a taxable year. For instance, if your payment is due at the beginning of each month and you made your January payment in late December, Form 1098 probably won't show that December payment. However, you are entitled to deduct it: Simply attach a statement to your return showing why your deduction is greater than the amount shown on Form 1098.

Meld several debts into one loan. "Consolidating your credit card debts into a home equity loan gives you two advantages: You'll probably get a lower interest rate, and you can deduct the interest on your federal return," advises Geller. Why? The IRS classifies the interest on credit card debt as personal interest. But the interest on up to $100,000 of a home equity loan—

Medical Expenses: The 7.5 Percent Problem

The tax code allows you to deduct medical expenses that have not been reimbursed by insurance. However, you can deduct only the amount that exceeds 7.5 percent of your adjusted gross income (your gross income minus certain deductions, like contributions to an individual retirement account).

Say that your adjusted gross income is $50,000 a year. Your medical expenses must exceed $3,750 before you get to write them off as a deduction—and you may write off only the amount over $3,750.

The trick here is to bunch enough expenses together in one year to break the 7.5 percent threshold. Let's say that it's December and you have outstanding medical bills. It may be a good idea to pay them before year-end. You also might want to make arrangements to pay some or all of your January medical expenses in advance. Some people even consider moving up their annual checkups or elective surgery to meet their tax needs.

The IRS classifies bills from doctors, dentists, and hospitals, and bills for prescription drugs, as medical expenses, says Stephen Pollan, an attorney, financial consultant, and author. But you may also be able to deduct travel to and from your doctor and, possibly, the cost of improvements to your home if they are primarily for medical reasons. (For example, widening doorways or installing ramps to accommodate a wheelchair.)

In some circumstances, the fees of acupuncturists, podiatrists, chiropractors, and physical therapists are deductible. A nice laundry list of what is and isn't deductible is available in IRS Publication 17, "Your Federal Income Tax."

Beyond the medical expenses incurred by you, your spouse, and your dependents, you can also deduct medical expenses that you contribute for someone who earns more than the personal-exemption amount ($2,550 in 1996) but would otherwise qualify as a dependent. Note that if you are divorced, you can deduct the medical expenses that you pay for your child, even if that child is claimed as a dependent by your ex-spouse.

essentially a second mortgage on your home—can be deducted in full as mortgage interest. Never mind that you took the proceeds of the loan and paid off the credit card bills that you ran up on your last vacation—you still qualify for a write-off.

Take credit for your generosity. Tote up your charitable contributions: They're deductible, and you may be surprised at how they add up. Remember that if you make a single gift of more than $250 to a charity, the organization is required to give you a receipt. Be sure to ask for it, since the IRS won't let you deduct a contribution this large without a receipt. (A canceled check isn't good enough.) All is well as long as you have the receipt in hand by the time you file your tax return.

Recycle old stuff. Instead of chucking out your old clothing or old furniture or old board games or old kids' toys, give them to a local charity—say, a thrift shop run by the Salvation Army or Goodwill. Make sure that you get a receipt from the charity when you drop off the items. Remember that you get a deduction only for the fair market value of the used goods (which, no doubt, will turn out to be a lot less than what you paid for them).

If the charity won't give you a receipt bearing its estimate of your donation's fair market value (this is the ideal policy), you must write in your own estimate. For help, ask the charity's staffers what price they expect to get for your donation. Even better, peruse the guidelines in IRS Publication 561, "Determining the Value of Donated Property." Rest assured that if you're audited, the IRS will take a hard look at the value that you claimed for these donations. Auditors love to knock these estimated values down, so don't be reckless.

Donate appreciated stock. Not only the Rockefellers but also people of modest income will feel the government's benevolence when they donate appreciated shares of stock or a mutual fund to charity. For one thing, you can usually get a tax deduction for the fair market value of the securities, which includes the appreciation since you bought them. Also, you avoid paying the tax that would be due if you sold the shares and then contributed the dollars left after paying the tax. If you want to use this maneuver, see IRS Publication 526, "Charitable Contributions," for more details about contributing appreciated stock.

Don't miss "Miscellaneous." This catchall category includes such items as safe-deposit-box rental, tax advice and preparation fees, and investment-related expenses like subscriptions to investment-advisory newsletters or investment-advisory fees paid to your broker or other such expert. If you meet certain requirements, you can also deduct job-hunting expenses, education expenses you incur in the process of upgrading the skills or knowledge you use in your current job, and expenses incurred on the job but not reimbursed by your employer. The best way to get an understanding of the specific rules is to review the instructions to Schedule A of your tax return or to order Publication 529, "Miscellaneous Deductions."

Note, however, that you can deduct only whatever portion of your miscellaneous expenses exceeds 2 percent of your adjusted gross income. So if you see your accountant in December to discuss year-end tax planning, you might want to pay the bill before December 31, if that payment will put you over the 2 percent threshold.

Log those miles. The feds allow you to write off, as a "miscellaneous" deduction, expenses that you incur when you use your car on the job and your employer doesn't reimburse you.

Note: You can't deduct the cost of traveling to and from your job.

The simplest way to take the write-off is to use the standard mileage rate—in 1996 it was 31 cents a mile for every business mile driven. Add to this the actual cost of tolls and parking fees incurred while on business.

LET UNCLE SAM HELP YOU SAVE FOR RETIREMENT

The government is so eager to have you put aside money for retirement that it gives you a write-off for every dollar you contribute to a plan like your company's 401(k).

"People who don't consider putting a hefty chunk of their income into a retirement plan are missing a golden opportunity not only to take a tax deduction but also to allow their money to grow dramatically," says Ted Tesser, a certified public accountant and head of Waterside Financial Services in Boca Raton, Florida. "A key factor is that the government gets no taxes on the appreciation of the funds in your retirement plan until you actually take the money out of the plan during retirement." The heftiest chunk that the feds allow you to contribute to a 401(k) is 15 percent of your wages, but not to exceed $9,500 (in 1996). Other types of retirement plans may allow you to contribute even more.

If your employer doesn't cover you under a retirement plan, you can usually put up to $2,000 a year in an Individual Retirement Account (IRA) that you can open for yourself at any bank or brokerage house. IRAs are great because you have until April 15 following the end of the tax year to make your contribution. You'll get the deduction (one dollar for every dollar you put into the IRA) just as if you'd made your contribution before year-end. For years after 1996, you can usually contribute an additional $2,000 on behalf of your wife, even if she doesn't work.

If your employer covers you under a retirement plan you may nevertheless be allowed to contribute to an IRA, but the rules are tricky. Check the instructions with your tax return under "Adjustments to Income." Nondeductible contributions to an IRA are possible as well. Even though you don't get a tax deduction for the contribution, the funds grow tax-free until they are withdrawn—usually at retirement.

Out on Your Own

Freelance writers and artists have always been with us, but downsizing has also begun to turn bank vice-presidents, computer systems engineers, and other forced-out executives into freelancers—in the form of consultants.

The government provides a few tax breaks for self-employed people who are savvy enough to find them in the tax code.

Note to the downsized: If you've stopped getting a salary and started working freelance, you'll need to ask your accountant how to file quarterly estimated tax payments, a procedure that will be new to you.

Two Big Items for Your Checklist

Anyone who's self-employed should take special note of two important tax write-offs: health insurance premiums and self-employment tax. Each qualifies as a deduction used in computing your adjusted gross income. Therefore, these deductions will reduce your taxable income whether you itemize or take the standard deduction.

Even if your medical expenses don't add up to more than 7.5 percent of your adjusted gross income, the feds offer you this nice benefit: You can deduct 40 percent of the money that you've paid in medical insurance premiums for you and your family. (The other 60 percent of your health insurance premiums are treated as medical expenses, so they aren't deductible unless they pass the 7.5 percent threshold.) The amount that you can deduct in this way rises to 45 percent for the years 1998–2002 and is scheduled to rise even more for later years.

You're allowed to write off half the self-employment tax that you've paid. Self-employment tax is, in effect, Social Security tax paid by a self-employed person.

There's also no better way to beat Uncle Sam out of dollars than to open a Keogh plan—a retirement plan for the self-employed.

"The tax advantage of a Keogh comes from the fact that the contributions to the plan are fully deductible and that the funds in the plan grow tax-free until they are withdrawn—usually when you retire," explains Bob Beckett, a specialist in structuring retirement plans at National Retirement Planning Associates in White Plains, New York. "It's also good to know that you have a lot of choices and flexibility in deciding what type of Keogh to implement."

Keoghs are broadly separated into defined-benefit Keoghs and defined-contribution Keoghs. You can usually put up to 25 percent of your earnings into a Keogh (and sometimes more). Your best bet is to ask your financial adviser which plan is right for you. Remember that most banks and brokerage houses have standard Keogh plans on hand, so it's fast, easy, and usually inexpensive to start up the Keogh of your choice.

Opening a "simplified employee pension" (also known as a SIMPLE—savings incentive match plan for employees), may be an even simpler alternative. It allows you to contribute as much as 15 percent of your earnings toward retirement.

Put Home-Office Deductions to Work for You

If you qualify, the home-office deduction provides a nice tax benefit. It gets the IRS to help you pay bills that are normally considered nondeductible personal expenses. For example, if you have a home office, part of

Entertaining Clients? Check Your Ws

If you intend to deduct the cost of business meals and entertainment, remember the four Ws.

1. Whom you entertained
2. Where the entertainment took place
3. When it took place
4. What the business purpose was

All this information should be written on the receipt (a restaurant stub or, better, a credit card bill). Remember that only 50 percent of the meal and entertainment expense will be deductible.

You can also deduct office supplies and books bought for your business. And travel to and from a client's office is also deductible, as long as it can't be considered commuting expense.

your utility bills and any other "indirect expenses," such as home insurance, become deductible.

How do you calculate what percentage of such bills you can write off? Figure out what percentage of the square footage of your home is used as your office. (You also get a deduction for depreciation for the portion of your home that is used as a business office.) For other expenses, like telephone bills, the rules are more complicated. Get publication 587, "Business Use of Your Home," for the details.

The most important question is, Do you qualify? Scan the instructions to Schedule C of your tax return to find out. In general, you can take the deduction only if the home office is used exclusively and regularly for your business—and if you're audited, the IRS will be very strict about these rules. Remember that the office must be the principal location of your business or a place where you regularly meet with customers or clients.

If you go for the Section 179 depreciation, the IRS will allow you an immediate deduction in 1997 for up to $18,000 of property (excepting real estate) that you acquire for your business during the year. You don't have to depreciate the property over several years. For example, if you buy a $3,000 computer for your business, you get to deduct the cost in the year that you begin using it in your business (usually the year that you bought it) rather than taking a depreciation deduction each year over the prescribed five-year life span of a computer. And it gets better: The amount of Section 179 depreciation is set to increase to $18,500 in 1998, with scheduled increases until 2003.

There are, of course, a few limitations. You can't use Section 179 depreciation if your business has a loss for the year, and you usually can't use it if you buy more than $200,000 of property during the year. For more information, check the instructions to the depreciation form (Form 4562), which gets attached to your tax return.

Home Owner Strategies

Your home will be your shelter—an actual shelter and a financial shelter—if you write off everything that's legitimately deductible. So if you really want to be handy around the house, nail down some of these write-offs.

CLEAN UP ON MORTGAGE INTEREST

Mortgage interest and real estate taxes are the home owner's two most important deductions. Any points that you pay to obtain a loan are usually deductible, too. (A "point" is a fee equal to 1 percent of the loan. The bank charges you this when you get the loan.) And remember that any interest you pay on up to $100,000 of a home equity loan is deductible, too.

Comb through in your closing statement. If you bought a new home during the year, don't fail to review your closing statement carefully for deductible points and real estate taxes. Points are deductible as long as:

- They are computed based on a percentage of the loan amount
- They are labeled as points on the closing statement
- You paid them at or before the closing

Real estate taxes are usually paid at the closing to reimburse the seller for taxes that he has already paid on the home, covering the period after you take over the house.

Make that new patio pay off. Each dollar that you spend on improvements to your home can translate into one less dollar of taxable gain when you sell. (The "gain" on the sale of your home is the difference between the price that you're selling it for and what you originally paid for the home, plus the cost of any improvements.) Patience, not sophisticated record keeping, is all that's required: Simply plop copies of receipts for every improvement that you make to your home into a folder. You'll get a tax break when you sell, even if that day doesn't come for decades.

Roll over, Fido. If you "roll over" all the proceeds of the sale of your home, the gain is tax-free. Rolling over the proceeds means that you invest the full amount that you obtained from the sale into a new principal residence and move in within two years of the date that you sold your old residence. Even if you can't roll over all the proceeds, try to plow as much as possible into a new home. At press time for this book, Congress was considering eliminating capital gains taxes for most people who sell their homes, so check with your adviser.

Get exclusive treatment—once. All home sellers over age 55 who have used the home as a principal residence for three of the past five years are entitled to a one-time exclusion of up to $125,000 of the gain on the sale.

Warning: You get only one exclusion, even if you use it to shelter less than $125,000 of gain. You'll never be able to use an exclusion again. This is another provision that Congress was considering revising at press time—in home owners' favor. Check with your tax pro.

THIS RENT REALLY PAYS

"This is one of the most generous freebies the tax code has to offer," says Tesser. "Just rent your home or vacation home for 14 days or less, and you'll pay zero tax on the rental income, no matter how steep a rent you charge."

Warning: If you rent your home out for more than 14 days, the IRS considers you a landlord. That means that you'll need to figure the net income or loss on the rental property (your rental income minus offsetting deductions like depreciation or the cost of repairs, maintenance, cleaning, or advertising the rental) and report it on your tax return. Of course, you still get to write off the real estate taxes and mortgage interest.

Since offsetting deductions must be apportioned between the rental period and the period when you make personal use of the property, your best bet is to refer to the instructions in Schedule E of your tax return and to IRS Publication 527, "Residential Rental Property." If you find the rules about using the deductions hard to fathom—and you won't be alone on this one—it might be wise to seek the advice of a CPA.

Where Credit Is Due

One surefire way to reduce your tax is to claim all the credits that you can. Remember that each dollar of credit is one less dollar of tax that goes to Uncle Sam.

CLAIM YOUR FOREIGN TAX CREDIT

"It's not unusual for someone to pay foreign taxes and not even realize it," says Jason Zweig, a mutual fund expert in New York City and columnist for *Money* magazine. "For instance, if you own shares in a mutual fund that has invested in a foreign security, you very well may have paid foreign tax that can be taken as a credit on your income tax return."

To know for sure, check to see if your brokerage house, mutual fund, or other issuer has made a notation of foreign tax withheld on Form 1099, the annual statement of interest and dividend income that it sends you. To find out more about the foreign tax credit, refer to Form 1116, the form used to claim this credit on your federal tax return.

While you're at it, make sure that you get any credit coming to you for child care. The amount of child care expenses that you can claim is figured as a percentage of the child care expenses that you incur. And the credit is scaled back as your income gets higher. Those whose adjusted gross income exceeds $28,000 can expect to be allowed a credit for only 20 percent of their child care costs, not to exceed $480 for one child or $960 if you have two. If you think that you qualify for the credit, refer to the instructions to IRS Form 2441.

CLAIM CREDIT FOR EXCESS SS

Check your W-2s to see if you paid more than the maximum required amount of Social Security tax. If you did, you get a dollar-for-dollar credit against your income tax for this excess.

"Excess Social Security tax is withheld from your paycheck in a year in which you work for more than one employer and you earned wages above the maximum amount to which the Social Security tax applies," explains Bob Philpott, a certified public accountant and partner in the accounting firm Philpott, Bills, and Stoll in Encino, California. In 1996, for example, that amount was $62,700.

"If you add up the Social Security tax withheld from your pay in 1996 as shown on your W-2s, and the amount exceeds $3,887.40, you get a dollar-for-dollar credit against your federal income tax for the amount over $3,887.40."

Since the maximum amount of Social Security tax increases each year, refer to the instructions on your Form 1040 for the precise amount applicable when you're filing.

Investment Income

One of the best ways to get an immediate bang for your buck is to cut the taxes you pay on investment income, advises Stephen Pollan, an attorney, financial consultant, and author. While only your financial adviser (someone like your broker, registered investment adviser, CPA, or certified financial planner) can tell you what investment moves you should make or what mix of investments is right for you, every investor should be on the lookout for the tax savings suggested here.

LOOK FOR TAX-FREE INVESTMENTS

Generally, municipal bonds are exempt from federal tax. But if you choose a bond issued by a municipality located in the state where you live, the interest will be "triple tax-free"—exempt not only from federal tax but also from state and local income tax. The interest on U.S. Treasury obligations like Treasury bills, notes, or bonds is subject to federal income tax but completely free of state and local tax. One of the best ways to get in on the action on "munis" or "Treasuries" is to buy shares in a mutual fund that specializes in either of those types of issues.

Use savings bonds to pay tuition. If you bought a U.S. savings bond after 1989 and were at least 24 years old on the date of purchase, the interest income can be completely exempt from tax (federal, state, and local) on whatever portion of it you use it to pay college tuition and fees for a dependent child. All you have to do is show that in the year that the bond matured you incurred college tuition expenses of at least as much as the full redemption price of the bond. (Obviously, parents should purchase bonds that will mature in a year in which it's likely that their child will incur substantial college tuition expenses.)

Note: This tax break is phased out if your income rises above certain levels. For instance, in tax-year 1995, if you filed a joint return, the exemption began to be phased out if you had an adjusted gross income above $63,450. And it completely disappeared when adjusted gross income reached $93,450. For single taxpayers, the phase-out range is an adjusted gross income between $42,300 and $57,300. Still, if you qualify for the exemption, or even a part of it, it's nice to get some help from the government in putting your child through college.

Record sales dates. If you sell an investment such as shares of stock or a mutual fund that you've held "long-term" (that is, for more than one year), you'll be taxed at a maximum federal rate of 28 percent. (And at press time, Congress was considering lowering that rate.) This is far lower than the top federal rate of 39.6 percent. Keep a record of the date, the cost, and the number of shares or face value of any securities that you've purchased.

Suppose you need to cash in some of your securities to come up with the money to redo the kitchen or make a tuition payment. You probably should opt to cash in an investment that you've held for more than a year rather than one that you've held for a shorter term.

Gain from your losses. Most of the property that you own and use for personal purposes, pleasure, or investment is a capital asset; and gains and losses from sales of capital assets are reported on Schedule D of your tax return, Form 1040. Check page 2 of the Schedule D of your tax return from the year before. See if you have net capital losses that can be carried forward to offset capital gains in the current year.

The tax code says that if you combine all your capital gains and losses for the year and this results in a net loss, only $3,000 can be deducted—the excess is carried over to future years to be used in calculating your net capital gains or losses for the year.

It's easy to overlook your carryover loss from a preceding year, so go to the files and look.

LEARN THE "BASIS" BASICS

The IRS generally considers your "gain" in the sale of securities to be the difference between the proceeds of the sale and your "basis" in the shares. *Basis* means "the amount that you originally invested in your shares." It is usually best when you sell shares to specifically identify which shares you're selling, for instance, "20 shares of IBM, which I acquired on June 15, 1993." That way, you choose exactly what basis is used for those specific shares when computing your gain.

If you don't specifically identify the shares that you sell, the IRS makes you figure your basis using the "first in, first out" method. That's usually to your disadvantage, since the basis or cost of those shares you acquired first is usually lower, resulting in more gain—and more tax going to the IRS.

If you use specific identification, it's a good idea to send a letter to your broker indicating which shares you want to sell, and keep a copy for yourself. And ask for a letter or some other statement confirming your instructions.

If you inherit property, make sure that you ask the executor of the estate to provide you with a written statement indicating the fair market value of the property as of the date of the decedent's death. This figure will allow you to "step up" your basis in the assets that you receive, explains Gary Ambrose, an estate and financial planning specialist with Personal Capital Management in New York City.

"The tax code says that when you inherit property, the basis that you generally take is the fair market value of the property as of the date of the decedent's death," says Ambrose. "That can translate into a tremendous tax saving for you."

Let's say that Uncle Howard leaves you 1,000 shares of Widgets, which he bought 50 years ago for 50 cents a share. If you sold those shares today for $10 each and used Uncle Howard's purchase price (50 cents each) as a "basis," your official capital gain—and your tax bill—would be huge. So don't do that. Instead, find out from the executor what Uncle Howard's shares were worth when he died. Say that they were worth $8 each. This "stepped-up" basis lets you pay tax only on the difference between the security's current value, $10, and what it was worth when your uncle died—$8.

Estate Taxes

The IRS gets to tax you on your yearly income when you're alive and, through the federal estate tax, takes a cut of the value of all the property you own when you die.

"Some of our clients don't realize it at first, but their estate tax is going to be more of a burden to them than their income tax," says Ambrose. "The rates on this tax are steep: They climb to the 30 percent level at $100,000 of the value of your estate. And they go up from there to a top rate of 55 percent on estates over $3 million."

Thankfully, there is a lot of maneuvering that you can do to minimize the tax that your estate will have to pay after you die. It just takes some planning, Ambrose says. Here's how to maneuver.

The Freebie and the Marital Deduction

Every taxpayer gets a freebie—a credit (called the unified credit) against his estate tax—for up to $600,000 of the property he leaves to his heirs. (That figure would increase under legislation that Congress was considering at press time.) This means that if the value of the estate you leave (the value of all your assets minus the value of all your liabilities) is less than $600,000, your estate will pay no estate tax. The marital deduction lets you (that is, your estate) pay no estate tax on property that you leave to your spouse. You'll find that a lot of estate planning focuses on using the unified credit and the marital deduction. More about that in a moment.

Size up the estate that you're leaving. Add up the fair market value of all your assets and subtract all the liabilities. If the resulting figure exceeds $600,000, your estate is going to pay some estate tax, so you have some planning to do. A good way to approach this task is to pencil in the numbers on IRS Form 706, "United States Estate Tax Return," which will provide a nice set of memory joggers for all the assets and liabilities that you have.

Make tax-free gifts. Gifts that you make during your lifetime remove property from your estate and reduce your estate tax accordingly. Usually, you'll want to make gifts that are free of the tax imposed on transfers of property made during your life. Gifts of $10,000 or less made during the calendar year to any one individual are free of gift tax.

If you are married, you can split your gifts: Treat half of the gift as made by you and half by your spouse. For instance, if you give $20,000 to your son and you and your spouse decide to split the gift, it will be treated as a nontaxable gift of $10,000 from each of you, even though the full $20,000 came from one bank account.

Retain appreciated assets. Sound estate planning often means that you keep appreciated property, making gifts only of property that has had no appreciation. Here's why. If you keep property that has gone way up in value, like a stock, your heirs will have a stepped-up basis (and, therefore, pay less capital-gains tax) when they go to sell the stock. If, on the other hand, you make a gift of this appreciated stock during your lifetime, there is no step up in basis—and the person you gave the stock to could be smacked with a large capital-gains tax when the stock is sold.

Pay for medical and education expenses. You can make an unlimited amount of payments for medical and educational expenses and not have them subject to gift tax. For instance, don't pay your daughter's college tuition by making a cash gift directly to her. A cash payment of over $10,000 during the year will be subject to gift tax (unless you and your spouse split the gift). But if you pay the educational expense directly to the institution, there is no gift tax due. The same holds true if you make direct payments of medical expenses.

Estate Planning: Update That Will

Remember that all of your estate planning efforts could be for naught unless you have put your wishes into writing. You aren't going to have a lot of say as to where your assets go after you die unless you do. If you already have a will but haven't had it reviewed in the last five years or so, have your attorney look it over to see if it needs to be updated for changes in the law or for changes in your personal circumstances.

Use a credit shelter trust. Trusts are for the Kennedys and the Rockefellers, right? Wrong. If you and your spouse have an estate valued at more than $600,000, you should discuss with your attorney the possibility of putting a credit shelter trust into your will in order to preserve your $600,000 unified credit against the estate tax.

GET LIFE INSURANCE OUT OF YOUR ESTATE

Life insurance may be an important financial tool, but if the value of your estate, including the life insurance policy, is greater than $600,000, owning a policy on your life may not be a good idea. When you die, the policy will be included in your estate and possibly subject to estate tax—meaning that the IRS could get a healthy cut of that insurance payout instead of your heirs.

If you already own a policy, you might want to give it to your spouse or to a child. However, if you die within three years of making the gift of the policy, the IRS will still tax it. You should also know that if you retain any "incidents of ownership," such as the right to change the beneficiary on the policy or the right to borrow against the policy, you will be treated as the owner and the policy will be subject to tax in your estate.

The best bet is never to own the policy in the first place. Have a child or spouse take out the policy on your life. You can make a cash gift to them each year to cover any premiums. Another sound idea is to create a life insurance trust. An irrevocable trust then owns the policy, and you make an annual cash gifts to the trust equal to the premiums. Before making any moves about changing the ownership of your policies or creating a life insurance trust, consult your attorney or CPA.

BOTTOM LINE

The more you scrutinize the tax code (dry as it is), the more loopholes you'll know about. The only way that you can beat the tax system legally is to find as many deductions as you're entitled to.

WORDS TO THE WISE

Basis: This is the amount originally invested in an asset. When you sell that asset, the difference between the sales price and the basis is your gain—potentially taxable income.

Fraud: Willfully and knowingly underreporting income or overdeducting expenses is a very serious matter. When the IRS smells out fraud, the best that can happen is that the taxpayer settles by paying a big penalty. At worst, he can go to jail.

Penalty: If the IRS decides that you haven't properly figured your tax, the penalty in store for you can go as high as 25 percent of the unpaid balance of your tax, plus interest.

ALLIES

The IRS: If you need more details about any part of the tax code, call 1-800-829-3676 (1-800-TAX-FORM) and you'll be sent whatever publication you request for free.

Still stymied after reading the forms? Call for "live" help from the IRS at 1-800-829-1040. (*Tip:* Write down the name of the person you talked to and the date and time of your call. If the information that you've been given turns out to be incorrect—and that does happen—penalties will not be imposed if you can show who at the IRS gave you this advice.)

Forging Your Audit Armor

How to Make IRS Scrutiny Less, Well, Taxing

Two little words—*IRS audit*—strike fear into the hearts of the most hardened businessmen and sophisticated investors in America. And rightly so.

The term conjures up the image of secretive, powerful agents of the government invading your home (albeit by appointment) and attempting to extract your hard-earned dollars through a rigorously detailed, stress-inducing, receipt-demanding, honesty-challenging examination of your tax return.

That mental image is highly realistic. In fact, tax experts say, more than 85 percent of tax audits result in the auditee's having to pay additional taxes. And knowing that, you'll naturally do what you can to lessen your chances of undergoing this kind of exhausting, intrusive investigation.

The IRS doesn't select its auditing targets at random. It has its suspicions about certain deductions (indeed, even about certain professions), and those suspicions are built into its targeting system.

To beat this system, you must know what the red flags are—and then avoid raising them. You must file an "audit-proof" return so that even if you do get targeted, your return will withstand the agent's attack. And you must know what to say and what not to say to the agent—and under what circumstances you'd be wise to stop representing yourself and hire a tax pro to be your spokesman.

Filing: Invest Time Up Front

Forging your audit armor means preparing a tax return as if you expected to be audited. It's eminently worthwhile to devote more time to filling out the form than you have in the past, adding explanations and documentation that you may never before have bothered to provide.

Why? If your return shows that you'll be able to substantiate every item and explain it to an IRS auditor, you'll greatly lessen the odds that you'll be selected for an audit in the first place, insiders say.

WHY DARE THE IRS TO AUDIT YOU?

Careless errors on your tax return have consequences. Innocent mistakes like math errors, incomplete returns, messy returns, failing to report any income, or reporting income on the wrong line are more serious than you'd think. In fact, they are audit flags, tax professionals say.

Get a calculator—and use it. Math errors on a tax return will at the very least generate a notice sent to you from the IRS assessing you additional tax (if you made the error in your favor) and will attract attention to your return. While a math error might not always cause a full-blown audit of the return, you don't want to invite any additional scrutiny of the return.

So double-check the math on your return each year to prevent math errors. If you prepare your return by hand, consider purchasing a small calculator that generates a paper tape to assist you with your math checking. Better yet, if you own a personal computer, consider using any one of several software packages to prepare your return so that you can avoid math errors altogether.

Yes, read those directions. If you file a return and omit a form, the IRS computers will flag your return and at the very least spit out a notice informing you that your return is incomplete.

To prevent this, review the instructions for every line that you fill out on your tax return. Make sure that there are no additional forms that the instructions state you have to fill out. Be especially on the lookout for instructions that provide lists of additional forms that you may have to file—and evaluate whether you are required to file them by checking the instructions of each form listed.

When you are ready to file your return, double-check that you have included in the envelope all the forms that you actually prepared. Forgetting to mail a form has the same effect as not preparing a required form, and you'll still attract IRS attention.

Tell all. Your employer, your bank, your brokerage house, and other third parties who send you income generally report that income to the IRS as well. If you don't show all the income on your tax return, it will be flagged by the IRS computers for a "correspondence audit" (more on that in a moment). It could also lead to a more in-depth investigation of your tax return.

So make sure that you properly report on your tax return all the wage income reported to you on W-2 forms by your employer. Be sure that you list all the income reported to you on Form 1099, such as dividends, interest, and miscellaneous income from self-employment. The IRS gets a copy of these forms, too, so they'll know if you slip up.

And be particularly careful to enter the income on the correct lines of your tax return. If you don't show the income on the right lines, you run the risk that the IRS computer won't find the income when it cross-checks the amounts—and you'll be flagged by the computer for a correspondence audit.

Remember: Neatness counts. Even if the IRS computers flag your return for audit, an IRS employee must then screen your return (that is, review it) and decide whether to refer it for an audit. A return that is messy can give the impression that it was hastily or improperly prepared, which could encourage the IRS reviewer to stick your tax return in the "audit" pile.

So prepare a nice, neat tax return for submission to the IRS each year. Don't submit a return that has illegible words or numbers or has stray marks on the forms. Consider purchasing a computer software package for preparing your return to get that crisply typed look. If you can't prepare your return using a personal computer, and you don't think that your handwriting is up to snuff, consider just typing the form.

Watch out for round numbers. Round numbers, like a deduction of an even $1,000, look suspicious on your return. "If you report a deduction that is a nice round number, you may attract the scrutiny of the IRS reviewer who screens returns for audit," says Ted Tesser, a certified public accountant and head of Waterside Financial Services in Boca Raton, Florida. "It's possible that he'll think that it's an estimate—and not a figure for which you have proper backup. This is particularly true if the round number represents an item that the IRS loves to challenge, such as business meals and entertainment, casualty losses, bad-debt expense, and medical expenses."

Schedule C stands for careful handling. If you are self-employed, you run a greater chance of being audited than other taxpayers. Self-employed people must report their business income on Schedule C of their annual tax return. IRS statistics for 1994 show that the audit rate for people who filed a Schedule C was at least three times greater than the audit rate for taxpayers whose incomes are under $100,000.

So if you file a Schedule C, make sure that any large or unusual items that you claim as deductions in figuring the profit or loss from your business are carefully documented. Consider attaching to your return explanations along with copies of any helpful backup, such as receipts and copies of canceled checks. Remember that the IRS loves to scrutinize deductions for travel and

Are You in the Danger Zone?

Amir Aczel, Ph.D., a statistics professor at Bentley College in Waltham, Massachusetts, made a statistical evaluation of audited tax returns. He believes that he has broken the top secret IRS code that is used to select tax returns for audit.

In his book *How to Beat the IRS at Its Own Game*, Dr. Aczel suggests these simple formulas for finding out whether your tax return is in danger of being flagged by the IRS computers for an audit.

Schedule A itemized deductions. Divide the total itemized deductions on your Schedule A (line 28 on the 1996 Schedule A) by your adjusted gross income (line 31 on the 1996 Form 1040). If the result is 0.34 (that is, 34 percent) or more, you are nearing the danger zone for an audit. If the result is 0.44 (44 percent) or more, Dr. Aczel believes that your return is almost sure to be audited.

Schedule C deductions. Divide your total Schedule C expenses (the sum of lines 28 and 30 of the 1996 Schedule C) by your Schedule C gross income (line 7 of the 1996 Schedule C). If the result is 0.52 (that is, 52 percent) or more, you are in the danger zone for an audit. If the result is 0.63 (63 percent) or more, Dr. Aczel believes that your return is almost sure to be selected by the IRS computers for an audit.

Of course, there are lots of other red flags for an audit, but these are like a bullfighter's waving cape. If you find yourself in the danger zone, take measures to minimize the risk that the agent who manually screens the returns will go ahead and pick your return for audit.

entertainment expenses, so consider attaching a nice summary of the breakdown of this item.

Also, consider forming an S corporation—a kind of corporation designed for small businesses—to carry on your business activities. That way, you'll avoid filing Schedule C altogether and decrease your chances of audit, tax experts say. Your financial adviser can tell you the costs of forming an S corporation (it should be well under $1,000). But tax rules vary from state to state, so ask whether running your business in corporate form will cost you additional taxes.

Look at your lifestyle. Where you live and what you do for a living may dramatically increase your odds of getting audited. For example, people in Nevada are three times more likely to be audited than people in North Carolina.

"The prominence of cash in Las Vegas probably raises the IRS's hackles, so Nevada residents must get closer scrutiny," says Cliff Shoolroy, a partner and certified public accountant with Frederiksen and Company, CPA, in Mill Valley, California, and former president of the State Society of Certified Public Accountants in Nevada.

Also, statistics show that a greater percentage of taxpayers in Western states get audited than those in Eastern states. While no one knows for sure why this is, Shoolroy, who has practiced as a certified public accountant (CPA) on both coasts, has noticed "a definite geographic bias by the IRS toward selecting taxpayers for audit on the West Coast."

The IRS has also zeroed in on certain professions through its Market Segment Specialization Program (MSSP), whose personnel get special training. Among the MSSP targets are lawyers.

What should you do? Well, you're hardly going to move out of state to avoid a tax audit. But if you are only nominally in one of the professions that trigger IRS scrutiny, list your job in a different way. For example, if you are an attorney by training, but really manage real estate for a living, don't list your occupation on any part of your tax return as "attorney"—list "real estate management" instead.

To find out what types of professions may be targeted by the IRS, ask your CPA or another financial adviser. Or contact the American Institute of Certified Public Accountants (AICPA) or the State Society of Certified Public Accountants where you live and ask how you can contact someone who sits on the committee that is the liaison with the IRS.

Get smart—file for an extension. Tax practitioners theorize that those who request an extension of the deadline for filing their returns lessen their chances of audit—and at least one study supports this conclusion. The idea is that since the vast majority of Americans file their tax returns by April 15 each year, the IRS fills most of its audit quota for the year shortly after this initial deadline. While a return filed after April 15 still could be flagged for audit, the argument goes, the odds of being selected decrease.

If you file a request on Form 4868 by April 15, you'll get an automatic extension until August 15 to file your tax return. There's one catch, though—with your request you must include a check for whatever amount you estimate you owe. Note that if you are due a refund, you pay nothing with your extension request; but by putting off filing your return, you'll delay getting the refund dollars in your pocket.

AVOID THE SPOTLIGHT

Being an individual means that your financial situation is like nobody else's. So remember that some peculiarities that show up on your tax return can be perfectly legitimate but still raise eyebrows at the IRS. You can go ahead and declare the deductions that you deserve, tax professionals say. Just keep these notes in mind.

Explain those extensive deductions. Uncle Sam is taking special notice when you take disproportionately high deductions. If your deductions seem too large for your income, you'll trigger an audit. Amir Aczel, Ph.D., a statistics professor at Bentley College in Waltham, Massachusetts, and author of *How to Beat the IRS at Its Own Game*, devised a way to show taxpayers just how strong a risk they are running. If the total itemized deductions reported on Schedule A of your tax return amount to more than 35 percent of your adjusted gross income (AGI), you are likely to be audited. On Schedule C, if the total expenses you claim exceed 52 percent of your income, your return may be flagged for audit.

"Blunt the IRS's skepticism about your unusually high deductions by attaching explanatory statements and backup—copies of receipts, canceled checks, photographs, or anything else that will demonstrate the validity of the amount deducted," says Tesser. "If you show the IRS that you are savvy about the deductions that you take, you'll discourage them from auditing you."

Be aware of sore subjects. If you claim unusual deductions, or deductions that are typically abused by unscrupulous taxpayers, your tax return can be flagged for audit. Here are a few to watch out for.

- Home-office deductions
- Casualty-loss deductions
- Theft-loss deductions
- Bad-debt deductions
- Medical-expense deductions

If you claim any of these deductions, tread carefully—and read all of the instructions for your return to make sure that you're entitled to deduct everything that you claim.

Explain that roller-coaster income. If your income shifts significantly from one year to the next—particularly if it drops suddenly—it could attract IRS attention and trigger an audit.

To blunt IRS interest in auditing your return, use the back-up-and-explain techniques previously outlined. If you show a logical explanation for a big income shift with your tax return, it could go a long way toward discouraging an audit.

Audits: Donning Your Armor

What if you get audited despite your prudent return preparation? Knowledge and good record keeping will be your shields.

There are three types of audits: correspondence audits (audits by mail), office audits, and field audits. You may be able to handle all three types of audits yourself, CPAs say, but you should know about the rights and resources that you can fall back on if you find your opponent too formidable.

A general rule is to never panic. The IRS is a behemoth bureaucracy, and there are ways of dealing with it. It makes mistakes, too: *Money* magazine once reported that 25 to 50 percent of all notices sent by the IRS were incorrect for one reason or another.

Remember that if you have forged your audit armor in advance, you have a good chance of getting through your audit unscathed.

LETTERS FROM UNCLE SAM

Correspondence audits are notices generated by the IRS computer and sent to you by mail. The notices usually ask you to send the IRS more information about specific items or deductions reported on your return.

Another type of notice comes to you on IRS Form CP2000, which is simply an additional tax bill. A CP2000 notice is usually generated when the IRS computer can't find on your tax return income that it thinks you should have reported. For example, the computer matches the income that you've listed on your return with all of the 1099s and W-2s that it received from your various bankers and employers. If one or more of these forms isn't matched by an equivalent entry on your tax return, the computer spits out a notice that you owe more taxes.

If you get one of these notices, don't panic. For one thing, such IRS notices are often incorrect. Sometimes the computer is looking for income on a certain line of the return, but you have reported it elsewhere on the form. Also, the notice could be incorrect because the IRS clerk entered your information into the computer incorrectly. Don't just presume that the IRS computer is right.

Gather your backup documents. Take out the information that you've stored in your tax file that will substantiate the income or deduction figures that the IRS is inquiring about. This includes copies of receipts, canceled checks, and any other documents issued by a third party that you used to prepare your return. Backup also includes documents that you generated yourself—business diaries, letters, or any other contemporaneous notes or documentation that you made at the time of a transaction.

"The IRS loves to see paper," notes Bob Philpott, a certified public accountant and partner in the accounting firm of Philpott, Bills, and Stoll in Encino, California. "So give them plenty of it, as long as it's relevant to the IRS inquiry."

Respond promptly, in writing. The paper trail is everything. "Unfortunately, a phone call just won't do the trick here," says Hal Peterson, a certified public accountant at the accounting firm of Martin Geller CPA P.C. in New York City. "You must respond in writing to an IRS notice to be absolutely sure that you've taken care of it. If you want to call the IRS at the phone number listed on the form to get some type of clarification, that's okay. But don't ever assume that a verbal response will get you off the hook."

Prepare a letter that states why you think the IRS notice is incorrect. Make reference to the amounts indicated on the IRS notice and compare them with the amounts that you actually reported on your return. Point out that you are substantiating your figures with copies of the enclosed documentation such as receipts or canceled checks. State clearly in your letter that you disagree with the IRS notice (if, in fact, this is so).

If you actually reported income on your tax return, which the IRS says it doesn't think you reported, make copies of the page or pages of your return (mark them "Copy") and enclose them as well. Include a copy of the IRS notice with your response.

Use certified mail. Always send correspondence to the IRS by certified mail. Peterson calls this the belt-and-suspenders approach. "You'd be ill-advised to send correspondence by regular mail," he says. "Using certified mail is the only way that you can prove that you actually responded to an IRS inquiry."

Get a PRO on your side. What if the IRS won't settle? Appeal to the Problems Resolution Office (PRO). If you have sent at least two letters to the IRS responding to the same notice and the IRS computer has not properly acknowledged or considered your thoughtful and thorough response, you are eligible to have your case referred to an IRS Problems Resolution Officer.

These special officers at the IRS help taxpayers resolve issues when the normal IRS channels don't do the job. If the IRS determines that you meet certain criteria, you will be assigned a case officer who is supposed to act as your advocate. The officer will consider the documentation that you produce and bring your case to a conclusion. You can contact these advocates by calling or writing to the Problems Resolution Office at your District IRS Center.

OFFICE AUDITS: GET ORGANIZED

For an office audit, you get a notice in the mail requiring your appearance at the IRS office at a specified date and time to meet face-to-face with an auditor. The letter usually asks that you bring certain documents that substantiate a few specific items of income or deduction reported on your return.

First, decide whether you should represent yourself or hire a tax pro. If the prospect of an office audit makes you feel that you're in way over your head, consult a professional like a CPA, an enrolled agent, or an attorney. An enrolled agent, although not a CPA or attorney, has passed an IRS exam about tax law and IRS procedures and is permitted to represent clients before the IRS. (See "Allies" on page 326.) If you prepare properly, however, you should be able to handle an office audit yourself.

Ask for a delay. Delay sometimes works in favor of the taxpayer who faces an office or field audit. Simply call the auditor listed on the notice and say that you need to reschedule the appointment because it does not allow you sufficient time to gather the information requested by the IRS. (Remember that it is your right as a taxpayer to have the meeting scheduled at a mutually convenient time.) As the next date approaches, call the auditor again and ask if you can reschedule.

The theory here is that IRS agents carry a heavy caseload and are under pressure from their supervisors to finish audits and move on. The longer you delay—within reason, of course—the more likely the auditor may be to accept the substantiation you produce on audit, close down your case, and move on.

"I've seen it work for my clients," says Tesser. "Usually, the longer a case stays open, the greater the desire to finish it up—even if it means that the agent has to compromise."

As always, round up your backup. As mentioned before, you'll want to make copies of all documentation to give to the auditor. And this is your second warning: Never part with the original documents that you keep in your tax file.

Prepare lists in advance. Make the auditor's job easier, and show him that you are well-prepared, by writing up sheets that clearly summarize the way that you arrived at the figure that you entered on your tax return.

"The mantra of preparing for a meeting with an auditor is 'organization,'" advises Peterson. "If you represent yourself at an audit and you are not well-organized, you'll become flustered."

RULES OF CONDUCT

Gulp. The day of truth comes: your sit-down with the auditor. Here are tactics that the tax pros say will make the experience as painless as possible.

Arrive on time. IRS auditors are usually on a tight schedule. Don't get off on the wrong foot by arriving late.

Take only documents for the auditor. Don't arrive at the audit with special "crib sheets" or other sensitive documents like diaries unless you are prepared to show them to the auditor. If you refer to documents at the meeting but try to shield them from the auditor's eye, he'll get the impression that you aren't being open.

Dress conservatively. Flashy jewelry or clothes could give the auditor the idea that you are wealthier than your tax form says you are—that you might not have reported all your income. IRS agents are human beings. How you look and act will help determine whether they trust you.

Don't let silence spook you. Auditors are trained to put subtle psychological pressures on you to make you uneasy and inclined to "fess up." Often this is done with a combination of silence and humor—perhaps a little friendly chitchat, followed by long periods of silence. Your best bet is to respond directly to questions if you can but never get chatty or make jokes—particularly about the IRS.

"Remember to look relaxed," says Tesser. "Your credibility is at stake here. Say little, smile a lot, and never volunteer information."

Adjourn the session if you need to. If you think that you're in over your head, the law gives you the right to adjourn the session at any time so that you can consult a tax professional.

Don't allow expansion. Don't encourage an expansion of the investigation beyond the few items that are specifically mentioned in the notice. For example, if you arrive at the audit ready to substantiate your real estate taxes but the auditor begins to question you about your charitable deductions, just politely but firmly say, "I'm not prepared to discuss my charitable deductions today. And how does this relate to the items specified on the notice?"

If the auditor asks about other tax years or other returns that you've filed, you're perfectly within your rights to say, "I'll have to check my records."

Review the auditor's report. Once the audit is finished, you'll get the auditor's report—usually several days or even a few weeks after your meeting. Review it carefully to make sure that the adjustments are exactly as the auditor discussed.

If you agree with the auditor's report, be it an assessment of some additional tax or a clean bill of health, sign it and return it to the auditor promptly. Remember, though, that if you sign the report and additional tax is due, you are giving up your rights to appeal the matter or go to tax court, and you are agreeing to an immediate assessment of the tax. So only sign if you are sure that you agree.

Don't be pressured to agree to any adjustments at the appointment. Sometimes auditors will print up their report at the end of your meeting and pressure you to sign. Never do this, no matter how much pressure you feel. If you are unhappy with the adjustments made at the audit, politely decline to sign the report and take a few days to think it over.

Voice your disagreement. "If you disagree with the audit report when you ultimately receive it, speak with the IRS auditor and let him know that you disagree and intend to appeal," says Shoolroy. "Remember that it's not illegal to have a difference of opinion with an IRS auditor."

This may make him interested in considering additional documentation that you may be able to present or in settling the matter for a lesser amount. But don't get your hopes up that this will always be the result. If you can't reach agreement with the auditor, don't sign the audit report—it will leave your case as "unagreed."

After a number of weeks, you'll receive a notice from the IRS specifying the additional tax due, and it will give you 30 days to file a formal appeal. If you believe that you've been unfairly assessed, your first step is to file an appeal. Your next step is to go to tax court.

FIELD AUDITS: THAT'S NO AVON LADY

Field audits are the most dreaded—with good reason. Statistics show that field audits are up to eight times as likely to result in an increase in tax as any other type of audit. Field audits are usually reserved for taxpayers who have their own businesses or taxpayers whose affairs are deemed too complex to handle in an office audit as described above.

A field audit is conducted by an IRS revenue agent. The name itself tells you that this person is out to generate revenue for the IRS. Revenue agents usually have more training and experience than tax auditors. Generally, you receive a notice in the mail from the revenue agent specifying the date and time that he would like to visit your home or business to go over the documentation that you have to support certain items on your tax return.

Call in the reinforcements. It's almost always advisable to consult a tax pro or even have one represent you for a field audit. If you draw a seasoned revenue agent, you can easily find yourself unprepared to do battle with this representative of the government.

Change the venue. If you hire a tax pro to represent you, he can have the audit changed from your home or place of business to the offices of your accountant. That will certainly reduce the amount of disruption of your day-to-day life.

Know what the agent will be looking for. The revenue agent is not restricted in his investigation to the few items of income or deduction that may be listed on the notice. You can bet that he will be looking for income that you didn't report on your tax return, or nonexistent expenses that you listed. Revenue agents will also be particularly interested in your lifestyle and "economic reality checks." So, watch out.

Resist the economic reality check. Revenue agents often try to flush out lifestyle information from you to see if the income and deductions that you reported seem appropriate to your apparent income level. For example, if you drive a Jaguar and live in a luxury-home area, but you've reported a paltry income on your tax return, the auditor's suspicions will be aroused. The agent will probably try to use some of the psychological pressures discussed above to get you to talk and, maybe, reveal that you've underreported your income.

To get more tangible results, the IRS has developed Form 4822, "Statement of Annual Estimated Personal and Family Expenses," which the agent may present to you at the audit. In fact, the IRS has abused the economic-reality-check technique so greatly in the past that the AICPA has advised taxpayers to consider not responding to lifestyle questions during an audit without a formal summons—a written request from the IRS auditor legally forcing the taxpayer to respond.

"The lifestyle check is to be used only if the agent suspects that you are a tax cheat. It's not to be used as a routine part of an audit," notes Peterson.

If the auditor tries to dig into your personal expenses and asks you to complete Form 4822, inquire how it relates to the items listed in the audit notice. If the agent is persistent about completing the form, respond by saying that you'll have to take some time to study the form at home and that you'll get back to him. Then, after your meeting with the agent, consult a tax pro to see if you're on safe ground playing "hardball" and refusing to fill out the form without a formal summons.

Gather your paperwork. The revenue agent will usually want to analyze your bank records because they present a fair picture of your tax situation. Accordingly, you should be prepared to substantiate that every deposit into your bank account is either income reported on your return, a gift from some kindly person or a transfer from another of your bank accounts. Likewise, you'll need to substantiate all the expenses that the agent investigates to verify that they are deductible for tax purposes.

It Pays to Appeal

If you disagree with your auditor's findings, take your case to the IRS Appeals Office. For a number of reasons, this is not at all an exercise in futility. IRS statistics show that appeals of audits result in a reduction of the auditor's assessment by more than 40 percent.

The appeals office is separate from the auditing division in the IRS, and the appeals officer usually has more training and experience than the typical auditor. Appeals officers also are judged based on their ability to settle cases, not by how well they hold up auditors' decisions.

"I have found appeals officers to be extremely fair and even-handed," says Peterson. "If they can't settle your appeal, there's a chance that your case will go to tax court—a lengthy and expensive process for the IRS, and something that it usually wants to avoid."

Swinging a Deal with the Appeals Officer

If the issues in your appeal are straightforward, you can handle the matter yourself. If not, consider hiring a tax pro such as an attorney, a CPA, or an enrolled agent to help you prepare or handle your appeal. Here are other moves that the tax experts recommend.

Prepare a letter. Unless the amount of the additional assessment is under $2,500, you must write a formal protest letter stating why you disagree with the auditor's findings. The auditor will send you a copy of IRS Publication 5, which will give you several items that must be included in the letter (such as your name, your address, and the tax period involved).

Also, your letter must include a statement, under penalty of perjury, that you believe the statements in your letter to be complete and true.

Meet with the appeals officer. Often you'll have to meet with an appeals officer—an "appeals hearing"—to settle the matter. In your meeting, use the tactics discussed above for dealing with an auditor. The businesslike manner that you show to the appeals officer will indicate how serious you are about responsibly defending your position.

"Treat the appeals officer civilly, and generally, if they have any kindness in their soul, they will listen," says Philpott. "Remember that the appeals officer wants to bring the matter to a conclusion. He is not likely to consider your case going to tax court a favorable result."

Strike a deal. The appeals officer may very well try to negotiate a settlement with you—say, by agreeing to accept a percentage of the deductions that the auditor disallowed. So work out in advance what you'd be willing to accept to get the matter behind you.

"You should probably be willing to give a little," advises Philpott. Negotiating in these circumstances is a delicate art, often best handled by a tax pro. But there's nothing wrong with negotiating with the appeals officer yourself if you feel up to the task.

FINALLY, YOUR DAY IN TAX COURT

IRS statistics show that only 15 percent of all taxpayers who appeal a tax audit wind up filing a petition in tax court. And once you file a petition in tax court, more than 80 percent of those cases actually get settled before going to trial.

It may be worth the effort, though. More than half of all petitions to the tax court result in some reduction of the tax assessment. You have 90 days to file a petition in tax court after you receive the "notice of deficiency" for tax due to the IRS.

Hire a tax pro. Most people are well out of their league by the time they reach the tax court level. You should really consult a tax pro before you consider going to court, even if you qualify for the small-case procedure discussed below.

Consider the "small" option. If the amount of the tax that you have been assessed after audit is $10,000 or less for any one tax year, you qualify for Small-Case Tax Court. This is pretty much like small-claims court. Your case will be heard by a judge who will listen to arguments and make a decision based on the facts presented.

If you elect to be a small case, you can't appeal the decision—period. But if you feel up to it, you probably will be able to represent yourself. And the court costs are less than $100. If you have a sound basis for your claim, just knowing that you can resort to tax court this way can give you leverage and confidence in handling your audit and appeals process.

If you don't qualify for the small-case procedure, you'll almost surely need a tax pro to represent you.

Bottom Line

Don't panic, and don't be afraid of the IRS. Knowing the auditing and appeals system is the surest way to beat it.

Avoid red flags for audits, such as careless errors, when you file your tax return. Any unnecessary attention that you draw to your return could be an invitation to an audit. Attach helpful explanations and other backup, such as copies of receipts or canceled checks, to your tax return. This could discourage the IRS from auditing you.

Words to the Wise

CP2000: A notice usually generated when the IRS computer can't find on your tax return income that it thinks you should have reported. Such notices are often incorrect.

Field audit: The dreaded session where a revenue agent—a highly trained IRS staffer—invites himself to your home or business.

Schedule C: The form that self-employed people use for reporting business income. Be careful—missteps here could invite an audit.

Allies

You may able—and willing—to handle a correspondence or office audit by yourself, but you really need a professional ally if you're summoned for a field audit. Consider these options.

Certified public accountant: A CPA almost always has a college degree and must be licensed by the state in which he practices.

Enrolled agent: Someone who has taken and passed an examination administered by the IRS, testing knowledge of tax law and IRS procedure. An enrolled agent is permitted to represent clients before the IRS, even though he is neither a CPA nor a tax attorney.

Tax attorney: A lawyer who specializes in tax matters and is licensed by the state in which he practices. Tax attorneys often have special tax-law degrees, such as an L.L.M. (a master's degree in law), which show that they have taken tax-related courses after law school.

Filing Frugally

It Takes a Year to Fill Out Tax Forms – If You're Doing It Right

One of the most daunting chores that you and 200 million other taxpayers face each year is filing your tax return. The trick is to file frugally—to minimize not only the amount of money that you pay but also the effort and anguish that you spend on the filing process.

Getting Started

Want to know the biggest secret to frugal tax filing? Treat tax preparation as a year-round project. The more systematic you are—gathering data throughout the year and forcing yourself to sit down and prepare your return in January or February—the less anxiety this obligation will cost you.

Chances are that your scrupulousness will also save tax dollars. (Note, however, that if you happen to be reading this only a few days before the deadline, there are still things that you can do to make the process easier on yourself.)

MAKE A YEAR-ROUND HOME FOR DOCUMENTS

Set up a tax folder at home. Throughout the year, drop in the income and expense records that you'll eventually need to prepare your return—documents like W-2s and 1099s, which show the income that you have received, as well as receipts for real estate taxes, charitable contributions, mortgage interest, and other expenses that you intend to deduct.

You may want to create a folder for each category. It is important that you save the records of all your banking and brokerage transactions, since they can be requested in an IRS audit. (After you've filed your return, keep these folders in a safe place.)

How Long Must You Keep Your Records?

Keep your tax records for six years from the date you file your return, tax pros suggest. In certain situations, the IRS can go back that far in an audit.

For example, if you file your 1996 tax return on April 15, 1997, you'll want to keep your tax records until April 15, 2003.

Never throw away the tax returns themselves (as opposed to the backup documents), or the certified-mail receipt that shows that you filed the return.

"You simply must maintain records such as brokerage statements, canceled checks, and purchase of tickets for six years after you file the tax return that reflects the sale of any such investment," advises Jeff Haveson, a certified public accountant with Martin Geller CPA P.C. in New York City. "If you never sell a particular investment, this means that you'll keep the records for as long as you live." Remember that if you don't keep the records that show how much you paid for, say, an investment in a stock or a bond, you won't be able to calculate gain or loss when you do sell.

Also never surrender to the garbage man any records that show the cost of your home or any improvements that you make to it. If you sell, those records will be invaluable for calculating your cost or basis in the home so that you can accurately figure your gain or loss on the sale.

If you own a computer, one of the best tools you can get is a software program such as Quicken or Microsoft Money, which will help you track and account for all important items of taxable income and expense during the year.

"There are a lot of decent software programs out there—so there's really no excuse for a lot of us not to use the computer to keep track of our personal finances," says Bob Philpott, a certified public accountant and partner in the firm Philpott, Bills, and Stoll in Encino, California. "The programs are easy to use and readily available, and you'll benefit from the financial information. They'll also help to keep your frustration level down."

The programs can be organized to track all your valuable itemized deductions by category as you pay them during the year. Just one "flip of the switch" and you can have a printout of where you stand with your tax deductions and income at any point in the year.

Tax preparation is not all about filling in numbers on IRS forms—it's also about forking over as little money to Uncle Sam as you legally can.

"I recommend a review of your situation around October," advises Cliff Shoolroy, a partner and certified public accountant with Frederiksen and

Company, CPA, in Mill Valley, California, and former president of the State Society of Certified Public Accountants in Nevada. "You'll probably be able to get a good idea of what your tax situation for the entire year looks like, yet you still have chance to switch tactics."

If you wait until the calendar year is over, you will have lost your chance to limit the amount of income that you must report or to increase the expenses that you mean to take as itemized deductions.

Preparing Your Return

When it comes time to actually fill in some figures on that tax form, get out those folders where you've been storing your receipts and records for this taxable year.

How Do Your Files Stack Up?

Make sure that your "Income" folder contains a record of everything that you've earned: W-2 forms, which show wages you earned during the year; and any 1099 forms, which report income such as interest and dividends, state tax refunds, or sales of stocks and bonds (to name a few). Your expense folder should have Form 1098 (which reports mortgage interest that you may have paid), receipts for payments of real estate taxes, and charitable contributions made.

Search for more deductions. Scour your checkbook for tax-deductible items that you may have forgotten about during the year. For example, it may have slipped your mind that early in the year you made a tax-deductible contribution to your favorite charity or made a payment of real estate taxes.

"Make a conscious effort to make notations in your checkbook for important tax-related items—even if you didn't cut a check for it," advises Shoolroy. "For example, if you donate old clothing to charity, make a note of it in your checkbook so that you'll be sure to remember to pick it up as a deduction."

If your checkbook is sloppier than it should be, pull out canceled checks for deductible items like medical expenses, real estate taxes, and charitable contributions.

Look to the past. Use last year's return as a memory-jogger. A line-by-line comparison is the best way to thoroughly review your new return for completeness.

"Match each of the items of income and deduction on last year's return with what you're reporting this year," says Jeff Haveson, a certified public accountant with Martin Geller CPA P.C. in New York City. "You should also 'check off' each Form 1099 and W-2 as you receive it, against the ones received and reported on last year's return to make sure that you aren't missing any."

If by January 31 you haven't gotten a 1099 or a W-2 for the previous year, contact the issuer (such as a bank or brokerage house) or your employer and ask for the form to be sent to you.

Sort your documents. If you haven't prudently kept your income, expense, and contribution items in separate folders, you'll now need to group your documents by category. For example, group all the interest income that will show up on Schedule B of your tax return by pulling together all the 1099 forms, which report interest income to you.

Buy a calculator. A calculator with a tape is one of the best investments that you can make. Use it to tote up the income that you received and the various categories of expenses that you'll be entering on your tax form. For example, run a tape of the interest reported to you on Form 1099. Check the numbers on the paper tape to make sure that you've added correctly. Then, when you fill out the section of Schedule B in which you report your income, make sure that the total on the tape matches the total interest income on the return.

If you use this procedure for each category on your return, you'll make sure that each item in your tax records has found its way to the return.

Leave a paper trail. Save those calculator tapes. They show how you arrived at the numbers that you entered on your tax return. And make sure that the records in this year's tax file stay organized by category and that you keep the file for the required length of time.

NOW SHARPEN A PENCIL

Ready to fill out the return? Don't just assume that the tax form is self-explanatory. Pore over the instructions. The instructions in your tax booklet not only tell you how to fill out the form properly but also alert you to common errors with headings titled "Caution."

Also provided in the booklet are tax-saving ideas and advice about documents that you should attach to your return to help the processing along.

Haveson suggests that you also order IRS Publication 17, "Your Federal Income Tax," by dialing 1-800-829-3676 (1-800-TAX-FORM). "The explanations in this IRS publication are thorough and really get to the heart of any question that you have," says Haveson. Your aim, of course, is to call as little attention as possible to your return as it moves through the IRS processing system.

Fill in the blanks. Now is the moment of truth—when you enter figures on the appropriate lines on your paper tax form or on the tax form that your software program has in your computer. If you are preparing your return by hand, use a pencil, not a pen, and then make a photocopy of each page for submission to the IRS. The photocopy has the permanence of a return prepared by pen, but your pencil copy can be corrected easily and photocopied over again, if necessary. A photocopy of most forms may be submitted to the

IRS. In the rare cases where this is not allowed, the face of the form will usually warn you about this.

Learn how to hide. It seems too simple—but it's true—that a neatly prepared return stands less of a chance for an audit. "A sloppy return indicates sloppy or careless preparation of the numbers on your return," says Ted Tesser, a certified public accountant and head of Waterside Financial Services in Boca Raton, Florida. "And that could make the difference between being audited or not."

So make sure that your return has no stray marks or illegible words or numbers. Fill out all the required forms. And double-check your math.

TOUCHING UP THOSE TOUCHY DEDUCTIONS

Speaking of not attracting the attention of the IRS, here's a rundown of the common deductions that the tax man tends to pay particular attention to. Go ahead and claim all the deductions that are due you, but proceed with care.

Home-office deduction. A deduction for a home office, reported on Form 8829, is a red flag to the IRS. The service has cracked down on taxpayers who take a deduction for maintaining a business office in their home, and the eligibility requirements have been tightened up.

So carefully review the rules in the instructions for your return to make sure that you qualify. If you do, consider attaching a description of the office space—or perhaps a photograph—to your return, as well as a note explaining why you believe that you qualify under the tax rules for the deduction.

If the amount that you'll save is small, it might be better not to risk drawing attention to your return by taking it—or consult a tax pro for advice.

You should also consider moving your office out of your home. The deductions associated with running an office outside the home—for instance, payments of monthly rent and utilities—are usually easy to justify and don't attract the high level of IRS scrutiny brought on by claiming these same expenses for an office in the home.

Medical expenses. If you take a deduction for medical expense, your return may be flagged for audit. Medical expenses that are unreimbursed by insurance are deductible only to the extent that they exceed 7.5 percent of your adjusted gross income (AGI), and fortunately, not too many of us incur this level of medical expense each year. That's why the IRS considers this to be an unusual deduction. It loves to investigate such deductions further, since it recognizes that taxpayers can be careless in this area by deducting medical expenses already covered by insurance or by deducting the expenses even though they don't reach the required minimum 7.5 percent AGI threshold.

What to do? If your unreimbursed medical expenses exceed the 7.5 percent AGI threshold, you'll want to attach an explanation to your tax return. State the nature of the expenses and the illness, and indicate what portion was covered by insurance. Consider attaching copies of medical bills or summary reports from insurance companies to your tax return. Also, make sure that you properly prepare Schedule A of your tax return, the form where your medical expenses are reported. Read the instructions carefully and don't be so imprudent as to deduct medical expenses if they don't reach the 7.5 percent floor.

Casualty or theft losses. Casualty and theft losses are deductible (to the extent not reimbursed by insurance) only if they exceed $100 and exceed 10 percent of your AGI. Not many people will ever have the opportunity to claim this deduction. It takes a major catastrophe like a flood or fire (in the case of a casualty) or a major swindle or robbery (in the case of a theft). Since this is an unusual item, it may attract IRS scrutiny.

So if you are taking a tax deduction for a theft or casualty loss, attach a well-organized summary of the amounts that you are claiming as a deduction, and also attach copies of insurance reports, police reports, and before-and-after photographs of the items involved.

Bad-debt expenses. The IRS is sure to pay attention if you claim a deduction for a loan that went bad and is uncollectible. This deduction is subject to taxpayer abuse or misinterpretation and is an easy challenge by the "feds." For example, the IRS might argue that you had never made a valid loan—that you had just made gifts to the person or entity that you loaned the money to.

If the instructions to your tax return indicate that you are entitled to this deduction, attach copies of loan documents (if they exist) to copies of the tax return to prove that the loan was bona fide. Attach a summary schedule indicating the date when the principal amount of the loan was made and all payments of principal and interest that have been made over the life of the loan. State why the loan is now uncollectible.

FINDING FUNCTION IN A SEA OF FORMS

The IRS gives you a number of options when it comes to filing your tax return. While Form 1040 may be the best-known form, there are actually no fewer than three versions among which to choose. If your tax affairs are complex, however, you probably won't be able to use the simplest versions of the form.

Go EZ on yourself. The 1040EZ is the simplest version of all the tax forms. And you can't miss it—it's pink. Preparing this one-page form is a snap. But to use the EZ, you must have:

- No itemized deductions
- No IRA deduction
- No dependents
- No dividends or capital gains
- No interest income in excess of $400
- No Social Security, alimony, or pension income to report

In other words, your tax and financial affairs are so easy that if you qualify to file the 1040EZ, you can file by touch-tone telephone. (More on that in a moment.)

Move up one level. If you don't qualify to use the 1040EZ, consider another simple form, the 1040A. This form lets you report interest, dividends, pension income, and Social Security income. There's a catch, though: Your total income must be under $50,000. Also, you can't report capital gains or alimony income, and you can't itemize deductions.

Join the big leagues. If you can't use the 1040EZ or the 1040A, you must file the "long" form, Form 1040. Also, if you have capital gains or income from self-employment or rent, you're forced to use the long form. While it is more complex, it also offers you the chance to use tax-saving strategies, like itemized deductions.

IN THE LONG RUN, YOU'LL NEED A SCHEDULE

If you file Form 1040, you'll likely need to file a number of other forms with it, so here's a schedule of the schedules.

Schedule A. This form is used for reporting itemized deductions: medical expenses, taxes, mortgage and investment interest, charitable contributions, theft and casualty losses, and other miscellaneous itemized deductions.

Certain Schedule A deductions are allowed only to the extent that they exceed a "floor"—a percentage of your AGI. Medical expenses, as we've seen, are deductible only to the extent that they exceed 7.5 percent of your AGI. Miscellaneous deductions, such as investment expenses, tax-preparation fees, and unreimbursed employee business expenses are allowed only to the extent that they exceed 2 percent of your AGI. When you prepare Schedule A, make sure that you carefully follow the instructions for figuring out whether you've reached the appropriate floor.

Schedule B. Interest and dividend income is reported on Schedule B, but you need to fill out the form only if either the interest or the dividends exceeds $400.

If you don't show all the interest reported to you on Form 1099-Int or all the dividends reported to you on Form 1099-Div, the IRS will, at a minimum, send you a notice and, at worst, will single you out for an audit. So be smart: Don't overlook any Schedule B income.

Schedule C. If you are self-employed, you are required to file Schedule C to report the earnings from your business.

Keep a separate bank account for your business and make sure that all your business receipts and disbursements are carefully reported on your tax return. Remember that if your income is under $100,000 and you file a Schedule C, your chances of audit are at least three times greater than those of other taxpayers, so be careful.

Schedule D. Capital gains and losses, such as those from the sales of stocks or bonds, are reported on Schedule D.

If you sell stocks or bonds through a financial institution like a bank or brokerage house, the proceeds will be reported to you on Form 1099-B after year-end. Check that you are reporting on Schedule D all the amounts reported to you on Form 1099-B. Otherwise, the IRS will be after you with a notice—or an audit.

Schedule E. If you have income from rental real estate, partnerships, or S corporations (a kind of corporation designed for small businesses), you'll have to file Schedule E.

If you own a piece of rental property, such as a home or an apartment, you'll probably be entitled to a deduction for depreciation. Depreciation is the write-off that you get for general wear and tear of the property. Remember that to claim depreciation as a deduction on Schedule E, you'll also be required to file Form 4562, the form used to track all your depreciation deductions.

Filing Your Return

Once you finish your return and it's ready to be filed, you're home free— well, sort of. Some of the worst mistakes that you can make, but the easiest to avoid, occur in the filing process. Here are a few to watch out for.

DOT THE I'S AND CROSS THE TS

Sign your return. Make sure that you sign your return before you file it. If you are filing jointly with your spouse, make sure that both signatures are in place. Remember that an unsigned return is considered incomplete and, at the very least, will attract some correspondence from the IRS.

Use the correct address. Mail your return to the correct address for the IRS. You are required to send your return to the IRS district processing center based on where you live, so read the "where to file" instructions carefully. Otherwise, your return will wind up at an IRS processing center that isn't expecting it. This could make processing of your return more difficult and result in additional handling and unwanted attention.

Include all required forms. Forgetting to mail a form is just as bad as not filling it out. Look at your filing copy page by page one last time to make sure that all the forms are there. Check that all attachments are in place, such as W-2s or a check for any balance of tax due. If you owe money to the IRS, make sure that your name and Social Security number are on the check and that the year and form number (for example, "1997 Form 1040") is written on the face of the check so that the payment gets credited to your account.

Use the peel-off label. The IRS sends you tax forms with a peel-off label showing your name, address, and Social Security number. Put the label at the spot at the top of page 1 of your tax return—where it says "Label Here."

What If You Can't Pay?

If you can't pay the balance of tax due by April 15, don't let yourself be paralyzed by fear. Instead, take quick action.

Fill out and attach to your return an installment agreement, Form 9465. The form asks the IRS to agree to let you pay off your tax over a period of time. The IRS won't even ask to look at your finances before considering whether to accept the agreement, as long as the amount due is under $10,000 and the period of time you take to pay it off is less than three years.

Note, however, that the IRS tends to charge interest at a hefty rate. You'll also pay a late-payment penalty of 0.5 percent per month on the balance of tax due. For example, if you file for an extension by the due date, but pay the $1,000 balance due after the due date, you'll be charged a late-payment penalty of $5 per month (0.5 percent times $1,000) plus interest at the going rate on the $1,000. The late-payment penalty can't exceed 25 percent of the tax due (in this example, $250).

Filing for an extension of the deadline works to your advantage in this scenario, too. "If it's April 15 and you are requesting an extension of time to file your tax return until August 15—but you can't pay the tax which you estimate is due—file your extension anyway," advises Jeff Haveson, a certified public accountant with Martin Geller CPA P.C. in New York City. "As long as you have made a good-faith estimate of the tax due, the IRS will accept your extension to file until August 15 even though you haven't forked over all the tax dollars that you owe the government."

You will be hit with penalties (0.5 percent per month) and interest on the balance of tax due. The advantage to filing the extension with a good-faith estimate of the tax due (even though you can't pay up) is that you avoid the dreaded late-filing penalty—a whopping 5 percent per month of the balance of any tax due.

Using the IRS label will make for faster and more efficient processing of your return.

Keep a copy of your return. If there is an inquiry into any aspect of your return, you'll want to be able to refer to the copy of the return that you filed. And, of course, you want to have something to refer to next year when you sit down to prepare your return.

Use certified mail. Always use certified mail to send your return to the IRS. Retain the receipt the post office gives you with the date stamp on it. That receipt is your only way to prove that you filed your tax return and that you filed it on time (your return is considered filed on the date that it is mailed.)

ALTERNATIVE WAYS TO FILE

The mail is no longer the only way to file your tax return. You may find advantages inherent in some of these alternatives.

File by phone. If you qualify to file Form 1040EZ, you can file using a touch-tone telephone. You needn't fill in lines on the form. All you need to do is punch in the numbers on your phone after dialing the specified toll-free number.

If you qualify for this option, the IRS will send you a package giving you the specifics. There's no extra cost, and it'll save you some paperwork.

Electronic filing. The IRS claims that electronic filing is the wave of the future. But think twice before you rush into filing that way. "Even if you file electronically, you must mail the IRS your W-2, as well as a signed Form 8453, which states that your return is accurate," Haveson points out. "If you owe tax, you'll also have to send a check for any balance due." Obviously, the process is not "paper-free."

Here are other points to consider about electronic filing.

• The upside: You'll get your refund faster. The IRS claims that you'll get your refund in 21 days if you file electronically, rather than the four to eight weeks that it takes to get a refund after filing a paper form.

• The downside: You'll have to pay to file. Yes, you'll have to pay a fee to an IRS-approved electronic filing center, such as H & R Block, to send your tax data directly to the IRS computers. That fee, which can run $15 to $40, will often wipe out any benefit of getting your refund sooner. So look before you leap.

• The IRS argues that since the tax preparer punches all the figures onto an electronic form, IRS employees do not have to transfer the figures from your paper form into their computers, and this reduces the likelihood of IRS keypunch errors on your return.

Calling In Reinforcements

So it's just you at the kitchen table with a stack of tax forms and a shoe box full of receipts and canceled checks. If beads of sweat are breaking out on your forehead, consider getting some help—either the electronic or flesh-and-blood variety.

LET SOFTWARE DO THE HARD JOBS

Tax software can take the headache out of the tax-preparation process. Not only are most software packages easy to use but also the most popular ones run in the $50-or-less price range.

Keep up your guard. "Think!" was IBM's old slogan, and you should take it to heart. Using tax-preparation software is no excuse to play dumb or be disorganized. "The product of the software, your tax return, is only as good as the information that you put into it," Tesser warns. "Garbage in, garbage out. You still have to organize your tax files, gather your tax information, and do some tax planning if you want to get the most bang for your buck."

On the other hand, your computer will spit out a nice neat tax return, usually free of math errors—two aspects of an audit-proof return. This will save you some sweat. And making changes on your return is a snap with a software package: Just punch in your changes and print. Calculations are done for you.

Use the help button. Most tax-preparation software comes with a built-in "help" button that gives you access to IRS instructions and usually some explanations in everyday language. If you run into problems, most packages offer technical support by phone or fax.

Skip the forms. Look for software packages that give you the option of preparing your returns by filling out tax forms on screen in the traditional way, or by going through an interactive interview process where the computer asks you a series of questions and where the responses you key into the computer are used to fill out the forms. It's not a bad approach if you feel daunted by the tax forms themselves.

Read the reviews. Tax-preparation software changes each year, and last year's most popular package could have slipped a notch. Get the latest reviews by reading about them in popular finance magazines.

Try the tried-and-true. Tax professionals say that it's hard to go wrong with one of these three software packages: TurboTax (Windows), MacInTax (Macintosh), or Kiplinger's TaxCut (Windows and Macintosh). All of them have the added feature of being able to import data from Quicken, a popular personal finance package. Each of these software programs comes with a money-back guarantee and will reimburse you for all penalties plus interest imposed should the software make a calculation error on your tax return. The price for each of these programs is under $50.

CONSIDER A TAX PRO

There's nothing wrong with choosing a tax professional to prepare your return. You just have to be smart about whom you choose and what services you really want.

Know the players. A certified public accountant (CPA) or an enrolled agent are the most likely licensed professionals to compete for your tax-preparation work. Tax attorneys usually don't handle tax preparation, except for their most valued and high-net-worth clients. The rest are just "commercial preparers"—not licensed or enrolled by any government body. Anyone can claim to be a commercial tax preparer—there's no law against it—so beware.

If your tax and financial affairs are pretty straightforward, you may need only a commercial preparer like H & R Block to drop the numbers onto the forms and correctly figure your tax. H & R Block is the country's largest,

States Want a Piece of Your Paycheck, Too

It's not just the "feds" you have to worry about when it comes to preparing income tax returns. Forty-one of our 50 states also levy an income tax.

As of 1996, the following states did *not* have an income tax: Alaska, Florida, New Hampshire, Nevada, South Dakota, Tennessee, Texas, Wyoming, and Washington. If you live in one of the other tax-happy states, you have to file a return.

Here are some things that certified public accountants say that you should look out for.

Watch for different rules. Take heart: Once you've determined what your income is for your federal tax return (on the Form 1040, for instance), many of the same income numbers will be used on your state return. But you have to read the instructions to be sure, since the rules can vary from state to state.

Read the instructions. States usually have their own rules about what income is taxable and how exemptions, deductions and tax are calculated. The instructions for your state tax return should be your starting point in preparing your state tax return properly. If your state does not send you tax forms automatically, call your state's Department of Revenue at the state capitol and ask for forms to be mailed to you.

Watch your deductions. Be careful: Not all states allow the same deductions in computing taxable income as the federal government does. For example, state and local taxes count as an itemized deduction for federal tax

and perhaps best-known, commercial tax-preparation service. Its fee for preparing the simplest tax returns runs under $100.

If, however, your financial and tax affairs are so complex that you feel that you want to engage a CPA or an enrolled agent, you'll pay fees ranging from perhaps as low as $50 per hour to as high as $250 an hour or more. A CPA or an enrolled agent will usually be interested in forging a relationship with you, and the best ones will be adept at exploiting complex areas of the tax code to your advantage.

Beware the independents. Every year, from January to April, all kinds of businesses from barbershops to drugstores offer "tax-preparation services." "You get what you pay for," advises Philpott. "You always need to be associated with competent, qualified people, and you should deal with the best professional available for your budget." Also, the preparer from your local barbershop or drugstore probably won't be able to help you much if your return is flagged for audit.

purposes, but they're not usually deductible in computing your state income tax. Again, check the instructions of your state income tax return to be sure.

Also, some states, notably Florida, have an "intangibles tax," which requires filing a form yearly. The tax is levied on the value of the intangibles, such as stocks and bonds, that you own. To find out just what your obligations are for paying state taxes, you should talk with a tax pro or call your state's Department of Revenue at the state capitol and ask for information about your state's requirements.

Be systematic. Be as systematic, organized, and diligent in state tax planning and return preparation as you are for your federal taxes. For instance, when you do an "October review" of your tax situation each year, make sure that you review not just your federal tax situation but also your state tax situation. Also, the advice to start your tax return preparation early—say, in January or February—applies to your federal and state tax returns equally.

Watch those due dates. Some states give you a break: Your state tax return may be due a little later than the federal return. Knowing the rules could take a little stress off you, so check those instructions for a date.

Buy time, if you need it. Some states don't even require that you request an extension of time to file your return past April 15—they'll grant it automatically without sending in a form, as long as your tax has been paid in full and you have requested an extension for federal tax purposes. Checking your state's rules on this could save you some paperwork around tax time.

Make it easy—and save. The more organized you are, the more money you'll save. You'll pay less in professional fees, and your tax pro will find it easier to suggest clever strategies rather than just wrestle numbers onto lines of the tax form. If you show up at the office of your CPA with a grocery bag of receipts and 1099s that he has to organize, you can bet that his fee will be much higher than it needed to be.

The early bird . . . Tax professionals are notoriously overworked from January through April 15. So the earlier you make an appointment with your CPA to hand over your tax files and get the preparation process going, the better.

Bottom Line

Filing frugally means treating tax preparation as a year-round project by systematically gathering data throughout the year and getting your tax files in order well before the deadline. This approach will minimize not only the amount of tax you pay but also the effort and anguish expended in the filing process.

Words to the Wise

Casualty or theft losses: Maybe a hurricane wiped out your home. Maybe a con man absconded with your life savings. Rest assured that the IRS will look closely at your resulting tax deduction.

Home-office deduction: One of the often-abused deductions that will prompt the IRS to scrutinize your return.

The "long" form: The longer version of the 1040 tax form may be more complex, but it also allows you to employ tax-saving strategies such as itemized deductions.

Allies

IRS live hot line: 1-800-829-1040, to talk an IRS employee.

IRS recorded tax information: 1-800-829-4477, around the clock.

IRS tax form hot line: 1-800-829-3676 (1-800-TAX-FORM).

"Your Federal Income Tax": Also known as IRS Publication 17. Information on your taxes and tax return. Fill out the order blank that comes with your tax forms, or call 1-800-829-3676 (1-800-TAX-FORM).

Part 9

WORK

Landing the Ultimate Job

Feel Like a Number? Make a Name for Yourself in Corporate America

Once upon a time, in the Land of Work, Mr. and Ms. Job Hunter went out in search of employment. They answered an ad in the paper, got hired by Company A and stayed with Company A for the rest of their working days.

Unfortunately, "once upon a time" has passed. And the Land of Work has drastically changed.

Big shifts in the corporate world have made finding, landing, and keeping your job a whole new ball game. In a nutshell, merger mania and downsizing, combined with the introduction of new technology, have made long-term careers with one company an anachronism. People now face short-cycle career paths, where movement from one company to another is the norm, says Douglas B. Richardson, a nationally recognized authority on career planning and development and president of his own career consulting firm, Richardson and Company, in Bala Cynwyd, Pennsylvania.

"We're now seeing a lot of people whose careers are made up of a lot of moves," he says.

This means that Mr. and Ms. Job Hunter—most likely that's you or somebody that you know—will be faced with finding a new job either now or sometime in the near future. If you're already there, you know that the scene isn't pretty. There are lots of others out there doing exactly the same thing you are—answering want ads, sending out résumés, networking, using headhunters, and doing whatever it takes to land one of the few challenging positions available. With more people using the same techniques,

Where Should Your Résumé Land?

When you're applying for a job at a company, there are at least two places to send your résumé—either to the human resources department or to a manager who has the power to hire you. So how should you address your letter?

This points to the cardinal rule of job hunting, says John Harahan, former president and owner of Telkom, a recruitment firm in Pennsylvania. "Try never to deal with human resources or personnel," he says. "Go directly to the hiring manager."

The reason is that if you mail to the same place that everyone else does, your letter will just get buried in a résumé landslide.

But human resources managers—like Donna Morgan, supervisor of associate relations in the human resources department of H & R Block in Kansas City, Missouri—point out that sending directly to a hiring manager can have its problems, too. A hiring manager could easily just shuffle your letter into an "in" bin where it will languish forever. Or the secretary could decide that the boss shouldn't be bothered with your letter and lay it aside.

Morgan's solution is to send a cover letter and résumé to both human resources and the hiring manager. But if you do mail twice to the same company, mention that fact in each cover letter, says Morgan. That lets both parties know what's going on and makes it clear that you didn't double up by mistake.

---

how do you set yourself apart? Let's take a look at several key job-hunting tools and see how you can use them in unique ways to put yourself ahead of the pack.

Employment Ads: How to Stand Out

One of the first places many job hunters turn when conducting their job search is the newspaper classified ads. After all, right there in black and white are descriptions of job openings and a blatant invitation to apply, right? Well, sort of.

One of the biggest problems with the classifieds is beating the numbers game. Chances are that anywhere from 25 to 200 other people are sending in résumés in response to the same ad that you are. And that means that your résumé becomes just one in a pile of 200 that lands on someone's desk—most likely a desk in the company's human resources department. Once there, your résumé becomes part of a review system in which the majority of résumés are weeded out and only a golden few get selected for the candidate pile.

MAKE YOUR RÉSUMÉ FLOAT TO THE TOP

Is there any way to rise to the top of this paper mountain? Any way to enhance your résumé's chances for selection? Here's the advice offered by a number of personnel experts.

Speed counts. "When you see an ad on Sunday, get your résumé in to us on Monday," says Carter Giles, a human resources executive with Front Range Medical Management in Denver. "We look them over right away. So if we find five or six in the first batch that look good, and yours is in the second batch that arrives, it might not even get looked at," he says.

Fire up the fax. Companies who put a fax number in an ad are generally looking for someone *immediately*, says Giles. So if there is a fax number in the ad, use it. If you don't own a fax, go to a stationery store, a business-supply outfit, or a photocopying service and use theirs to send your résumé.

Use the code. Many classified ads include a code, either with the address or at the beginning or end of the ad. Be sure to include it on your cover letter or résumé because that's what tells the employer what job you are interested in, says Giles. If you don't use the code, the employer may put your application in a slush pile where it never gets reviewed.

Cover your bases. Some job applicants send in their résumés without cover letters. Big mistake. "Without the cover letter specifying which job you are interested in, we can't tell which job you are applying to, and there's a chance that the résumé is going to land on the wrong desk," says Donna Morgan, supervisor of associate relations in the human resources department of H & R Block in Kansas City, Missouri.

Become a custom tailor. Whenever you respond to a want ad, imagine your résumé bobbing along in a river of other responses. If you want yours to float to the top and get noticed, forget about printing up dozens of copies of your résumé for every potential employer. Instead, custom-tailor your résumé on a word processor each time you send out an application, suggests Taunee Besson, president of Career Dimensions in Dallas and author of the book *Resumes*.

To do the custom tailoring, follow the ad's lead and be sure that your résumé gives priority to whatever skills and experience are most relevant to the job advertised. Also, do some research about the company and tweak your résumé to "fit." For example, if you know five software programs but Company A uses Program 1, be sure that your experience with Program 1 is highlighted most in your résumé.

The slogan to remember, says Besson, is "Tailor or Die."

Be ready for the phone screen. If you're applying for a position at a large company, be prepared for a spur-of-the-moment telephone interview. Some companies have a personnel staffer call to ask a series of questions to

Who's Scanning? A Quick Look

Here's a sampling of companies that use scanners to electronically manage and monitor the résumés of job applicants, according to the International Association of Human Resources Information Management.

- Aldus Corporation
- Avis Rent-a-Car System
- Blue Shield of California
- Citibank A.G.
- CompuServe
- Eli Lilly and Company
- General American Life Insurance
- Hallmark Cards
- Okidata
- U.S. Surgical Corporation
- Wisconsin Electric Power

Your résumé also is likely to be fed into a scanner at large companies, at recruiting firms, at big government agencies, and when you submit your résumé to job listings that appear on the Internet, says Taunee Besson, president of Career Dimensions in Dallas and author of the book *Resumes*.

weed out the field of applicants. Questions you can expect in a phone screen include:

- What is your salary range?
- Is the location good for you?
- Are the hours right for you?

The interviewer may also ask a number of technical questions about your field. So be prepared. Keep a script with your answers near the phone.

Read beyond the ads. While the classified ads do list job openings, read other parts of the paper for leads, says Tony Lee, editor of *National Business Employment Weekly*. Look for mention of companies that are expanding or introducing new products and send your cover letter and résumé their way, he says. These companies may have openings coming up.

Is a Machine Reading Your Résumé?

Scanners have invaded much of corporate America. No, this is not the plot of a science fiction flick. At many companies today, résumés are no longer read and reviewed by humans. Often the first reading and weeding is done by a résumé scanning machine, says Besson.

Scary? It doesn't have to be. If you know how scanners work, you can actually turn them to your advantage.

If your résumé goes to a company that uses a résumé scanner, or if you e-mail your résumé to a company, the document essentially becomes digital. That is, your résumé no longer exists as a piece of paper. Instead, it's an electronic file stored in a computer database.

Then, when the company wants to find the five top candidates for Position X, a computer program searches the résumés in the database for keywords that are specific to the requirements for that job. When the computer comes to your résumé, it hunts through it for preselected words, much like a spell-checking program scans a document for misspelled words. If your résumé contains a high number of keywords, it gets selected for the candidate pile, says Besson. The résumé with the *most* keywords goes to the top of the pile, she says.

This means that you have to write your résumé differently than you have in the past.

Play detective. Before sending in your résumé, find out if the company to which you are applying uses a résumé scanner and an applicant-tracking system. To do this, simply call the human resources department and ask.

Find the right words. Do some research and find out the appropriate keywords to include in your résumé, says Besson. Possible keywords to include are the buzzwords for your particular industry and any industry terms, skills, or qualifications listed in a job ad. Also, read about the company and talk to people who know the company to come up with more keywords.

Once you've compiled a hefty list of keywords, work them into your résumé—the more the better. You can weave them into the body copy of your résumé, of course. But some applicants even include a separate paragraph that simply lists keywords one after the other. In some systems, mentioning the same keyword more than once can get you more points, experts say.

Format carefully. Be sure to format your résumé in a way that's easy for a scanner to read, says Jay Ferriera, manager of the human resources department at PeopleSoft Corporation in Pleasanton, California. Here are some rules of thumb.

- Use standard type fonts, such as Helvetica and Courier.
- Avoid underlining or using bold or italic type.
- Use a 10-point type size or larger.
- Use white paper.
- Steer clear of boxes and fancy graphics
- If you e-mail your résumé to a company, be sure to send it as an ASCII file rather than a text file.

Allies: Enlist Others in Your Search

So many people fixate on answering classified ads and sending out their résumés, says Besson, that they ignore a crucial truth about hiring: Employers prefer hiring people that they already know and trust, she says.

New Job-Hunting Domain: Online Options

Maybe you thought that the Internet was nothing but a playground for self-absorbed cyberpunks. Well, job hunting is a pursuit in which the information superhighway can pay off big-time, says Taunee Besson, president of Career Dimensions in Dallas and author of the book *Resumes*. So if you have access to a personal computer and a modem, here are two powerful strategies. Turn on and tap in.

Online career centers. Surf the Net for online career centers and job posting centers, says Besson. A good place to begin is a site called, appropriately enough, The Online Career Center.

Company Web pages. Many companies are posting job openings on their pages on the Internet's World Wide Web, says Besson. So if you're interested in a particular company, track down its Web address, log on, and check it out.

Caution: If you respond to an online job opening by e-mailing your résumé, remember that it may not go just to the employer listed in the ad. It may end up posted on an electronic bulletin board somewhere, says Besson. So don't assume that your job-hunting efforts will remain confidential.

If you decide to launch your résumé into cyberspace anyway, be sure to send it as an ASCII file, says Besson. Otherwise, it will look like gibberish when it arrives at the other end.

That's why many career experts say that networking is the most powerful job-hunting tool. "The lion's share of employment since the days of the Pharaohs comes from informal, interpersonal contacts," says Richardson.

WHOM YOU KNOW REALLY DOES COUNT

Anyone can network, of course. So you need to know how to do it better than your competition. Here's how.

Spell out the details. "If you ask people that you know, they generally have no idea what you do," says Lee. So for your current network to function properly, you really have to teach your contacts specifically what it is that you do, what skills you have, and what type of job you want.

To do that, Richardson suggests two exercises. First, say to your friends, "Here's what I want you to keep an eye open for . . ." and then spell out exactly what types of opportunities you are interested in. Second, ask your contacts, "How will you describe me to others?" Listen to the description and edit it as you see fit. Then have your friend "play back" the edited version.

Keep it casual. During networking conversations, some people are so overly rehearsed that they sound like a Broadway production. Instead, keep your language conversational and casual, says Richardson. Look at net-working—whether you're talking with dinner party guests or asking some-one for a networking meeting—as an opportunity to set up an informal human relationship. Be professional but relaxed, focused but informal. And check your shtick at the door.

Set the agenda. When requesting a networking meeting, it's essential to set the agenda clearly at the outset, says Richardson. Remember that this discussion will be a tad more formal than cocktail party conversation but less formal than a job interview. Your mission is exploratory—to pick the brain of someone who's close to the business, field, or industry where you want to get a job.

When you call a contact to request a networking meeting, be sure to provide the following information.

- How you got the contact's name
- Why you are calling
- What kind of advice or information you are seeking
- What your situation is—are you actively conducting a job search, or are you just putting your toe in the water and gathering information?

If the contact asks how long the meeting will take, don't just volunteer 20 minutes, Richardson says—that's arbitrarily short. Just answer, "That's up to you," and let the contact call the shot.

Be reasonable. Remember that your contact isn't Santa Claus. So keep your requests for help within reason. Asking for information about an industry, for the contact's opinion about a trend, or even for names of other people to talk to are all within the realm of reason. Asking someone to actually find you a job or to solve the cosmic riddle of your working life is not reasonable, says Richardson.

The underlying arrangement in networking is that you are asking someone for a favor, he says. You are saying to your contact, "If you will give me a very short period of your life, I will give you the satisfaction of having helped me."

Treat 'em like experts. Another part of the networking arrangement is that your contact is supposed to be the expert, says Richardson. So give your contact plenty of opportunity to brandish his expertise, and keep your own chatter to a minimum.

Send your regards. A key part of the networking process is following up with your contacts. First, be sure to send a note thanking the contact for their time and effort, says Richardson. After that, you can follow up briefly and quickly in several ways.

- Send the contact an article that you think might be of interest.
- Call the contact with a very specific question.

Subtle Signals That Mean "Go"

You're deep into a job interview, and now you want to bring it home. What can you do to set yourself apart from other candidates?

"So much of the job-selection process is rapport," says Harvey B. Brickley, principal of Corporate Transition Solutions in Atlanta. Of course, you always need the technical competence; but if there are 10 other applicants in the running, it's building a good rapport that can sway the deal, he says. The way to do that is to read the positive signals that an interviewer sends you, respond to them, and build on them.

Watch for and respond to these positive signals, Brickley says.

Future speak. A subtle sign that an employer is gaining interest in you is when the interviewer shifts from talking about the past to talking about the future. Questions like "What do you want to do next?" or "Where do you see yourself in five years?" indicate a high degree of interest.

Linking your name directly with the job. When the interviewer starts verbally placing you in the job, that also indicates interest. For instance, the interviewer may shift from saying, "The person we hire will need to handle . . . " and start saying, "Sally, you need to handle . . . ." That's a sign that the interviewer is envisioning you in the job. You can build on this vision by switching your own language to more team-oriented phrases. Start talking in terms of "we," as if you were already a member of the team, says Brickley.

Long interview. If you were scheduled for an hour-long interview and it goes on for 90 minutes, that's a good sign, says Brickley. Likewise, if you find yourself being introduced to and interviewing with higher-ups who weren't on the original agenda, that's another clue that you're being considered seriously.

Request for references. People usually don't take the time to check references unless they are really interested, says Brickley. So if they ask for yours, that's a positive sign.

Spending money on you. If a company starts spending money on you, that's a clear sign of serious interest. Taking a psychological assessment or drug test costs money, so if you find yourself asked to do those things, don't be offended. It's a compliment.

- Call the contact to check in and let him know how your search is going.
- Send an updated version of your résumé.
- Send a holiday greeting card.

The key to an effective follow-up is to keep it short and simple, says Richardson.

Get regular. Some people wait until they're out of a job or ready to change jobs to actively network. Networking is something that should be done continually, even when you're employed, comfortable and happy with your job. "Stay in touch with everyone all the time," says Lee.

Be patient. Networking may be a powerful tool, but it's not always a speedy one. So don't fret if you don't get immediate results—the wheels are still turning. "The thing to remember is that just because you don't hear of a job opening right away doesn't mean that something isn't happening," Richardson says.

HEADHUNTERS: HIRE YOUR OWN ADVOCATE

Chances are that you've heard horror stories about those personnel recruiters commonly known as headhunters. Even recruiters themselves tell them.

Take John Harahan, former president and owner of Telkom, a recruitment firm in Pennsylvania that placed job seekers with such giants as Mellon Bank, Du Pont, and Signa. "In my nine years, I had three instances where clients had given their résumés to another headhunter, and that headhunter sent the résumé to the person's current boss," says Harahan. "Talk about embarrassing."

But using a headhunter doesn't have to be a nightmare. In fact, a headhunter can be a valuable tool in your job-hunting kit, says Harahan. But you have to know how to use it properly.

Check the reputation. Shop around and find a search firm that has a good reputation, says Eric Kropp, a recruiter with EHS and Associates in Minneapolis. A great place to get recommendations is also the most accessible—from your colleagues and friends, people that you know and trust.

Once you have a list of headhunters, "don't hesitate to ask the firm for names of people they have placed," he says. Call those people and ask about their experience with the firm. This will give you an idea of the level of service that you can expect. Keep in mind, though, that anyone to whom the firm refers you is bound to be happy with the service they received.

Zero in on the individual. When picking a headhunter, don't base your choice on the reputation of the firm alone. You need to go beyond checking out the company—check out the individual that you are thinking of signing up with, says Harahan. "You are using the headhunter, not the firm," he says, so know the specifics of that individual.

Pick a specialist. Stick with a headhunter who specializes in your field, says Harahan. The best way to find somebody like this is to talk with others in your industry, he says.

Interview the headhunter. Once you have identified several headhunters that come highly recommended, go out and interview them, says Harahan. Evaluate them and pick the one that you think is most appropriate for you.

During this process, remember that the headhunter is also sizing you up and evaluating how professional you are. Put your best foot forward when meeting with your headhunter and don't let your hair down too much, says Lynn Taylor, vice-president of Robert Half International, the world's largest executive staffing firm, headquartered in Menlo Park, California. Take the time to dress appropriately and present your best image.

Two headhunters are better than one. One headhunter alone cannot cover all the job opportunity bases. "I highly recommend that people use more than one recruiter," says Harahan. "I told my people, 'Don't limit your search to me.' "

Keep tabs on your résumé. When using headhunters, always know where your résumé is going before it goes, says Harahan. "Never give someone carte blanche to send your résumé wherever they please," he says. The reason is that some headhunters figure that the more they throw your résumé around, the more likely it is to "stick" somewhere. If the headhunter checks with you before sending out each résumé, you can stop it from being sent to the same place more than once—or from being sent somewhere that you don't want it to go, like your current boss.

Hang on to your wallet. Never pay a headhunter, says Harahan. "The headhunter is working for the company—not you—and is being paid by the company," he says. "You do not have to pay the headhunter a fee for the service." Also, you should never have to pay any expenses, such as travel costs, when being wooed by a company. The employer should pay all the expenses related to a job interview, Harahan says. And never offer to cover expenses—that just shows desperation.

Pocket your pen. Don't sign any contracts with a headhunter, says Harahan. When you land a job through a headhunter, some will ask you to sign a contract promising to pay the headhunter's fee if you leave the job before six months has passed. "That's bull," he says. "Do not sign anything and do not promise them anything."

Be sure to diversify. Headhunters are a valuable part of your job-search tool kit. But having one doesn't mean that you can rest your feet on your desk and wait for the job offers to roll in, says Taylor. Use headhunters as just one of several plans of attack.

BOTTOM LINE

The days are gone when you could update your résumé, print up a zillion copies, and drop them in the mail to personnel offices around the country. Use computer technology to tailor your résumé for each prospective employer. And act fast when you see an alluring job posted in the classified—particularly if there's a fax number listed.

WORDS TO THE WISE

Job code: A code carried in a "help wanted" ad. Be sure to put it on your letter or else it may never find the right home.

Keywords: Words that a computer scanner will spot in your résumé indicating that you have the right training and experience.

Phone screen: An out-of-the-blue telephone call from a personnel staffer. You'll be asked a list of questions intended to weed out the applicant pool.

ALLIES

Hoover's Handbooks: A comprehensive listing by Reference Press that rates corporations on different qualities and issues. Lists staff size, corporate structure, names of certain managers, and division heads.

National Business Employment Weekly: A weekly newspaper published by Dow Jones devoted exclusively to careers and job hunting.

National Business Employment Weekly Premier Guides: A series of books, available in bookstores, written by career experts. Each book focuses exclusively on a particular job-hunting or career issue, such as résumés, interviewing, networking, cover letters, and alternative careers.

Branching Out

How to Clock Out of the Rat Race for Good

Maybe Johnny Paycheck is your idol. Who hasn't entertained the fantasy of marching into the boss's office yodeling the country-and-western hit "Take This Job and Shove It"? Just quitting—no notice, no warning, no nothing.

Saying *"Hasta la vista, baby!"* to the daily grind has definite appeal. John McDorman, managing partner of Transition Consulting in Dallas, says that statistics show that a whopping 80 percent of us hate what we're doing day to day. So if you've thought about branching out and doing something new—changing careers, for instance; going into business for yourself; or retiring early—you're clearly not alone.

When to Throw In the Towel

Lots of us may fall into the Unhappy Puppy category when it comes to our jobs, but few manage to make the break to something new. When you look at people who've been laid off, says McDorman, 60 percent end up returning to the same line of work for a different employer. Just 20 percent will make a career change, and another 20 percent will explore entrepreneurial ventures.

If so many people are unhappy but so few make changes, something must be getting in the way. According to career experts, here's what keeps people locked into the same old routine.

Adversity to change. Psychologically, it's easier for people to accept the current state of affairs than to do something different, says David Urban, Ph.D., associate professor of marketing at the Virginia Commonwealth University School of Business in Richmond. The majority of people are just plain adverse to change, he says.

Commitment to family. Often people feel that a change will have negative implications for their family, says Dr. Urban. For many, this overpowers any willingness to take risks.

Fear of letting others down. Some people feel that they can't make a change because they will be letting others down, says Dr. Urban. They carry a sense of being indispensable, he says.

Financial issues. One big hurdle is money. Many people feel that they can't afford to redirect their careers, says Dr. Urban.

When workers fall short in the financial planning department, they often believe that they have few options when they consider job changes, says Richard H. Koonce, a career consultant in Arlington, Virginia, and author of *Career Power!*

American culture. "We come from a cultural background, a generation, that believes that in order to be a good person, you must have a job," says Jean Walker, executive vice-president of Pathways through Career Transition in Portland, Oregon. It's more than just being used to and wanting stability and security, she says. Baby boomers are people who grew up believing that to work is good and that an employed person is a good person, she says. So to leave a steady job for the risky or unknown goes against the cultural vein.

KNOCK DOWN THOSE OBSTACLES TO A NEW LIFE

So how do you shove those obstacles aside and charge on to a new and happier working life? Here's what experts recommend.

Stash your cash. While you are working at your steady-paying job, save and build up a financial war chest, says McDorman. Most people live on the financial edge, hardly earning enough to cover their spending habits, and that kind of financial bondage is what can prevent you from making a change, he says.

Let go of the security thing. If you've been in corporate America for 15 years, branching out on your own may sound like skydiving without a parachute. But in today's corporate world there *is* no security anymore, says John P. Creveling, a Philadelphia-based vice-president of the outplacement and consulting firm Drake Beam Morin. So let go of the idea that a corporate job is a protected, long-term, sure thing. It just isn't so.

Tackle your fears. If you sense that fear is paralyzing you, step back and ask, "What are my fears?" and "How real are they?" Jot your fears down, be as specific as you can and then look for ways to reduce or minimize them, says Creveling.

One way to do this is to look at your track record, he says. Review all the times in your life when you made transitions or changes successfully— when you left home, moved, got married, whatever—and give yourself credit for those. Doing this can help you realize that change is possible.

Watch for red flags. There's a whole slew of signals that indicate the need for change. They can range from boredom to cynicism to dawdling on the job, says Dr. Urban.

Leaping the Psychological Barriers

People contemplating a career change face two big psychological obstacles: their own psychology and the psychology of those with the ability to hire them into a new field.

Some people are distressingly mired in the rut syndrome, says McDorman. That's when people have comfortable positions, make good money, and enjoy the niceties of life but have no fulfillment or joy in what they do, he explains. Moving someone out of that generally takes a strong force from the outside. "One of the largest obstacles that people face is getting the internal motivation to change," he says.

The mind-set of hiring authorities in other career fields can also keep you landlocked. You may believe that your skills are transferable to a new field. But the person doing the hiring may consider you a bigger risk than someone who already has direct experience. They see you as a novice who will require an investment of time and money.

You can overcome these obstacles. Here's what experts recommend.

Use your springboard. The old notion still holds true: An employed person is a more attractive commodity. Therefore, the time to make a career change is when you have a job, not when you are out of work, says McDorman. So think of your current job as the "platform" that you'll use to spring into a new career.

Test-market your idea. While you are pulling down a paycheck from a full-time job, test-market your ideas about a career change, says McDorman. While many people are ready to say, "I'm gonna blow this pop stand," rarely do people know where they are going *to*, he says. So do your homework and get some sense of whether a change into your new field is feasible.

Size yourself up. In making a career change, take the time to evaluate your skills, aptitude, personality, and motivation, experts say. Finding your future focal point is not "microwave easy," says McDorman. It takes a lot of effort. So sit down, perhaps with a career coach, and identify the common threads in your past successes. You can find excellent exercises in books such as *Intercristo's Career Kit*, by Dick Staub and Jeff Troutman; Richard Bolles's *What Color Is Your Parachute?*; and Arthur F. Miller and Ralph T. Mattson's *The Truth about You*.

Write your own job description. Any public job listing that you run across is likely to be larded down with narrowly defined, stereotypical positions. If you are trying to make a change in careers, there's a good chance that you will not fit into these ready-made molds, says Walker. So categorize your skills and strengths, prioritize them, and write your own job

Breaking the Experience Barrier

Catch-22! You can't get a job in the new field that you want to enter because you don't have experience. And you can't get that experience unless you can get a job in the field.

So get creative, says Jean Walker, executive vice-president of Pathways through Career Transition in Portland, Oregon. Here's how she recommends that you get the necessary experience.

Give it away. Okay, so you won't be raking in the greenbacks at first, but volunteering in the new field that you're considering is one way to get experience. Lots of organizations would welcome no-cost labor in exchange for some hands-on experience.

Go on trial. A more unorthodox arrangement is to volunteer with a contingency. Offer your volunteer services at an organization for three months, with the contingency that if they like your work and hire you after the three months, you get paid for those three months, says Walker. This arrangement allows you and the employer to check each other out and gives you experience, and if all goes well, you'll be compensated for your efforts, too.

Gather credentials, not degrees. You don't necessarily have to go back to school to switch careers, says Walker. "I really discourage people from getting additional degrees," she says. Instead, just get a few educational credentials in the field that you're interested in.

A good, professional training course is often more useful than a college or graduate course anyway, she says. Look for training classes specifically designed for professionals. Say that you are thinking of switching into a new field that requires Internet experience. Call one of the companies that you're interested in and ask what training courses get their employees up and running online. Then sign up for the course yourself.

Call a meeting. Request informational interviews with experts in the new field that you are considering, says Walker. An informational interview is different from a networking meeting. You're not looking for job leads— you're gathering information to see if the field is right for you. Be sure that your intentions are clear, and be sure to follow up with a thank-you note.

description based on that. Then go out into the world and see if you can find or create that job.

Get that network working. Turn to your network for assistance in making your career change, says McDorman. If you have strong relationships with those people, chances are that they can help you.

Create a "loyal link." There's nothing like having an industry insider who is willing to lobby on your behalf. McDorman calls such allies loyal links—people in the industry who will argue your case to potential hiring managers. They work like an advance man who will actively try to sell you as a product, he says. You can find these loyal links in a strong network, if you have one. Be sure that your links know what you are looking for and point them in the right direction.

Quit When You're Ahead

John Graves, founder and owner of Bike Line, enjoys a level of entrepreneurial success that most of us only dream of. He started with the purchase of a single bicycle store and built the business into a virtual empire on wheels. In 1996, Bike Line was the largest retail bicycle chain in the country.

How do you know if going into business for yourself is the right move? It's important to remember that starting and running a small business is not a panacea for all your work problems, says William Fioretti, director of the University of Cincinnati Small Business Development Center. If you are doing it in an attempt to solve your problems at work, you need to rethink it, he says.

"The motivation should be that you are doing so well at work," Fioretti says. "It should be a positive motivation of wanting to do your own thing instead of a negative motivation of leaving a bad situation."

There are basically three options for entrepreneurs: starting up your own venture, buying an existing business, or buying a franchise.

START-UP BUSINESSES: MONEY AND MARKETING

Start-up businesses are generally the lowest-cost alternative for the fledgling entrepreneur, says Fioretti. They also enable you to control the business's growth and to satisfy your need to do your own thing, he says. But there are some big obstacles, or systems, that challenge folks who want to start up their own businesses.

The biggest hurdle is usually a lack of funds, says Fioretti. Often people want to go into business for themselves but just aren't sure whether they have the money to do it. A common downfall for new business owners is starting out with less money than they really need and then running out.

The second hurdle that people face is assessing whether there is a need for the product or service and whether people will pay your price for it, says Fioretti. Knowing that there is a market for your business is an essential factor, he says.

The third obstacle, says Fioretti, is lacking experience in the area of business that you are considering.

How can you ensure that your start-up business is successful? Here's what experts recommend.

Start with the market analysis. The first step is to find out how much demand there is for your product or service and whether people will pay for it. This is called doing a market analysis. You can conduct your own market analysis by reading trade journals and business magazines and by consulting with trade associations, says Fioretti. Most people don't even do a market analysis, but that's really the place to start, he says.

Do a mini-survey. Conduct a mini-survey about the product or service that you intend to offer, says Fioretti. "It doesn't have to be statistically sophisticated," he says. "It could mean talking to 20 people, asking them the same set of good questions and using their answers as a thermometer of the market for your service. I've seen business plans presented to banks that are based on very simple surveys."

Have a plan, Stan. It's absolutely essential that you write a business plan for your new venture, experts say. A good business plan will include a statement of purpose, a business section, and financial section. "If you look at successful businesses, they have business strategies and business plans," says Creveling. "It's important to do it, and it is important to be committed to it."

Stash the cash. Stockpile some savings to fall back on during the beginning phase of your new business. Some small-business experts recommend that you sock away enough money to cover your expenses for at least 18 months of business. Other experts say that that may be excessive padding—but you'd better prove it to yourself with careful paperwork before you launch your enterprise. Fioretti recommends that each prospective business owner do a detailed cash flow analysis that will give a realistic picture of how the new business will perform and then use that analysis to decide how much savings you need.

In addition to the money that you'll need for start-up costs—one-time expenses like equipment purchases, telephone lines, and initial inventory—you'll need what's called working capital. This covers monthly operating expenses like rent, salaries, insurance, taxes, and inventory resupply until the sales from your business can cover the costs of running it.

Pad your plan. Have you decided how much money you'll stash away for your new business? Now add in some more—a little margin for emergencies. For example, Creveling recalls that when he was in business for himself, the computer system that he'd inherited went on the fritz, costing him a couple thousand dollars in unexpected expenses. So play it safe.

Beware: There's no free lunch. If you are looking for a loan in order to get started, "there are really no grants or start-up funds out there from the government that come without stipulations," warns Fioretti. There are a lot of misconceptions and plenty of rip-off organizations that sell worthless information, he says. In particular, beware organizations that try to sell you $65 books on government sources of loan money, he says. There may be grant money available for start-up business, for instance, but often it's only available for research on narrowly defined subjects. And guaranteed government loan programs typically require that you have 20 percent of the start-up capital on hand and that you have collateral for the remaining 80 percent that's provided by the loan.

Scope out the "micros." The Small Business Administration (SBA) offers low-collateral micro-loans for up to $25,000, says Fioretti. Talk to your local Small Business Development Center, your local economic development company, or the chamber of commerce about such loans. The best time to apply for these loans is between October and December, when the funds are replenished, he says. These loan programs won't consider you unless you have already been turned down by a bank. So apply for a loan from a bank, get rejected, and then seek out the micro-loan, says Fioretti.

Ask for low-docs. Also ask around about "low-doc" (or low-document) bank loans, which are guaranteed by the SBA, says Fioretti. These programs are targeted to loans of $100,000 or less. They're issued through banks, require minimal paperwork, and can be decided upon within three business days (and for those reasons the banks really like them). In some rural areas, bankers may not be aware of low-docs, so you need to ask outright about them, says Fioretti.

Join the biz. If you're planning to open a business in an industry that's new to you, take the time to learn the business first, says Fioretti. Get a job, at any level, and observe everything. "There are very few places where you can go to learn about a business other than going there and working in it," he says.

Hire the experts. Recognize what expertise you don't have and then seek out and hire the people who can provide it, says Creveling. Consider hiring an attorney, accountant, or marketing person, he says.

Find a partner. Another way to address your lack of expertise in certain aspects of a business is to team up with a partner, says McDorman. "If you feel the itch to become an entrepreneur, don't jump into something that you don't know unless you jump in with someone who has experience in that area," he says.

SIZING UP AN EXISTING BUSINESS

Buying a business that already exists has its own advantages for the entrepreneur. For one thing, says Fioretti, you can see what you are buying into and analyze it. But going this route will generally require a fair amount of money, says Fioretti.

If you're contemplating purchasing a business, our experts recommend the following tips.

Ask why. Find out why the current owner is selling, says Creveling. Is it a financial reason—like a cash flow problem or heavy debt? Or is the reason more personal—perhaps relocating the family to the other side of the country?

Check the records. Ask to see the business's financial statements and be sure to analyze their past performance, says Fioretti. Look at a minimum of three years of statements and pay particular attention to the financial activity of the last year, suggests Creveling.

Consider location. Take a careful look at the location of the business, says Creveling. Have any new competitors arrived recently that could affect the business? Is the area one that you are ready to commit to for the long haul? Will you be able to relocate if need be?

Consult customers. Talk with customers about how the business has or hasn't served them, says Creveling. Get their feedback about its strengths and shortcomings.

Talk to employees. Interview people who have worked for the business, says Fioretti. They may give you a view from the inside that the owners aren't able to—or don't want to.

FRANCHISES: WORKING WITH A NET

Maybe you'd rather own a branch of a larger, parent organization. That's basically what you're doing when you buy a franchise. As the franchisee, you own and manage the business. But the store name, advertising, labeling, and marketing all come from the parent company (for example, Dunkin' Donuts, Boston Market, and Merry Maids).

One primary advantage to a franchise, says Fioretti, is that success rates are generally higher than they are for start-up businesses. But don't rely too heavily on success rate statistics. Often, if a franchise is verging on failure, the franchiser steps in and buys out that particular location.

There are several other pluses to buying a franchise, says A. Bernard Frechtman, a lawyer in Indianapolis who specializes in franchise law.

- If it's an established, successful franchise, you gain instant name recognition and identification.
- When you buy a franchise, the franchiser often provides employee screening, training, and preparation for you.
- The franchiser often provides you with the demographic information that you need to decide on a good location as well as plenty of research-and-development support.
- Franchises are often easier to sell than smaller mom-and-pop businesses.

All in all, buying and owning a franchise can be very much of a turnkey operation, says Frechtman. When you develop your own business from scratch, there's a lot that you have to figure out on your own. But with a franchise, the parent company provides you with a complete roster of what you need to do and a lot of support in getting it done, he says.

Whether that turnkey nature is for you depends. If you're looking to really beat the system that is corporate America, says Fioretti, starting a franchise may feel more like joining a system than beating one.

While you're investigating franchises, try the following tips.

Hit the books. Before you buy a franchise, do a careful, thorough investigation. Check out the individual franchise and the industry that it's in, says Frechtman. Find the industry studies. Ask people in the industry lots of questions. Consult the appropriate trade association for written materials and names of people to talk to.

Hit the bricks. When you've exhausted official industry sources, gather direct observations. Get on the phone to find out if there is any litigation in progress against the franchiser. Look up names of current franchisees and call them. Visit current franchisees in person.

Get a job. If you really want to know about a particular franchise, take a job in that business, says Frechtman. Go to Dunkin' Donuts or Sir Speedy, for instance, and get a minimum-wage job. There's no better way to learn the business, he says.

Break out the reading glasses. When you get close to deciding on a franchise, get ready to scrutinize some fine print—specifically, the Uniform Franchise Offering Circular (UFOC). This is not a document to skip through quickly, says Frechtman.

Hire the right lawyer. Chances are that your personal lawyer has little or no experience with franchises, says Frechtman. But your lawyer can help you find another lawyer who does. Ask your lawyer to call the Bar Association and ask for the directory of members of the Forum Committee on Franchising, says Frechtman. The directory lists its members alphabetically and by city, so your lawyer can identify a franchise lawyer in your area.

It should take the lawyer about five hours to adequately analyze the franchise agreement, or UFOC, says Frechtman. So for an analysis only (not including any negotiation by the lawyer) expect to pay the lawyer's hourly rate times five. Some lawyers charge a flat fee for such a review—anywhere from $500 to $750, says Frechtman.

Retirement: Unlimited Options

Ah, retirement: You snatch up a gold watch, toss your wing tips off a fishing pier, and head for Florida. Crack me a coconut, dear, I'm thirsty.

Well, maybe things were like that in your grandparents' day. But retirement is changing. Some career experts even recommend that you seriously question whether you should retire at all.

Attorney and financial consultant Stephen Pollan, co-author of *The Business of Living* and author of *Surviving the Squeeze*, calls retirement a failed social experiment, a relic of Franklin Delano Roosevelt's efforts to create job openings during a time of major unemployment. Moseying out to pasture at age 65 won't be practical for many of today's baby boomers, Pollan says, considering the instability of pensions and Social Security. Besides, why give up at what may be the most mature and productive phase of your life?

To stop working completely when you're still highly competent is a mistake—both for older people and for society in general, he says: "Sixty-five is not old anymore."

WHATEVER YOUR PATH, MAP IT OUT NOW

Does this mean that you have to continue working 60-hour weeks for the rest of your life? No. But it's a good idea to decide what you want your later years to be like—and to prepare for that now. Whatever your picture of retirement looks like, here are broad strategies that will help you get ready.

Expand your skill base. Learning new skills now will allow you more options 10 to 15 years down the road. They might enable you to change careers later in life or go into business for yourself, if that's what you want. Invest time and money in classes that interest you, read a trade journal regularly to expand your knowledge base, or join a trade association to learn about a new field, says Walker.

Pollan recommends learning a new language, becoming computer-savvy, and enhancing communication and writing skills.

Re-evaluate your lifestyle. As a planning exercise, make a study of your current lifestyle and the finances that support it, Walker suggests. And start talking about the lifestyle that you envision in your "retirement" years. Will you travel abroad every year? Will you cook all your own food? Will others be depending on you? What kind of finances will your new lifestyle require?

Build interests outside work. Now is the time to develop hobbies and other interests outside of your job, says Walker. That way, if you do partially or fully retire, you'll already have activities and interests integrated into your lifestyle. You are not going to suddenly develop outside interests the day that you turn in your office security card.

Think in segments. Take a creative approach to your retirement planning. Instead of viewing it as one big chunk of time, break it down into several phases. Maybe you want to travel for a year and then return home to do something different. Think in two-year blocks of time instead of one big 20- or 30-year span, says Walker.

Buy now, live there later. Start thinking now about where you want to live when you retire, says Alan Cohn, senior partner with Sage Financial Group in Bala Cynwyd, Pennsylvania. Consider buying a property there now, renting it out, and then moving there when you retire.

IT'S NEVER TOO EARLY TO PREPARE FINANCIALLY

Aside from those lifestyle considerations, naturally, there's a lot to consider about how your finances will work in your later years. Here's what the experts suggest.

Save, save, save. Even if you've decided never to retire 100 percent, you should save as much as you can while you have a full-time income, experts say. Your savings will take the pressure off and give you flexibility to roll back your work schedule late in your career. Try to save 15 percent of your salary each year, says Cohn. When you receive bonuses or unexpected financial windfalls, sock those away, too.

Get paid for your fun. Take a look at your leisure activities and see if you can translate them into income-generating pursuits, says Walker. Try to envision beyond the leisure activity itself: If you like golf, for example, maybe you'd like to run a golf shop. If you love bed-and-breakfasts, consider writing a bed-and-breakfast guide for your county or state.

Start your side business now. If your vision of retirement involves having a business of your own—allowing you to pursue your interests and to generate some income—think about starting it now, says Cohn. "Ten to 15 years before retirement is the time to plant the seeds for a new business," he says. Most new businesses take about 5 years to start generating a profit, he says. Starting now can allow you to get the business up and running and into the profit-generating phase before you leave your full-time job.

Develop your income stream. Put your money in places that will become a nonwork income stream for you during your retirement years, says Cohn. In addition to putting your money in stocks, consider a real estate investment in the form of a rental property, he says. This can be a good investment if you can hold onto it for 10 to 15 years, he says.

Save for health insurance. Set up a cash reserve now that you can use to pay for your health insurance later, says Cohn. In the old days, companies provided retirees with perks that included health benefits, he says, but now they are providing much less. So save for that expense on your own.

Insure your parents. One big expense that many baby boomers can expect to incur when they reach their fifties is eldercare for their aging parents. Consider taking out long-term care insurance on your parents, says Cohn. If you buy the insurance when your parents are in their sixties, you'll pay about $1,500 a year. If you wait until they're in their seventies, it will run you $4,000 a year.

Taking It All Home

Maybe your idea of branching out professionally means saluting the corporate environment good-bye and heading for home—to set up a home office for consulting or freelancing. Well, you're going to need a whole lot more than the new desk, fancy computer, and high-speed modem that you've been fantasizing about, experts say.

KEEP THAT STAFF OF ONE MOTIVATED

What's the biggest hurdle when you trade in the office watercooler for the kitchen spigot? Finding enough motivation and self-discipline, says Creveling. Lacking these attributes is a major factor in the failure of most would-be entrepreneurs, he says.

Given that these intangibles are likely to be your biggest bugaboos, Creveling recommends the following tips.

Set a schedule. Define a specific schedule of working hours, says Creveling. Whatever schedule you design, follow it for at least 21 days, he says. Once you've done something for 21 days, there's a higher chance that it will become habit and that you'll stick with it.

Get dressed. Are you having a rough time being disciplined enough to work at home? Then devise an outfit that you dub your work attire. When you have it on, that means that you are working. When you take it off, day is done.

Get a coach. Recruit a friend or relative to function as your "coach," says Creveling. Tell this person what your work objectives are and that you want to be able to call them for encouragement and discipline. Then call that person once a week to discuss your progress. If you have another friend who runs a business at home, "hire" each other for this purpose.

THAT HOBBY MAY BE YOUR FUTURE CAREER

Maybe you have a talent or lifelong passion that you've always thought of as a hobby—say, photography, wood crafts, or quilting. Some people manage to turn such pursuits into a business.

Look for the fire. One thing that sets successful entrepreneurs apart is a strong desire or motivation for what they are doing, says Creveling. "It is characterized by a burning desire," he says. That desire, that motivation, that fire in the belly is critical, he says. So ask yourself: What ignites your passion?

Take a trial run. If something is a hobby—like photography—and you think that you want to go professional, try it out on a limited basis, experts say. Keep your current job and enter a few photography shows on the weekends to see how you do. If customers are buying and you love doing it, maybe you're on to something.

Survey the market. Take a survey of people who you think might be customers for your product. Find out if there's a demand for your product and if people will pay enough for you to live off of.

Temp it. With all the downsizing and outsourcing that companies are doing, there is a tremendous demand for temporary workers. While you're trying to go professional with your hobby, consider supplementing your income with one of these flexible positions until you are up and running.

Bottom Line

If you're thinking about making a career change, you probably face two big obstacles: your own psychology (often laden with remnants of an outdated work ethic) and the psychology of those with the ability to hire them into a new field. Identifying those obstacles and knocking them down is essential to making a happy, effective switch in your working life.

Words to the Wise

Low-docs: A type of loan, issued through banks, that requires very little documentation, thus the name. These loans are available for $100,000 or less, require little paperwork, and can be issued in about three business days.

Micro-loans: Loans for up to $25,000, offered by the Small Business Administration.

UFOC: The acronym for the Uniform Franchise Offering Circular. This document outlines the terms of the agreement that you would sign when buying a franchise.

Allies

National Board for Certified Counselors: 3 Terrace Way, Suite D, Greensboro, North Carolina 27403-3660. Write for names of career counselors in your area.

What Color Is Your Parachute?, by Richard Bolles (Ten Speed Press).

Zen and the Art of Making a Living, by Laurence Boldt (Viking Penguin).

Powering Up Your Career

There's Still a Ladder to Climb— They've Just Rearranged the Rungs

In the 1980s it was called climbing the ladder. But in these days of corporate downsizing, the ladder just isn't what it used to be for ambitious workers. A lot of companies have "flattened out"—meaning that they eliminated layers of management, leaving you with fewer rungs to climb on, if any.

With the ladder so much shorter, it's harder to rise above the rest.

What's more, you still have all the traditional obstacles to career advancement: irascible bosses, promotion schedules, salary systems, office politics, and the like hamstringing your efforts to get noticed and move up.

But take heart. Here's how to get around these roadblocks and "power up" your career.

Problem Bosses: First, Know the Type

"Bad" bosses. It seems like the working world is just littered with them— incompetent twits with nothing better to do than make us honest-and-proud workers miserable. Just read a couple of "Dilbert" comic strips and you'll get the idea.

Like it or not, your relationship with your boss can make a big difference to your career. There are many types of bosses, and to deal with yours deftly, you should first determine which your boss is, says Richard H. Koonce, a career consultant in Arlington, Virginia, and author of *Career Power!*

This is what you really want in a boss: Somebody who's going to be collegial and who will help you grow and develop, Koonce says. This is the type that you have a strong personal chemistry with. You feel respect for him, and he treats you like a professional equal and tries to assist you in pursuing your own career objectives.

Koonce dubs this saint the professional colleague boss. The good news is that they can be great for your career. The bad news is that they're really hard to find.

A number of other kinds of boss can be more damaging to your career, Koonce says—namely, new bosses, control freaks, perfectionists, and macro-managers. Here are notes on identifying and dealing with each.

New Bosses: Get the Background

Maybe you're new to an organization. Maybe your old boss moved on. Now you're facing a new and unknown entity. Here's how to make a new boss work to your advantage.

Play sleuth. Interviewing for a new job is a great time to find out some information about your potential boss. During the interview process, ask to meet with the people who would be your colleagues and co-workers. If that request is denied, there's a red flag, Koonce says. If the request is granted, ask those other employees about their boss. Talk to as many people as you can (in case the first person you're directed to is nothing more than a company mouthpiece). Ask them all the same set of questions and listen carefully to what is said between the lines, Koonce says. The tone of their conversations and answers, whether they look you in the eye, and the general feel of the atmosphere will tell you a lot.

Conduct an interview. Sit down for a talk with your new boss and ask some key questions. Kelly Barrington, director of corporate and executive recruitment at McKesson Corporation and author of *The Be-All End-All Get Me a Job Book*, suggests the following:

- What are you responsible for?
- What are your stated duties and what are your real duties?
- What are your goals for the year?
- What is your style?
- What kind of people work the best with you?

Pay careful attention to what your new boss's needs are so that you can go about meeting those needs.

Check in. Once you have preliminary information about how your boss likes to work, schedule regular check-ins—say, at three months, six months, and nine months—to see that you are on track. This way, you can nip small problems in the bud before they become big ones, says Lorraine Colletti-Lafferty, Ph.D., co-chairperson of Human Synergistics International, a Plymouth, Michigan, training and development company that counsels executives and managers.

Here are questions to ask at check-in time: What can I do to help get the job done in a better or faster way? What things do I have to be aware of that might hinder getting the job done? What should I do more of? What should I do less of? Find out the boss's pet peeves and preferences, says Dr. Colletti-Lafferty. Remember that a large part of your job is to make your boss look good.

Perform at peak. One of the most important things that you can do when you get a new boss is do the best darned job you can, says Arnold Huberman, president of Arnold Huberman Associates, an executive search and management consulting firm in New York City.

"When someone new comes in, you may be dead in the water and not know it yet. So if you have a specific function, that is the time to be a star and do it the best that you can," he says. If your performance is stellar, then it's harder to be rousted out.

Zip your lips. Stop talking about your old boss, says Huberman. When you have a new boss, you have to show your loyalty to that new regime. For your own good, let the past go.

Run a "background" check. If you know where your new boss came from, call people at that company for information about him, says Huberman. Ask about management style and approach to work. It's perfectly innocent, he says, and it really shouldn't backfire on you.

THE CONTROL FREAK: SIDESTEP THE GATEKEEPER

Gatekeeper. Control freak. Power monger. Micromanager. This kind of boss has earned lots of names. Bosses in this category are often insecure, intrusive, have a need for control, and often treat employees in a parental manner, Koonce says.

If you're a self-starting or creative type, then dealing with this kind of boss can be rather hard, he says. A "control freak" boss can make it hard for you to get your work done, hamstring your efforts, and stonewall your career progress. Here's what experts recommend.

Accept the scene. Realize that this type of boss is not going to change, says Huberman. So you either resolve that their actions and attitude will not get to you or look for another job.

Play the anticipation game. Remember that this type of boss has a huge need to feel in control. Since it's always annoying to have this boss asking you for things or checking up on your progress, try to anticipate their needs and questions before they arise, says Huberman.

Pick your battles. If you have a control freak for a boss, chances are that you're going to butt heads at least sometimes. Remember that this boss has a strong need to know what's going on, to have a hand in everything, and to exert power and control over projects. A battle-a-minute environment won't do. So pick and choose your battles carefully, says Koonce. Decide in advance what issues you're going to fight over.

Consult with colleagues. One way to learn how to deal with the micromanager is to talk with others who have worked with him, says Koonce. Find out if others have been having the same problems that you are and ask for their suggestions. Maybe they have devised an effective way of working with this person.

Turn to a mentor. It really helps to have mentors in a company who can help you manage your boss, says Barrington. This mentor is not necessarily someone in your same area but someone in the company who can take you under his wing and advise you, she says. Don't burden a mentor with the details of the daily skirmishes. Use this person as a sounding board to understand the lay of the land at your boss's level of management, she says. If you can't find a mentor at your company, some cities have mentoring programs that hook you up with mentors at other companies, she says.

Invest elsewhere. Do your best to keep this particular job or boss from being the sole identifier of your identity, says Koonce. Try to maintain a certain degree of detachment, don't take every criticism that your boss renders to heart, and try to establish confidence and morale-boosting pursuits outside of your job. Remember that you are at this company voluntarily, says Barrington. If the situation becomes impossible, move—to another section of the company or to another firm.

THE PERFECTIONIST: PROTECT YOUR BEST IDEAS

If you have a boss who orders revisions on every letter or document you write and tends to throw most of your ideas out, you probably have an extreme perfectionist for a boss, says Dr. Colletti-Lafferty.

Read the writing on the wall. Understand that this is another type of person that you are not going to be able to change, says Dr. Colletti-Lafferty. It's up to you to learn to keep your sanity while working within a rigid system, she says.

Look for the pattern. Somehow, somewhere, ideas still must rise to the top. Your perfectionist boss may have a tendency to feed your first few ideas into the shredder and select the third or fourth idea you present as viable, says Dr. Colletti-Lafferty. If that's the case, recognize the pattern. If you know that your boss won't accept the first idea that you present, don't offer your best ideas first.

THE MACROMANAGER: WHEN YOUR BOSS IS AWOL

Sometimes bosses are so hands-off and uninvolved that you can't get the information that you need or the approvals necessary to get the job done. You're left floundering like a fish on dry land. With a boss who is so unstructured and out of contact, what can you do?

Take the initiative. If your boss isn't giving you the direction you need, then you need to step in and coral him in. "*You* have to be more structured," says Dr. Colletti-Lafferty. Set up breakfast meetings or lunchtime meetings and make sure that your communication needs are met, point by point.

Look elsewhere. If your hands-off boss won't schedule the meetings or cancels consistently, then you have to find a mentor who will give you the advice and direction that you need, says Dr. Colletti-Lafferty.

Keep record. If you've been working on a project and you're unable to get your boss's feedback and input, keep records of what you've been doing and of your efforts to talk with your boss. If you've been sending e-mails, save copies, says Huberman. Eventually, that documentation is going to be necessary, he says.

Recognition: First, Promote Yourself

Who doesn't love positive feedback and recognition of a job well-done? Receiving promotions and big raises are the grandest forms of recognition that you can receive at work.

But consider what the word *promotion* really means, says Barrington. It means "to move forward, to advance in station or rank." Well, in order to get promoted, you basically have to become a promoter and get yourself out there and noticed, she says.

WORKING THE PROMOTION SYSTEM

If your company has a standard promotion schedule, it can be tough to get around it. But it's worth a try. Here's what experts recommend.

Get your own promoter. "In order to get promoted, you have to have a mentor," says Barrington. This will be a person of enough stature that when he sings your praises, the right people listen.

Be visible. Put yourself in front of as many people as possible, says Barrington. And that doesn't mean just people in your department. Get involved in cross-departmental projects where others can work with you, see your talents and be aware that you're around. This gets you and your skills known across the entire company, she says. "You can't afford to be like a little starlet waiting to be discovered," she says.

Log your accomplishments. Make a special file and put in it a note about every one of your accomplishments over the year, says Barrington. Stick in there everything from casual e-mail notes complimenting you on your work to glowing notes from your boss, she says.

Also make lists, either daily or weekly, of the things that you've accomplished, says Troy Behrens, coordinator of career services at Roosevelt University in Chicago. Keep track of how many sales you make, how many clients you bring in, how many new contacts you make.

When you have your review at the end of the year, this file will enable you to talk concretely about your accomplishments, says Barrington. So add to the file continually. Don't try to piece everything together at the last minute—you won't remember all the crucial specifics.

Write it up. Before going in for your performance review, or when you're going in to ask for a promotion, write up your accomplishments in a format that you can present to your boss. You can write it all up as a list of accomplishments, or you can use a résumé format.

Dress a step ahead. If you want to move up to the next level, dress like it, says Barrington. We're very visual and we're constantly assessing people. It may sound superficial and vapid, but you will be judged on your appearance, she says.

Scope out the power base. If you want to get promoted, find out where the power is—both the obvious, stated power and the unstated but real power, says Barrington. One way to do this is to look for people who have been at your company for a while and who've moved up through the ranks. Interview them informally, asking how they got promoted.

Things to ask include: How long have you been with the company? What's your educational level and background? What kind of training have you had? Who were your mentors? What were your lucky breaks? This will give you valuable insight about how the system works, says Barrington.

Make sure that you come across to these people as an information gatherer, not as a gladiator who is out to steal their thunder, she says. Sometimes these very people will become mentors for you and will champion you throughout the organization.

Focus on the future. Always think ahead to what your next gig is, says Barrington. The time to start thinking about a promotion is not when you think you're ready for it. You should *always* be preparing for it, she says. Especially in today's corporate environment, anything and everything about your job could change tomorrow—so always keep in the back of your mind what your next step is going to be.

Broaden your horizons. To get ahead in any job, "I'm convinced that being a generalist is important," says Behrens. Get involved in other parts of the company by participating in projects that have overlap with your department, he says. Not only does this make you more visible but also it makes you more valuable.

For example, if you're in marketing, volunteer in human resources to help displaced workers market their skills, he says. Be creative, broaden your experience, and broaden your responsibilities, he says. If your regular duties are caught up for the moment, volunteer to help out someone in another department.

Move horizontally. If you find that you can't go up the ladder in your department—or don't want to—make a horizontal move within the company, says Behrens. Participating in as many company-wide projects as you can and finding ways to work with people in other departments will make a horizontal move easier to accomplish.

RAISES: STUDY THE SYSTEM AND CASH IN

Not only do raises provide positive reinforcement and padding to your wallet but also the higher salary makes you worth more on the job market. But landing a raise is not an easy task if your company follows a rigid compensation schedule.

There are two basic types of raises, Behrens says.

1. The cost-of-living raise, which is generally a raise of 3 to 5 percent. Some smaller companies tend to be more generous.
2. The merit raise, which is based on a performance review system. At a certain time each year, employees meet with their supervisors to assess their performance, and whatever rating they get determines the amount of raise. Raises under this system typically range from 5 to 20 percent, says Behrens.

The "Why I Deserve a Raise" Résumé

If you thought résumés were only for finding and landing jobs, think again. The résumé format can also be used while you have a job—to argue for a promotion or raise. This technique is called a WIDAR, the Why I Deserve a Raise résumé.

Borrowing the résumé format has several advantages, explains Troy Behrens, coordinator of career services at Roosevelt University in Chicago. It puts the information about your accomplishments into a format that looks familiar to people in your industry. That familiarity breeds comfort. It's also a format that you're familiar writing.

When bosses receive WIDARs, they usually react enthusiastically, says Behrens. It shows that the employee is taking initiative about his career, doing his homework, and taking the responsibility for monitoring his own progress.

Also, there are times when a worker's performance is reviewed by someone two or three levels removed from his daily work, Behrens points out. The WIDAR catalogs your activities and accomplishments on paper and gives documentation to back up your argument that you deserve a raise or promotion.

The only way that a WIDAR can work against you is if you present one to your boss too often, says Behrens. One every quarter is a bit much, he says. You want to keep the concept of the WIDAR fresh, new, and creative.

Once you've presented your WIDAR to your boss and made your verbal presentation of why you deserve a raise, ask your boss, "Do you agree that I

How can you beat the raise system at your company or at least use it to your full advantage? Here's what experts recommend.

Negotiate ahead. Have your performance review set up as part of your contract before you accept a job, says Behrens. Often review systems get overlooked or set aside. Negotiating it as part of your contract is one way to ensure that you will get reviewed on a regular basis. If the company policy only vaguely outlines an evaluation process, the contract-negotiation stage is a good time to get the details specifically stated on paper.

Get specifics. Get your supervisor to be as specific as possible about how the evaluation system will be applied to your performance. Ask: "What do I need to get a 5 percent increase?" and "What do I need to do to get a 10 percent increase?"

"In some companies, raises are all-or-nothing deals," says Behrens. Get it spelled out in a contract specifically what you have to do to get a specific percentage of raise.

Go above and beyond. Average performers are not going to make the compensation system ring like a personal cash register, says Barrington. The

have exceeded the expectations of my job?" Get your boss into a pattern of saying yes, so that eventually he will say yes to a promotion or raise.

Also ask if your boss can envision you in a different position, possibly one where you utilize more of your skills, says Behrens. This question prompts your boss to make statements recognizing your skills and to start agreeing that you could, in fact, be promoted to another position.

To write a WIDAR, write in a résumé format, including sections titled "Objective," "Achievements," "Experience," "Education," "Publications/Public Speaking," and "Membership." At the top of the résumé write your name, position, company name, and the period of time that the WIDAR covers. (This should be the time frame since your last raise or promotion or since you started with the company, if this is your first performance review.)

Achievements. List of your major accomplishments during the time frame listed at the top of the WIDAR.

Experience. Describe your daily responsibilities, spiced up with figures or stats to show your productivity.

Education. List your educational background, including any additional training that you've completed or courses that you've taken while on the job.

Publications/Public Speaking. List any outside activities that serve as good public relations for your company. Maybe you've written an article for a trade magazine or given a speech to an outside group.

only way to get ahead is to be an outstanding performer. Take on as much additional responsibility outside of your job description as you can. Get your fingers into as many pies as possible and go above and beyond what is expected of you.

Prepare for the review. If you want to get more in terms of a raise, be prepared for a negotiating process. Going in and asking for a raise or for more of a raise is really a presentation, Behrens says—one of the biggest presentations that you'll make all year.

So be prepared. Gather your facts and data. Just as with arguing for a promotion, regularly record all of your accomplishments. Write it all down and keep a running file.

Write it all up. Before your meeting with the boss, take the time to write up all your accomplishments in a clear, concise, and convincing form. Take this list of accomplishments with you to your meeting and leave a copy with your boss after you've argued your case.

HOW TO WIN A FLEXIBLE WORK ARRANGEMENT

Negotiating for a raise or promotion is one thing. Arranging to work a schedule that's out of the norm for your company is another. Some companies don't want to make an exception because they believe that it will set a precedent that every other employee will want to follow. Others may have a trust issue—they're not completely confident that you can do your job unless you're in-house like everybody else from 9:00 A.M. to 5:00 P.M.

If you're thinking about flextime, job sharing, or telecommuting, keep the following in mind.

Present a solution. Take solutions to your supervisor—not problems, says Barrington. So if you're requesting flexible working hours or a job-sharing arrangement, go in the door with more than one solution for how you could make it all work, she says.

For job sharing, for instance, write up a proposal that includes a job description, the logistics of making the job sharing work, who will share the work with you, how the responsibilities will be shared, how the hours will work, and how the money will work.

"You have to have it all scripted out," Barrington says.

Do your research. Talk to others who are working flextime, job sharing, or telecommuting and get the lowdown, says Barrington. Talk to people in other companies if you have to. Find out if the managers like it and why. (You may find that managers really love job sharing because it saves them money.) Then use your information as an argument in your favor.

Ask for a trial. Ask if you can try your proposal as a test, says Barrington. Suggest it as a pilot program, not something that has to be set in stone.

Include a check-in. Include in your proposal scheduled, regular check-in times. At three months, six months, and nine months you will check in

Put Power in Your Speech

A brush-up on communication skills could be just the career boost you need, says Lorraine Colletti-Lafferty, Ph.D., co-chairperson of Human Synergistics International, a Plymouth, Michigan, training company that counsels executives and managers from 400 of the Fortune 500 companies.

Defensiveness and a problem-based approach get in the way, she says. Do your best to communicate nondefensively, yet firmly. Here's how.

Listen actively. Response to co-workers isn't just verbal, says Dr. Colletti-Lafferty. It's physical, too. So do your best to maintain an open body posture. Use a lot of eye contact with the person to whom you are talking, she says.

Try an instant replay. One way to listen actively and maintain a nondefensive posture is to reiterate what the other person has said before you jump in with your idea or your approach, says Dr. Colletti-Lafferty. By saying, "So what you are saying is X, Y, and Z," you're confirming that you have heard and understood what was said.

Stick with strong language. Avoid weak, self-deprecating, and hesitant language on the job, says Dr. Colletti-Lafferty. "Put firmer words in your vocabulary," she says. Avoid such weak phrases as:

- "If I might suggest . . . "
- "If I could . . . "
- "Possibly . . . "
- "It's only a suggestion . . . "

Also, try not to end sentences with questions, such as "Right?" "Don't you think?" or Okay? This kind of language is indecisive and shows hesitancy instead of taking a firm, strong stand, she says. Just state your ideas or facts firmly, with no qualifiers.

with your boss about how the arrangement is working. You'll evaluate it, and if it's not working out, you can rearrange it or scrap the deal altogether.

Set goals. Set clear goals and objectives that your boss wants you to reach during the first month or two of the arrangement. This will serve as a benchmark to assess whether the new system is effective.

Politics: Do You Fight, Hide, or Retreat?

If you work, office politics are inevitable. They may be a murky business, but career experts agree on at least one thing: They're unsteady and unpredictable.

"The thing about office politics is that today's star could be tomorrow's fallen star," says Barrington. "And today's subordinate could be tomorrow's boss."

Here's the classic example, she says: The intern or young employee who leaves a company, only to return years later in a senior position. People who treated that young fledgling properly and with respect will have no problem. Those who ignored the youngster or, worse, treated him badly, will be quaking in their boots when he returns as their boss.

HARNESS THOSE POLITICAL FORCES

How can you survive such shifting winds? How do you weather the political maneuvering and posturing? Career experts recommend the following tips.

Keep positive. "Never say anything negative about anything, be it your boss, the company, yourself, or the job," says Barrington. Perhaps that sounds a tad too Mary Poppins. But the fact is that there's no functional reason for spreading around your negative thoughts and there are very good reasons not to.

"It is very dangerous to badmouth colleagues," says Koonce. This practice can come back to haunt you in career-damaging ways.

Limit the ammo. If you want to get ahead, don't put out information about yourself that people can use, says Koonce. "I used to think that it was important to present as full a profile of myself as I could," he says, "but while you want to be open, be careful about just how open you are. Don't share anything that you wouldn't be comfortable having broadcast."

Listen well. If you are a good listener, Barrington says, people will seek you out and share information with you. Be sure that you never pass along sensitive information to anyone else. Once people know that you can keep a secret, she says, they'll trust you and share even more.

On the other hand, there are two cautions about the art of office talk, says Koonce. First, you don't want to become known as the office psychoanalyst, because you may be perceived as having too much control. Also, when you're new, beware the person who comes by your office a lot, giving you the skinny on everybody else. If they gossip about other people, most likely they're doing it to you, too.

Don't triangulate. Beware getting entangled in other workers' political battles. If your work or performance isn't an issue in the battle, lay low and keep out of the squabble. If your performance is an issue and has become a punching bag for the two warring factions, try not to get "triangulated," says Barrington. A three-way skirmish creates an unproductive whirlwind of he-said, she-said bickering. Refuse to participate. Get all parties together in one room to talk about and resolve the issue.

Forget affairs. Having an affair with a co-worker can be a career catastrophe, says Barrington. And usually the woman involved suffers the most damage, she says.

Play free agent. Upon first glance, it might seem like a great idea, politically, to form fast friendships up and down the management ladder. But that can become uncomfortable and dangerous for all involved, says Barrington.

For a boss getting too friendly with the troops, it will get hard to maintain objectivity, she says. And for the subordinate getting too chummy with the boss, consider what will happen if the boss's career starts to sink—you'll be in trouble, too.

Staying detached is your best defense against getting sucked into the office politics quagmire, says Barrington. It helps to think of yourself as a free agent or consultant with benefits. After all, this collection of staffers is not your family. You are a professional who is paid to do a job and go home. Do not get 100 percent invested in the people and place where you work, she says.

GETTING YOUR IDEAS HEARD

One way to gain some ground in your career is to contribute fresh new ideas to your department or division. After all, good ideas can be worth money, and that's something that all organizations are interested in—making it or saving it.

But having ideas and getting them heard can be two different things. Sure, you could open a window and shout your ideas to a passerby. But what you really want is to have them heard by the right people, in a way that leads to them being effectively implemented in the organization—preferably with your name attached in flashing lights.

There can be several reasons why your ideas aren't being heard, says Huberman.

- The ideas are just no good.
- The ideas may be good, but they don't make sense in terms of your company's business plan. You may not be aware that they don't fit in, but nobody's taken the time to tell you that.
- Your boss is running interference—either your ideas are good and your boss is just stealing them and taking the credit, or your boss doesn't like you and isn't passing the ideas along because he doesn't want to make you look good.

Be relevant. You may have lots of good ideas, but the ones most likely to be heard are the ones that are really relevant to your company's goals.

"Think about what carries currency in your organization's culture," says Koonce. Most companies want bottom-line benefits, he says, as opposed to the "softer" human resources benefits. Take a step back, try to get the big picture on where your company is trying to go, and generate ideas that are pertinent to those goals.

Speak the language. "Couch your ideas in the language and culture of the company in which you work," says Koonce. The language used in the banking industry will be very different from that used in, say, architecture or advertising. Learn the lingo and present your ideas using the lingo. That way, they're more likely to be received.

Document, document. If you suspect that your boss is receiving your ideas but not acting on them or passing them along, be sure to document them, says Huberman. Keep copies of memos or e-mail that you send outlining your ideas. And follow up spoken conversations with a quick note, and keep a copy of that, too. If the ideas are ever acted on and your boss tries to take the credit, you'll have some evidence of your input.

Try a different forum. If you suspect that your ideas are on the mark but that your boss is stonewalling you, then try to get your ideas heard through a different forum. Try to write an article for a trade magazine about your idea, or try to express it during a meeting, workshop, or some other speaking environment, says Huberman.

Bottom Line

Even in a shaky corporate environment, some standard system-beating tools will serve you well in advancing your career. Do your research, understand the power centers, and know what you want and how to ask for it effectively. In the workplace, a bit of professional detachment will always serve you well. Think of yourself as a consultant with benefits rather than everyone's best buddy.

Words to the Wise

Cost-of-living raise: A raise given to employees, approximating an increase in the cost of living.

Merit raise: A raise determined by an employee's merit or performance.

Micromanager: The kind of boss who has to have a hand in everything, reviewing and approving every small detail.

Performance review: Usually a corporate-wide system that assesses performance of employees.

Allies

Career Power!: 12 Winning Habits to Get You from Where You Are to Where You Want to Be, by Richard H. Koonce (American Management Association).

Finding Your Perfect Work: The New Career Guide to Making a Living, Creating a Life, by Paul and Sarah Edwards (Putnam).

Working Woman magazine.

Part 10

OUT AND ABOUT

Making the Right Moves When You're on the Move

Grab Up Bargains in the Quickly Changing Travel Industry

You glance at the calendar and note that the family vacation is looming. Or your yearly convention. Or a visit to that client who's three states away. This means that it's time to make some big-budget decisions about how you're going to get yourself from point A to point B.

Chances are that you're going to make your moves on four wheels. Americans make more than a billion trips a year, 77 percent of them by automobile, 20 percent by airplane, 2 percent by bus, and 1 percent by rail, according to the Travel Industry Association of America. And all along the way, travel agents, rental agents, desk clerks, and salespeople have their hands out ready to grab up the hundreds of billions of dollars that Americans spend on travel each year.

Airlines:
The Ups and Downs of Pricing

With the rules changing rapidly in the travel industry, it's hard to know how to spend wisely on transportation—air travel in particular. In 1995 pleasure-seeking vacationers handed over $69 billion in revenues to the airlines. But purchasing those plane tickets is no longer a simple matter of calling your travel agent and making a reservation. The perplexed buyer must sift through such considerations as fare wars, new "discount" airlines, ever-changing rules, and flight-time restrictions.

Consumers can lose or save big bucks in this area. So let's take a look at how to plot out a prudent route in an industry that has rules and fees that are all over the map.

FLY WHEN DEMAND IS LOW

"Prices for airline tickets make no rational sense," says Gary Stoller, investigative editor for *Conde Nast Traveler*. "There's no obvious reason why an airline charges $800 to fly 500 miles and $300 to fly across the country."

There is an economic theory guiding the airline industry's pricing madness, however. It's called yield management. The airlines rely on sophisticated databases to keep track of reservations and historical travel patterns.

The goal is to fill every seat before the plane takes off. If the computer shows that people aren't buying enough seats on a particular route, or that historically the month of January is a slow time for travel, airlines will lower fares and initiate sales in an attempt to gain more customers.

With that in mind, here are some reliable strategies for getting good deals on air travel.

Fly at odd times. "Airlines are completely driven by supply and demand," explains James Glab, a contributing editor to *Travel & Leisure*. "When demand is high, prices stay high. The way to get the best deal is to play against those trends—fly in the middle of the week or late at night instead of during peak travel times."

Pray for war. Buy your tickets during airline fare wars, which are usually announced in the local newspapers on a Monday morning. Move quickly, though. These prices are typically available for a short window of time.

Plan well. Book your trip in advance, usually three weeks; plan a Saturday stay-over; and travel on a Tuesday, Wednesday, or Saturday to take advantage of the lowest, discounted economy fare.

WHAT GOOD IS A TRAVEL AGENT?

If finding a low airfare is as easy as that, you may ask, who needs a travel agent anyway? You do, travel experts insist.

"By all means, use a travel agent," says Betsy Wade, the "Practical Traveler" columnist for the *New York Times*. "They have access to extensive computerized reservation systems, they can prepare a detailed itinerary, and, most important, they can help if something goes wrong during your trip."

Be aware that travel agents are under economic pressures. The major airlines have imposed a cap of $50 on travel agent commissions for domestic tickets. And it costs the agent approximately $22.70 to book each domestic ticket, according to the American Society of Travel Agents.

Does this mean that travel agents are only interested in quick-and-easy bookings? Not at all. But it will work to your advantage if you develop a good working relationship with your travel agent by making wise and efficient use of the agent's time. Here's how.

Arm yourself with info. "To build an effective relationship with a travel agent," says Rudy Maxa, the Savvy Traveler on the public radio broadcast *Marketplace*, "you have to work with them. You have to do your homework and be a little smart yourself."

You want to choose an agent who specializes in your areas of interest. If you enjoy luxury travel to Europe, don't pick an agent whose expertise lies in South America or Asia. If you are thinking about taking a cruise, don't pick an agent who deals mainly with business travelers.

Be flexible. Ask about choices that you can make that will lead to a lower-priced ticket. Say that you want to travel from San Francisco to New York. It's not enough to ask which airline has the lowest fares. Tell your agent that you are willing to be flexible about which airport you use. On the West Coast, you can choose among Oakland, San Jose, or San Francisco airports. On the East Coast, you can choose among JFK and La Guardia (New York City), or Newark, New Jersey. The prices will differ greatly.

Also tell your agent if you can be flexible on your arrival or departure times. "Airlines allocate a limited number of super-saver fares per flight," says Joe Brancatelli, editor of *Frommer's Travel Update*, a monthly consumer newsletter. "These seats might be sold out on the 9:00 A.M. flight but still be available on the 7:30 or 11:00 A.M. flights."

Rewrite your ticket. What if airfares drop after you've purchased a ticket? Currently, airlines will let you rewrite your ticket for about a $50 fee. If you will still save money after paying this penalty, by all means, change your ticket. But make sure that you discuss it with your travel agent. Some have enough clout with the airlines to get the fee waived.

FLYING THE INTERNET HAS ITS LIMITS

If you can connect to the Internet, you'll find a wealth of travel information. The World Wide Web carries a vast number of destinations, including bulletin boards where people discuss their vacation plans and problems. You also will find several of the computerized online reservation systems that are used by travel agents. Among the most popular on the Internet are easySABRE, System One AMADEUS/One Link, ExpressNet, ITN, and PCTravel.

Not all airline fare schedules are listed on the computerized reservation systems, however, and you can't count on being led to the best deals. Many of the small, newer discount airlines depend on customers calling them directly.

"This is a fee-based system. People don't realize that the major airlines own the different reservations systems and charge their competitors a great deal of money to be listed," explains Brancatelli. "Since these smaller airlines are gaining market share by undercutting the major lines' fees, the big airlines are retaliating by raising the price to become part of the online reservation network."

As a result, neither the Internet nor the computers that your travel agent uses will guide you to the lowest fares. You have to know which upstart competitor is servicing the area that you want to visit and call them yourself.

UPSTART AIRLINES COULD BE JUST THE TICKET

Some people call them discount airlines. Others call them short-haul or no-frills carriers. But no matter what you call them, what they have in common is that they serve a small, niche market; offer discount fares; and provide bare-bones service—typically, no meals, no movies, and fewer cabin attendants.

"These discount airlines offer your best shot at a low-price plane ticket," says Wade. "They also drive down the prices of the major airlines whenever they enter a new market." For instance, competition between major airlines and the new upstarts reduced airfares by nearly $4 billion in 1995, according to the U.S. Department of Transportation.

The growth of discount airlines dates back to 1978, when the air travel industry was deregulated. Southwest Airlines, Midway Airlines, and People's Express pioneered the concept of a short-haul carrier servicing neglected passenger markets.

"Southwest established a template that everyone now follows," says Brancatelli. "First, don't compete with the big guys head-to-head. Establish a good base and grow slowly, relying on low fares and a frequent number of daily flights. And don't waste money on any frills. People always think that that just means no peanuts, but it really means that discount airlines offer basic, point-to-point service. They don't travel through a hub city, they don't schedule connecting flights, and they don't have interlinking agreements with other airlines."

Although People's Express and the original Midway Airlines have long since gone out of business, dozens more have sprung up in the last several years. Fare restrictions and service strategies differ according to airline. Some, such as Frontier and Reno Air, participate in frequent-flier mileage programs. Others, like Virgin Atlantic Air and Tower, provide first-class or business-class seating.

FLY OFTEN? GET WITH A PROGRAM

The best deal of all, of course, is to fly absolutely free. The introduction of frequent-flier miles in 1981 is considered one of the all-time greatest marketing innovations. "People never had 'brand loyalty' with airlines as they did with other products," says Brancatelli. "Before frequent-flier miles, they would buy a ticket with whomever offered the most convenient prices and departure times."

The program's popularity increased even more with the introduction of airline–credit card partnerships (also called affinity cards). In these programs, charges racked up on either a Visa, MasterCard, American Express, Diners Club, or telephone calling card earn the user mileage on a designated airline.

Be a frequent charger. Why pay with cash or a check when you could be building up mileage credits? "I charge everything that I buy on credit cards—groceries, doctor bills, gasoline—in order to earn mileage," says Stoller. "Although I pay an annual fee of $50 for my MasterCard, I earn two free trips a year. Two trips for $50? You can't beat it!"

Narrow your focus. The goal of all frequent fliers should be to concentrate on one or two airlines in order to quickly accumulate enough miles to earn a free trip. Be sure to read the program's fine print: Some airlines let mileage expire if not used within three or five years. Other airlines don't let mileage expire.

Join the elite. Most frequent-flier programs have what is called an elite level, or special awards for very frequent fliers. This means that you gain privileges like special reservations telephone numbers, first-class check-in service, priority baggage handling, liberal upgrade policies, and additional mileage. Elite membership is only earned from mileage actually flown, however, as opposed to miles earned via credit card purchases.

"Nonetheless," says Stoller, "there are tremendous benefits in being a frequent flier even if you don't get to the elite level."

Special Deals Are in the Air

Looking for even deeper discounts in air travel? You have to know where to look, and you'll probably have to put up with some form of inconvenience. Maybe you won't be assured of a seat until the last minute. Maybe you'll have to cope with a three-day departure window. Or someone else might even decide your destination for you. But if you're flexible and adventurous, there are some splendid travel deals to be had.

FOR SOLID SAVINGS, TRY CONSOLIDATORS

For foreign travel, the best option for inexpensive plane tickets is to buy a ticket through a consolidator. Because airlines cannot sell all their tickets even at discounted fares, they sell large numbers of seats to wholesalers—also known as consolidators—at bulk rates. The wholesaler resells these tickets to the public at a slightly higher markup. Savings can amount to 50 percent off full-fare tickets.

While consolidators do offer domestic tickets, the majority of their business focuses on international flights. Consolidators are especially popular in England, where such businesses are referred to as bucket shops.

"Occasionally, I'll use a consolidator to buy a ticket at the last minute," says Maxa. "A consolidator's ticket will cost less than a full-price fare in which you've missed the seven-day advance purchase requirement or if you can't stay over on a Saturday night."

There are several caveats to dealing with airline consolidators. "You may not receive your ticket until you arrive at the airport," says Robert Krughoff, publisher of *Consumers' Checkbook* magazine, based in Washington, D.C. "You will probably not earn frequent-flier mileage on these flights. And consolidators are working under great economic pressures. A widely advertised fare war can break out that will ruin a consolidator within 24 hours."

Conduct a background check. While it's perfectly safe and legitimate to use a consolidator, any problems that arise will occur during the process of buying the ticket, says Ed Perkins, editor of the *Consumer Reports Travel Letter*. To be safe, try to use a consolidator located in your hometown and ask how many years they have been in business. Check with the Better Business Bureau to see if any complaints have been filed against the business.

Protect yourself with plastic. Always pay with a credit card, which easily lets you to stop payment if the consolidator cancels or disrupts the service.

Work through an agent. For even better protection, get the flight information and price from a consolidator and purchase your ticket through a travel agent. Although you have to pay a commission, an agent can confirm your seat assignment and deliver the tickets faster than a consolidator. Many agents subscribe to the monthly newsletter *Jax Fax Travel Marketing Magazine*, a national listing of reputable consolidators.

ALTERNATIVE PATHS TO LOW AIRFARES

If you have a taste for adventure and a flexible schedule, try these ideas for low-cost air travel.

Be a courier and see the world. Courier travel is like taking a spur-of-the-moment magic carpet ride, says Wade. "Because prices drop dramatically the closer you get to departure, the system is geared to making a last-minute decision to go somewhere exotic," she says.

Courier travel is an outgrowth of the air freight industry. Companies promise to deliver documents, packages, and other air freight to international destinations within 48 hours. But these goods can't be sent as routine

---

Fly Solo at Charter Rates

You don't have to travel with a large group to take advantage of low-priced charter flights. Several organizations, such as Council Charter or Suntrips, sell individual charter tickets to the public. Charters usually service resort or tourist destinations, such as Hawaii, the Caribbean, and Mexico, or popular U.S. cities, such as San Francisco and New Orleans.

"With charters, you get the savings but lose the flexibility," says Gary Stoller, investigative editor for *Conde Nast Traveler*. "There are usually a limited number of flights scheduled during a week. Like consolidators, they probably won't have a backup aircraft if the flight is delayed for any reason."

---

cargo, which can get bogged down in transit for several days. When it's transported as passenger luggage, the freight can be claimed and picked up as soon as the flight arrives.

As a result you, the courier, are limited to carry-on baggage only. The courier company gets to use the checked-luggage space that goes along with your seat. Couriers must meet company officials in order to exchange documents and baggage-check claims. Your return date is usually fixed (trips often last a week to 10 days). And don't expect to travel with a companion. Companies usually need only one courier per trip.

Most courier flights depart from major international hubs, such as JFK in New York City, Miami, or LAX in Los Angeles.

Hitch a ride. Airhitch, with offices through the United States, originally provided standby tickets to students only. In business more than 20 years, Airhitch now serves the general public, but its essential service remains the same.

"If you can be flexible with your departure dates, Airhitch offers substantial savings," says Perkins. They are able to tap into unsold airline seats at the last minute. You provide the company with your destination and a three-day departure window. For flights from the United States to Europe, you must provide a five-day window of flexibility.

The company arranges flights to and from a number of destinations all across the United States, as well as Western Europe, the Caribbean, and Mexico.

Seniors, go by the book. If you are over age 62 and make at least two round-trips a year, senior coupon books offer an excellent travel value. Here's how they work. Airlines sell coupon books of four to eight one-way tickets. You pay a set price in advance (from $500 to $1,000, depending upon the airline and the number of coupons), and you must use them within a year's time. Before you choose an airline, ask if there are any travel restrictions or blackout days during which you cannot use the coupons.

Students, stand by for savings. "Compared with Europe, the U.S. travel industry has never provided many special privileges for students," says Perkins. "But there are several ways to save on airfare if you under the age of 26."

Low-fare charter and consolidator flights are offered by the Council on International Educational Exchange (CIEE), which has Council Travel offices throughout the United States. You must prove your age with a GO 25 card and your student status for an International Student Identity Card (both obtained through CIEE).

TWA sells coupon books to students that work the same way as a senior citizen ticket booklet. But the best deal for students can be found on international flights on any U.S. major airline. These carriers sell student fares to Europe on a standby basis.

Trains, Buses, and Autos

Train travel played a dominant role in the settlement of the western United States in the nineteenth century. Even today, the mention of a steam locomotive evokes images of leisurely travel past magnificent vistas of unspoiled wilderness, passengers in Victorian dress and finery, and maybe a quick glimpse of the Pony Express out the window.

While freight trains are still owned by privately held companies, passenger rail service was nationalized by the government, which created Amtrak in 1971. Today, "Amtrak is the only game in town for passenger rail service," says Perkins. However, if you love to ride trains for the simple pleasure of it, there are many short-haul lines that serve limited, regional areas throughout the United States, such as the Grand Canyon Railway or Roaring Camp and Big Trees Narrow-Gauge Railroad near Santa Cruz, California.

A plane will always get you to your destination faster than a train. But in a few situations, an intercity metro line could have the advantage. "I use the trains for short hops between New York City and Washington, D.C., when the weather is foul," says Maxa. "There's no traffic and no delay based on snow conditions."

"U.S. rail travel is a viable option only along certain routes," adds Wade. "In the Northwest corridor, the train will take you from city center to city center quickly and cheaply. East-west travel, however, can be slow and late, as the tracks are in a terrible state."

CROSS-COUNTRY TRAINS: SLOWER, BUT SCENIC

Despite this caveat, many of Amtrak's more scenic routes cross the country. That includes the California Zephyr, which takes in the Rocky Mountains, the Colorado River, and the Sierra Nevada as it travels between

Chicago and Oakland, California. Between New York City and Chicago, the Cardinal rolls through the Blue Ridge Mountains. The Pioneer (from Chicago to Seattle) climbs through the Pacific Northwest's Cascade Range.

Try a northern route. To the north, Rail Canada operates in much the same way as Amtrak. It also offers regional rail passes. Contact VIA Rail Canada, 2 Place Ville Marie, P.O. Box 8116, Montreal, Quebec, Canada H3C 3N3.

Mix 'em up. You can fly to your destination and ride Amtrak home. In a joint promotion with United Airlines, the rail service sells a round-trip ticket that combines one-way rail travel with stopovers and a one-way plane ride. Call Amtrak and ask about the American Vacations program.

Cash in on age. Age also counts on Amtrak. Students can get 15 percent fare discounts. Seniors older than 62 get a 15 percent discount. "Amtrak has some unusual pricing policies," says Herbert Teison, editor of the New York City–based *Travel Smart* newsletter. "Sometimes a round-trip fare will cost less than a one-way ticket if you travel on a weekday. So always ask if there's a weekend fare, a one-week fare, a one-month fare, or any seasonal discounts."

LEAVE THE DRIVING TO BUSES

At least 25 million people ride intercity buses each year. If you don't drive, bus service is frequently your only option to reach many rural communities.

A bus ticket even between major metropolitan areas is generally cheaper than air or rail travel, although you should factor in the cost of meals and overnight lodging to get an accurate price comparison. While there is no national bus service, the privately owned Greyhound bus service is the only major carrier still in business, with a national network of buses and city terminals. (Greyhound bought out its closest competitor, Trailways, in 1987.)

In an effort to attract more riders, Greyhound is renovating its downtown bus terminals; and newer buses offer more leg room, wider seats, and amenities such as onboard movies and vending machines.

Greyhound offers transit passes for unlimited travel anywhere in the United States within a specified amount of time. The program, called Ameripass, sells 7-day passes for about $180, 15-day passes for $290, 30-day passes for about $400, and 60-day passes for about $600. Also, if you and a partner purchase round-trip tickets on Greyhound three days in advance, the companion ticket will be free.

DEALS ON RENTAL WHEELS

Ten years ago, renting a car was pretty straightforward. Hertz was the most expensive, Avis tried harder, and companies such as Budget were the cheapest, just like the name suggested. Today, you can't count on one name-brand company to provide the lowest rate.

Of course, car agencies, like hotels, may provide discounts of 5 to 10 percent or more if you mention your affiliation with organizations like the American Automobile Association, the American Association of Retired Persons, the Government Employee Insurance Company—even Costco or Sam's Club. You can find out what kind of discounts are available by contacting the rental company directly. But you'll save more money by turning down expensive add-ons, such as ski racks, cellular phone rentals, baby seats, and, most important, insurance fees.

"The rental industry is losing money," explains Brancatelli. "Twenty years ago, when cars cost $3,000, rental companies charged $69 a week. Today, cars cost $20,000 and they're renting them for only $99 a week. The basic daily rate is so low that it's appalling. They make up the difference with extra fees and surcharges."

Pass on the insurance. If you need a baby seat and you can't bring your own, there's not much that you can do. But do you really need that extra insurance? In most cases, the travel experts say no.

"If you have a home owner's or renter's policy, you're already insured against the theft or loss of your personal items from, say, the trunk of the rental car. So turn down the personal effects insurance," says Charles Leocha, syndicated columnist and Boston-based author of *Travel Rights*.

The same principle works if you already own at car at home. Regular insurance policies often protect car owners against collision and injury. "That's because your auto insurance isn't specific to your car—it covers you as a driver," says Brancatelli. If this applies to you, turn down the collision damage protection.

Insure yourself with plastic. What if you live in a big city and don't own a car? You can still turn down the collision protection if you rent the car with a Diners Club card, some Gold Visa cards, some Gold MasterCard cards, American Express, or AT&T's Universal Card. These cards offer all the insurance protection that you'll need.

Skip the package deal. Don't fall for a rental agency's all-in-one inclusive rate. Too often they're throwing in things that you would decline, such as insurance and gasoline. According to *Consumer Reports Travel Letter*, all-inclusive rates are 30 percent higher than taking the basic rate and filling up the gas tank yourself.

Ask, "How do you define 'weekend'?" Weekend rates are usually cheaper than weekday rates. But before you make the reservation, ask the agent when their weekends begin and end. Some companies start the clock at noon on Friday. For others, it's noon on Saturday.

Lobby for a new car. Who doesn't prefer driving a newer car? Just speak up and the rental agency might be willing to give you the lowest-mileage auto available, says Christopher McGinnis, director of the Atlanta-based Travel Skills Group.

Give it a body check. Don't leave the rental agency lot without inspecting the car for scratches or dents. If you fail to note pre-existing damage, you'll be held liable, McGinnis notes.

Be Prepared: Heading Off the Hassles

When you're on the road, you're often on a tight schedule in unfamiliar territory. Which means that you are particularly vulnerable to a surprise downpour, a broken suitcase handle, or a gouging cab driver. Here's a guide to steeling yourself against the unexpected when you're away from home.

KEEP AN EYE ON THE SKY

No, you can't do much to change the weather. But the traveler who isn't attuned to the forecast is inviting disaster. How do the travel experts keep track?

"I always look at the weather column in *USA Today*," says Glab.

Brancatelli always tunes into the Weather Channel on cable television.

For $20 to $60, the truly dedicated can buy a weather radio, which transmits broadcasts from the National Oceanic and Atmospheric Administration.

Getting the information is only half the battle. After you hear the forecast, be sure to pack accordingly. "I always travel in layers," says Leocha. "I bring a rain hat instead of an umbrella, and a Gore-Tex windbreaker instead of a heavy raincoat. Then I'm ready for anything."

CELLULAR PHONES: A STRATEGY FOR SAFETY

"Cellular phones give me great confidence with I'm on a trip," says Wade. "I use mine as a safety tool in case I get lost or find myself driving through a bad neighborhood. It really does make a difference."

If you don't own a cellular phone and you're a single woman traveling alone, consider spending extra for a phone in your rental car.

You can also use your cellular phone to rendezvous with friends and family members. Since you must turn on your cellular phone not only to make but also to receive calls, set up prearranged times when family members can contact you while you're traveling or at your hotel. Also, use your cellular phone to avoid the access fees that hotels charge for long-distance phone calls made in your room. But remember that cellular phones charge for both outgoing and incoming calls.

HOW TO GET A HANDLE ON LUGGAGE

When shopping for luggage, don't buy the cheapest items. Strength and durability are just as important as price. Look for bags with heavy-duty stitching, zippers, padded handles, and metal buckles.

How to Get a Hot Seat

Say that you're visiting a city during the World Series, or when the Bolshoi Ballet is in town. A new Broadway play with your favorite actress is drawing rave reviews. These events have been sold out for months. Can you still get a ticket for the show?

The answer is yes—and you may not even have to pay a scalper's prices.

Major cities, such as New York City and San Francisco, have two-for-one ticket brokers. Here's how they work: You approach kiosks located downtown on the day of the event. Agents will sell half-priced tickets on a first come, first serve basis.

"The only downside is that you don't know which events they'll have tickets for on any given day," says Gary Stoller, investigative editor for *Conde Nast Traveler*. "Also, you can't be sure that it'll be the best seat." Like hotel and airline consolidators, theaters and sporting arenas sell their unused inventory to these brokers. That could mean anything from a single seat in the orchestra to one near the back of the balcony or behind a pillar at the sports arena.

There is, however, one other low-cost option. If you're willing to take a chance, show up at the box office about 15 minutes before the event. Tickets get returned to the box office for all sorts of reasons. Also, of the many tickets held by will-call, there are always a number of no-shows. Ask the box office if there are any unclaimed seats. They'll be happy to resell unused tickets at face value.

For the best seat at the last minute, try the concierge at your hotel. The concierge provides a wide range of services and can help with almost any request, from obtaining out-of-town newspapers to obtaining restaurant reservations, even (in some instances) providing notary service. Getting theater or sporting tickets through the concierge is a snap, since most hotels have arrangements with ticket brokers that buy up blocks of group tickets to popular events. You will have to pay a small premium for the ticket, but be assured that you'll get a good seat. And don't forget to tip.

Because luggage is often roughly handled, pick a dark color so that the scuff marks won't show. (And just in case your baggage looks like everyone else's, tie some colorful ribbon or fix a bumper sticker on your bags to make it easy to identify in an airport's baggage claim area.)

Also, consider buying luggage that comes with attached wheels. It's quite a relief to roll your bags through the airport without having to search for a luggage cart or lug them yourself.

Bags do get stolen and lost. Here are tips for heading off this traveler's nightmare.

Tag, you're mine. To be on the safe side, attach identification tags to the inside as well as exterior of your baggage.

Keep your guard up. "Don't let your luggage out of your sight," says McGinnis. "Don't leave it in the lobby or by your chair while you get up for a napkin or a cup of coffee."

Check the codes. When checking luggage at the airport, always double-check the three-letter airport codes that porters or gate agents attach to your bags. "The codes for some airports make sense, such as 'ATL' for Atlanta," says McGinnis. "But others are confusing. Washington-Dulles is 'IAD,' and Orlando is 'MCO.' "

If possible, save receipts. But what if you get off the plane and the worst has happened: Your bags are lost? Airlines are not responsible for carry-on luggage, but federal law requires that they reimburse you for lost checked baggage up to $1,250.

"But you will have to show receipts for every item you claim," says Brancatelli. "Sometimes it is easier to file a claim with your own insurance company than to go to the airline to recoup."

File a claim. Whatever else you may do when an airline loses your bag, don't leave the airport until you have filled out all the necessary forms, warns Leocha. "Even if airport personnel say that it's coming on the next flight, take the 10 minutes and fill out the forms. Otherwise, you have no way to prove that you didn't get your luggage."

Get your expenses paid. On the positive side, airlines will reimburse you for out-of-pocket expenses that you incur from losing your luggage, such as toilet articles or a change of clothing. While filing out your claim, ask the agent for these expenses.

SAFE BETS FOR A SECURE VACATION

"What's wonderful about travel," says Stoller, "is that you become open to new perceptions. You get into a different mind-set. In a word, you let your guard down. Unfortunately, that is precisely what makes you vulnerable to crime."

Now, succumbing to runaway paranoia would defeat the purpose of a vacation. But taking reasonable precautions will prevent a world of grief.

"Always be aware of what's going on around you," advises Leocha. "While strolling around a strange city, at least try to project the image that you know where you're going."

Ask about safe routes. If you walk or jog for exercise, ask ahead of time about safe neighborhoods or routes. Ask whether certain parks, no matter how pretty, have been the site of assaults during day or evening hours. In downtown areas, use common sense. Stay on well-lit, populated streets.

Wear your regular duds. "The best way to avoid muggers is to not look like a tourist," says McGinnis. "You can spot tourists by what they're wearing: middle-age couples in jeans, matching windbreakers, and new white sneakers." It may be tempting to buy a new wardrobe of casual clothing before your vacation, but you may be better served by wearing your regular weekend wear.

Don't flash that camera. "Don't invite problems by flashing around something valuable," says Stoller. Keep cameras in the bag. If you must bring valuables, store them in the hotel's safe. "Don't try to hide them in the room," says McGinnis. "There simply are no hiding places in a hotel room that the employees aren't familiar with."

Watch that laptop. Travelers going through airport security should keep an eye on valuables like laptop computers. Experienced travelers warn that if you put a compact computer on the x-ray conveyor belt and then stand in line at the metal detector, thieves may separate you permanently from your trusty keyboard. If you carry such valuables, wait until you're the next person in line before setting your computer on the conveyor belt, or hand it directly to the security agent for inspection.

Robbed? File a report. If your valuables are stolen, head straight for the nearest police station and file a report. The police are unlikely to recover your belongings. But you will need the paperwork to file an insurance claim.

Photocopy cards and papers. Teison advises travelers to make photocopies of passports, credit cards, and driver's licenses. Bring this material on your trip but don't pack it in your wallet or purse. Then, if you are robbed, you'll still have the necessary backup information.

BOTTOM LINE

Airfares are dictated by supply and demand. To get good deals, fly at the least popular times—during the middle of the week, for instance, or late at night. And even deeper discounts are available for travelers who are flexible about departure times and amenities.

WORDS TO THE WISE

Consolidator: A wholesaler who sells airline tickets to the public at a discount. Savings can amount to 50 percent off the full fare.

Discount airlines: Airlines serving small, niche markets and offering discount fares for bare-bones service.

Frequent-flier program: An airline's incentive program allowing customers to accumulate mileage credits toward free trips. Strategy tip: Concentrate on one or two airlines.

Allies

Air Courier Association: 191 University Boulevard, Suite 300, Denver, CO 80206. For information on courier flights.

Airhitch: 100 North Sepulveda Boulevard, Suite 903, El Segundo, CA 90245. Offers low-cost, standby air flights.

International Association of Air Travel Couriers: 8 S. J Street, P.O. Box 1349, Lake Worth, FL 33460. For information on courier flights.

U.S. Department of Transportation: Federal Aviation Administration, Flight Standard Service, Operational System Branch, P.O. Box 25082, Oklahoma City, OK 73125, attention AFS 624. To request information about a specific airline's safety record.

Fly for Less, by Gary Schmidt (Travel Publishing). Directory of airline consolidators.

Nailing Down the Best Room and Board

On a Hotel Bill, There's Always Room for Improvement

Most vacationers will fight tooth and toilet kit for the lowest possible air-fare, but they routinely ignore opportunities to reduce their hotel costs.

"During airline fare wars, the cost of one round-trip ticket from New York City to London can cost as much as the price of a one-night stay in a luxury London hotel," says Ed Perkins, editor of the *Consumer Reports Travel Letter*. "Obviously, the cost of your hotel room will be the biggest expense of your trip. It behooves you to work on lowering these costs rather than sweating the last dollar out of your airline ticket."

Where do you begin? "You have to bargain," says Gary Stoller, investiga-tive editor for *Conde Nast Traveler*. "You must call directly and ask for the cheapest rate—repeatedly."

Reservations: Beware "Rack Rates"

If you're calling a hotel chain, the toll-free number connects to a national reservation service. Don't book your reservation there. Use the toll-free number only to obtain general information about location, rooms, and amenities. The operator often quotes the highest, nondiscounted prices (also called a rack rate) from a computer screen and has no authority to bar-gain with you.

"That's like paying full fare for a first-class ticket on an airline and sitting in coach," says Stoller.

THE DESK MANAGER HOLDS THE KEY

After you have found out the full price from a hotel's toll-free number, call the hotel directly and ask for the desk manager, says Stoller. This person has the power to wheel and deal. After all, it's not in the manager's interest to have empty rooms. And remember, the less crowded a hotel is, the more leverage you have.

Work all the angles. Always ask for the weekend rate, specials, or a super-saver option. Be sure to mention if you are a member of the American Automobile Association or the American Association of Retired Persons. These memberships entitle you to additional discounts.

Go corporate. Take business letterhead or business cards to the hotel desk with you. That will help convince the desk clerk that you're on the job, and you'll be able to press for the corporate rate.

Ask for amenities. If the hotel won't budge on the price, ask if you can get more for your money—for example, a bigger room, a better view, or services such as free parking or breakfast.

Be persistent. You might be shocked at how flexible hotel rates are. In an experiment conducted by *Travel & Leisure*, it was revealed that room prices are in a constant state of flux. An editor booked a room one month in advance for a certain price. Then, he called back each day to get the prices on the same room. He discovered that the price of the room changed constantly—and not by just a few dollars.

The lesson is to book early if you want to feel secure, but keep calling at least once a week and see if the rate has gone down. Always make your reservation on a credit card—you have a confirmed reservation and you can obtain credit to your account much faster than if you wait for a cash refund.

Wait, if possible. The closer you get to the day of your reservation, the more likely it is that a hotel wants to be rid of excess inventory. But be careful about this strategy: Check whether there's a convention in town during your vacation. If so, you will not have as much room to negotiate, because hotels are likely to sell out.

GO FOR BROKERS

When Perkins surveyed readers, he found that a majority did negotiate hotel discounts up to 20 percent. But considerably fewer people knew to take advantage of even greater savings through hotel brokers or half-price hotel programs.

"There's a variety of discount programs available, which I view as a tool kit," says Perkins. "You must decide which tool works best for your trip. When I look over all the options, I believe that using a hotel broker is the most effective way to get substantial discounts on hotel rooms."

Hotel brokers operate in much the same way as airline consolidators. They have a prearranged agreement with hotels to fill a certain percentage of their rooms in exchange for a greatly discounted price. In some cases, the broker actually buys up blocks of rooms in advance, also at wholesale prices. Brokers, who specialize in specific cities, sell hotel rooms to the public at a substantial savings, considerably lower than what you could get by negotiating with the desk clerk.

What Do I Say?

Hotel Haggling

When you call to book a hotel reservation, ask to speak with the desk clerk or manager. Begin by asking, "What's the lowest rate that you have for the date of my arrival?" But when they tell you, don't stop there. Let them know that you will book a room only if you are offered a special deal.

"Hotel personnel are trained to give you the highest rate and then go down from there," says Joe Brancatelli, editor of *Frommer's Travel Update*, a monthly consumer newsletter. "They're trained to start at the top of the ladder and go down, in case they hit a high price that you can live with."

The only way to win is to be persistent. Tell them if you are a member of the American Automobile Association or if you're eligible for a senior citizen's discount. Again, don't stop there. Ask if there are any super-saver rates, weekend or weekday specials, or convention rates. Ask for the corporate rate and remember to bring your business card when you check in.

If you work for the government, ask if they give discounts to state or federal employees. If you are enrolled in the hotel's membership program or own stock in the corporate owner, tell them—it proves that you are a frequent visitor. Then ask about membership discounts or special shareholder rates.

Also ask what services are included in the room rate. "Maybe the rock-bottom rate won't save you as much money as a slightly higher price that includes free parking and breakfast," says Brancatelli.

How do you know when you've gotten the best rate? "When the reservations clerk is prepared to let you hang up rather than take your reservation," says Brancatelli. "As long as the clerk is still talking, there's still room to negotiate."

Hotels do not advertise brokers' services, however, because they don't want to drive away people who are willing to pay full price. Here are some other things to remember about brokers.

Gather the lists. When you call a broker, ask for a list of hotels and cities that the service specializes in as well as current prices. Some brokers offer hotel rooms in only one or two cities. However, others deal with hotels in a dozen or more cities.

Watch the fine print. You can make a reservation through a broker in advance, and always pay with a credit card. Ask about their cancellation policy, particularly how much advance notice is required. Some brokers do require prepayment for your rooms, while others let you pay the hotel directly upon checkout. As always, check the fine print.

Get with a Program

The travel industry is rife with special promotions—coupons, credits cards, "frequent-stayer" plans, and the like. These deals can produce substantial savings when they happen to mesh with your travel plans.

You've seen those coupon books, for instance, that offer two-for-one deals in your hometown on everything from restaurant meals to event tickets to hotel rooms. "What people don't realize is that you can buy one of these books for any city you plan to visit—just call their toll-free number and order one," says Perkins.

Hate Surprises? Beware Hotel Services

Even the best negotiator can't avoid a number of fees that crop up on the hotel bill. The biggest surprise hit for travelers is city-levied hotel taxes. New York City adds a 21.25 percent tax on all rooms more than $100. Chicago charges 14.9 percent tax, and Atlanta levies 13 percent on hotel stays.

Other costs that can appear on your bill include charges for overnight parking, incoming faxes, laundry service, telephone calls that you make from the room, and items that you take from the wet bar, says Stephen Pollan, an attorney, financial consultant, and author. Ask how much a service costs before using it. You may be able to find it cheaper elsewhere in the city.

As for telephone costs, always use your calling card for local and long-distance calls. Be sure to ask the front desk their fee for calling card access. They often charge 50 cents to $1 just to connect you to a carrier such as AT&T, MCI, or Sprint. When in doubt, use the pay phones in the lobby.

RESERVE ROOMS BY THE BOOK

Here's how coupon books work: The books typically cost $35 to $50 for a multitude of deals that expire in 12 to 18 months. A major player in the coupon book business is Entertainment Publications, which has signed up 1,600 hotels in the United States. Books are also available for worldwide locations such as Canada, Mexico, Europe, and Australia.

The books generally provide 50 percent off a hotel's rate. Again, you should bypass the toll-free number and contact the hotel directly (usually 30 days in advance) and give them your membership number. The rule is that if a hotel does not anticipate 80 percent occupancy during the time you want to book a visit, then they must offer you a discount. If the hotel has reached 80 percent occupancy, then they can refuse you.

Is there a catch? Yes: The discount is calculated against the highest list price and not the lowest one that you might have been able to bargain for yourself. Nonetheless, you will often get 20 to 40 percent off the room rate without having to test your ability to negotiate. That in itself is a bargain for some people.

REAP REWARDS FOR LOYALTY

If you travel a lot, make that repeat business work in your favor. *Consumer Reports Travel Letter* recommends considering one of the "frequent-stay" programs offered by hotel chains like Hilton and Marriott. They work in much the same way as the airlines' frequent-flier programs. By signing up with an individual program run by the hotel or by building points through credit card purchases, you eventually earn a free hotel stay at a later date.

Hilton, Marriott, and Ramada cosponsor credit cards through which you can earn hotel credit. American Express premium cards and Diners Club also have elaborate schedules of points to be earned and awards to be allocated. With all these plans, you earn program points for every dollar that you spend on hotel lodging. In some cases, you earn points for buying certain hotel services and merchandise. A few hotels will award points even if you have negotiated a discounted room rate.

Watch those fees. For the most part, membership in hotel-based programs is free—you simply sign up at the front desk. Often there are benefits simply for joining: free breakfast, free local calls, free parking, or late checkout times. Some hotels do charge fees for membership, however, so be sure to read the fine print before you sign up.

The credit cards also typically charge a yearly enrollment fee. Some credit cards ask that you decide upon enrollment whether you want your miles to build toward airline miles or hotel stays. The Hilton program allows members to earn credit for both air travel and lodging with a single hotel stay.

Check for the payoff. Don't settle for peanuts. "As you evaluate a program, make sure that they offer an award at least after staying 25 nights," says Perkins. "That's a reasonable goal for travelers. And be sure that you receive something tangible like a free night, a room discount, or a cash certificate. If all they offer is a room upgrade or free use of a health club, then it's not a good program."

Wilderness: Shouldering Your Way In

Since 1864, when California's Yosemite Valley was set aside for conservation, American vacationers have been grateful guests of the government in the great outdoors. Car and tent camping has long offered an affordable getaway amid unique landscapes and astonishing scenery, from silent deserts to alpine meadows, granite mountains and evergreen forests.

But if you have ever waited in a long line of cars to be admitted into a national park or been turned away during a popular three-day summer weekend, you know that America's national parks are almost too popular for their own good. How do you get into the most popular parks?

Work the phones. Reservations for campsites at national parks may be handled through a commercial computer ticketing system called Destinet. Reservations can be made one day to five months in advance. Some national parks do not take reservations (they operate on a first-come, first-serve basis). If you are unsure whether the park takes reservations, it is best to call the national park first. They will instruct you how they handle their reservations.

"If the computer system says that a park is full, it still pays to call the park directly and ask if there has been a cancellation," says Stoller. "Plans do change at the last minute, and things will open up."

Drive on the "shoulder." The most popular season to go camping is from Memorial Day weekend in May to Labor Day weekend in September. Naturally, that's when you'll find the longest lines, the biggest crowds, and the most difficulty getting into the park of your choice. However, if you can travel during the so-called shoulder seasons—late spring (March through May) and early fall (September through October)—chances are much better that you will get a reservation at even the most popular national park. And the weather is often warm enough for such activities as hiking, horseback riding, sailing, and swimming.

Apply for a pass. No, you can't bargain with the ranger over the usage fee at a national park. But if you are 62, you can apply for a Golden Age Passport. The pass costs $10. It's good for life and provides a 50 percent discount on all park facilities (except for those run by concessionaires). You can purchase the pass at any national park that charges an admission fee.

Disabled travelers can obtain the Golden Access Passport. There's no fee for this program and, as with senior citizens, you'll get a 50 percent discount on all park services.

Other campers should consider the Golden Eagle Pass. For $25, the Golden Eagle Pass entitles you and the companions in your vehicle to free admission to all national parks during the calendar year. You can inquire about all these passes at any national park.

TRY THE TRAILS LESS TAKEN

If you must travel during the summer months, consider alternative wilderness areas: state parks, national forest land, and national wilderness areas. These are administered by various state and government agencies.

Each state in the United States has an extensive system of state parks that are often less crowded than the better-known national parks. States classify protected land as either state parks, wilderness areas, ecological preserves, historical sites, recreation areas, or state beaches. Each one provides a memorable way to experience the country's rugged landscape.

Also under federal jurisdiction are national forests, many of which are located near national parks and have picnic tables and facilities for recreational vehicles and tent camping.

The Wilderness Preservation Act of 1972 set aside vast amounts of rugged landscape, under the administration of the Bureau of Land Management. While facilities are scarce in these natural resources—often no more than maintained trails, parking areas, and pit toilets—they do offer boundless scenery for the camper who is willing to rough it.

Get the lay of the land. The U.S. Geological Survey (USGS) maintains excellent topographical maps. Before heading out to any wilderness area off the beaten track, contact the USGS, P.O. Box 25286, Denver Federal Center, Denver, CO 80225, and request a map for the area that you plan to visit.

Go private. When all else fails, make a reservation in a privately owned campground, such as those administered by Kampgrounds of America (KOA). They can't compare with campsites in designated wilderness areas, but they're often open when the national parks are booked. You can stay overnight at a KOA and still pay a day-use fee ($3 to $10) that allows you to drive into the park for the day. For the best listing of such campgrounds, contact the KOA corporate office at P.O. Box 30558, Directory Department, Billings, MT 59114. They will mail you one of the directories (published annually) for about $3. Or, you can pick up a directory at any local KOA campground. The American Automobile Association can also provide you with a list of campgrounds in the area that you plan to visit.

Restaurants: Slicing That Tab

There are few things as satisfying as an excellent meal at a gourmet restaurant. But in many American cities, a meal at a four-star restaurant can easily run you $60 to $100 per person—not even counting drinks, taxes, and tip. Here's how to whittle that cost down to a reasonable sum.

Let's do lunch. Sure, you can choose more reasonably priced restaurants located in neighborhoods away from the high-ticket districts that attract tourists. But if you want to see how the other half eats, Stoller says, "pick any of the best restaurants in the city and make a reservation—for lunch. The menu is usually similar, the portions are almost as large, and the prices are much more affordable."

Play your cards right. Many of the strategies that help reduce the cost of hotel bills also will cut down on eating expenses. Two-for-one coupon books carry a substantial number of restaurant deals. And since you are paying a flat fee for the book, the more coupons you use, the more you save.

Several credit cards target restaurants specifically. One of the most popular cards is Transmedia. Headquartered in Miami, Transmedia offers 20 to 25 percent off the bill at member-restaurants, depending on which program you choose. "Don't forget Diners Club cards," says Perkins. "They also take 20 percent off the total bill." Call for their national directory of participating restaurants.

Ask an editor. Another good strategy is to call the local lifestyle-entertainment magazine that covers the city you are visiting. Ask the food and wine editor which restaurants have generous hors d'oeuvres and spreads of free food during happy hour. Also ask for recommendations of good restaurants in local neighborhoods. Then call those restaurants and ask if they offer early-bird prices. Often these restaurants offer 10 to 20 percent off between 5:00 and 6:00 P.M. for the locals in the neighborhood.

For more information on quality dining and good restaurant values, check out the Zagat Survey, pocket-size guides to restaurants in 35 major cities. Tina and Tom Zagat get input from nearly 30,000 diners across the country to develop their national and regional guides. They are available in some bookstores, or you can write for one at Zagat Survey, 4 Columbus Circle, New York, NY 10019.

Consult the concierge. Is the eatery of your choice jammed? You can always get the best table at a restaurant or a reservation even when it's full by dealing with the concierge of your hotel, says Herbert Teison, editor of the New York City–based *Travel Smart* newsletter. "Restaurants depend on hotels to send them a lot of business," says Teison. "They'll make special allowances if the reservation is called in by the concierge."

Stop by the concierge desk and introduce yourself. Try to give as much advance notice of your dinner plans as possible and be sure to tip the concierge generously.

Bottom Line

Hotel rates are shockingly flexible. So don't book your room through a chain's toll-free number for central reservations—call the specific hotel that you want to stay in, talk to the desk manager, and ask repeatedly for the best possible rate.

Words to the Wise

Frequent stay: The hotel industry's equivalent of the airlines' frequent-flier programs.

Rack rate: Read: "maximum rate." This is often the first price that you'll be quoted for a hotel room. Usually, you can bargain.

Allies

Here are addresses for hotel brokers, who rent out rooms for a price better than you'd ever get out of the desk clerk. Check the toll-free directory for phone numbers.

Accommodations Express: 801 Asbury Avenue, 6th Floor, Ocean City, NJ 08226. Books rooms only in the United States, with an emphasis on East Coast cities.

Express Reservations: 3800 Arapahoe Avenue, Suite 250, Boulder, CO 80303. They book hotel rooms in New York City and Los Angeles.

Hotel Reservations Network (HRN): 8140 Walnut Hill Lane, Suite 203, Dallas, TX 75231. They book rooms in 20 cities in the United States as well as London and Paris.

Quikbook: 381 Park Avenue South, New York, NY 10016. They book rooms in several cities in the United States.

RMC Travel: 424 Madison Avenue, Suite 705, New York, NY 10017. Serves 150 cities throughout the United States.

These membership clubs will open the door to huge discounts on lodging, meals, and entertainment.

America at 50% Discount: 1031 Cromwell Bridge Road, Baltimore, MD 21286. Focuses on businesses and services in the United States, Canada, and the Caribbean. It sells for about $20.

Carte Royale: 5605 Glenridge Drive, Suite 300, Atlanta, GA 30342. Strong listings in Italy. Membership costs about $40.

Encore: 4501 Forbes Boulevard, Lanham, MD 20706. Especially strong in the Caribbean and Canada. Membership with Encore costs about $50.

Entertainment Publications: 2125 Butterfield Road, Troy, MI 48084. They sell 160 different coupon books, including a U.S. hotel directory for about $30; and Entertainment International sells for about $43. Prices for coupon books range from $30 to $60.

Great American Traveler: P.O. Box 26573, Salt Lake City, UT 84127-0653. Strong in Germany, France, and northern Europe. Membership for the first year is about $100.

ITC-50: 6001 North Clark Street, Chicago, IL 60660. Substantial foreign listings, especially Canada, Asia, and the South Pacific. Membership costs about $49.

Privilege Card International: 201 East Commerce, Suite 198, Youngstown, OH 44503. Main strength is in Rome, Paris, and Singapore. Membership costs about $90.

Roughing it is one thing. Blundering into a park totally unprepared is foolhardy. These contacts will make your visit go smoothly.

Bureau of Land Management: For information on camping in wilderness administrated by the Bureau of Land Management, contact the Bureau of Land Management, Public Affairs Office, Department of the Interior, 1849 C Street NW, Room LS504, Washington, DC 20240.

Canadian Parks Service: Canadian Parks, 25 Eddy Street, 10th Floor, Hull, Quebec, Canada K1A 0M5. For information on the national parks of Canada.

Destinet: 9450 Carroll Park Drive, San Diego, CA 92121. To make a reservation in a national park or to reserve a campsite at any California State park.

National Park Service: For a copy of the "National Park System Map and Guide," contact the Consumer Information Center, P.O. Box 100, Pueblo, CO 81002-0100. It costs about $2.

U.S. Department of Agriculture (USDA) Forest Service: For information on camping on national forest land, contact the USDA Forest Service, Public Affairs Office, P.O. Box 96090, Washington, DC 20090-6090.

Part 11

LAW AND GOVERNMENT

Mastering Family Law

Armor Yourself—
And Then Stay off the Battlefield

Why don't sharks bite lawyers? Professional courtesy.

You've heard a million lawyer jokes, right? But when fate takes a cruel and unfair twist, when the deck is stacked and the stakes are mounting, your lawyer can be the best conceivable ally.

To master family law, you'll need to know how the process works, how to make it work for you, and how to enlist the help of others, including lawyers and other professionals.

In modern America, matters that you tend to consider your private business can easily become the law's business at one time or another—including such personal concerns as birth, marriage, divorce, support for children (both emotional and financial), illness, death, and even the way that your possessions are split up after you're gone. This becomes ever more pertinent when society is in a state of flux. For example, while married couples headed 87 percent of America's families in 1970, according to Census figures, that had dropped to 78 percent by 1994.

While you can beat some of society's "systems" with guile or sleight of hand, you have to approach the law with the utmost caution. No slick maneuvers. No shell games. The only way to beat the law is to develop a comprehensive knowledge of it, including the banana peels, sunken reefs, and outright booby traps.

"The law is the integral part of the glue that keeps society together," says David Weiss, renowned New York City criminal defense lawyer. "It's the compact that we've all agreed to live by so that we don't have a world consisting of survival of the fittest. The thing about the law is that if you don't learn it, you'll never beat it."

The legal system is designed to cover you like armor. But the secret to winning the war is to keep off the battlefield altogether. Learn how to use the law to your advantage, to recognize the pitfalls, and you have a powerful weapon at your disposal. But go into the world unarmed and you risk disaster. Here's a guide on dodging legal bullets.

Children: The Law of Life Cycles

The law's interest in your family begins on the day that you're born. By law, birth certificates must be issued to officially record the birth of a child. Normally, the hospital where the child is born will complete the necessary paperwork.

But take nothing for granted. One New York City lawyer had a newborn switched from one hospital to another because of a suspected heart ailment. In the confusion, the family never received a birth certificate, and it was months before all of the paperwork could be straightened out.

GET YOUR CHILD DOCUMENTED

To get your child toddling on the right foot in life, here's what legal experts advise.

Go to the source. If your newborn's paperwork slips through the cracks, or if you need to replace a lost birth certificate or have one changed, call the medical records office in the hospital or health care facility where your child was born. The hospital will be able to refer you to the appropriate town clerk's office or state bureau of vital statistics to obtain the copies that you need.

Get the real thing. Most people take birth certificates for granted—until they try getting a driver's license or passport without one. Remember that whenever you do need a birth certificate, you'd better have the actual document on hand. A photocopy won't normally do, not even notarized copies. So when you turn in the necessary forms, be sure to request several "certified copies," which are considered legal, duplicate originals. The copies usually cost a few dollars each, but they are worth it. Keep one in a safe-deposit box, one in a safe file, and one easily accessible for its various uses.

Take a number. Social Security numbers are now an indispensable form of identification in our society. Although the law does not mandate Social Security numbers for newborns, get one for your kid as soon as possible anyway. For one thing, the IRS won't allow you to claim a child over the age of one as a dependent unless he has a Social Security number. Besides, if you want Grandpa or Grandma to kick in with a savings bond, you'll want to make it easy and have the number on hand.

To obtain an application, contact the Social Security Administration (check the U.S. Government listings in the Blue Pages of your phone book). For an adult, you'll need a certified copy of your birth certificate, as well as some other acceptable form of identification, such as a driver's license or passport. For an infant, you'll need a birth certificate and another document, such as a hospital record with the baby's name on it. Some hospitals make this hassle-free. Ask the hospital in which your child was born whether they can get the Social Security paperwork rolling for you.

GUARDIANS: JUST IN CASE, NAME A BACKUP

If both you and your spouse died, who would take care of the kids? It's a heart-wrenching scenario to ponder, but as a parent it's your job to plan for the worst. Even before a child is born, would-be parents should draft a will that appoints a trusted friend or relative as legal guardian if both parents die while the child is a minor. If you're going to do this, however, be sure that your choice of guardians is a final one, says Stephen Pollan, an attorney, financial consultant, and author.

A legal guardian is someone other than a parent who has the legal right and authority to act as parent. Guardians can serve either permanently or on a short-term basis and are designated by the parent or approved by a court. Permanent appointments generally require court approval, and the best interests of the child are the chief priority.

Suppose a single parent fell seriously ill or were incapacitated for a while. In that case, a short-term guardianship might be necessary, and that can be accomplished less formally. Assuming that no other parent can step in, the ailing parent should designate a specific guardian in writing.

Although there is no universally accepted legal document for short-term appointment of a guardian, normally, a simple letter won't do. In fact, some states require that specific forms or affidavits be completed. While laws covering this vary from state to state, family law specialists say that some rules hold true for all situations.

- You have to spell out the precise nature of the appointment, specifying what decisions—medical and otherwise—you intend the guardian to make and the duration of the guardianship.
- The proposed guardian should always sign the document consenting to the appointment.
- The document should be witnessed and notarized.

If you believe that a third party is likely to object to your choice of guardian, get a lawyer involved.

ADOPTION: FINDING THAT NEW FAMILY MEMBER

Roughly 120,000 adoptions are completed in the United States in a year, most of them accomplished in one of three ways: (1) through an agency, (2) privately, or (3) from another country. Regardless of the method that you choose, networking beforehand will help immeasurably. Speak to other parents who have been through the process. They'll be able to refer you to reputable agencies, lawyers, and doctors; and they'll also tell you what states and countries have the "friendliest" systems.

It Figures

What Should Legal Services Cost?

Most attorneys charge an hourly rate for handling divorces, separations, will preparation, and estate planning. But you might be able to negotiate a flat-fee arrangement, particularly if the situation is straightforward.

Hourly attorney's fees generally range from as low as $100 per hour up to $400, depending on where you live, the size of the firm where your attorney works, and the attorney's experience. Discuss fees in detail when you first interview the lawyer (always do it in person) and get them memorialized in writing (typically called a retainer agreement or engagement letter).

Legal fees can typically run $1,500 or more for creating a basic trust and $2,500 or more for an uncontested divorce.

Family law experts say that you can lower your fees with these techniques.

Know the territory. Know how much services in your area typically cost. Learn this by asking friends and business associates who have experienced situations similar to yours.

Get an estimate. At the initial interview, ask the attorney to give you a budget based on an estimate of the number of hours that the job will take.

Get less costly help. Ask the attorney to farm out less technical or administrative work to paralegals or junior associates, whose hourly rates are lower.

Put a lid on it. Try to negotiate an hourly fee with a ceiling, an agreed-upon amount that the total bill will not exceed.

Retain the retainer. Though attorneys typically ask for retainers up front, see if yours is willing to forgo, reduce, or accept this amount in installments.

A number of organizations around the country provide information on all types of adoptions, including international and "special needs" children. You can also contact them for information on support groups in your area.

Parents adopting a newborn through an agency or privately can expect to pay $10,000 to $12,000 in fees, according to AdoptioNetwork, a volunteer group that has a World Wide Web site on the Internet. For a foreign newborn, costs can surpass $18,000.

Privately handled adoptions have less of a structured system in place than agency arrangements have. So if you decide to go the independent route, adoption specialists say, here are some tips to consider.

Set up a hot line. A New York City couple successfully arranged the private adoption of their two children by setting up a hot line in their home. With a lawyer's help, they carefully scripted classified ads listing a toll-free number. They installed a separate phone line in their house to receive the calls, and when the responses began to roll in, the lawyer also helped with the initial screening and investigative process.

A separate, dedicated telephone protects your privacy and ensures that your callers will always be able to get through. Consider using an answering machine to pick up calls when you're away from home. But remember that your callers are finding themselves talking to a machine under what could be emotional circumstances. Unless you're completely turned off by the message left, don't be too quick to write the caller off.

Handle with care. When you start to receive calls in response to an adoption ad, remember that the caller will probably be more nervous than you. Your main objective is to put the prospective mother at ease. In most instances, she will be have a lot of questions for *you*.

Small talk will usually help get the caller comfortable: Where are you from? What do you do? Are you in school? Once you've chatted a bit, you can begin to ask a few more pertinent questions like: When are you due? Why are you putting the child up for adoption? Have you been getting prenatal care? Is the child's father in the picture, and is he supportive of the adoption process?

Screen the responses. Certain signs warn you to rule a caller out right away. For instance, be wary of any caller who starts off the conversation by asking for money. That person could be involved in baby selling. If the caller is addicted to drugs or alcohol or has serious health problems, you should probably steer clear, says Pollan.

Turn 'em over to a pro. Once you've identified some likely adoption prospects, it's best to have your lawyer take over the discussion with your candidates. Yes, it's possible to screen callers without an attorney's assistance, but the process is so intricate and emotional that a lawyer who has experience with independent adoptions will be a big help. Such a lawyer will know what questions to ask, how to look into the caller's background in-depth, and what other local professionals—doctors, for instance—can help move things along.

Custody: The Kids Come First

When parents divorce, there's no set formula for deciding who gets custody of the children. But while equal opportunity is the rule in many areas of society, to this day the law still favors the biological mother. A father seeking custody faces an uphill battle.

But the issue isn't as gender-based as it once was, says Eleanor B. Alter, the nationally recognized family lawyer who has represented Mia Farrow (in her much publicized legal battle with Woody Allen) and actress Lori Singer. "Courts look to see which parent was the primary caregiver, and if that person has been functioning well, they're reluctant to upset the status quo," says Alter.

One exception is when an older child (age 13 or older) strongly prefers one parent over the other. In this case, Alter says, "most judges realize that they can't chain the child and force him to stay with the mother. If the kid comes into court and he's adamant about living with Dad—as long as he's not just mad at his mother for not letting him stay out late—often a judge will follow his wishes."

Not surprising, custody is often an emotionally charged, extremely contentious issue. How does the law approach the subject? Through the eyes of the youngster. At every juncture, the law poses the question, "What is in the best interests of the child?"

Remember that courts look for evidence of stability and predictability in deciding which parent will be awarded custody of minor children. You may need to consider certain lifestyle changes in order to measure up. Character references can also go a long way. So, if you're headed for divorce and you're afraid that you might lose custody, here are five things that custody specialists recommend you do to better your odds of at least winning joint custody.

Clean up. If you have a substance-abuse problem, get it under control. Join a 12-step group or consult your physician for other treatment options and forms of support.

Listen to experience. Ask your legal contacts to put you in touch with a custody advisory clinic. Also, talk to someone you know who has been through a custody battle and ask what helped and what hurt.

Get religion. Develop a relationship with a clergyman and become active in your church or synagogue.

Adjust your calendar. Arrange for future flextime at your job. This will demonstrate that you'll have the time necessary to properly raise your child.

Consider your partner. If you have someone else in your life, make sure that it's a relationship that can stand scrutiny. It's not enough that your own lifestyle be beyond reproach. Exposing your child to a significant other who is a drug addict, for instance, will destroy any chance that you have for winning custody.

Premarital Lex: Before "I Do"

You've decided to remarry. Both you and your spouse-to-be have your own assets, and you both have grown children who should inherit them when you die. So it's time to work out a prenuptial agreement.

These contracts are becoming an increasingly popular financial planning device, and they're especially common in these scenarios.

- When it is not a first marriage
- When the participants have complex business interests
- When one party's financial worth or income is significantly higher than the other's

Prenuptial agreements "are the only remedy that we as a society have for the epidemic of divorce litigation," says Raoul Felder, an internationally recognized family law lawyer whose clients have included Anthony Quinn's wife, Johnny Carson's first wife, Brian DePalma, and Martin Scorsese. "Given the present judicial and legislative environment in America, anyone who gets married without a prenuptial agreement should see a psychiatrist and not a lawyer."

Felder says that prenuptials are a good idea even for those entering marriage for the first time. "Those with money have always sought to insulate themselves," he says. "People who haven't yet made it should be equally concerned. Today's waiter will be tomorrow's restaurant owner. Today's hungry actor could become Hollywood's next superstar."

FORGING A STRONG AGREEMENT

A prenuptial agreement usually is an understanding between two people who want to marry. The contract establishes how property will be divided at three critical stages of the couple's lives: during the marriage, in the event of divorce, and when either spouse dies. (For that matter, the same ground can be covered after you've said "I do," in a postnuptial agreement. But the longer you wait, legal experts warn, the greater the potential for sticky problems.)

Virtually every state recognizes prenuptial agreements. But marriage is a powerful and intricate relationship, and therefore the law holds these contracts up to uncommon scrutiny. To create an enforceable agreement, lawyers recommend that you follow these guidelines.

Tell all. The law requires that both parties have complete access to all financial information concerning the other. Most states require that detailed net-worth statements be a prominent part of the prenuptial agreement. In most instances, failing to fully disclose assets or income is grounds for voiding the agreement.

How to Change Your Name

You might want to change your name for any number of reasons. For instance:

- A married woman may want to establish a separate and distinct name from that of her husband for use in the business world.
- A married woman may have taken her spouse's last name but decided to revert to her maiden name.
- When a couple separates or divorces, the wife might want to shed her ex-husband's name.
- Someone might just want to make a fresh start in life with a new name.
- Someone might have a name that is socially awkward.
- A name might have a stigma attached to it because it is similar to that of an infamous figure.

Every person has the right to choose any first or last name that he wants, so long as there is no intent to deceive creditors, avoid criminal prosecution, or commit fraud, legal experts say. But in most instances the task cannot be accomplished without wading through a myriad of legal procedures and red tape.

If you've ever lost a wallet, you know the torture of replacing credit cards, a driver's license, and other forms of identification. And replacing routine identification is just one of the hassles that occurs when you change your name.

Most states require a person changing names to work through the court system, but you needn't pay a lawyer. Contact the county clerk's office at your local courthouse and ask what the procedure is for obtaining a name change. Some forms of name changes, such as reverting to a maiden name following divorce, are fairly simple procedures. Forms can usually be mailed to you or picked up at the courthouse. Depending upon where you live, other name changes may require you to appear in court. Then, you might prefer an attorney's assistance.

To process a name change, you may need to submit supporting materials (including a certified copy of your birth certificate), pay a court filing fee, and arrange for publication of your new name in a recognized newspaper for a certain time—normally several weeks. Once a judge has issued a final order granting your name change request, you'll want to notify several parties, including the Social Security Administration, the IRS, the Department of Motor Vehicles, your employer, and any creditors.

If you're married, there is an additional hoop that you'll need to jump through. Most states require married people to obtain the spouse's written consent before the court will approve the change.

Talk business early. When there are signs of coercion, the courts take a dim view. And the closer to the wedding day that the prenuptial agreement is signed, the more likely it will seem that one of the parties was strong-armed. Maybe it doesn't fit your vision of romantic conversation, but it's best to talk about prenuptials even before you're engaged and to sign an agreement as soon as you are.

Get separate lawyers. Sure, the two of you want nothing but together-ness. But for your prenuptial agreement to hold up, you each need your own lawyer. If you both use the same attorney, there's a good chance that the agreement will be set aside if there's a dispute. In fact, it's a good idea for the agreement to name the attorneys that each of you used and for you and your future spouse to acknowledge that you've signed the agreement on the advice of independent counsel.

Be reasonable. Make sure that your premarital agreement makes sense in the real world. When one party is left destitute after many years of mar-riage, for instance, courts have been known to stretch to find a reason for invalidating the contract.

Divorce: Breaking Up Is Hard to Do

Starting a marriage is easy. Ending one is tough—not only emotionally but also legally.

If you and your spouse no longer want to be married, you can't simply trot down to the courthouse and untie the knot. Divorce is done much more slowly and deliberately—something akin to the cooling-off period that many states require before you can buy a gun. For better or for worse, the legal system is more interested in why you want a divorce than why you married in the first place.

So there are procedures to follow. First and foremost, you have to show a judge that there is a reason—commonly called grounds—for a divorce.

Grounds for divorce come under the heading of "fault" or "no-fault," al-though today fault is no longer an issue in all but four or five states, Alter says. The most common fault-based grounds for divorce are:

- Adultery
- Cruel and inhuman treatment (treatment that endangers the physical or mental well-being of a spouse)
- Abandonment
- Imprisonment for a crime
- Drug or alcohol abuse
- Fraud
- Physical or mental incapacity

In most states, the last two are grounds for annulment, a judicial pro-ceeding that completely voids a marriage, treating it as if it never existed.

Common no-fault grounds include:

- Separation. You and your spouse now live in separate homes.
- Irreconcilable differences. This is a catchall declaration that you and your spouse can no longer live together. Even in jurisdictions that require a judge's approval, irreconcilable differences virtually always get rubber-stamp approval.

Under certain circumstances it makes sense for couples to enter an interim stage—known as legal separation—rather than divorce. This is particularly true if the couple believes that there's a chance of reconciliation. A separated couple is still legally married, but a separation agreement or a court establishes certain rights between them—including rights to property and child support—just as if the parties were divorced.

DIVORCE MEDIATION: QUICKER, LESS COSTLY

To get divorced, you may not have to shell out for a lawyer at all. That decision should hinge on a number of factors, including the facts of your case and your financial wherewithal. But if there are disagreements over how property will be divided, who is responsible for alimony, how much the alimony will be, who gets custody of the children, and the amount of child support, divorce attorneys say that you'll most likely need to hire a lawyer who specializes in matrimonial law.

Even when the spouses are at odds, however, couples increasingly turn to alternative forums like mediation to resolve their differences without going to court. In mediation, both parties present their arguments to a trained mediator, who suggests alternatives that are tailored to the couple's situation. Mediation is almost always cheaper, less hostile, and quicker than paying lawyers to fight it out, which can take from several months to several years.

Mediation is also far more practical than court in many situations. If the only issue to be worked out is child custody, for example, the mediator may be able to help the parties fashion a "shared-custody" arrangement and a visitation schedule that is convenient for both parents. Under a judge, the divorcing spouses may be forced to accept a resolution that pleases neither party.

ALIMONY AND SUPPORT: HOW MUCH?

If you're going to be receiving alimony—or paying it—you'll naturally wonder how it's going to be calculated and what influence you have on that figure. Alter says that a court will typically consider these factors in deciding whether, how much, and for how long alimony will be paid.

- The income and assets of each party at the time of the marriage.
- Their income and assets at the time of divorce.
- The duration of the marriage. Typically, the longer the marriage, the greater the right to alimony (so-called rehabilitative alimony) until the nonworking spouse has time to get re-established in the workforce.

- The age and health of the parties. A 60-year-old woman is not usually expected to go out and get a career, for instance. But a 25-year-old can expect alimony for a limited period of time.
- The present and future ability of each spouse to be self-supporting.
- The time and training necessary for the spouse receiving alimony to become self-supporting.
- The presence of children in the home of either spouse.
- How assets are to be split. Certain assets generate income, and others don't. For example, a spouse may live with her children in a home that's worth $150,000, but that house does not provide any income. But $150,000 of invested cash would be generating interest.
- The standard of living or lifestyle established during the marriage.
- If either party is supporting a spouse or children from a prior marriage, affecting what's available for alimony in this marriage.

With those factors in mind, family lawyers recommend these techniques to make sure that your needs are met as the courts decide what alimony will be paid after your divorce.

Build a paper trail. The primary purpose of alimony is to support one of the spouses at the level to which he or she became accustomed during the marriage. Therefore, it will be necessary to document your lifestyle in sufficient detail to allow a court or mediator to determine what is appropriate. Be sure to retain credit card, clothing, and dining receipts as well as automated teller machine statements, vacation records, and other documents that demonstrate the style in which you lived.

Remember: Remarriage has a price. Be aware that alimony obligations usually cease if the spouse receiving payments remarries. Presumably, support is no longer needed.

Rise with the tide. If you're to receive alimony, make sure that your divorce decree provides for increases to offset rises in the cost of living as well as increases if your ex-spouse benefits from an increase in income.

One important exception is if your ex-spouse is self-employed or in a cash business. In this case, you won't want the award to be subject to adjustment, because it's too easy for the numbers to be manipulated. You'd be better off with a fixed amount.

State the rate. If you're to pay alimony, be sure to specify the rate of increases should your own income grow. Try to negotiate a ceiling on increases equal to the rate of inflation. Also, include a provision for a downward adjustment to protect yourself in the event that you get laid off or demoted.

CHILD SUPPORT: FUNDING THEIR FUTURE

Each state has a statute outlining what percentage of a parent's income must go to child support as well as other factors that should be considered in providing for the children of divorcing parents.

For example, Alter says that in New York that number is 17 percent of a parent's gross income up to $80,000—plus, in some instances, payment for private school and medical coverage. (Ask your attorney what your state's policy is.)

The Census Bureau says that among the 4.9 million women due to receive child support in 1991, those who did got an average of $3,011. Of the 443,000 men eligible, those who received support averaged $2,292 for the year.

Some factors in child support are consistent from state to state. Similar to alimony, child support is intended to allow children to continue to live in a style to which they became accustomed. And under that guideline, it's possible that children might be entitled to such luxuries as private school, vacations, and summer camp.

If you are going to be receiving support payments on behalf of your children, family law attorneys say that these techniques will ease the way.

List future needs. Child support is a one-time award that lasts until your children come of age, so when it's negotiated, you'll have to make sure that your children are covered for the future. How do you do this without a crystal ball? Anticipate needs rather than specific amounts of money. Requests for support should be stated in terms of a certain sum—plus such items as higher education, extended health insurance coverage, summer camp, and private school.

Keep it friendly. The better terms you're on with your ex-spouse, the more apt you are to collect child support. So maintain a good relationship with your ex-spouse, encouraging your ex-spouse to see the children regularly and to stay involved.

If you're paying support, consider having it automatically withdrawn from your paycheck to spare you the hassle. Ask your boss or someone in the human resources department at your company if this is possible.

Don't be shy. What if a court has awarded you child support but your spouse won't pay? State and federal laws protect spouses who are having trouble collecting alimony or child support. Remedies for collecting include attaching wages (having money withheld from a spouse's paycheck), having tax refunds withheld, seizing personal property or real estate, and requiring a delinquent spouse to post a bond or a security deposit.

How to Avoid a Nasty Court Battle

In vicious divorce court battles, the only winners are the lawyers. Such confrontations are expensive, painstakingly drawn out, and emotionally debilitating. Family law specialists recommend these approaches to diffusing a potentially nasty court battle.

Watch your tongue. It always pays to be civil with your spouse, no matter how difficult that might be, especially if there are children involved. Even if there are no children, your behavior toward your spouse during this

---

Got a New Love? Consider the Court's View

You've met the love of your life, but your divorce from your ex-spouse is still chugging its way through the court system. Does it matter whether you and your new partner live together? Or would it help to keep separate quarters, either for the sake of appearance or in computing alimony?

The answer is that it depends partly on where you live, say family law experts. Courts are not as concerned as they once were about issues of fault in a dissolving marriage. But remember that in court systems in cosmopolitan areas—where cohabitation is more openly accepted—you'll more likely fare better.

And there are other factors to consider. If your new partner is married, or half your age, that may raise the judge's eyebrows—which could prove costly if your state gives judges much discretion in awarding alimony. If this sounds like your situation, divorce attorneys say, try to keep a low profile and consider putting off cohabitation plans until the divorce is final.

---

period can significantly affect the eventual settlement. In fact, respectful, polite, and fair behavior is often the difference between settling amicably and going to court.

If you do end up in court, your prior behavior is likely to affect issues like visitation and custody. The last thing that you want is for the judge to take sides against you. Judges are typically hardened from experience with family matters, but it's still human nature to lean toward one person if the other is irrational or belligerent.

Show the judge respect. Keep in mind that judges are typically conservative, so you must watch your demeanor in court. Dress neatly: jacket and tie if you're a man, skirt or dress for a woman. When you stand, stand up straight. Always refer to the judge as Your Honor. Speak only when spoken to and with your lawyer's approval. And keep in mind that what you hear may make you angry. This is the time to show restraint. Don't act out. It can only work against you.

Call a conference. If at all possible, sit down with your spouse and try to work out the big issues yourselves. For many uncomplicated situations, the do-it-yourself divorce kits available in many bookstores and stationery shops will suffice in most states.

To some extent, involve a lawyer. If you're contemplating a divorce, you should speak with a lawyer before making any big moves. Say that it's uncomfortable for you to continue living in the same home with your spouse. No big deal—you'd move out, right? Wrong. Your spouse could accuse you of abandonment. And if you live in a state that still grants fault-based divorces—almost three-quarters do—your spouse might be entitled to a larger percentage of the property settlement.

Try mediation. In mediation, a neutral third party meets with the divorcing couple and helps them to work out their differences concerning alimony, child support, custody, and division of assets. The mediator, often a lawyer or retired judge, does not have the power to impose a decision on the parties but guides the discussion and helps the couple reach agreement. Most mediators will suggest that each spouse get his or her own lawyer to go over the agreement before it is signed to avoid challenges down the road.

Hire a therapist. It may sound like it's a tad late, but having a therapist work with a divorcing couple can be quite useful. Not to attempt reconciliation—to help the couple separate. If you and your spouse are having a tough time communicating, a therapist trained in couple counseling will assist you in opening the lines of communication. This will allow you and your spouse to discuss the issues that need to be resolved in order for you both to move on with your lives.

WHEN DIVORCE LOOMS: A TO-DO LIST

Here's what attorneys recommend that you do if you think divorce is inevitable.

Start photocopying. Since divorce is mainly about money—splitting up property, alimony, and child support—you'd better know all that you can about your spouse's finances. Make copies of all documents that you can get your hands on, including pay stubs, bank account statements, loan applications, insurance policies, deeds, and statements from stockbrokers, says Pollan.

Start an emergency fund. Since settling a divorce dispute can take months or even years, finances can get tight. So if you think that there's a divorce in your future, start mounting up a reserve fund in a separate account so that you'll be able to dip in as needed.

Divide the loot. If you have joint bank or other accounts with your spouse, now is the time to remove your share. But don't be a pig. Take half and move it into an account with only your name. If you take more than that, your actions and character will be questioned later on.

Protect investments. Send letters to stockbrokers instructing them not to sell jointly owned investments unless your signature is on the order.

Hire Sherlock. What if you suspect that your spouse has hidden assets? You can't possibly get a fair shake in a divorce settlement if all the cards are not on the table. It may be worth your while to hire a private investigator or asset search company to find misappropriated or hidden assets. Consider having the investigator look into the finances of your spouse's relatives as well, suggests Pollan.

It can be extremely difficult to track down money or assets if your spouse has had enough time to plot carefully. Your best defense is to keep your antenna up at all times and to keep tabs on your assets before marital problems even arise.

Size up the business. If your spouse owns a business, you are especially vulnerable to shady financial maneuvers. Hire an investigative accountant to examine your spouse's business records and tax returns. Also, you'll need to have an idea of what the business is worth in order to talk settlement. If your spouse is a doctor, lawyer, accountant, or some other licensed professional, this valuation should include the worth of the license itself. Since valuation can be a murky process, you'll want to make sure that you have an experienced professional on your side.

Parceling Out the Worldly Goods

When you die, what's going to happen to all your stuff? If you care, get a will made up. Now, preferably.

About 70 percent of Americans die without leaving a will, says Barbara Kate Repa, a California will and trust lawyer who created the software program called WillMaker. Many people just don't like to face the fact that one day they're going to die.

"Some people are afraid of making a will, and others are plain superstitious," says Repa. "They believe that by signing a will, they're tempting the gods."

WHEN THERE'S A WILL, YOU GET YOUR WAY

Basically, a will is a document that tells how you want all your worldly possessions to be dealt out to the living. To be valid, the document must be signed, witnessed, and perhaps notarized in compliance with the laws in your state.

Not only does a will allow you to choose which of your assets pass to which people but also you can provide for how those assets are given. That's especially important when children are involved—which raises another significant advantage to having a will: If you have minor children, a will is where you can appoint a guardian for your children and make specific provisions for their financial support.

Legal experts agree that not having a will is a big mistake. Without one (or a legal substitute such as a trust), there's no sure way to get your property into the hands of the people that you want to have it after you die.

If you die without a will, the state makes the decision for you. The consequences of dying intestate, as it's called, vary greatly depending upon the individual circumstances. For instance, state law generally provides that when one spouse dies without a will, the surviving spouse must share the decedent's property with the couple's children—regardless of the children's age or financial position or where that result leaves the surviving spouse. Also, dying without a will means that you can't leave property to friends, lovers, or even charities—all things that many of us would want to do.

Sure, a will is less important for some people than for others. If you're single with few or no assets, you probably don't need one. In fact, there are other ways to pass along assets, such as holding title to property jointly (for example, a bank account or real estate). But be sure to check the laws in your state before deciding that you can go that route. Contact the probate clerk at your county surrogate or probate court for information, or consult with a lawyer who specializes in trusts and estates.

Do You Need a Lawyer to Write Your Will?

If you want a do-it-yourself will, a plethora of books, guides, and computer software programs are available. Yes, it is possible for a layperson to draft a will that is legally sound and complies with state law.

But there also are big drawbacks in putting together a will without a lawyer. For one thing, just getting a document to comply with the formalities of state law does not ensure that it's going to accomplish what you hope it will. Neither does it ensure that *all* state laws and issues have been properly addressed. So if you have anything but the simplest of estates, you'll want to get a pro involved. Besides, it's not that expensive—usually $250 to $300 for the least complicated situations.

Experts in will drafting recommend that you keep these points in mind.

Find low-cost help. There is no central repository of information on will drafting, but most law schools have clinical programs where students, supervised by professors, provide "real-life" assistance to people in need. Your local city or county bar association can arrange a low-cost initial consultation with an attorney. Expect the cost to begin around $20 or $25 for the first half-hour. Also, some eldercare clinics can assist with estate planning.

If you have a trust and name a bank as trustee, or if you plan to name the bank as executor of your will, very often they'll have one of their lawyers prepare a will for you at little or no cost.

Make it available. Keep your will in a safe place where it can easily be found. It's often best to leave the original with your lawyer. A safety deposit could present problems: When someone dies, the safety deposit box is generally sealed until an estate representative is appointed. If the will is in the box, you have a bit of a catch-22.

Keep it current. Most people's lives change fairly regularly, so have a lawyer look at your will every five years or so just to be safe.

Why? Suppose that 10 years ago you and your spouse had wills drawn up. You each decided to leave $25,000 to your only close relatives, cousins Ruth and Sarah. Everything else would go to the surviving spouse. But in

Take Control with These Three Documents

Here's a quick guide to three powerful documents that will help you control life-and-death issues: living wills, health care proxies, and durable powers of attorney.

"They give people the ability to make choices about the type of medical treatment that they want at the end of life," says attorney Anna Moretti, former director of programming for Choice in Dying, a nonprofit organization based in New York City. "Over 20 percent of adult Americans have signed one or more of these advanced directives."

Living wills. A living will (sometimes called a medical directive or an advance directive) is a legal document in which you state whether you would want life support or other medical treatment if you had an incurable, terminal injury or illness. You can also describe the type of treatment that you'd want if you became so disabled that you couldn't give appropriate instructions at the time.

To be sure that your wishes are followed, give copies of your living will to your family, your doctor, and your lawyer.

Living wills are recognized in every state, but requirements and procedures for establishing them differ widely. Some states require living wills to be executed with the same formalities as a regular will. So contact your doctor, a local hospital, or Choice in Dying for details.

---

the past 10 years you've moved to a different state, you and your wife divorced, cousin Ruth died, and cousin Sarah married a man that you despise. Unless you want $50,000 going to someone you dislike or don't know, with the rest going to your ex-wife, you'd better change your will immediately. Out-of-date wills are a nightmare.

How do you update a will? If you're going on vacation in two days, or you only need to make one small change, this can be accomplished by way of "codicil," meaning an abbreviated modification. Codicils, however, must be signed with the same legal formalities as a regular will—you can't simply jot down your changes in a note. Typically, lawyers charge less for preparing a codicil than a full-blown will. But for anything more than a simple change or two, you'll want a brand-new will instead of an update.

Name backups. You'll want to name an executor of your estate, the person who sees to it that the terms of your will are carried out. The executors assemble property, contact creditors, and deal with heirs. They also work with estate lawyers and accountants, so your executor need not be a legal or financial expert.

Do pick someone who's trusted, reliable, and organized. Also list anyone that you'd like to serve as backup to your first choices for executor, guardian, and trustee. These people would fill in if your first choice refuses

For a few dollars, Choice in Dying will provide you with a package including state-specific forms for living wills and health care proxies as well as an instruction booklet. Check directory assistance for their toll-free number; write to 200 Varick Street, New York, NY 10014-4810; or locate their World Wide Web site on the Internet.

Health care proxy. A health care proxy allows you to name someone else who will make medical decisions for you if you can't someday. As with living wills, a health care proxy should include specific references to the type of medical treatment that you will and will not allow. Give copies to family members, your doctor, and your lawyer. Be sure to check your state's rules concerning the number of witnesses needed and whether the document must be notarized.

Durable power of attorney. A durable (or medical) power of attorney gives someone the authority to act legally on your behalf should you become disabled or incompetent. It would authorize your stand-in to do such things as pay bills, sign papers, and transfer property. Without one, a court may need to appoint a conservator or guardian to manage your affairs—which is complicated and often expensive. Generally, the durable power of attorney must be witnessed by two people and notarized.

to serve, dies, or becomes incapacitated. With this provision in place, if one of these things happens, you won't need a new will.

Tell the principals. You needn't tell anyone how your property is to be handled upon your death. However, you do want to inform anyone that you've chosen to act as an executor or trustee. And it's essential that you consult anyone that you want to name guardian of minor children. These people will be performing extremely important functions that will require time and energy. If they are unwilling or unable to serve for some reason, talking to them in advance will give you the chance to find alternatives.

Make other arrangements. If you have certain burial preferences—say, you'd like to be cremated—find another way to make your wishes clear. By the time your will is found, you could be long underground.

Trusts: An Estate-Planning Tool

Trusts were once considered the province of the very wealthy in our society, but today they're useful tools for people of widely varying means.

Living trusts—the kind that function during the creator's lifetime—fall within two basic categories: revocable, meaning that they can be changed at anytime, or irrevocable, meaning that once they are established, they cannot be changed. There are significant tax law differences between the two, and you should fully explore those consequences before you decide which suits your estate-planning needs.

Among other uses, trusts are good for:

- Managing assets during the lifetime of the person creating the trust
- Avoiding probate while passing along assets to beneficiaries
- Managing assets for children until they reach a certain age, generally structured so that income or principal from the trust can be used to meet the child's education, medical, and other needs
- In second marriages, managing assets for a surviving spouse while retaining property for children from the prior marriage

Now, trusts are highly technical legal devices. So before considering a trust, legal experts say, you're going to have to sit down with a lawyer who specializes in them to explore all legal, financial, and tax issues. Keep an eye on the advantages of a trust versus the start-up and maintenance costs.

SURRENDERING OWNERSHIP—TO YOURSELF

Living trusts are an increasingly popular estate-planning device.

Here's how they work. During your lifetime, you can place assets into a living trust. Upon your death, the trust distributes those assets according to your instructions. Typically, when you set up the trust, you're giving some or all of your property to yourself as trustee. Technically, you no longer own the property—your trustee does. It just so happens that your trustee is you.

While you're alive, you have control over the assets and investments, and you receive all the income and benefits. When you die, your trust executor distributes your remaining assets as specified in the trust.

By transferring your assets into a trust that survives you, you can protect against illness and incapacity, avoid probate, speed up distribution of your property, and preserve your privacy.

Sounds terrific, right? Well, yes and no. Some of the claimed advantages are, in fact, a bit overstated. Here's how family law experts describe the pros and cons.

Protecting against incapacity. True, if you set up a trust, you can select someone to manage your money in the event that you become seriously ill or mentally infirm. But a durable power of attorney, a document that gives someone the legal authority to act for you if you can no longer do so, does the same thing more simply and less expensively than a living trust.

Avoiding probate. Probating a will means filing the will in court, proving its authenticity and formalizing the appointment of an executor. For most people, the process is no longer the struggle that it used to be. In recent years, many states have adopted simplified laws that have streamlined the probate process. And the fees for probate aren't nearly as high as trust advocates would lead you to believe. In New York, for example, the maximum fee is $1,000.

Preserving privacy. If protecting your private affairs is a paramount concern, a living trust might be the right move for you. Unlike wills, which are a public record, living trusts are private documents. Nobody other than you and your lawyer needs to know its contents.

Speeding up distribution of assets. Again, many states have streamlined probate, so this may not be much of an advantage. But if you own a business and have made no provision for continued management after your death, then a living trust could be useful. It could designate someone to act immediately to keep the business going, providing beneficiaries with instant access to the business.

GIMME SHELTER, TAX-FREE

The credit shelter trust is a popular estate-planning technique that can prevent assets from being decimated by estate taxes.

It is designed to allow married couples, who can leave everything to each other tax-free, to take full advantage of the exemption that permits up to $600,000 in every estate (married or not) to pass free of federal estate taxes.

Here's how it works. Say that John and Joan are married. Their estate, including their house, investments, life insurance, and retirement accounts, is worth $1.2 million. Since they're married, each can leave everything to the other without triggering estate taxes. Joan dies first. When she does, everything goes to John tax-free. But when John dies, assuming the estate is still $1.2 million, the IRS will get $235,000—the estate tax on the amount in excess of $600,000.

But by creating a credit shelter trust, John and Joan could leave $600,000—in the trust—to be used by the one that survives the other, and eventually pass those funds to the kids—with no estate taxes.

BOTTOM LINE

Like it or not, from your birth to your death, the law involves itself in your personal life. Learning its particulars will save you enormous amounts of money, time, and aggravation. If you remain oblivious to the law, or if you try to circumvent it by sleight of hand, you'll be doomed to a life of costly surprises and frustration.

WORDS TO THE WISE

Guardian: A trusted friend or relative who will care for a minor child if both parents die. If you have children, name their guardians in a will—now.

Prenuptial agreement: A contract between people who intend to marry, establishing how property will be divided during the marriage, in the event of divorce, and when either spouse dies.

Surrogate parenthood: Having a third party contribute to creating a couple's child. A woman may carry a child for a wife who is unable. A man may contribute sperm when the husband is unable.

ALLIES

Academy of Family Mediators: 4 Militia Drive, Lexington, MA 02173. The academy requires every member to have at least 100 hours of actual experience, to meet certain training requirements, and to adhere to continuing education guidelines. You can also look for their Web site on the Internet.

AdoptioNetwork: A volunteer organization on the Internet committed to disseminating adoption information. Search for their World Wide Web site on the Internet.

Children Awaiting Parents: 700 Exchange Street, Rochester, NY 14608. National adoption and referral information service that seeks permanent placement for children awaiting homes, all of whom are in foster care. Cosponsors a World Wide Web photo listing of children awaiting adoption.

Child Welfare League of America: 440 First Street NW, Washington, DC 20001. Information on adoption, infertility, and many other child and family issues is available by mail or the organization's World Wide Web site on the Internet.

Department of Health and Human Services Administration for Children and Families: Office of Child Support Enforcement, Mail Stop OCSE/DCS/NRC, 370 L'enfant Promenade SW, Washington, DC 20447. For information on child support.

The International Concern Committee for Children: 911 Cypress Drive, Boulder, CO 80303. Publishes a report on foreign adoptions.

The North American Council on Adoptable Children: 970 Raymond Avenue, Suite 106, St. Paul, MN 55114-1149. A coalition of adoptive parents covering the United States and Canada. For information on adoption and support groups in your area.

Resolve, Inc.: 1310 Broadway, Somerville, MA 02144-1731. A national coalition for infertile couples.

A Legal Guide for Lesbian and Gay Couples, by Hayden Currey (Nolo Press).

Courting the Courthouse

How to Protect Yourself at a Reasonable Cost in This Litigious World

Talk to anyone who was in business in the 1950s and you're likely to hear the same tale of woe.

"When I first went into business, everything was done on a handshake. There were no contracts and no lawyers. If I gave someone my word, that was good enough. If there was a disagreement over a late shipment or damaged goods, we worked things out. Either we knocked a few dollars off the price or we gave the company credit against a future order—something. We never sued anyone, and we were never sued. It just wasn't done."

The days of handshake deals are now gone, replaced by long-form contracts, fine print, and complex legalese. People communicate by conference call, overnight courier, facsimile, e-mail, or worse, through their lawyers.

But you needn't retain a "hired gun" in an Italian suit to smooth over all of life's trouble spots. What you do need is a guide to the warning signs of trouble and the tools that you'll need to deal with it. And how to know when it really is time to call in a lawyer.

Before You Call the Lawyer

The average American has become conditioned to call a lawyer (or threaten to call one) to resolve virtually every legal or quasi-legal problem that he encounters. People have been trained to view lawyers as knights in shining armor—protector, defender, dad, and hired gun all rolled into one.

"The reality is that unless you've been arrested or accused or questioned in connection with a criminal matter, calling a lawyer should be a last resort," says attorney, financial consultant, and author Stephen Pollan.

While it might be nice to walk around with a lawyer in your pocket, "it's far from practical," says Pollan. In the first place, lawyers are expensive. What's more, while many of the problems that you encounter are frustrating, most don't involve big money. There simply is no reason to run for legal counsel every time you hit a bump in the road.

Lawyers are necessary in our society because of the complexities of life. Use them for big-ticket transactions, such as buying a home, selling or buying a business, or creating a complex estate-planning strategy.

Only get a lawyer involved when you've exhausted all other methods of resolving a problem, and understand that when you hire a lawyer, you've immediately added significant cost to your deal. Once you've raised the stakes by hiring counsel, odds are good that the party on the other side will, too. And that increases each party's resolve to win at all costs, legal experts point out.

FIRST, WEAR A WHITE HAT

Legal experts offer these tips for getting things done without a lawyer.

Launch a preemptive strike. If someone threatens to sue you, act quickly to defuse the situation. Start a dialogue with the person making the threat. A lawyer is ethically prohibited from calling your opponent directly, but you can and should do so—preferably before he has hired his own attorney.

If you're too late and a lawyer's already been engaged, show your opponent how you both can save money by settling matters yourselves. A savvy opponent realizes that lawyers typically charge 25 to 35 percent of the amount recovered in collection cases. And on your end, there will be the cost of defending yourself. So it makes good sense for both parties to sit down and agree on a settlement.

Do the right thing. The best and simplest way to avoid lawyers is to treat people fairly. If you're honest, keep careful records, and avoid overreaching, the people you deal with will be less inclined to use lawyers to resolve a dispute with you. Be careful and realistic about promising performance. Always allow for the unexpected. If you're borrowing money, don't agree to repay it more quickly than your circumstances will realistically permit.

Do your homework. A good way to avoid legal problems is to learn all that you can about the person with whom you're about to do business. If you're shopping for a car or an expensive antique, check with your local

Better Business Bureau, consumer agencies, and trade associations to re-search the business and its owner. If an acquaintance asks you to invest in a business deal, check the person out before handing over your money. You'll sleep better if you check business and personal references.

Get a Dun and Bradstreet report on any business in question and run a credit report on its owner. Hire one of the companies that runs background checks on individuals' assets, income, and financial standing. These searches may also turn up public information like a criminal record, past bankruptcy, and liens that have been placed on the individual's assets. Don't hesitate to walk away from an "opportunity" if you're the slightest bit un-comfortable with the information that you've turned up.

Do-It-Yourself Legal Matters

Legal experts say that it's reasonably safe for educated laypersons to handle the following situations on their own. Remember that several companies, most notably Nolo Press, publish how-to books on issues ranging from how to sue in small-claims court to fighting speeding tickets to child support. And some video stores have how-to sections with tapes on a variety of consumer-oriented topics, such as buying a house, getting a mortgage, and renovating your home. The advantage of a video over a professional consultation is that you can replay the advice again and again until the information sinks in.

Preparing a simple will. There are many self-help guides and kits avail-able at bookstores and stationery shops for those with uncomplicated estates and few assets. The best are computer programs that walk you through spe-cific questions regarding your estate. Even if you draft your own will, it's best to check with an attorney before signing to make sure that you're com-plying with your state's rules.

Incorporation. Likewise, there are incorporation kits that come complete with stock certificate forms, bylaws, corporate resolutions, and shareholder agreements. Start by calling your state's department of state. Ask for the di-vision or department of technical advice or assistance. With their help, and perhaps some assistance from your accountant or minor coaching from your lawyer, you should be able to handle the incorporation yourself.

Preparing a power of attorney. A power of attorney allows someone to designate another person to make decisions regarding their life and prop-erty in the event of illness or incapacity. These documents are fairly straight-forward, and forms come with instructional pamphlets to help you. Be sure to include only those specific duties that you want to delegate to the person that you're designating.

Small probate proceedings. Many states have simplified probate proceed-ings for the administration of small estates. The probate clerks at your local surrogate's or probate court are generally extremely helpful and can guide you through the process if the estate is relatively small—about $25,000 or less.

ASK FOR LOW-COST COACHING

Sometimes just a word with the wise is sufficient. You may want to handle a problem on your own, but attorneys say that you can still get a little advice or direction from a lawyer—sometimes for little or no money. Despite what many people think about lawyers, many will give you more than just the time of day without charging you a mint.

Ask whether your lawyer would be willing to act as your coach and assist in formulating your strategy. You might say, for example, "I have a problem, and because of time and financial constraints, I'm considering handling it myself. If things don't work out, I'll call back to retain your services. In the meantime, here's my strategy. What do you think?"

How to Get Out Of a Speeding Ticket

If you're like most people, you've exceeded the speed limit more than a few times without even thinking about it. But it's the time when a traffic cop catches you that will stick in your mind—and cost you in time, fines, and higher insurance rates. How can you minimize the chances of getting caught in the speed trap? Here are some fast tips.

Run with the pack. Even if you're exceeding the speed limit by 5 to 10 miles per hour (mph), the chances of getting pulled over decrease if you are simply keeping up with the flow of traffic, says Shawn Chase, a California Highway Patrol officer who has written more than 8,000 tickets in his 11 years on the force. But if a driver cuts and weaves through traffic at 5 to 10 mph over the limit, you're asking to get nailed.

Make the officer feel safe. The first step to getting in an officer's good graces is to make his job easy. So if you get pulled over, stop well off the road and even exit the highway if an off-ramp is near.

Officers are trained to suspect danger and don't welcome unexpected moves. "As an officer, you're thinking of your own personal safety first," says Chase. Wait for the officer to approach you—don't get out of the car. Keep your hands in sight on the steering wheel. Don't reach for your wallet, purse, or glove compartment until the officer asks you for information. Then, tell him what you are doing before you reach.

Be polite. As obvious as it sounds, being nice to the officer increases your chances of receiving a warning or at least convincing the officer to shave some speed off the citation.

Tell the truth. Traffic enforcers have heard all the lame excuses and can wait stone-faced through a river of tears. Stay calm and apologize for speeding. But if you have a legitimate excuse for speeding, tell the officer. "Some-

By setting things up this way, you'll get some valuable—and hopefully free—expert advice.

What to Do If You Get Sued

The odds are that sooner or later you'll be personally involved in a lawsuit. If you sue someone, of course, you've consciously decided to play the game. But what happens if you get sued?

Most people still react to lawsuits with fear, despite how common they've become in our society. In fact, legal experts say that the suing party is usually hoping to evoke precisely such a response.

---

times, if they're honest, I'll give them a break," Chase says. But if I think you're lying, forget it."

Ask for leniency. If you have developed any rapport with the officer, simply ask for a break, explaining that you can't afford the cost of the ticket or that you want to avoid points on your driving record.

"We're not Attila the Hun out there," Chase says. "We're human, just like everybody else."

Go to court. If you believe that the ticket was unwarranted or that you were cited for too high a speed, challenging it in court can be worthwhile. Again, don't bother lying.

"As long as most of us have been doing this job, if you try to fudge the facts or lie, it's usually readily apparent," says Dawson Muth, a district justice in suburban Philadelphia who has presided over many traffic-violation hearings in his career.

Make a good impression. If you go to court, dress neatly, speak calmly, and be respectful of the proceedings. "You catch a lot more flies with honey than vinegar," says Muth, who notes that rational defendants are much more credible. That's especially important in cases that come down to your word against the officer's. Also, Muth says, judges are more likely to reduce a fine or charge if they feel kindly toward a defendant.

Challenge the evidence. In many states, laws require that the police agency regularly document the accuracy of speed-detection equipment such as radar guns. The requirements vary widely from place to place, but some forces are expected to recalibrate equipment before each shift, while others check it monthly. Ask to see the most recent inspection forms for the device used to clock your speed. If it's not up-to-date, you're ticket may be dismissed.

Here are the two most important things to remember when someone serves you with a summons.

1. Don't panic. You'll need a clear head to respond intelligently. And keep in mind that the overwhelming majority of lawsuits never make it to trial. The fact that you've been served with a summons means only that the party suing has found an attorney willing to draw up the necessary papers and file them in court.
2. Unless you're being sued in small-claims court (where, by definition, the amount in dispute is small), call your lawyer immediately.

WITH A SUMMONS, THE CLOCK STARTS TICKING

A lawsuit can only commence if someone serves you with a summons—a legal notification that someone is suing you. It describes, usually briefly, what the other side is complaining about and how much money or other form of relief they are seeking.

You will typically have 20 to 30 days to answer the summons. Rules vary by jurisdiction, but the exact number of days will be spelled out in the summons, as will the name, address, and telephone number of the suing party's attorney.

Here are a few things to keep in mind, attorneys say.

• Don't be surprised if you receive a summons a long time after the incident in question has taken place. For example, in personal-injury cases, the injured party normally has two to three years to start up the suit before a court says that it's too late. This time period is referred to as the statute of limitations.

• In most instances, the party suing asks for far more monetary damages than what they're likely to receive even if they were to win in court. So don't overreact if the papers say that you're being sued for some outrageously high amount of money. It may be that your opponent's lawyer is trying to protect himself from being accused (by his own client) of not suing for enough. It's also a scare tactic, with the goal being to intimidate you.

• Read the papers carefully. At first glance, many legal papers look the same. For instance, it's easy to confuse a summons with a subpoena. A subpoena is an order to appear in court or at a deposition, either to give testimony or perhaps to deliver certain documents. The case may have nothing to do with you personally—rather, you are merely being asked to appear as a witness by one of the parties.

YES, NOW YOU NEED A HIRED GUN

While there are many instances when you may be able to handle a legal issue without hiring a lawyer, responding to a lawsuit is not one of them.

"The first thing that you should do if you're sued is immediately see a lawyer," says Conrad Johnson, clinical professor of law at Columbia Univer-

How to Hire an Attorney

Your attorney will take part in some of the most difficult and important decisions in your life. Because of the intimate nature of the relationship, it is essential that you find an attorney that you trust, that you have complete confidence in, and also with whom you have a personal rapport.

Legal experts recommend that you look for a generalist, not a specialist. Your personal attorney should be well-versed in most areas of the law, not necessarily an expert in any particular field. If he's worth his salt, he'll be able and willing to involve any other professionals necessary to get you the best possible results.

Legal professionals offer these tips for hiring the best lawyer for you.

Don't wait for an emergency. Choose a lawyer when you are in the proper frame of mind to make a calm, well-informed decision. So don't wait until there's a crisis to start your search.

Round up your candidates. Speak with friends, family, and business associates who are similarly situated and whose opinions you value. Other good resources for referrals include other professionals that you trust (your accountant, banker, or insurance agent) and your local or state bar association.

Run a background check. Once you've developed a list of candidates, try to find out as much background as possible on each. Your local law library should have a *Martindale-Hubbell Law Directory*, which is like an encyclopedia of lawyers. It will tell you the lawyer's education, specialty (if any), and perhaps how the firm is rated by other lawyers in the community.

Grill your candidates. Prescreen your candidates by calling each on the telephone. This will help you decide which ones you should interview in person. Here's what to ask.

- How long have you been in practice?
- Briefly describe your experience after graduating law school.
- Are you willing to give me the names of a few clients to call as references?
- Do you expect to be paid for the initial consultation, or will it be free?
- Do you work with other lawyers on a regular basis, and are you willing to make referrals if you encounter a problem outside your area of expertise?

Chances are that after listening to the answers, you'll know whom you'd like to meet in person.

Meet face-to-face. Always interview and meet a lawyer in person before hiring him. Conduct the interview at the lawyer's office during regular business hours. This way, you'll have the benefit of observing the office environment.

sity Law School in New York City. "Since you only have a certain period of time to respond, it's essential that you move quickly."

If you don't respond, the judicial system assumes that you are admitting everything alleged by the person suing you, and "default judgments" will be awarded against you. If this happens, the person suing you may attempt to take things from you—like money, personal property, and your home—in order to collect on the judgment.

So if time is running short and you're baffled by the process, the very least you should do is go to the courthouse where the suit was filed and ask to speak with the clerk of the court. Explain your problem—that you received these papers and aren't sure how to proceed. You'll want to file something with the court in order to preserve your right to defend against the accusations in the summons.

Johnson suggests filing what's called a general denial. "This tells the court that you don't know enough about all the specifics of the case—but that you're denying that the suing party is entitled to a judgment against you," says Johnson.

If you have a lawyer, send a copy of the summons and gather all pertinent information and documents for him to review. If you've chosen your lawyer wisely, he will be able to devise a prudent and cost-effective strategy for your defense.

In many instances, for economic reasons, a settlement is the best strategy. As emotionally charged as the situation may be, you still need to resist the temptation to throw good money after bad. It makes no sense to pay an attorney $5,000 so that you can save $1,500.

Contracts: Fine Print Is Everywhere

Say that you park your car in a public garage, and when you come back after dinner, the cashmere sweater that you left on the backseat is missing. Or the dry cleaner scorches your grandmother's turn-of-the-century wedding gown—the gown that your daughter expects to wear this June. When you try to recover for your losses, all too often someone will point to the back of a ticket or a sign on the wall and say, "You're out of luck."

Every day, you most likely enter into several legally binding contracts that are designed to limit the damages that you can collect when you suffer a calamity. And you do it unwittingly, without putting a signature on anything.

WATCH OUT FOR THOSE SUBTLETIES

When you think of a contract, your mind turns to an apartment lease or sales documents that you sign when buying or selling a home. But some contracts are created in subtler ways, and they need not be in writing. Accepting a claim check or receipt, a verbal agreement, or even a handshake can be enough, according to legal experts. Almost any time that goods or money change hands, a contractual relationship is formed.

Dazed by an explosion of lawsuits, businesses go to great lengths to protect themselves from liability. More and more, fine print and legalese are finding their way into everyday transactions. Often the language is too complex for even the most sophisticated person to understand. And sometimes consumers simply ignore the fine print in contracts, thereby surrendering valuable rights without even knowing that they've done so.

Gerald Frug, professor of law at Harvard University Law School, says that many everyday contracts are actually "take-it-or-leave-it propositions. Consumers are told simply to 'sign here.' Unfortunately, many people either fail to ask what 'it' is about or blindly take a businessperson's word for what an agreement says or means. And alarmingly, many consumers don't bother to read the contracts at all."

The terms of these contracts and bargaining power heavily favor one side—typically, the business enterprise that you're interacting with. Even if these contracts are so one-sided that they seem unfair, most courts are reluctant to interfere, legal experts note, still following the common law of caveat emptor: "Let the buyer beware."

But you don't have to sit still for this. Just because you are handed a piece of paper, you don't have to sign it, or even accept it, without making modifications. And even unwritten contracts can be modified.

CHANGE THE TERMS OF THOSE DAILY CONTRACTS

You may be told that an agreement is simply a "form" or "standard," or that it merely contains "boilerplate" language. If you remember one thing from this chapter, it should be that there is no such thing as a standard agreement. In fact, says Frug, these "form contracts" are anything but vanilla.

"They've actually been carefully written by professionals to protect business owners and service providers," he says.

Mark them up. Every contract can be negotiated, legal experts say. You can make changes to form documents, for instance, by simply crossing out unreasonable clauses or by adding language. For example, add the word "reasonable" to clauses wherever the other side's approval or consent is required in order for you to take some action or get some benefit.

Give yourself time. Increase the time periods in which you are required to perform an act or satisfy some condition. If a business accepts the forms with your changes, it will be bound by them.

Get a witness. Even if a businessperson refuses to allow you to make changes to the written or unwritten contract, you can still protect yourself. In the presence of a witness, make the statement that you are signing the contract under protest—that you do not agree with the terms or that you don't understand them but that you have no choice but to do as the business has required.

Protest the posting. If there is no contract—say, if you're giving an heirloom dress to a dry cleaner—tell a witness that you are accepting the terms posted by the business under protest. At the very least, these actions may help a judge side with you if the disagreement ever gets to court. What's more, your having taken this prudent step may prevent the dispute from getting that far.

Small-Claims: The Great Equalizer

Small-claims court is perhaps the most important tribunal in America. Truly the great equalizer of our legal system, it allows the average citizen, who otherwise would be left out in the cold, the opportunity to have a "day in court."

Small-claims courts make decisions in civil cases only, not criminal, and there is a dollar limit on the amount for which one can sue. In general, claims are limited to the $1,000 to $3,000 range, although amounts vary according to state law and can be as high as $5,000 or more. Some states also restrict small-claims court to individuals only and prohibit collection agencies or corporations from filing claims.

KNOWING WHEN TO GO IT ALONE

Anyone familiar with the card game euchre knows that going it alone can provide the game's ultimate thrill. In euchre, although each player has a partner, any one player can decide that he can win a particular hand without a partner's help.

Unlike a card game, however, legal disputes can be costly, time-consuming, and complex. An error in judgment could cost you both time and money. So if you're interested in going it alone—that is, working without a lawyer— here's a rundown, prepared by legal experts, of criteria that will help you determine whether you have a case for small-claims court.

Monetary loss. In small-claims court, the emphasis is on dollar limits and cash awards. Intangibles such as pain and suffering rarely come into play.

Liability. The concept of liability is the law's way of establishing blame. It's certainly possible that you could suffer a monetary loss without someone else being legally liable. To prevail in court, you must be able to show that the person that you are suing did something (or failed to do something) that caused your loss, and that he was legally obligated to do (or to refrain from doing) that thing.

Typically, liability can be shown in one of three ways.

Negligence. Here, the person suing (the plaintiff) must show that the accused party (the defendant) did not act with reasonable care and that the defendant's action or inaction was the cause of the plaintiff's loss.

Intentional acts. These are actions which, although not negligent, have caused monetary damage. Examples include assault and trespass.

Breach of contract. Most small-claims court cases involve contracts. A contract is any agreement involving an exchange of promises or a promise exchanged for some act or compensation. They can be either oral or written. To establish your case, you must prove three things: (1) that a valid contract exists, (2) that the party you accuse breached it, and (3) that you suffered a monetary loss as a result.

Now What Do I Do with These Papers?

Each small-claims court has its own district with specific geographic boundaries. It is vital to know how the court system in your state is subdivided when you are deciding where to file suit. Often you have a choice of districts in which to file because state requirements usually indicate where you *can* sue rather than where you *must*.

Consider your opponent's turf. Regardless of which state you live in, you can always sue in the district where the defendant lives or does business. By following this rule of thumb, you will head off the defendant's objection that it is too inconvenient to appear in court.

In more than 30 states, you can sue where the injury or damage occurred. And with contract disputes, you can sue where the contract was signed or, in some states, where the act specified by the contract was to be performed. If you are suing a large company that has many offices, you may be forced to file suit somewhere other than where you did business. It may even mean having to file in another state.

Start with the forms. Go to the courthouse in the district where you are filing, where you'll pay a filing fee (usually $5 to $10 but sometimes as high as $25 or more). You will also have to fill out a form that's often called the plaintiff's statement. The forms vary from state to state, but they seek the same basic information: your name, who you are suing, a brief description of your claim, and the amount that you are seeking.

Pick the right target. Always sue the person, persons, or business that harmed you. When you sue more than one person, be sure to name them individually (even if they're married).

For cases involving automobile accidents, always check to see whether the driver is the legal owner of the car. In most states, if the driver is not the registered owner, you must sue both the driver and the car's legal owner.

If the offender is a minor, you must also name a parent or legal guardian.

If you are suing a business, you must first determine what type of entity it is—that is, whether it is owned by an individual (a sole proprietorship), a partnership, a corporation, or what's known as a limited-liability company. If the business is a sole proprietorship, find out who owns it and sue the owner.

In most states, sole proprietorships are required to file what's called a DBA (doing business as) certificate, or fictitious name certificate, with the county clerk's office in the county in which the business is conducted. This certificate will give you the name and address of the person listed as the owner.

In a partnership, all partners are legally responsible for the acts of the business. Like sole proprietorships, partnerships must typically file a business certificate with the local county clerk's office. The certificate contains the names and addresses of all general partners. It's best to name all partners individually in your suit, as well as the partnership. Failing to name all the partners in the suit will not disqualify you, but it will result in fewer people that you can collect from should you win your case.

If you are suing a corporation, you should name the corporation only. Unless you can prove that the officers committed fraud, those individuals are typically not personally liable for the debts of their corporation.

Hand over the papers. All defendants of your small-claims suit must be served personally. For a corporation, one of its officers must be served. If the company is out of state, it may have a registered agent in your state. Check with the secretary of state's office.

You must serve the defendant within a specified number of days before the trial, not counting the day of service or the court date. Rules vary from state to state on which papers must be filed, who must get them, when they must be served, and how it must be done. Clerks at small-claims courts are generally very helpful in answering these questions.

THE TOUGH PART: COLLECTING

There are disadvantages to small-claims court. The process can be highly labor-intensive, for one thing. It's not unusual for the suing party to spend 10 to 30 hours researching and preparing a case. Remember that filing the case, serving the defendant, preparing the case, appearing in court on a business day, and collecting if you win are all part of the process.

But the biggest drawback is that it is often difficult to collect on your judgment. Winners stand the best chance of getting their cash when defendants earn salaries, have bank accounts, own property, or run a business.

You might get a check from the losing party on your way out of the courthouse—but don't count on it. If the appeal period has expired and it is clear that the defendant won't pay, you may have to take additional steps to collect your award. The small-claims court clerk will be able to tell you about collection rules in your state, but the task of collecting falls on you, not the court. The procedure can be time-consuming, complicated, and expensive. Lawyers says that these collection devices will help you get started.

Writ of execution. This is a court order that allows you to collect money or property, such as wages, automobiles, bank accounts, and real estate. To obtain such an order, fill out an application at the small-claims court, have a judge sign it, then take it to the county sheriff. Next, get an "abstract" (sometimes called a transcript) of the judgment and file it wherever the defendant owns real estate, usually at the county records office. This places a lien on the title to his property and prevents him from selling or refinancing until he pays you and title is cleared. When you notify the debtor and the bank that holds the mortgage that you have a lien on the property, it usually brings swift action.

Garnishing wages. In some states, you can have a sheriff or marshal contact the debtor's employer to order that wages be garnished to satisfy your judgment. Not all states allow wage garnishment, and those that do typically prohibit it where the wages are needed to support a low-income family.

It is also possible to subpoena a debtor to ask questions about the location and extent of his assets. He will be required to testify under oath to provide you with the information. Remember that you can always use a collection agency or lawyer to help you collect a judgment, but be prepared to pay the price if you do—typically a third to half of what's actually collected plus expenses.

SUITING UP FOR YOUR BIG DAY IN COURT

Anyone who has seen *The People's Court* on television has a pretty good idea of how small-claims courts function. As on the TV show, prevailing in a small-claims court case will frequently boil down to who is the best prepared and able to present his story in the most effective manner, attorneys say. Here are some tips from legal experts.

Get a preview. Visit the courthouse a week before your case is scheduled to be heard to observe how things work. This will familiarize you with court procedures and make you more comfortable when your turn comes.

Organize your evidence. It is essential that you arrange your evidence and what you'll say to the judge because your time will be limited to present your case—no more than a few minutes. You'll want to have documentary evidence, expert testimony, witnesses, and your own testimony.

Show the paper trail. Documentary evidence is likely to be the most important evidence that you can provide. Each side will have its own version of what happened, but documentary evidence—such as the damaged item, letters demanding restitution, receipts, police reports, photographs, canceled checks, contracts, warranties, evidence of financial loss, telephone call records, and returned envelopes marked "refused" or "unclaimed"—all provide independent confirmation of what you will later tell the court.

Have your documents organized so that you can readily access each one as needed. If you are missing a crucial piece of evidence, be ready to explain its absence.

Line up impartial experts. An expert is someone who is not involved in the case who testifies in court or submits a statement to the court on his official letterhead, describing things such as the problem, its cause, and the extent of damage.

Prepare your witnesses. Before you have witnesses testify on your behalf, discuss the case with them and prepare them for what your position is, what your opponent's position is likely to be, and what you would like them to say in response. To ensure that there are no surprises, ask your witnesses only questions to which you know what the responses will be.

Practice your delivery. Your own testimony in small-claims court should be clear, concise, and devoid of emotion. If at all possible, do not read from a prepared text. You will appear much more genuine if you speak naturally. And don't try to act like a lawyer or else the judge may start treating you like one. The judge's natural inclination to help you may disappear, and his sympathy may be transferred to the other side.

Leave the denim home. When you go to court, be sure to dress neatly. Judges tend to be conservative. They like to see people dressed appropriately for court appearances: for instance, jacket and tie, skirt, or dress. Not jeans and a T-shirt.

Mind your manners. Stand, unless you are instructed otherwise. Introduce yourself and your case. Be brief. Don't ramble. Stick to the facts and let the evidence speak for itself.

Be polite and address the judge as "Your Honor" at all times. When answering a question posed by the judge, use "Yes, Your Honor" or "No, Your Honor." Never interrupt or argue with the judge.

Listen to the judge. If the judge tells you to take a few minutes to try settling the case outside the courtroom, take the hint.

BOTTOM LINE

Sure, you want to have a lawyer that you can call on to protect you during big-ticket transactions like buying a business. But it's not economically practical to involve him in every one of life's hassles—even some of those that involve the court system. Instead, learn how the legal system works, what you can do for yourself, and what the warning signals are so that you can steer clear of sticky—and expensive—legal situations.

WORDS TO THE WISE

Coaching: Getting a few brief pointers from an attorney may be all the legal expertise you need for some situations. Your lawyer may provide coaching for little or no cost.

Contract: Just about any time goods or money change hands, there's a contractual relationship. You may enter into a contract several times a day without knowing it: Accepting a claim check, a receipt, or even a handshake can be enough.

Summons: A legal notification that someone is suing you. You typically have 20 to 30 days to respond. Unless it's for small-claims court, call your lawyer immediately.

ALLIES

Everyday Contracts—Protecting Your Rights: A Step-by-Step Guide, by George Milko, Kay Ostberg, and Theresa Meehan Rudy (David McKay Company).

Everybody's Guide to Small Claims Court, by Ralph Warner (Nolo Press).

Fight Your Ticket, by David W. Brown (Nolo Press).

How and When to Be Your Own Lawyer: A Step-By-Step Guide to Effectively Using Our Legal System, by Robert W. Schachner, with Marvin Quittner (Avery Publishing Group).

Enlisting Your Public Servants

You Pay Their Salaries, So Get the Performance That You Deserve

We Americans hate bureaucrats almost as much as we depend upon them.

From health care to housing to pensions, government bureaucrats play a big part in our daily lives. One American worker in five—18.6 million people—received a government paycheck in 1992. Despite the rhetoric about cutting bureaucracy, the government payroll is expected to swell to at least 20.8 million by 2005, according to the U.S. Labor Department.

So why can't this huge and growing "business" get anything done well? Why do the simplest chores take so long, if indeed they get done at all? Because, authors David Osborne and Ted Gaebler wrote in their best-seller *Reinventing Government*, bureaucracy "developed in conditions very different from those we experience today. It developed in a slower-paced society, when change proceeded at a leisurely gait."

The Rules of Bureaucracy

It's not that all bureaucrats want to be slow, inefficient, and unresponsive. But the rules of government—rules designed, in many cases, by elected officials to "bring the bureaucracy under control"—make it hard for even the most skilled public servants to act quickly. With little or no control over their budgets, their personnel, or even office procedures, government managers tend to focus on living within these constraints instead of concentrating on serving the public better.

YOU HAVE TO PUSH THE RIGHT BUTTONS

Government is a business unlike any other. Getting things done is an art form. Here are a few basic tips for dealing with bureaucrats.

Talk to the people who really do the work. In most cases, the hands-on worker won't be the person with the fanciest title. The principal, the police chief, or the planning director usually is too busy meeting with interest groups or dealing with budgets to see what's really going on in the classroom, the streets, or a zoning dispute.

Just ask them to be fair. Appealing to a sense of fairness works. Really. The true bottom line at many or most public agencies is not efficiency. It's equity—applying the same rules to everybody. As bureaucracy expert James Q. Wilson wrote in his book *Bureaucracy: What Government Agencies Do and Why They Do It*, "police administrators rarely lose their jobs because the crime rate has gone up. . . . They can easily lose their jobs if somebody persuasively argues that the police department has abused a citizen, beaten a prisoner, or failed to answer a call for service."

Work within the bureaucracy's rules. It may be gratifying to tell a bureaucrat how stupid you think the rules are. It is also pointless. Most government agencies were created to do the same tasks the same way over and over again.

Guarding Your Social Security

Everything about Social Security is big. Nearly 139 million workers and their employers pay about $400 billion in Social Security taxes each year. The agency, in turn, pays $335 billion each year to 46.7 million beneficiaries. For 38 percent of elderly households, Social Security is the difference between comfort and poverty.

It is much more than a retirement program. Social Security could change your life decades before you're ready to retire.

When he signed Social Security into law in 1935, President Franklin Roosevelt described it as a means to "give some measure of protection to the average citizen and to his family . . . against poverty-ridden old age." Today Social Security also provides benefits to disabled workers and their families as well as to millions impoverished by disability, age, or blindness.

In some respects Social Security is a model of bureaucratic efficiency. America's largest social welfare program scrapes by with 61,000 employees—one for every 765 beneficiaries. Administrative costs are just a penny of every tax dollar. Its employees have a sense of mission that's rare in government.

Fast Facts

Timing Is Everything

You can speed up your dealings with Social Security by watching the calendar. The agency mails or direct-deposits checks to beneficiaries on the third of every month. So every month, on the fourth, fifth, sixth, or seventh, a lot of people call the toll-free number or visit their local Social Security offices. Offices also tend to be busy early in the week. If you don't like crowds and if your business can wait, deal with Social Security later in the month.

Within a few years, Social Security plans to issue checks four times a month. That should end the delays.

But Social Security also is fraught with minefields for the uninformed. Take its telephone service, for example. In 1995, Dalbar, a company that provides analytical information for the financial services community, measured Social Security against such customer-service heavyweights as L.L. Bean (the big catalog marketer), Walt Disney Company, Nordstrom, and Southwest Airlines. Social Security beat them all. Its phone representatives scored the highest marks in the survey for knowledge and ability to respond to the customer. But to reach one of these world-class phone reps, the poor customer had to spend eight minutes on hold—nearly five times longer than the next slowest in the survey. That's assuming that the customer got through at all. In 1995, Social Security reported, nearly half the callers to its toll-free number hit a busy signal.

Disability insurance may be a lifesaver, but in 1994 Social Security took an average of 155 days to process a claim—and two years to resolve appeals.

PHONES AND STATEMENTS: TAP INTO THE SYSTEM

Social Security, in short, is a bureaucracy. Here are some ideas from the Social Security Administration for dealing with it.

Use the toll-free number. You can resolve most problems and start solving others by calling 1-800-772-1213. Automated services are available around-the-clock. People are standing by from 7:00 A.M. to 7:00 P.M. local time on business days.

Or use the Internet. Social Security has a site on the World Wide Web.

Social Security admits that it has had problems answering the 65 million calls a year it gets on its toll-free line. But it is trying. Between January and

March 1996, Social Security had reduced the proportion of busy signals from nearly a third to less than a tenth of all calls.

Once you get through, the toll-free number is a hassle-free way to handle many routine chores: replacing a lost or stolen card, ordering a first card for your child, reporting a change of address or a change of name. While you can't file a claim for benefits by phone, you can initiate the paperwork with a phone call and arrange an appointment at one of 1,300 local Social Security offices.

Know whom you're talking with. Social Security rotates calls to the toll-free number among dozens of offices nationwide. While an automated service handles millions of calls, the more complex questions go to genuine human beings. Errors are inevitable. So you should keep notes describing what you were told, when, and the name and office location of the person who told you. If Social Security decides later that you acted wrongly, you can point to someone inside Social Security at a particular time and place who told you differently.

Know what you're owed. If you're 60 or older, Social Security already is sending you a Personal Earnings and Benefit Estimate Statement. If you're under 60, Social Security will begin sending you a statement in the year 2000. Don't wait until then.

This form tells you how much in earnings Social Security has on record for you. It also tells you how large a monthly benefit you can expect, assuming that your earnings don't change. To get one, call the toll-free number. Social Security will send you a simple application that you can complete in a few minutes. You'll get a personalized benefits statement a few weeks later.

There are three good reasons to get this form. First, it's a great starting point for retirement planning. Current Social Security recipients depend upon the program for 42 percent of their retirement income on average. Look at your projected monthly benefit and ask yourself, if you were retiring today, how much more money you'd need to live comfortably.

"This is one of the most important things that Social Security can do," says Hans Riemer, a public policy associate at Save Our Security, a Washington, D.C., group that keeps tabs on the system. "Everyone should be thinking about retirement."

The form also lets you double-check Social Security's records of your earnings. That earnings record is one of the two factors that determines your eventual benefits. (The other is the number of years that you work.) The odds of a mistake in your earnings record are tiny. Of the four million people who requested statements from Social Security in 1994, just 25,162 spotted an error. But if you're part of the 0.6 percent with a mistaken record, it could cost you plenty. Normally, you have about three years to correct earnings records.

IS YOUR LIFE RAFT IN ORDER?

Social Security is important to you right now, even if your retirement is three or four decades away. The reason is disability. A 20-year-old worker stands a one-in-three chance of being disabled before reaching age 65. Disability insurance through Social Security is the life raft that supports 4 million disabled workers and 1.6 million dependents.

Act quickly if you're disabled. There is nothing easy about collecting disability under Social Security. For one thing, you qualify only if you are so disabled that you won't earn more than $500 a month for the next year. You must be disabled for six months before you can collect a penny in benefits.

And you may wait considerably longer than six months because you also must complete the application process. In 1994, that took 155 days on average. Social Security is trying to drastically shorten processing time to 40 days. But a spokesman admits that it could take five years to make the necessary changes. In the meantime, your best bet is to apply for disability just as soon as you get the bad news. Otherwise you could be waiting a long time for help.

Consider hiring a representative. Before awarding you disability, Social Security must collect evidence and decide if you really are disabled. It sounds complicated, and it is. You can appoint a representative (who may be a family member, a friend, or an attorney) to examine Social Security records, give evidence, question witnesses, and file appeals on your behalf. You must give Social Security your representative's name. The representative can't charge you without Social Security's consent. Fees are limited to 25 percent of past-due benefits or $4,000, whichever is smaller. Social Security sets the representative's fee, even if you lose.

Congress: Your Friends on the Hill

Sometimes the only way to deal with government is to find an ally: somebody who can get the bureaucrats' attention instantly and knows the system intimately.

Somebody like a congressman.

Sound improbable? It isn't. For many years, members of Congress have hired aides to work full- or part-time helping constituents overcome bureaucratic snags. State legislators and local elected officials often try to do the same thing. Senator William Cohen of Maine wrote in 1982 that constituent casework fulfills "one of the most important functions we serve as elected public officials—that of ombudsmen, of problem solvers for individuals who have been ignored, trampled upon, or treated arbitrarily by the government itself."

CASEWORKERS GET QUICK ANSWERS

Kathleen Hollingsworth is the district director for Representative Dana Rohrabacher. She has headed the Southern California Republican's casework staff for eight years.

The ever-growing size and complexity of the federal government make it hard for people to wend their way through the rules and regulations, Hollingsworth says. Congressional casework has evolved to meet the public's need for help.

The IRS is a good example. A constituent may pose the same question to different IRS offices and get different, and sometimes contradictory, answers. All the offices may be giving the right answers based on partial information, she says, but none of them has put all the facts together.

"From that, obviously, nightmares evolve," Hollingsworth explains. "The constituent will call or write to us and say, 'Help!'"

There are limits to what a congressional caseworker can do.

"A member of Congress cannot dictate to an agency or an agency staff member what sort of finding to make," Hollingsworth says.

But congressional caseworkers can get quick replies to questions. They can learn which precise rule or regulation has ensnared a constituent. They can clarify murky rulings. They can speed replies to long-neglected inquiries.

Caseworkers have to understand how government works, Hollingsworth says. In particular, they have to understand that there is no pecking order in government. A congressman can't settle a state tax issue. A state legislator can't resolve a local zoning dispute.

Fast Facts

Drop Your Rep a Line

You can call or write your congressman at his local office or in Washington, D.C. The local office is listed in the phone book.

If you'd prefer to deal with your congressman's Washington office, address letters to your representative at U.S. House of Representatives, Washington, DC 20515, or call (202) 225-3121. You can write your senator at U.S. Senate, Washington, DC 20510, or call (202) 224-3121. You must know your congressman's name if you're calling or writing to Washington since letters and calls are routed to a central mail room and switchboard.

Veterans Affairs: A Mammoth System

One American in three is potentially eligible for veterans' benefits. But they aren't easy to get.

The U.S. Department of Veterans Affairs (VA) "is an organization that's a big bureaucracy," says Bill Russo, director of benefits for Vietnam Veterans of America. "But my opinion is that with a little bit of knowledge a vet can raise the chances of winning significantly."

Veterans and their families have an immense stake in this system. The VA runs the nation's largest health care system, a network of 172 hospitals, 365 clinics, and 128 nursing homes. It supports 2.6 million disabled veterans and 716,000 of their surviving dependents. In 1995 it provided scholarships to 500,000 veterans and guaranteed home loans for another 600,000.

MANY VETS NEED ASSISTANCE AND PERSISTENCE

The VA's intricate rules make it tough for people to get the help they deserve. It's no wonder that Congress has chartered several organizations, including the American Legion and Vietnam Veterans of America, to help veterans deal with the VA. It is also no wonder that most states and counties have created their own veterans' departments to lend a hand.

Remember these strategies recommended by the Vietnam Veterans of America as you navigate the system.

Get expert help. All the major veterans' groups and many local veterans' offices employ veterans' service officers. Their job is to help veterans and their families get benefits. They get special training and VA certification. Best of all, they won't charge you a penny. You can find them through the veterans' organizations or at any VA office or medical center.

If you're seeking disability compensation, choose your adviser carefully. He will be representing you during the disability process. Look for someone with whom you feel comfortable. Keep in touch monthly.

Disabled? Apply quickly. The VA had a backlog of 378,600 pending claims for disability compensation or pensions in 1995. It's a long line, and you're doing yourself no favors by waiting to sign up. Don't wait until you've gathered all the evidence.

The VA grants disability compensation for conditions that are service-connected. These need not be old war wounds. If a veteran is hobbled by a knee that he injured during an off-base, off-duty softball game, he's potentially eligible for veterans' disability compensation.

The VA bases compensation on the degree to which a veteran is disabled. If the VA judges that a veteran is 10 percent disabled, he qualifies for $94 per month in compensation. A totally disabled veteran gets $1,924 per month.

The VA sometimes decides that a veteran has a service-connected disability but is 0 percent disabled. That sounds like a catch-22, but it isn't. A disability finding, even a 0 percent rating, automatically qualifies a veteran for free health care in VA hospitals.

Generally, the only other way into the door of a VA hospital is to have a thin wallet. Single veterans without a service-connected disability can be treated if their annual income is $21,001 or less. Higher-income veterans can get medical care only if there's space available and if they're willing to pay an amount equal to the Medicare deductible, $736 in 1996.

Gather evidence yourself. The VA is supposed to collect your service and medical records. Usually, it does. But often it misses something. Keep every bit of correspondence between you and the VA. If you're requesting help and you don't hear from the VA for several months, call. Don't assume that they're working on your case. They might have forgotten about you.

You can get copies of your personnel and medical records from the military as well as your medical records from all VA facilities that have treated you. Just be sure to invoke the Privacy Act and to identify yourself clearly in your written request for those records. You also should gather your private medical records.

Don't give up. A veteran can ask a hearing officer to review a disability claim if the initial reviewers reject it. Nearly 40 percent of the time, hearing officers rule in disabled veterans' favor. If a veteran loses at that stage, he still can appeal to the Board of Veterans Appeals and from there to the U.S. Court of Veterans Appeals.

USE THAT TUITION BENEFIT WITHIN 10 YEARS

While health care, disability compensation, and pensions for impoverished veterans consume most of VA's $39 billion budget, its educational and housing programs have had a huge impact on American life. Since passage of the original GI Bill in 1944, the VA has sent 20.8 million veterans to college or training schools. VA-guaranteed loans have helped put a roof over the heads of 14.6 million veterans. Unlike the disability program, there is nothing elaborate involved in getting these benefits. Still, many veterans miss out.

Since 1985, the U.S. has offered people in the military a can't-lose investment: Give up $100 a month in compensation during the first year of service ($1,200) and get $15,000 in educational benefits after an honorable discharge.

But somehow many veterans do lose on this deal. "We're finding that about two-thirds of all service members who contribute don't use the GI Bill," says Phil Budahn, media relations manager for the American Legion and author of a 1994 book *Veteran's Guide to Benefits*. "And the way the system is structured, they can't get the $1,200 back."

Educational benefits are a use-it-or-lose-it deal. And generally, they run out, forever, 10 years after a veteran's discharge.

Information: Laws Provide Access

Government is a treasure trove of information—most of it available to the public.

News reporters and lobbyists for big companies have been mining this treasure for years. You can, too. The key is to learn about a couple of important federal laws, the Freedom of Information Act and the Privacy Act. The states have similar measures.

THE FACTS OF LIFE IN A FREE SOCIETY

The Freedom of Information Act of 1966 requires federal agencies to "make records promptly available" to anyone who asks. The requester must reasonably describe the records and agree to pay a fee if necessary. (More on that later.)

The Privacy Act of 1974 ordered federal agencies to let citizens see what the government has on them. It also gives people the right to correct errors in their records. This is the ultimate antibureaucracy law: Government can no longer tell you that facts and allegations about you are none of your business. Under the Privacy Act, if you ask, they have to tell.

Of course, like everything else, requests under the Freedom of Information and Privacy Acts can get complicated. The Privacy Act spells out several ways that an agency can deny you records. Among the most important: to protect law-enforcement investigations, trade secrets, and national security. The Freedom of Information Act also allows agencies to exempt records to protect personal privacy.

HOW TO OPEN UP THOSE FILES

When it comes to dealing with government, information really is power. The government has it. Here's how you can get it.

Figure out what you want and who has it. You need to be specific about what you want, and you need to ask the right agency. No law requires the Bakersfield, California, office of the Farmers Home Administration to call the energy department in Casper, Wyoming, so that you can get a copy of an oil field study. Nor does the government have to create a record for you.

Ask politely. Often this is all you have to do. No letters, no lawsuits, no screaming matches. If the answer is that you must file a written request, ask for the name and address of the office's top local manager or the person who handles requests for information. But don't let someone tell you, "That isn't public."

Cite the law. Early in your letter, mention that you're seeking information under the Freedom of Information Act or the Privacy Act. If the information you want might be covered by either law, mention both. It will speed processing if you also put the words "Freedom of Information Act request" or "Privacy Act request" on the envelope. Remember that these laws apply only to the federal government. If you need information from your state, county, or city, cite your state public records act. A sympathetic bureaucrat may tell you about the local law. If not, someone at the local newspaper is sure to know about it.

Identify yourself clearly. The Privacy Act was intended to protect your privacy. To prevent somebody else from requesting your personal information, the act requires requesters to identify themselves. Include your full name, address, Social Security number, and date and place of birth. You may want to get your signature notarized, too.

Set a limit on what you're willing to pay. Tell the agency from which you're requesting information what the maximum fee is that you're willing to pay. Include your daytime phone number so that the agency can call you if costs exceed that limit. You can cut or eliminate costs by agreeing to inspect records rather than ask for copies. You also can seek a fee waiver. The Freedom of Information Act allows waivers for several reasons, including a catchall: if disclosure would serve a significant public interest.

Get First-Class Postal Service

The U.S. Postal Service really does want your stamp of approval.

Faced with competition for its more lucrative services, the Postal Service is trying to be friendlier to its customers. As part of that effort, it has developed an elaborate system to inform consumers and to make sure that every complaint is answered within days.

HOW TO ADDRESS POSTAL PROBLEMS

The last time you walked into your post office, you may have noticed a small display inviting your comments on a special form. This is no simple suggestions box. The Postal Service being the Postal Service, it has given every postmaster detailed, written instructions on the proper care and handling of each "Consumer Service Card."

From the time a consumer fills out one of these cards, the local postmaster has 24 hours to acknowledge receipt and 14 days to give an answer. The postmaster has to send a copy of the raw complaint and a copy of his reply to a central office in St. Louis. In 1995, the Postal Service logged 612,000 contacts with its customers.

Don't like the local postmaster's answer? Go over his head to the nearest regional office. Each of the 85 regional offices has a Consumer Affairs and Claims office. They report to the Consumer Advocate, a Postal Service vice-president in Washington, D.C. In 1995, the Consumer Advocate handled 100,000 customer complaints and compliments.

Stamping Out Mail Fraud

It's a crime what some people send in the mail. The name for this crime is mail fraud, and it carries a five-year federal prison sentence.

The Postal Service's in-house police department, the U.S. Postal Inspection Service, investigates mail fraud as well as mail theft and the use of the mail to ship drugs. Its beat ranges from penny-ante bunco schemes to massive securities frauds.

Mail fraud can be blatant—"cures" for AIDS, sexual come-ons—or it can be subtle. The operators of First Pension Corporation, a California-based Individual Retirement Account administrator, quietly stole $136 million from 6,000 customers. They disguised their theft by sending customers phony account statements in the mail. First Pension's mastermind pleaded guilty to two counts of mail fraud in 1994. He is serving 10 years in federal prison.

If you think that you've been defrauded through the mail, write your postmaster or ask him to direct you to the nearest office of the U.S. Postal Inspection Service.

MAIL ASSISTANCE MADE EASY

Here are other ways the Postal Service can deliver for you.

Stop objectionable mail. If someone's mailing you obscene material, the Postal Service can stop it at the source. Ask for Form 2201 at your post office. This will give the mailer notice under federal law to take your name off his mailing list.

Let your fingers do the waiting. You don't have to stand in line at the post office to find out how much it will cost to mail a package overseas or what the difference is between registered mail and certified mail. You can get the facts through the automated Postal Answer Line. It handles an average of 3.6 million calls annually.

Postal Answer Lines are operating in 81 metropolitan regions. Eventually the Postal Service hopes to create a single, nationwide toll-free "Customer Care Center" to provide information and deal with complaints. It's testing the concept in selected areas in the East and Midwest.

Seek payment for mail damage. You don't have to stew silently because your children's Christmas gifts were broken in the mail. If the package came by insured, registered, COD, or Express Mail, you can seek compensation from the Postal Service. You must fill out a claim form and bring the packaging, mailing container, and damaged goods (if you received them) to the post office for inspection. Bring your original mailing receipt and proof of value, too.

Local Government: Close to Home

Local government gets you where you live.

Local schools teach, or fail to teach, your children. A local cop tickets you when you run a red light, finds your stolen car, and speaks to your Neighborhood Watch. A local zoning board decides what kind of business you can run in your home and whether to permit a big apartment complex nearby.

Collectively, state and local governments employ 15 million people—five times more than the federal government. So this is a huge and incredibly diverse bureaucracy. Here are some tools that you can use to get what you want, whether you're dealing with a big city or a tiny water district.

· GET THE NEIGHBORS ON YOUR SIDE

Rallying neighbors to your cause might be easier than you would first think. The federal government deals mainly with individuals. State and local governments tend to deal with areas. If the IRS denies you a deduction for your last Christmas party, you'll suffer alone. If city hall increases the speed limit on your street, your neighbors will be just as upset as you are. Organizing your neighbors or working within an existing neighborhood group will give you a louder voice in local government.

"For those who do not have access to power, I think that organizing is the only way" to get results, says Pablo Eisenberg, executive director of the nonprofit Center for Community Change in Washington, D.C. He has made a career of organizing low-income groups—"people who are fairly voiceless and have been locked out of the system." But organizing has worked for people of all income levels in all parts of the country. The basic elements are to rally people around an issue, force local officials to pay attention, and lobby for a solution. Perhaps the best-known example is MADD, Mothers Against Drunk Driving.

Hundreds of local groups have used the same principles to influence local planning. The American Planning Association reported in 1993: "In the last several years especially, there has been a dramatic upsurge in citizen involvement activity (in planning) across the country." Scarcely a city in America has avoided a public revolt over planning—a revolt so universal that it has earned its own acronym: NIMBY, Not in My Backyard.

NIMBYs and other citizens' groups are putting old-fashioned, from-the-top-down local government on the defensive. Dozens of cities and counties are looking for ways to anticipate citizens' demands and defuse their anger.

"There's a prevailing sea change in the way that citizens approach governments to get things done," says Bill Potapchuk, executive director of the Program for Community Problem Solving, an arm of the National Civic League in Washington, D.C. The new approach, he suggests, is less adversarial and more collaborative. Instead of dictating results, he says, city officials are trying to work with citizens to get things done.

YES, YOU CAN FIGHT—OR WORK WITH—CITY HALL

Here are more strategies for getting satisfaction out of your local government.

Meet the key bureaucrats. Worried about cars racing down your street? Look for the city planner or road official who studies traffic in your neighborhood. Upset about kids loitering in front of your house at midday instead of sitting in a classroom? Talk to the local principal or to the police sergeant who supervises patrols in your area.

"Meet with the key bureaucrats first and try to get them to respond to the needs of the residents," says Bud Kanitz, executive director of the National Neighborhood Coalition. "Then, if there is no positive response, go to the local elected council member. . . . Try to work with the line official and get them to respond."

Offer ideas. Be ready with a workable solution to your problem. "Even if it's a tentative one," says Eisenberg, "it's better than just identifying the problem."

This doesn't mean that you have to shout at a crowded city council meeting. Many local agencies have reacted to bruising, public fights with their constituents by forming dozens of formal and informal advisory groups. Their common job is to forge consensus on difficult issues. If you really care about an issue, you can help shape a solution by joining one of these groups.

Follow the money. Local governments have a pocket of money reserved for solving neighborhood problems. There's $4.6 billion in this pocket nationwide. It comes from federal tax money, and it's known as the Community Development Block Grant Program. Federal rules require local governments to stage public hearings before they distribute the money.

Congress is cutting back on this program and simultaneously loosening the purse strings, giving local officials more control over how the money is spent. Because of these changes, Kanitz says, "citizen participation is, if anything, even more important."

Get your name on mailing lists. Did you get a notice before the local zoning board approved a new strip mall four blocks away? How about the decision to drop funding for a traffic light at the busy intersection that your kids cross every day? Local governments make scores of decisions that might affect you. In most states they have to notify the public, but they don't have to try very hard. They may post a notice of an impending construction project on a light pole near the site. Or they may publish legal notices in small type right next to the obituaries in your local paper.

The solution is to ask your local government to notify you if something comes up on a particular issue. A few local planning departments routinely notify neighborhood associations of every zoning proposal near their turf. Your city, or a sympathetic bureaucrat, may be willing to notify you before acting on an issue that concerns you.

Bottom Line

Governments are bigger and balkier than most bureaucracies. But if you're patient, and if you know how they work, you can make them work for you.

Words to the Wise

Freedom of Information Act: This 1966 law requires federal agencies to make records available to anyone who asks. You must reasonably describe the records and agree to pay a fee if necessary.

NIMBY: Acronym for "Not in My Backyard." This widely used phrase testifies to the power that neighborhood groups exercise across the country. NIMBY has made it into the dictionary because city hall really can be beaten.

Privacy Act: This 1974 law orders federal agencies to let citizens see what information the government has on them.

Allies

Veterans Affairs (VA): Information line: 1-800-827-1000, or write to the U.S. Department of Veterans Affairs, P.O. Box 8079, Philadelphia, PA 19101. You can also visit the VA Web site.

Postal Crime Hot Line: 1-800-654-8896, or report crimes directly to your local postmaster or the nearest office of the postal inspector.

Congressional caseworkers: These people, and their counterparts in state legislatures and city councils, know government inside-out. They're paid to help you solve your problems with government. Check the Blue Pages of your phone book for the number of your representative. The office should be able to connect you with a congressional caseworker.

Your neighbors: One citizen with a complaint is a grouch. Ten citizens with the same complaint are a voting bloc.

Part 12

LIFESTYLE

Keeping the Faith

In the Business of Beliefs, Beware Emotional Spending

How do you "shop smartly" when spending money on something as personal as a charitable organization or religious community? Or something as emotionally driven as your own wedding or the funeral of a loved one? What you're purchasing, after all, is not a commodity to one day be discarded but a symbol of your core values.

It isn't easy, but when the heart leads, the head better not be far behind. The business of beliefs is big business indeed. Consider that in 1994 alone Americans gave nearly $130 billion to charities, with almost half going into the coffers of religious organizations. Furthermore, the average cost of a funeral is about $6,000, and the cost of a wedding exceeds $15,000.

Weddings: Vendors Unveiled

Your wedding is something that you don't so much *think* about as *dream* about. And dreams are not inhibited by the constraints of reality. Unfortunately, neither are wedding merchants, and many are more than eager to fill your dreams even if it means emptying your pockets.

"The bride and groom are excited about the prospect of marriage but ignorant about the process," says consumer advocate Alan Fields, who with his wife, Denise, has authored nine books on the wedding industry. "Unscrupulous vendors, knowing this, will pepper their pitches with loaded phrases like, 'Well, you only get married once,' or 'You *do* want the best, don't you?' There's a lot of money at stake in weddings. You have to stay on your toes."

In an Unregulated Field, Protect Yourself

Indeed, a number of factors play to the vendor's favor: the amount of money to be made on a wedding, the couple's vulnerability to a smooth

To Prevent Those Wedding Bell Blues . . .

Here are some ideas for ensuring a hassle-free wedding, according to consumer advocate Alan Fields in his book *Bridal Bargains*. Fields and his wife, Denise, have authored nine books on the wedding industry.

- For flowers, try a local horticulture school.
- Don't look at a photographer's "greatest hits" album. Ask to see the last wedding shot. Do the same with florists.
- Small local restaurants can make for great caterers.
- Whenever possible, don't use the word "wedding" when shopping. Vendors hear it as "sucker."
- In the final days, have a surrogate "bad cop" (trusted friend, relative, convicted felon) shadow you and intervene whenever a vendor is causing hassles or failing to deliver.

sales pitch, and the fact that there are no government regulations or guidelines overseeing the industry. But with a little information and the right attitude, you can have the wedding of your dreams at a price that won't keep you up nights. Here are some tips from *Bridal Bargains*, by Denise and Alan Fields and from the Better Business Bureau.

Get it in writing. An oral agreement is worth nothing. Every contract you enter into, be it with a photographer, caterer, gown maker, florist, limousine company, or musician, should be detailed in black and white. Assume that they have only *their* best interest at heart. Be annoyingly specific about dates, products, promises of service, times of delivery, and penalties for failure to deliver. And don't go along with their "standard contract" if it misses something.

Pay with plastic. Weddings are often pay now, receive later. You're generally purchasing goods or services that will be delivered well after you put down at least some of your money. Credit cards allow you to withhold actual payment if there is a problem or dispute between you and your vendor.

Keep down payments low. You're going to be dropping a lot of down payments all over town, so negotiate them down as far as possible. Remember that the higher the percentage of money you pay a vendor up front, the lower your leverage if a dispute arises later.

VOW TO STUDY THE DETAILS

With wedding vendors, the devil's often in the details. But a little foresight can help you avoid getting swallowed up in a sea of add-ons. Here's an example: You purchase your wedding gown from a bridal shop but find out in the fine print that an additional charge for alterations is excessively high.

You might be better off locating your own seamstress (check at a local fabric store or garment workers union). Similarly, accessories like handbags and veils are highly priced "extras" that the shop owner might try to finesse into your package. They're generally cheaper elsewhere.

Likewise with caterers and banquet halls. You agree on a price for food, but late in the game you discover that the price doesn't include the cost of extra dishes, glasses, napkins, tablecloths, chairs, and such. Or the staff to set up, operate a buffet, refill wine glasses, cut your cake, and so forth. Some vendors (most notably, florists) try to tack a "consultation fee" onto their bills regardless of whether you ultimately do business with them.

Look for the tags. The Fields say that most wedding-related complaints are leveled at bridal-gown shop owners. One common practice is ripping the tags out of a sample gown so that you don't know who has manufactured it. This allows them to charge premium prices for a gown that could well be of inferior quality or to pass off a counterfeit gown as a designer model. It also prevents you from comparison-shopping.

If you encounter this, demand that the owner prove to you the identity of the manufacturer. If need be, cite the Textile Fiber Productions Identification Act of 1960, which requires all apparel to be so marked.

Get the specifics. Some bridal shops attempt to charge you hidden markups for large sizes, small sizes, rush orders, ironing, delivery, and accessories. Again, you want to comparison-shop and you want to negotiate fees ahead of time. Have every single cost and a guaranteed delivery date delineated in the contract you sign. When a shop owner balks and tells you, "This is not how we do things," reply, "It is if you want to see a penny of *my* money!"

A "steal" might be just that. Beware the sort of "liquidators" who round up last year's models, sample gowns, and overstocks from defunct gown shops and then stage a bang-up, closeout sale at some local hotel. The problem is that many of them make all sorts of promises about service delivery and then blow town with your money.

The solution is to steer clear of such sales. If you want to go the discount route, look into operations like the Maryland-based Discount Bridal Service or the Pennsylvania-based David's Bridal. These companies operate nationwide and eliminate frills and services (and about 25 percent of the markup).

Funerals: Plan for the Inevitable

"None must be counted happy till his last funeral rites are paid."
—Ovid, in *Metamorphoses*

Perhaps the only consumer more vulnerable to professional predators than the bride and groom is the bereaved. In a state of grief, you're not exactly thinking strategically. You're easily soothed by a gentle word and an assuring smile. You may have little or no experience with the expenses and protocols of funerals. And you may have only a day or two to make the necessary arrangements.

In short, you're in no position to discern how best to manage what—on average—is about a $6,000 investment.

While none of us can avoid that last exit on life's little highway, with a little forethought and planning you can at least beat some of the tolls. Keep in mind that you are purchasing a ritual that meets the desires of the dead and the needs of the living. You don't want to pay for unnecessary accoutrements, but you also don't want to compromise others' values, beliefs, or wishes just to save a buck. Instead, you want to satisfy those wishes without paying more than you need to.

STUDY THE LOWER-COST FUNERAL OPTIONS

Despite what funeral directors might tell you about rules and protocols, services don't have to be conducted in a funeral home. A church, mosque, or synagogue with which the deceased was affiliated might be a less expensive and a more intimate venue. You can even use a private home.

And if at the service you want the casket to remained closed, you need not incur costs for "preparation" (embalming, makeup, and such). The local clergy should help you think this one through.

Consider cremation. Cremation is another option, either with or without the body first being available for viewing. And regardless of what you are told about funeral "requirements," if the latter is the case, there is no need for a casket. (Casket price tags usually reflect a markup of about 400 percent over wholesale.) You can even purchase your own urn for the ashes, which can be a good bit less expensive and more creative than what most funeral homes offer.

Have a viewing, skip the burial. If you choose cremation but want the body available for viewing first, there will be costs for making the body presentable and for a casket. (You may want to rent one, but rental prices are sometimes exorbitant.) But you will save on the cost of a grave-site burial, which can be considerable—transportation, burial plot, casing, and upkeep.

Help a school. Yet another option is to donate the body to science, through either a medical school or a teaching hospital, each of which will gladly accept your donation. When its usefulness is exhausted, the institution will return the ashes to a designated survivor. Not surprising, funeral directors balk at this option and may tell you that hospitals either don't need the bodies or won't return the ashes. But neither is true, says Karen Leonard, a San Francisco researcher who studies the funeral industry and a consultant on the subject for the American Association of Retired Persons.

KNOW YOUR RIGHTS: A MORTICIAN'S MIRANDA

The bad news is that funeral directors have been known to prey upon the grief-stricken with strong-armed sales tactics ("I know you'll want to see the very best"), leading questions ("Harry wouldn't want it done *cheaply*, would he?"), and misleading information ("A solid brass 16-gauge burial vault runs a little more, but it's the *only* way to protect your loved one's remains.")

The good news is that the Federal Trade Commission (FTC) has written rules and regulations to prevent this sort of stuff. Not all funeral directors adhere to those rules and regulations. But you can force them to if you know what they entail and know how to close any loopholes.

FTC's "Funeral Rule," first issued in April 1984, is a set of stringent guidelines requiring all funeral directors to provide consumers with accurate, itemized price information and various other disclosures about goods, services, options, and expenses. Here are the highlights.

Price list. Funeral directors must hand you an itemized price list of goods and services as soon as you begin to discuss a funeral, the goods and services attendant to a funeral, or the prices of those goods and services. They also must hand it to anyone who asks for it.

The choices. The list must include the fact that the consumer has a right to select only the goods and services desired, the fact that embalming is not legally required, the availability of alternative containers for cremation, the basic services fee (fees for professional services that the funeral home will add to your bill), the casket price list, and the "outer burial container" price list.

Service prices. It must also delineate prices for all services (such as limousines, direct cremation, transportation of body to funeral home, and cosmetic preparation) for which you might be charged.

The truth. The rule also specifically prohibits misrepresentations common to the funeral industry. These include:

- Embalming. It is *not* required by law.
- Casket for direct cremation. This is also not required by law. All that is required is a simple box, usually made of pressed cardboard.
- Outer burial container. Also not required by law in most areas of the country but required by many cemeteries to avoid having the graveside cave in at a later date.

Protection claims. This may seem a little ghoulish, but funeral directors have been known to try to sell customers on high priced burial vaults by scaring them into thinking that the remains will decompose in a particularly hideous manner if a cheaper vault is used. This not only preys upon the fears of the squeamish but, according to Leonard, it's blatantly untrue.

Don't buy their scare-laced sales pitches, Leonard says. A body with minimal extra "protection" will decompose more naturally, more quickly, and without the kind of parasitic invasions attendant to a slow decomposition process.

Your best bet may be to have a copy of the regulation, which can be obtained from FTC headquarters in Washington, D.C., or from one of its several regional offices. Ask for their publication "Complying with the Funeral Rule." Write the Federal Trade Commission, Public Reference Branch, 600

Pennsylvania Avenue NW, Washington, DC 20580. And when you go to meet with a funeral director, bring it with you. Let *them* get nervous.

PROTEST THE "COVER CHARGE"

The tough part of the FTC rule, Leonard points out, comes with the non-negotiable cover charge that funeral homes are allowed to charge for their services. Your wiggle room on this is small but worth knowing about. Essentially, you have two options.

First, though the fee is nonnegotiable, you can *try* negotiating or, in Leonard's jargon, protesting. When they say, "I'm sorry, but this is how we cover our overhead," you point out that the overhead includes facilities that you're not using, like the embalming room, parking spaces for limousines, and upkeep of their large chapel.

Second, it may be possible to eliminate the funeral home altogether. If, for instance, you have chosen immediate cremation with a memorial service at a place other than the funeral home, the body can be removed to a crematorium by just about anyone who has secured the necessary permit. (State regulations vary, so check with your state representative.) Survivors can retrieve the ashes or have them mailed back and—voilà!—no need for the funeral home to profit at all from your grief.

PLAN YOUR TRIP TO THE SHADOWED VALLEY

Author and radio personality Garrison Keillor once said he rued the thought of his funeral. He was sorry that so many people would be gathered to say nice things about him at an event that he would have to miss by only a few days. Although you can't attend your own service, you can save an awful lot of headaches and hassles for the folks gathered to say nice things about you—if you plan. Such planning solves three problems.

1. It allows you time to shop around, get the best prices and the services you want. No one is pressuring you to "close the deal" in a day or two.
2. It can be done with a clear head and a light heart. No one is extending any open wounds to the salt lick of the funeral industry.
3. You leave no room for confusion about what your wishes and intentions are. You take your survivors off the hook about giving you a bells-and-whistles send-off extravaganza.

But one final caveat: Plan well in advance but don't prepay. As with weddings, prepayment takes the leverage out of your hands and puts it in the hands of the funeral directors.

Charities: Of Paupers and Pirates

You open a magazine or flip on the TV. Suddenly, your eyes are met by the sunken gaze, at once pathetic and accusatory, of a waiflike child with tattered clothes. For just a few bucks, you're told, you can play messiah-of-the-month and save this little lamb from certain starvation. How can you say no?

How indeed. On the other hand, what do you know about the pipeline that runs from your wallet to her stomach? Does it put your money where her mouth is? How many leaks will it spring before it reaches her? How much did that ad cost, anyway? Giving generously to a cause close to your heart is good. Giving wisely is better.

REACT WITH YOUR MIND, NOT YOUR EMOTIONS

Instead, respond to it. Here's the deal: Very often charities intentionally design their appeals to strike a chord so quick and decisive that you instinctively reach for your checkbook to alleviate either someone else's suffering, your own guilt, or both. ("You can help feed little Sally, or you can turn the page . . . ").

But just because the cause is compelling, don't assume that the organization is. Take a minute to do a little research. See if they're as legitimate as the problem that they claim to be alleviating.

Pay particular attention to a charity's spending habits. (Allow for some flexibility—the percentage of funds spent directly on programs could change from one year to the next.) Say that you wanted to help provide health care and shelter to drug-addicted infants and training and counseling to teen mothers. In New York City, for instance, your research using the Better Business Bureau's *New York Giving Guide (Winter '95)* would show that in 1994 Hale House devoted 47 percent of its budget to such programs themselves, as opposed to the 84 percent spent by the Children's Aid Society, which does much the same work.

In general, when you want to know what a particular nonprofit organization is up to, you have three solid resources to rely on.

National Charities Information Bureau (NCIB). This group collects and critiques information from more than 300 charities and evaluates them on the basis of these criteria: governance, purpose, program content, accuracy of promotional materials, fund-raising practices, use of funds, thoroughness of annual report, accessibility of accurate financial statements, and accessibility of an accurate, detailed budget. The NCIB is itself a nonprofit organization founded in 1918.

Better Business Bureau (BBB). Your local office often bird-dogs charities in your vicinity using similar criteria. Many local offices research and evaluate local charitable organizations and make their information available to the public either in printed reports or in voice recordings, says Jeannette Kopko, senior vice-president at the Dallas office of the BBB. If you want to find out more about this service, contact your local office or write the BBB's Philanthropic Advisory Service, 4200 Wilson Boulevard, Suite 800, Arling-

What Do I Say?

When Charities Go Dialing for Dollars

Your home phone rings, and you get an earful of scripted fast talk about a charity with a name that's strangely similar to that of a well-known organization. How do you respond without falling into a trap? Here's what the National Charities Information Bureau suggests.

- Ask the caller to send you literature about the organization, especially if it's one that you're not familiar with.
- Don't make any commitment over the phone.
- Don't send anybody any money simply in response to a call.
- Don't give out your bank account number (you'd be surprised how many people do).
- Don't give out your credit card number unless you've placed the call.

ton, VA 22203-1804. Their reports on national charities are available online through their World Wide Web site.

The charity itself. The charity that has aroused your interest should be in a position to supply you with an annual report, an annual budget (including its allocation of expenses), a list of programs, its board of governance, and, of course, documentation of its legal status as a nonprofit organization. Beware any charity that is as stingy with its figures as it is generous with its promises.

ROOT OUT THE RACKETS

Some charities are run better than others, some are better than others at putting your dollars to good use, some manage to do more with less, while others do less with more. But some are simply out-and-out rackets. So be careful.

Pay by check. Never give cash to anyone soliciting on behalf of a charity, Kopko says. Always make out a check, payable to the organization. Along with preventing fraud, the check becomes your receipt at tax time.

Look twice at that name. Don't be fooled by a charity's name, Kopko says. It might just look impressive. Or it might closely resemble the name of a well-known organization. Do your homework.

Fend off phone callers. Be very wary of "telefunding" appeals, especially telephone fund-raisers who target seniors, says Dan Langan, public information director of the NCIB.

"Catastrophes breed scams," he says. "If there's a flood, an earthquake, or a bombing somewhere, the scammers will be calling vulnerable people and

---

'Tis a Gift to Be Simple

Want to make holiday gift giving a simpler, less costly endeavor? Consumer experts offer these suggestions.

- Strike an agreement among family and friends: No gifts that have to be plugged in or are battery-driven.
- Agree to donate a percentage of your gift-giving budget to charities and include that information in your holiday cards.
- Consider exchanging only handmade gifts.
- Consider exchanging only gifts made from recycled materials.
- Draw names out of a hat—each person buys only one gift for another.

---

soliciting money for relief programs that either don't exist or never see the money solicited."

Religion: What Price Glory?

One of the most personal (and, by extension, most ticklish) questions that people grapple with is the question of what constitutes a fair and sufficient pledge of support for their local church or synagogue.

There are rarely issues of fraud or unsavory solicitations. But neither is there a hard-and-fast rule or set price tag for participation or membership in a community of faith. So you wonder: What *are* some of the variables that you ought to take into consideration when offering manna to the heavens? How much bread do you cast upon the waters?

MAKING THE CONNECTION: VALUES AND LIFESTYLE

Churches and synagogues form no consensus on the question of giving, in part, because each one is its own community with its own personality, history, culture, and financial expectations. Within Protestantism alone there are 150 to 200 *denominations*, says Philip Williams, executive director of Indianapolis's Ecumenical Center for Stewardship Studies. And even within those denominations you're bound to find broad ranges of attitudes on the subject, from the extremely informal to the near-legalistic.

Among Hebrew congregations, while there is not such a wide spread of affiliations, each synagogue is more or less free to design its own dues structure. Emily Grotta, director of communications for the Union of American Hebrew Congregations, notes that while many synagogues have a specific, determined set of dues (often either a flat rate or a percentage of income), they are almost always negotiable, depending upon family circumstances, crises, and such. And, as both Williams and Grotta are quick to note, a family is almost never forbidden from joining a congregation because of a lack of ability to pay.

The broader issue, for both congregation and congregant, is understanding their financial pledge in the greater scheme of things—as "one's overall sense of stewardship," says Williams. This means that congregations want their members' donations to reflect a commitment to living less materialistically and to caring for others.

"The congregation," says Williams, "is a community of faith that helps the individual make a connection between their religious beliefs and their lifestyle."

But, Williams readily admits, it can be hard for a church or synagogue to stress simplicity of lifestyle and rejection of material impulses when the institution itself is bedecked in enough gold and silver to make Solomon jealous. Or when—as in some cases—it feeds off an endowment in excess of $100 million.

INVEST WISELY IN YOUR BELIEFS

So, how does an individual discern how best to support a church or synagogue? Here are a few ideas offered by religious experts.

Target your money. Consider designating a portion of your pledge to a particular program within the congregation that you believe is particularly worthwhile.

Study the figures. Consider the overall finances of the institution. Does it have an endowment? Does it have other means of generating income? Study its budget. How much does it spend on administration, overhead, and salaries? How much on missions, education, and social outreach? What, specifically, are you being asked to support, and how does this jibe with *your* values and interests? The less the organization invests in your particular areas of interest, the more specific you may want to be in designating how your giving is to be used.

Bear a reasonable load. Think of giving to your community of faith the way that you might think of weight lifting: If you're doing too little, you probably won't even break a sweat, and it won't do you much good. But if you're trying to do too much, you're probably just going to hurt yourself. So look for the right amount of tension.

Contributed services. Remember that there are also ways to contribute that go beyond finances and that are equally valuable and worthwhile to the institution. These might include volunteering your time as a teacher, caretaker of property, committee member, or outreach worker or donating your professional skills in service to the congregation.

BOTTOM LINE

When an investment is tightly bound to a subject of high emotional content, take a step back and lead with your head, not your heart. Plan before spending so much as a dime. Avoid slogans meant to push your buttons and sales pitches laced with a lot of sentimental jargon. Remember that scrupulous causes are infiltrated by unscrupulous characters. Get everything in writing. And if you don't like someone else's rules, make your own.

Words to the Wise

Funeral Rule: The Federal Trade Commission list of consumer protection regulations that all funeral homes must abide by.

Truth in Lending Act: This federal law protects you in the purchase of any goods or services that are charged to a credit card. Especially useful with wedding purchases.

Telefunding: Direct telephone solicitation on behalf of nonprofit organizations. An effective means of raising funds but also a highly effective tool for scam artists to get money and credit card numbers from unsuspecting marks.

Allies

National Charities Information Bureau (NCIB): 19 Union Square West, New York, NY 10003.

Bridal Bargains, by Denise and Alan Fields (Windsor Peak Press).

Health Clubs

Before You Sign Up, Exercise Your Detective Skills

There's something about getting out of the house and going to a sports club that makes exercising easier. Maybe it's the state-of-the-art equipment. Maybe it's the routine. Maybe it's the sauna afterward. Or maybe you just feel guilty about all the money that you sank into a membership.

Whatever the appeal, millions of Americans join health clubs, fitness centers, YMCAs, and gyms every year. But finding the best one for you—a facility that meets your needs and your budget—can be tricky.

That's partly the nature of the beast. There are workout facilities for every taste, from posh fitness temples to humble iron-pumping gyms, from specialty racquet clubs to women-only exercise centers.

Then there's the darker side of the industry: slick sports clubs that demand long commitments and hefty "initiation fees," only to shortchange members with crowded facilities or, worse, close their doors without an apology—or a refund.

But with a little planning and some inside knowledge, this is an eminently beatable system.

Find a Club That Fits

The key to a healthy relationship with your health club is to choose one using a sensible step-by-step process. Assess your needs, know the choices, investigate potential clubs, then make sure that you get a square deal.

"Health club shoppers tend to be worse than car shoppers," says Stephen Tharrett, co-author of the *ACSM Health/Fitness Facility Consumer Selection Guide*, published by the American College of Sports Medicine. "They don't know what they want, and they can end up getting persuaded by a high-pressure sales job."

Don't Become a Statistic

Low-end clubs with large memberships bank on members dropping out. To avoid becoming a statistic, choose a club with varied programs and make it a goal to incorporate working out into your overall lifestyle. How many drop out and why? Check out these numbers.

- 50 percent of new members drop their workout habit in the first 90 days.
- Half of those remaining quit exercising within six months.
- Most people will not stick with a club that requires more than a 15-minute commute.

FIRST, KNOW THYSELF

Start by answering two crucial questions about yourself: First, what four or five health club attributes are most important to you? Do you want unlimited aerobics classes? Free weights with no waiting? Self-defense instruction? A swimming pool that opens at 5:00 A.M.? On-site masseuse?

Second, estimate how much you are willing to pay for your top priorities. How much extra—if any—are you willing to pay for top-notch service? Remember that the ideal club membership will become part of your lifestyle. Make sure that you can afford it.

Once you have these answers in mind, you're ready to check out a few facilities and assess their offerings and cost.

But before you head out the door or pick up the phone, ask yourself one final question: Why do I want to join a club in the first place? "If your goal is to get into your bathing suit for the summer, a health club is probably not for you," says Shirley Rooker, president of the consumer advocacy group Call for Action, in Bethesda, Maryland. "Your goal should be long-term health. It has to become part of how you live your life if you're really going to get your money out of it."

KNOW THE TERRITORY

The world of health and fitness clubs breaks down into four rough categories: high-end, mid-tier, low-end, and specialty clubs. In general, the more money you spend, the better facility you'll get. Don't expect to get pampered on the cheap. At the top of the price pyramid are the high-end clubs that have few members, the latest equipment, many workout options, and often amenities like in-house dry cleaning, restaurants, and free towels and soap. They are also, of course, the most expensive.

Mid-level clubs offer almost as many workout options—expect swimming, racquetball, indoor basketball, weight training, and aerobics—but give less personalized service.

Low-end clubs get by with small staffs. And some of them have 10,000 to 12,000 members on their rolls. These no-frills outfits often count on members losing their taste for exercise after a few weeks.

Specialty clubs aim to fill one niche in the market, such as the demand for aerobic dance, racquetball, or tennis.

Deciding On a Club

After scouring the countryside for a health club, you think that you've found the perfect venue. But don't get distracted by the dazzle of chrome weights and thumping aerobics music—it's not yet time to write that membership contract.

TIME FOR A CHECKUP

If the health club that you're interested in still passes muster, it's time to really put the facility through its paces. Here's how to go about a thorough checkup, according to consumer advocates and health club experts.

Go at the right time. Visit the club that you're interested in at the same time when you expect to work out. A club that's virtually deserted at 10:00 A.M. might be swamped at 5:30 P.M.

Ask about staff. Check on the number of staffers available and find out what training they have.

Try a test-drive. Most reputable clubs will give you a free two-week or monthlong trial membership. Take advantage of it, but make sure that it doesn't obligate you to sign up for membership at the end of the tryout. In fact, it's a good idea to write "two-week trial only" on the sign-up form.

Inspect the gear. Look for equipment that's relatively new and in good shape. Ask how much the club spends on updating its equipment. A responsible facility will invest 4 to 8 percent of its yearly revenue on new equipment.

Check their reputation. Make a call to your local Better Business Bureau to find out if the club has been the target of consumer ire.

NOW, WORK OUT THE BEST DEAL

Once you know that you've found the right health club, you still need to pay careful attention to the details of the membership contract. Here's what consumer experts recommend.

Sleep on it. Always take the membership contract home to look it over. "A good club will always let you leave without buying a membership," says

Can You Take It with You?

If you travel often and like to work out on the road—or if you think that you might move in the near future—look for a club that has links with other facilities. These links come in three variations.

Large chains. Organizations such as Bally Total Fitness, which has clubs nationwide, and 24-Hour Fitness Centers, found on the West Coast, operate hundreds of clubs. A membership in one will allow you access to the organization's clubs in other areas.

Note: You may have to pay extra or join at a "higher level" to take advantage of this privilege.

YMCAs. With more than 2,168 facilities in the United States, you're likely to find a "Y" wherever you travel. More than 900 take part in the non-profit organization's AWAY ("Always at Home at the Y") program, which allows members to work out away from home if they show the membership card of their home facility. Most AWAY participants will charge a small guest fee—$3 to $5—for a workout. Some limit the hours and facilities that guests can use.

Affiliated clubs. Even small clubs can give you access to other facilities—if they are affiliated with a trade group such as the International Health, Racquet, and Sportsclub Association (IHRSA). IHRSA's passport program links 2,700 clubs, some of them in Europe and Asia. The program allows members of affiliated clubs to work out for a guest fee, usually in the $5 to $10 range.

Tharrett. "A bad club will want you to sign up on the spot. You don't want to join that club."

Don't rush. Don't be fooled by the hype of a "special" that just happens to be running when you consider membership. Most clubs have regular specials. If you miss one, the next one will be along soon.

Check the rate card. Be wary of clubs that won't show you their rates up front. Except for initiation fees, which are sometimes open to bargaining, rates should be standard for all members.

Keep it short. Choose shorter membership terms and especially avoid lump-sum payments for long-term membership. If the club goes under, you're likely to lose your investment. That's true even in states that require sports clubs to post a bond—a lump of cash to pay off members in case the club folds. Often the bonds end up paying only pennies on the dollar.

Look for the exit. Make sure that the contract contains a cancellation clause, which allows you to change your mind within a specified period, usually two weeks or 30 days. Regardless of the contract, many states protect consumers with a "cooling off" law, which allows cancellation of a contract as long as the buyer's remorse strikes within two or three days.

Bottom Line

To be worthwhile, a health club membership has to be integrated into your lifestyle. So do your homework and make sure that you're absolutely comfortable with the staff, the other members, the equipment, the services, the location, and the regular payments that you'll have to make.

Words to the Wise

The professional staff of a health club can be the key to a safe, effective, and lasting workout program. But when you look for staffers' credentials, you're likely to find yourself up to your ears in alphabet soup. The following acronyms indicate recognized, professional organizations.

ACE: American Council on Exercise

ACSM: American College of Sports Medicine

AFAA: Aerobic and Fitness Association of America

AFB: Association for Fitness in Business

CIAR: Cooper Institute of Aerobic Research

IDEA: International Dance Exercise Association

NIRSA: National Intramural Recreational Sports Association

NSCA: National Strength and Conditioning Association

YMCA: Young Men's Christian Association

Allies

American College of Sports Medicine: Publishes a helpful guide to finding the right health club. Request one from Human Kinetics Publishers, Box 5076, Champaign, IL 61825-5076.

International Health, Racquet, and Sportsclub Association (IHRSA): 263 Summer Street, Boston, MA 02210. Publishes a useful guide to sorting through health centers.

Dressing for Less

Keep Yourself and
Your Bottom Line Looking Great

You want to look your best, to portray in your dress the self-confident and capable person that you are. But if you're like most people, your wardrobe is a mysterious collection of clothes and accessories that happened to you virtually by accident, in a fit of impulse buying.

Sure, you've made attempts at imposing rules and reason on your wardrobe purchases, but chances are that you ended up confused by a sea of choices and convinced that what little money you had to spend on clothes could not possibly make any difference in the quality of your wardrobe.

These common problems stem from a decades-old fashion system designed to separate consumers from their money, season after season, and thrust them into endless, meandering quests for the right somethings to wear. Meanwhile, the bull's-eye on the fashion target keeps moving.

Learning to beat the fashion system, as in the rest of your life, means gaining fiscal control and doing things right the first time. *You* take control of your own appearance—not entrust it to a designer, a salesclerk, or your hairdresser. And *you* decide what and when you will spend to create your personal image.

Find Your Style

Dressing well need not break your budget, nor should shopping trips be overly time-consuming or confusing. Three key steps can put you on the road to tasteful wardrobing, helping you quickly reach a point where you need only invest a limited amount of time once or twice a year to maintain your wardrobe and assure worry-free dressing.

BEATING THE FASHION SYSTEM

The fashion industry thrives only when people spend money on clothes and accessories, not once but throughout the year. It does this by promoting change. New styles, colors, and fabrics are introduced at least every three months, and many stores today turn over their merchandise every six weeks. No sooner does your eye adjust to one color scheme, one hemline, or one lapel width before it is time to move on to another.

Learning to beat this system is important not only to your pocketbook and to your presentation of a consistent and appropriate image but also to your self-confidence. Knowing that you are well-dressed and that you look your best are secret weapons in achieving your goals, whether as chairman of the board or head of the Parent-Teacher Association. And basically, you have to outsmart designers and retailers in order to build your wardrobe.

The fashion industry fell on hard times in the early 1990s as consumers took to shopping less and spending less. Whether consumers didn't like what they saw in the stores or couldn't afford the pricey fashions is still being argued by the industry. Either way, you can turn retailers' problems and continuing uncertainties into advantages for you.

The very chic say that less is more, but how do you go about boiling your wardrobe down to less, to the essentials? And that done, how do you keep it from becoming boring?

The solution to dressing for less, in less, lies in three basic steps.

1. Window shopping
2. Closet shopping
3. Real shopping

The procedure outlined here is the gospel according to Gayla Silva Bentley. A former director of Saks Fifth Avenue's personal shopping service in Houston, Bentley is well-known on Houston television as Dr. Styles, whose down-to-earth approach to fashion and shopping has molded the wardrobes of thousands of women across the United States.

Her three-step process is simple. Once completed, maintaining your wardrobe becomes virtually effortless. And the good news is that the first two steps require absolutely no cash expenditures.

FIRST, DO SOME WINDOW SHOPPING

This first step in building a wardrobe is fun—a license to read fashion magazines and browse the best shops in town. It's a form of shopping, says Bentley, only you won't be spending any money.

The most tasteful wardrobe—one with staying power—steers clear of high fashion, so your first step is to learn to spot trends in order to help you avoid mistakes when the real shopping begins.

Dropped out? Tune back in. If you normally ignore your newspaper's fashion section or tune out the fashion channels on television, spend a week or two tuning in. Listen and watch for information on jacket styles and lengths, color and pattern prognostications, and skirt and pant styles. Something as simple as pleated-front pants, as opposed to flat-front pants, can date an outfit. Look for the details that make one designer "hot" and another yesterday's news. Your wardrobe will neither ignore nor embrace the latest fashions, but you have to know the rules before you can break them.

Check out the library. Save money by reading fashion magazines free of charge at your local library, which probably stocks more than you'll need.

Peruse the best. Visit the best fashion stores in your area and study the merchandise and displays. It costs nothing to look as you educate yourself on what fashions are current, what they cost, and how all the pieces fit together.

Wake up to work styles. If you work outside your home, observe the people at your office, especially your boss and your boss's boss. Do they wear suits, or is more casual dress the norm? Do the women wear dresses and high heels, or are pantsuits popular? Are bright colors and dramatic or creative dressing encouraged, as they are in fields such as advertising and the arts, or is your workplace more conservative? What is it about these people that defines their unique styles?

Know thyself. Also spend time getting to know yourself. Discovering your best clothing colors, your face and body shapes, and if you are a woman, your best palette of makeup colors helps you go directly to choices that will work for you. Much has been made of the seasonal color system—fall, winter, spring, and summer skin and hair tones—used by image consultants. But remember that this is a helpful guide, not a set of hard-and-fast dressing rules. If your shopping has been totally without guidelines in the past, just knowing the most flattering colors for your skin tone can narrow your field of choices by up to 75 percent.

Try a counter attack. Makeup counters at many large department stores have personnel trained to do color analyses and makeup applications for free and supply you with samples to take home. With a little prompting, they can also advise what clothing colors will go best with your skin and hair colors.

Now Do Some Paperwork

The next task, says Bentley, is to analyze the types of activities in your life. Do you need dressy or casual clothing for work—or both? Do you have frequent or infrequent activities that require special clothing, such as board meetings, charity or cultural arts balls, sporting events, an annual world-class rodeo, a corporate Christmas party, or class reunions?

"What we are attempting to identify here," says Bentley, "is the lowest common denominator wardrobe that can not only take you through every

Clothing Styles: The Winners and the Duds

That neon-paisley zoot suit probably looked like a real bargain when you bought it at 50 percent off. But now that it's hung idle in a dark corner of your closet for a couple of years, you have to admit that it never earned its keep. Stick to this checklist, style watchers say, and your clothing purchases will always be a good investment.

ALWAYS IN GOOD TASTE

Traditional Business Dress

Dark blue or gray pinstripe suits

Taupe or beige for warm weather

White or blue dress shirts or blouses

Slim or flared skirts

Wingtip shoes for men

Mid-heel pumps for women

Traditional Evening Wear

Black tuxedos or very dark suits for men

Black dresses or tuxedo looks for women

Classic Casuals

Navy blazer, chino pants, polo shirt

Chambray or denim shirts, jeans (in good repair)

Conservative knit separates for women

Preppy Casuals

Sweaters over shirts

Jeans or chino trousers

Walk shorts

Twin sweater sets for women

Loafers, espadrilles

PROBLEMATIC PICKS

Overly feminine, masculine, or sexy styles

Overly short or long hemlines

Plunging necklines

Any garment with tears or portholes

Asymmetrical necklines or hemlines

Sheer or ultra-lightweight fabrics

Wrap or high-slit skirts

Western outfits, riding clothes, or boots

Florals, polka dots, or animal prints

Pastels or overly bright colors

Sequins or shiny fabrics

Angora sweaters

Slogan T-shirts

White shoes

Fringe

day of the week, every week of the year, but also do it in style. But you can't do this without some thought and planning. No one can."

Bentley tells her clients to make a list of the regular activities in their lives, estimating the minimum number of outfits required for each. Because this list will eventually accompany you on shopping trips, include it in your personal organizer or a separate notebook.

How to Choose a Reliable Set of Threads

Fabrics are undergoing a revolution. Technological advances continue to improve once-problematic fabrics, such as rayon, viscose, acrylic, and polyester. Microfiber, for example, is a polyester fabric woven in such a way that it breathes. Look for the latest information on new fibers and blends on clothing hangtags and care labels, or ask sales associates to explain fabric properties.

To guide your clothes shopping, clothing experts offer this checklist of reliable and notoriously unreliable fabrics.

RELIABLE	UNRELIABLE
Wool, worsted wool, or wool crepe	Dry-clean-only daytime silks
Lightweight and Tasmanian wool	Dry-clean-only linens
Merino wool sweaters	Wool/nylon blends
Gabardine	Polyester
Cashmere	High-polyester-content blends
Washable silk	Ramie
Washable linen (for casual wear)	Flannel
Cotton	Satin
High-cotton-content blends	Metallic fabrics
Denim, twill, or chino (casual dress)	Exotic leathers
Tencel	
Microfiber	
Silk or velvet (dress and evening wear)	
Fleece (outdoor wear)	
Gore-Tex (outdoor wear)	

"A good rule of thumb," says Bentley, "is that your basic wardrobe should include at least one outfit per season for each of the regular activities in your life. Obviously, if you work five days a week, you'll need more work clothes."

When you make out that list of activities, make special note if there's a special occasion coming up, such as a wedding. Mark an asterisk by the space where that outfit would fit into your wardrobe—daytime, dress, or evening. This will remind you that perhaps a new outfit is in order, one that might require more of your wardrobe investment dollars. But it will also help you to visualize how that clothing will fit into the rest of your wardrobe plan. While an outfit may be perfect for that special occasion, you should be able to wear it more than once.

GO SHOPPING—IN YOUR OWN CLOSET

Once you know what you need, Bentley says, you need to know what you have. Pessimists might refer to this operation as closet cleaning, but now that you have identified and listed your wardrobe needs, shopping in your own closet can actually be a satisfying way to fill in some of the blanks on your wardrobe list. Very few people can afford to buy an entirely new wardrobe, even if they need one. This step helps you identify the "keepers" in your closet.

Another important part of this process is getting in touch with your personal style. This does not mean that you must delve into your psyche for the inner fashion child who envisions herself as Sharon Stone or himself as Don Johnson. Identifying your personal style simply means determining what kinds of clothes you feel most comfortable wearing.

Name your style. Is your style traditional, classic, dramatic, trendy, sporty, or romantic? While it is not important to cast your style in stone, you may have aspects of all six in your closet. But this is the time for a wardrobe reality check. It will help you determine if your present style fits the image that you need or hope to project.

Factor in your personality. Remember that it is possible to change your image by changing your clothes, but changing clothes does not necessarily change your personality. While black is considered a power color for women, if black makes you uncomfortable or depressed, it does not suit your personality. Midnight navy or taupe might be better choices for achieving the same purpose with your dress.

Identify the 20 percent. Imagine that a black hole suddenly opens in the back of your closet and sucks in 80 percent of your wardrobe, beginning with the clothes you wear least often. Chances are that you probably would not notice a change in the way you dress. Wardrobe experts agree that most people regularly wear only about 20 percent of the clothing and accessories that they own. This means that the majority of their wardrobe dollars are poorly invested. By identifying the clothing that you wear most often, you will have invaluable clues to your own style.

GIVE YOUR WARDROBE A WORKOUT

Now comes the most physically challenging part of learning to be a savvy dresser, the step that Bentley says most people resist. But remember that you only have to do it once.

"Try on all—yes, every single one—of the clothes in your closet, complete with shirts, ties, shoes, and other accessories," says Bentley. In doing so, you evaluate each and every garment—for fit, color, style, and comfort—and figure out whether you have the proper accessories.

In their book *Instant Style*, Emily Cho and Neila Fisher recommend asking yourself about each garment: "Does it make me feel good?" If the answer is an emphatic "no," out it goes.

Begin with the clothes that you wear most often, for these are the basics in your wardrobe. Your two most helpful tools in this process are a full-length mirror and good posture. Hey, not only is good posture free but also it automatically gives you an air of confidence. Poor posture, on the other hand, changes the fit of your clothes.

Select the unexpected. With each outfit, include a touch of the unexpected. Lynn Wyatt, an internationally known hostess and a member of numerous best-dressed halls of fame, says that she always dresses, checks her look in a full-length mirror, then adds a whimsical piece of jewelry or a bright or contrasting scarf.

Tough it out. If, like most people, you have amassed a closetful of clothes that you rarely wear, having to deal with each and every item in your closet will seem a formidable task. As you get the hang of it, however, the process will go quickly. Some things you may be able to discard without trying them on; others may go directly into a resale pile. Be ruthless in your evaluations.

Ask for an audience. Ask a trusted friend or relative whose taste you admire to help in the evaluation, providing them with a comfortable chair and something to eat and drink. Chances are that they'll help by making notes for you, and the process will be more fun.

Sell, then reinvest. No matter how much you paid for a piece of clothing, if you don't wear it, it has zero value in your wardrobe. Clothing sold in a garage sale or on consignment in a resale shop can yield dollars for wiser wardrobe investments. Sell three or four things that you rarely wear and invest the proceeds in something that you love and will wear often. There are almost as many resale shops these days specializing in clothes for men as there are for women.

RESTOCK YOUR CLOSET—ORGANIZED THIS TIME

When an article of clothing passes all of your tests, get out the list of wardrobe needs that you started at the beginning of this process. Find the appropriate category of wear on the list and write in that approved piece. But don't jump the gun here: Do not put anything back into your closet until you have completed your analyses and thoroughly cleaned your closet. When you are ready to restock the closet, group clothing first according to color, then further according to type: black jackets, black skirts, black pants, and black tops, for instance.

Let nothing hide. Everything in your closet should be visible. Discard cleaning bags. Arrange shoes and accessories on open shelves, label boxes, or consider clear plastic boxes. If you can't see an item in your closet, you might as well stuff it into a time capsule. It won't emerge again for eons.

Size up the rejects. Clothing that does not measure up goes into piles to be given away, sold, or altered. This is where your prior research can pay off. Will changing the buttons on a suit update it? Can you add new shoes or a new shirt and tie, a colored shirt, or a turtleneck sweater; raise or lower a hemline; narrow a pair of full pants?

Pin or clip a note on each garment to be altered. Add items to your wardrobe list that you need to purchase, but in parentheses or underlined, as they are suggestions at this point.

Eventually, the items in parentheses will be entered on a separate list of potential purchases, a list that will become your game plan when the real shopping begins.

Store it, then decide. If you are uneasy about parting with a garment, even though you haven't worn it for some time, store it away for a year. At the end of that time, if you have not worn it, give it to charity. Think tax deduction.

Real Shopping

Shopping for clothing is a learned art. Bentley says that few untrained consumers possess the knowledge and discipline necessary to keep their wardrobes on track. You, on the other hand, now possess a wardrobe list and the beginnings of a shopping list.

Just as going to the grocery store without a list is a mistake, shopping for clothing without a clear idea of what you need is a mistake—and since clothes cost considerably more, it can also be a budget disaster. If you tend to be an impulse buyer, tell yourself that you're on a clothing diet: You can't have anything that isn't on the approved list.

As you complete your shopping list, filling in the blanks of your list of basic wardrobe needs, be specific. For example, "White tailored, long-sleeved shirt to go with blue pinstriped pantsuit; dark suit to double for board meetings and dining out." If you need a suit, what color, style, and fabric? If you need a dress, should it fill both daytime and evening needs? Should a blouse be summer weight or long-sleeved? Should a tie be "power red" or a casual print? In a large store, faced with dozens of choices, an annotated list helps keep your shopping focused.

"Strive to make every single piece of clothing and accessory in your wardrobe do double duty," says Bentley. "This is the smartest way to stretch your wardrobe dollars."

Now it's time to plan how much you will spend on your various needs. If you have a long list, don't set out to fill all your needs at once. Quality fabric, construction, and style translate into more wearings per garment; therefore, more of your wardrobe dollars should be spent on the clothing that you will wear most often or for your most important occasions.

On Your Mark, Get Set...

A major wardrobe overhaul, while not as costly as buying a new automobile, can nevertheless benefit from careful financial planning.

Check all the angles. Consider the shopping possibilities before you begin. Outlet malls, discount stores, mass merchandisers, and catalogs are good resources for savings on wardrobe basics, such as shirts, undergarments, shoes, and other accessories.

It Figures

Calculate the Cost per Wearing

Figuring the cost per wearing of a garment is more than a mathematical rationalization of an expensive purchase. It helps you understand, in precise figures, the old adage, "You get what you pay for." It allows you to quantify the value of quality fabrics, workmanship, and design.

For example, a lightweight wool suit by a respected yet relatively conservative designer fits you perfectly, fulfills your need for a dark blue suit, and would make a heck of an impression on your banker. The price is $800. You estimate that with its serviceable fabric and conservative cut and color, you could wear the suit once a week, 52 weeks per year in your climate, for at least six years. Therefore, the cost per wearing would be approximately $2.56.

Consider a discounted $300 suit that looks okay and fits you well, although it has a garish lining and lapels that border on being labeled wide. The fabric is a polyester and wool blend, with polyester being the higher percentage of fibers. This means that it may tend to retain perspiration odors, may shine after repeated dry cleaning, and is too lightweight for the three months of coldest weather in your area. You estimate that you would wear it weekly, 39 weeks per year for three years, the cost per wearing comes to approximately $2.56—exactly the same as the more expensive suit.

Faced with these figures, you would be better off buying the more expensive suit if you can afford it. The intangible yet unquantifiable benefits that it would add to your wardrobe tip the balance.

Consider knockoffs. Consider your wardrobe budget in deciding where to shop. Certain stores and brands blatantly copy well-known designer clothing, shoes, and accessories at much lower prices. Some designers and stores even "knock off" themselves with secondary lines that offer less expensive fabrics and notions with lower price tags.

Target the right departments. If you're a woman shopping high-fashion retailers, first get a handle on which departments are likely to fit your budget, says Rose Marie Bravo, president of Saks Fifth Avenue in New York City. If you expect to be outfitted head-to-toe for $600 or less, consider a store's private-label merchandise, she says. If $1,000 is your budget ceiling, look in the bridge department. Designer merchandise would generally run you $2,000 or more.

Call ahead. If it is possible to set appointments with sales associates or wardrobe consultants at the stores where you plan to shop, do so. Many retail stores today will agree to meet customers before or after hours for wardrobe consultations. Always tell the salesperson what you will be looking for and be as specific as possible so that the salesperson can save time by pulling merchandise before you arrive.

Take it on the road. Consider wardrobe shopping while on vacations or business trips. Not only will you find a different and perhaps larger selection of clothing in other cities but also you may be able to ship your purchases home from another state and avoid paying state sales taxes.

Follow the rules. Final preparations should include memorizing these shopping rules.

- Don't buy anything that you don't love. If you love it, you'll wear it.
- Buy less, buy better.
- Buy the best that you can afford—unless it's something trendy.
- Less is more—and you save money.
- Don't buy anything unless you know where you'll wear it the second time.
- One good white shirt is better than a peck of prints.
- For women: If in doubt, buy black. It's very forgiving. Even the cheapest fabric looks better in black.
- For men: Your best suit should be darkest blue.
- When trying on a garment or accessory, ask yourself, "What message is this sending?" Make sure that it's the proper one.
- Never buy anything in anticipation of losing pounds or inches. Consider that a jinx.

BE AN INFORMED SHOPPER

Let the shopping begin but never leave home without your list. This does not refer only to shopping trips. You never know when the urge or opportunity to shop may present itself. If you are prone to impulse buying, make sure that you carry a list in your wallet. If you spot something that you truly need, it's not impulse buying—it's serendipity. If you made a picture file of clothing that would be appropriate for you, take the file with you. It will help to explain your needs to sales associates.

First, think big. Always shop for your major needs first, Bentley advises. Suits, dresses, and evening clothes are major purchases. Those expenditures will affect how much remains for other items. You may find that a suit in a high-quality "cool-wool" fabric costs more than you had planned to spend but will do double seasonal duty in your wardrobe. This could mean that you need only one suit instead of two and one set of accessories, in which case you may have more money to spend on quality accessories.

Use a go-between. Let the sales associate or your wardrobe consultant do the running while you remain in the dressing room. Besides the obvious reason that you won't have to dress to go out in the store, an added advantage is that you might be coaxed to try on merchandise that you might not have chosen yourself. Be adventurous—it costs nothing to try on a garment.

Use color control. "If your wardrobe budget is tight—and whose isn't?—choose clothes that allow you to stick to a single shoe and handbag color, usually black, navy, brown, or taupe," says Bentley. "Then next season or next year, choose a second color. Remember: Buy less, buy better."

Build on the basics. Bentley earned her reputation as a shrewd shopper by snaring designer finds at a fraction of their original costs and using that one fabulous piece as the focal point with a handful of basics. "Basics alone are not memorable. It's what you do with them that counts, that adds your

Danger Signals

A Reality Check, Before You Buy

Unless you are evaluating a wedding gown or tuxedo—and even if you are—spotting any of the following in a garment should set off warning bells about a potentially bad wardrobe investment.

- Color is very bright, drab, or unusual.
- Fabric is shiny, very sheer, or very thick.
- Fabric is a print or patterned.
- Cut is radical, seaming is unusual.
- A designer logo is prominent.
- Garment is overly short or long, tight or full.
- You have no plans for a second wearing.

personal style. Basics focus the attention on the individual—where it belongs—while add-on pieces and accessories provide the spice."

Try an odd size. When shopping sales, try sizes larger and smaller than your normal size. There must be some reason that absolutely smashing suit ended up on the sale rack.

Branch out your search. Check out different departments. Women should look for evening wear in the lingerie department—camisoles, bodysuits, nightgowns, robes—and jackets, vests, work shirts, rain gear, and navy blazers in the young men's department. Men should check the sportswear department for colored or striped shirts to wear with suits in today's more casual atmosphere.

Consider doubling up. Sometimes it pays to buy two. Not that Imelda Marcos was always right, but when you find the perfect pair of black pumps, purchasing a second pair could save time and frustration later when they are no longer available. The same argument applies when buying walking shoes, little black dresses, anything white, any pants or jeans, dress shirts, hosiery and tights, undergarments, or lipsticks.

Put accessories to work. Buy the best shoes and handbags that you can afford. These accessories telegraph your taste. Save money by buying these items on sale or from designer outlet stores. Even when buying designer fashion jewelry, it is important to buy fewer pieces and better pieces, says Bentley. "A woman can get years of use out of a dynamite Chanel brooch, and the man can do the same with a pair of Gucci loafers or a belt."

Coats, a major expenditure in most wardrobes, should be limited to three: an all-weather coat, a dress coat for day and evening, and a casual coat or jacket. Women can take a tip from fashion editors and buyers, purchasing a solid-color shawl to match a jacket or suit, a move that in some climates can avoid buying a coat.

Watch for seasonal hosiery "box" sales and check out stores' hosiery "clubs," which often provide a free pair for every 10 to 12 purchased.

Ask about discounts. Before concluding a purchase, always ask the salesperson, "Are there other savings or discounts available?" Some stores have established a practice known as preselling, in which you may choose garments and even decide on alterations days or weeks before a specific sale. The garments will not be charged to you until the day of the sale, at which time you will receive a lower price. Sometimes savings coupons may also be used against the presale prices.

If a salesperson asks if you have a coupon for a discount and you don't, ask for one. Some states require that these be made available and some nice salespeople make sure that they are.

If your total purchases at one store add up to a considerable amount—say, $1,000 or more—ask for a discount. While some stores have set no-discount policies, you may be surprised to find that even the largest specialty stores will give a discount if pressed.

Play your cards right. Most stores offer 10 to 25 percent discounts on a day's purchases if you open a charge account, a process that, thanks to the electronic age, usually takes no more than 5 to 15 minutes.

Be aware, too, that large stores, such as Neiman Marcus and Saks Fifth Avenue, have their own valued customer programs in which you can earn points toward travel, dining, and merchandise rewards. Or by charging your purchases to major credit cards, you can earn points in reward programs as well as make it easier to return merchandise should that become necessary.

Save those tags. Even after you have completed your shopping, leave the tags on your purchases until time comes to wear them and continue watching for news of sales. Most stores have policies that allow for refunds on purchases made a week to two weeks prior to a sale.

Bottom Line

In a closet stocked with flattering basics purchased at reasonable prices, you will never again have nothing to wear. Research, closet cleaning, and planned shopping help you get in touch with your personal style, evaluate your present wardrobe, and establish a shopping routine that will continue to build an investment-quality wardrobe. Learn how to conduct reality checks to keep your shopping on track and curb impulse buying.

Words to the Wise

Cost per wearing: A method of quantifying the actual value of an article of clothing—dividing its price by the number of times that it's likely to be worn.

Impulse buyer: A shopper who snaps up merchandise without much thought toward need, practicality, or the message that the clothing will telegraph. The best cure is a specific list of wardrobe needs.

Knockoffs: Clothing that blatantly copies well-known designer clothing, shoes, and accessories at much lower prices. Some high-ticket designers even knock off their own designs to provide low-cost alternatives.

Allies

Chic Simple, a series of fashion books by Kim Johnson Gross and Jeff Stone (Alfred A. Knopf). *Accessories* (1996) contains a glossary and reference sections on how to know whether accessories are worth the cost, their care and storage, accessory wardrobe basics, and sources. *Women's Wardrobe* (1996) contains reference sections on the basic wardrobe, clothing first-aid, storage tips, a fashion and fabric glossary, dress codes for various events and cities worldwide, tips on fitting clothes, and how to shop and where. *Body* (1994) contains reference sections on first-aid, skin, makeup and hair, and easy manicures and pedicures.

Fabulous You!: Unlock Your Perfect Personal Style, by Tori Hartman (Berkley Books). Includes "Style Wheels" for determining personal dressing styles for men and women.

Instant Style: 500 Professional Tips on Fashion, Beauty, and Attitude, by Emily Cho and Neila Fisher (HarperCollins). Quick tips on what to wear and how.

Spreading the Word

In a Roiling Sea of Information, How to Reel In Your Audience Every Time

You don't have your own television talk show or your own newspaper column. You can't afford expensive advertising, and you don't want to hire a publicity agent. So how do you get the word out about your small business, your nonprofit group, your neighborhood association, your opinion on government spending, or the garage sale that you're planning?

Publicity Basics: Plan for Success

Here's the real beauty of using publicity to spread your message: Much of the exposure will be free.

Not that getting that exposure is easy.

"You're competing with a lot of other folks doing the same thing," says Steve Erickson, Counselors Academy director and spokesman for the Public Relations Society of America in New York City. Thousands of professionals spend their careers working to influence the public's perception of their clients. But with planning and inside knowledge, beating this system is utterly possible and handsomely rewarding.

BECOME YOUR OWN MARKETING PRO

Whether you're planning a media campaign for the next Olympics or spreading the word about a Cub Scout pancake breakfast, a few basic principles should guide your work. Marketing and media professionals say that following these principles—which emphasize planning, strategy, and discipline—will put you ahead of many of your potential competitors.

Define your goals. Decide what you want to accomplish through publicity and come up with a specific way to measure it. Maybe you want to sell

How to Write a Press Release

Editors and news directors receive wheelbarrow-loads of press releases daily. They flip through their mail, giving each a fraction of a second to strike a chord.

In crafting a press release, you need to walk a fine line. You want your message to sound distinctive and important enough that it will inspire an editor to take action. But at the same time your press release needs to follow certain rules so that the editor doesn't have an easy excuse for flipping it into the trash can.

Write a snappy headline. The headline should be clear and tell the editor the angle on the story. If it's not effective, it will likely be the only part of your release that gets read, says Jay Conrad Levinson, a San Francisco marketing consultant and author of *Guerrilla Marketing Online Weapons*. Try it out on a few friends and colleagues and be willing to rewrite it if the reaction is not positive.

Have a real contact. In the upper right corner, designate a "contact" name and phone number. Make sure that the person—you or someone working with you—knows more about the subject, can refer a reporter to even more information, and is accessible at the phone number given.

Put the news first. The first paragraph of the news release should focus on the news at hand, not you or your company. Cover the five journalistic Ws—who, what, when, where, and why—and fill in the details in subsequent paragraphs.

Deliver hot stuff. Call to find out what editor or reporter covers stories similar to yours, then hand-deliver the release. If that's too difficult or time-consuming, fax the release. That way the recipient won't have to open an envelope.

1,000 copies of your self-published book. Maybe you want 500 people to attend the neighborhood street fair that you are helping to organize.

Define your audience. Knowing whom you want to reach will help you narrow your efforts and concentrate on the right outlets. If you're trying to bring attention to a neighborhood pothole problem, your only necessary audience may be the city administration, or it may be your neighbors. So look for a local newspaper to carry your message.

Think like your audience. Do some research to find out what your audience reads, what it watches, and what influences it. If you want tennis enthusiasts to find out about your line of breathable sports clothing, consider that tennis players may read magazines on tennis, bulletin boards in tennis clubs, and the local newspaper's tennis column.

Make a plan. Once you've targeted an audience and determined the best channels to reach it on, take the extra step of planning your publicity. This means making a list of the target media—specific reporters and editors, newsletter chairpeople, corner kiosks—and then creating a schedule for approaching those outlets. "Ninety-nine percent of marketing is done without following a plan," says Jay Conrad Levinson, a San Francisco marketing consultant and author of the *Guerrilla Marketing* book series. "It's spontaneous—and that's why it usually doesn't work."

Let's say that you're hoping to get your handmade ballpoint pens mentioned in a Sunday supplement's yearly holiday gift guide. Now you have to investigate the publication's schedule. Many magazines have a lead time of two months or more, which means that your information should be in the editor's hands long before Thanksgiving.

EMPHASIZE HOW THE AUDIENCE BENEFITS

Now that you've fully researched your audience and the vehicles for spreading your message, you're ready to put your plan into motion. The marketing pros say that these pointers will help you out.

Ask what's in it for the reader. When it comes to getting media coverage, the key to success is pitching a story that readers or viewers want to know about.

The editors that you approach are not just looking for information that will fill space or airtime. They want information that is also attractive to their audience. They aren't in the business of doing favors for sources.

Neatness counts. Busy editors look for reasons to toss unsolicited material in the round file. So when you approach media outlets, make a point of giving them clear, professional, and well-organized materials. Press releases should follow a standard format, photographs should be reproducible, and the source of past press clippings should be identified.

Look for allies. Other groups and businesses may share your goal and be willing to help you get the word out. For example, if you're promoting a 5-K race to raise money for a children's hospital, local merchants may be willing to hang fliers in their windows, since they hope to be perceived as community-minded. TV and newspapers may be willing to run public service announcements about your event. The local Kiwanis club may be willing to bring you in as a luncheon speaker.

Swaying the Public

Suppose that you find yourself in the middle of a dispute with the local, state, or federal government. Maybe you and your neighbors are unhappy about an epidemic of speeding cars in the neighborhood. Or maybe you want to fight the construction of a miniature golf course next to your church. How do you mobilize public interest and support? Here's what public relations specialists say.

To Fight City Hall, Start at the Top

Before you call *60 Minutes* to investigate your cause, try calling the government officials in charge. Write a letter to the mayor, the head of the planning commission, or the administrator of the local Environmental Protection Agency office.

Ask for a brief meeting. Lay out your concerns and make sure that the official knows that you are ready to mobilize public support in your effort, publicity specialists say.

Write a letter to the editor. The letters column is one of the best-read sections of any newspaper, Levinson says. Make your letter brief and of interest to readers (not just to you). Summarize the main points of the letter in the first paragraph. Put a two- or three-word headline at the top that says what the letter is about and follows the style of the newspaper that you're sending it to. The headline may not be used, but it will help separate your letter from the rest.

Form a group. A single voice may not carry much weight in a public debate, but a "neighbors alliance" can command instant respect—and news coverage. Use the publicity techniques that you've learned in this chapter to bring the issue to your neighbors' attention, then encourage them to join in the effort to fight for a better neighborhood.

Events: How to Attract a Crowd

One of the best uses of publicity is to draw participants and customers to one-time events. It might be a fund-raising car wash, a bluegrass festival, or the opening of a new park. By their very uniqueness, one-time events tend to be newsworthy, and they often catch the attention of community-oriented groups. You can use that to your advantage, publicity experts say.

Ask for help. Let's say that you're promoting an annual street fair. Many businesses in the area will be willing to hang flyers in their establishments. Such collaborative marketing is effective—and free, Levinson notes. Get a list of community organizations from the chamber of commerce. Ask the organizations to alert members to the event in newsletters and at meetings.

Target the best media. Your music festival may be the highlight of the suburb that you live in, even if it doesn't cause much of a ripple in the big city nearby. So concentrate your press campaign on the local newspaper, television, cable, and radio outlets. They are more likely to be in touch with your target audience than the big-city outlets. Study the broadcasts and news pages of targeted outlets. Notice how they cover stories similar to yours and which stories never get covered. When you make your pitch, aim it at the busy reporter who has covered similar stories.

Post your message. Community bulletin boards have become enormously popular in the United States in the past decade. For example, there are more than 600 in the San Francisco Bay Area alone, says Levinson, who lives there. In some communities you can even find small companies that will post your flyer for a modest fee. Depending on your target audience, hiring one of these companies is a worthwhile investment.

Designate a charity. Helping worthy causes will benefit the community and help you get attention for an event. Local media are more likely to cover a street fair, for example, if some of the proceeds are to be donated to a public park. Other businesses and community organizations are also more likely to lend a hand in getting the word out.

Go online. Depending on the type of event, posting an announcement on computer bulletin boards and Internet Web sites may help attract attention to a one-time event. Remember the basic rule: Seek a target audience wherever it may lurk.

WHEN YOU'VE MADE A BETTER MOUSETRAP...

Getting publicity for a small business's product or service is undoubtedly more challenging than putting the spotlight on a community problem or event, Levinson says. Media expect businesses to pay for advertising.

But that doesn't mean that some products and services aren't newsworthy. And, as we've seen, there are other low-cost and free channels through which to spread the word about a business. Consider these strategies.

Go directly to customers. Imagine that you've invented a small device that will help golfers improve their swing. Go to where the golfers are and get help spreading the word about your product from golf pros, golf shops, and driving ranges. For a percentage of the sale, arrange for your device to be displayed where golfers congregate.

Give away samples. Word of mouth is one of the strongest ways to get the word out about a product or service. If your product is inexpensive enough, start off by giving away lots of free samples. If it's a more costly product, target only opinion leaders with free samples. "The more you give away for free, the more you'll sell," Levinson says.

Become the expert. Smaller newspapers, television stations, and many club and association newsletters will welcome free columns from experts on everything from insurance to bird-watching. As a columnist or commentator, make sure that you emphasize your credentials and where you can be reached, but don't try to pitch your product or service directly. When readers, viewers, or listeners need someone in your business, your name will likely be the first to come to mind.

GET IT OFF YOUR CHEST—EFFECTIVELY

Sometimes you just need to get something off your chest—to the world. Maybe you're upset about the high price of peaches or have something

---

Cable Access: Become a TV Star for Free

Television coverage can be as close as your local cable cooperative. There are thousands of groups and channels across the country that will help you produce your own TV spots, specials, and series—often for little or no fee.

"If you hate the media, become the media," says Barry Forbes, executive director of the Alliance for Community Media, an umbrella association of cable access groups based in Washington, D.C.

You might find a local cable access organization by calling your area cable companies. Also, the alliance publishes a community resource directory ($60 for nonmembers) that contains more than 1,000 listings of public education and government access organizations. Reach the alliance at 666 11th Street, Suite 806, Washington, DC 20001-4542.

---

pressing to say about international politics. Or maybe you just want to tell the touching story of your family reunion.

Study the forum. Say you decide that you'd like to publish an opinion piece in your city's newspaper. Study the op-ed section for a week or two. Take note of what topics crop up. What length are the articles? What writing style do they use? Then write your piece to match. Most newspapers and magazines have writers' guidelines that they'll send you.

Get the little things right. Before sending your piece, call first to find out the name of the editor who will review it. Then spell the editor's name correctly. If the space in the publication has a specific heading, like *Newsweek*'s "My Turn," make sure that you add that—correctly. "When you're getting hundreds of submissions a week, and some of them are sent into the 'Your Turn' column, it's an indication to an editor making snap decisions that the person is not very conscientious and might just be clueless," says George Hackett, who edits the column for *Newsweek*.

Write it for the readers. Remember that an editor wants to please his readers, not you. Make sure that what you have to say will interest the audience. Newspapers and magazines are looking for the "voice on the street" to add to the mix of expert commentary.

Be yourself. Good, clear writing goes a long way toward impressing editors. But if you're not a professional writer, don't try to sound like one. "We're looking for stuff that isn't slick or overdone," says Hackett. "People should try to be direct, conversational, colloquial. We're not expecting it to read like a George Will column."

Use humor. A light touch and some wit will make your writing and opinions go down easier. It will also set you apart from the dour, preachy screeds submitted by many would-be editorialists.

BOTTOM LINE

You want to get the word out—say, about the widgets that you invented or about the dangerous intersection near your child's school. Remember that you're casting your message out into a large, roiling sea of information. And many of your competitors are savvy professionals. To succeed, create specific goals, study the audience that you want to reach, determine which channels of communication influence that audience, then devise and implement your plan.

WORDS TO THE WISE

Audience: The people you want to reach with your message. Defining it specifically will help you decide how to craft your message and how to deliver it.

Bulletin board: Whether you mean the traditional cork and wood variety at the grocery store entrance or the electronic version online, bulletin boards are an easy, free way of hooking a specific audience.

Marketing plan: A detailed plan for getting your message out. Take into account the audience, the media channels that you will target, and the timing of all of your moves.

ALLIES

Guerrilla Marketing for the Home-Based Business, by Jay Conrad Levinson and Seth Godin (Houghton Mifflin).

Guerrilla Marketing Online Weapons: 100 Low-Cost, High-Impact Weapons for Online Profits and Prosperity, by Jay Conrad Levinson and Charles Rubin (Houghton Mifflin).

Professional's Guide to Publicity, by Richard Weiner (Public Relations Publishing).

Gambling

A Sure Bet: What You Don't Know Will Hurt You

Imagine, for a moment, the world's simplest game of chance: a beautiful gold coin, perfectly weighted so that each side is equally likely to land facing up; a somber official, who tosses it straight in the air so that it twirls evenly throughout its flight. Heads you win, tails you lose.

Ah, but our imaginary game has a cruel twist. If you lose, you pay $1. Win and you get 20 cents. For atmosphere, add flashing neon lights, along with bells that clang each time you win. A crowd gathers, gambling with you and watching you gamble; they cheer your victories and mourn your losses. Instead of a dour bureaucrat, a friendly, attractive woman tosses the coin. She roots openly for you to win. A waitress brings you free drinks. In this version of our game, you get 90 cents each time the coin lands on heads.

Would you play? What if you win 95 cents each time the coin comes up heads? What if, instead, you are paid $1 but the coin is weighted unevenly so that it lands on tails 52 percent of the time?

What if you could choose from among these various payoffs in the same building—which would you pick? Would you be content with the lower figure?

Alas, our fictional game is deeply flawed, in that it would be horribly boring, so you're unlikely to see it copied by a casino this side of Siberia. But it's also instructive: In essence, the same unequal payout occurs every time you play the lottery, make a legal bet with a "sports book" on a football game, or gamble at a casino.

Wagering: Against All Odds

Put bluntly, games of chance are rigged against you. The casino, lottery commission, sports book, or track either takes its share of money before

It Figures

The House Edge

When figuring the casino's advantage over the gambler, experts calculate how much money the casino will keep, on average, for every $100 that you bet. A coin toss in which you win 20 cents but risk $1 is similar to a relatively high-paying lottery, which returns 60 percent of all money gambled in prizes. The game with a 90-cent return is comparable to roulette, where the "house edge" is 5.3 percent.

Here's the math on the "lottery" scenario:

Number of coin tosses: 100

Money wagered: $100

Expected winnings: $10 (50 — $0.20)

Expected losses: $50 (50 — $1)

Casino gross revenue: $40

House edge: 40 percent ($40/$100)

paying bettors or makes rules in its favor to assure the same thing. In roulette, for example, the ball can land on any of 38 numbers (from 1 to 36 plus 0 and 00), but a $1 bet on one of them, where the odds are 37 to 1 against you, earns $35. In gambling parlance, the difference is called vigorish; with roulette, the casino will typically keep 5.3 percent of all money bet.

You'll probably be better off if you keep your wallet in your pocket. In the long run, if you gamble you're almost certainly going to lose money—unless you're a skilled poker player, you can predict the future in sports or at the racetrack, or you can count cards at blackjack (while avoiding detection—it's not illegal, but casinos strongly discourage it).

GAMBLING IS THE NEW NATIONAL PASTIME

If only the decision to gamble was as simple as knowing your odds. Whether drawn by excitement, neon, the lure of potentially vast wealth, or simply the conviction that they'll beat the odds, Americans spend a phenomenal amount of money on gambling—legal and illegal.

In 1995, they spent $32.1 billion on state-run lotteries alone, according to the trade journal *La Fleur's Lottery World*. They won $17.3 billion, roughly what the federal government spent on elementary and secondary public school education in 1992 (the last year for which such figures are available). The District of Columbia and 36 states have lotteries.

As recently as 1988, only two states, Nevada and New Jersey, had gambling casinos; now you can gamble legally at casinos in more than 20 states. Legal gambling enterprises enjoyed gross revenues of almost $40 billion in 1994, according to *International Gaming and Wagering Business* magazine—almost four times as much as in 1982.

Lottery: The Longest Odds

For a moment, though, forget the casinos and bookies. Think about your neighborhood convenience store, where your very own state government probably offers what is the worst legal bet in America: the lottery.

On average, state lottery commissions pay 54 cents of every dollar gambled in prizes. Because the odds against winning are so high, that works out to less than our 20-cent coin flip. Even the best rate of return, 69 percent in Massachusetts, is far lower than you'll find at any casino or racetrack. (In fairness, an average of 34 percent does go to state governments, presumably allowing them to charge lower taxes or improve services.)

Having trouble resisting the urge to play the lottery? Consider the odds: In Powerball, the multistate lottery that once gave a $111 million prize, your chance of winning the jackpot—hitting 5 of 45 regular numbers in any order, plus the sixth "powerball"—with a single ticket are roughly 1 in 55 million. "If you have to drive 10 miles to buy a lottery ticket, you're three times more likely to get killed in a car crash on the way than you are to win the jackpot," says gambling authority Mike Orkin, Ph.D., associate dean of the School of Science at California State University in Hayward, who for years taught a statistics course called Games of Chance.

Still can't resist the urge to play the lottery? Here's some practical (and some not-so-practical) advice.

Burn a bill. The next time that you're tempted to buy a ticket, hold a dollar bill in your hand, close your eyes, and imagine burning it. (This will probably be more exciting than the actual lottery.) Then ask for change, put 50 cents in your pocket, and donate 50 cents to charity. Everyone comes out ahead.

Stop burning cigarettes. Quit smoking and use your cigarette money to buy tickets. That way, you're guaranteed to win big—with better health. If by some slim chance you also win money, all the better.

Let the computer pick your numbers. "People tend to pick numbers 1 through 31—they choose birth dates, anniversaries, and other numbers that are important to them," explains Bruce La Fleur, senior vice-president of *La Fleur's Lottery World*. "You don't get a true random sampling, because you ignore roughly a third of the matrix (all numbers above 31)."

Go to Boston. If you have a choice, play a lottery with a better rate of return. The drawback is that a portion of the money you lose benefits another state, not your own.

Can You See Past the Thrill?

The analysis of gambling odds is a coolheaded, rational endeavor; gambling itself is anything but. If people made the decision whether and how much to gamble on an entirely rational basis, casinos would go out of business. Obviously, they don't.

"To a gambler, there is nothing so compelling as a gambling table," says Marvin Karlins, Ph.D., psychologist and professor of business administration at the University of South Florida in Tampa and author of *Psyching Out Vegas*. "Nothing. The thrill of gambling, for me, is going up against the odds. With every roll of the dice, the odds are against you. You're giving up control. It's like getting in an airplane. You don't control the outcome."

Don't be blinded by the thrills of gambling. Know your opponent, especially the casino. Remember that casinos are designed to take your money. The people who work there have devoted vast amounts of time to figuring out how to help you lose as much of it as possible. There are no clocks or windows to remind you of the outside world. You bet chips, not cash—it's easy to forget that they're real money, just like what's in your savings account. Waitresses bring you free drinks.

"If you underestimate your enemy, you're going to lose the war," warns Dr. Karlins. "Don't underestimate how powerful that force can be."

Herewith is some of Dr. Karlins's advice, culled as much from the craps table as the classroom.

- Never gamble money that you can't afford to lose.
- Decide in advance how much you're willing to lose—the maximum cost of your entertainment. Then stick to your limit. Religiously.
- Set a time limit—tired gamblers make foolish bets.

THE RANDOM NATURE OF CHANCE

Take this pop quiz.

1. At the roulette wheel, the ball lands on red six times in a row. You're tempted to make a large bet on black. What are your chances of winning?
2. You watch someone play a slot machine for an hour without winning a significant jackpot and figure that it's primed to pay a big one. Is it?
3. Your neighbor at the craps table, who has been charting dice rolls, tells you that no one's hit a 12 in the past 100 rolls. You consider putting $5 on the 12 (potential payoff: $150). Is it a good bet?

- Decide in advance how much you'll be satisfied with winning. Dr. Karlins walks away if he increases his stake 50 percent. (If he brought $200, he'd quit when he won $100.) But don't walk away from a winning streak—they're as real as they are utterly unpredictable. Leave your money on the table until you lose a hand. The dice may have no memory, but there is such a thing as pure, blind luck.

Another way to handle winning: Pocket the $300 (your original stake plus 50 percent) and continue gambling with what's left. Take more money off the table if you're lucky enough to continue winning. Then walk away a winner. Sure, you might triple your stake if you stay. More likely, you'll end up broke: You can't beat the house in the long run. With luck, in the short run, you sometimes can.

"You're looking for a short-term deviation—what we call a random walk," Dr. Karlins says.

- Don't be afraid to gradually increase bets when ahead. If you're playing craps and win three times in a row, add 25 percent to your usual wager. Think of it as reinvesting the casino's money in your name.
- Never, ever increase the size of your bets when losing. Do not try to gamble yourself out of a hole, and don't borrow money so that you can try to do so. If you have trouble following this rule, leave your credit cards, ATM cards, and blank checks at home or in your hotel room.

"The real test of character is when you're losing," Dr. Karlins says. "It's hard to walk away without trying to get your money back right away. That's when you start losing houses."

Here are the answers.

1. The same as always (18/38—that's assuming that the wheel is balanced).
2. No.
3. It's still a terrible bet, because the odds of rolling a 12 with fair dice always and forever remain 35 to 1 against you, while the casino pays either 29 to 1 or 30 to 1.

"The dice have no memory," says Marvin Karlins, Ph.D., psychologist and professor of business administration at the University of South Florida in Tampa and author of *Psyching Out Vegas* (and an avid craps player). For that matter, neither does a roulette ball or slot machine.

The Four Least Onerous Lotteries

For every dollar that the Massachusetts lottery takes in, it pays 69 cents in prizes. (Neighboring New York, in contrast, pays only 49 cents.)

Rhode Island returns 62 percent of its revenue to players in prize money. Idaho and Missouri pay 60 percent.

The average for all states is 54 percent.

In games of chance, what happened in the past has absolutely no bearing on the future. No system can predict the future any more than you can tell a person's fortune with tea leaves. Short of staying home, you can only choose better bets and handle your money more carefully.

Choosing Your Game

Another basic truth is that most people leave a gambling establishment with less money than they had when they arrived. But then, most people also leave restaurants and movie theaters with less money. The difference, of course, is that with a casino you don't know how much you're going to pay for your entertainment. And what you don't know can hurt you.

In a casino, the house edge—its gross revenue expressed as a percentage of money wagered—varies wildly from game to game and even at the same table, from lows of 1 to 1.4 percent at craps (on certain bets) and 1.19 percent at baccarat to 16.7 percent on the worst craps bets and 25 to 50 percent across the board at keno. (A house edge of 5 percent means that, on average, a bettor will lose $5 for every $100 he bets.)

NARROW THE HOUSE'S EDGE

Only in blackjack can a bettor truly gain an advantage over the casino, but in order to do so, he must keep track of every card that has been played so that he knows what remains in the deck. At best, that's a tedious and not-very-profitable task. By following simple rules of strategy, though, you can decrease the casino's edge to around 1 percent.

Playing properly, you can cut the house edge to less than 2 percent in three casino games: blackjack, craps, and baccarat. Remember, though, that the casino still has an advantage. The longer you play, the more likely you are, overall, to be behind. And craps especially is a fast game in which losses can mount quickly.

But even keno, with its house edge of more than 25 percent, has its saving grace, says Dr. Orkin, the statistics wiz. Keno is a bit like the lottery—you select numbers on a card and hope that they match the numbers on balls blown through the chute of the keno machine. The game unfolds slowly, with a break between each one. This slow pace tends to limit your losses. In his book *Can You Win?* (his answer is no), Dr. Orkin calls keno "the casino version of getting the highest hourly wage. Relax in the keno lounge. Make a $2 bet. Drink a free toast to the suckers at the craps table who are playing a better game than you but are somehow losing more money."

In addition to picking your poison, pick your poisoner, too—if you can. "The simple rule of thumb is that where there is the most competition there is the best available product," says Charles Anderer, editor of *International Gaming and Wagering Business* magazine. "It's a simple rule of capitalism."

In Nevada, for example, slots machines must, by law, return at least 75 percent to gamblers, but competition drives the average return up to 95 percent, with a few casinos featuring machines that return 97 percent or even 98 percent. In contrast, the slots at a casino in Connecticut with no competition for many miles, pay about 88 percent. That means that you'll lose an average of $7 to $10 more for every $100 you bet. In Nevada, and especially Las Vegas, some casinos do put up signs telling people which are their high-return slots. Others that advertise high-paying slots won't put up signs but will tell you if you ask. In Atlantic City, New Jersey, however, casinos are forbidden from advertising specific payoffs.

POKER: THE OTHER CASINO GAME

Poker is an entirely different animal—a game of skill hidden in the random jungle. What you win or lose at poker depends greatly on your skill and your opponents'. The casino or card room makes its profit by either skimming a share of the pot (in low-stakes games) or charging an hourly seat-rental fee.

"Poker is the only game in the casino that you can win at consistently if you play well," says Linda Johnson, publisher of *Card Player* magazine. "In any other game, such as blackjack or craps, the house has an edge. If you're the best poker player at a table, you're going to win far more than you lose. If you take the time to learn the odds and study the psychology, you can be a good player."

Never played poker at a casino? Here's Johnson's advice.

Hedge your bets. Start out in low-stakes games, where the minimum and maximum bets typically range from $1 to $3 or $1 to $4. You'll limit your potential losses and usually won't run into really good players who are likely to take your shirt. Move up slowly. When bets increase to the $10 to $20 range, you start running into better players.

Size up the competition. How can you tell a good player? Patience, Johnson says: Good players fold when they have a poor hand and play aggressively when they have good cards (or when they bluff). After folding,

Better Blackjack

Unless you are a professional gambler, forget card-counting in blackjack. It's tedious to master and profitable only if you make large bets. Besides, do you want some large casino employee mad at you?

This table outlines a much simpler approach commonly called a basic strategy, which narrows the casino's edge to around 1 percent, says gambling authority Mike Orkin, Ph.D., associate dean of the School of Science at California State University in Hayward. Photocopy it and take it to the table with you—that's allowed.

"Soft" hands are hands containing an ace, in which the ace can be counted as 11 points without bringing the total over 21. "Hard" hands are hands that are not soft. The "hard doubles" portion tells you when to double down (double your bet and get only one more card). You also can double your bet by splitting a pair.

Your Hand	Dealer's Up Card									
	2	**3**	**4**	**5**	**6**	**7**	**8**	**9**	**10**	**Ace**
Hard Totals										
12	S	S	S	S	S	H	H	H	H	H
13	S	S	S	S	S	H	H	H	H	H
14	S	S	S	S	S	H	H	H	H	H
15	S	S	S	S	S	H	H	H	H	H
16	S	S	S	S	S	H	H	H	H	H
17	S	S	S	S	S	S	S	S	S	S

they don't sit back and daydream. Instead they study opponents, searching for "tells" (ways that individual players tip their hands), and they watch carefully in the hope of noticing something that can help them on a future hand. Follow their lead: Know thine opponent.

Sports Gambling

The other game that can be beaten is sports betting. In theory.

Clearly, lots of people believe this theory. Americans legally bet a record $2.1 billion on sporting events in 1994, according to *International Gaming and Wagering Business* magazine. (Nevada is the only state with legal sports

Your Hand	Dealer's Up Card									
	2	**3**	**4**	**5**	**6**	**7**	**8**	**9**	**10**	**Ace**
Hard Doubles										
8	H	H	H	H	H	H	H	H	H	H
9	H	H	D	D	D	H	H	H	H	H
10	D	D	D	D	D	D	D	D	H	H
11	D	D	D	D	D	D	D	D	D	H
Split Pairs										
2-2	H	H	SP	SP	SP	SP	H	H	H	H
3-3	H	H	SP	SP	SP	SP	H	H	H	H
4-4	H	H	H	H	H	H	H	H	H	H
5-5	D	D	D	D	D	D	D	D	H	H
6-6	S	SP	SP	SP	SP	H	H	H	H	H
7-7	SP	SP	SP	SP	SP	SP	H	H	H	H
8-8	SP	SP	SP	SP	SP	SP	SP	SP	SP	SP
9-9	SP	SP	SP	SP	SP	S	SP	SP	S	S
10-10	S	S	S	S	S	S	S	S	S	S
A-A	SP	SP	SP	SP	SP	SP	SP	SP	SP	SP
Soft Hands										
A2-A3	H	H	H	D	D	H	H	H	H	H
A4-A5	H	H	D	D	D	H	H	H	H	H
A6	H	D	D	D	D	H	H	H	H	H
A7	S	D	D	D	D	S	S	H	H	H
A8	S	S	S	S	S	S	S	S	S	S
A9	S	S	S	S	S	S	S	S	S	S

KEY: H = Hit, S = Stand, SP = Split, D = Double

gambling. Americans bet far more illegally, with bookies large and small scattered across the country.)

Compared to 1993, gross revenues from legal sports gambling in 1994 skyrocketed. Here's how *International Gaming and Wagering Business* magazine assessed a 63.3 percent increase: "The players got creamed. In the 13 years we've reported these statistics we've never seen anything like it. There must be some very, very unhappy sports fans in Nevada."

THE RISK IS YOURS—NOT THE BOOKIE'S

As we said, in *theory* you can win at sports gambling. In theory, sports gamblers can win because they don't face the intractable laws of probability that doom them in games like craps and roulette. All you have to do is predict more winners than losers, manage your money well, and. . . .

In reality, it's complicated. To begin, you must contend with the ubiquitous vigorish. Legal or illegal, most sports gambling works the same way: You bet $11 to win $10. Thus, the sports book typically keeps 4.5 percent of every dollar bet. Because of that, you must win 52.4 percent of the time (if you bet equal amounts) simply to break even.

What makes that difficult is the point spread. Throughout basketball and football season, an expert in Las Vegas imagines how many points one team (the underdog) might need to tie its opponent (the favorite). Take the underdog and, for betting purposes, those points are added to your score; take the favorite and they're subtracted.

Like bookies, the people who run sports books (often casinos) don't really care which team wins and which loses. They want to make a profit. For them, the surest way to make a profit is to see that an equal amount of money is bet on each side. Then the casino pays winners with the losers' money and pockets the difference.

For sports like baseball and boxing, the betting is different, with odds fixed by the line maker. Win on the underdog and you get back your original bet plus somewhat more than you wagered. (If the odds were 1.5 to 1, you'd win $15 for a $10 bet.) Choose the favorite and you get less. (You might, for example, have to risk $15 in order to win $10.)

SOME ADVICE: BEWARE ADVISERS

Over the years, Las Vegas oddsmakers have proven to be remarkably adept at devising odds and point spreads, which makes it far more difficult to win by betting at sports than it might appear.

But if you enjoy obsessively reading about sports and don't bet more than you can afford to lose, sports betting can be entertaining. You may win. You're more likely to lose. Betting will give you a reason to care about obscure teams playing meaningless games. Because of the point spread, you'll often care about games long after the outcome has been decided. That may or may not be a good thing.

That said, here are few nuggets of advice.

Decide your own bets. Don't rely on "touts," the so-called experts who hawk picks, often via toll-free and 900 phone numbers. There may be good ones who consistently pick more winners than losers, but the industry is a quagmire of misleading ads and broken promises. Be especially wary of those who boast about winning records (against the point spread) of 60, 70, or even 80 percent.

As Dr. Orkin points out in *Can You Win?*, a gambler who wins 65 percent of his bets could turn $1,000—a tiny stake by Las Vegas standards—into more than $25,000 in just 100 bets if he used a common money-management system designed to minimize the chance of going broke. If these guys were so good, why would they need to share their picks with you? And besides, what's the fun of letting someone else tell you how to bet?

Beware useless statistics. Desperate to gain an edge, sports bettors massage statistics in myriad ways and devise a seemingly infinite number of systems for betting. But many of these so-called trends, when examined closely, turn out to be meaningless. If someone advises you to bet teams with green jerseys when they're favored on the road in the Central time zone because they win against the point spread 75 percent of the time, be skeptical.

Bottom Line

If you're going to gamble, you're virtually certain to lose over the long haul—unless you're psychic or phenomenally good at poker or blackjack. If you're just wagering for entertainment, compare your losses to the cost of a movie or a nice dinner.

Words to the Wise

Lottery: Probably the worst legal bet in America.

Vigorish: The percentage of all wagers that a gambling establishment keeps.

Allies

National Council on Problem Gambling: 1 Nall North, 10025 Governor Warfield Parkway, Suite 301-B, Columbia, MD 21044. Disseminates information about problem gambling and promotes development of services for problem gamblers.

Gamblers Anonymous: P.O. Box 17173, Los Angeles, CA 90017. A nationwide self-help group modeled after Alcoholics Anonymous.

Gambler's Book Club: 630 South 11th Street, Las Vegas, NV 89101. If you gamble at any but the simplest of games, you'll do better if you read about them. If you can't find what you need at the library or bookstore, try the Gambler's Book Club. They've been in business since 1964 and publish an extensive catalog of books, computer programs, and videos on gambling.

Index

Underscored page references indicate boxed text.

A

Underscored page references indicate boxed text.

<u>Underscored</u> page references indicate boxed text.

Underscored page references indicate boxed text.

Underscored page references indicate boxed text.

Underscored page references indicate boxed text.

Underscored page references indicate boxed text.

<u>Underscored</u> page references indicate boxed text.

<u>Underscored</u> page references indicate boxed text.

Underscored page references indicate boxed text.

Underscored page references indicate boxed text.

Underscored page references indicate boxed text.

<u>Underscored</u> page references indicate boxed text.